Wholesale
by Mail
and Online
2000

Wholesale by Mail and Online 2000

by the Print Project

Lowell Miller, Executive Producer
Gail Bradney, Executive Editor

Contributing Editors:
Joëlle Francis and Kathryn Gleason

 A HarperResource Book
from HarperPerennial

Wholesale by Mail and Online 2000 is a resource for use by the general public. Companies in this book are listed at the sole discretion of the editors, and no advertising fees are solicited or accepted. All products and brand names are trademarks of their respective companies or owners.

HarperCollins books may be purchased for educational, business, or sales promotional use. For information please write to: Special Markets Department, HarperCollins Publishers, Inc., 10 East 53rd Street, New York, NY 10022.

ISSN 1049–0116
ISBN 0–06–273676–0

99 00 ❖/RRD 1 2 3 4 5

Contents

Editor's Introduction

With the advent of the new millennium, virtually everyone in the print, radio, and television media is taking the opportunity to look back over and comment upon the last 100 years. It got me thinking about this book and how it too has evolved over its long life.

Few books in the publishing world have survived as long as this one. It's hard to believe that the *The Wholesale-by-Mail Catalog,* as it was then called, began in 1978, nearly a quarter century ago, and has been published and updated annually ever since. Back in the 1970s, shopping by mail was a revolutionary idea, a concept about as novel, seemingly ill fated, and even ominous to most folks as shopping over the Internet would seem twenty years later. Vendors were discovering they could sell goods to consumers a heck of a lot cheaper through the mail because they could avoid some of the overhead associated with owning a storefront or dealing with middlemen. Consumers, for their part, realized the benefits of shopping this way as well: avoiding sales tax, having goods delivered right to their front door, and enjoying the convenience of shopping at home, to name a few. The trick was getting these vendors and buyers together.

Wholesale was the first book to present this hard-to-find information to consumers. *Hard to find?* you say. Absolutely. People weren't getting barraged with mail-order catalogs each month in those days. In fact, if you wanted to buy something by mail, you'd have to do quite a bit of detective work to dig up vendors willing to sell this way. We even had to convince some retailers to offer mail-order service just to fill out our categories! *The Wholesale-by-Mail Catalog* was the first book of its kind, and the fact that its popularity continues twenty-some years later is a testament to its intrinsic value and smartness. The message we're getting is: *Readers of all kinds still love this book.*

The 2000 edition includes some important changes that parallel those in the direct-mail industry. To be successful in mail-order retailing today, companies have to keep up with the latest consumer trends—namely, consumers' increasing interest in and demand for Internet shopping opportunities. (I myself shopped for and bought snow tires on the Internet this year—a first for me!) In just a year we've seen the percentage of companies with websites jump threefold. Therefore, readers of *Wholesale by Mail and Online 2000* will find a great number of vendors in every category offering high-quality products to consumers at discount prices *on the web*.

Does this mean print catalogs will become extinct? No. Just as there are people who prefer the tactile experience of handling the goods they buy, there are also those who prefer to pore over catalogs, look at the pictures, and dog-ear the pages. And then there are the impatient, insomniac 3 A.M. shoppers—busy people who don't have the time or desire to go malling and who can't stand "junk mail" filling up their trash bins. For those of you who like Internet shopping, you'll enjoy this book. If you're a holdout and still don't own a computer, never fear. There are plenty of companies in this edition that still prefer to sell their goods the old-fashioned way: by chatting with the customer on the phone or by getting to know you through mail correspondence.

We've also spent time and thought making this edition of *Wholesale by Mail and Online* fun to read and more consumer-friendly. Among other things, we've added some new chapters—"Luxuries," for instance, where you can indulge all your senses at bargain prices. And we've greatly expanded others—take the new and improved "Travel" chapter, for one, which has really novel and exciting companies that can broaden your horizons without busting your wallet. We also reorganized and redesigned the table of contents and greatly expanded the "Find It Fast" and "Related Products/Companies" sections throughout to anticipate your query "Now where would I find . . . ?" We aim to keep our book as fresh and fast-paced as the buying times so it will remain your bible to discount shopping by phone, mail, and online for at least *another* quarter century.

Finally, if you're creatively challenged when it comes to figuring out what to give your college-aged kid, your father-in-law, or your darling but demanding wife, check out "The Gift Guide," new this edition. Each year I have a lot of fun reading hundreds and hundreds of mail-order catalogs—in print and on the Internet. I get a tremendous kick out of some of them, and have often wished I could tell readers about specific products that sparked my imagination. Many times I'd think, *Wow, my mother would flip for this,* or *I must get one of these for my son,* or *I've gotta tell my best friend about this—her husband will love it.* Eureka: "The Gift Guide" was born. I guarantee you'll be entertained and inspired by it.

My eventual goal is to do all my shopping in pajamas. I hope this book helps you do the same.

—G.B.

How to Use This Book

The aim of *Wholesale by Mail and Online 2000* is to help consumers find great deals on products when buying by mail, phone, fax, or on the Internet. The term *wholesale* refers to discounts of 30% or more on list or comparable retail on some of a firm's products or services, which is how they qualify to be in this book. Many of the companies here sell at even deeper discounts. If you're interested in buying in quantity, some of the firms here will negotiate with individuals or small businesses to sell to you on a wholesale basis, often involving a minimum order, and sometimes but not always requiring you to have a resale number. Those firms are denoted with a star in the icon line in their listings. For details, see "The Wholesale Star," page xix.

There are other icons that will help you get the most from the information, so before sending for a catalog or placing an order, please read the key to the symbols in "How to Read the Listings," pages xviii–xix. For more detailed information on mail-order shopping, see "A Guide to Buying by Mail," beginning on page 625.

Following is a guide to several of this book's features that will help you make the best use of the material.

Table of Contents

I have sympathy for retailers who must find the right aisle and shelf in their store for oddball items. If you were searching for table pads, for instance, would you automatically think to look in the household furnishings department? Think of this book as a print version of a mall. Each chapter comprises a group of companies that make up a wing of the mall selling similar or related goods. Sometimes within a wing (chapter) where there are companies selling very general goods in that product category, there will also be three or more companies that specialize in one particular aspect of that category. When this occurs, I've further divided the chapter into themed subsections (for example, "Ceramics," "Jewelry-making," and "Textile Arts" in the "Crafts and Hobbies" chapter).

The Table of Contents is designed to help you narrow your product search—or at least to land you into the correct wing of the mall—with brief descriptions of the type of goods found in each chapter or section. These should serve as cues to guide you to the right chapter, where the "Find It Fast," individual company descriptions, and "Related Products/Companies" will assist further.

"Find It Fast"

Okay, so you've gotten to the right chapter. To continue the "shopping mall" metaphor, you're now standing in the wing that has store after store of desired goods. But if you're in the "Animals and Pets" chapter looking for tropical fish supplies, you don't need to read every single company listing. Go first to the "Find It Fast" listings, located immediately after the introduction to that chapter or chapter section. This at-a-glance guide tells you which companies sell the item you're looking for, and outlines different types of products offered by the firms in that section or chapter.

Company Listings

At the top of each company listing under the firm's name is an information slug that includes physical and online addresses, contact phone and fax numbers, and other information such as what they sell; forms of payment they accept; whether they issue a print catalog; and how much it costs, if anything. For a line-by-line rundown and decoding of the symbols and abbreviations I've used in these information slugs, see the section following this one, "How to Read the Listings," pages xvii–xix.

About the listings more generally, I have the benefit of seeing the catalogs firsthand or talking to the owners in person. There's a lot of information one can glean from a catalog—ranging from the management's sense of humor to the company's general sense of design and organization. Sometimes owners have stayed on the phone for half an hour regaling me with their business philosophy and vision. As much as possible we've tried to capture the company character (or characters!) in the listings, as well as to accurately portray their inventory. Obviously one cannot list everything a telephone-book-sized catalog of tools, for instance, sells. So if a company description seems a bit general but leaves you intrigued, go ahead and write or call them with your questions, log onto their website, or request a print catalog.

"Related Products/Companies"

Each firm is listed in the chapter that best reflects its business focus, and *cross-referenced* in the "Related Products/Companies" sections at the end of other chapters, as appropriate. For example, Frank's Cane and Rush Supply is listed in the "Crafts and Hobbies" chapter because that's where it belongs. But go to the "Related Products/Companies" listings at the end of the "Garden, Farm, and

Lawn" chapter and you'll find Frank's Cane and Rush listed there as well. Why? Because this company sells tropical fencing panels as well—perfect for that Oriental stone-and-herb garden you're planning!

I have a lot of fun compiling the RP/C listings, and you'll understand why when you read them. In these listings you'll find interesting or unusual items that aren't necessarily sold by that chapter's firms, but that you'll get inspiration from nevertheless. These listings provide great gift ideas as well.

A Caveat

Wholesale by Mail and Online 2000 is compiled as a resource for consumers to help you to find good values available by mail. Even if prices or a specific product are mentioned in a listing, *never order directly* from a company based on the listing in this book without first contacting the company. *Don't request extra discounts or wholesale prices, unless the listing states they are available. Attempting to bargain with these firms makes the vendors quite unhappy.* All of the information in this book is based on research and fact-checking as of press time, and is subject to change.

If you have product or company ideas, or positive or negative feedback concerning your experiences with these companies, I encourage you to contact us. See "Feedback," page 654, for more information.

How to Read the Listings

Some of the information in the listings is presented in a simple, coded form at the head of each entry, formatted as follows:

1. **Company/Contact Information**

   Company name, mailing address, and phone numbers, including toll-free (800, 888, and 877), fax, and TDD (telecommunications device for the deaf) lines

2. **Information**

   This first line tells you right away what form of information you can expect from a company. If the firm issues print material, it might be in the form of a catalog, brochure, flyer, leaflet, price list, or individual manufacturer's brochures. The form of print material is followed by its price, if any, and "refundable" or "deductible" if you can redeem the cost by placing an order. In some cases a company will send you printed information for free as long as you send them a SASE: a long (business-size), self-addressed envelope with a first-class stamp (unless more postage is requested). The text then might read "free with SASE." If the catalog is online only, the information line will read "website only, no print catalog." Many companies have both print and online catalogs. This is usually detailed in the main body of the company listing. See the "Online Catalog" symbol, page xix, for further explanation.

3. **Pay**

   Methods of payment accepted for orders (catalog fees should be paid by check or money order unless the listing states otherwise):

   - **check:** personal check
   - **MO:** bank or postal money order
   - **MC:** MasterCard credit card
   - **V:** VISA credit card
   - **AE:** American Express/Optima credit cards
   - **CB:** Carte Blanche credit card
   - **DC:** Diners Club credit card

- **DSC:** Discover/NOVUS credit cards
- **JCB:** JCB credit card
- **BRAVO:** BRAVO credit card

4. **Sells**

   The general type of goods and services sold by the company

5. **Store**

   If there's a physical location—be it a storefront, warehouse, farm, outlet, or factory—the address and hours of operation or visitation are listed. If the line reads "mail order only" or "website only," this business doesn't sell to customers in person; often their phone hours will then be listed.

6. **E-mail**

   E-mail addresses are included if the company doesn't currently have a website. If there's a website, no e-mail address is listed. To e-mail the company, log onto the website and e-mail directly from the site. Every website has a hot button that, when clicked on, makes an e-mail form pop up. Usually that button is named something like "Contact Us" or "E-Mail Us."

7. **Online**

   URL address on the Internet; for simplicity's sake and space considerations, we list all addresses beginning with *www* (www.onlineaddress.com), omitting the http:// prefix.

The Maple Leaf

This symbol means the firm will ship goods to Canada. Canadian shoppers should ask the vendor about current import restrictions and tariffs before placing an order, and request shipping charges or an estimate before finalizing the order. *Please note:* U.S. firms generally request payment for goods *and* catalogs in U.S. funds, and may stipulate that payment be drawn on a U.S. bank or paid via postal money order.

The Flag

A small U.S. flag on the symbol line means the firm will ship goods to APO and FPO (U.S. military) addresses. For more information, see "Shipments Abroad," page 637.

The Globe

A small globe on the symbol line means the firm has stated that it will ship goods worldwide. Readers having goods delivered abroad should read the listing before sending for a catalog; check with local authorities to make sure products can be imported, what restrictions may apply, and what tariffs may be charged. For more information, see "Shipments Abroad," page 637.

Spanish Spoken Here

This icon means the firm has Spanish-speaking sales representatives on staff. Before calling a company so indicated, read the listing and the "Special Factors" notes, since the person's availability may be limited to certain hours or days.

The TDD Symbol

This symbol indicates that the firm can communicate with a TDD (tele-communication device for the deaf). In most cases, the firm uses a separate phone line for the equipment; sometimes it's combined with a fax line.

The "Wholesale" Star

Firms so marked will sell at wholesale rates to *qualified individuals or other firms.* To sell to you at genuine wholesale, most firms require proof that you're running a company—a business card, letterhead, resale number, or all three—and may impose different minimum orders and sell under terms different from those that apply to retail purchases. Please note that, unless specified, all information in these listings applies to consumer transactions only. For more information, see "Buying at Wholesale," page 629.

The "Online Catalog" Symbol

The computer symbol indicates that this company has a website that features online ordering. In some cases the online catalog represents the company's entire inventory. In other cases, it may be a special online catalog that features just that firm's best-selling items or maybe just specials or closeouts. Since online catalogs are still a relatively new phenomenon, companies are experimenting with this form to different degrees. They may offer website-only specials to encourage you to buy online (thus saving themselves a bundle; print catalogs cost money, whereas electronic catalogs are much, much cheaper). Since many companies were still developing their websites at press time, it's always a good idea to log on and see if their website has online ordering capabilities yet, even if you don't see the "Online Catalog" symbol. Just because a company's website features electronic ordering doesn't mean you have to do it. Usually firms offer still-wary customers another option: downloading a form and faxing or mailing it in, calling in your order, or e-mailing it.

A Guide to Buying by Mail

This primer on mail-order shopping, which begins on page 625, will answer other questions you have on everything from sending for catalogs to interpreting warranties. If a problem arises with a mail-order transaction, look here for help in resolving it.

Wholesale
by Mail
and Online
2000

Animals and Pets

*Supplies and equipment for
livestock, horses, and household pets;
pet medications; pet doors; humane
animal traps; equestrian supplies*

Perhaps the four words we mothers dread most are "Can I keep him?" I once spent $170 on a homely box tortoise that a "friend" had given us when my son was just a toddler. There was the aquarium, the plug-in heated rock, the heat lamp, the fresh worms, the organic strawberries, the tortoise-friendly bedding material, the trip to the vet . . . Well, if you're an old softy when it comes to animals, as I am, you'll understand my dilemma. The problem was, when I'd look deep into Harry's cold-blooded reptilian eyes to see if he appreciated me (or even noticed me, for that matter), it wasn't at all clear that he did. Most pets, however, are as rewarding to own as they are expensive. And the rewards don't stop with a lick on the cheek. Being around pets has been shown to help people with depression and various illnesses, and has even been linked with lower mortality rates in the elderly.

Is a baby alligator an appropriate pet for a toddler? Will a pot-bellied pig be a good companion in a small city apartment? Will a rabbit gnaw the legs off my antique furniture? Am I likely to outlive my koi carp? If you're thinking about getting a pet, you might want to first check out "The Veterinarian's Way of Selecting a Proper Pet," a brochure put out by the American Veterinarian Medical Association (AVMA). The brochure is available upon request; send a long, stamped, self-addressed envelope with your request to the American Veterinary Medical Association, Suite 100, 1931 N. Meacham Rd., Schaumburg, IL 60173–4360. Or log onto their website, where you can read this and other brochures put out by the AVMA (www.avma.org).

For an all-around great resource that will lead you to humane organizations or concerned individuals who can help you find a shelter (for adopting unwanted animals of all species) or animal hospital in your area, offer more information on pet care, and provide material about specific animal welfare issues, check out ASPCA's website (www.aspca.org). There you'll find a comprehensive list of national and state-by-state organizations with websites, as well as links to indices with lots more references and resources. If you're a snail-mail enthusiast, you can also call or write ASPCA Public Affairs, 424 E. 92nd St., New York, NY 10128–6804, 212–876–7700, ext. 4650, to request their information packet.

I'm a believer in self-education, and almost all of the companies in this chapter carry books, videos, and CD-ROMs so you can become expert on just about any kind of animal and pursue any number of related subjects (training, breeding, care, etc.). Several of the firms listed in this chapter are owned by or retain veterinarians who will answer your questions on products and use, but usually won't give specific medical advice. Whether you're seeking discount food for your alpaca or a miniature entertainment center for your favorite hamster, you'll find nearly everything for the winged, scaly, furry, fuzzy, stinky, prickly, or slimy loved one in your life—for a lot less in some cases than you'll pay locally.

Find It Fast

Birds
- Jeffers, KV Vet, Omaha Vaccine, That Fish Place/That Pet Place, Tomahawk Live Trap, UPCO

Dogs and Cats
- Drs. Foster & Smith, Jeffers, KV Vet, That Fish Place/That Pet Place, UPCO, Valley Vet Supply

Equestrian Clothing, Footwear, and Gear
- State Line Tack, Valley Vet Supply

Fish
- Jeffers, Omaha Vaccine, That Fish Place/That Pet Place

Horses
- Jeffers, KV Vet, Omaha Vaccine, State Line Tack, UPCO, Valley Vet Supply

Livestock
- Jeffers, KV Vet, Omaha Vaccine, Valley Vet Supply

Pet Doors
- Patio Pacific

Reptiles and Small Animals
- Jeffers, KV Vet, That Fish Place/That Pet Place, UPCO

Traps (Humane)
- Tomahawk Live Trap

Vet, Kennel, and Groomer
- Drs. Foster & Smith, KV Vet, Omaha Vaccine, UPCO, Valley Vet Supply

Drs. Foster & Smith

2253 Air Park Rd.
P.O. Box 100
Rhinelander, WI 54501-0100

800-826-7206
715-369-2821
Fax: 800-776-8872

Catalog: free
Pay: check, MO, MC, V, AE, DSC
Sells: dog and cat supplies
Store: mail order only
Online: www.drsfostersmith.com

Doctors Race Foster and Marty Smith, both practicing veterinarians, personally select every product in their catalog to assure high standards for qualilty and value. Their 76-page color catalog includes pet furniture, treats, toys, vitamins, products for skin and hair, vaccines, cat trees, carriers and crates, grooming tools, leashes, training aids, and much more. Helpful sidebars dot the pages on subjects ranging from caring for your older dog to clipping your pet's nails. You'll also find an excellent selection of reference books on breeds, guides to traveling with your pet, health manuals, and other useful reading sources. Although many of the products in the catalog are Drs. Foster & Smith brand, a spot check of several major brands carried at other discount pet stores showed this company's prices to be the same or lower than its competitors. If good prices and the handpicked selection of products isn't enough, on Tuesdays and Thursdays you can speak to a staff vet on general pet issues and health care. The special vet hotline number is in the current issue of the catalog. By the way, the website is comprehensive, easy to use, and features online ordering.

SPECIAL FACTORS: Satisfaction is guaranteed; returns are accepted.

Jeffers

P.O. Box 100
Dothan, AL 36302–0100

800–JEFFERS
Fax: 334–793–5179

Catalog: free
Pay: check, MO, MC, V, DSC
Sells: pet care supplies
Store: 353 W. Inez Road, Dothan, AL; 6 A.M.–7 P.M. daily
Online: www.1800JEFFERS.com

If you're seeking products for your furry, scaly, or feathery little bundles of joy, Jeffers' "Pet Catalog" may be your new favorite source. Jeffers specializes in products for the health and care of your pet, at prices that are hard to beat.

The jam-packed 80-page color catalog has photos and descriptions of hundreds of products for the care of cats, dogs, ferrets, birds, fish, exotic pets, and other animals. From alcohol preps (for administering shots) to Zoom Groom (for combing out loose hair), you'll find it all at Jeffers. Jeffers has a livestock and an equine catalog as well, which you can request along with or instead of the "Pet Catalog." If you prefer shopping online, the website has a no-frills online catalog that lists the products and offers secure electronic ordering.

SPECIAL FACTORS: Money back if not completely satisfied; customs restrictions may apply to certain medicines shipped outside the U.S.; quantity discounts available.

KV Vet Supply Co., Inc.

3190 N. Road
David City, NE 68632-0245

800-423-8211
402-367-6047
Fax: 800-269-0093

Catalog: free
Pay: check, MO, MC, V, AE, DSC
Sells: vet and pet supplies and equipment
Store: South Hwy. 92 and 15, David City, NE; Monday to
Friday 8–5, Saturday 9–12 CT
Online: www.kvvet.com

KV Vet Supply is a family-owned and -operated business founded in 1979 to bring the very best products to owners of animals, large or small (the animals, not the owners!). Co-owners Drs. Metzner and Porter, both veterinarians, sample and review thousands of new products each year and then hand-select them for the catalog. The prices here are excellent—discounted by as much as 45% off retail.

The "Master Catalog" is the company's yearly 280-page color catalog that includes every category of product for almost any animal one could imagine—from house pets to horses to livestock. If web surfing is your thing, you can view the entire inventory on their website, although you can't order online.

SPECIAL FACTORS: Certain shipping restrictions and requirements may apply to vaccines and hazardous materials; authorized returns accepted within 30 days; satisfaction guaranteed.

Omaha Vaccine Company, Inc.

P.O. Box 7228
3030 L. St.
Omaha, NE 68107

800–367–4444
Fax: 800–242–9447

Catalog: free
Pay: check, MO, MC, V, AE, DSC
Sells: dog, cat, bird, reptile, small animal, horse, and
livestock supplies
Store: several locations in NE, SD, MO, and MN; call for
addresses and hours
Online: www.omahavaccine.com

For over 30 years Omaha Vaccine has been serving veterinarians and pet owners with great service, competitive prices, and a broad selection of products for household pets as well as horses and livestock. As you'll see in the catalog, this is a company that values its customers; contests, customer mail, the Pet Birthday Club, various reward programs—all are designed to win and keep your loyalty.

The "Best Care" catalog presents 130 well-designed pages of prescription and over-the-counter drugs and medical treatments, pet beds and clothing, food, kennels, doors, leashes, odor- and tick-control products, grooming tools, toys, cages, training aids, chewies, and many other items for the most common pets, including birds, reptiles, and fish. The "First Place Equine/Professional Producer" catalog focuses on gear, supplies, and equipment related to raising livestock and horses. Both catalogs have a comprehensive selection of health-care products. On the website you can view products, but there's no online ordering.

SPECIAL FACTORS: Some medical items may require an authorized prescription from your veterinarian; a $10 charge is added for hazardous materials being shipped by ground delivery; call for other special fees and requirements for shipments outside the U.S.; satisfaction guaranteed; authorized returns accepted within 30 days.

Patio Pacific, Inc.

America's Pet Door Outlet
1931 N. Gaffey St. #C
San Pedro, CA 90731-1265

800-826-2871
Fax: 310-547-3715

Catalog: free
Pay: check, MO, MC, V, DSC, AE
Sells: pet doors
Store: same address, Monday to Friday 8–5, Weekends
9–3
Online: www.petdoors.com

Patio Pacific, Inc., also known as America's Pet Door Outlet, solves a problem every pet owner has contemplated: How can I remain in bed eating bonbons, my feet toasty warm, while Fido braves the blizzard outside so he can "do his business"? Easy, according to Patio Pacific. Buy a pet door. Here you'll find the largest selection in the world, the lowest prices (guaranteed), 24-hour shipment, and free installer referral service.

There are a number of models to choose from: sliding glass door pet doors in semipermanent or temporary installations, some designed for extra security, others for quick installation, still others dual paned for extra warmth; pet doors for doors and walls; electronic pet doors; pet doors for screens and even windows. When you request a catalog you'll receive Patio Pacific's brochure along with a collection of manufacturers' brochures that detail features, installation, and warranties. The helpful staff is on the other end of a toll-free call to help you with questions you might have about measuring your pet. Before placing your order, ask the sales rep or check the website for Bargain Bin items. Sometimes you can get an even better discount on items that have been returned or lightly damaged in shipping.

SPECIAL FACTORS: Complete satisfaction guaranteed.

State Line Tack

1989 Transit Way
P.O. Box 935
Brockport, NY 14420-0935

800-228-9208
Fax: 716-637-8902
TDD: 800-468-8776

Catalog: free
Pay: check, MO, MC, V, AE, DSC
Sells: equestrian clothing and supplies
Store: ten stores in AZ, CA, CO, DE, NH, NV
Online: www.statelinetack.com

State Line Tack bills itself as the world's largest tack shop. If you're a member of the horsey set, you'll love browsing through the 236-page glossy catalog that features color photographs, detailed descriptions, and State Line's prices next to suggested retail prices so you can readily calculate your savings. Items are discounted anywhere from 15% to 40% off.

The attire section has proper riding breeches, jodhpurs, chaps, tights, jackets, coats, shirts, and boots for men, women, and children of all shapes and sizes, designed particularly for those who want to dress for competitions (or royal foxhunts!). There's also plenty of less formal footwear and outdoorsy clothing here as well, including some great hats and caps, rain gear, gloves, and protective riding gear such as helmets and vests. Lest we forget what riding is all about, State Tack has a large selection of wearable items for the horses too, from horse blankets and mane tamers to traveling boots and even horse pajamas. The gear, equipment, and supplies just keep going: medical and therapeutic aids, shipping and trailering equipment and accessories, grooming tools, portable sheds, feeding equipment, barn and stable supplies, fly and pest control items, nutritional, hygiene, and medical products, bridals, saddlery, horse-themed jewelry and gift items, books, videos, and much more. This catalog is kid-friendly too, with lots of products designed for very young riders and their ponies. By the way, State Line Tack has clothing and gear for people of *all* sizes, as well as for people with disabilities. The website features online ordering.

SPECIAL FACTORS: Complete satisfaction guaranteed; returns accepted for refund, exchange, or credit.

That Fish Place/That Pet Place

237 Centerville Rd.   717–299–5691
Lancaster, PA 17603   Fax: 717–295–7210

Catalog: free
Pay: check, MO, MC, V, AE, DSC
Sells: supplies for aquariums, reptiles, birds, dogs, cats,
  and ponds
Store: same address; Monday to Saturday 10–9, Sunday
  11–6
Online: www.thatpetplace.com

That Fish Place bills itself as the world's largest discount aquarium supplier. If you're an aquarist, you'll find a comprehensive selection of aquarium-related products at the guaranteed lowest prices. Among the dozens of name-brand manufacturers represented in TFP's 96-page color catalog, you're bound to find everything you need to keep your fish healthy and their environment beautiful (including live plants). Check out the separate 40-page "Ponds & Water Gardens" catalog from TFP for good deals on books, plants, fountains, and other supplies for lily ponds, koi ponds, and even patio or balcony ponds for urban dwellers (cool gift idea!). That Pet Place, a division of That Fish Place, offers three catalogs, each with a different focus: "The Bird Book," which includes food and feeders for wild birds as well as pet birds, "Dog & Cat," and "Reptile & Small Animal." Got a question? Call Dr. Jeszenka, TFP/TPP's on-staff veterinarian, who will answer any of your pet questions *for free* if you call him during the appointed times: Tuesdays 3–6 and Thursdays 5–8, EST, at 717–299–5691. That Fish Place/That Pet Place has a website where you can view inventory or download a catalog, but there was no online ordering at press time. Between the quantity discounts and good pricing, you can save up to 70% by ordering through these catalogs.

Please note: Specify which catalog you're interested in when you call to request one, and be sure to mention *Wholesale by Mail and Online*.

SPECIAL FACTORS: Authorized, unused returns accepted (a 15% restocking fee may be charged).

Tomahawk Live Trap Co.

P.O. Box 323
Tomahawk, WI 54487

715–453–3550
Fax: 715–453–4326

Catalog: free
Pay: check, MO, MC, V, DSC
Sells: humane animal traps and animal handling
  equipment
Store: Tomahawk, WI; Monday to Friday 8–5
Online: www.tomahawklivetrap.com

Q: What's this company doing in the "animal supplies" chapter? A: These are *humane* traps. Tomahawk's box traps are used all over the world by state and federal conservation departments, dog wardens, universities, and others who want to trap animals without harming them. (Capture and then drive that lettuce-eating varmint over to your feuding cousin's down the road.) The prices here are about 30% under retail, and discounts are even greater if you can order six or more of the same trap.

Established in 1925, Tomahawk manufactures over 80 different traps and cages for just about any animal of any size: fish, turtle, beaver, grackle, pigeon, raccoon, opossum, skunk, muskrat, cat, dog, rat, mouse, squirrel, chipmunk, armadillo, badger—and many more. Rigid box traps with rear-transfer doors, collapsible traps that fold to one inch in height, double-door traps that capture the animal entering from either direction, thumb traps, fish traps, and others are available here. Since trapping requires bait and sometimes special handling equipment as well, such as snake hooks, animal-handling gloves, and pole syringes, Tomahawk carries these items too. You can check out the entire inventory and also order online at Tomahawk's website.

SPECIAL FACTORS: Quantity discounts available; returns must be authorized and may be subject to a 15% restocking fee.

UPCO

P.O. Box 969, Dept. WBM
St. Joseph, MO 64502–0969

816–233–8800
Fax: 816–233–9696

Catalog: free
Pay: check, MO, MC, V, AE, DSC
Sells: supplies for dogs, cats, horses, birds, and small
animals
Store: 3705 Pear St., St. Joseph, MO; Monday to Friday
7:30–6, Saturday 7:30–5
Online: www.upco.com

United Pharmacal Company's 194-page color catalog lists the top ten reasons that you should buy here, including quantity discounts, same-day shipping, and special discounts for licensed wildlife rehabilitators. In business for over 45 years, UPCO has managed to carve out a niche for itself in this highly competitive arena by offering fair pricing and good selection and service. You'll find health and grooming products, toys, training items, and practical pet supplies for nearly every type of animal except fish: dogs, cats, reptiles, horses, birds, and small animals such as rabbits, hamsters, and ferrets. Notable are the hundreds of books on dog care, training, and breeding in the UPCO Library. UPCO has a searchable website with hundreds of products, but no online ordering.

SPECIAL FACTORS: Quanitity discounts available; returns accepted within 20 days; minimum order is $10.

Valley Vet Supply

1118 Pony Express Hwy.
P.O. Box 504
Marysville, KS 66508-0504

800-360-4838
Fax: 800-446-5597

Catalog: free
Pay: check, MO, MC, V, AE, DSC
Sells: vet and pet supplies for dogs and cats
Store: mail order only
Online: www.valleyvet.com

What distinguishes one pet supply catalog from another? Well, in the case of Valley Vet, it's free shipping on most items, excellent prices (discounts up to 30% aren't unusual here), online ordering, Internet specials, and three separate catalogs, each with a different focus.

Valley Vet's "Pet Catalog" offers 84 pages of supplies for mainly dogs and cats as well as their owners, including homeopathic remedies, pet vacuums, dog- and cat-themed doormats and other gift items, and of course the standard leashes, collars, food, cages, pet clothing, toys, grooming tools, and the like. The "Equine Catalog" boasts the best selection of horse blankets and sheets anywhere, and also features an extensive selection of riders' boots and clothing as well as some equine-themed toys, games, and gifts. Here you'll find everything you might need to outfit and care for Mr. Ed. Finally, there's the "Farm and Ranch Catalog," geared toward livestock and their owners.

SPECIAL FACTORS: Satisfaction guaranteed; authorized returns accepted within 30 days.

Related Products/Companies

Bat houses
- Mellinger's

Bird-watching binoculars
- Ewald-Clark, Mardiron Optics, Orion Telescope Center

Dog backpacks
- Campmor

Fly traps
- Mellinger's

Horse blankets
- Gohn Bros.

Natural products for livestock
- Ohio Earth Food

Pet life preservers
- Defender Industries

Pond liners and pond supplies
- Bob's Superstrong Greenhouse Plastic

Saddlery
- Weaver Leather

Art, Antiques, and Collectibles

*Fine art, antiques, Americana
and militaria collectibles,
pop culture memorabilia*

This is one of my favorite chapters to research and explore. The companies here prove you don't have to be rich to decorate your home with rare or unusual items. In my twenties I had a filmmaker friend who lived in a run-down top-floor loft in Manhattan's downtown seaport district. I loved to visit him because every square inch of his loft was covered with oddities: a 1950s U.S. Army recruitment poster; cracked and yellowed circus flyers; a row of Aunt Jemima syrup bottles; Mr. Peanut banks; cartoon-character salt and pepper shakers—it was fabulous!

The firms listed here offer an eclectic selection of the rare and unusual, from World War II pinup calendars to fruit crate labels, valuable antique maps to candlestick telephones, Simpsons neckties to Vietnam-era camos. Some of these products have excellent resale value; others don't. But because you're buying directly from the dealer, these items are less expensive than if you found them in an antique shop or gallery.

If you're serious about collecting, there are hundreds of reference books available to help you negotiate the antiques minefield. Perhaps the best known is Ralph and Terry Kovels' annual *Kovels' Antiques and Collectibles Price List*. I'm a big fan of Amazon.com (www.amazon.com), where you can search by topic and find this and other books about collecting art, antiques, and memorabilia—at a discount, no less!

If you like the feel of a Sunday-morning country auction, your heart racing as you bid $5 on a dusty box full of junk from somebody's attic, you'll love Hake's Americana & Collectibles in this chapter, and Ebay, in the "General Merchandise and Good Deals" chapter. Both companies require that you bid for their merchandise; both carry an eclectic assortment of collectibles, some valuable, some not. Hake's operates as a phone/fax/mail auction, while Ebay is strictly online. (Ebay sells a lot of new merchandise as well, which is why they're not in this chapter.)

If you acquire old maps, photographs, advertisements, or other items that need protection from air and moisture, be sure to check out University Products (in the "Office, Business, and Professional" chapter), an excellent source for display binders, albums, boxes, and restoration materials for artworks, books, manuscripts, photographs, textiles, posters, and postcards.

All of the merchants in this chapter are in their field because they love it. Since most of what they sell are one-of-a-kind items, don't be afraid to ask the merchant questions if you're seriously interested in one of their pieces, but are unsure of its value or just want more information about it.

Find It Fast

Ad and Poster Reproductions
- Desperate Enterprises, PosterNow

Labels
- Miscellaneous Man, Original Paper Collectibles

Maps and Prints
- American Prints and Maps, Hake's Americana, John W. Poling

Militaria
- John W. Poling

Phones
- Phoneco

Political Memorabilia
- John W. Poling

Pop-Culture Collectibles
- Hake's Americana, John W. Poling, PosterNow, Sunway

Rare/Vintage/Pop Culture Posters
- Hake's Americana, Miscellaneous Man, PosterNow

Simpsons Collectibles
- PosterNow, Sunway

Buy original, antique art from a price list, by mail? Yes, insists Gary Kunkelman, owner of American Prints and Maps. Art and antique collectors, historical researchers, and major museums do just that. This company sells authentic, antique American prints and maps from the 1500s through the 1800s. These are original vintage prints—lithographs, engravings, or etchings—not reproductions or restrikes. Each is guaranteed genuine. While inventory is constantly changing, it customarily includes several hundred Currier and Ives lithographs priced from $35 to more than $5,000; maps of America, some printed within decades of Columbus' discovery of the New World, others documenting Colonial America and early nationhood; old steel engravings of heroes and events in American history, including the Revolutionary and Civil wars; images of Native Americans; and more. Recent lists have also included other original graphics such as bird prints by Audubon and old Ringling Brothers circus posters. Operating exclusively by mail, American Prints and Maps is priced below retail galleries on most items. Kunkelman keeps his overhead modest in order to pass the savings on to his clients. Items are described in the 8- to 12-page lists, which come out four to five times a year. Subscription is $2/year, and photos or color photocopies are provided on request.

SPECIAL FACTORS: All items guaranteed original; returns are accepted for any reason within seven days for prompt refund.

Talk about a fun catalog to browse . . . Back in 1987, Desperate Enterprises owner Bob Secrist, a nut for advertising collectibles, saw prices for these items going sky high, and saw diminishing supplies of originals falling into the hands of a very few wealthy collectors. He decided to reproduce some of the most popular images onto tin and make them available at modest prices, thereby sharing his passion with ordinary folks like us. The rest is history.

To get an idea of what this company is all about, check out the website, which features online ordering, color graphics, product updates, and a free electronic newsletter announcing new products and special promotions. Or browse the 70-page color print catalog that presents hundreds of nostalgic images from movies, television, sports, and popular culture adorning tin signs, daily magnetic reminders, light-switch plates, paper posters, refrigerator magnets, reproduction canning tins, key chains, and neon signs and clocks. Some of the themes include gasoline images, Marilyn Monroe, Lionel trains, baseball heroes, John Deere, and famous beverage brands. The back pages feature nostalgic originals. This is a great source for gifts or inexpensive home decor. The prices are a fraction of what the original items would cost—if you could even find them—and Desperate Enterprises offers significant discounts when you order in modest quantity.

SPECIAL FACTORS: Satisfaction guaranteed; C.O.D. orders accepted; quantity discounts.

Hake's Americana & Collectibles

P.O. Box 1444　　　　　　　　　**717–848–1333**
York, PA 17405–1444　　　　　　**Fax: 717–852–0344**

Catalog: $4 and up (see text)
Pay: check, MO, MC, V, DSC
Sells: pop culture/nostalgia collectibles via auction by
  phone/fax/mail
Store: mail order only
Online: www.hakes.com

Ted Hake is known as "the grandfather of collectibles." Since 1967 he's been running a wildly popular worldwide mail-and-phone auction of pop culture and nostalgia collectibles—from action figures to watches and everything in between. The 168-page catalog comes out five times a year, and you can order a onetime sample catalog for $4, or subscribe to a year's worth for $30 (U.S. and Canada, or $45 if you live overseas).

This is really fun stuff. Hake's offers original, one-of-a-kind collectibles that are *affordable*—as little as $5 and as much as $4,000. Each item is photographed in black and white, described in minute detail, and coded as to "Estimated Value," which represents that item's current retail value. Bids placed prior to closing days may be higher or lower than the estimated value, and the highest bidder gets it (bids below the estimated value are accepted at the discretion of the seller). All bidding is done by mail, by phone, or by fax (no online bidding). In the catalog and website are complete terms of the auction, including the closing time and date, rules and suggested procedures, as well as a bidding sheet—all clearly and carefully spelled out and explained.

Hake's Americana & Collectibles is known and revered by collectors around the world. You'll have lots of fun imagining having your very own Mickey Mouse eggcups, silent movie posters, Li'l Abner and Daisy Mae juice glasses, tin toys, 1950s lunch boxes, and more. The website has links to related sites, a wonderful biography of Ted Hake (described as "Santa Claus and the Wizard of Oz combined"), and thousands of items priced for immediate sale (not for bidding). Why shop the ordinary way when you can get caught up in a global mail/phone/fax frenzy and land yourself a deal on some great stuff to jazz up your house or office?

SPECIAL FACTORS: Layaway plans are available on purchases of $75 or more; see catalog or website for terms-of-sale details and auction schedules; auction is not conducted online; mail, phone, and fax bids are accepted.

Miscellaneous Man

P.O. Box 1776–BWBM   717–235–4766
New Freedom, PA 17349–0191   Fax: 717–235–2853

Catalog: $7
Pay: check, MO, MC, V
Sells: rare and vintage posters and labels
Store: mail order only; phone hours Monday to Friday
10–6

Miscellaneous Man, established in 1970, sells *original* vintage posters on theatrical, movie, military, sports, labor, travel, and advertising themes, *original* pinups and pinup calendars, and handbills, graphics, and product labels. The selection at Miscellaneous Man is far better than that of New York City dealers—at prices ranging from 30% to 70% less. George Theofiles, the "man" in Miscellaneous Man, maintains a 3,000-item catalog of ephemera including collections of cigar box labels and luggage stickers. The catalog indicates item size and condition beside a small black-and-white photo of each item; for a more detailed view, larger photos are available ($2 each). Sale catalogs with reductions beyond the usual 30% are sent to regular customers.

While some posters are sold already mounted on linen or conservation paper, referrals are made to firms that specialize in poster mounting, which aids in preservation without reducing value. Miscellaneous Man also buys vintage posters and ephemera.

SPECIAL FACTORS: Layaway available; returns accepted within three days; minimum order on credit cards is $50.

Original Paper Collectibles

700-W Clipper Gap Rd.   916–878–0296
Auburn, CA 95603

Brochure, Sample Label: free with SASE
Pay: check or MO
Sells: original, vintage product labels
Store: mail order only

Some are charming, some amusing, others hip—I'm talking about American fruit and vegetable crate labels. Original Paper Collectibles has been in business since 1970, when founder William Wauters noticed that American commercial art was one of the hottest collectibles at antique shops. Mr. Wauters sells his labels for roughly half what you'd pay from an antique dealer. All labels are original American commercial art, not used for a variety of reasons.

The current stock described in the price list and flyer includes labels originally intended for brooms, soda pop cans and bottles, canned fruits and vegetables, tea and spice containers, and produce crates. There's also an interesting selection of "Negro-theme" labels. The collections offer the best per-label prices: 150 different fruit crate labels for $25, for example. Imagine walking into a sunny kitchen decorated with framed antique labels or labeled cans perched on the windowsill. Original Paper Collectibles is a great source for fun, inexpensive decorating ideas.

Please note: Payments for orders should be made to William Wauters, not Original Paper Collectibles. Request for brochures must include a long, self-addressed, stamped envelope.

SPECIAL FACTORS: Satisfaction guaranteed; quantity discounts available; wholesalers should inquire about terms; inquire by mail, not phone.

Go retro. Phoneco, Inc. has been repairing, restoring, and selling old telephones since 1971. You can buy old working phones as well as hard-to-find phone components through the 46-page color catalog. Many of the models are as much as 30% cheaper here than elsewhere, and if you buy an "as is" model and restore it yourself, you can save even more.

The selection varies over time, of course, but current and past editions have featured art deco phones from the twenties, candlestick phones, antique pay phones, European crank models, rotary desk models, Snoopy models, hot-pink "princess" models for your talkative teen, and many others. Looking for parts? Phoneco carries a great selection of cord including cloth-covered ones, magnetos and ringer boxes, dials and touch pads, receiver parts, line jacks and adapters, and even original decals and nameplates. You can also find original GTE Communications Handbooks, vintage phone books, and books on collecting and repairing old phones.

SPECIAL FACTORS: Price quotes by phone or letter; authorized returns accepted within 30 days for refund, exchange, or credit.

John W. Poling's three catalogs—"Military Collectibles," "Political Collectibles," and "Miscellaneous Catalog"—may turn you into a collector once you see how reasonably priced his merchandise is. The first two catalogs are $2 each, and the Miscellaneous Catalog is sent along for free with either or both. The catalogs consist of pages of typewritten descriptions and black-and-white photocopies.

What are political collectibles? Mostly campaign buttons from local and national elections, but also gems such as Mikhail Gorbachev's Official Soviet Government Portrait, an old issue of *National Geographic* with an article by Richard Nixon, a "Senator Sam" T-shirt made during the 1972 Senate hearings, and campaign bumper stickers. There's also a selection of political books at rock-bottom prices. Militaria is Poling's forte—clothing, helmets, insignias and emblems, patches, field equipment, and printed material galore, including used and rare books and manuals, maps, magazines, and newspapers. In the "Miscellaneous Catalog" bargain hunters will find key chains, banners, posters, coffee mugs, shot glasses, and other items commemorating such events as the World's Fair of 1962 and the Seoul Olympics, and such celebrities as the "typical Boy Scout" and Elvis. Description after description of antique postcards, Vietnamese Communist Government Ration Coupons, 1950s motel soaps, and other such gems will keep you entertained for hours and brimming with good gift ideas.

SPECIAL FACTORS: Satisfaction guaranteed; returns accepted within ten days for exchange or refund.

PosterNow

Information: website only, no print catalog
Pay: check, MO, V, MC
Sells: posters, postcards, calendars, fan articles, T-shirts
Store: online only
Online: www.posternow.com

A reader recommended this company, and I'm so happy he did. PosterNow, a gang of German-based entrepreneurs, sells new, high-quality posters at way less than anywhere else. Their selection is fantastic, prices moderate, and shipping very inexpensive—$3.90 flat rate for orders under $43, free on orders $43 and over, as of this writing (by regular mail, which may take two to four weeks). Posters come rolled in a cardboard tube. The website has a searchable database that's easy to use; categories include animal, art print, calendars, cannabis, comic, fantasy, fractal/virtual, fun, movie, music and personality, pinups, planet earth/nature, postcards, sports, and T-shirts. All items are pictured in full color and described (size, price, etc.). What I love about these posters is that they don't have a lot of writing on them—just clear, beautiful images for the most part. If you wanted to decorate a child's room with animal posters, buy your teen a portrait of his favorite basketball or movie star, or spruce up a college dorm with fine art prints, you'd find interesting, unusual examples here. The movie and "fan" poster selections are awesome. If there's a poster or fan article you seek, be sure to e-mail the friendly folks at PosterNow. They're very responsive to customers. They'll even throw in a free poster on orders of $100 or more.

Wholesale customers: Please inquire about terms.

SPECIAL FACTORS: Quantity discounts available; shipping by regular mail could take two to four weeks (faster service via UPS, which costs extra, is available for U.S. customers).

Sunway Co.

2115 Ashby Ave.
Berkeley, CA 94705

510–843–4019
Fax: 510–845–4148

Catalog: website only, no catalog
Pay: V, MC
Sells: Simpsons collectibles, gifts, clothing, and toys
Store: mail order only
Online: www.sunwayco.com

In the early days of the Simpsons, most of the licensed merchandise was kid stuff: inexpensive plastic toys and dolls, novelty items, and fast food "kid's meal" giveaways. Today Simpsons fans are likely to be both adults and serious collectors. When Mark Tarses, founder of Sunway Co., tried to find high-quality Simpsons items for his own collection, he was dismayed that there was no single company that sold them, and found that much of the merchandise out there consisted of cheap knockoffs (which, he points out, may be inexpensive but also have no resell value). So he started his own online company for the "serious Simpsons collector." Sunway promises that every item bears a Matt Groening and/or Twentieth Century-Fox trademark. Since Tarses handpicks and buys everything he sells directly from the manufacturer, his prices are lowest and his products are of the highest quality. My conversation with Tarses convinced me that this is one committed Simpson's collector! A sample of the current inventory on the website might include a Simpson's chess set (Marge, of course, is queen); a Christmas necktie; a 100% cotton Bart Simpson T-shirt with the logo "What homework?"; frosty mugs; salt and pepper shakers; refrigerator magnets; clocks; and silk boxers. The website is sure to entertain Simpsons fans.

SPECIAL FACTORS: Satisfaction guaranteed or your money back (except on custom-made or special-order items).

Related Products/Companies

Animal figurines and tchotchkes
- Cook Brothers

Antique/rare books
- Strand Book Store

Archival-quality storage and mounting materials
- University Products

Fine art books
- Hacker Arts Books, Strand Book Store

Heirloom/estate silver pieces
- Beverly Bremer Silver Shop, The Silver Queen

Miniature woodstove replicas
- Lehman's

Miscellaneous collectibles
- Ebay

Old-fashioned porcelain signs
- Lehman's

Porcelain figurines
- Alberene Royal Mail, Replacements, Ltd., Nat Schwartz

Prints of dogs, many breeds
- Jeffers Pet Supply

Rare and vintage film/TV (video-recorded)
- Video Yesteryear

Vintage fountain pens
- Fountain Pen Hospital

Vintage fretted instruments
- Elderly Instruments, Mandolin Brothers

Vintage LPs and 45s
- Berkshire Record Outlet, Record-Rama Sound Archives, Harvard Square Records

Vintage radio shows
- Adventures in Cassettes

Auto, Marine, and Aviation

Tires, parts, and equipment for cars, vans, trucks, motorcycles, RVs, marine and air craft; auto brokerage services

There are certain goods you don't normally associate with mail order—auto parts among them. I used to think that way, but no more. I've purchased four new snow tires by mail as well as a needed part for my old Honda through two of the companies in this chapter. In both cases I had the satisfaction of knowing that I saved myself some money, and enjoyed the thrill of coming home from work one day to find my purchases waiting for me on the front porch. Don't think you have to visit a testosterone-fueled auto parts store to get what you need, or that you have to depend on your mechanic's sources (my mechanic's "best" local source—a junk parts supplier—was going to charge us 25% more for my part!). The companies in this chapter thrive in the mail-order business because they can get it to you for less—in some cases up to 70% less. Even with shipping costs factored in you'll save. The firms listed here sell all kinds of used and new parts and supplies—including wheels and tires—for cars, vans, trucks, motorcycles, and RVs. You'll even find parts for other types of vehicles such as tractors, snowmobiles, and riding mowers. Some of these companies offer the convenience of ordering online.

The Internet is a wealth of information when it comes to automobiles. You can get price quotes on new and used cars, read reviews, check out model specifications, compare cars by two different makers side by side, discover dealers' "real" sticker prices, get general automobile information, learn how to haggle intelligently, check out related links, access bulletin boards, join chat groups, get safety and recall information, and much more. One place to start is AutoSite, a free service provided by the Automotive Information Center (www.autosite.com). This excellent clearinghouse for automobile information takes pride in being constantly updated.

The Internet also offers consumers a whole new way to approach car-buying. For a good overview of virtual auto dealers and their relative merit, see Internet Shopper's "In the Driver's Seat," a report of online car buying that's archived in their "library" (www.internetshopper.com/library). Always right on is Esmarts (www.esmarts.com), which finds good consumer deals in just about every category, including "cars." Here you'll be able to read no-nonsense mini-reviews of auto-related websites offering the best deals to consumers. If you're looking to buy a new car and are willing to do a lot of the initial legwork, American Automobile Brokers, listed this chapter, rewards your efforts by quoting you a price that's less than the one you got locally.

Perhaps the best known reference for used car pricing is the *Kelley Blue Book Used Car Guide*. The latest consumer edition is less than $10. Or check your local library, which will probably have the book or can get it for you. This company also has a fantastic website (www.kbb.com) where you can find out the value of your used car and motorcycle *for free*.

If you're into boating, you know all too well about insurance, dock fees, and the expense of upkeep and new equipment. But did you know you could save 30% routinely on the cost of maintenance products, gear, and electronics by buying from the marine suppliers listed here? Their vast inventories include every type of coating, tool, electronics, hardware, and instrument you need to keep your vessel shipshape. There's also plenty here for landlubbers, including foul-weather clothing and nifty gadgets for the outdoorsman.

Private pilots will also save on some of the parts, supplies, and electronics from the aviation discounters in this chapter. Like the marine suppliers, these firms also sell goods of interest to those on terra firma, at savings of up to 50%.

Find It Fast

Aviation
- Aircraft Spruce

Boating Supplies and Equipment
- Defender

Car Parts and Accessories
- The Benz Bin, Car Racks Direct, Cherry Auto, Clark's Corvair, Honda Parts Wholesale, Trollhattan Auto Parts

Farm/Construction Equipment Parts
- Central Michigan

New Vehicles
- American Automobile Brokers

Racing Equipment
- Racer Wholesale

RV Equipment and Supplies
- RV Direct

Tires
- Discount Tire, Tire Rack

Aircraft Spruce & Specialty Co.

225 Airport Circle
Corona, CA 91720

800–824–1930 (West Coast)
800–831–2949 (East Coast)
Fax: 909–372–0555 (West)
Fax: 770–229–2329 (East)

Catalog: $5, refundable (see text)
Pay: check, MO, MC, V, AE, DSC
Sells: small aircraft and pilot equipment
Store: West, same address; East, 900 S. Pine Hill Road,
  Griffin, GA; call for hours
Online: www.aircraft-spruce.com

Since 1965 Aircraft Spruce & Specialty has been selling aircraft parts and supplies to aviation enthusiasts worldwide. If you know what you're looking for, call for a price quote. Otherwise, $5 buys you a phone-book-size resource (or $20 if you live overseas) with 500-plus pages listing everything under the sun; the catalog fee is refundable with a purchase of $50. You'll find an exhaustive inventory of composite materials, aircraft kits, wood products, metals/plastics, airframe parts, landing gear, engine parts and accessories, covering supplies, instruments, electronics, tools, avionics, books, maps and charts, and other pilot supplies at prices that meet or beat other major aircraft supply discounters. There's even nifty stuff here for the nonflyer, such as pedal planes for kids, wall thermometers, and aviator sunglasses. Be sure to take a look at their full online catalog for more specials.

SPECIAL FACTORS: Satisfaction guaranteed.

American Automobile Brokers, Inc.

24001 Southfield Rd., Suite 110   248–569–5900
Southfield, MI 48075   Fax: 248–569–2022

   Information: price quote
   Pay: check or MO (see text)
   Sells: new vehicles
   Store: same address; Monday to Friday 10–6

Let your fingers do the walking next time you're ready to buy a car. In business for over 30 years, American Auto Brokers, Inc. sells and leases domestic and foreign cars, trucks, and vans at discounted prices and has your dream vehicle factory-delivered to a new-car dealership near you with the paperwork done, ready to drive away. The customer, be it an individual, business, or corporate fleet account, typically knows the kind of vehicle he or she wants. You call or write with complete details of the auto, including options, and American Auto Brokers will arrange the buy or lease transaction for less money than you'd get elsewhere. Your savings depend on the prices in your area. Test-drive your car and get a quote from a local dealer, then see how much American Auto Brokers can save you. The price includes dealer prep, full factory warranty, and manufacturer's rebates and incentives when applicable. Financing is also available. Most domestic and foreign makes are brokered. The first quote is free; extra quotes are $5 each. *Be sure to send a self-addressed, stamped envelope when requesting a quote form, and when sending it back for the quote.*

SPECIAL FACTORS: Price quote by phone or mail with American Automobile Brokers quote form (include SASE); checks and money orders are accepted for deposit only—balance payable by certified check, cashier's check, or wire transfer.

The Benz Bin

888–MB–TECHS   **Fax: 609–883–3178**
609–883–9316

Information: website, no print catalog
Pay: check (see text), V, MC, AE, DSC,
Sells: Mercedes Benz auto parts
Store: online only; phone hours Monday to Friday 9–5:30
  EST
Online: www.thebenzbin.com

When I clicked on "Officecam" at The Benz Bin's website, I saw three guys—one happily chatting on the phone, another engrossed in his computer, and a third on the phone listening intently. The images are updated live during business hours every ten seconds. (I'm glad the world isn't watching *me* work.) At Benz Bin it's obvious that what you see is what you get: one-on-one, personable service. This company specializes in selling parts and accessories for Mercedes Benz automobiles at wholesale prices. If you order your part through The Benz Bin, you'll save up to 50%. One nice feature of the website: the list price and Benz Bin's price side-by-side so you can readily see your savings. Check out the website specials and online catalog, then call the guys at The Benz Bin to ask questions or place your order. There's no online ordering, but the website does feature a form you can fill out to register the part you need (in case you don't see it online) that you can submit electronically.

SPECIAL FACTORS: Free technical advice given; satisfaction guaranteed.

Car Racks Direct

80 Danbury Rd.
Wilton, CT 06897

800–722–5734
Fax: 203–761–0812

Catalog: free
Pay: check, MO, MC, V, AE
Sells: vehicle racks
Store: same address; Monday to Friday 10–6 EST
Online: www.outdoorsports.com

For seven years, Car Racks Direct, the mail-order division of Outdoor Sports Center in Wilton, Connecticut, has been selling racks, parts, and accessories for carrying skis, canoes, kayaks, bikes, sailboards, luggage, and lumber on motorized vehicles. In stock are products by such recognized manufacturers as Thule, Yakima, and Rhode Gear, and if you find a lower published price on any product, Car Racks Direct will match it—even after 30 days. A visit to the website presents a clear explanation of the products available, the list and discounted prices, and information on how to order, whether you choose to do so online or by printing out the onscreen form and mailing your order in. Car Racks Direct has over 500 fit kits in stock to accommodate "any VW Bug, hummer, or land yacht."

SPECIAL FACTORS: Prices quotes by phone or letter; authorized returns accepted.

Central Michigan Tractor & Parts

2713 N. U.S. 27
St. Johns, MI 48879

800–248–9263
517–224–6802
Fax: 517–224–6682

Catalog: free
Pay: check, MO, MC, V
Sells: used, new, and rebuilt parts for tractors, combines, and cotton pickers
Store: mail order only; phone hours Monday to Friday 8–5:30, Saturday 8–3
Online: www.worthingtonagparts.com

The bad news is that your tractor or combine is ailing. The good news is that when you buy new, used, reconditioned, and rebuilt parts from Central Michigan Tractor & Parts, you're likely to save as much as 50% and get a 30-day guarantee to boot. Central Michigan stocks items from starters to cylinder blocks and overhauls rebuilt parts so completely as to get them functioning as well as new ones. While they stock parts for machines made by every major manufacturer, if you need a part that isn't in stock, Central Michigan, a member of the "Parts Express Network," can place the item on a list that circulates among twelve other member firms. The website has a number of interesting features, including an online appraisal form for your equipment, a free classified ads section, and information on antique tractors. There's no online inventory or ordering, however.

SPECIAL FACTORS: Price quote by phone or letter; C.O.D. orders accepted.

Cherry Auto Parts

5650 N. Detroit Ave.
Toledo, OH 43612

419–476–7222
Fax: 419–470–6388

Information: price quote
Pay: check, MO, V, MC, DSC
Sells: used and rebuilt parts for imports and Chrysler-Jeep-
Eagle cars and trucks
Store: same address; Monday to Friday 8:30–5, also
25425 John R Rd., Madison Heights, MI (Detroit area);
Monday to Friday 8:30–5
Online: www.cherry-auto.com

I have to admit that I was skeptical about buying a car part through the mail. But earlier this year when I was spiffing up my old Honda to sell, it turned out I needed a part that was going to set me back more than $200—and that was from a local junkyard. Once I discovered that Cherry Auto Parts had the same part for $50 less—including shipping—I was a convert. With access to more than 1,500 cars a year for parts, this company can supply you with just about any used part for up to 70% off the price of new ones, as well as rebuilt and new parts. For half a century Cherry Auto has specialized in late-model imports, and more recently in Chrysler-Jeep-Eagle drivetrain components (engines, transmissions, axles, steering gears) and electrical, glass, and body parts. You'll find major discounts on parts for Acura, Audi, BMW, all the Chrysler imports (Colts, Raisers, Vistas, etc.), Honda, Hyundai, Isuzu, Jaguar, Land Rover, Lexus, Mazda, Mercedes, Mitsubishi, Nissan, Porsche, Saab, Sterling, Toyota, Volkswagen, and Volvo. For the history of Cherry Auto, log on to their online "Yard Tour," which provides a link to the most recent "Cylinder Head Catalog." You can also access that catalog directly for the thrill of comparing a $300 retail price for a 90–91 Lexus cylinder head with Cherry Auto's $50 CORE price. You can read the plain-language Warranty Information ("A warped or cracked head is the result of a problem—not the cause of one.") and fill in an online Part Inquiry Form. Cherry Auto will contact you when the part comes in.

SPECIAL FACTORS: Minimum order $20; price quote by phone (preferred), e-mail, and letter; all parts "guaranteed in stock at the time of quotation, guaranteed to be the correct part, and in good condition as described."

Clark's Corvair Parts, Inc.

Dept. WBM
Rt. 2, 400 Mohawk Trail
Shelburne Falls, MA 01370

413-625-9776
Fax: 888-625-8498

Catalogs: $5 in U.S. (see text); $6.95 in Canada;
  elsewhere inquire
Pay: check, MO, MC, V, AE, DSC
Sells: Corvair parts
Store: mail order only
Online: www.corvair.com

The world's largest Corvair parts supplier, Clark's Corvair Parts, Inc., has been in business for more than a quarter century. If you own one of these classic cars, you should know that Clark's can save you up to 40% on mechanical parts, upholstery items, trim, and more for your Corvair. When you order a print catalog, you'll receive about three pounds of material: the more than 400-page main catalog, a 170-page specialty catalog (NOS, Performance, and Used Parts), and the current 40-page price list. Clark's stocks nearly every part for Corvairs, some from the original suppliers and others specially made for them, in a number of categories including engine, directional, shifter, transmission, instruments, sheet metal, clutch, harnesses, power top, differential, locks and ignitions, door latches, suspension, turbos, nuts and bolts, steering, generator/alternator, exhaust, brakes, VW conversion, and tools. Clark's also has a good selection of shop manuals, assembly manuals, and other reference books, as well as upholstery sets produced just like the originals, door panels, padded dashes, carpets, top boots for your convertible, cardboard kick panels and package areas, trim and emblems, weather strips, armrests, sun visors, and more. You can order online at the informative and interesting website (read all about the history of Corvairs, including Ralph Nader's unique role), but you still have to have a print catalog to do so, as the inventory is not on the website. If you're a Corvair owner, this catalog will no doubt become your bible.

SPECIAL FACTORS: Price quote by phone or letter; returns accepted; minimum order $10.

Defender Industries, Inc.

42 Great Neck Rd.　　　　　800–435–7180
Waterford, CT 06385　　　　Fax: 800–654–1616

Catalog: free (see text)
Pay: check, MO, MC, V, DSC
Sells: marine supplies, gear, equipment, and clothing
Store: same address; also Defender Marine Supply NY,
　321 Main St., New Rochelle, NY; Monday to Friday
　9–5:45, Thursday 9–8:45, Saturday 9–4:45 (call
　914–632–2318 for hours, October to February)
Online: www.defenderus.com

Defender Industries, marine outfitter since 1938, claims to have the largest selection in boating and "the lowest prices all year long." Sit back with the phone book–sized catalog from Defender and you'll find that many of the hundreds of products offered here are priced 35% or more below retail.

What will you find here? The question more properly should be "What won't you find here?" Defender offers just about anything related to boats and the boating lifestyle: fabrics, knives, paint products, railings, cover accessories, shoes and boots, fishing equipment, pumps, marine stoves and dishes, hammocks, antennae, safety equipment, inflatables, outboard engines, fuel products, navigation instruments, radar systems, books and videos, winches, electrical products, binoculars—and that's just skimming the surface. From anchors to Zodiac life rafts, there's a lot here for those who own or live on a boat, and plenty for those who don't. By the way, if you're needing sunbrellas, boat or sail covers, netting, awnings, pool covers, or the like, Defender has a canvas shop where they've made custom and standard sizes of sewn products in canvas, Naugahyde, Dacron, nylon, and other synthetic fabrics for 60 years. Send a template and sketch for their low price quote.

SPECIAL FACTORS: Minimum order $25; returns accepted within 20 days for refund or exchange.

Discount Tire Direct

7333 E. Helm Dr.
Scottsdale, AZ 85024

800–589–6789
Fax: 602–483–9230

Information: price quote
Pay: check, MO, MC, V, AE, DSC
Sells: tires, wheels, and suspension
Store: call for locations
Online: www.tires.com

Discount Tire Direct is the mail-order division of Discount Tire Co., which has been in business for nearly 40 years. You can call, e-mail, or write for price quotes on wheels and all-season, high-performance, snow, and light-truck tires by name-brand manufacturers. In fact, I did just that last winter to see how buying tires through the mail compares with my local tire discounter. Surprise! Even with shipping added in, this company was less expensive. Getting product and price information at the website is an easy proposition; search available products by the make and model of your car or truck. Special promotions are also featured on the website so it's worth checking out. There's no online ordering; sales reps need to personally check your order to make sure the tire you want is suitable for your vehicle.

SPECIAL FACTORS: Satisfaction guaranteed; returns accepted within 30 days for exchange, refund, or credit.

Honda Parts Wholesale

888–53HONDA

Information: website only, no print catalog
Pay: V, MC, DSC
Sells: new parts for Hondas
Store: phone hours Monday to Friday 8–5 EST
Online: www.hondacarparts.com

You don't have to be a grease monkey to buy discount auto parts. I've never done anything more complicated than check the oil on my Honda, yet I now shop around for the best prices when I need a new part. Let's face it: Unless you're related to your mechanic, chances are he's obtaining car parts from his usual source, which isn't always in *your* best interest. Honda Parts Wholesale sells and ships genuine Honda parts at discount prices to the public. When you call the toll-free number you'll get a helpful sales rep on the other end who can quote you prices on every Honda part. Or check out the website to find listings of accessories and parts for Honda Civics, Accords, Preludes, CRVs, and Passports, as well as current specials. List prices and your cost are side-by-side so you can calculate the savings—around 25% in most cases. If you don't find what you're looking for, call for a price quote. There was no online ordering at the website as of this writing.

SPECIAL FACTORS: Parts shipped within the continental U.S. only.

Racer Wholesale

1020 Sun Valley Dr.,
Dept. WBM
Roswell, GA 30076

770–998–7777
Fax: 770–993–4417

Catalog: free
Pay: check, MO, MC, V, DSC
Sells: auto racing safety equipment
Store: same address; Monday to Friday 9–6 EST
Online: www.racerwholesale.com

Racer Wholesale, in business since 1985, is known among amateur and professional auto racers for impressive discounts—up to 70% off list prices—on auto equipment, safety equipment, and accessories by name-brand manufacturers. Racers can shop here for professional driving suits, gloves, boots, and helmets, and other catalog items such as harnesses, mufflers, canopies, towing equipment, and wide-view mirrors. The catalog runs about 80 pages, so you're sure to find here the auto-racing equipment you need. On the website you can view and order current closeouts and other specials.

SPECIAL FACTORS: Except for special orders, authorized (and unused) returns accepted within 45 days for exchange, refund, or credit (restocking fee applied).

RV Direct

P.O. Box 1499, Dept. 17032
Burnsville, MN 55337–0499

800–438–5480
Fax: 612–894–0083

Catalog: free
Pay: check, MO, MC, V, AE, DSC
Sells: RV equipment and accessories
Store: mail order only

Is a recreational vehicle a means of transportation or is it a state of mind? One wonders when browsing the latest catalog from RV Direct. If you own a camper or RV, this is a great source for enhancing your mobile lifestyle with both utilitarian and really fun luxury items sold at the lowest price anywhere (guaranteed). Here you'll find RV covers, awnings, solar batteries, generators, air conditioners, vents, fans, heaters, security items, water pumps, sanitation accessories, camp stoves and other cooking equipment and accessories, satellites and antennas, lighting, cleaning supplies and machines, automotive and towing parts and accessories, cargo units, electronics, books, and much more.

SPECIAL FACTORS: Authorized returns accepted within 30 days for refund, credit, or exchange.

The Tire Rack

771 W. Chippewa Ave.
South Bend, IN 46614-3729

800-428-8355
219-287-2345
Fax: 219-236-7707

Catalog: free
Pay: check, MO, MC, V, AE, DSC
Sells: tires, wheels, and packages
Store: same address; Monday to Friday 9-4, Saturday 9-3
Online: www.tirerack.com

Tires by mail? That's what I said until I did it myself. Now I'll never schlep over to the discount automotive joint again. My tires were less expensive-including shipping—than the ones I priced locally and arrived in three days to boot. Had I purchased these same tires locally, I would have had to wait seven to ten working days for them to come in. But don't believe me. Check out Tire Rack's website, which is easy to use and will give you all the information you crave—photographs, descriptions, ratings, reviews, tips, and more. You're also welcome to browse the print catalog or call the helpful people at The Tire Rack, who've made serving mail-order customers their main focus. In fact, Tire Rack's own staff tests and rates all new tire models and can offer informed advice on the best tire for your style of driving and your climate. Besides tires, Tire Rack also sells wheels, packages (tires and wheels together, "expertly balanced"), and accessories.

SPECIAL FACTORS: Satisfaction guaranteed; returns of unused merchandise are accepted within 30 days for exchange, refund, or credit.

Trollhattan Auto Parts, Inc.

813 Eastern Blvd., Ste. 102
Baltimore, MD 21221

800–328–7655
410–682–2827
Fax: 410–682–4739

Information: website only, no print catalog
Pay: check, MO, MC, V, AE, DSC
Sells: new parts for Saabs and Volvos
Store: mail order only; phone hours Monday to Friday 8–6
EST
Online: www.cybertroll.com

Everybody and his uncle drives a Saab in Woodstock, New York, where I live. Saabs handle great in wintry conditions, and besides, they're super cool. However, you'll never see me driving one; they're too darn expensive to service. Cruising along the information superhighway the other day I came upon Trollhattan, which will make all Saab and Volvo owners happy. Why? Because this company is devoted to selling Saab and Honda parts at 20% to 50% off dealer list. The website tells you what Trollhattan does sell (lighting, brake, suspension, tune-up, transmission, fuel-injection, air-conditioning, heating, cooling, electrical, drive train, and clutch components) and doesn't sell (body parts, high-performance accessories, trim parts, interior parts, audio equipment, parts for cars older than 1975). They offer 24-hour shipping; orders delivered to home, office, or shop; a few different ordering options (by phone, fax, online, or mail); and free technical support via phone or e-mail. The folks at Trollhattan are friendly and knowledgeable. Give 'em a call next time a deer hoof knocks out your Saab or Volvo's headlight.

SPECIAL FACTORS: Personal checks must clear before your order is shipped; 12-month or 12,000-mile warranty on all parts.

Related Products/Companies

Airline and auto seat belt extenders
- Amplestuff

Auto body refinishing supplies
- Red Hill Corporation

Automotive accessories
- Damark, Overton's, The Sportsman's Guide

Automotive repair/maintenance equipment
- Camelot Enterprises, Harbor Freight Tools, Northern Hydraulics

Boats and water sports gear/equipment
- Bart's, Campmor, Mohawk Canoe, Overton's, SOAR Inflatables

Car security systems
- Crutchfield

Car stereos/speaker systems
- Crutchfield, Gold Sound

Cleaning supplies
- The Cleaning Center

Dog seat belts, car safety barriers, seat covers
- Drs. Foster & Smith, Jeffers, Omaha Vaccine, That Fish/Pet Place, UPCO, Valley Vet

Farm equipment
- Northern Hydraulics

Fishing equipment
- Overton's

Fuel tanks
- Overton's

Horse-themed mudflaps and auto sunshades
- Valley Vet

Infant car seats
- Bennett Brothers

Marine equipment/accessories
- Bart's, Northern Hydraulics, Overton's

Marine optics and weather instruments
- Mardiron

Motorcycle, ATV, minibike, and snowmobile parts
- Manufacturer's Supply, Northern Hydraulics

Online car buying
- Netmarket's AutoVantage

Original vintage political bumper stickers
- John W. Poling

Radar detectors and police scanners
- Beach Sales, J&R Music World, LVT Price Quote Hotline, Percy's

RV equipment
- Northern Hydraulics

Sailboard car racks
- The House

Sheepskin seat and steering wheel covers
- Sheepskin Station

Trailers, trailer jacks, trailer parts
- Northern Hydraulics, State Line Tack, Tool Crib of the North, Valley Vet

Books, Audiobooks, and Periodicals

*Books of all kinds for
all ages; books on tape; and
discount magazine subscriptions*

If there's one thing you should learn from this book, it's that paying full price for books and magazines is absolutely unnecessary. Every company in this chapter offers deals on books of every kind—from elegant coffee-table art books and multivolume encyclopedias to best-sellers and children's books. You'll find brand-new books as well as antiques; you can shop online or through old-fashioned booksellers who deal strictly through the mail and are willing to personally answer your questions and offer recommendations. There isn't a book in existence you won't be able to find here for substantially less than you'd spend at your local bookstore.

Remember that a bookstore is more than just a place to buy books. Many of the vendors in this chapter offer the same kind of service you get at your local bookshop. They'll help you locate out-of-print titles, for example, or recommend books you need or desire on a specific subject.

You won't find every subject category of book listed in the "Find It Fast" section below. Unless the bookseller specializes in one particular genre of books (cookbooks, say, or fine art), you should assume that the general booksellers in this chapter will have books on your topic of choice. If you're looking for mysteries, for example, you'll find them in many forms here: as brand-new books, as unused but "remaindered," or as used books.

If you find yourself commuting or traveling a lot, have vision problems, or just love to keep your hands free while improving your mind, you'll enjoy the audiobook offerings, some of which you can rent instead of buying.

Finally, shave dollars off every magazine subscription you're now carrying with the subscription-services firms. If you have a business that subscribes to several magazines, your savings will be substantial.

Please note: Many if not most of the firms in *Wholesale by Mail and Online* carry books, booklets, guides, and even newsletters on subjects relevant to their businesses. Although some are listed in the "Related Products/Companies" section at the end of this chapter, to list every firm that sells one or two books would be impossible. Therefore, use common sense: If your interest is cooking, see the

"Food and Beverages" chapter for companies that stock cookbooks; for books on health-related subjects, check out the listings in the "Health, Beauty, and Fitness" chapter; for how-to and do-it-yourself books, try some of the firms in the "Home: Building, Renovation, and Upkeep" section, or the "Tools, Hardware, and Shop Machines" chapter, and so on. Happy reading!

Find It Fast

Alternative Culture
- Essential Media

Audiobooks
- Bargain Book Warehouse, Blackstone, The Family Travel Guides Catalogue, Reader's Digest

Children's Activity Books
- Dover Publications

Consumer Publications
- Consumer Information Center, U.S. Govt. Superintendent of Documents

Cookbooks
- Jessica's Biscuit, Reader's Digest, Storey Books

Country Wisdom Manuals
- Storey Books

Do-It-Yourself Books
- Reader's Digest, Woodworkers' Discount Books

Encyclopedias
- Amazon.com, Barnes & Noble, Reference Book Center

Family Travel Guides
- The Family Travel Guides Catalogue

Fine/Applied Arts Books
- Hacker Art Books, The Potters Shop

Graphic Arts Books/Manuals
- Print Bookstore

Hardcover Books
- Edward R. Hamilton, Tartan

Large-Print Books/Magazines
- Reader's Digest, Tartan

Magazine Subscriptions
- Barnes & Noble, Below Wholesale Magazines, Delta Publishing Group

Old, Rare, Used Books
- Strand, Tartan

Publishers Overstock/Clearance/Remaindered
- Bargain Book Warehouse, Barnes & Noble, Bear Mountain Books, Daedalus, Edward R. Hamilton, Tartan

Underground Comics
- Essential Media

University Press/Scholarly Publications
- Barnes & Noble, Daedalus, The Scholar's Bookshelf

Amazon.com

P.O. Box 80387
Seattle, WA 98108-0387

800-201-7575 (not for orders)
206-346-2992
Fax: 206-346-2950

Information: website only, no print catalog
Pay: check, MO, MC, V, AE, DSC
Sells: books, CDs, and videos
Store: online only; phone hours Monday to Friday 8–7 PT
Online: www.amazon.com

Amazon.com figured out early on that many of us busy consumers would rather shop in our pajamas. This virtual bookstore has 2.5 million titles, a wealth of reviews, personal recommendations, author interviews, excerpts, and much more. Plus you'll enjoy savings of 20% to 40% on hundreds of thousands of titles at Amazon.com. The "Gift Center" offers recommendations for readers of all tastes and ages, as well as Amazon.com accessories such as mousepads, T-shirts, and hats. When I recently bought three books at Amazon.com, they were in my country mailbox two days later! Not only is this a good place to buy books at a discount, but it's a godsend for writers and others who are looking to find references and sources on any subject, since you can search by author, title, subject, or keywords. Amazon.com has branched out into the entertainment field with CDs and videos in addition to books. The CDs are especially of interest, as shoppers can hear selections before buying (assuming that you have audio capabilities on your computer). Neat, huh?

For those of you who are wary about shopping on the web, Amazon.com guarantees that every credit card purchase is 100% safe. But if you prefer, you can complete the order form except for the credit card information and then call that number in, or fax or mail the order form the old-fashioned way. The website has an extensive FAQ section and customer service information, but unlike other web-only shopping sites, you can also call the Amazon.com staff to have a real human being answer your questions.

SPECIAL FACTORS: Satisfaction guaranteed; returns accepted within 15 days for exchange, refund, or credit.

Bargain Book Warehouse

Soda Creek Press
P.O. Box 8515
Ukiah, CA 95482–8515

800–301–7567
707–463–1351
Fax: 800–949–4946
Fax: 707–463–2072

Catalog: free
Pay: check, MO, MC, V, AE, DSC
Sells: clearance and publisher's overstock books
Store: mail order only
Online: www.sodacreekpress.com

The "Bargain Book Warehouse" (BBW) catalog from Soda Creek Press offers 88 pages of current and out-of-print titles priced up to 80% off regular retail. Mysteries and whodunits, adventures and thrillers, Westerns, biographies, historical novels, romance, science fiction, fantasy, books for kids—these are a few of the genres you'll find here. Each title's listing includes a brief plot summary, page count, the publisher's price, and BBW's discounted price. There's also a small selection of books on cassette and videos here. The website offers daily specials, online ordering, as well as a larger and more up-to-date inventory.

For mystery and romance lovers out there, Soda Creek offers two other catalogs: "Mysteries by Mail" and "Manderley." While the savings aren't as great as those in Bargain Books Warehouse, there are a number of ways the avid reader can still save. You'll still get 10% off all hardcovers, and 20% off best-sellers. And a "Baker's Street Dozen" will get you a thirteenth book free if you order a dozen romance or mystery novels. You'll find these two catalogs on Soda Creek's website alongside Bargain Books Warehouse.

SPECIAL FACTORS: Satisfaction is guaranteed; returns are accepted for exchange, refund, or credit.

Barnes & Noble Books by Mail

One Pond Rd.
Rockleigh, NJ 07647

800-THE-BOOK
Fax: 201-767-9169

Catalog: free
Pay: check, MO, MC, V, AE, DC, JCB
Sells: books, cassettes, videos, gifts, etc.
Store: call main number for nearest location
Online: www.barnesandnoble.com

For more than 120 years Barnes & Noble has been presenting readers with the best in new and unusual titles featuring the latest hardcover releases, hard-to-find paperbacks, publishers' overstocks, remainders, and books from small publishers and university presses at savings up to 80%. Every issue of the catalog offers hundreds of books in a spectrum of subject categories including history, mystery, the arts, science, literature, film, medicine, biographies, satire, juvenilia, current fiction, linguistics, religion, reference, crafts, self-help, and photography. Keeping pace with technology, Barnes & Noble has a fabulous website as well, where browsers can find books, magazines, and software at the same great discounts. Subscribing to your favorite magazine through Barnes & Noble will yield savings around 79%.

SPECIAL FACTORS: Satisfaction guaranteed; returns accepted; library and school discounts available.

Bear Mountain Books

Woodbury Common   **914–928–7565**
Central Valley, NY 10917   **Fax: 914–928–3396**

Information: website only, no print catalog
Pay: check, MO, V, MC, AE
Sells: books, music CDs, videos, and CD-ROMs
Store: same address; Sunday to Wednesday 10–6,
  Thursday to Saturday 10–8
Online: www.bargainbooks.com

Bear Mountain Books & Music, which has been in business since 1974, sells all their books at 20% to 70% off, music CDs for $4.98 each, videos at $2.98, and CD-ROMs for as little as $3. The selection is broad but not deep. It only takes a moment to scroll through the website to see what's currently in stock. It's a little bit like shopping your favorite bargain store—worth checking out because from time to time you'll find what you've desperately wanted at a price that's a real steal. The book categories include art/photography, business/investing, children's, cooking, computers, fiction, history/biography, self-enlightenment, and more. *USA Today* was "stunned and awestruck" by the classical CDs at only $4.95. The music categories run from dance, ethnic, and international to jazz, blues, and big band, with lots in between. The CD-ROM selections included children's, general, graphics, utilities, and entertainment and game. If you're into exercise videos, the current site had a long list of available videos for less than $3 each. By the way, if you want the bookstore to order a title not listed on the website, you'll still get a discount: 20% off paperbacks, 30% off hardcovers.

SPECIAL FACTORS: See website for list of foreign countries to which company can ship, as well as other shipping policies and costs; order by fax, mail, phone, or online.

Below Wholesale Magazines

1909 Prosperity St.,
Dept. WBM
Reno, NV 89502

800–800–0062
Fax: 702–785–7509

Price List: free
Pay: check, MO, MC, V, AE, DSC
Sells: magazine subscriptions
Store: mail order only
Online: www.magazinediscounts.com

With access to over 1,000 magazines, Below Wholesale Magazines offers "the deepest discounts in America. Period." This translates into savings up to 90% off newsstand prices. If you order from them and then find a lower authorized price, they'll match it or credit you with 125% of the difference! With this kind of deal, it seems crazy to subscribe to magazines the normal, old-fashioned way, doesn't it? Below Wholesale has a four-page brochure they'll send you for free, or you can check out the website with its alphabetical listings and online ordering capabilities. Either way, if you don't see what you're looking for, call; chances are Below Wholesale Magazines can get it for you. Self-employed professionals such as doctors, dentists, lawyers, etc. are offered even deeper discounts here and should inquire about the terms.

SPECIAL FACTORS: Satisfaction guaranteed; gift service available; allow 12 weeks for first issue to arrive.

When my mother, an avid reader, had cataract surgery, she was unable to read for several weeks. I wish I had known about Blackstone Audiobooks, with the guaranteed lowest prices on full-length (unabridged) high-quality audiobooks. The 148-page catalog is closely printed, with hundreds and hundreds of titles. Blackstone's catalog is organized alphabetically by category, including 20th-century fiction, poetry, children's (great for those long car trips or troubled sleepers), science fiction and fantasy, baseball, business, religion, speeches, plays, Civil War, biography, and many others. The cassettes are for purchase or for rent—usually for 30 to 45 days, depending on the book length. The rentals average around $8 to $10 for children's, or $10 to $15 for adults', which isn't much per day. Owner Craig Black says his audiobooks are about 15% to 20% lower than comparable recordings, and he also offers used audiobooks for 50% off. There are quantity discounts for individuals on purchases and rentals (rent three books, get an additional 10% off, for example), monthly specials, and discounts for libraries and wholesalers (inquire). See the catalog for details on shipping and returning rentals. Blackstone's user-friendly website features online buying or renting, whichever you prefer, and an easy-to-access table of contents.

SPECIAL FACTORS: Different shipping rates apply outside the contiguous 48 states.

Consumer Information Center

P.O. Box 100
Pueblo, CO 81002

888–878–3256
Fax: 719–948–9724

Catalog: free
Pay: check, MO, MC, V, DSC
Sells: consumer publications
Store: over 1,300 Federal Depository Libraries nationwide
  (see text)
Online: www.pueblo.gsa.gov

Established in 1970, the government's Consumer Information Center "helps federal agencies promote and distribute useful consumer information." Its 16-page "Consumer Information Center" is full of booklets and manuals on subjects including cars, children, employment, federal programs, food and nutrition, health, housing, money, small business, and travel. Most of the booklets are a dollar or under, and many are free! For example, the "Consumer's Resource Handbook" lists contact names and numbers of trade associations, consumer advocacy organizations, and government agencies where you can seek help with consumer complaints and problems. Or there's "A Guide to Disability Rights Laws" that describes your rights regarding housing, public accommodations, telecommunications, education, and more. Both free! For a mere 50 cents you can obtain "How You Can Buy Used Federal Personal Property," which tells about used equipment and industrial items sold by the government. If your ex is a deadbeat dad, there's a booklet describing whom you can contact to get that back child support. If you're concerned about the Y2K problem and how it might affect you, there's a booklet on that too. From pruning your trees to saving energy costs, help is here and it's quite inexpensive. Log onto the website to see the full selection as well as the full text of most of these booklets, view the text of other consumer publications, get the scoop on current consumer news, find links to other helpful websites, and order the Center's booklets online.

Spanish-speaking consumers: A Spanish-language catalog is available.

SPECIAL FACTORS: A $2 handling fee is charged on all orders.

Daedalus Books and Music

P.O. Box 6000 (WBM)
Columbia, MD 21045–6000

800–395–2665
Fax: 800–866–5578

Catalog: free
Pay: check, MO, MC, V, AE, DSC
Sells: book overstocks and remainders, music CDs
Store: mail order only
Online: www.daedalus-books.com

There's a lot of competition out there between booksellers, so a company has got to be good to make it these days. Daedalus has been around for nearly two decades selling new and remaindered books up to 90% off the original publishers' prices. Why buy books hot off the press? If you can defer your gratification, you'll be able to buy the best books around at unbelievable savings. Daedalus has books of fiction, poetry, and literature, books for children, books on travel, food and health, gardening, crafts, the arts, history, religion, politics, science, and more. The 48-page catalog has cover photos and detailed reviews, as does the website, which also features online ordering. Audiophiles will love the selection of music CDs: classical, jazz, hard-to-find European recordings, and more offered at greatly discounted prices.

SPECIAL FACTORS: Institutional accounts available; returns accepted within 30 days.

Delta Publishing Group/Magazine Warehouse

1243 48th St.
Brooklyn, NY 11219

800–SEND–LIST
718–972–0900
Fax: 718–972–4695

Catalog: free
Pay: check, MO, MC, V, AE, DSC
Sells: magazine subscriptions
Store: mail order only

How can Delta Publishing Group, a.k.a. Magazine Warehouse, sell you the same magazines for much lower prices than the publishers and clearinghouses? Delta's brochure explains: (1) their warehouse is stocked with over 850 titles, rather than devoted to only one title; (2) they don't spend money on glitzy ads, spokespersons, or gimmicks (read: sweepstakes); (3) they save money by requiring prepayment to avoid good customers subsidizing "deadbeats"; and (4) they cut down on paperwork and staff because 90% of their customers order several magazines for several years, and therefore only get one infrequent renewal notice. Now that you know why it's cheaper, know also that Delta will save you up to 80% on just about any magazine subscription. If you're getting magazines for your office waiting room, Delta will keep track of all your subscription renewals for free. Membership in Delta's 800–SAVE–SAVE Club also gives you discounts on how-to videos, self-help books, CD-ROM software, travel, and phone calls, and more.

Please note that some titles require a "trade" address as well as a business name, letterhead, and/or business card. Magazines will be mailed to that address only. Be sure to mention WMO when you call 800–SEND–LIST or write for price list.

SPECIAL FACTORS: Lowest price guaranteed.

Dover Publications, Inc.

31 East 2nd St., Dept. MC   **516–294–7000**
Mineola, NY 11501–3582

Catalog: free
Pay: check or MO
Sells: Dover publications
Store: same address; Monday to Friday 8–4; also 180
    Varick St., 9th Floor, New York, NY; Monday to Friday
    9–4:30

One would think I'd become jaded after reading hundreds of mail-order catalogs. But when a good one comes along that offers interesting products and great value, it stands out from the crowd and I only hope I can relay my enthusiasm to the reader. Dover Publications has a really neat catalog. For over 50 years this publisher has specialized in producing imaginative original and classic reprint editions of books in art, photography, commercial art and design, children's books, needlecraft, music, cookbooks, fiction, science, mathematics—you name it. And prices here average—ready for this?—around $5. Many books can be found for $1! Perhaps more exciting even than the great selection of fiction and nonfiction books are the other items. For example, if you're in charge of your organization's newsletter, Dover has copyright-free books of illustrations on every topic, copyright-free photographs, clip-art in books, electronic clip-art, copyright-free graphics specially designed for your copier, instant art stickers, and more. There are books galore on design, ornamentation, calligraphy, every kind of craft and fine art, as well as sheet music, language books, and even wrapping paper, gift cards, postcard books, stickers and seals, and toy, game, and activity books for children, including an entire selection of those old-fashioned delights: paper doll books. This is a great source for parents.

SPECIAL FACTORS: Satisfaction guaranteed; returns accepted within ten days for refund.

Essential Media Counterculture Catalog

P.O. Box 661245
Los Angeles, CA 90066-1245

800-490-5350
310-574-1554
Fax: 310-574-3060

Catalog: $2
Pay: check, MO, MC, V
Sells: alternative/underground books, comics, videos,
   music CDs, etc.
Store: mail order only; phone hours Monday to Friday
   9:30–5 PST
Online: www.essentialmedia.com

In these days of political correctness, it's nice to find folks who are willing and eager to push the envelope on bad taste, rudeness, outrageousness, off-the-grid intellectualism, revolutionary plotting, adolescent thinking, misanthropic behavior, and just plain shocking ideas. The first impression one gets from Essential Media's Discount Counterculture Catalog is that it's smart. The second, that it's fun. If you're a fan of cult videos, underground music, unusual books, comics, and 'zines, you've come to the right place. Some of the notables featured here include Robert Crumb, William S. Burroughs, Marquis de Sade, John Waters, and Timothy Leary. "Queer Culture," UFOs, pirate radio, tattooing, hip-hop, alternative histories, the occult—it's all here in various forms at a discount. The 26-page catalog is a lot of fun to thumb through, and the website, which features online ordering, is equally titillating. Are you a kitsch-hound? A vampire? A computer geek? A drag king? The questionnaire on the back of the catalog is almost as kooky as everything else put together (filling it out entitles you to a free gift). Check it out.

SPECIAL FACTORS: Satisfaction guaranteed; returns in original condition accepted within 30 days for exchange, refund, or credit.

Traveling with children is like having a broken leg: You don't realize how difficult or inconvenient it is until it happens to you. This is due in large part to the fact that the world isn't geared toward children. Wouldn't it be nice to know all the great places that welcome children with special activities, facilities, and rates?

Carousel Press has put together a collection of really helpful, valuable, and inexpensive books that focus on making your next family vacation a memorable one—for the *right* reasons. A current review catalog had books on the best zoos in America, adventuring with children (backpacking, sailing, bicycling, etc.), European trips, great family vacations in every region of the U.S., how to organize a baby-sitting cooperative so you can spend free time *away* from your kids, scary campfire story collections, a child's vacation diary book, and many more. There are a number of clever activity books, educational games, and even children's audiocassettes that would make great gifts. Carousel Press has clearance books that are half-price, although there's nothing offered here that's expensive to begin with. This little catalog is a must for every parent. By the way, a free vanity plate diary is included with every order.

SPECIAL FACTORS: Satisfaction guaranteed; returns accepted for refund, credit, or exchange; international orders must be paid by credit card.

Hacker Art Books

45 W. 57th St.	212–688–7600
New York, NY 10019–3485	Fax: 212–754–2554

Catalog: free
Pay: check, MO, MC, V
Sells: books on the fine and applied arts and related topics
Store: same address; phone hours Monday to Saturday
9:30–6 ET
Online: www.hackerartbooks.com

An avid scholar and publisher, Seymour Hacker opened his Greenwich Village store in 1947. More than a half-century later, Hacker Art Books continues to thrill and impress serious art scholars with its renowned collection of books from America, Europe, and the Far East on the fine and applied arts, architecture, archaeology, and books for collectors. Prices here are from 30% to 60% less than the original publishers' price, welcome news for those of us who love coffee-table art books but can't justify spending the big bucks. This bookstore takes a personal approach to bookselling with thoughtfully written descriptions of each book in the 64-page catalog as well as photographs. On the website you can view the current selection, but at press time there was no online ordering capability.

SPECIAL FACTORS: Minimum shipping charge on international orders is $12.50; maximum shipping charge on orders sent within the U.S. is $25; institutional accounts available; refunds or credits on books returned in good condition.

Edward R. Hamilton Bookseller

Dept. 5166
Falls Village, CT 06031–5000

> Catalog: free
> Pay: check or MO
> Sells: new, closeout, and remaindered books
> Store: mail order only

Bargain books! New, hardbound books are mostly what you'll find in Edward R. Hamilton's monthly catalog, which lists hundreds of high-quality books selling for 75% or more off the original price. Categories include biography, crime, sports, U.S. and world history, politics, Native American culture, religion, travel, archaeology, the occult, gardening, hobbies, animals, cooking, fashion, collecting, fine art and crafts, photography, music, children's books, current fiction, classic literature, science fiction, self-help, psychology, reference, and much more. Hamilton still does business the old-fashioned way—by mail. He keeps costs down by requiring all orders to be prepaid.

SPECIAL FACTORS: Satisfaction guaranteed or your money refunded; shipment to U.S. addresses only.

Jessica's Biscuit Cookbooks

The Cookbook People
P.O. Box 301
Newtonville, MA 02460

800–878–4264
617–965–0530
Fax: 617–244–3376

Catalog: free
Pay: check, MO, MC, V, AE, DSC
Sells: cookbooks and food and wine reference
Store: mail order only
Online: www.jessicas.com

Here's a great idea: a whole catalog devoted to nothing but cookbooks offered to you at up to 50% below original price. Just about everyone can use a cookbook. Jessica's Biscuit Cookbooks has something for everyone: books on ethnic, regional, and international cooking, classic cookbooks from well-known chefs and celebrities, books on desserts, baking, vegetarian cuisine, wine and beer, cake decorating, children's cookery, and many others. The 40-page color catalog is fun to read and even features recipes. Jessica's also sells calendars and food-related posters. Check out the website, where you'll find the entire inventory and be able to order online.

SPECIAL FACTORS: Satisfaction guaranteed; returns accepted.

The Potters Shop

31 Thorpe Rd.   **781–449–7687**
Needham Heights, MA 02194   Fax: 781–449–9098

Catalog: free
Pay: check, MO, MC, V, DSC
Sells: books and videotapes on ceramics and pottery,
  ceramics tools
Store: same address; Monday and Friday 9–12, Tuesday,
  Wednesday, and Thursday 11–5:30
E-mail: sbranfpots@aol.com

Established in 1977, The Potters Shop issues a poster-size catalog that lists hundreds of pottery-related books discounted between 15% and 25%. This is a great source for anyone interested in the subject, in categories that include technical books (clay, glaze, kilns, firing), throwing, hand-building/sculpture, tiles/mosaic, decoration/casting/mold-making, porcelain, health/business/marketing, potters' philosophy, world pottery, children's books, and much more. Dolan tools are also sold here discounted 10%.

Spanish speakers: There are books in Spanish here too.

SPECIAL FACTORS: Defective products will be exchanged; other returns accepted for credit; schools and institutions should inquire about discounts.

Print Bookstore

3200 Tower Oaks Blvd.　　　　**301–770–2900**
Rockville, MD 20852–9789　　**Fax: 301–984–3203**

Catalog: free
Pay: check, MO, MC, V, AE
Sells: books on the graphic arts
Store: mail order only
Online: www.printmag.com

I know a thirty-something waitress who just quit her job to become a full-time freelance graphic designer. These days, if you have talent and the right equipment and software, you can compete with the big design houses right from your own home. The Print Bookstore is a great source for the most important books on graphic design—offered at discounts up to 30%. The 16-page catalog features books on web design, desktop publishing and computer graphics, graphic design, trademarks and corporate ID, type and typography, design and layout, business and careers, computer graphics–training CD-ROMs, and Pantone color manuals. All books are pictured and described in detail. In other words, Print Bookstore is like browsing the best and most up-to-date computer graphics section of an excellent bookstore. You can also subscribe to *Print* magazine here. Check out the website if you'd like to order online or just get a quick view of the books this company carries.

SPECIAL FACTORS: 100% satisfaction guaranteed.

Reader's Digest Association, Inc.

Pleasantville, NY 10570–7000   800–310–6261
TDD: 800–735–4327

Information: website only
Pay: interest-free installments
Sells: magazines, books, audiobooks, CD-ROMs, videos, music CDs
Store: mail order and online ordering only
Online: www.readersdigest.com

Reader's Digest is as American as apple pie. But if you think this company is old-fashioned and only fit for killing time at the dentist office, you haven't checked out the Reader's Digest website. What a fun place to visit! Here you'll get a taste of the various Reader's Digest book, magazine, music, video, and CD-ROM offerings. There's a large-print version of *Reader's Digest*, as well as editions in Swedish, Czech, Portuguese (Brazil), Dutch, and other languages. You'll find the links here to the international Reader's Digest websites, as well as information about how you can subscribe to the magazine, get the "All Products Catalog," or find out about other aspects of the company and what it offers.

This company is really strong on cooking, do-it-yourself, and offering titles on various subjects, from gardening, to do-it-yourself, to children's books, for 20% off—are features of the website. But what really makes the site stupendous is all of the free stuff.

For example, click into How-To Library and you'll find 400 creative projects to make your life easier. The "Home Projects" button lets you search by category to find articles about everything from Asphalt Driveway Repair to Choosing Contractors. Click into "Backyard" to see articles such as How to Play Croquet and Creating Window Boxes. "In the Kitchen" offers advice on Low-Fat Ways to Thicken Stews and Making Herbed Ice Cubes, among other subjects. "Your Health" features short articles on topics from Caffeine and Your Health to Beauty and the Heat ("preventing makeup melt-down").

In another section of the website you can list the ingredients in your cupboards and they'll suggest a recipe to fit what you have! You can also search for any of hundreds of Reader's Digest recipes, or browse the tools, techniques, and tips of chefs and cooks. For the handyperson there's more great (free) stuff here. For example, "Ask the Family Handyman" has answers to just about any problem you have on any topic—in the form of short articles—which you can search for by category.

To find out more about this fascinating company and all of what they offer, check out the website. "Bookmark" this site when you do; you'll be visiting it often.

SPECIAL FACTORS: Online ordering available; any item is returnable; pay in interest-free installments.

Reference Book Center, Inc.

175 Fifth Ave.
New York, NY 10010

212–677–2160
Fax: 212–533–0826

Catalog: $2
Pay: check and MO
Sells: new and used encyclopedias and reference books
Showroom: Monday to Friday 9–5

When it comes time to make that big investment for your youngsters—the family encyclopedia—here's the place to call first. The Reference Book Center is well known to schools and institutions, but few consumers know that this is a great source for current and used encyclopedias and other references—many at bargain prices. Here you'll be able to purchase new sets at less than normal retail—sometimes considerably less; the used sets are even better deals. The 20-page catalog also includes every other type of reference book: English and foreign language dictionaries; children's history, geography, and other reference books; atlases; Shakespeare collections; the Great Books; Indians; mythology; astronomy; and references on many more subjects. But the best bargains are the encyclopedias. If you're into rare or older references, be sure to see the last pages of the catalog for some interesting deals.

SPECIAL FACTORS: Call for details on return policies and shipping rates; wholesale rates to qualified buyers who purchase in quantity (inquire if interested); no C.O.D. orders accepted.

The Scholar's Bookshelf

110 Melrich Rd.
Cranbury, NJ 08512

609–395–6933
Fax: 609–395–0755

Catalog: free
Pay: check, MO, MC, V
Sells: scholarly and university press books
Store: mail order only
Online: www.scholarsbookshelf.com

Here's a bookstore that specializes in university press and scholarly imprint remainders on a wide range of subjects for the serious reader, researcher, teacher, and student. The Scholar's Bookshelf, in business since 1974, sweetens your scholarly pursuits with discounts that average 30% below the publisher's price, although savings can run up to 75%. You'll also find wonderful videos here at a discount.

The general sale catalog has concise descriptions of volumes on philosophy, religion, history, travel, literature, cinema, music, science, reference, and more. Throughout the year The Scholar's Bookshelf produces themed catalogs as well, including "Literature," "Fine Arts Books," "Military History," and "History." The videos offered are the kind of documentaries that would make wonderful teaching or presentation aids on subjects such as World War II and African-American history. If you prefer to shop online, The Scholar's Bookshelf's website features the full inventory and online ordering.

SPECIAL FACTORS: Returns accepted within 30 days for exchange, refund, or credit; minimum order is $10.

Storey Books

Schoolhouse Rd.,
P.O. Box 445
Pownal, VT 05261

800–441–5700
Fax: 800–214–1438

Catalog: free
Pay: check, MO, MC, V, AE
Sells: Country Wisdom Bulletins, books, and videos
Store: mail order only
Online: www.storey.com

Even though I'm a mother myself, I still sometimes call my mother halfway across the country for reminders on how to can tomatoes or how to pleat curtains. Somehow she always knows the answer. But if you're not lucky enough to have a mother like mine, get yourself a copy of Storey Books' catalog of "How-To Books for Country Living." John and Martha Storey have compiled a catalog full of titles "offering good, solid advice to help to achieve a simple, more rewarding style of life." Subject categories include gardening, herbs, natural beauty and health, crafts, cooking, beer, wine, and cider, kids, animals, horses, building, country wisdom bulletins, kits, and videotapes. From raising a calf for beef to creating natural water gardens to making your own perfume, you'll find low-tech approaches to enhance your new-millennium lifestyle. The website features online ordering.

SPECIAL FACTORS: Satisfaction guaranteed; returns accepted for exchange, refund, or credit.

Strand Book Store

828 Broadway   212–473–1452
New York, NY 10003–4805   Fax: 212–473–2591

Catalog: free
Pay: check, MO, MC, V, AE, DSC
Sells: new, old, rare, and used books
Store: same address; Monday to Saturday 9:30–9:30,
   Sunday 11–9:30; also Strand Book Annex, 95 Fulton St.,
   New York, NY (212–732–6070); Monday to Friday
   8:30–8, Saturday and Sunday 11–8
E-mail: strand@strandbooks.com

"Eight miles of books!" The largest used bookstore in the world, Strand stocks thousands of high-quality hardbound books and sells them at the guaranteed lowest prices anywhere. Some are remainders, others "fine secondhand," still others hard-to-find or out of print. Americana, art, children's books, cookbooks, fiction, film and drama, history, literature, medical, music, natural history, religion, science, sports, and travel are among the subject categories. Strand is also known for its rare book collection. The discounts here are really exceptional—up to 50% off publisher's prices. Why buy new? Once you've perused the catalog with succinct, well-written descriptions of every title, that's what you'll be asking yourself.

SPECIAL FACTORS: 100% satisfaction guaranteed; appraisals are available; used books also bought.

Tartan Book Sales

500 Arch St., Dept. 5N	**800–233–8467, ext. 6508**
Williamsport, PA 17705	**Fax: 800–999–6799**

Catalog and Brochure: free
Pay: check, MO, MC, V
Sells: used books
Store: same address (Brodart Outlet Bookstore); Monday
  to Wednesday 11–5, Thursday and Friday 10–6, Saturday
  10–4

Tartan Book Sales, in business since 1960, can bring you the latest in hardcover popular books at discounts up to 75% off the publisher's price. That means if you see a title from "Oprah's Picks" or an author from a best-seller list—John Grisham, Stephen King, Danielle Steel, or Patricia Cornwall, for example—the title is probably listed in the most recent catalog, along with books from such genres as biography, crime, sports, health and self-help, business and finance, and politics. As a direct-mail division of Brodart Co. (a consultant to libraries with collections ranging from less than 1,500 titles to more than 3 million titles), Tartan sells only books that have circulated in libraries across the United States and that have been inspected before being shipped. Sales terms for books purchased for resale or use by an institution are explained in the catalog.

SPECIAL FACTORS: Quantity discounts available; institutional and retail accounts available.

U.S. Govt. Superintendent of Documents

U.S. Government Printing Office
P.O. Box 371954
Pittsburgh, PA 15250-7954

202-512-1800
Fax: 202-512-2250

Catalog: free
Pay: check, MO, MC, V, DSC
Sells: federal government publications
Store: 24 U.S. government bookstores in AL, CA, CO, DC, FL, GA, IL, MA, MD, MI, MO, NY, OH, OR, PA, TX, WA, and WI (see catalog for locations)
Online: www.access.gpo.gov/su_docs

Have you heard about the "IRS Audit Technique Guides"—originally written for IRS revenue agents, but now available to the rest of us—which outline the books and records you must maintain in your industry, and business practices you should follow to avoid a nasty audit? This is just one of the offerings in the current catalog from the U.S. Government Superintendent of Documents. The list of CD-ROMs, periodicals, pamphlets, and books available from the U.S. government is fascinating. The 28-page catalog offers everything from the "Americans with Disabilities Handbook" to the 420-page *Alternative Medicines: Expanding Medical Horizons.* There are handbooks about the history and natural beauty of about four dozen vacation destinations across the U.S.; books on business, health, education, family issues, history, government and public affairs, environment, science, and defense. This is a great source for research materials (for example, the *Census Catalog and Guide),* government information (with an $8 annual subscription to *Consumer Product Safety Review,* you can keep abreast of the latest federal safety actions, studies, and standards involving consumer products), and more. None of the books or pamphlets are free, but many cost under $10 and are real treasure troves of useful information. (Quantity discounts of 25% on orders of 100 of the same title—with some exceptions—are available.) Subscriptions to consumer magazines published by the government can be ordered through the catalog, and there are calendars and a number of posters of American artists' work as well as space shots and maps. The catalog also lists the various website addresses where you can access free government information. On this company's website, you can read about the brochures and pamphlets available, but you have to call or fax your order.

SPECIAL FACTORS: Quantity discounts are available; authorized returns due to government error are accepted within six months for exchange or credit; institutional accounts are available.

Woodworkers' Discount Books

735 Sunrise Circle	**719–686–0756**
Woodland Park, CO 80863	**Fax: 719–686–0757**

Catalog: free
Pay: check, MO, MC, V, AE
Sells: woodworking books, videos, and plans
Store: mail order only
Online: www.discount-books.com

I am looking forward to being old and having time. When I have the time, perhaps I'll pick up a copy of the current Woodworkers Discount Books catalog, or log onto the website, and get myself a book to teach me how to do fine woodworking. This catalog has every kind of book and manual for beginners and experts alike on subjects ranging from furniture-making, clock-making, and boxes, to design philosophy, power tools, and fine home-building. Book prices are discounted an average of about 20%. The website features the full catalog with online ordering, and includes current specials and the very latest editions, so it's worth checking out.

SPECIAL FACTORS: Satisfaction guaranteed; shipping free on three or more items.

Related Products/Companies

Antique phone books
- Phoneco

Art-related books and manuals
- Cheap Joe's Art Stuff, Jerry's Artarama, Daniel Smith, Utrecht

Astronomy atlases, star charts
- Orion Telescopes

Aviation-related books
- Aircraft Spruce & Specialty

Beekeeping books
- Brushy Mountain Bee Farm

Bicycle-repair manuals
- Bike Nashbar

Billiards, game of pool, and darts books
- Mueller Sporting Goods

Boating books
- Defender Industries

Build-it-yourself machines and power tools handbooks
- Poor Man's Catalog

Ceramics/pottery/sculpture books
- Axner Pottery Supply, Bailey Ceramic Supply

Children's books, encyclopedias
- Cook Brothers

Cleaning manuals
- The Cleaning Center

Computer-related books
- H&R Company

Cookbooks and cooking-related books
- ChuckWagon Outfitters, A Cook's Wares, The CMC Company, Gohn Bros., E. C. Kraus, Mountain Ark, New England Cheesemaking Supply, Professional Cutlery Direct, Rafal Spice, Sultan's Delight

Country skills and self-sufficiency themed books
- Lehman's

Craft and hobby books of all kinds
- The Artist's Club, Glass Crafters, Micro-Mark, National Artcraft, Warner-Crivellaro Stained Glass Supplies

Equestrian subjects
- State Line Tack

Field guides, survival and outdoor guides
- Campmor, Mass. Army & Navy

Floral and bridal design, dried-flower and herb craft books
- Billiann's, Caprilands Herb Farm

Gardening, herbs, and farming books
- Butterbrooke Farm, Caprilands Herb Farm, Fedco Seeds, Johnny's Selected Seeds, Mellinger's, Turner Greenhouses

Hatmaking books
- Manny's Millinery

Health-related topical books
- American Health Food, Essential Products, Mountain Ark

Kites and kitesmithing books
- BFK Sports

Knife-use and knife-collecting books
- The Cutlery Shoppe

Large-print books and reading aids for the visually impaired
- Independent Living Aids, The New Vision Store

Library marking tools
- Hot Tools

Logging books, manuals on chain-saw use, etc.
- Bailey's

Military and political topical books
- John W. Poling

Music-related books
- Elderly Instruments, Giardinelli Band Instrument Co., Mandolin Brothers, Metropolitan Music Co., Musician's Friend, Weinkrantz Musical Supply, West Manor

Pet food cookbooks
- Jeffers Pet Supply

Pet subjects of all kinds
- Drs. Foster and Smith, KV Vet Supply, That Fish Place/That Pet Place, UPCO, Valley Vet

Photography references
- B&H Photo-Video–Pro Audio, Poor Man's Catalog, Porter's Camera Store

Preservation supplies for old-book collections
- University Products

Resources for special-needs children
- Special Clothes

Resources related to size-acceptance movement
- Amplestuff

Road-travel guides
- RV Direct

Science and astronomy books
- Orion Telescope Center

Seat-weaving, basketry, upholstery books
- The Caning Shop, Frank's Cane and Rush Supply

Shop, construction, contractor manuals and books
- Fidelity Products, Poor Man's Catalog, Tool Crib of the North, Tools on Sale, Wholesale Tool Co.

Teaching aids for playing bridge
- Baron Barclay Bridge Supplies

Textile arts–related books/manuals
- Atlanta Thread and Supply, Connecting Threads, Dharma Trading, Gohn Bros., Great Northern Weaving, Newark Dressmaker Supply, Sewing Machine Super Store, Sewin' in Vermont, Webs

Water sports–related books
- The House, Overton's Sports Center, World Wide Aquatics

Woodworking, woodcraft reference texts
- William Alden Company, Poor Man's Catalog, Tool Crib of the North, Tools on Sale

Cameras, Photographic Equipment/Services, and Optics

*Cameras and darkroom equipment,
film and film-processing
services, optical instruments*

The companies in this chapter sell cameras, lenses, filters, tripods, lighting equipment, screens, splicers, batteries, and everything else for the amateur or professional shutterbug, including basic darkroom supplies (chemical, paper, film, etc.), darkroom equipment and furnishings, and digital imaging supplies and equipment. Some of the firms here also provide services, from very low cost film processing and custom touch-up work on your prints and slides, to full-scale digital imaging and graphic design for complex photo presentations. And one can't talk lenses without including other optics such as microscopes, spotting scopes, telescopes, and binoculars. If you're looking for just about anything related to cameras and optics, you're in luck—you can save up to 48% by buying through the mail from the companies below.

If video is your thing, you'll find most of the companies that sell video cameras, camcorders, videotape, VCRs, and other video-related goods in the "Music, Audio, and Video" chapter.

The Gray Market and Other Concerns

Years ago, the camera and electronics industries came up against some problems caused by the *gray market*—a market that legally circumvents authorized channels of distribution to sell goods at prices lower than those intended by the manufacturer (the trademark owner); these gray-market goods were originally produced to be sold in other countries. Less expensive than their "authorized" counterparts, gray-market goods have one major disadvantage: They definitely don't come with a warranty that's honored in the United States. They may also be of lesser quality and contain ingredients not approved for use in the United States.

I spoke to one of the oldest firms in this chapter to find out why the term *gray market* has such negative connotations. In short, she explained, companies that sell gray-market goods are unethical *unless they inform customers about what they're buying*. In other words, a gray-market product isn't necessarily bad in and of itself as long as the customer understands the gamble: Buy cheap and take your chances, because there's no manufacturer's warranty. She told me you should be very suspicious of a name-brand camera, for example, that's sold for a hundred dollars less in one place than another. Find out why, she urged. A vendor who doesn't advertise the product's real origins up front isn't worthy of your business.

If you see such an item sold at an unbelievably low price, just make sure the vendor is an authorized distributor and that the product has a valid warranty honored by the service centers of the U.S. manufacturer. Some merchants offer gray-market products with a store warranty equal to the original manufacturer's, which may end up being a good deal as long as you're happy with the quality of the product. Don't forget: Buying by credit card is always a good way to get certain protections under the Fair Credit Billing Act.

While gray-market activity has abated somewhat, another form has become prevalent—"diversions" of products from the authorized path, say by a wholesaler or mass merchant. In this case, the product was intended for the U.S. market, but not for the store in which it's sold. This isn't always bad; the consumer benefits, for example, when major department stores buy in enormous quantities to get the lowest possible price, and then resell the surplus "out the back door" to other stores and discounters. The problem is that the manufacturer might not assume any liability for the product's poor performance if that product wasn't sold to you by an authorized dealer. If you're a lot more cautious than I am— Where did I put that warranty?—take the time to contact the manufacturer about the model you've chosen and find out what's normally included with the item— case, lens, cap, strap, coupons, etc.—and especially if there's a manual that's supposed to come with it explaining proper use and care. Most manufacturers have toll-free numbers and websites.

Find It Fast

Binoculars, Telescopes, Microscopes
- Ewald-Clark, Mardiron, Orion

Cameras and Photography/Darkroom Equipment
- B&H, Ewald-Clark, Mystic, Porter's

Digital Imaging Equipment
- B&H, Porter's

Digital Imaging Services
- ABC Photo

Film and Slide Processing
- ABC Photo, Ewald-Clark, Mystic, Owl Photo

ABC Photo & Imaging Services, Inc.

9016 Prince William St.,   703–369–1906
Dept. WBM   Fax: 703–631–8064
Manassas, VA 22110

Catalog: $3, refundable
Pay: check, MO, MC, V, AE
Sells: film processing services
Store: same address; Monday to Friday 9–4:30
Online: www.imageabc.com

Maybe you have a friend with a high-quality scanner. Maybe you know someone else who's a whiz with the computer and has some fancy graphic design software. And maybe there's a photo studio in the next town over with a retouching genius who's there on Fridays. That's all well and good, but if you're needing to create high-quality presentation materials bringing together slides, posters, photographs, and graphic design, you're going to need photo and imaging services all under one roof. I have to confess that some of the language in ABC ("Always Better Color") Photo & Imaging Services' catalog and website were a bit too technical for me. However, what came through loud and clear were ABC's commitment to excellent service, competitive pricing, and attention to detail.

ABC is a full-service professional and commercial mail-order photo and digital imaging lab that offers computer graphics; scanning and digital imaging; large-format digital prints direct from digital files; total exhibit support services for trade shows and exhibits; extensive film processing and photo-finishing services; customized printing and production including complicated photo-composite displays; large-volume print orders; and finish and detail work including mounting, laminating, and production. Whether you're a professional wedding photographer or a business person launching a new campaign, this company can give you the personal service you require from the comfort of your own home or office, at prices that rival a comparable metro-area lab—if you could even find one this good. The website is informative, but you still need to talk to a customer service person by phone.

SPECIAL FACTORS: Liability for damaged or lost film is limited to replacement with unexposed film; call customer service to obtain special free mailers.

B&H Photo-Video-Pro Audio

420 Ninth Ave.
New York, NY 10001

800–947–9950
212–444–6600
Fax: 800–947–7008
Fax: 212–239–7770

Catalog: free
Pay: check, MO, MC, V, AE, DSC
Sells: equipment and supplies for photography and imaging, video and pro-audio
Store: same address; Monday and Tuesday 9–6, Wednesday and Thursday 9–7, Friday 9–1, Sunday 10–4:45, closed Saturday
Online: www.bhphotovideo.com

If you're a photographer living in the New York metropolitan area, you already know about B&H. This company has been "the professional's source" for more than two decades. Today you'll find low prices, good service, and one of the largest inventories of photo, video, audio, and imaging equipment on the face of the globe.

Whether you prefer the website or the print catalog (104 closely printed pages at last count), B&H caters to the mail-order crowd with an experienced sales force ready to help you negotiate the incredible spectrum of products: photography equipment, including large-format options for both studio and field operations; every imaginable accessory, from tripods and lights to umbrellas and stands; darkroom equipment and supplies; video equipment suited for professionals as well as home hobbyists; computer equipment such as scanners, nonlinear editing apparatus, and hardware and software; and pro audio equipment such as high-end microphones, earphones, and mixing devices. The used division is where you'll find incredible deals, as well as the Specials section only found on the website.

SPECIAL FACTORS: Gray-market goods are not sold without the consumer's knowledge, and these come with a B&H warranty; satisfaction guaranteed; authorized returns accepted for refund, credit, or exchange.

Ewald-Clark

17 W. Church Ave.
Roanoke, VA 24011

540–342–1829
Fax: 540–345–9943

Information: price quote only, no catalog
Pay: MO, MC, V, AE, DSC
Sells: cameras, darkroom equipment, optics, services, and repairs
Store: same address; Monday to Friday 8:30–5:30; also Bedford, Blacksburg, and Salem, VA

Since 1949, photographers have turned to Ewald-Clark, a full-service photography center, for the latest in cameras, lenses, accessories, darkroom equipment, and finishing services. A source for binoculars as well, Ewald-Clark offers an average discount of 30% off list prices. They carry major brands including Amphoto, Beseler, Bogen, Bronica, Canon, Fuji, Gitzo, Gossen, Gralab, Ilford, Kodak, Logan, LowPro, Minolta, Nikon, Novatron, Olympus, Pelican, Pentax, Polaroid, Quantum, Ricoh, Samyang, Tamrac, Tamron, Tiffen, Varta, and Vivitar. But you won't find them in an Ewald-Clark print catalog. That's because there is no catalog: Prices on specific models (including digital cameras) are *quoted by phone or by letter* (be sure to include an SASE). Rates and specifications on custom photofinishing services are available the same way. A website was in the works at press time. As long as you've done the footwork, it can't hurt to call; shopping by price quote can save you a bundle.

If your purchase is being shipped to a destination outside the United States, it will be subject to regulations covering hazardous materials.

SPECIAL FACTORS: Prices quoted by phone or by letter, with self-addressed stamped envelope.

Mardiron Optics

The Binocular Place　　　　　781–938–8339
4 Spartan Circle, Dept. WBM
Stoneham, MA 02180–3230

　Manufacturer's Brochures and Price List: $1, refundable
　　with first order
　Pay: check or MO
　Sells: binoculars, telescopes, microscopes, etc.
　Store: mail order only

I love companies with attitudes like this one. Mardiron sells high-quality products at a discount—up to 48% off—in the belief that "a customer well served is often a source of future referrals." Look no further (pardon the pun) if you're in the market for binoculars, spotting scopes, astronomical telescopes, range finders, microscopes, theater glasses, night vision binocs and scopes, rifle and pistol scopes, and marine and weather instruments from the best-known manufacturers.

　　Mardiron carries all models in current production. If you can't find what you need, they'll have it shipped to you directly from the manufacturer. Recently discontinued or superseded models are further discounted, are in perfect condition, and are sold with the manufacturer's new-product warranty. At this time Mardiron does business the old-fashioned way: by phone or mail.

SPECIAL FACTORS: Price quote by phone; shipping free within the continental U.S.

Mystic Color Lab

Mason's Island Rd.　　　　　800–367–6061
P.O. Box 144　　　　　　　　860–536–4291
Mystic, CT 06355–9987　　　Fax: 860–536–6418

Catalog and Mailers: free
Pay: check, MO, MC, V, AE, DSC
Sells: film-processing and enlargement services
Store: same address; Monday to Friday 9:30–5:30
Online: www.mysticcolorlab.com

I'll often hold onto a roll of exposed film for months before I get around to taking it to the local drugstore, filling out the form and mailer, and then returning several days later to pick up my envelope of poor-quality pictures. As I'm learning, there's a better way. Although perhaps not as cheap as your local drugstore counter that runs frequent twofer and other specials, Mystic Color Lab nevertheless beats most other competitors' prices. (It was about 20% cheaper than other online photo labs I price-checked at press time.) Best of all, the whole photofinishing process can be accomplished by mail. Since 1969 this film lab has wooed customers with free mailers and shipping, a 24-hour turnaround time, and good prices and policies. The website has some nifty features, including an option that allows you to send Mystic your film, which they scan onto their computer so you can view the images, order reprints, download images into your PC, even have images e-mailed to family and friends. Cool, huh? Besides standard film processing, Mystic also offers custom-printable photo mugs, mousepads, greeting cards, and calendars.

SPECIAL FACTORS: Free shipping; Mystic Print Pledge guarantees your satisfaction—see company's Internet or printed material for details.

Orion Telescope Center

P.O. Box 1815, Dept. WBM   800–676–1343
Santa Cruz, CA 95061–1815   Fax: 831–763–7017

Catalog: free, $5 outside U.S. and Canada
Pay: check, MO, MC, V, DSC
Sells: telescopes, binoculars, and accessories
Store: 89 Hangar Way, Watsonville, CA; also Cupertino
and San Francisco, CA
Online: www.oriontel.com

Orion is America's largest direct source for outdoor optics, namely, telescopes and binoculars. The 104-page color catalog also offers lenses, books and software, finder scopes, monoculars, sporting scopes, mounts and tripods, and lots of other optics-related equipment and accessories. All items in the catalog and full-service website aren't discounted, but with an inventory this large and focused Orion is able to run frequent specials and closeouts that make shopping here worthwhile for the bargain hunter. You can find fantastic deals on the website on seconds (not quite new but otherwise fully functional) and discontinued (new but unused) merchandise; both come with warranties. If you're thinking about dropping some serious bucks on a telescope for your kid, why not save about 45% and buy her last-year's model (just in case she was really hoping for gymnastics lessons).

SPECIAL FACTORS: Satisfaction guaranteed.

Owl Photo Corp.

701 E. Main St.　　　　　　　580–722–3353
Weatherford, OK 73096　　　　Fax: 580–722–5804

Mailers: free
Pay: check, MO, MC, V
Sells: film processing and reprinting services
Store: same address; Monday to Friday 7:30–5, Saturday
　9–1

Talk about great deals! It would be hard to find any place—mail order, Internet, or local one-hour joint—with prices lower than Owl's for color and black-and-white film processing. Just give them a call with your name and address and they'll send you free mailers and their current price list. Reprints and film are available here as well. Owl uses high-quality Kodak paper and chemicals. Give the friendly staff a call if you need a price quote on other photo-finishing services.

SPECIAL FACTORS: Satisfaction guaranteed; free shipping.

Porter's Camera Store, Inc.

P.O. Box 628　　　　　　　888–PORTERS
Cedar Falls, IA 50613　　　319–268–0104
　　　　　　　　　　　　　Fax: 800–221–5329

Catalog: free (see text)
Pay: check, MO, MC, V, DSC
Sells: photographic, darkroom, video, and digital-imaging
　equipment and supplies
Store: 323 Viking Rd., Cedar Falls, IA; Monday to Saturday
　9:30–5:30
Online: www.porters.com

Porter's Camera Store has been selling photographic and darkroom equipment since 1914. The 128-page tabloid-style "Photo Video Digital" catalog pictures thousands of items both amateur and professional shutterbugs and videoheads will appreciate—including many hard-to-find and unusual items—at prices slashed by 60% and more on many products. Porter's makes the shopping fun by running contests (the review catalog at the time of this writing featured a free "Dream Photo Kit" worth $1,239), by giving away free stuff (folding scissors on an order of $65 or more, for example, or free film when you order paper), and by offering ridiculously low prices on items with "seven thousand" numbers—coded as such to indicate that Porter's bought these in large quantity and is reselling at greatly reduced prices. Professionals and serious hobbyists will find the major manufacturers and supplies represented here, but there's photography-related stuff here for everyone else too, from kids' craft projects to gifts for grandma.

A click onto Porter's website will give you a taste of what this mail-order enterprise is all about, and you may find some great buys in the final clearance sale items, "priced down to the bone." Orders are taken over the phone or fax; the site isn't set up for online ordering at this writing.

Canadian and other foreign customers, please note: For Canadian customers, the catalog costs $3 in Canadian funds, but orders must be paid in U.S. funds. For other foreign customers, the catalog is $10 payable in U.S. funds.

SPECIAL FACTORS: Authorized returns are accepted; institutional accounts are available.

Related Products/Companies

Archival-quality storage materials for photographs, slides, film, negatives, microfiche, etc.
- University Products

Binoculars and marine optics
- Cook Brothers, Damark, Defender Industries, Hidalgo, RV Direct

Building your own camera and photo equipment handbooks
- Poor Man's Catalog

Cameras
- Bennett Brothers, Damark, J&R Music World

Digital imaging and slide processing
- Visual Horizons

Film
- Beach Sales

Hunting optics and binoculars
- The Sportsman's Guide, Wiley Outdoor Sports

Microscopes
- American Science and Surplus, H&R Company

Night-vision goggles
- RV Direct

Photo storage sheets and albums
- 20th Century Plastics

Scanners
- Affordable Photocopy

Slide Projectors
- Visual Horizons

Surplus optics
- H&R Company

Telescopes
- Damark

Underwater cameras
- Berry Scuba, Central Skindivers

Clothing

Women's apparel and hats;
men's and women's outerwear
and work clothing; wedding gowns;
dance wear; army surplus

I recall a famous ex-wife boo-hooing because the alimony payments from her multimillionaire husband would prohibit her from maintaining the lifestyle to which she had grown accustomed. Among her *monthly* expenses: $4,000 for clothing and shoes. Gulp! I've never spent that much on clothing in a year. Then again, *my* goal is to eventually live in a pair of pajamas full-time so I can do all my shopping by mail.

If you're reading this book, dearie, take heart. The companies in this section sell all kinds of clothing for exercising at the gym, knocking about town, tending your garden, dressing up for that important date, accessorizing with flair, and even for getting married in—assuming you have the stomach for it the second time around. If you've had it with rich guys and opt to go slumming downtown incognito, you can even gear up in some army camos. All at tremendous discounts—some as deep at 75% off!

Although there are lots of offerings for men and children in this general section of the "Clothing" chapter, be sure to check out the more specialized "Men's Business Attire" and "Babies and Children" subchapters that follow on pages 124 and 102, respectively. Likewise, if you're specifically shopping for men's or women's shoes or boots, see "Footwear," page 110. Underneath it all, you still need hosiery and underthings. You'll find incredible deals in the subchapter called "Intimate Apparel," page 117.

Those searching for work uniforms (chef's whites, hospital scrubs, janitorial jumpsuits) or everyday clothing such as polo shirts and caps on which to imprint your company slogan should see the "Uniforms and Promotional Products" section of the "Office, Business, and Professional" chapter.

Many other companies in this book offer clothing and footwear. For example, you'll find outdoor and athletic clothing of all kinds in the "Sports and Recreation" chapter; foul-weather gear in "Auto, Marine, and Aviation"; and safety and protective clothing in "Office, Business, and Professional." There's assorted clothing in the "General Merchandise and Good Deals" chapter, and of course many companies sell themed T-shirts. So don't limit yourself to the companies below, and be sure to read the "Related Products/Companies" listings at the end of this and the other sections of the "Clothing" chapter for more ideas.

Find It Fast

Bridal Attire
- Carla's Vintage Wedding Gowns, Discount Bridal Service, Manny's Millinery

Dancewear
- Dance Distributors

Hats
- Manny's Millinery

Men's Clothing
- Bridgewater, Cahall's, DesignerOutlet, Gohn Bros., Mass. Army & Navy, Sportswear Clearinghouse, The Ultimate Outlet, WearGuard

Warm- and Foul-Weather Gear
- Cahall's, DesignerOutlet, Gohn Bros., Holly Raal Textiles, Mass. Army & Navy, The Ultimate Outlet, WearGuard

Women's Clothing
- Bridgewater, Chadwick's of Boston, DesignerOutlet, Holly Raal Textiles, The Ultimate Outlet, Willow Ridge/Bedford Fair

Work Clothing
- Cahall's, Gohn Bros., WearGuard

Bridgewater

Box 1600
Brockton, MA 02403–1600

800–525–4420
508–583–7200
Fax: 800–448–5767
TDD: 800–978–8798

Catalog: free
Pay: check, MO, MC, V, AE, DSC
Sells: women's, men's, and children's clothing and
accessories
Store: mail order only

Bridgewater, a division of Chadwick's of Boston (also listed this chapter), offers fashions for men, women, and kids too at reasonable prices. The ladies' clothing comprises classic separates in nice fabrics such as cotton and rayon, simple dresses for home and office, and casual attire. The men's lines include such basics as chambray shirts and linen/cotton pants. In the children's clothing you might find cotton overalls, bicycle pants in pretty pastels for girls with matching tops, and durable cotton T-shirt/pants combinations. The overall look in Bridgewater is clean, comfortable, tailored, and classic—at prices that are about 25% to 30% lower than the better-known mail-order catalogs.

SPECIAL FACTORS: Satisfaction guaranteed; returns accepted for refund, exchange, or credit.

Cahall's Work Wear

P.O. Box 450–WM

Mount Orab, OH 45154

937–444–2094

Fax: 937–444–6813

Brochure: free

Pay: check, MO, MC, V, AE, DSC

Sells: work clothing and footwear

Store: Cahall's Work Wear Store; 112 S. High St., Mount
Orab, OH; Monday to Saturday 9–6

The Cahall family opened its department store in 1946 and took the leap into mail order nearly 30 years later with heavy-duty apparel and footwear. I love the four-page brochure, which has an old-timey feeling with pictures and descriptions of no-nonsense work items. Cahall's can supply your favorites—jeans, shirts, jackets, two-piece rainsuits, union suits, hats, lined snap-on hoods, overalls, and more—at savings of up to 30% on suggested list or retail prices. Popular lines from Carhartt, Hanes, Key, and other well-known manufacturers are available. Cahall's also offers an excellent selection of work shoes and boots for men and women from Carolina, Danner, LaCrosse, Wolverine, and other names, in hard-to-find sizes. Hush Puppies and Rocky Boot sport boots are also stocked, as well as heavy-duty socks, work gloves, bandannas, T-shirts, and even nail aprons. If you don't find what you're looking for in the brochure, call them and Cahall's may stock it or be able to get it.

SPECIAL FACTORS: Satisfaction is guaranteed; returns are accepted for exchange, refund, or credit.

Carla's Vintage Wedding Gowns

Catalog: website only, no print catalog
Pay: check or MO
Sells: vintage wedding gowns
Store: website only
E-Mail: Gowns4you.com
Online: members.aol.com/gowns4you/index.html

Carla Michaels loves vintage clothing and so do I. In fact, I got married in a gorgeous lace gown circa 1906. It didn't belong to my grandmother; I actually bought it in an antique store in SoHo. Browsing Carla's website reminded me of the fun I had shopping for my dress. Click onto Carla's Vintage Wedding Gowns and you'll be treated to full-color photographs of a variety of gowns from every era and for *every dress size*. Carla explained to me that many of the vintage gowns she seeks out are perfect for women who aren't necessarily built like Twiggy. In other words, women with real busts, waists, hips, and thighs.

The website allows you to sample a few of the gowns currently available. On a recent visit to the website I was treated to a Titanic-era sheer lacy number— definitely for a super-romantic; a satin and lace gown from the 1930s; a shimmering cream-colored satin dress with a long cathedral train, probably 1940s, that you'd almost have to be poured into; even an understated but hip 1960s sleeveless brocade dress. Carla photographs and describes the gowns, including the condition they're in and whether they'll require special cleaning, mending, or care. The dresses are really inexpensive, most well under $500 at this writing. The website is updated regularly, and Carla keeps a supply of photographs if you need to see more goods that aren't on the website before making your decision. (Send your request by e-mail.) You'll be able to afford a fabulous honeymoon with the money you'll save if you fall in love with one of these dresses. If there's a type of dress you're looking for, e-mail Carla's Vintage Wedding Gowns and they'll do their best to find it for you—at a reasonable cost. This small company wants you to be a satisfied customer, so if you have special requests or problems with your purchase, Carla urges you to get in touch with her right away.

SPECIAL FACTORS: Dresses will be reserved for seven days, then shipped once your check has cleared; returns accepted on unaltered dressed within two days of receipt.

Chadwick's of Boston, Ltd.

Box 1600
Brockton, MA 02403–1600

800–525–4420
Fax: 800–448–5767
TDD: 800–978–8798

Catalog: free
Pay: check, MO, MC, V, DSC, JCB
Sells: women's clothing, shoes, and accessories
Store: mail order only

Chadwick's of Boston, "the original off-price catalog," is full of tremendous deals for women. You'll save up to 68% here on darling sweaters, khakis, skirts, jumpers, jeans, trousers, dresses, business suits, blazers, and coats, in materials such as silk, cotton, suede, wool, and rayon. There's also a nice selection of footwear: coordinated-colored pumps, flats, boots, boiled-wool clogs, and more. You won't find a lot of loud prints or outrageous styles in the 82-page color catalog. Chadwick's clothes are appealing, to me at least, because they're classic and understated. You'll find items such as cotton cardigans, mix-and-match silk separates, knock-around rayon dresses, and tea-length A-line skirts—most of them in solid colors, and all very inexpensive. You could build a seasonal wardrobe here for very little money by mixing and matching separates.

Note to plus-sized readers: Chadwick's of Boston has clothes to fit women of every size. If you're 14W to 26W, ask for the "Jessica London" catalog.

SPECIAL FACTORS: Satisfaction guaranteed; returns accepted for exchange or refund; deferred billing available.

Dance Distributors

P.O. Box 11440, Dept. WBM
Harrisburg, PA 17108

800–333–2623
Fax: 717–234–1465

Catalog: free
Pay: check, MO, MC, V, AE, DSC
Sells: dancewear and accessories for men, women, and
   children
Store: mail order only
E-mail: dancedstr@aol.com

Here's a no-fuss catalog that will appeal to anyone looking for an excellent selection of dance shoes, body wear, and accessories for men, women, and children at prices that are consistently about 25% off list. (Regular retail prices are listed alongside Dance Distributors' prices so you can see the savings.) The 38-page black-and-white catalog features photographs and descriptions of shoes (ballet, pointe, dance sneakers, gymnastic, jazz, tap, and more); a wide variety of dance bodywear from the top-name manufacturers; and dance-related accessories such as dance bags, foot-comfort products, and an interactive CD-ROM entitled *Ballet Is Fun*.

SPECIAL FACTORS: 24-hour ordering line; returns accepted, except special orders, within 30 days of receipt, with a $3 reshipment charge for exchanges.

DesignerOutlet

800–923–9915   **Fax: 212–367–7679**
212–989–0778

Information: website only, no catalog
Pay: V, MC, AE, DSC
Sells: designers' overstocks on women's, men's, and
   children's clothing, footwear, jewelry, and accessories
Store: online only
Online: www.designeroutlet.com

Once you discover this site you'll never want to shop anywhere else. If you're a boutique shopper, you've now died and gone to heaven, because DesignerOutlet has ingeniously come up with a way to buy top designer overstocks and sell them to you at greatly reduced prices. This Internet-only store, started by a 15-year fashion industry veteran, can avoid incurring high overhead costs of real estate, catalog printing, and personnel, so the savings are real—to the tune of 35% to 75% off retail. The site is updated every two weeks with new merchandise, new designers, and new categories. Quantities are limited, so if you see something you love, you'd better buy it right away before it disappears into the ether. All items are first quality and guaranteed, and all merchandise is current season.

The site is really easy to use. Just select men's, women's, or kid's, then a designer. Up will pop the current selection—an evening gown, a sweater, a tie, a shirt, a handbag, a watch, pajamas, jewelry, etc. It's kind of like shopping at a rich person's yard sale. Keep in mind that a designer gown here might be marked down 55%, but it's still not going to be cheap. An informed consumer will find this a great place to shop. If you're looking for a specific designer, e-mail your request and the staff will act as your personal shopper and try to find it for you. Happy shopping!

SPECIAL FACTORS: Order by phone, Internet, or fax; company will gladly exchange or credit any purchase that doesn't satisfy you completely; returns must be made within two weeks (details on website).

Discount Bridal Service, Inc.

9037 E. Larkspur Dr.
Scottsdale, AZ 85260

800–874–8794
Fax: 602–998–3092

Information: call for referral (see text)
Pay: varies (see text)
Sells: women's bridal attire
Store: see text
Online: www.discountbridalservice.com

What's the first thing your girlfriend from college asks you when you call to invite her to your wedding (well, maybe the second thing)? "What are you wearing?" And indeed, choosing the right dress is one of the hardest decisions, partly because this is your big day and you want to look flawless, and partly because it will likely end up being one of your biggest expenses. Discount Bridal Service (DBS) can help out. Recommended by dozens of consumer publications and organizations, this is a network of international dealers who live and work in your community. Your part is to thumb through the national bridal magazines until you find one or more dresses you like. Your local DBS dealers can help you select the style, material, fabric colors, and size for you and your bridesmaids. Once you've made your decision, they'll order the dress on your behalf and have it shipped directly to you. Ordering through DBS can save you from 20% to 40%, which translates into hundreds of dollars. DBS can recommend local seamstresses if you need alterations. Since delivery can take from 6 to 30 weeks, start early! If you have access to the Internet, I recommend checking out the website, which has a "frequently asked questions" section that explains this company in detail and how it all works.

SPECIAL FACTORS: Consult with your DBS rep for terms of your sales policy; satisfaction guaranteed.

Gohn Bros. Mfg. Co.

105 S. Main   219–825–2400
P.O. Box 111
Middlebury, IN 46540–0111

Catalog: $1
Pay: check or MO
Sells: general merchandise and Amish specialties
Store: same address; Monday to Saturday 8–5:30

If there's such a thing as a mail-order company that will melt your cold, cold heart, this is it. Gohn Bros. has been offering Amish and plain clothing to everyone for 94 years. I really enjoy getting Gohn's 12-page print catalog every year. It's like stepping into another world, a world where straw hats "for the summer heat," ear muffs, drop-front work pants, men's garters, suspender web by the yard, ladies' black shawls, and children's bloomers are everyday items. Everything sold by Gohn Bros. is reasonably priced; many are items you just can't find anymore. You'll find thermal and regular underwear, work and dress clothing, hosiery, and outerwear for men, women, and children. The women's intimates section has a number of items for nursing mothers. There's also an extensive section for infants. The footwear ranges from men's leather work and dress shoes to women's high-top shoes to children's canvas sneakers. What you'll also love at Gohn are the hard-to-find items such as white crocheted doilies, buggy blankets, flour sack towels, and wooden spool holders. The sewing notions and yard goods are a find unto themselves, featuring cheesecloth, 60-inch-wide denim, and even bandanna fabric.

SPECIAL FACTORS: Satisfaction guaranteed; C.O.D. orders accepted.

Manny's Millinery Supply Center

26 W. 38th St.   212–840–2235/2236
New York, NY 10018   Fax: 212–944–0178

Catalog: $5
Pay: check, MO, MC, V, AE
Sells: hats, millinery supplies, gloves, bridal trimmings
Store: same address; Monday to Friday 9:30–5:30,
    Saturday 10–4:30

Please trust me when I tell you that you're going to fall in love with Manny's Millinery Supply Center when you get the catalog. As soon as I received mine I wanted to buy and make hats, throw a hatmaking party, and change my whole image. Some catalogs merely show products; this one *inspires*. Owner Howard Manny, a real character, will get you smiling with his introductory text.

Manny's has two catalogs. (Your $5 with catalog request will get you both.) The "Basic Supply Catalog" offers millinery items such as straw, felt, hat pins, beading, feathers, tapes, sizing, veiling, ribbons, and other professional millinery supplies and equipment, including horsehair braid, hat stretchers, display heads and racks, hatboxes and travel cases, and cleaning products. The 62-page "Hat" catalog is fabulous and features 400-plus photographed hats—with and without trim. The styles are many, in materials including pari sisol, chenille, velour, felt (both fur felt and wool felt), twisted toyo, and others. Scores of "frames," or fabric-covered hat forms, are offered. The satin frames are suitable for bridal outfits, and the buckram frames provide a base for limitless flights of fancy.

In addition, Manny's hat catalog offers a variety of jeweled, feather, and beaded hat pins; flowers (hat pins) of every conceivable type; trimmings in a dazzling variety, including cording, wired ribbon, wired mesh, lace, and pleated stretch velvet in many designs, colors, and textures; bead, sequin, and rhinestone trimmings; wooden hat blocks and basic crowns; oversize hat forms; and hat trees. Savings vary from item to item, but average 33% below regular retail. By the way, if you're into hatmaking or other crafts projects, check out Manny's five "Surprise Grab Bags" (Rounding Assortment, Feather Surprise, Millinery Madness Surprise, Flower Surprise, Triple Flower Surprise). These are 19 by 19-inch plastic bags crammed full of one-of-a-kinds, remnants, flawed, seconds, or shopworn items, and worth "5 to 10 times the face value of what's in them." They vary in price and are described in detail in the catalog. You can buy them individually, or get three for $35. Manny's also sells two, at this writing, truly excellent books on hatmaking.

Please note: If you're buying hats only, the minimum order is three; if you buy one or two hats, you must also buy $15 in assorted items (frames, trims, etc.); if you're buying assorted items only, the minimum order is $25. There is no minimum book order.

SPECIAL FACTORS: Price quote by phone; minimum order on certain items (see text).

Mass. Army & Navy Store

15 Fordham Rd., Dept.   800–343–7749
BWBM   617–783–1250
Boston, MA 02134   **Fax: 617–254–6607**

Catalog: free
Pay: check, MO, MC, V, AE, DSC
Sells: government surplus apparel and accessories
Store: 895 Boylston St., Boston; Monday to Friday 9:30–8,
    Saturday 12–8, Sunday 12–6; also 1436 Massachusetts
    Ave., Cambridge, MA; Monday to Saturday 10–9, Sunday
    12–8

When I moved to New York City in my early twenties I used to love going down to Canal Street and milling around the army/navy surplus stores looking for deals. Mass. Army & Navy issues a 64-page color catalog full of items that in stores like the Gap command big bucks—such as cargo pants and bomber jackets. But the prices here are a lot less. Because this is surplus, there's no telling what you'll find from month to month. Past catalogs have included items such as camouflage clothing and gear, French and Spanish army raincoats, East German guard boots, U.S. Air Force sunglasses, and Yukon hats. You'll also find bandannas, Levi's jeans, Dockers, knapsacks, camping and survival gear, mess kits, and more. If a vintage gas mask is your idea of a fashion statement, don't shop anywhere else.

SPECIAL FACTORS: Satisfaction guaranteed; returns accepted for exchange, refund, or credit.

Holly Raal Textiles

344 Rt. 28A
Hurley, NY 12443

914–340–1352
Fax: 914–339–2229

Brochure: free
Pay: check, MO, V, MC
Sells: handwoven chenille and hand-dyed velvet scarves
  for women and men
Store: mail order only; phone hours Monday to Friday
  9:30–6 EST

I feel *so lucky* to have found this company. Holly Raal Textiles is a small family business whose handwoven and hand-dyed scarves are sold in famous East Coast boutiques for big bucks. There are still a few, rare business people like Holly who want ordinary people to enjoy beautiful, hand-crafted goods too, even if it means less profit for her company. Holly is permitting readers of this book to buy her scarves at the wholesale price, or 50% off. She's making two of her lines available by mail: handwoven chenille scarves and hand-dyed velvet (60% silk/40% rayon) mufflers and scarves.

In the last few years people have discovered rayon chenille, which is incredibly soft but *weighty*, giving it a luxurious drape. Holly's chenille scarves are extraordinarily plush, densely woven pieces with hand-knotted fringe in an exotic array of colors. The four-page color brochure shows 15 patterns ranging from dark, elegant plaids in earth tones and muted purples to mysterious black-and-sapphire combinations. What's really nice about Holly's weaves is that they're perfectly appropriate for either gender. The chenille scarves are a generous 11 by 70 inches, so they'll drape around your neck more than once and lend warmth or elegance whether worn with a coat or sweater.

The other line consists of scarves (14″ × 70″) and mufflers (8″ × 58″) hand-dyed by Holly in a special process that gives the velvet (in upraised floral or leaf patterns) and smooth silk background contrasting hues. Holly lines them with crepe de chine for weight, warmth, and a finished look. I bought a Holly Raal velvet muffler in black and gray for my sophisticated and choosy New York sister—and she was thrilled. These beautifully accent plain dresses and sweaters. Both mufflers and scarves are available in three textured patterns (leaves, morning glory, and ivy) and 14 hues. You can buy a silk muffler for only $30 here, a silk scarf for $45. The woven chenille scarves are $80 at this writing. Trust me when I tell you you'd be lucky to find chenille scarves of this quality for less than $200 in stores. I'm treating myself to one, and I'm looking forward to having it for a lifetime.

SPECIAL FACTORS: French and Arabic spoken here in addition to English; authorized returns accepted within 15 days of receipt.

Sportswear Clearinghouse

P.O. Box 317746-BWBM　　　　**513–522–3511**
Cincinnati, OH 45231–7746

Brochure: free with SASE
Pay: check, MO, MC, V, DSC
Sells: printed sportswear overruns
Store: mail order only

This is the place for printed sportswear—and I don't mean floral and checkered. Sportswear Clearinghouse sells such items as T-shirts, caps, casual sports shirts, and socks imprinted with company logos, team names, and advertising slogans for 70% less than you'd find in a store. Okay, so you'll be a walking billboard, but you'll save big on clothing you can wear to the beach, on the golf course, when exercising, to school, etc. Blank (nonimprinted) items such as sweatshirts and baseball caps are also available here at good prices. Sizes run from youth XS to adult XXXL.

SPECIAL FACTORS: Satisfaction guaranteed; unused returns accepted within 30 days for refund, credit, or exchange.

The Ultimate Outlet

A Spiegel Company
P.O. Box 182557
Columbus, OH 43218–2557

800–332–6000
781–871–4100
Fax: 800–422–6697
TDD: 800–322–1231

Information: website and free catalog
Pay: check, MO, MC, V, AE, Spiegel charge card
Sells: clothing for men, women, and children, and
   department store goods
Store: Spiegel Ultimate Outlet Stores in CO, FL, GA, IL,
   IN, MI, MN, MO, NV, OH, PA, TX, and VA; call
   800–645–7467 for addresses and hours
Online: www.ultimate-outlet.com

If you're a fan of Spiegel, as American as a BLT on white with mayo, you'll love The Ultimate Outlet, the clearance division of Spiegel. Log onto the website for deals galore on women's and men's apparel, bed and bath items, even children's toys. Selection will vary depending on the time of year and what's being cleared out for the next season, but savings here are fantastic—up to 50% on many items. The emphasis is on name-brand fashion apparel, and the website is one of the nicest around. Just click on a category (women's dresses, for example) and you're transferred to a page of photographs accompanied by descriptions and was-versus-now prices. Want to see that dress in more detail? Just click on the image to zoom in. Ultimate has one of the best returns policies I've seen anywhere, including the option to return the item to any one of 4,000 supermarkets nationwide. I like this company a lot, as you can tell, and particularly because their online store features secure electronic ordering and is so consumer-friendly.

SPECIAL FACTORS: Satisfaction guaranteed; returns accepted for refund or credit.

WearGuard Corp.

Longwater Dr.
Norwell, MA 02061

800–388–3300
781–871–4100
Fax: 800–436–3132

Catalog: free
Pay: check, MO, MC, V, AE, DSC
Sells: work clothing, outerwear, and accessories for both
  genders
Store: mail order only
Online: www.wearguard.com

WearGuard Corp., a national seller of work clothes, uniforms, and outerwear since 1952, offers a full line of durable work clothes and outerwear for both genders at up to 30% off. You'll find even greater savings at the website, where overstocks and clearance items are reduced as much as 50%. WearGuard's offerings include jackets and parkas, work shirts, T-shirts, knit shirts, heavy-duty pants, jeans, coveralls, thermal underwear, gloves, and rainwear. There are items for women too, such as stonewashed jeans and three-season jackets. Boots and work shoes by major manufacturers are available as well as footwear under Wear-Guard's own label.

Since many of WearGuard's products are ordered as employee recognition awards, sales incentives, trade-show giveaways, and logowear for company stores, WearGuard maintains a Custom Logo department that does screen printing and direct embroidery of original logos and designs; in-stock logos and lettering are available too. At the website you can order a catalog, view specials, and see the kinds of items that your company might want to put its logo on, such as blankets, Swiss army knives, and travel mugs.

SPECIAL FACTORS: Satisfaction guaranteed; returns accepted.

Willow Ridge/Bedford Fair Lifestyles

421 Landmark Dr.
Wilmington, NC 28410

800–388–8555, Dept. WBM
(Willow Ridge)
800–964–1000, Dept. WBM
(Bedford Fair)
Fax: 910–343–6859
TDD: 800–945–1118

Catalog: free
Pay: check, MO, MC, V, AE, DSC
Sells: career and casual women's apparel
Store: mail order only

"Unbeatable values!" exclaims text on the cover of Bedford Fair catalog. This source for swingy, inexpensive clothing for women will make you happy with its well-balanced selection of colorful suits, skirts, dresses, and shirt/trouser combos for work and weekends, not to mention shoes, sweaters, stirrup pants, and jackets. Some of the best deals here are the basics—plain acrylic knit turtlenecks, silk blouses, cotton sweaters, A-line skirts, or rayon jumpers that make up the foundation of a fall or winter wardrobe, yet cost about 25% less than what you might pay in stores. Past summer catalogs have featured pastel party dresses, silk blazers, and crocheted sweaters. Sizes range from petite (starting at size 4) up to misses size 20, and women's 18 to 28; a handy measuring table is included in the catalog to help insure proper fit. Look for the sales catalogs, where items are marked down as much as 50%.

SPECIAL FACTORS: Satisfaction guaranteed; returns accepted for exchange, refund, or credit; deferred payment available.

Related Products/Companies

Archival hat boxes
- University Products

Auto-racing suits
- Racer Wholesale

Bathrobes
- Clothcrafters

Bee-themed T-shirts
- Brushy Mountain Bee Farm

Bicycling and other sports apparel
- Bike Nashbar, Performance Bicycle, Spike Nashbar

Bridal lace, silk flowers, and wedding veil fabric
- Billiann's, Newark Dressmaker Supply

Camouflage clothing
- Bowhunters Discount Warehouse

Carhartt clothing
- Valley Vet

Costumes
- Oriental Trading Company

Dog sweaters, parkas, rain slickers
- Drs. Foster & Smith, Jeffers, KV Vet Supply, Omaha Vaccine, That Fish/Pet Place, UPCO

Equestrian clothing
- State Line Tack

Extra-large clothing hangers
- Amplestuff

Faux fur coats and accessories
- Fabulous-Furs, Monterey

Feather marabous, boas, and fans
- Gettinger

General clothing
- Ebay, Make Us An Offer

Government surplus and vintage military clothing
- John W. Poling

Hats and headwear
- Beauty by Spector, Billiann's Floral and Bridal, Lehman's

Hunting and camouflage clothing
- Bowhunter's Warehouse, The Sportsman's Guide, Wiley Outdoor Sports

Outdoor wear
- Bailey's, Campmor, Defender, Sierra Trading Post, The Sportsman's Guide, Wiley Outdoor Sports

Plain, undyed cotton and silk clothing
- Clothcrafters, Dharma Trading Co.

Sheepskin mittens and hats
- Leather Unlimited, Sheepskin Station

Simpsons collectible T-shirts & neckties
- Sunway Co.

Special-needs clothing for adults
- Special Clothes

Stain remover
- The Cleaning Center, Solo Slide Fastener

Swimming and other water sports clothing
- Bart's, The House, Overton's, World Wide Aquatics

T-shirts, sweatshirts, hats
- Cook Brothers

Uniforms for the restaurant, medical, and other industries
- Cheap Aprons/Allstates Uniform, Clothcrafters, Cotton Scrubs, Tafford

Women's apparel
- Make Us An Offer, One Hanes Place, Thai Silks, Utex Trading

Wool and mohair shawls
- Mangham Manor Farm

Work clothing
- Northern Hydraulics, Omaha Vaccine, Tool Crib of the North

Babies and Children

Diapering needs; baby clothes and supplies; clothing and accessories for children; school uniforms

When my son was born, I spent a fortune on tiny matching outfits, little cardigan sweaters, miniature high-top sneakers, down-filled sleeping bags, and on and on. Now that he's a bit older and in school, I'm appalled at how expensive clothing is, and I've definitely learned that buying $30 shoes that he'll fit into for only half a year is fruitless. Thank goodness for some of the companies in this chapter. You can save up to 60% on everything from disposable diapers to velvet-and-lace dresses for your little tykes.

For a wealth of companies in other chapters that offer children's and maternity clothing and accessories, browse "Related Products/Companies" at the end of this section. There are also numerous firms in other chapters that carry various and sundry child-related goods—from children's crafts projects to games and toys to tiny-sized protective beekeeping suits to kids' vitamins. It would be impossible to list them all here, so be sure to browse the relevant chapter if there's something specific you seek (e.g., for children's computer software, see the companies listed in the "Computer Hardware and Software" section of "Office, Business, and Professional"; for children's furniture, see the "Furnishings" section of the "Home" chapter, and so on).

Find It Fast

Baby Slings and Carriers
- Baby Bunz

Cloth Diapers and Covers
- After the Stork, As a Little Child, Baby Bunz

Disposable Diapers
- Diaper Warehouse

Infants' Clothing
- Baby Bunz, Rubens & Marble

School Uniforms
- Iuniforms.Com

Toddlers' and Children's Clothing
- After the Stork, Olsen's Mill Direct

Toddlers' and Children's Shoes
- After the Stork, Olsen's Mill Direct

After the Stork

P.O. Box 44321
Rio Rancho, NM 87174–4321

800–441–4775
Fax: 505–867–7101
TDD: 800–505–1095

Catalog: free
Pay: check, MO, V, MC, AE, JBC, DSC
Sells: children's clothing
Store: mail order only
E-mail: storkmail@afterthestork.com

If you're like me, nothing's too good for your little one. From the time my son was an infant, I've dressed him in 100% cotton. Call me crazy. Now that he's soccer, tree-climbing, kickball, and sledding age it's more important than ever to find high-quality clothes that are affordable since he either outgrows them or wears out the knees in no time. Enter After the Stork. This great company has sturdy, attractive clothes for boys and girls (and even a few things for Mom) at about 30% to 40% less than that well-known Swedish company. For instance, you can get thermal-knit long johns in solid colors for $18.50, and if you buy three sets the fourth is free. T-shirts and shorts, sweatshirts and sweatpants, leggings, long-sleeve tees, jeans, snow boots and snowsuits, corduroy pants, rain slickers, socks, shoes, underwear—you'll find it all here at very affordable prices. This is my kind of company.

SPECIAL FACTORS: Satisfaction guaranteed; returns accepted.

As a Little Child

10701 W. 80th Ave., Dept. W   **303–456–1880**
Arvada, CO 80005

> Brochure: free
> Pay: check or MO
> Sells: diaper covers and cloth diapers
> Store: mail order only

If you want to save money and do something nice for the environment and your baby, use cloth diapers. I did with my son, and it was great. He never had diaper rash and I actually enjoyed being outside in the mountain air hanging up the many white cotton diapers on our long line, my baby cooing beside me in a basket or wrapped next to my body. It's not for everyone, but if you're the all-natural type, you'll want to know about this company. As a Little Child sells just a few items, pictured and described in the brochure: the Wabby, which is the only diaper cover made of soft, breathable Gore-Tex; cotton diapers as part of the Wabby diapering system; and cotton washcloths and miniwipes. The Wabby comes in a variety of sizes to accommodate babies from 5 to 34 pounds, and in several colors and prints. At $12.95 each, the diaper covers are a bargain. But the per-Wabby price goes down the more you buy. The same is true of the cotton diapers.

SPECIAL FACTORS: No credit cards taken.

Baby Bunz & Co.

P.O. Box 113–WB00
Lynden, WA 98264–0113

Catalog: $1
Pay: check, MO, MC, V
Sells: cloth diapering supplies, layette items, toys, books,
  etc., for infants and toddlers
Store: mail order only

It all started in 1982 when Carynia, founder of Baby Bunz, was looking for a diaper cover for her newborn son and wanted to make them available to other parents like herself. Nearly two decades later, Baby Bunz is a grown-up company that specializes in a variety of natural diapering and other products for babies at below-retail prices, with a best-price guarantee to sweeten the deal. This company offers Nikky diaper covers in a range of styles—some with waterproof liners, others all-cotton, still others lambswool or breathable poly. The lovely 20-page catalog features detailed descriptions, photographs, and even diagrams for cloth-diaper folding (different for boys and girls). A careful selection of infant items—baby buntings, baby caps, blankets, footies, etc.—in all-natural cotton, as well as baby basics, from baby's first books and toys to classic coveralls, are here. Moms—if you're looking for discounted Weleda products such as that heavenly calendula cream (that I still use on my hands now that my baby isn't a baby anymore), Baby Bunz has them too.

SPECIAL FACTORS: No wholesale orders please; satisfaction guaranteed; returns accepted within 30 days for refund, credit, or exchange.

5635 S. Mingo
Tulsa, OK 74146

888–791–2229
918–249–8888
Fax: 918–249–8889

Brochure: free
Pay: check, MO, V, MC
Sells: disposable diapers
Store: same address; Monday to Friday 10–6, Saturday
10–2
Online: www.diaperwhse.com

Here's a company that came up with a great idea: inexpensive diapers by the case. If you're a frugal parent with infants and toddlers, or maybe run a day-care center, you know how quickly a case of diapers disappears. And when you're toting a sleeping baby in your arms while pushing a fussy toddler in a stroller, the last thing you need is a trip to the supermarket to buy one of those suitcase-size packs of diapers. The folks at Diaper Warehouse imagined such a scenario when they figured out a way to sell diapers at 35% to 50% less than what you pay at discount stores. These are first- and second-quality name-brand diapers produced by leading manufacturers of disposable diapers. Tests have shown that these diapers are just as absorbent as the leading brands. The minimum order is one case (that's 240 diapers in the smallest size, or 120 in X-large). You can call or write for a brochure, or get the exact same information off the website. Whether your child is 7 pounds or 37 pounds, you won't be paying much here. Shipping is free, so if you have the storage space, buy several cases. Order by phone, fax, or online.

SPECIAL FACTORS: Diaper Warehouse unconditionally guarantees their diapers; wholesale orders possible (inquire); shipping within the continental U.S. only.

Iuniforms.com

888–563–6398

Information: website only, no print catalog
Pay: V, MC, AE, DSC
Sells: school uniforms for boys and girls
Store: website only; phone hours Monday to Friday 9–5
  EST
Online: www.iuniforms.com

One of my sisters converted to Catholicism and proceeded to have seven children. Each one of those kids goes to private school. That's a lot of little navy-blue pants, plaid skirts, and button-down shirts! While school uniforms can be a big expense, they needn't be. Iuniforms.com was founded on the idea that since shopping for school uniforms is a no-brainer, this company could save parents of school-age kids a lot of money—20% or more—by selling their uniforms on the web. This no-frills company understands that parents don't need their hands held when shopping for school uniforms; they already know everything about the uniforms beforehand: size, style, quantity, etc.

Log onto the Iuniforms.com website and you'll find a good selection of shirts, pants, shorts, sweaters, jackets, ties, and skirts in solid colors (navy, burgundy, khaki, green, gray, and black) and plaid, for boys and girls of all sizes—from 4X to 20.5 plus. Items are pictured and described; you choose the size and style you want and then order online. At press time all shirts and blouses were two for $10, and all pants were $9.99. Now that's a deal! Iuniforms.com wants to be your only school uniform source, and offers a lowest price guarantee to win your loyalty.

SPECIAL FACTORS: All products carry a one-year money-back guarantee; special orders taken.

Olsen's Mill Direct

1641 S. Main St.
Oshkosh, WI 54901–6988

800–537–4979
Fax: 920–426–6369

Catalog: free
Pay: check, MO, MC, V, AE, DSC
Sells: children's clothes
Store: same address, 11–4 daily

It's wonderful to find a source for high-quality children's clothing discounted about 45% off normal list price. Olsen's Mill Direct, located in the heart of the Midwest, issues a 48-page color catalog filled with well-made, sturdy, adorable dresses, sweaters, overalls, pants, leggings, socks, outerwear, pajamas, shoes and boots, and even some clothing for mothers. From everyday school clothing to velvet and lace dresses, Olsen's Mill Direct could very well become your main kid-shopping source.

SPECIAL FACTORS: Satisfaction guaranteed; returns accepted within 30 days for refund, exchange, or credit.

Rubens & Marble, Inc.

P.O. Box 14900-A
Chicago, IL 60614–0900

773–348–6200

Brochure: free with SASE
Pay: check or MO
Sells: infants' clothing
Store: mail order only

Chances are, the first clothes you or your baby wore were made by Rubens & Marble, Inc. That's because Rubens has been supplying hospitals with infant garments since 1890. You can purchase these same items at very low prices directly from their "Baby Wear Factory" flyer. The double-sided flyer shows baby shirt seconds (with small knitting flaws) in snap-front, tie-front, and slipover, in short or mitten-cuff sleeve, at less than a dollar apiece. There are also first-quality all-cotton baby shirts, gowns and kimonos, sheets for crib, bassinet, and porta-cribs, stretch diapers by the dozen, training and waterproof panties, and terry bibs. Shirt sizes range from preemie and newborn up to 36 months (29–32 pounds).

SPECIAL FACTORS: You must include a stamped, self-addressed envelope to receive the price list; all seconds clearly indicated; minimum order one package (number of items varies depending on item).

Related Products/Companies

Allergy-free nap sets and stuffed animals
- National Allergy Supply

Baby lambskins
- Sheepskin Station

Boy Scout gear and clothing
- Wiley Outdoor Sports

Camouflage clothing for children
- Bowhunters Discount Warehouse

Children's bedding
- Chock, Clothcrafters, Gohn Bros.

Children's equestrian gear
- Stateline Tack

Children's pajamas
- Chock

Children's socks, tights, and dancewear
- Asiatic Hosiery, Chock, Dance Distributors

Children's sweatsuits and long underwear
- Chock, One Hanes Place

Children's water sport and water safety gear
- Bart's Water Sports

Cloth diapers
- Chock, Gohn Bros.

Designer children's clothing
- DesignerOutlet

Diaper-changer baby backpack
- Campmor

Layettes and infant clothing
- Chock, Gohn Bros., Lady Grace

Maternity clothing for health professionals
- Cotton Scrubs, Tafford

Maternity hosiery
- One Hanes Place

Nursing bras and accessories
- Gohn Bros., Lady Grace, The Smart Saver

Special-needs clothing for children
- Special Clothes

Sterling silver baby gifts, silver spoons
- Silver Queen

Tiny beekeeping suits
- Brushy Mountain Bee Farm

Toddlers' and children's clothing and outerwear
- Bridgewater, Chock, DesignerOutlet, Gohn Bros., Wiley Outdoor Sports

Undyed baby clothing
- Dharma Trading

Footwear

Men's and women's casual and dress shoes and boots; work boots; sheepskin moccasins

These firms offer everything from doctor-designed women's comfort shoes to lace-up pole-climber boots for men. You'll find a wide (pardon the pun) selection of shoes in hard-to-find sizes and widths, and even some luxurious sheepskin moccasins—all at discount prices that will knock your socks off. With savings as high as 50%, it would be hard to find a better way to buy footwear. There's still the problem of fit, however, unless you're ordering more of the same model you've worn before. Here are some tips that might improve your odds of success:

- If you can find the shoes you're buying at a local store, try on a pair before ordering them by mail. Afternoon is the best time, when your feet have swollen slightly.
- Carefully unwrap the shoes or boots and save the packaging. Also, walk around in your new shoes on carpet to avoid scuffing them.
- Try out your new shoes for at least 30 minutes. If they fit, think about ordering a second pair while they're still in stock.

- If the shoes don't fit, return them in the original packaging, according to the firm's instructions.

A brochure with fitting guidelines and information on foot problems is available from the American Orthopedic Foot and Ankle Society. Send a long, stamped, self-addressed envelope to AOFAS, 1216 Pine St., Suite 201, Seattle, WA 98101; request the "Ten Points of Proper Shoe Fit" brochure. Or call them at 206–223–1120, or log onto the website (www.aofas.org). There's lot of foot and shoe information online.

If your shoes and boots need professional help and you don't have a good cobbler locally, contact the friendly folks at Houston Shoe Hospital, 5215 Kirby Dr., Houston, TX 77098; 713–528–6268. This firm overhauls worn footwear and handles mail-order repairs.

Even though the companies in this section specialize in footwear, there are many others in the book that have shoes and boots in their inventory. Basketball sneakers, steel-toed logger's boots, watershoes, ski boots, hiking boots, tap shoes, old-fashioned ladies high-tops—this is just a sampling of the footwear you can find elsewhere in the book. Take a good look at the "Related Products/Companies" listings at the end of this section for companies selling footwear and related goods such as leather-care and waterproofing items.

Find It Fast

Athletic Shoes
- Gene's Discount

Men's Dress and Casual Shoes
- Altman's, Gene's Discount, The Shoe Shack

Men's Work Boots
- Altman's, Gene's Discount, The Shoe Shack

Sheepskin Footwear
- Sheepskin Station

Women's Shoes
- Gene's Discount

Altman's

120 W. Monroe St.   312–332–0667
Chicago, IL 60603   Fax: 312–332–1923

Manufacturer's brochures: free
Pay: check, MO, MC, V, AE, DC, DSC
Sells: men's shoes and boots
Store: same address, Monday to Friday, 8:30–6, Sat.
  8:30–4:30

Since 1932 Altman's Shoes and Boots for Men has provided men of all sizes and walks of life with the largest selection of sizes—5 to 19 in widths ranging from AAAA to EEE—and one of the most complete selections of men's footwear available. I really enjoyed chatting with the people at Altman's, who were friendly, sincere, and helpful. Discounts range from $15 to $65 off the regular price, and the top-name brands here include Bass, Birkenstock, Dan Post, Dansko, Ecco, Frye, Hush Puppies, Justin, Naot, New Balance, Rockport, Timberland, Tony Lama, and many others. If you like real, old-fashioned service and high-quality shoes, you'll love Altman's.

SPECIAL FACTORS: Special orders are welcome; phone hours the same as store hours; satisfaction guaranteed.

Gene's Shoes Discount Catalog

126 N. Main St., Dept. BWBM   800–807–4637
St. Charles, MO 63301   314–946–0804
                                        Fax: 314–946–0804

Catalog: $1
Pay: check, MO, MC, V, DSC
Sells: men's and women's dress, casual, and athletic shoes
Store: same address; Monday to Saturday 9–5:30
Online: www.genesshoes.com

For half a century Gene's Shoes has been helping men and women walk a little easier by offering comfortable shoes in hard-to-find sizes. Whether you browse the print catalog or now the website, you'll find shoes by Soft Spots (the "doctor-designed footwear"), Supremes, New Balance, Selby, Trotters, Ecco, Bostonian, Rockport, Hush Puppies, Easy Spirit, and many others. Savings here run from 20% to 30% on some styles; if you're on the web check out the "Internet Specials." Women's shoes are available in AAAA to EEE widths, sizes 3 to 13; men's shoes are here in AA to EEEEE widths, sizes 5 to 18.

SPECIAL FACTORS: Satisfaction guaranteed; unworn, salable returns accepted within 30 days for exchange, refund, or credit.

Sheepskin Station

3628 E. Marginal Way S.   206–343–5345
Seattle, WA 98134   Fax: 206–621–7675

Information: website only, no print catalog
Pay: check, MO, V, MC
Sells: sheepskin footwear, auto seats, rugs, and
  accessories
Store: same address, Monday to Friday 9–5
Online: www.sheepskinstation.com

When Sheepskin Station, a major wholesaler of sheepskin products, sorts through their merchandise to ship to the likes of L. L. Bean, Hammacher Schlemmer, and other big-name mail-order outfits, there are always products that may not be perfect enough to sell to these customers. Because sheepskins are natural they may have blemishes where dyes don't take evenly, different textures of wool sewn together, or an obvious seam. None of these things affects the overall quality of the products, and, in fact, may not even be noticeable. That's good news for us, because Sheepskin Station then sells these items to us at deep, deep discounts. Just log on to the website and you'll gasp at the prices, which are about 50% less than you'll find anywhere else. Just about anyone can afford to have their front and back car seats covered with sheepskin (starting at only $29!) in many sizes, styles, and colors. Besides auto seat covers, this company carries steering-wheel and seat-belt covers, a beautiful selection of sheepskin slippers in five styles; large (7' × 4') and small (4' × 2½') rugs; baby lambskins; and assorted other accessories, such as regular and exercise bicycle-seat covers and wash/dust mitts. Sheepskin Station makes it easy to order directly online, or by e-mail, phone, or fax. There's no print catalog, so if you don't live in the Seattle area, your best bet is to see the website for inventory and specials.

SPECIAL FACTORS: Orders shipped in the U.S. only.

The Shoe Shack

1167 Shady Grove Rd.　　　　　　800–634–1468
Martin, TN 38237–8109

Catalog:　free
Pay:　check, MO, MC, V, DSC
Sells:　men's work boots and shoes
Store:　mail order only, phone hours Monday to Friday 8–5
　CST

Owner Bennie Castleman had a good idea that grew and grew. He started out selling men's pole climbers: those no-nonsense, lace-up leather boots worn by the handsome telephone guys who cause me to nearly wreck my car when I see them perched up high near the treetops. By selling 'em cheap, his fortunes rose and so did his reputation. The philosophy at The Shoe Shack hasn't changed much since those simpler days: low overhead (Bennie works out of his backyard); factory-direct shipment (no money tied up in inventory); and low prices that get passed on to you. The inventory has expanded, however, and now includes work boots from DuraShocks and Carolina Gold, as well as some oxfords, walkers, and dress shoes from Hush Puppies and Bostonian. Whether you're a logger looking for steel-toed protection or a teenager trying on the macho look, any fellow who browses the no-frills fliers from The Shoe Shack can't help but spot a pair of boots or shoes he's gotta have. This little company is a real gem.

SPECIAL FACTORS: Give a second choice when ordering.

Related Products/Companies

Army surplus shoes and boots
- Mass. Army & Navy

Bicycle shoes
- Performance Bicycle

Children's boots and shoes
- After the Stork, Olsen's Mill Direct

Dance shoes
- Dance Distributors

Designer shoes and boots for men and women
- DesignerOutlet

Doggy boots and paw protectors
- Jeffers, KV Vet Supply, Omaha Vaccine

Equestrian boots
- State Line Tack, Valley Vet

Extra-long shoe horns
- Amplestuff

Golf shoes
- Golf Haus

Medical-profession clogs and shoes
- Cotton Scrubs, Tafford

Men's dress and business shoes
- Huntington, The Ultimate Outlet

Outdoor footwear, and work and hiking boots
- Bailey's, Cahall's, Campmor, Defender Industries, Gohn Bros., Holabird Sport, Omaha Vaccine, Sierra Trading, The Sportsman's Guide, Valley Vet, WearGuard, Wiley Outdoor Sports

Running shoes
- Sierra Trading

Shoes for any sport
- Holabird

Slippers
- Chock, One Hanes Place

Snowshoes
- The Sportsman's Guide

Soccer shoes
- Acme Soccer, Soccer International

Volleyball shoes
- Spike Nashbar

Water shoes
- The House

Women's shoes
- Bridgewater, Willow Ridge, The Ultimate Outlet

Women's support and comfort shoes
- Support Plus

Intimate apparel

Undergarments and hosiery for women, men, and children

I was not destined to wear hose. When I have a special event to go to and have to look like a million dollars, I'll often visit the local boutique that sells fancy underthings and buy a $16 pair of panty hose. By the end of the affair I'm more likely than not to have an unsightly run spoiling my look. Recent consumer studies have shown that "cheap" hose will last you as long and possibly longer than the pricy ones I buy. Fortunately, the companies in this section sell high-quality hosiery of every kind—including socks for men and children's items such as tights—at bargain prices. Problem solved.

As for bras, panties, and other unmentionables, you'll find them here too. I know many of you out there hold on to your old friends with the holes, tattered lace, and yellowed armpits (you know who you are). Go ahead and treat yourself to some brand-new intimate apparel that's affordable for a change.

Find It Fast

Nursing and Post-Mastectomy Bras
- Lady Grace

Sleepwear—Men's and Women's
- Chock, Lady Grace

Socks and Hosiery—Men's, Women's, and Children's
- Asiatic Hosiery, Chock, No Nonsense Direct, One Hanes Place

Women's Lingerie
- Chock, Lady Grace, One Hanes Place, The Smart Saver

Women's Swimwear
- Lady Grace

Asiatic Hosiery Co.

P.O. Box 31
Little Falls, NJ 07424–0031

973–872–2111
Fax: 973–872–2114

Catalog: $2, $4 outside U.S., refundable
Pay: check, MO, MC, AE, DC, DSC
Sells: hosiery for men, women, and children
Store: mail order only
Online: www.sensationshosiery.com

We writers don't have to put on panty hose every day and look presentable in office attire. But I can tell you if I did I'd be buying them by the dozen. The reason is that I don't believe I've ever had a pair of panty hose last longer than one wearing. I'm hexed. Along comes Asiatic Hosiery, which prides itself on fast delivery and good prices and service. This company, nearly four decades old, distributes quality, affordable hosiery for the entire family. Here you *must* buy by the dozen, and the offerings include knee-highs, ankle-highs, footies, thigh-highs, panty hose, ladies' and girls' socks, men's and boys' socks, opaque panty hose, and girls' and ladies' tights. The eight-page black-and-white catalog features one- or two-line descriptions that include size parameters for each item, but no pictures. If you're not fussy about brand names, you'll save a lot of money here. For example, sheer panty hose are less than a dollar a pair. The website is bare-bones and doesn't feature inventory or online ordering, although you can e-mail the company from there.

SPECIAL FACTORS: Minimum order 12 items of one style and color.

Chock Catalog Corp.

74 Orchard St., Dept. WBM　　212–473–1929
New York, NY 10002–4594　　Fax: 212–473–6273

Catalog: $2, $5 outside U.S.
Pay: check, MO, MC, V, DSC, JCB
Sells: hosiery, underwear, sleepwear, and infants' layettes
Store: same address; Sunday to Thursday 9:30–5:30,
　Friday 9–1
Online: www.chockcatalog.com

Guys: Here's a little secret. Although we say we like sexy lingerie, what women actually buy and wear most of the time are practical cotton panties. And there's no better source for this and other underwear and hosiery than Chock Catalog, in business since 1921 bringing top-brand merchandise directly to consumers at prices discounted about 25%.

There's something quite old-timey and reassuring about Chock's 66-page catalog that features underthings for men, women, and children, sleepwear, socks, and hosiery, and a small selection of toiletries and gifts. The women's items include briefs, camisoles, bras, pajamas, socks, and hosiery. For men there are boxers, briefs, undershirts, long underwear, bathrobes, socks, and more. Chock also carries boys' and girls' socks, underwear, and sleepwear, as well items for infants including sleepwear, onesies, receiving blankets, and waterproof sheets. The manufacturers include Calvin Klein, Hanes, Carters, Bali, Vanity Fair, and others. There's a small section of nonapparel goods that includes Montgomery Schoolhouse wooden toys, Caswell-Massey soaps and lotions, well-priced mineral-salt-crystal deodorant stones, slippers, umbrellas, and handkerchiefs. By the way, there's nothing old-fashioned about the website, which allows you to view the full selection of products and then order online.

SPECIAL FACTORS: Satisfaction guaranteed; unopened returns with manufacturer's packaging intact accepted within 30 days.

Lady Grace has been "serving the needs of America's women" since 1937, offering a wide range of women's intimate apparel in all sizes, including hard-to-find sizes. The everyday prices are good, but Lady Grace has semi-annual sales where you can find items discounted about 25%: bras (underwire, soft-cup, full-figure support, minimizers, nursing, post-mastectomy, strapless, low-back, back-support, etc.), underpants, long underwear, nightgowns, slips, swimsuits, girdles, and more. Bra sizes run up to 54, cup sizes up to J. The 32-page color catalog includes photographs, descriptions, and measuring guides. On the website you can order a print catalog and view some of the inventory, but there's no online ordering. If you prefer, Lady Grace's "intimate apparel buying staff" can assist you by phone.

SPECIAL FACTORS: Satisfaction guaranteed; authorized returns accepted within 30 days for exchange, refund, or credit.

No Nonsense Direct

P.O. Box 26095   800–677–5995
Greensboro, NC 27420–6095   Fax: 336–275–9329

Catalog: free
Pay: check, MO, MC, V, AE, DSC
Sells: slightly irregular hosiery
Store: mail order only
Online: www.legwear.com

Want to save money on hosiery and socks? Take the no nonsense approach: Buy through the mail or over the Internet with No Nonsense Direct. You can save up to 65% through this mail-order factory outlet, a subsidiary of Kayser-Roth Corp., by choosing Practically Perfect legwear and hosiery including support hose, knee-highs, opaque colored tights, everyday panty hose, full-figure panty hose, men's and women's socks, and more. What does "practically perfect" mean? This is second-quality merchandise that's slightly irregular: Perhaps a seam isn't exactly straight or maybe the toe reinforcement is too long, for example. If you're a fan of the No Nonsense and Burlington legwear lines, this is a good way to save money. Sizes offered accommodate women up to 300 pounds. The website has secure online ordering. Or you can call for a flyer and mailer and order the old-fashioned way.

SPECIAL FACTORS: Satisfaction guaranteed on all first- and second-quality products; returns accepted for refund, exchange, or credit.

One Hanes Place Catalog

P.O. Box 748
Rural Hall, NC 27098-0748

800-300-2600
Fax: 800-545-5613
TDD: 800-816-4833

Catalog: free
Pay: check, MO, MC, V, AE, DSC
Sells: first-quality and "slightly imperfect" women's
  hosiery and underwear
Store: mail order only
Online: www.ohpcatalog.com

Bras and other intimates, cotton leggings, panty hose, panties, socks, indoor slippers, exercise outfits, even casual wear such as cotton sweater/stirrup pants combos can all be bought at a discount through the One Hanes Place outlet catalog and website. Bras by Bali, Playtex, Hanes Her Way, Hanesport, Just My Size, Wonderbra, Champion, and Jogbra are here in a variety of styles discounted as much as 50%. I don't remember the last time I saw a bra under $10, but you'll find some here. The hosiery selection comprises the many Hanes lines (of which L'eggs is one) for up to 50% off if you can buy in quantity—a dozen pair of the same style. Besides undergarments and hosiery, the One Hanes Place catalog and website offer some nice casual wear such as cashmere/cotton sweaters with matching skirts at very good prices. The website features online specials and secure online ordering.

SPECIAL FACTORS: Free shipping; "slightly imperfect" merchandise is clearly indicated; returns are accepted; TDD service is accepted Monday to Friday 8 A.M. to midnight.

The Smart Saver

P.O. Box 105   800–554–4453
Wasco, IL 60183

Catalog: free
Pay: check, MO, MC, V
Sells: bras, girdles, shapers, and panties
Store: mail order only

If The Smart Saver carries the intimate apparel you love best, you're in luck. This company has first-quality, fine intimates at 35% off (no seconds, no irregulars). Their catalog calls these "styles for the forgotten lady." These aren't the racy numbers worn by Janet Jackson and Madonna. The bras you'll find pictured in Smart Saver's 20-page black-and-white catalog are the classics by Playtex, Exquisite Form, Crown-ette, Bestform, Glamorise, Vanity Fair, Venus, Perfect Comfort, Goddess, and Lollipop. You'll find girdles, bras, and panties in real women's sizes—ranging from S to 9XL. There are girdles and shapers for bottoms, thighs, midriffs, and full leg; bras for women who need extra support and room; good, old-fashioned 100% cotton waist-high briefs; and more. There are also bras for nursing mothers and for women who've had mastectomies. You'll see the suggested retail price alongside Smart Saver's, a feature I always appreciate. The owner, who's had the business for 16 years, says her customers are "very loyal."

SPECIAL FACTORS: 100% satisfaction guaranteed; will ship to all 50 states, Canada, and locations with postal zip codes (for example, Guam, U.S. Virgin Islands, etc.).

Related Products/Companies

Extra-wide socks
- Amplestuff

Men's boxers and underwear
- America's Shirt, Huntington's

Post-mastectomy bras and forms
- Bosom Buddy Breast Forms

Socks, hosiery, underwear for men, women, and children
- Gohn Bros., Huntington

Sports bra patterns, shoulder pads
- Newark Dressmaker Supply

Support hosiery, socks
- Essentials, Support Plus, The Support Shop

Undyed silk and cotton slips, camisoles, boxers, etc.
- Dharma Trading Co.

Women's lingerie
- Beauty Boutique, Gold Medal Hair Products, Thai Silks, The Ultimate Outlet

Men's Business Attire

Shirts, ties, suits, and traditional menswear and accessories

Lest they get lost in the general section of the "Clothing" chapter, I decided to separate out these firms dedicated to outfitting America's businessman for less. Why? Because high-quality men's clothing at bargain prices isn't all that easy to come by, and I figured you guys deserved a section of your own. To misquote the disco tune, you work hard for your money so I'd better treat you right. You'll find great deals on everything from imported Italian silk ties to custom-sewn Egyptian cotton shirts. As always, remember to consult the "Related Products/Companies" listings at the end of this section for other companies that carry men's office attire.

Find It Fast

Shirts
- America's Shirt and Tie, Huntington, Quinn's Shirt Shop

Ties
- America's Shirt and Tie, Huntington

Other Traditional Menswear
- America's Shirt, Huntington

America's Shirt

546 S. Meridien St., Ste. 205
Indianapolis, IN 46225

800–259–7283
317–321–9999
Fax: 317–639–2029

Information: website only, no print catalog
Pay: check, MO, V, MC
Sells: shirts and ties
Store: online only
Online: www.hugestore.com

America's Shirt is a remarkable company. Carl Levinson, president, began his Internet-only store after the longtime family clothier business closed. He launched America's Shirt in 1994 with the idea of creating a virtual company that would sell high-quality business and casual attire for men at the lowest prices. Without advertising, print catalogs, and a huge staff, he's been able to do it successfully. Log on to the website and you'll get to read the many kudos America's Shirt has received from such notables as the *Wall Street Journal* and *Los Angeles Times*.

You'll save about 40% on shirts (casual, dress, golf, and T-shirts), pants (dress, casual, and jeans), sports coats, suits, T-shirts, ties, and boxers. Click onto the shirts, for example, and checkmark your size, color, fit, and brand, then hit the search button. Your choices will come up with a picture and price. If you like what you see, put it into your shopping cart. It's as simple as that. If you can get a group at your office to order a total of twelve items of any mix, you'll get an additional $2 knocked off each item. For larger quantities there are greater discounts you'll want to check out here.

SPECIAL FACTORS: 100% satisfaction guaranteed; all items returned for any reason will be refunded.

Huntington Clothiers

1285 Alum Creek Dr.
Columbus, OH 43209-2797

800-848-6203
614-252-4422
Fax: 614-252-3855
Fax: 800-848-0644
(international)

Catalog: free, $3 outside U.S.
Pay: check, MO, MC, V, AE, DC, DSC, JCB
Sells: traditional menswear
Store: same address; Monday to Friday 10–6, Saturday
10–5
Online: www.huntingtonclothiers.com

I have a dear friend with a problem. His neck size is, well, huge. Yet if he buys a shirt off the rack with the proper neck dimensions, the shirt, proportioned for a very large person, balloons out like a circus tent. My friend just doesn't have an off-the-rack kind of body. Yet to have shirts custom-made would cost him a fortune. Thankfully I can now tell him about Huntington Clothiers and Shirtmakers. This remarkable company, in business for two decades, custom-sews men's shirts and sells them directly to the individual, skipping the middleman and passing the savings on to you.

The catalog and website make the process easy: Select from one of 15 premium fabrics; select the neck and sleeve sizes; choose from two body styles (full cut or trim cut); select one of six collar styles and the type of cuff. *Voila!* You'll have yourself a handsome, custom-made shirt in about three weeks at about half what your local tailor would charge. Huntington Clothiers is all about classic, conservative men's clothing made from the best materials (cashmere, Egyptian cotton, pure lambswool, silk, tweed, etc.). The 52-page color catalog also has ready-made shirts, ties, sport coats, tuxedo shirts, trousers, shoes, white cotton underwear, bathrobes, luxury items such as genuine Dopp travel kits and cufflinks, and much more. Secure online ordering is available for your convenience.

SPECIAL FACTORS: Satisfaction guaranteed; a two-shirt minimum is required for custom shirt orders.

Quinn's Shirt Shop

Rte. 12, P.O. Box 383   508–943–7183
N. Grosvenordale, CT 06255

     Price List: $2 with SASE, refundable (see text)
     Pay: check or MO
     Sells: Arrow shirts
     Store: 245 W. Main St., Dudley, MA; Monday to Saturday
       10–5

Quinn's Shirt Shop is for all you guys who love Arrow shirts and know exactly what you want. According to the owner, this company deals "strictly with Arrow Irregulars in top grade (best of the irregular line) with savings from 40% to 50%." If you know the line (Dover, Brigade, Bradstreet, Kent Collection, etc.), specify the size, SS (short sleeve) or LS (long sleeve), the sleeve length if long sleeve, and color preference. Collars come in regular or button down. Big and tall sizes are available here too. There's no print catalog, and all orders are C.O.D. The price list is $2 with a self-addressed stamped envelope, and is refundable with your first purchase. Or you may call for a price quote.

SPECIAL FACTORS: Minimum four shirts per order; only C.O.D. accepted; returns accepted for exchange.

Related Products/Companies

Dress shoes
- Altman's, The Shoe Shack, The Ultimate Outlet

Men's shirts and officewear
- Bridgewater, DesignerOutlet, Gohn Bros., The Ultimate Outlet

Socks and suspenders
- Lehman's

Suits and Ties
- DesignerOutlet

Crafts and Hobbies

*Materials, supplies, tools,
and equipment for
craftworkers and hobbyists
of all kinds and ages*

The firms in this general section of the "Crafts and Hobbies" chapter can provide the materials for nearly any artsy diversion—miniatures, stenciling, basketry, embossing, caning, clock-making, stained glass, tole, decoy-painting, floral and potpourri, doll-making, music boxes, lamp-making, candle-making, woodworking, papermaking, and much more. There's a lot here for everyone: children, elderly people, summer-campers, schools, and professional craftspeople.

I get a tremendous kick out of thumbing through some of these catalogs. If you had nothing but time on your hands, you could braid your own rugs, weave your own baskets, make heirloom Teddy bears and music boxes for your children, create all of the clocks in your house, throw your own pots and dishes, hand-dip candles to place in your handmade candlesticks, paint your own picture frames, turn your windows into stained-glass masterpieces, make a gorgeous heirloom quilt, fill your drawers with hand-made sachets, create your own embossed stationery, and generally have a house full of homemade, crafty knickknacks. Whew! If you're like me, you'll agree that many of the craft catalogs here are as valuable for ideas and inspiration as they are for the goods they sell.

The companies listed in this section are either general crafts suppliers with a very broad selection spanning many disciplines or are firms specializing in one item or type of goods—feathers, parts for stuffed bears, stained glass supplies, basketry and caning, etc. For help in locating a particular item, see "Find It Fast," below.

If you're looking for ceramics, pottery, or sculpture supplies, you'll find some here. But for companies that *specialize* in these goods, see the section in this chapter called "Ceramics," page 149. If creating wearables such as earrings and necklaces is your thing, check out the "Jewelry-Making" section, page 153. And if you're looking for materials and equipment for the arts of spinning, weaving, knitting, sewing, quilting, soft sculpture, or other fabric and fiber art or craft, you'll find many such companies in "Textile Arts," page 158. Leather crafters should see the "Luggage and Leather Goods" chapter, page 392, for leather-by-the-piece and leather-crafting tools.

Depending on where you draw the line between art and craft, you're likely to find useful and related goods in the "Fine Art Supplies" chapter, page 179, as well.

Find It Fast

Caning, Basketry, Gourd Craft
- The Caning Shop, Frank's Cane and Rush Supply

Clock-Making Supplies
- Creative Clock, National Artcraft, Turncraft Clocks

Craft Kits
- The Artist's Club, The Caning Shop, CR's Bear and Doll Supply, Frank's Cane and Rush, Gramma's Graphics, Vanguard Crafts, Warner-Crivellaro Stained Glass

Doll- and Bear-Making Supplies
- CR's Bear and Doll Supply, Craft Catalog, Craft King, National Artcraft

Feathers
- Gettinger

Floral and Potpourri
- Billiann's Floral and Bridal Supply, Craft Catalog, Tom Thumb Workshops

General Crafts Supplies
- Craft Catalog, Craft King, National Artcraft, Sunshine Discount Crafts, Vanguard

Glass Crafts
- Craft Catalog, Glass Crafters, Warner-Crivellaro

"Sun-Printing" Supplies
- Gramma's Graphics

Thermography and Embossing
- Think Ink

Tole and Decorative Painting
- The Artist's Club, Craft Catalog

The Artist's Club

P.O. Box 8930
Vancouver, WA 98668-8930

800-845-6507
Fax: 360-260-8877

Catalog: free
Pay: check, MO, MC, V, AE, DSC, JCB
Sells: tole and decorative painting supplies
Store: mail order only

The Japanese love this company—so much so that there's a Japanese-language catalog as well as a store (see below). Tole is the name of the game here. For those of you who are unfamiliar with the term, *tole* is the American folk craft of hand-painting things. If there's something you want to decorate, The Artist's Club no doubt carries it, and discounts run up to 40% on items in the 88-page catalog and the sales fliers published ten times a year. Unpainted items include wooden holiday decorations, picture and mirror frames, napkin holders, tic-tac-toe boards, end tables, bulletin boards, boxes, plant stands, jewelry boxes, children's step stools, and much more. This is *the* source for books on tole projects and techniques, which make up about half of The Artist's Club business. There are also project kits and of course tole supplies such as tiny brushes, paints, and stencils. At press time a website was in the works.

Japanese customers, please note: A Japanese-language catalog is available. For information call the store in Japan Monday to Saturday, 9 to 5, 045-510-4221, or fax 045-510-4065.

SPECIAL FACTORS: Satisfaction guaranteed; returns accepted within 30 days for exchange, refund, or credit.

Billiann's Floral and Bridal Supply

P.O. Box 35
Atlanta, IN 46031

765–292–6388

Catalog: $4 (see text)
Pay: check, MO, V, MC
Sells: satin and silk floral and bridal supplies
Store: 125 W. Main, Atlanta, IN; Tuesday, Thursday,
Friday 9–5, Wednesday 1–8, Saturday by appointment

Here's a great source of silk and satin flowers, bridal accessories, and floral supplies at wholesale prices—about 30% or more below what you'd pay in a retail store. Billiann's sells satin and silk flowers that are so lifelike in the photos I had to call and verify that they weren't real. Roses and rosebuds, carnations, lilies, daisies, orchids, spider mums, calla lilies, gardenias, and other romantic delights are all available in one of 39 colors, or they can be custom-dyed to match your gown. There is also "greenery" here: ferns and ivy of many kinds, plants and bushes among them, in addition to assembled cascades and nosegays with greenery and lace.

Besides flowers and greenery, Billiann's sells jeweled and flowered bridal wreaths, caplets, headbands, unadorned hats, fans, wristlets, baskets, and parasols, as well as all the floral supplies and accessories to decorate your own wedding: pearl strands, sequined flowers, laces, wire door-wreath hangers, Styrofoam cones and wreaths, floral adhesive, tape, wire, wood wire picks, and more. If you're saving money on your wedding by doing the flowers and decorations yourself, be sure to check out Billiann's collection of wedding and floral-design books. There's no minimum order on merchandise, and the price of the catalog is refundable with your first purchase.

SPECIAL FACTORS: No minimum order; C.O.D. orders add $4.50.

The Caning Shop

926 Gilman St., Dept. WBM
Berkeley, CA 94710-1494

800-544-3373
510-527-5010
Fax: 510-527-7718

Catalog: $1, refundable
Pay: check, MO, MC, V, DSC
Sells: seat-reweaving, gourd-crafting, and basketry
  supplies
Store: same address; Tuesday to Friday 10–6, Saturday
  10–2
Online: www.caning.com

To explore the catalog from The Caning Shop is to become immersed in a world of natural materials and quiet industry. Founded by caning expert and author Jim Widess in 1969, The Caning Shop repairs woven furniture, holds crafts workshops, and sells tools, supplies, and instructional materials for furniture repair, basketry, gourd crafts, and egg decorating. Prewoven cane webbing (in traditional and modern patterns), rawhide (especially for chair seats), genuine Danish seat cord (for Danish chairs of the 1950s), and rubber webbing (for modern Danish chairs and sofas) are some of the repair materials detailed in the catalog, along with reed splint, fiber rush, and Hong Kong grass, which can all be used on chair seats and in basketry. Pressed fiber (imitation leather) seats, easily cut and suitable for staining, are available in square, round, and quilted patterns. Professionals can pick up caning tools—awl, caning chisel, hooked spline chisel, hand clamp, utility knife, caning nippers, spline cutters, and sliver gripper; weaving tools— small, regular, heavy-duty and extra-long tools, with straight and bent tips; and electric tools—a miniature jig saw and a high-speed drill. Also available here are Danish nails, upholstery tacks, and "official" caning pegs (to replace those golf tees!) as well as bone and stone fetish assortments, long leaf pine needles, and kits for making baskets and keepsake pouches. About half of the 40-page catalog is devoted to instructional books and videos on many crafts topics including papermaking, bookbinding, and Native American designs. You can get a print catalog from the website, but online ordering is not possible.

SPECIAL FACTORS: Satisfaction guaranteed; C.O.D. orders accepted.

Craft Catalog

P.O. Box 1069
Reynoldsburg, OH 43068

800–777–1442
Fax: 800–955–5915
Fax: 740–964–6212

Catalog: $2
Pay: check, MO, V, MC, DSC
Sells: general craft supplies
Store: 2087-K Rt. 256, Reynoldsburg; Monday to Friday
  10–9, Saturday till 6, Sunday 12–5
Online: www.craftcatalog.com

Here's a catalog that will get you thinking about all the projects you wish you had time for. This would be a great resource for camp counselors, people who work with the elderly, and others looking for a one-stop craft supply source. The 188 pages are filled with supplies and equipment for virtually every kind of crafts discipline: woodworking, miniatures, clocks, dolls, sewing, tole, fabric-painting and dyeing, wood antiquing, glass crafts, papier-mâché, box-making and decorating, ornament-making, stenciling, needlework, quilting, candle-making, floral design, decoupage, jewelry-making, potpourri, lamp-making, rub-on art, and more. And there are scores of books peppered throughout on everything from window design to foil finishing. The catalog is well indexed and organized, and the prices here are excellent, about 20% to 50% less than normal retail. You'll find coupons for certain items that bring greater savings, and if your order is over $30, Craft Catalog will send you a free surprise gift of their choosing. At press time the website was under construction, but promised to be up soon offering secure online ordering, so check it out.

SPECIAL FACTORS: Free shipping on orders of $60 or more; no C.O.D. orders accepted; quantity discounts available.

Craft King

P.O. Box 90637
Lakeland, FL 33804

1-888-CRAFTY
Fax: 941-648-2972

Catalog: free
Sells: general craft supplies
Pay: check, MO, MC, V, DSC
Store: 3033 Drane Field Rd., Lakeland, Monday to
Saturday 9–5
E-mail: craftkng@gate.net

Craft King is a family business and one of the largest discount craft suppliers in the country. For over fifteen years, this company has been making customers happy with savings averaging around 20% on all kinds of craft-making items. Craft King entices bargain hunters by offering free shipping on your first order over $50 (within the continental U.S.), and an additional 5% discount when you reorder within a time specified on your order receipt. Miniatures, music boxes, beads, flower presses, lamp-shade frames, rubber stamps, wreaths, sequins, straw hats, doll parts and accessories, fabric paint, rabbit skins, yo-yos, charms—these are just some of the supplies you'll find in the 64-page catalog. When you place your first order, you'll receive the "Full Catalog," which is issued annually and has 160 full-color pages. This is a good source for hobbyists who like to dabble in a number of different crafts.

SPECIAL FACTORS: Satisfaction guaranteed.

Creative Clock

Box 565
357 High Street
Hanson, MA 02341

800–293–2856
781–293–2855
Fax: 781–293–0057

Catalog: $1, refundable
Pay: check, MO, MC, V
Sells: battery-operated quartz clock movements, dials, and
   clock-making tools and supplies
Store: mail order only

Creative Clock is a small, personable company whose main objective is to keep its customers happy. The company issues a 14-page catalog at wholesale prices that's for everybody—from do-it-yourself hobbyists and schools to clock and craft shops. The only requirement is a minimum order of $15. The prices at Creative Clock are already good, and if you buy in quantity, the discounts deepen. Additionally, Creative Clock says if you can find someone else selling the same item for less, they'll try to meet or beat that price. Here you'll find a variety of movements (mini-quartz, thermometer, high torque quartz clock, 24-hour—even specialty movements that operate in reverse!); clock hands and sweeps of all shapes and sizes in black, white, red, and brass; weather instruments; fit-ups; clock faces and painted clock dials; clock face components ranging from old-fashioned Arabic numerals to minimalist dots; and accessories and supplies galore—bits, hex nut drivers, magnets, saw-tooth picture hangers, corner ornaments, clock stands, polymer coating and brushes, dial templates, and much more.

SPECIAL FACTORS: Unconditional lifetime guarantee on all clock movements; C.O.D. orders add $4.75; some shipping restrictions apply; see catalog for details.

CR's Bear and Doll Supply Catalog

Box 8-WBM
Leland, IA 50453

515–567–3652
Fax: 515–567–3071

Catalog: $2 (see text)
Pay: check, MO, MC, V, DSC
Sells: doll- and bear-making supplies
Store: 109 5th Ave., Leland, IA; Monday to Friday
8:30–3:30 CT
Online: www.crscraft.com

I have to admit that it's a tad disconcerting to thumb through pages of disembodied doll heads and doll arms, but when you see the finished products, you'll be enchanted. CR's Crafts puts out a 152-page color catalog of kits, patterns, supplies, and accessories for making priceless, collectible teddy bears and dolls. Here you'll find wigs, miniatures, doll-clothes patterns and books, and accessories for 18-inch girl dolls (such as the American Girl Collection), as well as fabrics, clays, sculpting books, and ready-to-dress porcelain dolls. CR's also offers quality vinyl doll kits and sculpting videos. You'll find everything you need to make delightful dolls and bears, including heads and faces, squeakers and voice boxes, fabric and fur, eyelashes, stuffing, hats, and more. Prices are competitive with other toy-making suppliers, and very low when you factor in the cost of buying one of these little dears brand new. The website offers online ordering of some limited items, but by no means represents the full inventory.

Please note: Catalogs are $2 in the U.S.; $4 in Canada (U.S. funds only); and $7 outside the U.S. and Canada (U.S. funds).

SPECIAL FACTORS: Orders shipped outside the continental U.S. are sent via U.S. Parcel Post.

Frank's Cane and Rush Supply

7252 Heil Ave., Dept. WBM   714–847–0707
Huntington Beach, CA 92647   Fax: 714–843–5645

Catalog: free
Pay: check, MO, MC, V, AE, DSC
Sells: seat-reweaving supplies, furniture, kits, books,
    natural fiber matting, grasses, tropical fencing, etc.
Store: same address; Monday to Friday 8–5
Online: www.franksupply.com

For 25 years, Frank's Cane and Rush Supply has supplying craftspeople and shop owners with the materials and tools for chair-caning and seat-weaving, wicker repair, hat-making, basketry, and other fiber arts. The 40-page newsprint catalog is practically a handbook on how to repair furniture and select the right materials for different jobs, with several pages devoted to instructional and reference books, posters, and topical instruction sheets ($1.50 each). Frank's recommends ordering a materials sample for any product you're not sure of—for example, reed spline, oak and ash splints, Shaker tape, flat, round, and oval reeds, and colored rush— and suggests *sending in* samples to match weaves or widths. Frank's sells cane webbing, strand and binding cane, fiber and wire-fiber rush, fiber wicker, and Oriental seagrass in twisted or braided coils, matting, and carpet. While some items, such as tissue flex and welt cord (braided or twin), require a minimum yardage (10 yards), most products receive discounts when ordered in quantity or large sizes (rubber webbing: $.68/foot, $32.00 per 100-foot roll). The catalog depicts wood hoops and handles, wire handles, rattan rings, broom corn, wheat straw, fleece twine (for hamper repairs), sisal, jute roving, sugar plum and raw coconut fiber, and an assortment of raffia. The section on rattan poles, bamboo poles, and bamboo splits and cuts provides detailed information about sizing, condition, and uses, and offers discounts on bales of 10, 25, and 100 poles. Seat-weaving kits are a simple low-cost way to learn flat-fiber seating, hand-caning, and rush-weaving (stools from $12.95 complete), and pages of furniture kits (rockers and ladder-back chairs), standard tools, wood parts, and hardware provide a complete shopping opportunity. The website gives the same information and tips as the printed catalog, and orders can be placed by e-mail.

SPECIAL FACTORS: Minimum order $10 on credit cards; C.O.D. accepted; authorized returns accepted (no exchanges on bamboo).

Founded in New York City in 1915, Gettinger Feather Corp. is one of the leading suppliers of feathers for carnivals, theatrical companies, fashion designers, Indian crafts, and general craftspeople. This is a fine source of turkey, guinea hen, pheasant, peacock, rooster, marabou, and goose feathers, as well as feather boas, feather pads, and ostrich plumes. First-quality ostrich plumes, 20 to 24 inches, run $180 per pound, but second quality, 22 to 28 inches, in assorted colors, go for $125 per pound. An "A" quality marabou boa is $2 per yard; "B" quality, $1. Turkey feathers, packaged in one-, five-, and ten-pound units, start at $29 for one pound and drop to $16.50 for ten pounds. Solid-color quills range from $35 per pound to $19.75 for ten pounds. Goose feathers, in loose-soft, strung-soft, loose-stiff, and strung-stiff biots range from $59 to $72 for 20-pound units. Those coque tail feathers, either white or bronze, strung or loose, cost a pretty penny, in one- or five-pound units, but they are so impressive! For something more affordable and fun, the four-page price list shows a marabou fan of 12-inch feathers for $8.50. If you're seeking a good source for bedding feathers to replenish your comforter or pillow, this is the place.

SPECIAL FACTORS: Accounts welcome; minimum order $25.

Glass Crafters

398 Interstate Ct.
Sarasota, FL 34240

800–422–4552
941–379–8333
Fax: 941–379–8827

Catalog: free
Pay: check, MO, V, MC, AE, DSC
Sells: stained glass and other glass craft supplies
Store: mail order only
Online: www.glasscrafters.com

Whether you're new at stained glass or a professional craftsperson, Glass Crafters is a godsend. In business since 1975, Glass Crafters offers a wide selection of instructional videotapes, pattern books, projects, tools, supplies, and, of course, stained glass. Their 66-page catalog lists a unit price for most items, and a discount price even if you buy in small quantity, which usually nets a 15% savings or more. On many of the items, you can "mix and match" and still get the quantity discount. Bimonthly eight-page sales flyers offer specials that will save 30% to 50% on selected items (these flyers can be viewed on the company's website). But even the routine prices are better than most everyone else's—some as much as 50% better—this verified by a local glass artist who constantly bargain hunts for the best suppliers.

The catalog features all kinds of glass-crafting equipment and accessories: glass cutters, diamond glass grinders, specialty cutters, soldering tools, copper foil and tools, lead and brass came, glass mosaics, and more. There are sections devoted to lamp-making, bead-making, clock-making, and box- and frame-making, with all the tools, parts, and hardware you'll need. You'll find cast figures, etching stencils, paints, markers, jewels, and a wide selection of patterns and pattern books for projects ranging from mosaics to quick-and-easy lamps to distinctive vases.

SPECIAL FACTORS: Satisfaction guaranteed. Returns within 14 days of receipt, not including glass, lead came, or videotapes, unless defective; air-mail postage is $2 for Canada, $4 for Europe, $5 for Asia/Pacific Rim.

Gramma's Graphics, Inc.

20 Birling Gap,
Dept. TWBM-P9
Fairport, NY 14450–3916

716–223–4309
Fax: 716–223–4789

Brochure: long SASE and $1; $3 outside U.S.
Pay: check or MO
Sells: blueprint cloth-imaging materials and Sun Print
 diazo paper
Store: mail order only
Online: www.frontiernet.net/~bubblink/donnelly

The "Gramma" of Gramma's Graphics is Sue Johnson, coauthor of *Grandloving: Making Memories with Your Grandchildren,* which features over 200 innovative and inexpensive activity ideas to do with grandchildren or to send in the mail. An expert on fun craft projects, Johnson built an entire business around Sun Print kits, which "blueprint" an image on prepared fabric, creating a photographic representation in shades of blue that can be toned to brown, charcoal, tan, amethyst, or green. You must use 100% cotton or other natural fiber, since the imaging solution will bead up and roll off synthetics, sizing, or resins. Gramma's Graphics sells all the Sun Prints ingredients—from the imaging solution to the fabric—as well as instructions for creating the prints, assembling a pillow, and making an heirloom quilt. The six-page brochure suggests a number of subjects for projects—family portraits, wedding invitations, certificates and degrees, treasured photographs—and other applications including clothes, banners, wall hangings, doll faces, place mats, tote bags, and more. This quick-and-easy printing process can be done right in your own backyard and results in permanent prints. With a Sun Prints kit you can make unique, unforgettable, *inexpensive* gifts.

The website allows you to view color photographs of some finished products made with Sun Prints, such as a vest, a wedding pillow, and a keepsake quilt, and has other information about Sun Prints, but no online ordering.

Wholesale buyers: Minimum order for wholesale prices is 24 kits.

SPECIAL ORDERS: Satisfaction guaranteed; quantity discounts available.

National Artcraft Co.

7996 Darrow Rd.　　　　　　330–963–6011
Twinsburg, OH 44087　　　　Fax: 330–963–6711

Catalogs: $3 for "Main"; $2 for "Doll"; $1 for others (see
　　text); $5 for any combination without "Doll"
Pay: check, MO, MC, V, DSC
Sells: musical movements, lighting and electrical parts,
　　doll-making, ceramics/sculpture, clock-making supplies,
　　and general craft supplies
Store: mail order only, phone hours Monday to Friday
　　8:30–6, EST
Online: www.nationalartcraft.com

If you're a hobbyist or craftsperson, or you have your own craft business, get yourself a three-ring binder, 'cause National Artcraft has a main catalog as well as five satellite catalogs designed to bind for easy reference again and again. National Artcraft is a wonderful find if you love to make dolls, lamps, clocks, music boxes or carousels, ceramic and pottery items, and just about anything else. You can buy any item singly at a good price, but the prices are really great—up to 50% less—when you buy in larger quantity. Price breaks vary for each item, and unit prices are listed under each quantity so you can calculate the discounts. National Artcraft sells "wholesale direct"—they ship directly from their warehouse—but anyone can buy here as long as you meet the $25 minimum.

The 112-page "Main" catalog has an eclectic selection that includes all types of craft accessories: embroidered angel wings, beveled glass mirrors, ball-point desk pen sets (you make the base), flatware parts (you design the handles), lotion pumps, teapot handles, oil lamp and candle accessories, doll components, decorative egg stands, fountain pumps, jewelry parts, gold leaf, blank china ready to decorate, brushes of all kinds, special scissors for greeting card edges, and much, much more. If you specialize in ceramics, pottery, or sculpture, request the comprehensive 64-page "Ceramic & Pottery" catalog. There you'll find supplies and equipment (including kilns) for almost any related medium, at great prices. The "Music & Sound" catalog is 32 pages of wind-up and electric musical movements in over 400 melodies and sound effects (voices, animal noises, laughing ghosts, etc.) with parts that rotate, spin, seesaw, fly, throw, twirl, rock, nod, and wave. You'll find all the components here to create an heirloom music-maker for that special loved one. If you're wired into lamps and lights, you'll find what you need in the 32-page "Electrical & Lighting" catalog's collection of components and accessories. The 12-page "Clocks" catalog serves clock-makers with a good selection of movements, clock components, and accessories. Finally, the "Doll-making Supplies" catalog is 48 color pages of eyes, hair, teeth, and other body parts, as well as head and body molds, armatures, and frames, footwear, hosiery, eye wear, hats, clothes, parasols, movements, tools, and supplies for making dolls of every kind. There are also doll-making books here. You can order electronically off the website, but you won't find the full inventory there.

SPECIAL FACTORS: Satisfaction guaranteed; returns made within 30 days will be fully refunded; quantity discounts available; C.O.D. orders add $4.75; shipping within 24 hours.

Sunshine Discount Crafts

P.O. Box 301, Dept. WBM   727–538–2878
Largo, FL 33779–0301   Fax: 727–531–2739

Catalog: $2 for U.S.; $4 for Canada; $10 international
Pay: check, MO, MC, V, AE, DSC
Sells: general crafts and hobby supplies
Store: mail order only
Online: www.sunshinecrafts.com

Leafing through Sunshine Craft's 176-page, closely printed catalog gave me the feeling of being in a giant warehouse, where one might find buckets of plastic animal eyes, barrels of colorful beads, aisles of paints, and cases of polymer clays and mosaic tiles. In fact, this catalog boasts over 14,000 products for the craftsperson and hobbyist, and you won't be disappointed by the prices—25% to 35% below regular list, with better prices on some items when you order in small quantity. There are supplies here for doll-makers, clock-makers, jewelry crafters, home decorators, glass artists, woodworkers, tole fanatics, and more. There's also plenty here for the kids—rubber stamps, memory scrapbook kits, beading, glitter, feathers, barrettes, baskets, and on and on. Whether you're making a stuffed animal, creating Easter ornaments, or decorating your own bridal headpiece, you'll find what you need here. The website is informational only; there's no online ordering of products here, although you can order a print catalog on the site.

Wholesale orders: Please inquire about price lists and policies.

SPECIAL FACTORS: See catalog for returns policy; orders under $20 require an additional $2.50; quantity discounts available on some items; wholesale buyers should inquire for terms.

Think Ink

7526 Olympic View Dr.,   425–778–1935
Suite E-W   Fax: 425–776–2997
Edmonds, WA 98026

> Catalog: $2, refundable with first order
> Pay: check, MO, MC, V, DSC
> Sells: thermography/embossing powders, GOCCO
>   printers, supplies, etc.
> Store: same address; Monday to Friday 9:30–5:30
> Online: www.thinkink.net

If you're part of the rubber-stamp-art craze, you're going to be very happy to find out about Think Ink. This company, says the enthusiastic owner, has perhaps the largest selection of embossing (also called thermography) powders anywhere—171 colors and counting at press time—at prices that are about 50% to 60% less than you'll find anywhere else. When we think of rubber stamps, most of us think "Return to Sender!" or "Second Notice!" in red block letters. But today's rubber-stampers are creating beautiful, masterful art. This is an unbeatable source.

In addition to stocking embossing powders, Think Ink sells GOCCO printers, supplies, and creative accessories for printing your own colorful flyers, bulletins, cards, tote bags, T-shirts, and nearly anything else made of paper, card stock, fabric, leather, or wood. More than 7 million GOCCO printers have been purchased in Japan and elsewhere for home use since their introduction a generation ago. (In Japan, serious artists use large-format GOCCO printers to produce limited-edition, fine-art prints, an art form known as Shin Kohanga.) Think Ink sells two models of Print GOCCOs, the B6 model (with a 4″ × 5¾″ image area, $99) and the B5 (6″ × 9″ image area, $300), both sold for less here than you're likely to find elsewhere. These printers work by creating a master of your design that can be inked like a silkscreen and printed. Until I had a good look at the catalog and website, I wasn't exactly sure what these printers were capable of. Now I'm tempted to buy *The New GOCCO Guide,* a 245-page guide penned by none other than Think Ink's owner Claire Russell, that offers project ideas, steers you through tricks and traps, and generally aids you in getting the most out of this marvelous home printer. The website, which offers online ordering, is a good place to find out more about these extremely cool presses and the bargain embossing powders.

SPECIAL FACTORS: Wholesale orders accepted; inquire for terms.

Tom Thumb Workshops

14100 Lankford Hwy.   757–824–3507
P.O. Box 357–WBM
Mappsville, VA 23407

Price List: free with a long SASE
Pay: check, MO, MC, V
Sells: potpourri, spices, herbs, oils, etc.
Store: same address (Rt. 13); Monday to Friday 9–5
Online: www.tomthumbworkshops.com

With a catalog from Tom Thumb Workshops you could make your own personal massage oil or create beautiful pressed-flower art. Or you could order herbs and dried flowers, labels and stickers, fabric sachets, and potpourri boxes and then make heartfelt Christmas gifts throughout the year—at prices 20% to 45% below those charged elsewhere. Tom Thumb carries booklets and crafting designs, patterns and illustrated how-tos, and full-sized texts to help take the mystery out of potpourri crafts, card crafting, wreath-making, herbal soap-making, blending of essential oils, and many more activities that are good for the soul and have practical application. An additional saving of 25%, except for books and items from the "bulk oil list," applies on orders $100 and higher. Founded in 1975, Tom Thumb will decoratively package your selection of potpourri in four-ounce bags, with a ribbon bow and botanical elf, as gifts ($9.50 each). Do check out the nice website, where you can view inventory, order merchandise online, obtain a print catalog, and just see what's available.

SPECIAL FACTORS: Satisfaction guaranteed; returns accepted within 30 days; minimum order $15; $30 with credit card.

Turncraft Clocks, Inc.

P.O. Box 100–WBM   800–544–1711
Mound, MN 55364–0100   Fax: 612–471–8579

Catalog: $2
Pay: check, MO, MC, V, DSC
Sells: clock plans and movements
Store: 4310 Shoreline Dr., Spring Park, MN; Monday to
    Friday 8–5
Online: www.nonni.com/woodhobby

With nearly 30 years of experience, Turncraft Clocks continues to offer wood-workers and clock-makers plans for cabinets (curio, jewelry, gun), humidors, coffee tables, desk sets, and floor, wall, mantle, and patio clocks. They also stock the parts (but not the wood, in most cases): a full selection of movements—regular mini-quartz, pendulum, dual chime, six melody chime—decorative tubes, clock hands, clock dials, numbers, hardware, and decals. The 32-page color catalog offers precision-cut laser clock frames in assorted subjects (fisherman, teacher, farm scene, cat in window) that can be paired with quartz fit-ups (sized from $1^7/_{16}''$) in solid brass or brass or silver finished bezels. Clearly written catalog descriptions help with selecting correct sizes and appropriate styles. Lamp parts packages (basic, universal, and three-way), drill bits, glue, stains, and router books are also available. A print catalog can be ordered online at Turncraft's website, but there's no electronic ordering of inventory at this time.

SPECIAL FACTORS: Satisfaction guaranteed; school accounts with purchase order.

Vanguard Crafts

P.O. Box 340170, Dept. WBM   718–377–5188
Brooklyn, NY 11234–0003   Fax: 888–692–0056

    Catalog: $1, refundable
    Pay: check, MO, MC, V, DSC
    Sells: crafts, kits, and materials
    Store: 1081 E. 48th St., Brooklyn, NY; Monday to Saturday
      10–5

If you manage a classroom, an after-school program, a day-care center, or a household of children, the catalog from Vanguard Crafts can help you plan instructive, interesting, even "cool" projects—not only for the kids! Since 1959, Vanguard has made crafts kits and projects affordable while updating the inventory to keep pace with current fads. This year it's friendship pins and trade bead bracelets—easy, inexpensive, and fun to make (a 45-project pack of friendship pins, $7.75; a 12-pack of bracelets, $13.45). The colorful 76-page catalog introduces fantasy masks complete with decorating materials, mini-tote kits, preassembled wooden boxes ready for finishing and decoration, papier-mâché dance rattle kits ($16.89 for a 12 pack), and the popular s'getti strings (50 assorted 50-yard spools, $94.30). Vanguard has kits and supplies for tissue art, printmaking, tie-dyeing, weaving, basket-making, sponge-painting, modeling, calendar-making, crocheting, beading, and almost every art or craft you can think of, including leather and woodworking, calligraphy, and stenciling. Brushes, artists' supplies, and tools are also available—for example, brush packs ideal for classrooms, art papers, paints, craft scissors, knife sets and snips, and jewelry pliers. Institutional accounts from accredited organizations are welcome, and bids and quotations are invited.

SPECIAL FACTORS: Institutional accounts welcome; minimum order $25.

Allentown, Pennsylvania, is home to Warner-Crivellaro's 40,000-square-foot warehouse and showrooms of glass, bevels, filigree, wooden boxes, flowers, lamp prisms, and more for the stained-glass enthusiast. The 178-page catalog and the comprehensive website bring the quality and service of Warner-Crivellaro into your home. At the website, "Technical Tips" offers lessons on working with lampshades, copper foil, soldering, leading, and glass-cutting. Online sales run limited-time discounts of 10% to 30% off Warner's usual prices, and web specials offer additional reductions. Free patterns for night-lights, quilt squares, and Pennsylvania Dutch designs are available online too.

Catalog and online shoppers can order boxed sample sets of glass (2″ × 3″) marked with a manufacturer's color number and representing everything available from a particular manufacturer. "Bargain Boxes" are an economical way to stock up on first-quality glass (10 sheets, 8″ × 10″ or 12″ × 12″) at great prices. Bevels—plain, engraved, in holiday and seasonal themes—drop in price when ordered in mix-and-match quantities; nuggets, nugget foilers, marbles, jewels, night-light filigrees, and videos receive quantity price breaks too.

If you're looking for a grinder, a soldering iron, a tubing cutter, or an electric engraver to fashion your own tables, windows, and lamps, all are here in name-brand models. Ready-made brass and antiqued lamp bases and wrought-iron table and plant stands, with optional tops, can cut decorating costs. Kits (kaleidoscope, lamp, candle shell), books, stencils, chemicals (cement, sealant, fluxes, grinder coolant), chain, and even gift wrap can be found here too.

SPECIAL FACTORS: Phone orders available 24 hours a day; call about matching glass and making special orders; authorized returns accepted; minimum order $25.

Related Products/Companies

Arts and crafts supplies
- Make Us An Offer

Battery-operated pottery wheels for kids
- Ott's Discount

Books on country crafts
- Storey Books

Candle-making supplies
- Brushy Mountain Bee Farm, Ott's Discount

Clock-making supplies
- Eloxite

Doll-making
- Newark Dressmaking Supply, Oppenheim's, Taylor's Cutaways and Stuff

Dyed mohair locks for doll wigs
- Mangham Manor Fiber Farm

Feathers and trim
- Manny's Millinery

Flower-drying equipment
- Johnny's Selected Seeds

General craft supplies
- Axner Pottery, Oppenheim's, Ott's Discount, Pearl Paint

How-to craft books
- Dover

Jewelry craft
- Eloxite, Fire Mountain Gems, Hong Kong Lapidaries, House of Onyx

Kite-building
- BFK Sports

Leather craft
- Leather Unlimited, Weaver Leather

Model-building tools, supplies, plans
- Micro-Mark, Poor Man's Catalog

Native American beadery and craft supplies
- Leather Unlimited

New and surplus tools and machine/gizmo parts
- H&R Company

Papermaking materials
- Daniel Smith

Soap-making supplies
- Brushy Mountain Bee Farm

Stencils
- Stencil House of N.H.

U-Build power tool plans
- Poor Man's Catalog

Wood-burning kits for kids
- Ott's Discount

Woodworking books
- Woodworkers' Discount Books

Woodworking tools, hardware, and supplies
- Camelot Enterprises, Econ-Abrasives, Hot Tools, Northern Hydraulics, Ott's Discount, Tool Crib of the North, Tools on Sale, Woodworker's Supply

Wreaths, pomanders, sachets, essential oils, herbs, etc.
- Atlantic Spice, Caprilands Herb Farm, Taylor's Cutaways and Stuff

Ceramics

Materials, supplies, tools, and equipment for pottery, sculpture, and other ceramic crafts

Most people think of mugs, pots, and bowls when they think of ceramics. But people who love to work with clay also make lamps, clocks, jewelry, mirrors, tile, ornaments, sculptures, candlesticks, porcelain boxes—the list is as endless as the craftsperson's imagination. For all of the little parts, tools, and accessories you'll need to create these items, look to the companies below, but don't forget that many of the general craft companies in the previous section, starting on page 128, carry them too. You'll find ceramics supplies, tools, and even heavy equipment such as kilns carried by the companies in this chapter. Because they want your mail-order business, most companies will give you incentives to buy kilns and other heavy goods by offering free or very inexpensive shipping.

Find It Fast

Books on Ceramic Art and Technique
- Aftosa, Axner, Bailey's

Clays, Slips, and Glazes
- Axner, Bailey's

Craft Project Supplies
- Aftosa, Axner, Lou Davis Wholesale

Large Equipment (Wheels, Kilns)
- Axner, Bailey's, Lou Davis Wholesale

Aftosa

1034 Ohio Ave.
Richmond, CA 94804

800–231–0397
510–233–0334
Fax: 510–233–3569

Catalog: free
Pay: check, MO, MC, V, AE, DSC
Sells: pottery accessories and craft supplies
Store: mail order only
Online: www.aftosa.com

Aftosa is the place to shop if you're looking for pottery and craft supplies at wholesale prices. There are supplies here for all your ceramic projects. Dispenser pumps; pin frogs for flower arranging (you create the container/base); wire, cane, and rattan handles for ceramic baskets, teapots, and other vessels; metal stands for candle holders; bottle spigots and stoppers; cotton and fiberglass wick, as well as oil burners and glass chimneys; wooden accessories such as honey sticks and salad servers; mirrors; clocks and jewelry parts; display stands; cork (composition, bark-top, and natural); metal and glass shades; wooden trivet boxes; and, of course, potter's tools and supplies can all be found here at prices that are 35% to 50% less than retail. There's no minimum, but if your order is under $50, there's a $5 surcharge. Shipping is free! The website has some useful company information, but no online ordering.

SPECIAL FACTORS: Orders to Hawaii, Alaska, and Canada add 15%; other international orders, see catalog for details; returns are subject to a 10% restock fee; see catalog for complete returns policy.

Axner Pottery Supply

P.O. Box 621484
Oviedo, FL 32762–1484

800–843–7057
407–365–2600
Fax: 407–365–5573

Catalog: free
Pay: check, MO, V, MC
Sells: pottery supplies, books, and videos
Warehouse/Showroom: 804-A Eyrie Dr., Oviedo, FL;
 Monday to Friday 9–5, Thursday till 7, Saturday 9–2
Online: www.axner.com

A professional potter recommended Axner Pottery Supply as a good source with reasonable prices. Axner's goods average about 20% less that what you'd find in a ceramic supply shop—if you're lucky enough to live near one. The 192-page newsprint catalog has a lot of explanatory text alongside the photographs of products, which makes it a good resource. Quantity price breaks are included for many items, and suggested retail prices versus Axner's prices are also listed on some, but not all, products. Here you'll find equipment, tools, and supplies for making tile, jewelry, pots and dishes, lamps, clocks, and more. You'll find the big equipment here—kilns, wheels, and mixers, for example—as well as clay and glazes of all types. (There's an eight-page color insert for the glazes.) Axner claims to have the largest supply of pottery supplies and equipment "in the known universe," so just about any tool, finishing supply, or other pottery-related item you seek will be here. Be sure to leaf through the pottery/ceramics books and videos section, for which Axner is renowned. The website has information about the company, but currently no online product ordering.

SPECIAL FACTORS: Satisfaction guaranteed; 30-day return policy; wholesale orders accepted; no C.O.D.'s.

Bailey Ceramic Supply

P.O. Box 1577
Kingston, NY 12402

800–431–6067
914–339–3721
Fax: 914–339–5530

Catalog: free
Pay: check, MO, MC, V
Sells: professional ceramic supplies and equipment
Showroom: 62 Ten Broeck Ave., Kingston, NY; Monday to
Friday 9–12, 3–4:30; call beforehand. Mail-order phone
hours: Monday to Friday 9–5 ET

Jim Bailey and his wife Anne Shattuck Bailey are dedicated ceramists. Since 1984, Bailey has been supplying professional potters with great products that are up to 25% less than retail when you buy in quantity, and major name-brand pottery equipment at "the lowest prices in the USA." Bailey also manufactures many of its own products, such as extruders, slab rollers and wheels, and kilns, and sells them at factory-direct prices. The 188-page black-and-white catalog offers chemicals, clays, and glazes; small tools and accessories; hand-building equipment; wheels and wheel accessories; mixing equipment; kilns; safety, production, storage, and spray equipment; packing materials; display and accessory items; lamp and jewelry accessories; an extensive video and book library; and much more.

SPECIAL FACTORS: Satisfaction guaranteed on every order; five professional potters on staff to answer questions; most orders shipped within 48 hours.

Lou Davis Wholesale

N3211 County Rd. H   414–248–2000
P.O. Box 21   Fax: 414–248–6977
Lake Geneva, WI 53147

Catalog: $2
Pay: check, MO, MC, V, AE, DSC
Sells: ceramic and craft supplies
Store: mail order only

If you've seen one crafts supply catalog, you've seen 'em all, right? Well, no, not exactly. For instance, I found that Lou Davis Wholesale, in business for over 40 years, stood out from the pack by being a straightforward company presenting real savings to ceramicists by offering a lowest-price guarantee, quantity discounts, and a good selection of basic supplies for lamps, music boxes, clocks, dolls, and small sculptures with moving parts, among other things. The 40-page newsprint tabloid-style catalog has hundreds of products drawn or photographed, with descriptions and different price breakdowns—the lowest when you order in quantities such as one or two dozen. If you're serious about saving, you can even phone and ask for higher quantity discounts.

SPECIAL FACTORS: Complete satisfaction guaranteed; returns accepted within 90 days.

Related Products/Companies

Books and videotapes on ceramics and pottery
- The Potters Shop

Ceramics tools
- The Potters Shop

Clay and kilns
- Ott's Discount

Jewelry-Making

Beads, stones, gems, findings, and supplies for making fine and craft jewelry

There are some mail-order catalogs that make you dream. I've really enjoyed reading and learning about cultured pearls, Czechoslovakian beadery, Native

American silversmithing, investment-grade stones, and many other eclectic and fascinating subjects you'll find in this section's company literature. If you've ever considered making your own earrings, rings, pendants, bracelets, pins, and necklaces, or wanted to turn an ordinary item such as a pillbox, barrette, or money clip into something valuable and precious, the firms below will provide you with many-faceted avenues to do so, from inexpensive materials, tools, and accessories to rare and precious metals and cut gems. Have fun.

Find It Fast

Beads
- Fire Mountain Gems, Hong Kong Lapidaries

Gemstones
- Eloxite, Fire Mountain Gems, Hong Kong Lapidaries

Jewelry-Craft "Blanks" (Nonjeweled Items)
- Eloxite

Jewelry Findings
- Eloxite, Fire Mountain Gems

Pearls
- Fire Mountain Gems, Hong Kong Lapidaries

Thread and Silk
- Eloxite, Fire Mountain Gems, Hong Kong Lapidaries

Eloxite Corporation

806 10th St. 307–322–3050
P.O. Box 729 Fax: 307–322–3055
Wheatland, WY 82201

Catalog: free
Pay: check, MO, MC, V, DSC
Sells: jewelry craft supplies
Store: 806 Tenth St., Wheatland, WY; Monday to Friday
  8:30–4, Saturday 8:30–3
Online: www.eloxite.com

Eloxite has been selling wholesale jewelry findings, cabochons, beads, and other lapidary supplies since 1955. Prices here are up to 75% below those charged by other crafts sources for findings and jewelry components. Jewelry findings with a Western flair are featured in the 88-page catalog: bola ties and slide medallions, belt buckles and inserts, and coin jewelry are prominent offerings. Also shown are pendants, rings, earrings, lockets, tie tacks, jewelry boxes, money clips, barrettes, pins, and more, made to be set with cabochons or cut stones, as well as jump rings, chains, pillboxes, screw eyes, and ear wires. The stones themselves are sold—cut cubic zirconia and synthetic gemstones and oval cabochons of abalone, agate, black onyx, garnet, opal, obsidian, jasper, and malachite. There's also a full range of jewelry supplies and equipment, including tumblers, soldering tools, grinding wheels, and more.

Sandwiched between the pages of jewelry components are quartz clock movements and blanks for clock faces, clock hands, and ballpoint pens and letter openers for desk sets. Discounts are available on most items, and specials are usually offered with orders of specified amounts.

SPECIAL FACTORS: Quantity discounts are available; undamaged returns are accepted within 15 days for exchange or refund (a $2 restocking fee may be charged); minimum order is $15; C.O.D. orders are accepted.

Fire Mountain Gems

28195 Redwood Hwy.	800–423–2319
Cave Junction, OR 97523–9304	Fax: 800–292–FIRE

Catalog: free
Pay: check, MO, MC, V, AE, DSC
Sells: beads, jewels, gems, and supplies for jewelry-making
Store: mail order only

I knew I'd found a gem of a company when I read this mail-order catalog and wanted to meet the owners, who share their philosophy about working cooperatively with village people in 14 developing countries to obtain interesting products ethically and constructively. Fire Mountain Gems has been around for 25 years and publishes a 244-page color catalog that's a jewelry-maker's dream come true. We're not talking plastic beads here. This is a serious source for serious artisans. Price breaks are listed for each item; buying a single item in small quantity can net you a savings of 40%. Czech glass beads; Austrian crystal beads; seed beads; shell strands; porcupine quills; porcelain beads; pewter pendants; freshwater cultured pearls of every size, color, and description; gem beads; gold, silver, and other metal beads; cloisonné beads and pendants; faceted gems; cabachons; findings; tools; supplies such as beading twine, hemp cord, and suede thong—the list of what you'll find goes on and on. Suffice it to say that if you want to make jewelry, Fire Mountain Gems will have what you're looking for at prices you can live with.

SPECIAL FACTORS: Any unaltered item can be returned for refund, credit, or exchange; see catalog for details; orders under $50 incur a $5 charge.

Hong Kong Lapidaries, Inc.

2801 University Dr.
Coral Springs, FL 33065

954–755–8777
Fax: 954–755–8780

Catalog: $3, $5 outside U.S.
Pay: check, MO, MC, V
Sells: jewelry supplies, beads, cabochons, and loose stones
Store: mail order only

Hong Kong Lapidaries, established in 1979, sells a wide range of precious and semiprecious stones in a variety of forms. The 58-page catalog lists items of interest to hobbyists as well, and the prices run as much as 70% below comparable retail. Thousands of cabochons, beads, loose-faceted and cut stones—heart shapes and charms, flowers and leaves, rings, donuts, and more—mosaic stones, and strung chips of pearl, garnet, amethyst, onyx, abalone, and other kinds of semiprecious stones are offered through the catalog, which comes with a separate 12-page color brochure that shows representative pieces. Egyptian clay scarabs, coral, cameos, cubic zirconia, yellow jade, cloisonné jewelry and objets d'art, 14K gold-filled and sterling silver beads, and ball earrings are available. Hobbyists should note the necklace thread—100% silk or nylon—in a score of colors and 16 sizes, as well as stringing needles.

SPECIAL FACTORS: Satisfaction is guaranteed; price quote by fax; quantity discounts are available; returns are accepted within 12 days; minimum order is $50; C.O.D. orders are accepted.

Related Products/Companies

Diamond broker
• Simply Diamonds

Investment-grade loose stones
• House of Onyx

Jewelry-making supplies
• Newark Dressmaker Supply

Textile Arts

Supplies and equipment for sewing, spinning, knitting, weaving, quilting, needlework, and other textile arts

Once upon a time—and not so long ago, either—sewing, quilting, and knitting were common activities in most homes. Today, making your own clothes, curtains, tablecloths, blankets, and other home accessories is a great way to save money, assuming you have the time. The companies in this chapter can help you find all the right tools and materials for your projects. You'll find everything from raw fleece for spinning and large looms for rug-weaving to professional dress forms for designing your own gowns and undyed silk for batiking. There's also lots here for the everyday knitter or mender just looking for some bargain supplies. Every kind of textile artist will find plenty here to love—at huge savings.

Other chapters in this book sell textile-related supplies and equipment, particularly "Fine Art Supplies" and two sections of the "Home" chapter: "Appliances and TVs" and "Wall and Window Treatments, Decorator Fabrics." Be sure to check out "Related Products/Companies" at the end of this section to find suppliers of sewing machines, fabric dyes, upholstery fabric, and more.

Find It Fast

Batting, Pillow Inserts, Fiberfill
- Buffalo Batt & Felt, Connecting Threads, Monterey, Oppenheim's

Custom-Made Zippers
- The Button Shop, A. Feibusch

Doll-Making Supplies
- Newark Dressmaker Supply, Oppenheim's, Taylor's Cutaways and Stuff

Drapery Hardware
- Atlanta Thread

Fabric
- Connecting Threads, Fashion Fabrics, Oppenheim's, Taylor's Cutaways and Stuff, Thai Silks, Utex Trading

Fabric Dyes
- Dharma Trading

Fake Fur
- Monterey, Oppenheim's, Taylor's Cutaways and Stuff

Looms
- Great Northern Weaving, Webs

Quilting Patterns and Supplies
- Connecting Threads, Oppenheim's, Taylor's Cutaways and Stuff

Rug-Making Supplies
- Great Northern Weaving

Sewing and Pressing Machines, Sergers, Dry-Cleaning Equipment
- Atlanta Thread, The Button Shop, Solo Slide Fasteners

Sewing Notions and Tools
- Atlanta Thread and Supply, The Button Shop, A. Feibusch, Newark Dressmaker Supply, Solo Slide Fasteners

Undyed Fabric and Clothing Blanks for Dyeing
- Dharma Trading, Thai Silks

Yarns and Raw Fiber for Spinning
- Smiley's Yarns, Bonnie Triola, Mangham Manor Fiber Farm, Webs

Atlanta Thread & Supply Co., a division of National Thread & Supply Corp., has been in the business of providing professionals with sewing equipment and supplies since 1948. Extremely competitive pricing and a high level of customer service make this a worthy company to know about, particularly if you can buy items in quantity, where deeper discounts apply.

The 67-page catalog presents photographs or line drawings with no-nonsense product descriptions. Tailors, upholsterers, dressmakers, and those who do serious sewing at home will appreciate the wide selection of threads (all-purpose, embroidery, serging, buttonhole, etc.), dress and tailoring forms, sewing supplies, linings, buttons, scissors, cleaning items, drapery-making supplies and hardware, crinolines, tapes, irons and pressing tables, professional and at-home sewing machines and machine parts, and more. I liked the "Uniquely New" dress form and pant/skirt forms; when you lose or gain weight, adjust the form's cover and it will compress or expand to your new size! Don't be looking for cutesy arts and craft stuff in this catalog. This is a serious supplier of top-name products for professional-caliber sewing.

SPECIAL FACTORS: Satisfaction guaranteed; returns accepted for refund or exchange; quantity discounts apply; C.O.D.s accepted; same day shipping on orders received before 2 P.M. EST.

Buffalo Batt & Felt Corp.

3307 Walden Ave., Dept. WBM   **716–683–4100, ext. 130**
Depew, NY 14043   **Fax: 716–683–8928**

Brochure and Samples: $1, refundable
Pay: check, MO, MC, V
Sells: fiberfill, quilt batts, pillow inserts, decorative "snow"
Store: mail order only
Online: www.superfluff.com

We always wondered what made cloth dolls and hand-crafted pillows so springy, washable, *and* affordable! Buffalo Batt & Felt Corp. probably has the answer, with its "Super Fluff" bouncy polyester stuffing; Ultra Fluff, a premium fiberfill; "Soft Heart" Quallofil pillow inserts; and "thermabonded" quilt batt. With an array of desirable properties (high loft, nonallergenic, flame-retardant, machine washable, easy to sew), Buffalo Batt's fiberfill, quilt batts, and pillow inserts are available in convenient small sizes as well as bulk at substantial savings on normal retail prices. Buffalo Batt & Felt also sells "Buffalo Snow" products—Christmas tree skirts, loose flakes (for window or display decorating), snow blankets, and other items. The sample-laden catalog gives details about thicknesses, sizes of rolls and inserts, and the differences among products. The website has lots of information, as well as excellent photographs and descriptions of their products and a FAQ section that textile artists especially will appreciate. You'll have to order a minimum of any two cases to receive wholesale pricing, so team up with a friend.

Please note that orders are shipped, via UPS, only within the 48 contiguous states.

SPECIAL FACTORS: Quantity discounts available; two-case minimum order; C.O.D. orders accepted.

The Button Shop

P.O. Box 272   **Tel/Fax: 847–818–8420**
Des Plaines, IL 60016–0272

Catalog: free
Pay: check, MO, MC, V
Sells: buttons and sewing supplies
Store: mail order only
E-mail: ButtonShop@aol.com

The Button Shop calls itself "America's source for discount sewing supplies for over 98 years." Among the items offered in the 18-page black-and-white catalog are zippers (cut to any size and color-matched to your fabric if you send in a two-inch fabric swatch), a good selection of top-name scissors, odds and ends such as vest buckles and suspender clips, Coats & Clark thread, thread for serger machines, interfacings, tapes, binders, elastics, shoulder pads, pins and needles, hooks and eyes, sewing machine parts, miscellaneous sewing gadgets, and of course, buttons. Buttons for children's wear and craft projects, plain white buttons, make-your-own covered buttons, buttons of glass or wood, military-style buttons, colored buttons, gold-rimmed buttons, peacoat buttons, fancy ladies' buttons—you name it. In spite of the fact that the catalog lacks detailed descriptions or colors, I like this company's old-fashioned approach to mail-order, which relies more on its customers' being knowledgeable than it does on glitsy layouts. The Button Shop's prices are about 30% to 40% below what you'd find at retail.

SPECIAL FACTORS: Minimum $10 with credit card orders; returns accepted within 30 days.

Connecting Threads

P.O. Box 8940
Vancouver, WA 98668–8940

800–574–6454
Fax: 360–260–8877

Catalog: free
Pay: check, MO, MC, V, AE, DSC, JCB
Sells: quilting patterns, materials, and supplies
Store: mail order only

Newfound respect at auctions these days for traditional early-American quilts has spawned a resurgence in the art of quilting. Connecting Threads is an invaluable source for "the busy quilter" with its 48-page color catalog of patterns, instructional books on quilting and other textile arts, and a full inventory of quilter's handy tools and basic supplies: quilting stencils, frames and batting, cotton thread, slash cutters, slice rulers, bias tape, flexible-angle lamps, thread, basting guns, cutting mats, pencil remover solution, and much more. Prices here are about 20% less than retail.

SPECIAL FACTORS: Satisfaction guaranteed; returns accepted for credit, refund, or exchange.

Dharma Trading Co.

P.O. Box 150916
San Rafael, CA 94915–0916

800–542–5227
415–456–7657
Fax: 415–456–8747

Catalog: free
Pay: check, MO, MC, V, DSC
Sells: textile craft supplies and clothing "blanks"
Store: 1604 Fourth St., San Rafael, CA; Monday to
  Saturday 10–6
Online: www.dharmatrading.com

It's a pleasure to pass along information about firms like Dharma Trading Co. This consumer-friendly company sells undyed fabric, garments, hats, and accessories for women, men, and children of all sizes, and the dyes, fabric paints, batik supplies, markers, and tools to color and decorate them. Dharma's policies are as plain as their goods: prices are discounted from list about 20%, and the per-unit prices drop even more if you can order in small quantities. Quantity discounts apply to the total amount ordered, not the type or style, which means you can mix and match and still get the best prices. The wearables in the 121-page catalog include silk items: baseball caps, sun visors, hair bows, neckties, T-shirts, ponchos, tank tops, skirts, over vests, boxers, chemises, and camisoles; cotton, jersey, and hemp items: infant rompers, toddler T-suits, short- and long-sleeved shirts, underpants, baby wraps, bubble suits, kids' caps, shorts, shirts, dresses, tights, all types of outer- and underclothing for men and women; and other fabric "blanks," including gloves, tablecloths, laundry bags, place mats, tote bags, aprons, bandannas, tea towels, sarongs, headbands, silk fans, silk-covered earring blanks, pillow covers, muslin dolls, and much more. There are books galore on every aspect of the textile arts, and of course the supplies you'll need to turn these textiles into one-of-a-kind masterpieces. The catalog is full of useful information such as safety tips, how-to articles, and information on such topics as shrinkage and fabric types. The website is well-designed, informative, and offers online ordering.

SPECIAL FACTORS: Satisfaction guaranteed; returns accepted within 30 days with some conditions (see catalog for details); C.O.D. orders accepted.

Fashion Fabrics Club

10490 Baur Blvd.   800–468–0602
St. Louis, MO 63132   Fax: 314–993–5802

    Membership: $10 (see text)
    Pay: check, MO, MC, V
    Sells: dress fabric
    Store: 10512 Baur Blvd., St. Louis, MO; Tuesday to
      Saturday 10–5, Sunday 12–5
    Online: www.fashionfabricsclub.com

One of the best moments in mail-order shopping occurs when already low fabric prices, like those at Fashion Fabrics Club, are further reduced for clearance. So if you're a home sewer who already enjoys Fashion Fabrics' 50%-per-yard savings on name-brand polyester crepe, cotton velvet, cotton chambray, wool, and cotton/Lycra blends, you know the joy of opening the mailbox to find the latest monthly sampler with clearance prices on the back. On nonclearance items, you can use the rebate bonus coupons you accrue with each mailing.

How does a home sewer receive a monthly selection of coordinated swatches? For an annual fee of $10, you become a member of Fashion Fabrics Club, and during special promotions the fee is waived if you buy one or more fabrics. One introductory newsletter offered new members fabrics at $1.99 per yard, with a five-yard maximum per fabric, and threw in one year's free membership! Members also have access to a professional thread-matching service from a selection of 262 colors by Gutermann Thread (for regular machines and sergers, $1.25 per spool). There's never an obligation to buy, and all uncut fabrics will be accepted for return anytime. At press time the website was just being launched, so check it out.

SPECIAL FACTORS: Satisfaction guaranteed; returns accepted; club membership available only in the United States and possessions.

A. Feibusch

27 Allen St.　　　　　212–226–3964
New York, NY 10002　　Fax: 212–226–5844

Information: price quote
Pay: check or MO
Sells: zippers, thread, notions, and garment supplies
Store: same address; Monday to Friday 9:30–5, Sunday 10–5

Write a company to buy a zipper? Not so silly once you realize that this company, A. Feibusch, regularly handles mail and telephone orders and has been doing so since 1941. A. Feibusch carries all kinds of sewing notions—"everything but buttons"—and sells them for about 50% less than anywhere else. From tiny doll's zippers to heavy-duty zippers for luggage, A. Feibusch either stocks your zipper or can have it custom-made for you. This is a good source for just about any color of all-cotton and polyester thread. If you know what you want, mail your request, with a fabric swatch if matching is necessary, or call, since there's no catalog. The salespeople here speak many languages, including Spanish, French, Chinese, and German.

SPECIAL FACTORS: Price quote by letter.

Great Northern Weaving

451 East D. Ave.   **800–370–7235**
P.O. Box 462   **616–341–9752**
Kalamazoo, MI 49004–0462   **Fax: 616–341–9525**

Catalog and Samples: $2.50
Pay: check, MO, MC, V
Sells: rug-making supplies and tools
Store: same address; Monday to Friday 9–4

Ask a rug-weaver for a great source and they're likely to cite Great Northern Weaving. That's because Great Northern offers high-quality supplies and equipment for rug-weaving, braiding, and crocheting at prices that are below everyone else's. The 12-page catalog features rug warps (cotton/poly, 100% cotton, spun nylon, and multifiber); rug wefts (rag coils, loose rags, wool rags, cotton rag filler, poly rug filler, rug roping, fuzzy loopers, colored loopers, and white loopers); weaving equipment such as shuttles, warping board, rag cutters, and spool racks; and loom parts. Braiding and rug-crocheting supplies can also be found here, as well as small-frame looms for little projects, the "incredible rope machine," and other items.

SPECIAL FACTORS: $4 handling fee for orders under $40; add $5 on C.O.D. orders.

Mangham Manor Fiber Farm

901 Hammocks Gap Road   804–973–2222
Charlottesville, VA 22911   Fax: 804–973–7108

> Catalog: free
> Pay: check or MO
> Sells: raw fleece from sheep and Angora goats, yarn, dyed
>   mohair locks, wool and mohair socks, shawls, blankets,
>   etc.
> Store: mail order only; farm visits by appointment; phone
>   hours Monday to Friday 10–4 EST
> E-Mail: MangManor@aol.com

The Manghams of Mangham Manor Fiber Farm, in the foothills of the Blue Ridge Mountains, have been raising naturally colored sheep and Angora goats for 16 years. This is a great place to know about if you're a spinner, knitter, or weaver because you'll get the finest quality raw wool and mohair here for 50% less than what you'd pay in a retail shop. In fact, it's likely that the Manghams are your supplier's supplier.

Chatting with Michelle, half of the Mangham husband-wife team, reminded me that shepherds see themselves as loving caretakers of a large family—in this case 250 breeding head with *triple* that number in the spring! The Manghams are careful to practice "green" farming techniques to insure that the soil and animals remain healthy for the next generation of Manghams and beyond. Many of their "girls" have names and have been with them for many years. (Spinners from all over the globe have favorite animals they know by name whose fleece they reserve each year!) The fleece comes in various shades of gray, black, white, red, and brown. The Manghams sell washed and dyed mohair; raw mohair; raw wool; 50% wool/50% mohair carded, batted, and in roving form; white or black mohair socks (the softest and warmest socks I've ever worn!); and white or chocolate brown mohair blankets. Other products include gorgeous dyed mohair locks (great for yarn, doll wigs, tassels, felted hats, etc.), mill-spun yarn (dyed mohair and soft gray wool—perfect for tweeds), long tail hairs from the horses that work on the farm, and "how to" felt ball packages (popular with the school kids who regularly tour the Manghams' farm). Samples are available by request. Languages spoken at the farm include Spanish, German, and French.

SPECIAL FACTORS: C.O.D. orders accepted.

Monterey Incorporated

1725 E. Delavan Dr.
Janesville, WI 53547

800–432–9959
608–754–8309
Fax: 608–757–3312

Price List: free with SASE
Pay: check, MO, MC, V
Sells: fake-fur fabric
Store: same address; Monday to Friday 8–4:30; Saturday
 8–12 (April to September), 8–4:30 (October to March)
Online: www.montereyoutlet.com

For over 25 years, Monterey Incorporated has been able to sell fake fur fabric at discount prices—up to 50% off—because it manufactures the popular deep-pile fur fabrics it sells. It supplies toy, apparel, craft, costume, and pet markets as well as the over-the-counter market. Here you'll find the country's largest selection of knitted deep-pile fabrics in first quality, closeouts, overruns, discontinued, and substandard items.

You can order such "fun" furs as seal, giraffe, dalmation, and jaguar by the cut yard ($11 to $19 per yard), by the roll (15 to 20 yards per roll), and, for remnants, by the pound ($4.50 per pound or $4 per pound over 35 pounds). A carton of fake-fur remnants would keep an elementary-school art teacher happy for a year. Monterey carries basic plush, "kurl," and shag, as well as remnant chosen by the mill. A sample set is available for $5 in the U.S., $10 to addresses in Canada. Inexpensive stuffing (from 85 cents per pound) for crafts projects is also available. Do you love furs but love nature's critters more? Then get a fake fur coat from Monterey. Wow! Wait till you see the luscious full-length hooded cheetah coat for only $160! And finally, Monterey sells 100% Merino wool sleepers (mattress pads). This company is a great find. But don't believe me. Log onto the excellent website and see for yourself. There's no online ordering, but you can download an order form here and then mail or fax it in.

SPECIAL FACTORS: Minimum yardage one yard; minimum order $25, on C.O.D. orders, $100.

Newark Dressmaker Supply Inc.

6473 Ruch Rd. Dept. WMJ
P.O. Box 20730
Lehigh, PA 18002–0730

610–837–7500
Fax: 610–837–9115

Catalog: free
Pay: check, MO, MC, V, DSC
Sells: sewing notions, crafts, and needlework supplies
Store: mail order only

If you think Newark Dressmaker Supply, Inc., only serves home sewers, get ready to cheer because the 68-page color catalog also has some unusual products for year-round and theme-based craft-making. Two-thirds of the catalog, not surprisingly, is devoted to sewing needs: thread, specialty zippers, machine accessories, and tools such as rotary cutters and scissors. There's even a mini–vacuum attachment kit ($8.95) for cleaning tight spots in computers and sewing machines. There's no shortage of interfacing and interlining, home-decor items (tassels, fringe, Shir-rite tape, plastic rings), upholstery tools, and clothing and utility fabrics (gingham check, waterproof flannel, broadcloth; mosquito netting, Jiffy-grip, duck). For home sewing of bridal outfits you'll find several pages of heirloom, cluny, and eyelet lace, ribbon, sequins and pearls, wired flower garlands, and $7/16$-inch metal boning.

Crafters and workshop students will appreciate the pages of supplies and how-to books for paper crafting, toy- and doll-making (animal fabrics, eyes and noses, 18-inch doll patterns and clothes), beading (alphabet beads, 100 pack, $1.40), jewelry-making (rhinestones, spangles, findings), and decoration. So many unexpected items pop up throughout the catalog—decorative glass bottles, regular and heavy-duty glue guns, miniatures for florals and dollhouses—that it's worth a look. You're likely to find something you'd given up ever finding.

Wholesale customers: request wholesale order form with catalog; $125 minimum; no other specials or bonuses apply to wholesale orders.

SPECIAL FACTORS: Satisfaction guaranteed.

Oppenheim's

P.O. Box 29
120 E. Main St.
North Manchester, IN
46962–0029

219–982–6848
Fax: 219–982–6557

Catalog: free
Pay: check, MO, MC, V, DSC
Sells: yard goods, notions, crafts materials
Store: mail order only

"Ladies' Book," Oppenheim's 64-page newsprint catalog, invokes the quaint timelessness of hand-crocheted doilies and shelf sitters, with prices reminiscent of days gone by. Home sewers, quilters, and crafters know that Oppenheim's, in business since 1875, is an excellent source of mill remnants—by VIP, Concord, Joan Kessler, Peter Pan, and others—in assortment packages (24 print patterns), craft print or plain quarters (18″ × 22″), and slightly irregular broadcloth, muslin, sheeting, denim, chambray, and flannel. The catalog lists so many fabrics and prints that it's best to see for yourself. It's also packed with quilt and pillow tops, quilting hoops and frames, organizing and cutting tools, doll-making kits (notably mop head, bottle doll, and muslin), apron and vest kits, sewing notions, lace by the yard, woven name labels, and ready-made items suitable for decorating and painting. You'll also find standard and unusual buttons sold by the bag and by the dozen. I liked the intriguing "Patented PALMLOOM," a hand-held device that turns remnants of wool, cotton, or nylon "into rugs, coasters, table pads, rosettes, and hats." At $4.50 each, instructions included, it just might prove irresistible.

SPECIAL FACTORS: First five swatches free with SASE (additional, 50 cents each); satisfaction guaranteed; returns accepted within ten days for exchange, refund, or credit.

92–06 Jamaica Ave., Dept. W　　**718–847–2185 (mail order)**
Woodhaven, NY 11421　　　　**718–849–9873 (store)**

Brochure:　free with SASE
Pay:　check or MO
Sells:　yarn for hand-knitting and crocheting
Store:　same address; Monday to Saturday 10–5:30 (closed
　Wednesdays)
Online:　www.smileysyarns.com

Smiley's Yarns, a yarn source since 1935 for the serious knitter and crocheter, serves more than 25,000 customers through its "Yarn of the Month" mailings. To receive a sample of each month's featured top-quality, name-brand yarn, at a discount of 25% to 75% off list price, you only need to place your first order. (If you want occasional samples, send Smiley's a long, stamped, self-addressed envelope.) Among the manufacturers represented are Bernat, Hayfield, Lion Brand, Patons, Phildar, Plymouth, Reynolds, Schaffhauser, Unger, and Wendy. One month the featured yarn was Reynolds' "Frivoli," a 70% mohair blend (25% wool, 5% nylon) from Italy, priced at $3.99 a ball (suggested retail, $10). Patons' "Nature Fleece" and "Ram's Wool" from Canada, and Hayfield's "Jive" from England (a new wool blend chunky) have also been featured. Many features come with a free pattern. The website is informative in that it presents specials, but there's no online ordering.

SPECIAL FACTORS: Prices quoted by phone or with SASE; quantity discounts available; wholesale customers inquire about terms.

Solo Slide Fasteners, Inc.

8 Spring Brook Rd., Dept. WB   **800–343–9670**
P.O. Box 378   **Fax: 800–547–4775**
Foxborough, MA 02035

Catalog: free
Pay: check, MO, MC, V, AE, DSC
Sells: dressmaking and dry-cleaning equipment, sewing
   and alteration supplies
Store: mail order only
Online: www.soloslide.com

This family-run business has been supplying cleaners, tailors, dressmakers, bridal shops, hospitals, hotels, and schools with sewing and alteration supplies, large and small, for nearly half a century. And they've kept up with the times by offering online ordering at their website of some popular items, although by no means their whole inventory. To take advantage of Solo's excellent wholesale (50% off retail) prices, the minimum order is $30; many items are further discounted if you can order them in quantity. The 66-page catalog has everything from Ace staplers (used by dry cleaners) to zippers, and everything in between—large (pressing machines, for example) and small (suspender buttons, for example). Even if you're not a professional, there are many useful items here for home use, such as lint brushes and thread organizers.

Please note: Solo Slide has a Korean-speaking sales rep.

SPECIAL FACTORS: Authorized returns accepted (except custom-ordered or cut goods); minimum order is $40; free shipping on orders over $100; C.O.D. orders accepted.

Taylor's Cutaways and Stuff

2802 E. Washington St.,
Dept. WBM
Urbana, IL 61802–4660

Catalog: $1
Pay: check, MO, MC, V
Sells: cutaways and patterns
Store: Mail order only

Started in 1977, Taylor's Cutaways and Stuff has based its business on the fabric that's left when garment pieces are cut away—to the benefit of doll- and toy-makers, quilters, and sachet-lovers. Instead of saving up your own scraps, you can order from an assortment of packs: calico, Christmas, solid, doll clothes, and mini-calico, each filled with different prints, some generously sized at 9 by 44 inches. Remnants of polyester, satin, velvet, velour, felt cutaways, and craft fur come in half-pound to four-pound bundles, in sizes suitable for quilts, toy animals, and baby clothes. Fifty satin squares (4″ × 4″) sell for $3, 20 white cotton blend (9″ × 9″) for $3.50, and if you don't care what fabric is in the packet, 50 assorted colors (4″ × 4″) can be had for just $.99. Taylor's simplifies toy- and doll-making with precut items such as hearts, stockings, and teddy bears; teddy patterns and kits (a mini teddy kit including eyes, nose, buttons, and outfit flannel: $1.29); and soft toy patterns, all full-size and complete with instructions. The 16-page catalog abounds with surprise bargains and items you won't find in your local store: fashion doll clothing patterns (for Barbie-sized dolls), instructions for making an apple-head doll, patterns for high-button leather doll shoes, recipes for making your own pet food ($.98), satin rosebuds ($2.50 for ten), elastic assortment (woven edges, picot, and grosgrain, $2.50 per bag), crochet patterns, precut stencil books, iron-on transfers, bags of buttons, animal (or doll) joints, animal noses, and eyes for toys. And be sure to check the specials sheet for "buy two get one free specials."

SPECIAL FACTORS: Quantity discounts available.

Thai Silks

252 State St.
Los Altos, CA 94022

650–948–8611
Fax: 650–948–3426

Brochure: free
Pay: check, MO, MC, V, AE
Sells: silk and other all-natural fabrics, silk scarves, silk
    clothing, etc.
Store: same address; Monday to Saturday 9–5:30
Online: www.thaisilks.com

With direct access to foreign loomers, Thai Silks brings artists, clothing-makers, interior decorators, and upholsterers savings of 30% to 50% on regular retail prices for silks, velvets, satins, and accessories. An assorted sample set, $40 plus $3 for shipping, is not a bad idea when you consider the wide choices and low prices (or choose a specialty sample: bridal, $15; artists', $5). For $20, you can enroll in the silk fabric club and receive quarterly mailings of Thai Silks' newest colors, prints, and fabrications and a sample of the current closeout.

The easy-to-read fold-out catalog details the popular habotai silk (40 selections, 8 momme weight) used for flower-making, silk charmeuse (with and without crepe back), many fancy silk chiffons, "stretch" silks (92% silk/8% Lycra), and the wrinkle-resistant silk noil. Scarce satins such as Silk Duchesse and tapestry "silk" brocades (traditional, yarn-dyed, and soft finish) are available here, although delivery is slow and supplies are limited. A favorite two-ply taffeta Thai silk for bridal gowns ($40.30/yard) has the same iridescent quality that moved Colonel Morgan to go into the silk business after he encountered the fabric in Bangkok in 1964. Indeed, perusing the catalog brings the far reaches of the world close to hand. Heavier 14 momme to 18 momme silk prints in the best patterns and colors of European and U.S. designers sell here at prices ranging from $14.95 to $29.60 per yard. Assorted white silks, pongees, and hand-hemmed white silk scarves for batiking and hand-painting are available in wide selections and sizes. There is also a limited selection of 100% hemp, 100% cotton batik, and 100% ramie. Novelty scarves, white silk shawls, men's silk neckties, sarongs, T-shirts, tank tops, habotai pants, hand-embroidered handkerchiefs, and pincushions and sewing kits round out the catalog. For current sale and closeout items, check the online site, where orders and sample requests can be made.

SPECIAL FACTORS: Wholesale orders subject to yardage and price minimums;

discounts (one yard minimum) for artists, dressmakers, boutiques; minimum order half a yard; C.O.D. accepted.

Bonnie Triola Yarns

343 E. Gore Rd.
Erie, PA 16509–3723

814–825–7821
Fax: 814–824–5418

Catalog and Samples: $10 (see text)
Pay: check, MO, MC, V
Sells: yarns
Store: mail order only
Online: www.moose.erie.net/~btriola

For those of you who love to use knitting machines, looms, and even embroidery machines, you should know about Bonnie Triola. She tests and works with all of her yarns and will happily answer any of your questions regarding their use. For $10 you receive a year's worth of mailings with yarn samples, price lists with special closeout sales, and newsletters full of helpful hints, resources, seminar notices, and new product reports and reviews. On top of Bonnie's already discounted prices, many of her yarns are eligible for quantity discounts where you can save up to 25% additionally. She also has a wholesale catalog (no minimums) for qualified buyers, with deep discounts on everything. She carries her own lines of natural and synthetic fibers, overruns from New York designers, and yarns by Tamm, Millor, and Sunray. (Samples and color cards on these latter three are not included with the $10 catalog; inquire for prices.) Her metallic yarns are popular with people who use embroidery machines, but almost any textile artist or craftsperson will find great choices and buys here. Most of Bonnie's yarns are sold as full cones only, and many of the markdowns are close to 75% less than retail. The website will give you a good idea of Bonnie's selection and discounts; however, there's no online ordering.

SPECIAL FACTORS: C.O.D. accepted; net 30 billing for qualified wholesalers (request the wholesale price list).

UTEX Trading Enterprises

826 Pine Ave.   Tel/Fax: 716–282–8211
Niagara Falls, NY 14301

Price List: free with SASE
Pay: check, MO, MC, V
Sells: imported silk fabric
Store: same address; by appointment only
E-mail: utextrade@aol.com

If you're a decorator, seamstress, tailor, or textile artist, you'll want to know about UTEX, America's largest silk source. Since 1980 this company has been importing silk fabric directly from mills around the world and passing the savings on to the public by selling fabric as well as silk sewing thread, silk knitting/weaving yarns, silk neckties, and silk scarves directly through the mail. UTEX issues a no-nonsense price sheet with the discount schedule, fabric selection table to help you locate the right fabric for your needs (wedding gowns, evening wear, casual clothing, suits, interior decoration, etc.), and fabric weights, widths, and swatch numbers. Once you select the sample(s) and send in a deposit (to cover the cost of the samples), you have 20 days to make a decision to purchase or return, after which you get a partial refund. This is a great source for people knowledgeable about silk, since the flyer descriptions are minimal. The more you order, the more you'll save, as quantity discounts apply to both scarf and fabric orders.

SPECIAL FACTORS: Sample deposits refundable, less handling charges; C.O.D. orders accepted.

Webs

P.O. Box 147, Dept. WBM   413–584–2225
Northampton, MA 01061–0147   Fax: 413–584–1603

Price Lists and Samples: $2 (see text)
Pay: check, MO, MC, V, DSC
Sells: yarns, and spinning and weaving equipment and
  books
Store: Service Center Rd. (half a mile off I–91),
  Northampton, MA; Monday to Saturday 10–5:30
Online: www.yarn.com

Webs keeps the world of fibercrafts spinning with yarns discounted up to 80% off suggested retail prices and equipment for weavers, spinners, and knitters at all levels of development. The already-low yarn prices receive additional discounts of 20% and 25% on purchases of $60 to $119 and $120 or more, respectively, and looms and wheels are shipped freight-free. In business since 1974, Webs stocks books and hard-to-find publications as well as current and back issues of major fiber-arts magazines, and runs classes in fibercrafts.

The catalog and the online site cover Webs' four merchandise categories: "Specials," which include mill ends, closeouts, and odd lots (advertised through bimonthly mailings); "Webs' Yarns," which is a high-quality in-house product line; "Name-Brand Yarns," which are sold at discount; and "Equipment and Supplies," which includes looms, loom kits, spinning wheels, and knitting needles. Webs' constantly expanding inventory includes worsteds, cottons, silks, rayons, blends, and several lines of specially made yarns such as mohair, dyed and natural linens, rayon chenille, and woolen spun wools. Shoppers can receive samples of yarns through the ten mailings each year, and only need to make a purchase once every four months to remain on the mailing list. Individual color cards can be ordered for $5; the complete loose-leaf binder color book, with generous samples, is $37.50. Some items, such as yarns imported from Great Britain, are subject to a one-pound minimum purchase; others are available only in one-pound cones, but these details are evident in each product description. Webs is oriented toward providing the right equipment and yarns, so indicate your specialty (hand- or machine-knitting, weaving, spinning) in correspondence and look forward to some getting-to-know-you questions when you shop for equipment. The website features online specials, but no electronic ordering capability as of yet.

SPECIAL FACTORS: Shipping not charged on looms, spinning wheels, or drum carders; quantity discounts available; authorized returns accepted within 30 days, with possible 15% restocking fee; minimum order $20 on credit card orders.

Related Products/Companies

All-cotton woven fabric for upholstery, linens, draperies, etc.
- Homespun Fabrics

Blank textile goods for dyeing and decorating
- Clothcrafters

Decorator fabric, trim
- The Fabric Center, Hancock's of Paducah, Shama Imports, Silk Surplus

Doll-making supplies
- CR's Bear and Doll, National Artcraft

Fabric
- Campmor, Gohn Bros.

Fabric-painting supplies
- Jerry's Artarama

Faux fur
- Fabulous-Furs

Feathers and trim
- Gettinger Feather, Manny's Millinery

Needlepoint/embroidery supplies and kits
- Sewin' in Vermont

Photographic transfers for T-shirts
- Porter's Camera Store

Quilting and needlecraft books
- Dover

Quilting supplies
- Gohn Bros., Hancock's of Paducah

Sewing machines
- Discount Appliance Centers, Sewin' in Vermont, Sewing Machine Super Store

Sewing notions
- Gohn Bros., Sewin' in Vermont, Sewing Machine Super Store

Silk-screening/fabric painting supplies
- Jerry's Artarama, Ott's Discount Art Supply, Pearl Paint

"Sun-printing supplies"
- Gramma's Graphics

Thermography/embossing supplies
- Think Ink

Woven chenille and hand-dyed silk velvet scarves
- Holly Raal Textiles

Fine Art Supplies

*Materials and equipment
for fine artists*

If you're an artist living in New York City, you're lucky to have access to large, well-stocked art-supply stores that sell art materials of all kinds at reasonable prices. The rest of us would be stuck with tiny retail stores that might as well be selling liquid gold in those tubes of oil paint if it weren't for mail order. Art supplies are one area in which you can get *excellent* deals by mail. Mail-order art-supply discounters routinely offer savings of 20%; some of the vendors this chapter can save you as much as 70%. The firms listed here sell supplies and materials for fine arts and some crafts: pigments, inks, drawing material, paper, brushes, canvas, mats and frames, stretchers, studio furniture, vehicles and solvents, silk-screening supplies, carving tools, and much more.

The Art Materials Labeling Act of 1988 together with the Consumer Products Safety Commission have created standards for the art materials industry and banned hazardous materials from being used in elementary schools. Although many art materials have been reformulated to conform to the legal standards, toxic ingredients are still an unavoidable problem. Most artists are aware of the risks, but for more information about art materials in general, as well as toxicity issues, pick up a copy of *The Artists' Handbook of Materials and Techniques*, by Mayer and Sheehan. Another book, Michael McCann's *Health Hazards Manual for Artists*, has become something of a classic and is a must for every artist's studio library. The fully revised edition has the most current information on safety, labeling, and new chemicals. It outlines the dangers for artists in such fields as painting, photography, ceramics, sculpture, printmaking, woodworking, textiles, and many others, and has a special section on health hazards for children working with art materials. Both of these titles are available from many of the bookstores listed in this book.

If you're a commercial artist, you'll be glad to know some of the firms in this chapter sell graphic design-related software and computer goods, but you'll do well to consult the computer section of the "Office, Business, and Professional" chapter as well. Some of firms in the "Crafts and Hobbies" chapter carry supplies for fine artists and graphic artists too. See "Related Products/Companies" at the end of this chapter for relevant company listings found elsewhere in the book.

Find It Fast

Art and Graphic Design Books/Videos
- Cheap Joe's, Jerry's Artarama, Daniel Smith, Utrecht

Computer Graphics Supplies
- Utrecht

Framing Supplies
- American Frame Corporation, Graphik Dimensions, Jerry's Artarama, Pearl Paint, Daniel Smith, Utrecht

General Art Supplies, Tools, and Equipment
- Cheap Joe's, Jerry's Artarama, Ott's Discounts, Pearl Paint, Utrecht

Specialty Papers
- Daniel Smith

Studio Furniture
- Pearl Paint, Daniel Smith

American Frame Corporation

400 Tomahawk Dr.
Maumee, OH 43537–1695

800–537–0944
Fax: 800–893–3898

Catalog: free
Pay: check, MO, MC, V, AE, DSC
Sells: preassembled and sectional frames and supplies
Store: same address; Monday to Friday 8:30–6 EST
Online: www.americanframe.com

I confess: I have friends' valuable artwork tacked on my wall with push pins. But now that I've taken a gander at American Frame Corporation's 36-page color catalog of frames, mats, and framing hardware, I'm thinking of changing my ways. I need this catalog! And you do too if you've looked at frame prices recently. I can save up to 50% off retail prices on all types of frames and mats, and the excellent website, with the complete inventory, offers another way to view the selection and place an order.

American Frame's catalog boasts that it's "more than just a catalog. It's a handbook." The print and online catalog are chock full of tips to help the novice like me through the tricks and traps of framing, such as how to choose the right frame and mat color for the artwork, how to determine the mat's border size, and other nifty snippets. The catalog offers more than 200 metal and wood frames in a variety of styles and gorgeous colors, and more than 150 mat colors. Color photographs, precise cross-section line drawings, and clearly written descriptions guide the reader through the world of framing. You'll also find the framing hardware and accessories you'll need. All frames and mats are cut to your specification, and if the detailed instructions on how to measure them aren't clear enough, there's a friendly support staff on hand to answer your questions.

The website is a joy, not only for its complete online catalog and ordering, but because of "Framer's Forum" where technical terms are explained and shoppers' questions answered.

SPECIAL FACTORS: Measure twice, cut once is the rule, as a restocking fee applies to all returns, and custom-cut mats cannot be returned.

Cheap Joe's Art Stuff

374 Industrial Park Rd.
Boone, NC 28607

800–227–2788
704–262–0793
Fax: 800–257–0874
Fax: 704–262–0795

Catalog: free
Pay: check, MO, MC, V, DSC
Sells: art supplies and equipment
Store: Boone Drug Co., 617 E. King St., Boone, NC;
Monday to Saturday 8–6; phone hours Monday to
Thursday 9–7, Friday and Saturday 9–5 EST
Online: www.cheapjoes.com

The Joe behind Cheap Joe's Art Stuff has a heart of gold. Just visit his website for a glimpse at listings of national and regional arts organizations, mini-art lessons in different genres presented by practicing artists, and inspiring artist's statements. Joe also sponsors Vincent's Brushes, a charity venture to collect art supplies (damaged but usable goods and pass-alongs) for distribution to children who can't afford to buy them.

The catalog—more than a hundred colorful pages—features papers, paint, and brushes by well-known manufacturers as well as Cheap Joe's own line. A 30% discount is typical throughout the catalog, with 60% possible on quantity purchases of select items. Cheap Joe's also sells easels, shrink-wrap systems, projection equipment, canvas, and print racks. Since equipment and materials work best if you know how to use them, Joe plants tips throughout the catalog and carries books and videotapes on painting and art history. Cheap Joe, whose artistic medium is watercolor, invites questions and suggestions regarding materials and equipment. You can order a print catalog on the website, but there's no inventory or online ordering.

SPECIAL FACTORS: Satisfaction guaranteed; no shipping charged on brushes; institutional accounts available.

Graphik Dimensions Ltd.

2103 Brentwood St.
High Point, NC 27263

800–221–0262
910–887–3700
Fax: 910–887–3773

Catalog: free
Pay: check, MO, MC, V, DSC
Sells: sectional and custom-made frames and accessories
Store: same address
Online: www.graphikdimensions.com

For 40 years the husband-and-wife team of Joan and Stephen Feinsod has been stocking a huge inventory of quality framing materials and selling them to artists and photographers at discount prices. Graphik Dimension's 36-page color catalog has a frame to suit every kind of artwork and every kind of surrounding, from castle to rustic cabin, austere and minimal to youthful and cheery. There are standard-depth frames for use with glass as well as "canvas" depth—for paintings on stretchers. Whether you seek a gilded, ornate frame for an heirloom painting or a glossy, gulf-blue frame for that whimsical print to hang in your bathroom, you'll find it here. Graphik Dimensions offers framing kits in your choice of wood frames, including the glass (or acrylic), backing board, retainer clips, hanging screws, and wire—no tools necessary. Sample corners are available for most frames (free in some cases, $5 to $30 in others, depending on the frame), and most come with a gift certificate that you can apply to your purchase. The website was under construction at press time, but it looked promising, with online ordering and web specials to come.

SPECIAL FACTORS: Satisfaction guaranteed; quantity discounts available; authorized returns accepted.

Jerry's Artarama, Inc.

P.O. Box 58638, Dept. BWBM   919–878–6782
Raleigh, NC 27658   Fax: 919–873–9565

Catalog: $2
Pay: check, MO, MC, V, AE, DSC
Sells: art supplies, picture frames, etc.
Store: stores in West Hartford, CT; Bellerose and
   Rochester, NY; Deerfield Beach, FL; and Fort Collins, CO
   (call for hours and addresses)
Online: www.jerryscatalog.com

In business since 1968, Jerry's Artarama promises you'll "always save up to 75% off manufacturer's list prices" on commercial and fine arts materials and furniture, and there's a lowest-price guarantee to boot. The 110-page catalog details name-brand easels, canvas, paints, pastels, brushes (individual and in sets), palette knives, gold finishes, drawing and sketch media, film and frame hardware, portfolios, files, and heavy-duty studio equipment. Prices drop on quantity purchases of such items as brushes, palette cups, Gessobord, unprimed linen, and stretcher bars. Some minimum order requirements apply.

Fabric artists can save from 33% to 50% on silk scarves and ties, Niji fabricolor marker sets, wax pots, and many dyes and paints. For airbrush painters, Jerry's has top-name equipment at hefty savings (compressors that list for $610 sell here for $429). Jerry's carries equipment for mat- and glass-cutting, shrink wrapping, and even graphite and ink erasing. Products by TV artists Bob Ross and Susan Scheewe, instructional videos, and classic books (*Drawing on the Right Side of the Brain, The Artists' Handbook*) are discounted. Components for the Walker Display system can be found here too. For everything from Academy watercolors to Zippy art totes, Jerry's Artarama is the place. At press time the website was under construction.

SPECIAL FACTORS: Satisfaction guaranteed; color charts and product specifications available on request; quantity discounts available; minimum order $20 by mail, $50 by phone.

Ott's Discount Art Supply

102 Hungate Dr., Dept.
BWBM
Greenville, NC 27858–8045

800–356–3289
Fax: 252–756–2397

Catalog: free
Pay: check, MO, MC, V
Sells: art, graphics, and craft supplies
Store: mail order only
Online: www.otts.com

Since 1972 Ott's Discount Art Supply has catered to the supply needs of artists and arts programs with regular savings of 30% to 64% off manufacturers' list prices and discounts up to 70% on closeout items. Ott's carries standard artist's supplies—sketch books and parchment, charcoal, and pastel papers; drawing inks; synthetic or natural-bristled brushes—by Liquitex, Grumbacher, Winsor & Newton, Strathmore, Canson, and others; and studio equipment such as projectors, magnifiers, lamps, and light boxes. Ott's 60-page catalog also carries products geared toward the student, the child artist, and craftspeople. It includes a page devoted to "kids activity sets" by NSI, priced to make fun and educational gifts (Master Woodburning kit, $13.56; battery-operated kids' pottery wheel, $28.42), and a section on origami and rice papers, design-your-own greeting cards, pottery tools and clay, felt sheets and glue, natural sponges, and modeling compounds by Sculpey and Fimo. Ott's has added basic tools for jewelers, a deluxe hobby tool set for woodworking, and devices that magnify while freeing up your hands. Ott's inventories more items than shown in the catalog, so call if you don't see what you need. Catalogs can be requested at the website, but there's no online ordering.

SPECIAL FACTORS: Satisfaction guaranteed; returns accepted within 30 days; institutional orders accepted; see catalog for additional fees or shipping charges on heavy or flammable items.

Pearl Paint Co., Inc.

308 Canal St., Dept. BWBM   800–221–6845
New York, NY 10013–2572   212–431–7932
                                  Fax: 212–274–2290

Catalog: $1.50
Pay: check, MO, MC, V, AE, DSC
Sells: art, craft, and graphics supplies, studio furniture,
   etc.
Store: same address, also 16 other locations in CA, FL,
   GA, IL, MA, MD, NJ, NY, TX, and VA; call for locations
Online: www.pearlpaint.com

Pearl Paint Co., Inc., knows that although New York City teems with artists, not all artists live in New York. That's why in addition to 16 store locations (listed in the print and online catalogs), Pearl Paint makes its many craft, fine arts, and graphic arts products available through the mail. Strolling through Pearl was one of my quintessential New York experiences some years ago, and Pearl has managed to transfer its hip, well-organized, service-intensive atmosphere to the catalog and website as well. You'll find great values at Pearl, with discounts that go as high as 50% on some items. Pearl Paint also stocks studio furniture and, yes, house paint.

In business for over 60 years, Pearl Paint is the place for tools, canvas, manuals, handmade drawing and writing books, poster paper, foam core, frames and framing supplies, pens, stretchers—you name it! If you need an item that's not listed in the catalog or on the website, call, fax, write, or e-mail for information. Pearl Paint's weekly online specials will save you a bundle, so it pays to check in frequently if you have Internet access.

SPECIAL FACTORS: Quantity discounts available; all orders under $50 will incur a $4.95 handling fee; all flat-wrapped paper will incur an additional $2.50 packing charge.

Daniel Smith

P.O. Box 84268
Seattle, WA 98124–5568

800–426–7923
206–223–9599
Fax: 800–238–4065

Catalog: $5 with rebate; supplements free
Pay: check, MO, MC, V, AE
Sells: fine-art supplies and equipment
Store: 4150 First Ave. South, Seattle, WA; Monday to
Saturday 9–6, Wednesday 9–8, Sunday 10–6
E-mail: dsartmtrl@aol.com

After thumbing through dozens of discount mail-order catalogs with blow-out, blast-off deals and enough exclamation points in the text to give you a headache, it's always a great relief to settle back each year and open up the most recent catalog from Daniel Smith. The 194-page reference catalog is an example of informed design, respect for an artist's intelligence, well-written and informative text, fabulous selection, and wonderful prices. Although it doesn't look like a discount catalog, it is; prices here are well below list in most cases, and there are many items you just won't find anywhere else. Daniel Smith manufactures their own paints (oils, acrylics, and watercolors), etching and lithographic inks, painter's canvas and linen, and other products. As a friend to many serious artists, I've heard these products are some of the best in the biz. You'll also find an extensive selection of paints of every kind by top-name manufacturers, as well as brushes and other painting tools, drawing and printing supplies, an incredible variety of paper and canvases, framing supplies, studio furniture, books, and much more. If you're a paper freak, check out the single-sheet papers from all over the world—German etching paper, Italian intaglio paper, Japanese woodblock print paper, French marble paper, Nepalese block printing paper, and others too exotic and gorgeous to believe.

SPECIAL FACTORS: Satisfaction guaranteed; authorized returns accepted for exchange, refund, or credit; minimum order on paper is ten sheets.

Utrecht

33 35th St.
Brooklyn, NY 11232

800–223–9132
718–768–2525
Fax: 718–499–8815

Catalog: free
Pay: check, MO, MC, V, AE, DSC
Sells: general art supplies
Store: nine locations in NY, MA, CA, DC, MI, IL, and PA;
   see catalog for addresses and phone numbers
Online: www.utrechtart.com

It's so rewarding to have looked through and rejected a great many art-supply mail-order catalogs and found one that truly deserves to be in this book. Utrecht is something of an institution for New York City artists as a great source for discount artist's paints. (Utrecht manufactures their own paints and sells them directly to the customer, saving you a bundle.) But the paints by top-brand manufacturers such as Winsor & Newton, Rembrandt, and Liquitex, are also discounted 40% and more. Brushes, canvas, drawing implements and supplies, paper, framing supplies, printmaking tools and inks, portfolio/presentation cases—these and other artists' needs can be found in Utrecht's 52-page color catalog as well as on their website, where you can view a large part of the inventory and order online. On many items savings run as high as 66% off. If you're a serious artist, you'll definitely want to check out Utrecht, if you haven't already.

SPECIAL FACTORS: Institutional accounts available; quantity discounts available.

Related Products/Companies

Art books
- Dover, Hacker Art Books

Cardboard tubes for storing and shipping art
- Yazoo Mills

Children's art and crafts supplies
- Toysmart.com

Clip-art
- Dover Publications

Commercial and fine arts books and manuals
- Hacker Art Books, Print Bookstore

Computer graphics hardware and software
- Computer Discount Warehouse, Dartek

Digital imaging and slide processing
- ABC Photo & Imaging, Visual Horizons

Photographic colored postcards, business cards
- Lighthouse Colorprint, Mr. Z's Print Services

Scanners
- Affordable Photocopy

Studio furniture, drafting tables, and equipment
- Fidelity, OfficeMax

Food and Beverages

*Bulk foods; health, ethnic,
and gourmet foods;
cheese-making supplies; coffee and
tea; beer- and wine-making supplies*

Sales of mail-order food are in the billions of dollars annually, reflecting an increase in the demand for good foods not available locally, as well as hard-to-find cooking ingredients. In this chapter you'll find savings up to 80% on bulk foods such as dried fruits, nuts, and candy; gourmet and ethnic ingredients; organic meats; and health food items. For the industrious types, there are kits and ingredients to make your own cheese, beer, and wine at home. And you'll find great deals on coffee and tea too.

Food makes the perfect gift. If you want to maximize your savings, choose something like tea or dried fruit, buy it in bulk, and repackage it yourself in gift tins. You can save a lot of money by going in on an order with friends and buying in large quantities. Dry goods like grains and beans keep almost indefinitely if tightly sealed, as do dried fruits. Nuts should be kept in a sealed container or zipper-lock bag and refrigerated at all times; nuts' high oil content makes them susceptible to rancidity.

If you're seeking out companies that primarily sell herbs, spices, condiments, extracts, and other flavorings, see the section that follows entitled "Spices, Condiments, and Flavorings," page 205. For super-luxurious food items such as caviar, truffles, and foie gras, check out the "Luxuries" chapter, page 400.

In my neck of the woods, friends belong to food co-ops. Co-ops are great ways to meet people with like interests—in this case, healthy food, "green" lifestyle, and cooking—and great ways to save money since you team up with friends, buy in bulk, and then split up the orders yourself. You're also doing nice things for the environment by cutting down on unnecessary individual packaging. To find out who's running a food co-op near you or to get information on starting your own co-op, call or write Co-op News Network, Box 57, Randolph, VT 05060, 802–234–9293. The nice folks there can look up your locale in the *National Co-Op Directory* to find one in your area.

There are a couple of helpful websites as well. You can access the Directory of U.S. and Canadian Food Cooperatives (www.prairienet.org/co-op/directory). To click into the world of online food co-ops, try www.columbia.edu/~jw157/

food.coop.html. Both of these sites have wonderful links to other kinds of co-ops (e.g., banking), nutrition newsletters and information, agriculture sites, and much more.

A good source of information that sorts food facts from fallacies is Ralph Nader's *Nutrition Action Healthletter*, published by the Center for Science in the Public Interest (CSPI). This is the newsletter that broke the stories about the high-fat content of Chinese and Mexican restaurant food. Subscriptions are currently $24 per ten-issue year; write to CSPI-Circulation, 1875 Connecticut Ave. NW, Suite 300, Washington, DC 20009, or call 202–332–9110 for a subscription. Better yet, log onto the website (www.cspinet.org) for an online subscription or to find lots of other interesting health news.

With Deepak Chopra and Dr. Andrew Weil occupying the best-seller lists, it's clear that people across America are looking for ways to enhance their own body's ability to heal itself and to stay healthy. Even if you're not particularly New Agey or spiritual, there's a great book out there that even my mother loved. It's called *Food—Your Miracle Medicine*, by Jean Carper (HarperCollins). Here you'll find out the results of the most recent scientific studies on different foods, and how they can help cure or prevent particular health problems. (My mother cured her chronic back pains by ceasing her daily orange juice!) Another excellent resource with a "mentor" section that cites numerous other food, nutrition, and health resources is Nikki and David Goldbeck's *The Healthiest Diet in the World*. Most of the companies in the "Books, Audiobooks, and Periodicals" chapter will carry these wonderful books or be able to get them for you.

Since food safety is a big concern among consumers, here's a short list of experts who can answer just about any questions you have:

- To find a registered dietitian in your area, or to order brochures on improving your health, call The American Dietetic Association at 800–366–1655; Monday to Friday 8 A.M. to 8 P.M. CT.
- USDA Meat and Poultry Hotline answers your questions on the safe handling of meat and poultry; 800–535–4555, in DC 202–720–3333, and TDD is 800–256–7072; Monday to Friday 10 A.M. to 4 P.M. EST. Or check out the website (www.usda.gov/fsis).
- "How to Help Avoid Foodborne Illness in the Home," published by the FDA, covers risks and safety precautions for buying, handling, storing, and preparing food. A copy can be ordered from the Consumer Information Center, listed in this book.
- The FDA's Seafood Hotline dispenses answers to your specific questions on fish-related safety issues; call 800–FDA–4010, 24 hours a day. If you have Internet access, the FDA website is extremely user-friendly—even fun. There you can look up articles on all kinds of food- and health-related issues. The online address is www.fda.gov.

Find It Fast

Candies
- Bates Bros., Bulkfoods.com

Cheese
- Deer Valley Farm, Gibbsville Cheese, New England Cheesemaking Supply

Coffee and Tea
- Catskill Mountain Coffee, Northwestern Coffee Mills

Cookbooks
- A Cook's Wares, Beer and Winemaking Supplies, Inc., E. C. Kraus, Mountain Ark, Sultan's Delight

Dried Nuts and Fruit
- Bates Bros., Bulkfoods.com, Deer Valley Farm, Jaffe Bros., Mountain Ark

Gourmet Foods
- A Cook's Wares, Deer Valley Farm, Mountain Ark, Sultan's Delight

Grains, Beans, Cereals
- Bulkfoods.com, Deer Valley Farm, Jaffe Bros., Mountain Ark

Herbs and Spices
- Bulkfoods.com, Deer Valley Farm, Jaffe Bros., Mountain Ark, Sultan's Delight

Meat and Fish
- Deer Valley Farm, Gibbsville Cheese

Sugar-Free Candy/Confections
- Bulkfoods.com, Mountain Ark

Wine- and Beer-Making Supplies
- Beer and Winemaking Supplies, Inc., E. C. Kraus

A Cook's Wares

211 37th St.	**724-846-9490**
Beaver Falls, PA 15010-2103	**Fax: 800-916-2886**

Catalog: $2
Pay: check, MO, MC, V, AE
Sells: gourmet ingredients, cookware, and cookbooks
Store: same address, Monday to Friday 9–4, Saturday 9–1
Online: www.cookswares.com

Back when I was a cookbook editor I can remember seeing a fabulous recipe that called for champagne vinegar. "Now where would I get that?" I wondered from my Catskill Mountain cabin. Now I know: A Cook's Wares. If you live in an area where the nearest gourmet shop is 50 miles away, or even if you don't, this is a great source for gourmet ingredients, cookware, and cookbooks—many of them marked down from suggested retail price by as much as 50%.

I liked the 64-page text-heavy catalog illustrated with line drawings. There's nothing pretentious here—just good values throughout. For instance, if you're looking to outfit your kitchen with chef's-quality cookware and bakeware, you'll find such brands as Mauviel, Demeyere Apollo, All-Clad, Cuisinart, Sitram, Calphalon, Le Creuset, and others. Other items include top-name cutlery, appliances, utensils, and gadgets, as well as wondrous, hard-to-find gourmet ingredients and condiments (vinegars and oils, sweet sauces and biscotti, spices and herbs, extracts and vanillas, to name a few). On the company's website you can view the full inventory and then download an order form and fax or telephone your order.

SPECIAL FACTORS: Complete satisfaction guaranteed; returns accepted within 30 days for exchange or refund.

Bates Bros. Nut Farm, Inc.

15954 Woods Valley Rd.   760–749–3333
Valley Center, CA 92082   Fax: 760–749–9499

Catalog: free
Pay: check, MO, MC, V, DSC
Sells: nuts, dried fruits, and candy
Store: same address; daily 9–5; also Terra Nova Plaza,
  358 E. H St., #604, Chula Vista, CA; daily 10–7:30

"Nuts from all over the world meet here," according to Bates Nut Farm's catalog. Okay, so they might not win prizes for their cutting-edge wit, but when it comes to fresh roasted nuts, dried fruits, candies, and gourmet treats, you won't go wrong by shopping here, where prices average 20% to 30% below most others. Bates Nut Farm is a roadside attraction complete with ducks and geese for the kids to feed, sheep and goats for them to pet, crafts fairs, the "famous Pumpkin Patch," and more. But if you're on the other coast, as I am, you'll get the same down-homey feeling by browsing their mail-order catalog. The Bates family does all the roasting and packaging themselves to insure the freshness of their nuts, which include a dazzling array of raw or roasted nuts and seeds (almonds, cashews, pumpkin seeds, sunflower seeds, Virginia peanuts, filberts, macadamias, pistachios, etc.). Bates also offers dried fruit (apples, banana chips, papaya spears, sweet-tart cherries, pitted dates, cranberries, etc.) as well as candy and other confections for those with a sweet tooth (cashew brittle, yogurt peanuts, party mints, candy corn, malted milk balls, gummy worms, etc.). Specially made fruit-and-nut mixes, glazed fruits (for baking), and an impressive presentation of gift packs round out the inventory.

SPECIAL FACTORS: C.O.D. orders not accepted; gift packs available year-round, but please order four weeks in advance if for Christmas.

Before the home beer- and wine-making craze took hold, aptly named Beer & Winemaking Supplies, Inc., set up shop in 1976 in the New England town of Northampton and they've been there ever since. Keeping up with the times, they've launched a wonderful website (no print catalog) where you can shop online for kits to make beer, wine, vinegar, and soda pop, as well as all the ingredients and supplies necessary to bottle your own brand of fizz and buzz. Although Beer & Winemaking Supplies isn't a discounter, you'll spend less on the equipment, which can be used over and over, and the ingredients than you would buying your own beer and wine. Plus it's more fun! I found the website to be very well organized and easy to use. Click into different sections of the site for wine-making ingredients, beer-making ingredients, vinegar-making and soda kits, and starter kits for beer/wine and other equipment such as corks, bottles, labels, and much more. You can also check out the Recipe of the Month and read about brewing history in Western Massachusetts. Don't worry if you're just getting started; the website offers an array of books on wine, beer, cider, mead, and other delightful diversions. If you're not comfortable ordering online, there's a toll-free telephone number for orders only listed on the web. You can also call the store and have questions answered by a real human being.

SPECIAL FACTORS: Orders shipped within the continental U.S. only.

Bulkfoods.com

Fax: 888–BULK–COM

Information: website only, no print catalog
Pay: V, MC, AE, DSC
Sells: nuts, grains, cereals, sugar-free candy, penny candy, etc.
Store: online only
Online: www.bulkfoods.com

For my companion's big birthday bash, I filled a giant punch bowl with peanut M&Ms. The guests were more impressed with that than with the catered food and two bands. I guess it just proves that we're all kids at heart. It's hard to imagine too many occasions one might need 33 pounds of M&Ms. But if you did, Bulkfoods.com would gladly fill your order. This Internet-only store sells health-food items such as rolled oats, 12-grain cereal, and beans; great candy including "Gummies" in every conceivable shape, chocolate-covered raisins and peanuts, lollipops, licorice, etc.; an unusual selection of sugar-free candies, including such items as sugar-free chocolate-covered peanut butter cups; dried fruit, including unsulfured bananas and apricots; a large selection of nuts—roasted and raw, salted and not; herbs and spices; and assorted baking goods such as sprinkles, milk chocolate drops, and cherry bits. If you order here, be ready to order in huge quantities—5- to 33-pound bags. You'll pay shipping based on weight (via UPS ground in the 48 contiguous U.S.; this is not a good source if you live in Hawaii or Alaska), the amount of which is clearly shown at the bottom of your order form before you have to commit to buying. But even with the shipping cost added, the prices here checked out to be at least 20% less than supermarket prices, and some sale items on the "Specials List" page were 40% less than the local health food store prices. This would be a good place to consider for a church or school fund-raising event where you could repackage bulk candy in small bags to resell.

SPECIAL FACTORS: Credit cards only; no check or money orders accepted.

Catskill Mountain Coffee

906 Rt. 28
Kingston, NY 12401

914–334–8455
888–SAY–JAVA

Information: Brochure
Pay: check or MO
Sells: organic, cooperatively grown coffee
Store: mail order only
Website: www.catskillmtcoffee.com

Please pinch me so I can wake up from this delicious dream. And be sure to have a cup of Catskill Mountain Coffee ready when I do. I was so delighted when I discovered that this wonderful company is now selling their coffee directly to consumers. The good news is that all of the coffee is organic *and* kosher. The better news is that the prices here are about 40% less than what you'd pay in a store.

The coffee is roasted, flavored, and blended in small batches to ensure high quality and freshness, and certified kosher by the Vaad Hakashrut of the Capital District, Albany, New York. Proprietor and master roaster Emma Missouri is committed to the principles of organic farming, which helps to replenish and rebuild our world's topsoil while protecting human and animal life. In other words, you can feel good about buying this coffee. The two-sided brochure lists the available beans—from Colombia, Ethiopia, Papua New Guinea, El Salvador, Peru, and so on; the blends, imaginatively named and described (for example, Dancin' On the Ceiling, Wired!, and Black Bear Brew, to name three); and flavors, including old favorites such as hazelnut and Irish creme as well as less common ones—Mud Pie (Chocolate, Pecan, and Vanilla) and Butter Rum, for instance. There are also a variety of decafs. Ms. Missouri custom-roasts the beans to one of the five choices you specify—American, Viennese, Full City, French, or Espresso, all described in the brochure. This is without a doubt the least expensive organic and kosher coffee anywhere; the current wholesale prices at this writing were $5.80/pound for beans, blends, or flavors, and $6.80 for decafs. The only catch is that you have to order three pounds of one type to get these prices. No problem! The website is informative, but there's no online ordering.

SPECIAL FACTORS: Minimum order is three pounds of one type.

Despite the growing market for them, "organically grown" meats are not easy to come by. Deer Valley Farm, certified by New York State Organic Farmers, has been selling organically grown meats—hamburger, trimmed sirloin, veal, pork, and lamb—as well as fish since 1947. Also available are baking ingredients, grains, nut butters, herbs, fruits, pastas, and raw milk cheese, all at wholesale discounts of 25% to 40%, as long as you place a minimum order of $150. With a normal-sized refrigerator and enough storage jars, that should be an agreeable endeavor! If you want less, however, and are willing to forego the discounts, the minimum order is only $15.

SPECIAL FACTORS: Delivery in NYC area by Deer Valley truck; elsewhere, via UPS; minimum order $15; $150 for wholesale prices.

Gibbsville Cheese Company, Inc.

W–2663 CTH–00
Sheboygan Falls, WI
53085–2971

920–564–3242
Fax: 920–564–6129

Price List: free
Pay: check or MO
Sells: Wisconsin cheese and summer sausage
Store: same address (five miles south of Sheboygan Falls
on Hwy. 32); Monday to Friday 7:30–5, Saturday 7:30–4

My companion claims there's a part of the human brain that requires the "snap" of cheddar once a day to function properly. Gibbsville Cheese Company is the place where all cheese addicts can satisfy their needs at standout prices. For example, at this writing a pound of mild cheddar is $2.80/pound if you purchase it in five-pound bulk packaging. Gibbsville offers several types of Wisconsin summer sausage (regular, beef, or garlic) and beef sticks too, in addition to well-priced gift boxes to suit every budget and taste.

In business since 1933, Gibbsville produces the most popular kinds of cheese, including cheddar (mild, medium, aged, supersharp white, and caraway), Monterey Jack (including garlic and pepper versions), two-tone cheese, Swiss, Muenster, Colby (including reduced-fat Colby and Colby with salami), Parmesan (chunks and grated), provolone, Romano, and much more. If you're into flavored processed cheeses or cold-packed cheese spreads, you'll find them here ranging from hot pepper-, pizza-, and bacon-flavored cheeses to port wine, garlic-and-herb, and horseradish cheese spreads. Dieters will appreciate the lower-fat varieties, clearly marked in the catalog.

Please note: Gibbsville won't ship during the summer months—from approximately June to September—as UPS doesn't have refrigeration.

SPECIAL FACTORS: Price quote by letter with SASE.

Jaffe Bros. Natural Foods

P.O. Box 636-W
Valley Center, CA 92082–0636

760–749–1133
Fax: 760–749–1282

Catalog: free
Pay: check, MO, MC, V, DSC
Sells: organically grown food
Warehouse: (call first) 28560 Lilac Rd., Valley Center, CA;
   Sunday to Thursday 8–5, Friday 8–3
E-mail: jb54@worldnet.att.net

With all the competition out there, it's good to find a source selling comparatively inexpensive natural foods. Jaffe Bros. has been doing it for half a century through their 24-page catalog. Prices here average about 30% below retail and dip even further if you can go in with a friend and buy in large quantities. Organic dried fruit (Fuyu persimmons, Black Mission figs, kiln-dried apricots, sliced kiwi, whole bananas, etc.); raw, unbleached nuts of every kind; peas, beans, flours, grains, and cereal; organic pasta (wheat and nonwheat) and sauces; dehydrated vegetables; organic apple sauces (such as raspberry-apple and peach-apple); health-food snacks and treats; cooking oils; Organica brand home-maintenance products—these and many other items can be found at Jaffe for less. If you don't live in a Manhattan closet and can afford the space, take advantage of the bulk discounts here and buy untreated, natural foods from Jaffe. You'll feel good about supporting this family business.

SPECIAL FACTORS: Quantity discounts apply; problems with your order should be reported to Jaffe within ten days of receipt; C.O.D. orders accepted.

E. C. Kraus

P.O. Box 7850-WC
Independence, MO 64054

816–254–7448
Fax: 816–254–7051

Catalog: free
Pay: check, MO, MC, V
Sells: wine- and beer-making supplies
Store: 733 S. Northern Blvd., Independence, MO; Monday
to Friday 8–4:30 CT

Save up to half the cost of wine, beer, and liqueurs. How? Make them yourself! I well remember the gals in my college dorm whipping up batches of "Kahlua" made from vodka, instant coffee, and nonfat sweetener. Yuck! We would have downed anything back then. Fortunately my palate has gotten more sophisticated, and E. C. Kraus would be just the place to get started with a home wine-making hobby. For over 30 years they've made it simple by selling kits through their "Home Wine and Beer Making Equipment and Supplies" catalog that include everything you need to make four gallons of beer, or five gallons of wine, including ingredients and instruction books. This is a one-time investment, after which you need only buy the ingredients and a few other supplies, sold here as well. Yeast (for beer and wine), fruit acids, wine clarifiers, purifiers and preservatives, grape concentrates, fermenting vats, malted barley grains, kits for specific beers and soft drinks, liqueur extracts, measuring tools and gauges, and a great selection of books and manuals are a few of the items E. C. Kraus sells.

SPECIAL FACTORS: Please check your local ordinances regarding home production of alcoholic beverages; shipment to APO/FPO addresses "at buyer's risk"; C.O.D. (UPS) orders accepted; shipping free in the continental U.S.

Mountain Ark Trading Co.

799 Old Leicester Hwy.
Asheville, NC 28806

800–438–4730
828–252–1221
Fax: 828–252–9479

Catalog: free
Pay: check, MO, V, MC, DSC
Sells: Japanese and macrobiotic natural foods
Store: same address; Monday to Friday 9–5:30
Online: www.mountainark.com

This is a great source for persons who are on macrobiotic diets or who love to cook Japanese-style. Mountain Ark was recommended by a reader who regularly orders her grains, seaweed, and nuts in bulk from this company. The 38-page black-and-white catalog has a reader-friendly table of contents that will guide you from aduki beans to yuku vinegar. Beans, lentils, seeds, and grains of every kind; Chinese herbs and Taoist tonic herbal formulas; teas; vinegars; seaweeds; noodles; flours and cereals; sugar-free candies, cookies, and syrups; an array of miso; dried fruits; soy and other sauces; and cooking oils are among the fine foods listed here. There are plenty of obscure and hard-to-find items, such as dried daikon, spelt pasta, and mugwort mochi. Mountain Ark also has cookware and kitchen items such as steamers, tempura pots, sushi-making kits, and Japanese knives. A full line of Weleda personal-care products (sage deodorant, salt toothpaste, calendula baby soap, green clay powder, etc.) are available, as well as a number of intriguing books about healing, alternative approaches to diet and health, and Japanese and macrobiotic cooking. The prices are excellent, about 20% to 25% less than you'd find at stores, but are dependent to some degree on the dollar's strength against the yen and other foreign currencies. The minimum order is $35. Japanese is spoken here, as well as English. If you prefer to shop online, you'll find Mountain Ark's website wonderfully user-friendly.

SPECIAL FACTORS: Returns are accepted, but see catalog for terms; quantity discounts and wholesale orders available; C.O.D. orders are accepted; Canadian orders must be made in U.S. funds.

New England Cheesemaking Supply Co.

P.O. Box 85, Dept. WBM
Ashfield, MA 01330–0085

413–628–3808
Fax: 413–628–4061

Catalog: $1
Pay: check, MO, MC, V
Sells: cheese-making supplies and equipment
Store: Main Street, Ashfield, MA; Monday to Friday 8–4
(call first)
Online: www.cheesemaking.com

Making cheese at home is easier than you might think. It's also economical. The only problem is, according to Ricki, owner of New England Cheesemaking Supply, once you've tasted your own freshly made cheese, the store-bought variety will never taste quite the same again. There are two ways to get to know this company—through the free 20-page newsprint catalog or through the adorable website (wallpapered with cheery Swiss cheese polka dot holes), where you can order online, get recipe ideas, and link to related sites. Either way, you'll immediately feel at home with the wonderful products for beginners (Basic Cheese Kit), books, equipment such as cheese presses, molds, and pasteurizers, supplies such as cheesecloth and cultures (starters), and much more. What kinds of cheese can one make at home? Cheddar, Gouda, Monterey Jack, cottage cheese, buttermilk cheese, ricotta, mozzarella, mascarpone, gourmet soft cheeses, crème fraîche, chèvre—you name it, and you'll find everything necessary to do so right here.

SPECIAL FACTORS: A 10% restocking fee applies to all returned items.

Northwestern Coffee Mills

Middle Rd., Box 370　　　　715–747–5825
La Pointe, WI 54850　　　　Fax: 715–747–5405

Catalog: free, $2 outside U.S.
Pay: check, MO, MC, V, AE
Sells: coffee, tea, herbs, spices, coffee filters, coffee
　　flavors, and syrups
Store: same address, and 217 North Broadway, 2nd Floor,
　　Milwaukee, WI; Monday to Friday 10–5:30, Saturday
　　10–4
E-mail: nwcoftsp@win.bright.net

Northwestern Coffee Mills has had long experience in their specialty coffee and tea business, which began 120 years ago as Robertson's, the first coffee roaster in Wisconsin. Their landmark Milwaukee roasting mill has been roasting coffee with the same vintage equipment since 1914. But to keep pace with today's coffee and tea drinkers, not to mention the competition, Northwestern offers a selection that's broad and deep, good prices that become even better when you order in quantity, flat-rate shipping, and excellent service. Using gas-fired, slow-roasting ovens creates especially delicious coffee. Whole bean or ground to order, the coffees here include blends, estate straights (Brazil Serra Negra, Guatamala Antigua, Mexican Custapec Altura, Ethiopia Harrar, to name a few), natural decaffeinated (CO_2 or Swiss water-processed) blends and straights, and dark roasts. Teas include black-tea single estates and blends, oolong and green teas, flavored and herb teas, and decaf, loose or bagged. Interesting gift packs and samplers are available here, as well as coffee flavors and syrups and an assortment of coffee filters. If you're an unabashed caffeine fiend, get a "coffee subscription" from Northwestern Coffee Mills, and save even more (see details in catalog). You'll be thrilled to have incredible coffee delivered right to your door for less. Now if only someone would make it for you each morning!

SPECIAL FACTORS: Satisfaction guaranteed; quantity discounts available.

Sultan's Delight

P.O. Box 090302
Fort Hamilton Station
Brooklyn, NY 11209–0302

800–852–5046
718–745–2121
Fax: 718–745–2563

Catalog: free with SASE
Pay: check, MO, MC, V, AE, DSC
Sells: Middle Eastern and Mediterranean foods and gifts
Store: mail order only
Online: www.sultansdelight.com

Sultan's Delight is frequently cited in magazines and cookbooks as a source of Middle Eastern and Mediterranean foods and ingredients. The prices here are good and in some cases tremendous—at least 30% below what they'd be in gourmet specialty shops. Whether you familiarize yourself with their products over the Internet or by requesting a catalog (include a self-addressed stamped envelope), Sultan's Delight provides a very smart and convenient way to stock your kitchen with ready-to-serve Middle Eastern specialties, grains and beans, spices, dried or candied fruit, preserves and syrups, bread and pastry dough, Turkish coffee and tea, tahini, flower water, olives, and specialty oils. Sultan's Delight also carries Italian items (such as olive oil, sun-dried tomatoes, and black olive sauce), henna, and even Turkish coffee cups. If you're into cooking, this is a company you'll want to get to know.

The many cookbooks here offer introductions to cooking with spices, cooking Indian cuisine, Armenian, Greek, Lebanese, and Moroccan cuisine. For the kitchen there are also mortar and pestle, falafel molds, and corers. Ordering can be done by secured e-mail, fax, toll-free call, and regular mail.

SPECIAL FACTORS: Minimum order $20; inquire about shipping options other than UPS.

Related Products/Companies

Animal-themed food gifts (Dark Horse chocolates, for example)
• Valley Vet

Bulk creamer/sugar, bar snacks, coffee
• Paper Wholesaler, Party & Paper Worldwide

Bulk nuts and seeds
• Atlantic Spice

Butter churns, ice cream makers, and other nonelectric kitchen gadgets
- Lehman's

Cookbooks
- Jessica's Biscuit Cookbooks

Decorative gift boxes and bags for food
- Sally Distributors

Dehydrated bulk vegetables
- Atlantic Spice

Food safety guidelines
- Consumer Information Center

Fortune cookies
- Paradise Products

Freeze-dried camper's food
- Campmor

Gourmet foods
- Caviar and Imported Gourmet Foods Warehouse, Le Jardin du Gourmet, Make Us an Offer, Zabar's

Guides to preserving, home brewing, canning, etc.
- Storey Books

Herb essential oil, Chinese tea
- East Earth Trade Winds

Honey products and mead-making supplies
- Brushy Mountain Bee Farm

Penny candy
- Party & Paper Worldwide, Sally Distributors

Tea
- Alberene Royal Mail, Atlantic Spice

What's-in-your-cabinet recipe ideas
- Reader's Digest

Zipper-lock bags in every imaginable size
- Plastic BagMart

Spices, Condiments, and Flavorings

Bulk herbs and spices; international condiments; flavoring oils and extracts

The companies in this section carry all the little items that jazz up our palates, whether it's exotic and unusual oils for flavoring, Cajun spices, Indian chutneys, or Vermont maple cream. These are some of the best items to buy mail order, since they're often sold in bulk—which can mean up to 90% savings. Just be sure that you store your herbs and spices in airtight bottles or jars, away from heat and light.

See also the listings in the previous section for other firms that sell gourmet condiments, spices, and herbs.

Find It Fast

Condiments
- The CMC Company, Palmer's Maple Products, Wood's Cider Mill

Ethnic Seasonings, Sauces, Condiments
- The CMC Company

Flavorings, Essential Oils, Extracts
- Bickford, Rafal

Herbs and Spices
- Atlantic Spice Co., Rafal

Tea and Coffee
- Rafal

Atlantic Spice Co.

P.O. Box 205
North Truro, MA 02652

800–316–7965
508–487–6100
Fax: 508–487–2550

Catalog with Potpourri Recipes: free
Pay: check, MO, MC, V, DSC
Sells: culinary herbs and spices, teas, potpourri ingredients
Store: Junction of Route 6 and 6A, North Truro, MA;
  Monday to Friday 9–5, Saturday 10–2
Online: www.atlanticspice.com

Atlantic Spice Co. will add spice to your life whether you're cooking up gourmet meals; healing with herbs, botanicals, and essences; or creating scented wreaths and potpourri. All ingredients are free from irradiation. Most of the items are sold in bulk and wrapped in one-pound packages made of biodegradable plastic. Cooks will find spice blends (apple pie, curry powder, pickling spice, etc.); culinary herbs and spices; extracts and flavors; bulk teas; baking items; dehydrated vegetables; and shelled nuts and seeds at savings of 50% and more. There's lots here for the New Ager, such as St. John's Wort, Valerian root powder, goldenseal root powder, and ginseng powder, not to mention those essential oils used by aromatherapists. Craftspeople will appreciate the fragrance oils, potpourri ingredients, and fabulous detailed recipes for potpourri, sachets, pomander balls, and simmering fragrances.

Rounding out the double-sided, maplike catalog are related supplies and equipment—muslin sachet bags, potpourri jars, self-seal teabags, spice jars, gel caps and capsule fillers, plastic gallon jars, and the like. The listings are flagged to note items that shouldn't be used in food or drink. Atlantic's low prices drop 10% on orders of five pounds of the same item (based on the one-pound rate), 15% off on 25 pounds, and shipping is free on orders over $200 (subject to some restrictions). If you're a web shopper, you'll like Atlantic's site, where you can view the full inventory and order online.

Please note: If you wish to buy in smaller quantities, contact Atlantic's sister company, San Francisco Herb Co., which offers the same selection and prices, but in four-ounce sizes. Their phone is 800–227–4530; web address is www. sfherb.com.

SPECIAL FACTORS: Satisfaction guaranteed; quantity discounts available; minimum order is $30; add $5 to C.O.D. orders.

Bickford Flavors

19007 St. Clair Ave.
Cleveland, OH 44117–1001

800–283–8322
216–531–6006
Fax: 216–531–2006

Price List: free
Pay: check, MO, MC, V
Sells: flavorings
Store: same address; Monday to Friday 9–5

If you or someone you know objects to foods that have alcohol as an ingredient, you've just found an unusual and excellent source for nonalcoholic flavorings.

Established in 1914, Bickford Laboratories makes and sells their own concentrated flavorings from naturally derived oils. You won't find any sugar or alcohol here; you will find a dizzying selection of flavors—over 100 at last count—in their flyer, as well as food colorings and the odd ingredient, such as vanilla powder, corn syrup, carob syrup, citric acid solution, and glycerin. Get a load of some of these flavorings (in a soy oil or propylene base): apple maple, boysenberry, champagne, cheesecake, cranberry, guava, maraschino, onion, raisin, root beer, and watermelon. Among the exotically flavored oil extracts are blueberry oil, cinnamon oil, coffee oil, kiwi oil, peanut butter oil, and tangerine oil. Imagine the unusual hard candies or lollipops you could make! If you're looking for vanilla (pure, dark, or white), it's here too in a variety of sizes. All flavorings are sold in one-ounce bottles, the oils in half-ounce and one-ounce sizes. The selection here is unparalleled and the prices are good. If you can buy in larger sizes (16 ounces and up) the prices go down even further.

SPECIAL FACTORS: Flavorings are free of alcohol and sugar; wholesalers should inquire about terms.

The CMC Company

P.O. Drawer 322
Avalon, NJ 08202

800–CMC–2780
Fax: 609–624–8414

Catalog: $1, refundable with first order
Pay: check, MO, MC, V, AE, DSC
Sells: gourmet seasonings and ethnic specialties
Store: mail order only
Online: clever.net/wwwmall/cmc

If English is your second language and you're living in Snowfalls, Minnesota, you may have a problem. Namely, where are you going to find that crucial Pakistani, Malaysian, Mexican, or Thai ingredient to make your family's favorite dish? Don't worry, because The CMC Company specializes in hard-to-find ingredients and food specialties for both gourmet and gourmand, and they're less expensive here—by 10% to 50%—than in most gourmet shops.

Some of the items CMC carries include dried, powdered, and canned chiles for Mexican cuisine, Mexican hot sauce, hot chile peanuts, tomatillos, Mexican dried shrimp, and more. If ingredients from Thailand, Malaysia, Singapore, or

Indonesia are what you seek, check out the sambals, sauces, spices, curry pastes, and rice at CMC. You'll also find ingredients for the following cuisines: Chinese, Indian, Pakistani, Japanese, Creole, Cajun, Jamaican, French, Greek, and Middle Eastern. The 38-page catalog from CMC offers the very best ethnic cookbooks from around the world, and special implements needed in preparing such cuisine such as a tortilla press, a food smoker bag, and more. "It is our hope," says the catalog text, "that we can help you prepare authentic ethnic dishes without resorting to unsuitable substitutions or unfortunate omissions."

Wholesale customers, please note: Discounts are given to resellers and food-service professionals.

SPECIAL FACTORS: Keep the catalog, since it's updated with inserts from printing to printing.

Palmer's Maple Products

72 Maple Ln.   Tel/Fax: 802–496–3696
Waitsfield, VT 05673–9710

Brochure and Price List: free with long SASE
Pay: check, MO, MC, V
Sells: maple syrup, cream, candy, and jelly
Store: Mehuron's Market and Bisbee's Hardware,
  Waitsfield, VT

Maple-syrup harvesting is an art that's been passed down from generation to generation. How does one know when it's time to head out into the woods and begin the arduous process of tapping the trees? The Palmers of Waitsfield, Vermont, claim "a certain scent is in the air." Delbert Palmer, the fourth generation to be involved in producing this all-American nectar, along with his wife, Sharlia, their two children, Shawn and Susan, and even their grandchildren (that's six generations!), run a world-renowned maple farm complete with a new sugar house that's wheelchair accessible. The brochure details the process of sugaring, relates the history of the Palmers' operation, includes happy-customer testimonials as well as recipes, and presents the wonderful products they make on their farm. You can buy grade-A maple syrup (light amber, medium amber, dark amber) in various sizes and formats, including a log cabin and a gift jug; maple cream in two, four, eight, and 16 ounces; maple jelly; a variety box of maple candy; and even honey. Prices here are excellent, especially when you buy in larger quantities. If you have a kid who eats oatmeal, waffles, and pancakes, as I do, you'll go through that half-gallon in no time! Talking with the Palmers was a lovely experience, and their company literature reflects their old-fashioned integrity and family values. Visitors are welcome to drop by.

SPECIAL FACTORS: Be sure to include a long, self-addressed, stamped envelope when you request a price list and brochure.

Rafal Spice Company

2521 Russell St.   313–259–6373
Detroit, MI 48207   Fax: 313–259–6220

Catalog: free
Pay: check, MO, MC, V, AE, DSC
Sells: spices, herbs, coffee, tea, flavorings, cookbooks, etc.
Store: same address; Monday to Saturday 7–4

Rafal is a good source for a wide variety of flavoring items: spices and herbs, food specialties from anchovy paste to Wright's Liquid Smoke, extracts (pure, imitation, and alcohol-free), and coffee flavorings, among others. On select items you can save as much as 30%, and even more when you buy in bulk. If ethnic cooking is your thing, be it Cajun or Chinese, you'll find a wide range of unusual ingredients here, such as Creole seasonings; French beignet mix; fiery condiments with saucy names like Dis Stuff Really Hot Mon!, Endorphin Rush, and Ass Kickin' Sauce; cellophane noodles; Swiss spaetzle dumplings; Thai satay (spicy peanut) sauce; and much more. Rafal also sells coffee beans by the pound, teas, cookbooks, spice jars, and essential oils.

SPECIAL FACTORS: Satisfaction guaranteed; allow three weeks for delivery.

Wood's Cider Mill

R.D. 2, Box 477　　　　　　　**802-263-5547**
Springfield, VT 05156

Brochure: free with SASE
Pay: check, MO, MC, V
Sells: cider jelly and syrups
Farm: call for appointment

Willis and Tina are the Woods behind Wood's Cider Mill. Their small southern Vermont farm, on which they keep cows, sheep, chickens, and a vegetable garden, has been in the family since 1798. Luckily for us, the Woods produce four items that they sell by mail. The first two are cider jelly and boiled cider. They grind and press apples on the original 1882 screw press to make sweet cider, then evaporate it in a wood-fired stainless-steel evaporator to make boiled cider. Boiled cider is concentrated to about 7 to 1, and cider jelly about 9 to 1. Use boiled cider with hot water for a delicious drink, in cooking, or as a topping for pancakes, yogurt, or ice cream. Cider jelly is great with peanut butter on sandwiches, on bagels, or along with stews and meats. (The Woods will send you a recipe sheet if you request one with a SASE.) You'll also find maple syrup here, for which Vermont is famous, and the Woods' own cinnamon cider syrup—half maple syrup, half boiled cider with a stick of cinnamon in each bottle. Yum! Some say it tastes like apple pie in a bottle. The prices here are excellent, especially if you order larger-format bottles and jars.

SPECIAL FACTORS: Satisfaction guaranteed; quantity discounts available.

Related Products/Companies

Condiments
- A Cook's Wares, EDGE Distributing, Jaffe Bros., Le Jardin du Gourmet, Mountain Ark, Zabar's

Ethnic seasonings, sauces, and condiments
- A Cook's Wares, Mountain Ark, Sultan's Delight

Flavorings, extracts
- Northwestern Coffee Mills

Spices and herbs
- Bulkfoods.com, Caprilands Herb Farm, A Cook's Wares, Deer Valley Farm, EDGE Distributing, Mountain Ark, Northwestern Coffee Mills

Garden, Farm, and Lawn

Seeds, bulbs, and live plants;
supplies and equipment for home
gardens, nurseries, beekeeping,
and land- and waterscaping

While the rest of the country was waiting every year to see if Punxsutawney Phil would see his shadow, my grandmother would already be well into her plans for spring and beyond. Why? Because as soon as the first seed catalog had arrived at year's beginning, she had big decisions to make. I have nothing but wonderful memories of working in my grandparent's huge garden in Illinois, not to mention the bounty of fresh vegetables that graced every meal and the giant bouquets of roses, gladiolas, zinnias, and snapdragons in every room. If you've never experienced gardening, I highly recommend it. Ask anyone who grows vegetables, tends flowers, or just putters around the yard taking pride in weedless borders: Working the land is a proven cure for malaise.

Print and online catalogs provide one of the best ways to extensively plan your garden. Not only can the companies in this chapter bring you a fantastic selection of bulbs, plants, flowers, herbs, and seedlings, as well as tools and equipment, but they can do so at considerable savings compared to your local farm and garden centers.

If you're a beginner, don't fret. Most of these firms have catalogs or websites jam-packed with tips and information. Many also sell great reference books as well. And all are staffed with people who want to answer your questions and offer advice. Gardening isn't hard as long as you buy plants, bulbs, and seeds appropriate to your climate, conditions, and soil. Ohio Earth Foods, listed in this chapter, will test your soil for $17, which is less than half the price of the best-known home gardener kits. Want to start a new hobby? Why not take up beekeeping? Brushy Mountain Beekeeping Farm listed in this section can help you get started.

If you're ready to quit that corporate job and begin a whole new life, move out of the city and start a Christmas tree farm. Flickinger's sell evergreen seedlings at wholesale prices. Or you can order tree seedlings and transplants to plant around your new country home from Carino Nurseries.

From tractors to garden tools to lawn furniture, there are plenty of companies located elsewhere in this book that sell goods related to farming, landscaping, and gardening. Check out the "Related Products/Companies" at the end of this chapter for a comprehensive listing.

Find It Fast

Beekeeping Supplies
- Brushy Mountain Bee Farm

Bulbs
- Daylily Discounters, Dutch Gardens, Mellinger's, J. E. Miller, Pinetree Garden, Van Bourgondien, Van Dyck's, Van Engelen

Flower, Vegetable, Herb Seeds
- Burrell's, Butterbrooke Farm, Caprilands, Fedco, Johnny's, Le Jardin du Gourmet, Mellinger's, J. E. Miller, Pinetree Garden, Rohrer's Seeds, Twilley Seeds

Garden and Lawn Decor and Furniture
- Caprilands, Florist Products, Turner Greenhouses

Gardening Books
- Burrell's, Butterbrooke Farm, Caprilands, Daylily Discounters, Fedco, Johnny's, Le Jardin du Gourmet, Mellinger's, Pinetree Garden, Turner Greenhouses

Greenhouses
- Bob's Superstrong Greenhouse Plastic, Burrell's, Florist Products, Mellinger's, Turner Greenhouses

Live Plants
- Brittingham, Carino Nurseries, Fedco, Flickinger's, George's Plant Farm, Le Jardin du Gourmet, Mellinger's, J. E. Miller, Nor'East Miniature Roses, Pinetree Garden, Prentiss Court

Pond Liners and Pond Equipment
- Bob's Superstrong Greenhouse Plastic

Tools and Supplies
- Burrell's, Daylily Discounters, EON Industries, Fedco, Florist Products, Johnny's, Mellinger's, Ohio Earth Food, Pinetree Garden, Rohrer's Seeds, Van Bourgondien

Trees
- Carino Nurseries, Flickinger's, J. E. Miller Nurseries

Bob's Superstrong Greenhouse Plastic

Box 42-WM, Neche, ND 58265   204–327–5540
Box 1450-WM, Altona, MB,   Fax: 204–327–5527
R0G 0B0, Canada

Brochure: $1 or two first-class stamps
Pay: check or MO
Sells: greenhouse plastic and fastening systems, and pond
  liners
Showrooms: Neche, ND, and Altona, Manitoba, Canada
  (by appointment)
E-mail: northerngreenhouse@mb.sympatico.ca

Bob and Margaret Davis started their business in 1980 when they decided to combine his gardening experience with her business management skills to market their UV-stabilized superstrong woven poly, the only greenhouse plastic they found that was strong enough to resist the violent winds, hail, and temperature changes on their Manitoba prairie farm. Their 32-page newsprint catalog is a joy to thumb through; the Davises show us the many uses for this miracle stuff and wax poetic on their missions to aid troubled teens through promoting greenhouse projects in the U.S. and Canada, to encourage solar heating and wind power, and to help ordinary folk get the most out of their gardens in every season.

The woven poly comes in 10-, 12-, and 18-mil thicknesses, in clear, translucent, or opaque. The catalog text describes the different properties and possible uses for each. There are two anchoring systems to choose from: the Cinchstrap, a plastic lath to nail down the poly, and Polyfastener, a two-part plastic channel-and-insert strip. Prices for the woven poly run from 16 cents to 27 cents per square foot. Custom-made barn curtains, tarps, plastic mulching, terrariums, and greenhouse kits are also offered here. Besides the detailed measurement and price charts and descriptions, there are testimonials from happy customers who've used Bob's Superstrong Poly for everything from sails and water-tank liners to boat sheds and skywalks.

Canadian readers: Please write to Canadian address for literature.

SPECIAL FACTORS: Phone hours are from 6 A.M. to 8 P.M. CST; C.O.D. orders accepted.

This family business, which has been around for more than half a century, specializes in berries: strawberries, blackberries, raspberries, grapes, and blueberries. The 32-page color catalog tells you everything you need to know about cultivation and handling. Brittingham participates in Maryland's strawberry certification program, which assures you virus-free strawberry plants. Strawberries are king here, with over two dozen varieties in the current catalog, for early through late yields. Prices begin at $10.50 for 25 plants, and the per-plant price goes down the more you buy. In addition to berries, Brittingham sells asparagus and rhubarb. Quantity price breaks apply to everything Brittingham sells.

Please note: Plants are not shipped to AK, CA, HI, NM, or outside the continental U.S.

SPECIAL FACTORS: Satisfaction guaranteed; replacements, refunds, or credits are offered within a specified date (see catalog); minimum orders vary, depending on item; C.O.D. orders accepted.

Brushy Mountain Bee Farm

610 Bethany Church Rd.
Moravian Falls, NC
28654-9600

800-233-7929
336-921-3640
Fax: 336-921-2681

Catalog: free
Pay: check, MO, V, MC, DSC
Sells: supplies for beekeeping, candle-making, soap-making, etc.
Store: same address; Monday to Friday 8:30-5
Online: www.beeequipment.com

You'll like this company, whether you're a seasoned beekeeper or merely interested in the subject. The 72-page catalog makes for a great read. For example, did you know that queen-marking colors are internationally standardized so that any queen's age can be easily determined? Did you even know that queens are marked? (I didn't.) The catalog is jam-packed with articles, calendars, suggested references, product descriptions, personal anecdotes, checklists, and advice. Best of all, prices here are about 20% to 30% below retail. The owners, who've been in business since 1978 have a friendly attitude toward their customers. You'll find beekeeping supplies and equipment aplenty, from complete hives to all necessary components, tools, and accessories; protective clothing for adults and children; mite treatments; queens and package bees; bee food; queen-marking kits; honey-producing presses, extractors, and other equipment; honey jars, bears, and bottles in every size and style; honey and beeswax products; mead-making books and equipment; candle molds and supplies; soap-making supplies; beeswax products such as furniture polish; children's bee-related books, games, and puppets; and books and videos on many subjects, from instructional videos to a natural cosmetics primer. There's so much more, but you'll want to discover all the goodies in this catalog yourself. By the way, the website is wonderful as well, and features online ordering.

SPECIAL FACTORS: Wholesale orders available to qualified buyers (inquire); satisfaction guaranteed; unused merchandise must be returned within 30 days (see catalog for details).

D. V. Burrell Seed Growers Co.

P.O. Box 150–WBM
Rocky Ford, CO 81067

719–254–3318
Fax: 719–254–3319

Catalog: free
Pay: check, MO, MC, V
Sells: flower and vegetable seeds, and growing supplies
Store: 405 North Main, Rocky Ford, CO; Monday to Friday
8–5

If you have dreams of turning your home garden into an income-producing road-side stand, Burrell's Better Seeds is a great source to know about. This company, which has been serving commercial growers and florists since 1900, sells vegetable, fruit, and flower seeds in large quantities (100 pounds), tiny quantities (individual packets), and everything in between. There are price breaks at 1, 5, 25, 50, and 100 pounds. Naturally, if you can go in with a friend and buy more, your prices will be lower and you'll save on shipping costs as well. The 105-page catalog pictures and describes everything one would want to grow, from artichokes to watermelons. You get the feeling everything in Burrell's catalog has been carefully and thoughtfully selected for its hardiness and reliability. And in fact, the catalog's introductory text says it all: "No seedsman can hope to survive the critical judgment of the trade unless his product consistently delivers satisfaction." The back of the catalog features some useful items: a garden seeder, backpack sprayer, germinator greenhouse kit, and reference books.

Customers outside the United States, please note: Catalogs cost $5 (in U.S. funds), and orders must be paid in U.S. funds.

SPECIAL FACTORS: Shipping included on certain items; quantity discounts are available; institutional accounts are available.

Butterbrooke Farm Seed Co-Op

78 Barry Rd.   **203–888–2000**
Oxford, CT 06478–1529

> Price List: free with long SASE
> Pay: check or MO
> Sells: seeds
> Store: mail order only

Butterbrooke Farm, where helping you become "seed self-reliant" is their goal, is a membership organization of organic farmers, home gardeners, and seed savers. While you don't have to become a co-op member to buy from Butterbrooke, the membership fee is low ($15/year at this writing) and with it you receive a lot of benefits: 33% discount on all seeds, a quarterly newsletter, access to unlimited free advice, and the opportunity to buy heirloom seeds, among others. The price list, free when you send in a self-addressed stamped envelope, has many varieties of seeds available in small packets (enough for one or two 20-foot rows) and larger packets (for planting four to six 20-foot rows), both at extremely reasonable prices. All seeds are fresh and chosen specifically for short growing seasons. Be sure to check out Butterbrooke's booklets on everything from mulching to making compost.

SPECIAL FACTORS: C.O.D. orders accepted.

Caprilands Herb Farm

534 Silver St.   **860–742–7244**
Coventry, CT 06238

> Brochure: free
> Pay: check, MO, MC, V, AE
> Sells: live herbs, freeze-dried herbs, spices, and gifts
> Store: same address; daily 9–5 except holidays
> Online: www.caprilands.com

Founded in 1929, Caprilands Herb Farm, with vast offerings of standard and hard-to-find herbs and less common plants, gives herbal collectors, natural magic practitioners, and cooks good reasons to cheer. As with all successful ventures, there is a person behind Caprilands' reputation and vision—Mrs. Simmons, a life-long herbalist who runs the farm and shares her professional passion with visitors during luncheon talks at her 18th-century farmhouse. (See the brochure for details about the program and reservations.) Mrs. Simmons has distilled her knowledge of herbal horticulture into the classic *Herb Gardening in Five Seasons*, and has authored guides on how to cultivate and use herbs. These and other Caprilands Press books detailed in the brochure are available to wholesale customers, herb societies, and garden clubs at varying rates of discount.

Caprilands sells over 300 kinds of culinary and less common herbs in plant form (available only at the farm) and in seed form, available in individual packets or in larger quantities (four ounces and one pound); freeze-dried herbs such as basil, Italian parsley, shallots, and garlic; teas and tisanes; botanicals; oils; potpourris and fragrances; herb- and garden-related goods (sachet pillows, spice necklaces, wreathes, sundials, "good luck crows"); and a honey made by the intriguing "Buckfast Bee," bred for its resistance to arcine, a deadly bee disease. The website lists many of the offerings and has other interesting information about the farm, but no online ordering is available.

SPECIAL FACTORS: Some items in catalog are available only at the farm.

Carino Nurseries

P.O. Box 538, Dept. WBM   800–223–7075
Indiana, PA 15701   724–463–3350
      Fax: 724–463–3050

Catalog: free
Pay: check, MO, MC, V, DSC
Sells: tree and shrub seedlings and transplants
Store: mail order and nursery pickup only
Online: www.carinonurseries.com

Located in Indiana County, Pennsylvania, "the Christmas tree capital of the world," Carino Nurseries has been around since 1946 and is now run by the third generation of Carinos. Here you can get evergreen and deciduous seedlings and transplants direct from the grower *at wholesale prices*. To get an idea of what this nursery has to offer, check out the website. There you'll see the many varieties of trees, in transplant and seedling form, you can buy here: all kinds of spruce, fir, pine, hemlock, chestnut, walnut, butternut, dogwoods, locusts, olive, ash, oak, and birch, among others. Carino's trees are suitable for Christmas trees, ornamentals, windbreaks, noise barriers, landscaping, timber, wetlands restoration, wildlife food, and cover. Or maybe you're like I am and just want to be around trees of every kind. The website specials are great deals and come with the added benefit of free shipping. The print catalog includes details about the variety, age, and approximate height of the plants, and other relevant information regarding shipping, planting zones, pruning, and selecting the right tree.

SPECIAL FACTORS: Shipments made by UPS; some minimum orders apply; shipping takes place October 1 to November 15 and March 20 to May 15 only.

Daylily Discounters International

One Daylily Plaza   904–462–1539
Alachua, FL 32615   Fax: 904–462–5111

 Catalog: $2
 Pay: check, MO, MC, V, AE, DSC
 Sells: daylilies
 Store: mail order only
 Online: www.daylilydiscounters.com

Start with a clear-cut goal, stick to it, and you're likely to succeed. That's what the folks at Daylily Discounters did when they aimed to offer the public special hybrid daylilies that weren't generally available, at prices far below the collector's market. Now, ten years later, business is booming, and it's easy to see why when you look through the company's 78-page glossy color catalog.

Dozens of hybrid lilies grace the pages of this catalog photographed in up-close detail and vivid color. Each lily has accompanying text describing size, growing specifications, and price. The catalog also features helpful pages about the history of daylilies, advantages, soil needs, hardiness, when and how to plant them, selecting varieties, and much more. There is a small selection of other items here too, such as seaweed powder, plant tags, liquid humus, and other fertilizers especially suited for daylilies. These resilient and popular flowers are great values since a single bulb keeps giving year after year; the price per bulb improves when you order in quantity. Be sure to look at their website—the full catalog is online, with online ordering available.

International customers, please note: Import permits required before you can order; call or write for details.

SPECIAL FACTORS: Minimum order is $25; all plants guaranteed for up to one year from shipping date.

Dutch Gardens

P.O. Box 200, Dept. WBM   **800–818–3861**
Adelphia, NJ 07710–0200   **Fax: 732–780–7720**

Catalog: free
Pay: check, MO, MC, V, AE, DSC
Sells: Dutch flower bulbs and perennials
Store: mail order only

If you've seen one bulb catalog you've seen 'em all, right? Not exactly. The 180-page color catalog from Dutch Gardens is a stunner that stands out from the pack. This catalog features page after page of gorgeous photographs of over 200 varieties of flower bulbs and perennials, shipped grower-direct from Holland at prices that are 30% and more below retail. Everything is guaranteed to grow, and there are quantity price breaks that help you save more money when you buy in larger quantities.

What's lovely about this catalog, besides the presentation, is the amazing selection. For example, there are 35 pages devoted to daffodils and narcissi alone, with detailed and interesting text about the history of these flowers, the types of conditions each is best suited for, height, blossom size, and more. Dutch Gardens keeps creative gardeners in mind with wonderful collections, such as the "Peach Collection"—60 bulbs comprising eight different types of tulips, narcissi, and hyacinths, all in luminous peach and salmon hues. The catalog is also a treasure trove of information ranging from fertilizing your bulbs to forcing bulbs indoors. If you want to design a garden, rather than just plant one, look to Dutch Gardens for inspiration and good prices.

SPECIAL FACTORS: All bulbs guaranteed to bloom; additional 10% discount applies to orders over $125.

Eon Industries, Inc.

P.O. Box 11, Dept. WBM   419–533–4961
107 W. Maple St.
Liberty Center, OH
43532–0011

Brochure: free
Pay: check or MO
Sells: metal garden markers
Store: mail order only

Since 1936, the family behind Eon Industries has focused on the production of one thing: metal plant markers. This focus allows them to give their personal attention to each detail of the process, which results in a superior product—at half the price of those shown in upscale garden catalogs! These simple yet elegant markers come in a number of styles and lengths—Rose Markers and Nursery Markers for larger, easy-to-read labels, and the smaller Swinging Label marker and Staff marker for the more understated areas in your garden. Eon also sells a variety of marking pens and pencils, and has advice on the most weatherproof methods for labeling the markers.

SPECIAL FACTORS: Markers are sold in multiples of 25 and 100 only.

Fedco Seeds, Inc.

P.O. Box 520-WBM   Tel/Fax: 207–873–7333
Waterville, ME 04903–0520

Catalog: $1 (see text)
Pay: check, MO, V, MC
Sells: seeds, trees, seed-starting and cultivation tools, etc.
Store: mail order only

In 1978 the Fedco garden seed cooperative was formed, working with the now-defunct Maine Federation of Cooperatives and the still-thriving Maine Organic

Farmers and Gardeners Association. Now, nearly a quarter century later, Fedco is going strong, providing high-quality seeds at the lowest possible prices (20% to 70% less than you'll pay elsewhere).

This isn't your ordinary seed catalog. Fedco doesn't have an individual owner or beneficiary: "Profit is not our primary goal." Consumers own 60% of the cooperative, and workers 40%. About half of Fedco's customers are individuals, and the other half are cooperatives. The inside spread of their catalog explains how you can form a buying cooperative with friends, neighbors, and family, and indeed the savings when you order in bulk are substantial. There are separate order forms for individuals and groups, and a strict schedule by which you must place your order. Once you've read all the fine print, it makes a lot of sense to buy this way, and you'll get a good feeling that you're participating in keeping prices low by doing some of the work normally handled by a team of employees on the other end of the phone line. Once you've filled out the form (and double-checked it for errors), you can either mail or fax it (no phone orders).

One of three catalogs—"Fall Bulbs," "Trees and Spring Bulbs," and "Seeds, Organic Growers Supply, and Moose Tubers"—will come to you at the appropriate time of year with an ordering deadline. Each of these catalogs is a labor of love and intelligence, chock full of standard and interesting varieties, some heirloom, with valuable descriptions, historical sidelights, instructions for growing, plenty of witty and wise philosophy, and good, sound advice. There are books, mostly of the "politically green" variety, about medicinal herbs, organic gardening, earth-friendly insect management, coloring and comic books, and more; T-shirts; and tools, supplies, and accessories, particularly for the organic gardener. You get a year of mailings for the $1 fee, which is usually $2, so be sure to mention WMO when you order.

Canadian readers, please note: Only seeds are shipped outside the United States (no live plants), and payment is required in U.S. dollars.

SPECIAL FACTORS: Satisfaction is guaranteed; handling is included on orders over $50; quantity discounts are available.

Flickinger's Nurseries

P.O. Box 245   800–368–7381
Sagamore, PA 16250

    Catalog: free
    Pay: check, MO, MC, V
    Sells: evergreen and deciduous tree seedlings
    Store: same address; daily 8–4:30

For three generations, Flickinger's has supplied landscapers, nurseries, and Christmas tree farms with quality seedlings and transplants at wholesale prices. Their new price list features over 18 species of pine, fir, and spruce trees suitable for Christmas tree, ornamental, and reforestation uses, and includes hemlock, arborvitae, paper and European birch, white and red dogwood, and European larch trees. These top-quality seedlings have excellent root systems, thick stems, and good color, and will be freshly dug for your order. Seedlings and transplants are sold per 100 and per 1000, but their low prices hold for quantities as low as 50 (their smallest order amount). These people move a lot of trees, which is what makes their thrifty prices possible.

SPECIAL FACTORS: Orders under $30 include $5 handling fee; pickup orders notify them three days in advance.

Florist Products

P.O. Box 3190   800–828–2242
Barrington, IL 60011   Fax: 800–252–4022

    Catalog: free
    Pay: check, MO, V, MC, AE
    Sells: greenhouse and nursery supplies
    Store: mail order only

You'll save up to 40% on your gardening supplies by shopping with Florist Products. The 42-page "Hobby & Homegrower Catalog" offers a wide selection of equipment, tools, and supplies for professional growing at home. Among the 4,500 items available are hanging baskets, flats, and pots; fertilizers and injectors; greenhouse structures, benches, and heating and ventilation systems; labels; pesticides; plant supports; safety equipment; soil testers; sprayers; thermostats; gardening tools; and watering and irrigation supplies. Florist Products runs frequent specials and offers quantity discounts as well, where the savings are greatest.

SPECIAL FACTORS: Satisfaction is guaranteed; wholesalers should request the Commercial Price List.

George's Plant Farm

**1410 Public Wells Rd., Dept.   Tel/Fax: 901–587–9477
BWBM
Martin, TN 38237**

Flyer: free
Pay: check, MO
Sells: sweet potato plants
Store: mail order only; January through April phone hours
2 P.M. to 10 P.M. CST, Saturday 7 A.M. to 10 P.M.; May
through June, 7 A.M. to 10 P.M. seven days

The Dellingers of George's Plant Farm have been growing sweet potato plants and selling them at grower-direct prices to people all across the United States since 1985. George's Plant Farm is a small-timey operation that values its customers and guarantees all plants will have strong stems, healthy roots, and can withstand cross-country shipping. Making these sweet potatoes ever sweeter is the fact that prices here are well below everyone else's, there are quantity price breaks offering even greater savings, and there's free shipping. The current flyer has seven varieties to choose from, each described in detail as to best features: color, yield, flavor, cooking characteristics, etc. Growing instructions and recipes come with your sweet potato plants, as well as "George's guarantee."

SPECIAL FACTORS: No plants shipped to California or outside the continental U.S.; C.O.D. orders accepted, but call first.

Johnny's Selected Seeds, Inc.

R.R. 1, Box 2580
Albion, ME 04910

207–437–4301
207–437–9294
Fax: 800–437–4290

Catalog: free
Pay: check, MO, MC, V, AE, DSC
Sells: seeds, roots, tubers, seed cultivation supplies
Store: Monday to Saturday 8:30–5; phone hours June to
  December, Monday to Friday 8:30–5; January to May,
  Monday to Friday 8–7, Saturday 8–5
Online: www.johnnyseeds.com

Johnny's Selected Seeds, Inc., established in 1973, is a firm that cultivates both customer satisfaction and an inventory of exemplary-quality seeds, equipment, tools, and supplies at good prices. Customers appreciate the easy-to-use catalog and outstanding rate of seed germination. When they're in Albion, Maine, they enjoy the seasonal workshops and summertime open house. Seeds—flower, vegetable, legume, grass, and herb—are sold in fractions of an ounce as well as by the pound (1, 5, 15, 50, and, for corn, 100). To make sure you benefit from the fruits of your labors—and to help keep them coming—Johnny's also carries food mills and dehydrators, flower-drying materials, seed-station supplies, weather instruments, pest control products, and all kinds of books. If you prefer to shop online, you can visit Johnny's helpful and comprehensive website. There you'll also pick up gardening tips and find links to related sites as well.

SPECIAL FACTORS: Satisfaction guaranteed; no shipping charges (continental U.S. only) on orders over $100; quantity and volume discounts given; returns accepted for exchange, refund, or credit.

Le Jardin du Gourmet

P.O. Box 75-WC
St. Johnsbury Center, VT
05863

802–748–1446
Fax: 802–748–9592

Catalog: 50 cents
Pay: check, MO, MC, V, AE, DC, DSC
Sells: seeds, plants, and gourmet foods
Store: mail order only
Online: www.kingcon.com/agljdg

Le Jardin du Gourmet was started by a New York City chef who moved to Vermont where his fondness for growing shallots became a successful business, today run by his daughter and her husband. The 16-page print catalog offers herbs, plants and seeds, garlic, and small shallots for planting and large ones for cooking. For cooking, frog-leg shallots are available monthly and bimonthly. Other culinary delights include chestnut spread, fancy meats, chutney, and herbal teas, along with books on growing and cooking with herbs and preserving food through canning and pickling.

But what's really neat about this company is their 30-cent "sample" seed packets of culinary herbs. Fenugreek, lemon balm, German chamomile, spearmint, caraway—these are just a few of the hundreds available. The tentative gardener/cook can grow these in her kitchen windowsill for pennies; order as many as you like, add $2 for shipping/handling, and you've still got yourself a good deal.

Available by request is the Christmas catalog, which features wreaths, shipped directly from the manufacturer, for $23 inclusive of shipping (20 to 22-inch wreath, with pine cones, waterproof bow, and matching ornaments).

At the time of this writing, the website was rather limited in scope, and featured online ordering of only one item.

Canadian customers: Only products *other than* plants and bulbs can be shipped, and payment must be in U.S. funds.

SPECIAL FACTORS: Minimum order on credit cards is $15.

Mellinger's

W. South Range Rd., Dept.
WBM
North Lima, OH 44452-9731

330-549-9861
Fax: 330-549-3716

Catalog: free
Pay: check, MO, MC, V, DSC
Sells: seeds, bulbs, live plants, and home and garden
supplies
Store: same address; Monday to Saturday 8:30–5 (June 16
to April); 8–6 (April to June)
Online: www.mellingers.com

For 72 years, the Mellinger family has been committed to going the extra mile for their customers. Their business has been built on offering the very best products at the best possible prices, backed with knowledgeable salespeople who take the time to help their customers. This company sells everything you need for successful ornamental and vegetable gardening—terra cotta pots, arbors and trellises, greenhouse accessories and greenhouses, pest control products, bat houses, bird feeders, plant fertilizer, and more. Most of the catalog, however, is reserved for the many types of vegetable, flower, fruit and grass seeds that they sell. You'll find all your old favorites here, as well as some rare and unusual tropical plant seeds. Mellinger's also sells a collection of gardening books and useful kitchen gadgets. Their website was still under construction at press time and looked promising, so do check it out.

SPECIAL FACTORS: Plants are warranted for 13 months (see catalog for terms); authorized returns accepted (a 10% restocking fee may be charged); $1 service fee charged on credit card orders under $10.

If you're like me, there's nothing more beautiful than an arbor trailing with grapevines and heavy with bunches of frosty purple fruit; or aisles of ruby-red raspberries, ready for the picking. There's just something satisfying about being surrounded by the bounty and sweetness of nature. For over a century, the Miller Family has provided access to nature's bounty in the form of 65 varieties of crisp, hardy "Olde-Tyme" apples; strawberries, raspberries, blackberries, and blueberries; pears, cherries, nut trees, grapevines, and much more, at a 50% discount from typical nursery prices. Miller Nurseries is a major supplier of trees, shrubs, and vines for the backyard fruit and nut grower. They even provide possible garden layouts, suggesting that edibles can be a beautiful, productive, and cost-effective part of any landscape. Miller Nurseries also offers shade trees, ornamental grasses, and decorative flowers, and rounds out the catalog with mulches, wheelbarrows, and other gardening supplies and equipment. This family-owned, family-operated nursery is dedicated to their customers, and each purchase is backed with Miller's "Canandaigua Quality" guarantee. Visit their website to order a free catalog and for directions to their garden center.

SPECIAL FACTORS: Some stock is shipped only in spring.

Nor'East Miniature Roses, Inc.

P.O. Box 307–WB
Rowley, MA 01969

978–948–7964
Fax: 978–948–5487

Catalog: free
Pay: check, MO, MC, V
Sells: miniature roses
Store: 58 Hammond St., Rowley, MA; also 955 W. Phillips
St., Ontario, CA; Monday to Friday 8–4, both locations
Online: www.noreast-miniroses.com

One never tires of the beauty of a rose. Nor'East Miniature Roses, Inc., one of the largest miniature rose nurseries in the U.S., makes miniature roses available at prices significantly below those of other dealers. The pricing is simple: all minis are $5.25; all miniature tree roses are $21.95; and collections are priced as marked (starting at five plants for $19.95). In addition, quantity discounts apply, so the more you order, the less you spend per flower. Great service is a hallmark of Nor'East, whether you're buying through the catalog or off the website.

The approximately 30-page color catalog details the specifics of many kinds of miniature bush roses (micro-minis, climbers, and tree roses). To help you plan a suitable garden for your climate and landscape, the catalog describes plant height at maturity, blooming pattern and coloring (roses come in solid colors and blends), best conditions for growth, and scent. The well-designed website has gorgeous color images of all rose offerings, with descriptions, cultivating suggestions, online ordering, and more. Nor'East helps novices enjoy the rewards of growing roses by offering easy-to-cultivate choices. If Nor'East selects the roses for you, or if you order in quantity, additional savings will apply. Gifts and vases are also available.

SPECIAL FACTORS: Plants that don't perform are accepted for replacement within 90 days.

Ohio Earth Food

5488 Swamp St., NE
Hartville, OH 44632

330–877–9356
Fax: 330–877–4237

Catalog: free
Pay: check, MO, V, MC, DSC
Sells: natural fertilizers and natural pest controls
Store: same address; Monday, Tuesday, Thursday, Friday
8–5; additional days and hours between March 30 and
June 6

Ohio Earth Food has been serving gardeners and farmers since 1972 with natural fertilizers and pest control products. The 16-page catalog offers dozens of products certifiable for organic crop production by Ohio Standards at the time of this printing. If you have a summer roadside vegetable stand, participate in farmer's markets, have a large garden, or even own a full-scale farm, Ohio Earth Food has great prices when you buy in bulk. (Growers' price breaks include ton lots.) You'll find natural fertilizers such as Re-Vita Compost Plus, Jersey greensand, cottonseed meal, diatomaceous earth (made of ground fossil shell), liquefied seaweed, fish products, rock phosphate, and others; insect and disease controllers such as rotenone and milky spore powder—great for Japanese beetles; herbicides for killing weeds and grass; natural products for livestock; growing supplies such as potting soil, compost makers, soil test kits, and powdermill dust applicators; and a small selection of books about bio-friendly growing. Detailed contents and descriptions accompany each product listing, as well as quantity price breaks. Send in a soil sample and Ohio Earth Food will analyze it for $17 with the base exchange capacity of your soil, organic matter content, levels of nitrogen, potassium, phosphorous, calcium, magnesium, and sulfur, and the amount of lime needed, if any.

Wholesalers: Ask for the grower price list with your catalog.

SPECIAL FACTORS: Shipments over 500 pounds are generally shipped by commercial truck; see catalog for all shipping rates and requirements.

Pinetree Garden Seeds

P.O. Box 300
New Gloucester, ME 04260

207–926–3400
Fax: 888–52–SEEDS

Catalog: free, $1.50 outside U.S.
Pay: check, MO, MC, V, AE, DSC
Sells: seeds, bulbs, plants, garden equipment, and books
Store: mail order only
Online: www.superseeds.com

Remember those beautiful old-fashioned cornucopias, luscious-looking and brimming over with fruits of the harvest? That's what you'll find in this catalog, a cornucopia of over 800 varieties of vegetable and flower seeds, bulbs, plants, tools, and a distinguished selection of gardening books—all at old-fashioned prices! Established in 1979 to serve home gardeners with the best products at the best prices, Pinetree Garden Seeds has grown into a larger company that has kept its original philosophy. They believe their typical customer is a sophisticated gardener who wants to try many of the things he or she has heard or read about, hence their line of "vegetables from around the world." This amazing selection includes traditional vegetables from France (haricots vert, cornichon cucumbers, dandelion greens), the Orient (snow peas, daikon, Thai peppers), Italy (artichokes, eggplant, fennel), Latin America (black beans, cilantro, many chiles), and also includes Native American vegetables such as blue corn, gourds, and squash. Where else could you find this variety at the best prices around, and all backed with their ironclad guarantee? If you're computer-savvy, be sure to check out their full catalog online.

SPECIAL FACTORS: Satisfaction guaranteed; returns accepted for exchange, refund, or credit.

Want to spend less time mowing the lawn? Would you like a visually interesting, easy-care carpet to cover "difficult" areas around your home? Or are you just looking for wide sweeping beds of color, lush borders, and sunny expanses of daylilies? Well, look no further than Prentiss Court Ground Covers for all of this at a very reasonable price. In business since 1978, Prentiss Court currently offers over 50 varieties of ground cover, at savings of up to 50% below nursery prices. The types of plants offered range from the shade-loving hosta (four varieties) to the sun-loving daylily (eight varieties), and include jasmine, Japanese honeysuckle, liriope, and traditional and Algerian ivy, as well as ornamental grasses, Virginia creeper, bronze-improved ajuga, dianthus, and cotoneaster, among others. Cost ranges from 39 cents for bare-root ornamental grasses to $2.74 for the dramatic "Sammy Russell Red" daylily. Plants are "pampered" by the skilled horticulturists at Prentiss Court, packed carefully, and shipped quickly. Plants are available in pots or bare root.

SPECIAL FACTORS: Minimum order varies with bare-root or potted orders.

Rohrer's Seeds

P.O. Box 250
Smoketown, PA 17576

717-299-2571
Fax: 800-468-4944

Catalog: free
Pay: check, MO, MC, V, DSC
Sells: flower and vegetable seeds, gardening supplies,
    lawn seed, forage, crop seed, etc.
Store: 2472 Old Philadelphia Pike, Smoketown, PA; call or
    see the catalog for directions and hours
E-mail: pl_rohrer@compuserve.com

For flowers and vegetables with an historic twist, simply flip through the pages of Rohrer's seed catalog. Our great-grandmothers grew many of the heirloom seeds listed here, and probably paid a similarly low price. For larger agricultural interests, Rohrer's supplies pasture mixtures, grasses and crop seed, and both organic/natural and conventional herbicides and fungicides. Most of the catalog, however, is devoted to the home gardener, and highlights the local, organically grown historical heirloom variety seeds of the Landis Valley Museum, grown by Pennsylvania settlers from at least the mid 18th century. These include the sweet Amish Moon and Stars watermelon, extra-white German Gilfeather turnips, and green Jenny Lind cantaloupes. Rohrer's guarantees that every seed, old-fashioned or modern, must satisfy you, or you will get your money back.

SPECIAL FACTORS: Orders of 15 or more seed packets are shipped free; returns accepted for exchange, refund, or credit.

Turner Greenhouses

P.O. Box 1260, Dept. 131
Goldsboro, NC 27533–1260

800–672–4770

Catalog: free
Pay: check, MO, MC, V, DSC
Sells: greenhouses and accessories
Store: mail order only
Online: www.turnergreenhouses.com

As an avid gardener, I once thought greenhouses were only found at wealthy estates or commercial growing operations. But after receiving Turner's catalog, I now believe that with prices over 35% less than their competitors, the day is not far off when I will be the proud owner of a Turner greenhouse—"the affordable greenhouse that grows with you!" The three expandable types of greenhouses Turner sells are backed by three generations of expertise in the manufacture, care, and setup of greenhouses. They believe that your purchase is too important not to make a thorough investigation, so they encourage potential customers to look at their competitors' catalogs and compare price and service. Turner provides a list of Turner greenhouse owners in your area for you to talk to, and each greenhouse kit comes with a free video that walks you through the simple assembly process. And best of all, they don't forget you after the sale. They promise a lifelong relationship of service, and will take time to answer any questions you may have as long as you own your greenhouse. The catalog includes useful greenhouse accessories such as circulators, benches, misters, thermometers, and cooling units, as well as handy items like propagation mats and the gardener's phone pack, which allows you to take your phone wherever you go! Make sure to check out the website for more information about Turner greenhouses, including photographs. At this time there's no online ordering.

SPECIAL FACTORS: Satisfaction is guaranteed; authorized returns in original condition are accepted within 30 days for refund or credit.

Twilley Seeds

121 Gary Rd.
Hodges, SC 29653

800–622–7333
Fax: 864–227–5108

Catalog: free
Pay: check, MO, MC, V
Sells: seeds and small-grower supplies
Store: mail order only

If you're a truck farmer, u-pick, or bedding plant grower, Twilley is the place to buy your seeds in bulk. Claiming they sell "the best seeds your money can buy," Twilley puts their money where it counts—back in your pocket. Prices for small quantities are comparable to most seed catalogs, but if you buy in quantity—from 1 to 500 pounds of seed, the price quickly drops from 40% to 50% off the original. Twilley's carries everyone's favorite garden vegetable seeds, and both annual and perennial flower seeds. Symbols in the catalog will alert the discerning grower to All-America Selections winners, Twilley's own "Professional Seed Series" and seeds that are particularly well suited to roadside stands or u-pick operations.

Organic growers, please note: Twilley is unable to supply untreated seeds.

SPECIAL FACTORS: Discounts for bulk orders over $100; minimum $25 on credit card or C.O.D. orders.

Van Bourgondien Bros.

P.O. Box 1000
Babylon, NY 11702

800–622–9959
Fax: 516–669–1228

Catalog: free
Pay: check, MO, MC, V, AE, DSC
Sells: flower bulbs and perennials
Store: mail order only
Online: www.dutchbulbs.com

This catalog takes me back to my grandmother's flower garden filled with poppies, forget-me-nots, and bachelor's buttons. I could almost hear bees buzzing over the blooms as I flipped through its pages! The prices in this catalog would have made my frugal grandmother very happy—Van Bourgondien, in business since 1919, sells Dutch bulbs and perennials at discounts of 40% less than usual prices. The variety here is exciting. The typical bulbs—iris, hyacinth, tulip, amaryllis, narcissus, daffodil, muscari, crocus, peony, and allium—are represented, along with a lovely selection of perennials, which include Greek windflowers, jonquil, bluebells, poppies, phlox, asters, astilbe, lavender, lupins, and much more. Be sure to take a peek at their online catalog for early bird bonus specials, as well as many articles, tips, and gardening tricks from the Bulb Lady herself—Debbie Van Bourgondien!

SPECIAL FACTORS: Goods are guaranteed to be as described, and to be delivered in perfect condition; quantity discounts available.

Van Dyck's

P.O. Box 430
Brightwaters, NY 11718-0430

800-248-2852
Fax: 800-639-2452

Catalog: free
Pay: check, MO, MC, V, AE, DSC
Sells: flower bulbs and perennials
Store: mail order only
Online: www.vandycks.com

If you're looking for a company that's serious about flowers, Van Dyck's is the place to start. The Van Dyck family has sold bulbs in Holland for generations, and has been doing business in the U.S. since 1990. The family tradition continues today with discounts of at least 40%, excellent service, and their "no quibble" guarantee of satisfaction. Their catalog blooms with pages and pages of full-color photographs of tulip, crocus, iris, hyacinth, lily, narcissus, allium, daffodil, muscari, amaryllis, hosta, and peony flowers. As with most companies, the more you buy, the more you save—so Van Dyck's recommends combining orders with friends and family or with a garden co-op to get the lowest prices possible. You can order a print catalog on the website, but there's no online ordering of inventory.

SPECIAL FACTORS: Bulb bonuses available with quantity orders, quantity discounts available; satisfaction guaranteed.

Van Engelen, Inc.

23 Tulip Dr., Dept. WBM
Bantam, CT 06750

860–567–8734
Fax: 860–567–5323

Catalog: free
Pay: check, MO, MC, V
Sells: Dutch flower bulbs
Store: mail order only
Online: www.vanengelen.com

Over 650 varieties of exhibition-quality Dutch flower bulbs grace this catalog, which is the only wholesale collection of Dutch bulbs in the U.S. Since this is a wholesale catalog, the bulbs are sold in multiples of 50, but if you're looking for a large number of bulbs at a very low price, this is the catalog for you (you can always go in on an order with friends). The types of flower bulbs sold include varieties of tulip, narcissus, crocus, daffodil, anemone, allium, freesia, iris, fritillaria, hyacinth, amaryllis, and lily. The height of the plants and colors of the flowers are described in detail, so you can get the type of plant that would complement your garden perfectly. Van Engelen also offers special collections of bulbs in selected combinations priced below their listed wholesale prices, so you can experiment with smaller quantities of bulbs than are offered elsewhere in the catalog. You can order a print catalog—but no merchandise—directly from the website.

SPECIAL FACTORS: Satisfaction is guaranteed; quantity discounts are available; minimum order is $50.

Related Products/Companies

Antique tractor appraisal
- Central Michigan Tractor & Parts

Bamboo and other natural fencing panels and supplies
- Frank's Cane and Rush

Birdhouses and birdfeeders
- Tender Heart Treasures

Chain saws and logging equipment
- Bailey's

Farm and garden equipment
- Northern Hydraulics

Fertilizers and insect control
- Deer Valley Farm

Gardening books and manuals
- Reader's Digest, Storey Books

Gourd craft books and supplies
- The Caning Shop

Granite pet memorial stones
- That Fish/Pet Place

Grower-direct fresh-cut flowers
- Evergreen Farms, Hand-Tied Flowers

Hand-powered wagons, lawn mowers, cultivators, seeders, and other gardening implements
- Lehman's

Havahart traps
- Lehman's

Lawn and patio furniture and decor
- Bennett Brothers, Ellenburg's Furniture, Fran's Wicker & Rattan, Loftin-Black Furniture, RV Direct

Lawn repair sprays
- Drs. Foster & Smith, Jeffers

Logging and forestry books and equipment
- Bailey's

Multipocketed aprons for gardening and yard work
- Clothcrafters

Patio furniture covers and canopies
- RV Direct

Planters
- Tender Heart Treasures

Porous plastic sheeting for frost protection
- Clothcrafters

Posthole diggers
- Harbor Freight Tools

Snow throwers
- Beach Sales

Swimming pool equipment and supplies
- Water Warehouse

Thermopane panels for greenhouses and cold frames
- Arctic Glass and Window Outlet

Tires for mowers and wheelbarrows
- Manufacturer's Supply

Tractors and farm equipment
- Central Michigan Tractor & Parts

Woodpile covers and firewood carriers
- Clothcrafters

General Merchandise and Good Deals

Surplus goods; online auctions and garage sales; great values on a wide range of products

Most of the companies listed in this chapter offer such a wide range of products it might be confusing to put them elsewhere: Everything from electric mattress warmers to cleaning supplies to snowblowers turns up. These are some of my favorite catalogs to browse, the print equivalents of a big Sunday-morning six-family yard sale. Go through the listings carefully since there are some real finds here. You're bound to get lots of gift ideas for Christmas, birthdays, and other occasions.

You'll find some interesting Internet sites here as well—Ebay, an online real-time auction where you can bid for great steals and deals on everything under the sun; Make Us An Offer, which lets you "haggle" electronically for prices on a variety of products; and Andy's Garage Sale, which is exactly as it sounds, only virtual.

For online malls that "house" many different discount stores and offer significant discounts on a multitude of products, see the section following this one, "Internet Malls," page 253.

There are a number of other fantastic general-merchandise companies that for various reasons fall in other chapters of this book, so be sure to check out this section's "Related Products/Companies" listings.

Find It Fast

Arts and Crafts
- Make Us An Offer

Cleaning Supplies
- EDGE Distributing

Cloth Goods
- Clothcrafters

Educational Gifts
- American Science & Surplus, Cook Brothers

Food
- EDGE Distributing, Make Us An Offer

Jewelry
- Bennett Brothers, Ebay, Make Us An Offer

Nonelectric Tools and Household Aids
- Lehman's

Online Auction and Haggling Sites
- Ebay, Make Us An Offer

Overstocks and Closeouts
- Andy's Garage Sale, American Science & Surplus

Paper Goods
- Current

Personal Care Items
- Cook Brothers, Damark, EDGE Distributing, Make Us An Offer

Tools, Electronics, and Gadgets
- American Science & Surplus, Bennett Brothers, Cook Brothers, Damark, Make Us An Offer

---

American Science & Surplus

3605 Howard St., Dept. WBM   847–982–0870
Skokie, IL 60076   Fax: 800–934–0722

Catalog: free
Pay: check, MO, MC, V, DSC
Sells: industrial, educational, and scientific surplus goods
Store: Milwaukee Ave. at Foster, Chicago, IL; Rte. 38, East
  of Kirk Rd., Geneva, IL; 15138 S. LaGrange Rd., Orland
  Park, IL; and 6901 W. Oklahoma Ave., Milwaukee, WI
Online: www.sciplus.com

"Incredible stuff, unbelievable prices," is their motto, and the 64-page black and white catalog from American Science and Surplus doesn't disappoint. This collection of kits, tools, toys, teaching aids, arts and crafts, models, gadget parts, and miscellaneous useful products is a bargain hunter's dream come true, with savings reaching over 75% on some items. Junior inventors, teachers, students, and tag-sale aficionados will find lots to love about this catalog.

Established around 1937, American Science and Surplus issues a catalog every two months. Because quantities are finite, the inventory is always changing, and therefore defies description somewhat. However, past catalogs have included such items as science projects both wacky (Rubber Flubber and Goofy Gel) and serious (ecology kits to test pond water, make-your-own geodes), magnets, toys, tools, batteries, electronic parts, computer educational software, arts and crafts kits and supplies, microscopes and telescopes, film mailers, talking door mats, fanny packs, hospital robes, seasonal decorations, and on and on. Line drawings and amusing descriptive text make this indescribable spectrum of surplus goodies the catalog equivalent of strolling through an exceptional flea market. The website has the full inventory and features online ordering.

SPECIAL FACTORS: Minimum order is $10; phone hours are Monday to Friday, 8–5:30 CT; returns accepted within 30 days; quantity discounts apply.

Andy's Garage Sale, Inc.

25 Mcleland Rd.　　　　800–711–ANDY
St. Cloud, MN 56395–2007　　Fax: 320–654–7565

Information: website only, no print catalog
Pay: check, MO, MC, V, DSC
Sells: manufacturer's overstock, closeouts, etc.
Store: online only; customer service phone hours Monday
　to Friday 8–8 CT
Online: www.andysgarage.com

When is online shopping as much fun as rummaging through a yard sale? When you visit Andy's Garage Sale, a bounty of ever-changing products at discounts of up to 70% off original prices. The red-letter signs arouse all the excitement a bargain-seeker craves—"Hot Buys," "Top 20," "Big Deal of the Day"—and spotlight items you may secretly be hungering for: a Lava lamp for $34 from the Lava Lamp-0-Lator Assortment, and a Weider Zone Tone Exerciser, at $20. Andy's site offers so many products—from toiletries to kitchenware—that curiosity keeps you hunting through the thousands of items with real gusto. You can even enjoy a laugh by clicking on Jokes, get answers to your shopper's questions at Questions or from Andy, via e-mail, or sneak into the "Attic" for last-minute buys.

The website makes a paper catalog obsolete, yet ordering is just as easy thanks to the options explained online. You can order online or by fax, by mail, and toll-free by phone. If you have a printer and prefer not to send credit information over the computer, you can print out a form Andy provides onscreen and mail in your order the traditional way. Bargains, variety, and easy shopping are what Andy's Garage Sale is all about.

SPECIAL FACTORS: Satisfaction guaranteed; authorized returns accepted within 30 days for exchange, refund, or credit.

Bennett Brothers, Inc.

30 East Adams St.　　　　800–621–2626
Chicago, IL 60603–5676　　Fax: 312–621–1669

Catalog: free
Pay: check, MO, MC, V, AE, DSC
Sells: jewelry, appliances, electronics, luggage, furnishings, etc.
Store: same address; Monday to Friday 8:15–5 (see catalog for holiday shopping hours); also 211 Island Rd., Mahwah, NJ; Monday to Saturday 9–5:30
Online: www.bennettbros.com

Once a year Bennett Brothers, in business since 1906, issues their "Blue Book," a 148-page glossy color catalog filled with brand-name products including jewelry, watches, silver, housewares, appliances, electronics, cameras, luggage, toys, sporting goods, and more—all at prices well below retail, up to 45% below on some items. The three Bennetts (father and two sons) smile out at you on the inside page, and promise that their honest and equitable business practices will make you a loyal customer.

What's this catalog all about? Gifts, gifts, and more gifts—from luxury items such as diamond and gold jewelry for people with discretionary income to sterling silver flatware and Black Forest cuckoo clocks. And then there are more modest and practical items, such as gourmet gadgets, cordless telephones, and even toys. Everything here is name brand and high quality, and the suggested retail price (provided in most cases by the manufacturer) is listed alongside Bennett's so you can see the savings. Corporate buyers should contact Bennett Brothers for details on the firm's "Choose-Your-Gift" booklets for employee award and incentive programs at price levels from $16 to $1,000.

SPECIAL FACTORS: Authorized returns are accepted within ten days for exchange or credit.

Clothcrafters, Inc.

P.O. Box 176, Dept. WBM
Elkhart Lake, WI 53020

800–876–2009
Tel/Fax: 920–876–2112

Catalog: free
Pay: check, MO, MC, V
Sells: home textiles
Store: mail order only, Monday to Friday 7:30–4 CT
Online: www.clothcrafters.com

Since 1936 Clothcrafters has been sewing "useful, durable, reuseable" products for home and professional use and selling them to consumers at factory-direct and wholesale prices. Here's some of what you'll find in the catalog and website: denim dog-bed covers, storage bags and dust covers, cloth garment bags, laundry bags, terry-cloth towels, chef's white or denim aprons, tote bags, children's bibs, place mats, pot holders, cotton coffee filters, cotton dish towels, canvas wood carriers, flannel sleeping-bag liners, and more. Get the idea? This company is like having a handy aunt who hand-sews useful cotton items for your home. This is a lovely find for those who like high-quality, no-frills decor—such a 100% white cotton shower curtain—and products that can be washed and reused rather than thrown away, such as supermarket produce bags. While the website can give you a good idea of what Clothcrafters is all about, it only features a small sampling of what's in the print catalog. Wholesale prices kick in when you order the minimum amount of a single item, which varies for each item; for example, a minimum of three shower curtains gets you an additional 17% off; a dozen aprons saves you 28%, and so on.

SPECIAL FACTORS: Satisfaction guaranteed; quantity discounts available.

Have you ever seen a fur-wrapped lady walking the narrow cluttered aisles in one of those bargain-blowout stores in the mall? We all have a secret—or maybe not-so-secret—fascination for these stores, which seem to carry a little bit of everything, and sometimes a lot of junk as well. Cook Brothers is a catalog you'll find yourself captivated by since there are unbelievable deals to be found if you look hard enough. There are plenty of items you probably don't need: 16-inch porcelain oriental dolls in geisha dresses, lava lamps, classic rooster weather vanes, rhinestone necklaces and matching earrings, and decorative wire bird cages; many items you didn't realize you needed until you saw them: beaded curtains, a soda-can caddy for your refrigerator, a gold-plated manicure set, and a cordless nose-hair trimmer; and a number of things you can't live without, now that you think of it: a digital scale, a braided black leather whip, a new travel bag on wheels, and a set of Blue Willow doll dishes for your daughter. Believe me, you'll find something to buy at Cook Brothers, and you'll save a lot of money when you do—as much as 60% off suggested retail. Become a member ($19.95) and save an additional 10% on every purchase for the next year. This is a good source for inexpensive educational toys and games, knives, kitchen and cooking items, costume jewelry, perfume, luggage, and all kinds of household gadgets. The website has contact information only; no online catalog or ordering.

SPECIAL ORDERS: Notify customer service within 15 days of invoice for returns authorization; C.O.D. orders not accepted.

Current

1005 E. Woodman Rd.,   800–525–7170

Keycode DM24   Fax: 719–593–5900

Colorado Springs, CO 80920   TDD: 800–855–2880

Catalog: free

Pay: check, MO, MC, V, AE, DSC

Sells: stationery, gifts, wrapping paper, cards, etc.

Store: outlets in CA, CO, and OR

Online: www.currentcatalog.com

Looking through the Current catalog and website, I was struck by the interesting and somewhat out-of-the-ordinary items carried here in addition to the company's great-priced stationery, cards, and other paper goods, for which it is generally known. I decided to put Current in this "general merchandise" chapter because there's a lot more here worth checking out.

Don't get me wrong: This is still a good source for gift-wrap items (paper of every conceivable pattern and theme, ribbons and bows, gift boxes and bags), invitations, note cards, greeting cards, stationery, and calendars. Current has a three-tier price-break: one to four, five to seven, eight and up. If you can order eight items (for example, an assortment of cards and gift wraps can be mixed to add up to eight items) you'll save around 50%. Orders of $30 and up automatically qualify you for the lowest-listed price. Here's a sampling of what else you'll find at Current: the lowest-priced mail-order checks I've seen; postage meters; household items such as shower organizers, refrigerator magnets, vinyl shower curtain–hole reinforcers, leather tear menders, tiny vases, produce bin liners, garage-sale stickers, and wooden furniture repair crayons; and gifts for children and others such as scrapbook kits, hinged wooden shadowboxes to create your own hanging memento display case, holiday ornaments, candle holders, magnetic picture frames, and more. The website features online ordering and the full inventory.

SPECIAL FACTORS: Satisfaction guaranteed; quantity discounts apply.

Damark International, Inc.

7101 Winnetka Ave. N.　　　　**800–827–6767**
P.O. Box 9437　　　　　　　　**Fax: 612–531–0281**
Minneapolis, MN 55440–9437

Catalog: free
Pay: check, MO, V, MC, AE, DSC
Sells: computers, home/office furniture, home
　　improvement items, sports/fitness equipment, etc.
Store: mail order only
Online: www.damark.com

Damark, via the print and online catalogs, is a good source for great deals. In business since 1986, Damark International, Inc., has built a loyal mail-order customer base through its catalog and Preferred Buyers Club, which provides discounts on travel, food and lodging, entertainment, and merchandise purchased through the catalogs or online. If you're a basic club member, which costs $59.99 a year at this writing, you get 10% off all purchases, discount coupons galore, and special deals through the membership-only catalogs. (See catalog or website for more information on other Damark clubs and membership benefits.)

Happily, you don't have to be a member to order through Damark. What's fun about Damark is the eclectic selection—something like a modern-day general store with a high-tech slant. The website and catalog—for all shoppers, not just members—offer discounts up to 60% on such items as snowthrowers, radar detectors, office shredders, stainless steel flatware, electric blankets, portable PCs, telephones, VCRs, industrial garment racks, folding creeper/shop seat (for automotive repair), fog machines, inflatable mattresses, acupressure clips to suppress your appetite, vacuum cleaners, Wonder Forms figure-enhancer bras, televisions, calculators, two-room tents, Lionel train sets, parking meter banks, cappuccino makers, office furniture, magnifying lamps, Cuisinart 13-piece heavy-duty cookware, and more. Some of the best deals on electronics here are the factory refurbished items—not brand new, but they still come with warranties. Damark's website has received good marks from BizRate (see listing in next section), which means that Damark shoppers think highly of the company's products, prices, and service.

SPECIAL FACTORS: "Easy Pay Plan" allows customer to pay over the course of four or six months (minimum purchase for "Easy Pay" is $99.99 as of this writing;

see catalog for details); satisfaction guaranteed; 30-day return policy (see packing slip for complete details).

Ebay

Information: website only, no print catalog
Pay: seller's discretion (see text)
Sells: collectibles, gadgets, jewelry, shoes and clothing, electronics, etc.
Store: online only, 24 hours/day
Online: www.ebay.com

This is the largest person-to-person trading area on the Internet and functions as an online auction where you bid for goods and the highest bidder wins—sometimes at significant savings. It is also the longest running and the most innovative, with over 300 categories divided into easy-to-use subcategories, from antiques, collectibles, and computers, to magazines, jewelry, toys, and dolls. A perusal at the time of this writing had the site featuring close to 2 million items for sale in over a thousand categories!

Ebay recommends that you make phone or e-mail contact with the seller before you begin bidding. People interested in buying from a vendor can look up the vendor's selling history, a collection of actual buyers' reviews of this vendor. If the vendor turns out to be reliable, get started! Friends who have used this site love it. It's best if you have a general idea of how much an item costs before you catch the bidding bug. For example, a pair of women's suede boots starting at $1 looks promising, but not if the winning bid eventually exceeds the boots' suggested retail price!

Ebay's site map is a table of contents that links you to pages that will explain the whole bidding or selling process, will give you tips on how to have the best experience, will offer hints on how to find what you're looking for, etc. Bidding time spans and starting bids vary for each item. Most items are pictured, which is helpful if not necessary. Credit card payment, shipping requirements and procedures, and warranties and guarantees will vary from seller to seller.

SPECIAL FACTORS: Valid e-mail address is required.

EDGE Distributing, Inc.

760 Busse Hwy.

P.O. Box 307

Park Ridge, IL 60068

800–373–3726

847–696–1623

Fax: 847–696–9284

Price List: free

Pay: check, MO, MC, V

Sells: pantry items—spices, prepared foods, cleaning and personal care products

Store: mail order only

Occasionally I telephone my mother in the Midwest and ask her to mail me a seemingly normal product—a common ink remover or my favorite condiment for fresh turkey sandwiches. Why? Because the supermarket in my small town in Woodstock, New York, doesn't carry them. And have you ever discovered that a product such as your favorite-brand floor wax just disappears? That's because of competition for supermarket shelf space, and the story behind *that* would take up its own chapter, complete with multinational companies that muscle out the mom-and-pop brands. Well here's help: EDGE Distributing carries many common brands—Mop & Glo, Old English, Snowy, Woolite, Wizard, Zout, Easy Wash, Lysol, Chore Boy, Easy-Off, Spice Island, Durkee, Dec-a-Cake, French's, Rid-X, Cool Blues, Binaca, D-Con, and Gulfwax, among others—at prices that average 15% below list. The catch is that you have to buy at least a case. However, if you can't live without your brand, you'll end up using a case of it eventually anyway. The product lists include the product name, size, number per case, and case weight, but you must call for current prices and shipping costs.

SPECIAL FACTORS: Minimum order one case.

Lehman's Non-Electric Catalog

One Lehman Circle, Dept.
BWBM
Kidron, OH 44636

330–857–5757
Fax: 888–780–4975

Catalog: $4 to U.S.; $5 to Canada
Pay: check, MO, V, MC, DSC
Sells: nonelectric appliances and products for self-sufficient living
Store: same address; Monday to Saturday 8–5:30, Thursday 8–8
Online: www.lehmans.com

Want to get "off the grid"? Worried about Y2K? Or are you like me: someone who just loves old-fashioned, high-quality products and ingenious gadgets that hark back to simpler days? You're going to *love* Lehman's, which began in 1955 as a hardware and appliance store catering to the Amish population in Ohio. With the year-2000 bug creeping up, Lehman's received a barrage of calls and publicity from those interested in products that don't depend on electricity. Lehman's has the country's largest display of wood cookstoves and a huge selection of nonelectric appliances including gas refrigerators and wringer washers, as well as people-powered products. You'll find cooking aids (butter churns, nonelectric yogurt incubators, grain mills for making flour, giant cast-iron kettles on legs, nonelectric toasters); household items (doorbells, oil lamps, wind-up flashlights, composting toilets, water pumps, solar power systems), children's toys and games, farm and garden tools and equipment, snowshoes, a terrific assortment of books, and more. I don't think there's anyone over the age of 40 who won't look through Lehman's Non-Electric Catalog and exclaim, "Wow! I haven't see one of those in years." Lehman's itself is very much "on the grid," as witnessed by their fantastic website, which features online ordering. This company is included here not so much for their discount prices (although products that are people-powered do save money on electricity) but for the range of hard-to-find products they carry.

SPECIAL FACTORS: Free shipping on most orders within the U.S.; satisfaction guaranteed; authorized returns accepted within 30 days; order by phone 24 hours, seven days/week.

Make Us An Offer

Catalog: website only, no print catalog
Pay: check, MO, V, MC
Sells: name-brand collectibles, decor, electronics, fashion
  and beauty products, housewares, etc.
Store: website only
Online: www.makeusanoffer.com

Have you ever left a store without the item you were interested in because the price was too high? You left disappointed, and the store didn't win either since it didn't get your business. Make Us An Offer was launched on the idea that if you get to haggle a bit about the price, then both you and the merchant leave happy: You get a lower price for your merchandise, the merchant makes the sale.

At Make Us An Offer, you choose the items you're interested in and then begin a discussion with Chester, a friendly, portly, suspender-wearing cartoon salesman, about the price. You propose a price to Chester and Chester tries to find a price that you both can agree on. Chester (a friendly face for a computer program) makes his decision on how low he'll go based on a complex calculation of supply and demand, cost of labor, and inventory. But Chester has been known to give generous discounts to attract a first-time customer or to reward a loyal customer.

There are many types of merchandise available at this site. The At Home section includes appliances, arts and crafts (collectibles, music boxes, sculptures, vases, etc.), and bedroom and kitchen items. There's also an At Work category with electronics, gadgets, home audio and video, and office equipment; Having Fun (books and music, toys and games, gourmet food, sporting goods, etc.); Looking Good (clothing, jewelry, personal care, and watches); and On the Road (auto, binoculars, cameras, and luggage). These products are all brand name, so you can be assured of their quality. Now all you need to do is decide what you're looking for and make Chester an offer!

SPECIAL FACTORS: Merchandise in its original condition may be returned within 15 days of receipt, minus a 20% restocking fee.

Related Products/Companies

Appliances, electronics, tools, and gadgets
  • All Electronics, Coastal Tool, Harbor Freight Tools, Percy's, Poor Man's
    Catalog

Bags and containers for everything imaginable
- Associated Bag

Earth-friendly cleaners and personal care products
- Cal Ben

General department-store goods
- Gohn Bros., The Ultimate Outlet

Surplus clothing, electronics, camping equipment, etc.
- Mass. Army & Navy, The Sportsman's Guide

Internet Malls

Highly rated virtual malls for online shopping of every kind

If you're like I am, the idea of online shopping is appealing, but the reality may be altogether different. There are too many people out there in cyberspace selling too many products. Some online stores have great sites with an "About Us" page, a customer-service phone number where you can actually speak with a human being, and searchable inventory with a shopping and purchasing system that's easy to use and to understand. Other stores I've browsed are slow, confusing, and oblique. (One I visited recently didn't have a company address, phone, fax, or even an e-mail; my only option would have been to submit my credit card information and purchase!)

The Internet "malls," for lack of a better word, that I've selected to list here are some of the best, and the shops they "rent space to" or manufacturers they represent are likewise reputable. Each "mall" takes a slightly different approach, which you'll discover when you read the descriptions, but most have two things in common: consumer-friendly formats and reviews of the online stores they house. In other words, if you're looking for furniture, you can go to one of these malls and find "their" stores that sell furniture. You'll be able to read a little blurb about each store to decide whether it has the kinds of prices and inventory you're looking for, rather than wasting time visiting each one.

Now that I've "bookmarked" the sites in this section, I find Internet shopping to be really fun and convenient. I've also discovered it's a wonderful way to save time and money.

Find It Fast

General Merchandise
- Esmarts, Mall 21, Netmarket

Membership Benefits
- Mall 21, Netmarket

Reviews of Web Merchants
- BizRate, Esmarts, Internet Shopper

BizRate

Features: consumer and staff reviews/ratings of web shopping sites, with links to same

Online: www.bizrate.com

It's nice to know that someone is looking out for the consumer in the big, anarchical world of web shopping. Luckily, BizRate's practices also help the Internet shops themselves, so it's a win-win situation for everyone. If shopping on the Internet is intimidating to you, it just got less so. BizRate is dedicated to helping shoppers find quality online merchants by providing a site where you can view the results of consumer and BizRate staff reviews and ratings. This is a free service to both consumers and the businesses that get listed here. (To find out why Bizrate does it for free, see their FAQ page.)

Here you'll find the top 25 companies—those that scored highest in overall customer satisfaction—updated weekly. You can also search by category (apparel, computers, food and drink, hobbies and collectibles, to name a few) and see how different Internet vendors fared in the ratings. What's good about this site is that it's not just an Internet mall, but a living, changing compendium of companies with descriptions of their products and services, as well as links to their home pages.

BizRate makes it simple to find companies offering significant discounts, since you can search by "price" within categories, which then sorts the companies in that category in descending order (highest-scoring companies are those that consumers were most satisfied with vis-à-vis their pricing). There's lots more here, including a nice reference section about consumer rights and company responsibilities. This is a site with which all Internet shoppers should become familiar.

Esmarts

Features: proprietary reviews and rankings of Internet shopping sites, shopping links, newsletter, message board, etc.
Online: www.esmarts.com

There's something about Esmarts that's friendlier than most web malls. For one thing, Esmarts doesn't even call itself a mall, but rather "a *community* of bargain shoppers." You get a good feeling when you log onto the aptly named Esmarts. Click on a category (flowers, groceries, music, travel, etc.) and you don't just get a list of vendors with links. Instead you get thoughtful and well-researched short essays about Internet merchants in that category, along with Esmarts' rankings according to price, service, etc. It's really a consumer guide that's designed to help the wary e-shopper find reputable vendors selling at a bargain. And you'll feel a sense of community with the other clever web-surfers who've found this site because there's a message board that Esmarts encourages everyone to use. Here you can find out about good and bad experiences shoppers have had with different vendors. I liked the downloadable coupons for merchants in my area, the reward programs that allow me to collect points on my purchases, and the Esmarts newsletter, which keeps me abreast of shopping news, discounts, and specials. Go to Esmarts and you'll see that web shopping can be fun, enlightening, inexpensive, and—yes—even friendly. I really like this site and recommend it to anyone looking for intelligent life along the information superhighway.

Internet Shopper

Features: online reviews and articles about Internet sites offering goods and services, and links to these sites
Online: www.internetshopper.com

Internet Shopper has changed a bit. It began as a print magazine with a sister website. Since then Internet Shopper has dropped the print magazine and is now, at least at this writing, only a website.

The Internet is vast and overwhelming, especially for beginners. So how do you find the great shopping sites? How can you distinguish the good from the dreck? Internet Shopper's stated goal is to serve "consumers who want to get the most out of their Internet investment—who want to use the Internet to make better purchasing decisions, get better information, and be smarter consumers."

Internet Shopper's staff of writers continually searches the web for the most interesting sites and then writes excellent, comprehensive articles and reviews for the rest of us. For example, one might read where and how to buy a PC on the net; perfect gifts for movie buffs; shopping for wine; best ornaments and trinkets; advice for parents looking to buy educational games for their children; travel bargains; fitness equipment online; and much more. In fact, every day there's a new article, and these are archived so that you can spend endless hours reading about Internet shopping tricks and traps. It's just a great way to weed through the chaos, and it's free. Let's hope this excellent website won't meet the same fate as the print version.

Mall 21

Features: listings of stores selling merchandise of every
   kind, and links
Online: www.mall21.com

So you need to go to the mall, but you only have an hour before you have to pick up the kids? Don't despair. Now you can go malling on the web. Mall 21 is a megasite that houses hundreds of mail-order companies selling brand-name merchandise at wholesale prices and deep discounts. There are similar mega–shopping sites on the web, but I like this one because it's comprehensive and user-friendly. The categories include holiday specials, audio/video, camera, Christian, computer, electronics, fashion, garden, health, home, jewelry and watches, personal care, sporting goods, and travel service. Although you don't have to register to shop here, you're eligible for special member discounts and other benefits if you do.

When you click on a category (or search by store name), you'll be taken to a page with company listings and small descriptions of each. The brief blurbs give you enough information about what each store offers to decide if you should enter or not. I like this feature. There's nothing worse than sitting in front of your computer screen waiting for the pictures and text to come in only to find that you didn't want to be there in the first place. All of the stores housed at Mall 21 offer great prices. Discounts of 50% to 60% off normal retail prices aren't uncommon here. If you need assistance of any kind, there's a real human being on the other end of Mall 21's toll-free number (displayed at the website) who can answer questions about payment, shipping, policies, etc.

Netmarket

Features: general merchandise, auto brokering, travel packages, online auctions, member services, etc.
Online: www.netmarket.com

This is a mammoth web shopping mall that proudly offers "name-brand merchandise at wholesale prices!" Netmarket's parent company has been a pioneer in online shopping since the early 1980s. With more than 60 million customers, Netmarket connects directly to manufacturers and passes the savings on to you—no warehouse, no middleman. From *Business Week* to *Motor Trend* to television's *20/20,* this site gets high marks if you're shopping for a car (at AutoVantage, www.autovantage.com) and want to shave a couple thousand or more off the usual dealer's price.

There are dozens of shopping categories to go to, from Apparel and Babies to Sports and Video Games. Besides great customer support and excellent products and prices, NetMarket also has some fun options, some for members only, others for anyone. For instance, there's an online auction, a flea market, a "haggle" zone, and downloadable coupons. If you're a Netmarket member, you can also take advantage of the Personal Shopper or Gift Finder. Details about membership are on the site, but some basic benefits include additional savings of 10% to 50% off, cash back on qualified purchases, 135% low-price guarantee, and free extended warranties for active members.

Related Products/Companies

Online auction and haggling for general merchandise
- Ebay, Make Us An Offer

Health, Beauty, and Fitness

Eye Care and Eyewear

Contact lenses and supplies, eyeglasses, and sunglasses

If you're a contact lens wearer, you know how much you spend every year on lenses, eye checkups, cleaning and soaking solution, contact lens insurance, etc. You'll still need to see your doctor once a year, but you can save a great deal of money—up to 75%—by using the companies in this section for replacement lenses and contact lens supplies. You'll also find firms here that specialize in eyeglasses and sunglasses at a discount. If you don't think buying attractive, well-fitting eyeglass frames by mail is possible, think again. Some of the companies below have made mail order their sole venue for many years, and that means customers who've been satisfied with both the end result and the price they paid for the services.

Find It Fast

Contact Lenses
- Contact Lens Replacement Center, Lens Express, National Contact Lens Center, Prism Optical

Lens-Care Products
- Lens Express

Prescription Eyeglasses
- Hidalgo, Prism Optical

Sunglasses
- Contact Lens Replacement Center, Hidalgo, Lens Express, Prism Optical, Shades.com

Contact Lens Replacement Center

P.O. Box 1489, Dept. 00　　　**800–779–2654**
Melville, NY 11747　　　　　**516–491–7763**
　　　　　　　　　　　　　　　Fax: 516–643–4009

Price List: free with long SASE
Pay: check, MO, MC, V, AE, DSC
Sells: contact lenses and sunglasses
Store: mail order only
Online: www.clrc.com

That's it: After the last bill I got from my eye doc I'm joining the ranks of savvy consumers who visit their eye-care professionals for medical checkups, but purchase their lenses elsewhere. That bill was a real eye-opener, especially when I saw the prices in Contact Lens Replacement Center's current brochure. I could have spent 50% less had I ordered through the Center.

This company is for experienced lens wearers like me—people who have a current prescription, brand, and style, and wish to save money by ordering the lenses themselves (instead of paying their eye doctors to do it, and suffering the consequent markup). The Center offers gas permeable and hard lenses, soft lenses, disposables, and program replacement lenses from the best known manufacturers. You provide a current prescription, the Center's staff can help you from there. The prices here are so low that it may make sense to discontinue your lens insurance and rely on this service if you lose or damage your lenses. And there are no membership fees. In addition to contact lenses, the Center sells fashion sunglasses by Bollé, Maui Jim, Ray-Ban, Serengeti, REVO, Vuarnet, and Gargoyles. If you find a pair of sunglasses from one of these manufacturers in a store, try them on, note all the pertinent information, such as model number or SKU number, frame color, lens type, temple style, and price. Then call Contact Lens Replacement Center for their price. All sunglasses come with cases and the manufacturer's warranty.

SPECIAL FACTORS: Lowest price guarantee; quantity discounts apply.

Hidalgo

45 La Buena Vista, Dept. WM   512–847–5571
Wimberly, TX 78676   Fax: 512–847–2393

Catalog: free
Pay: check, MO, MC, V, AE, DSC
Sells: prescription eyeglasses, sunglasses, binoculars,
    watches, knives, etc.
Store: Wimberly North Too Shopping Center, Wimberly,
    TX; Monday to Friday 10–6

Although you might need glasses to read Hidalgo's 56-page closely printed black-and-white catalog, you'll be glad you made the effort. Here's an honest company that's been in the mail-order eyewear business since 1967. They've done it by offering their customers, whom they characterize as "sharp, intelligent, careful shoppers," eyeglasses and prescription and nonprescription sunglasses at 40% to 50% less than you'd pay at your ophthalmologist's, and by making excellent customer service a given.

The catalog functions as a manual. Take the section on sunglasses, for example, where you'll find lengthy, descriptive text about how to select the right darkness, frame size, tint, etc. for the appropriate activity (a pilot, for example, has very different needs from a skier, a backpacker, or a skeet shooter). Hidalgo has a wide selection of frames (titanium, nylon, memory metal, plastic, etc.) in many styles and sizes, as well as a full range of lens choices—plastic, glass, single-vision, bifocal, antireflection coatings, tinted, thin, etc. When you're shopping for frames from Hidalgo, be sure to take part in the "Try-On" program, which allows you to try on three frames before you decide, and then qualifies you for a refund in case they don't turn out to be satisfactory once you make your choice. In addition to eyewear, Hidalgo also sells an eclectic assortment of other goods: binoculars, sun visors, desktop airplane models, watches, and eyeglass accessories.

SPECIAL FACTORS: Satisfaction guaranteed.

Lens Express, Inc.

350 S.W. 12th Ave.　　　800–USA–LENS
Deerfield Beach, FL 33442　954–422–8181
　　　　　　　　　　　　Fax: 954–480–6419

Catalog: free
Pay: check, MO, V, MC, AE, DSC, DC, CB
Sells: contact lenses, lens-care products, sunglasses
Store: mail order only
Online: www.lensexpress.com and on AOL: keyword LENS
　EXPRESS

Lens Express sells 80,000 contact lenses a day, which is why they can sell you the same brand-name lenses prescribed by your doctor for much less than you'd pay elsewhere—from about 35% to 45% less—and this includes the "one-hour" discount vision stores at the mall. (Lens Express offers a "lowest price guarantee"; see catalog for details.) You can call the company with your prescription information, order online, or have Lens Express staff call your doctor to get the prescription.

The 24-page color catalog offers contacts by Ciba, Bausch & Lomb, Wesley-Jessen, PBH, CooperVision, and Johnson & Johnson, from exotic tinted lenses to bifocal disposables, and every style and type in between. Lens Express also carries a full line of their own brand saline solutions and cleaners at prices that are nearly half what the famous-name-brand items sell for at your local drugstore. If you become a member of the Lens Express Discount Club—$29 for a three-year membership—you'll receive discounts on eye care through a network of national participating providers; eyeglass frames and lenses at savings up to 50%; additional discounts on eye-care products; automatic lens replacement at regular intervals; and more. (See catalog for details.)

Lens Express has another catalog that features sunglasses. Here you'll find all the best manufacturers—Ray-Ban, REVO, Giorgio Armani, Calvin Klein, and Gargoyles among them—in a range of styles, at prices, like their contact lenses, that are up to 45% off list. Swiss army knives in their various configurations are also available here at good discounts.

SPECIAL FACTORS: Lowest price guarantee; satisfaction guaranteed (see catalog for special conditions on gas permeable and toric lenses); quantity discounts available.

National Contact Lens Center

P.O. Box 1953
Santa Ynez, CA 93460

805–686–9440
800–326–6352
Fax: 805–686–5330

Brochure: free
Pay: check, MO, MC, V, DSC, JCB
Sells: soft and gas-permeable contact lenses
Store: mail order only
E-mail: mtalmadg@interserv.com

I've been wearing hard contact lenses since high school. I won't tell you how long ago that was, but suffice it to say that gas permeables hadn't been invented yet. I'm a lens wearer who doesn't need her hand held when fitted with new lenses. Yes, I get an eye checkup each year. But as far as replacement lenses go, I'm just the type of customer who should shop at National Contact Lens Center. Why? Because it's a no-nonsense way to save money—a lot of money—if you're already accustomed to contact lenses. Savings approach 75% on top-brand disposable, daily wear, extended wear, opaque, gas-permeable, and planned replacement lenses. If you don't find your contact lenses listed on NCLC's flyer, feel free to call for a price quote or any other assistance you might need.

SPECIAL FACTORS: Satisfaction guaranteed; returns accepted (with the exception of disposable color contacts) within 30 days for refund, credit, or exchange.

Prism Optical, Inc.

10992 NW 7th Ave.,
Dept. BWBM
N. Miami, FL 33168

800–637–4104
Fax: 305–754–7352

Catalog: $2, $5 outside U.S.
Pay: check, MO, MC, V, AE, DSC
Sells: prescription eyeglasses, contact lenses, and
   sunglasses
Store: same address; Monday to Friday 8:30–5
Online: www.prismoptical.qpg.com

"Save up to 75% on your next pair of eyeglasses, sunglasses, or contact lenses." That's what Prism Optical promises, and they've been doing it for nearly 40 years. At Prism you can get precision eyewear ground to your doctor's prescription with "painstakingly precise" workmanship; a full-range of men's, women's, and children's frames in popular sizes, shapes, and colors; just about every kind of lens made—single-vision, bi- and trifocals, invisible progressive lenses, tinted, plastic, super-lite polycarbonate, etc.; custom-fit glasses with lenses made to fit *your* eye size, and bridge and temples made to fit *your* face; and a complete line of contact lenses.

So how do you get great-fitting frames by mail? You can either send in your present frames for duplication (Prism's specialists will duplicate temple and bridge size, frame width, and lens size) or use Prism's Precision Frame Fitting Guide, which has diagrams against which you can place your current frames to determine these measurements. There are pages of Prism's frames to choose from; Prism can also get you a good deal on designer frames not listed in their catalog if you call or fax them with the manufacturer's name, frame color, and size (information found on the inside of the frame, usually the temple). Service is quick, and all glasses are guaranteed, so what do you have to lose? The website, by the way, does not offer online ordering.

SPECIAL FACTORS: If not satisfied with glasses within one-month trial period they can be returned for full refund.

Shades.com

714 Main St.
Yarmouthport, MA 02675

800–467–4233
Fax: 508–362–4220

Information: website only, no print catalog
Pay: check, MO, V, MC, AE, DSC
Sells: sunglasses
Store: online only; phone hours Monday to Friday 7–9,
   Saturday 10–2 EST
Online: www.shades.com and on AOL: keyword
   SUNGLASSES

Shades.com calls itself "The Sunglass Supersite," and indeed one would be hard pressed to find a source for top-name sunglasses with a better selection or better prices. You'll save up to 50% here on 15 major brands, at this writing, including BluBlocker, Eagle Eyes, Gargoyles, Gucci, Guess, H2Optix, Polaroid, Ray-Ban, Reebok, REVO, and Serengeti. At press time Shades.com carried nonprescription shades only.

With fierce competition out there for your Internet shopping dollar, companies have to be good to stay in business. Shades.com has been around since 1990, has received dozens of favorable reviews and ratings, which you can read about at the website, and specializes in fast, easy service, a user-friendly online catalog, a lowest price guarantee, good return policies, customer service by phone, and other nice amenities such as free gift wrapping. When you log onto the website, you'll be greeted with Shade.com's current specials. Click onto these for more details, or use the search function where you can either find your sunglasses by model number or create a custom search where you specify brand, frame color, lens color, price, etc. Suggested retail prices are listed alongside Shades.com's so you can see how much you're saving. The website also has cartoons, scientific articles, manufacturer links, repair information, and much more. Once you've made your selection, Shades.com offers you options: Order online, order by phone, or download an order form and order by mail or by fax.

SPECIAL FACTORS: 30-day satisfaction guarantee.

Related Products/Companies

Fashion/sports/aviation sunglasses
- Aircraft Spruce & Specialty, Defender, Holabird Sports, Mass. Army and Navy, Sierra Trading Post, Spike Nashbar, The Sportsman's Guide

Magnifiers and other aids for the visually impaired
- Comfort House, Independent Living Aids, The New Vision Store

Optic lens cleansers
- Orion

Fitness and Exercise

Exercise machines; body-building equipment and supplements; health monitoring devices

My grandmother, who was born at the end of the nineteenth century, was disgusted by joggers. When she would see early-morning joggers in gay-colored outfits running along her road past red barns and pigsties, she'd snort. "Why don't they jist pick up a shovel an' hoe?" It's a different world now. She'd be cursing me too if she had lived to see the day when her own granddaughter would spend hard-earned money for the privilege of running *indoors* on a treadmill three times a week. If you're into exercise machines, free weights, and other indoor workouts, this is your chapter. Some of the firms here sell professional-quality machines at factory-direct prices. They won't be cheap, but they'll be less expensive here than elsewhere. You can also find related supplies here, including heart-rate monitors, body-building supplements, and even dance studio setups.

Find It Fast

Body-Building Supplements
- Fitness Systems Mfg. Corp.

Free Weights and Exercise Machines
- Better Health Fitness, Creative Health Products, Fitness Factory Outlet

Health/Fitness Measuring Devises
- Creative Health Products

Health, Fitness, and Training Videos
- Creative Health Products

Better Health Fitness

5302 New Utrecht Ave.   718–436–4693
Brooklyn, NY 11219   718–436–4801
                                Fax: 718–854–3381

Information: brochure and catalog (see text)
Pay: check, MO, MC, V, AE
Sells: fitness, dance, and playground equipment
Store: same address; Monday to Wednesday 10–6,
   Thursday 10–8, Sunday 12–5 (closed Friday and
   Saturday)

Since 1977, Brooklyn has been home to Better Health Fitness, sellers of exercise equipment and gear for individual and commercial use. If you've got the space, Better Health has the treadmill, ballet barre, massage equipment, ski machine, locker-room equipment, sauna, and even indoor/outdoor resilient flooring—at up to 20% off regular prices. Whether you seek a single stationary bike or multi-station units, free weights and benches, boxing equipment, or the makings of a dance studio, Better Health Fitness will give you a price quote with your faxed request. The Better Health Fitness brochure is brief and to the point; it lists the manufacturers and type of fitness equipment the company represents. You do the rest by shopping around for the equipment you seek, then getting a quote from Better Health. If you're looking for playground equipment, either institutional or for home use, you can request the free 50-page playground equipment catalog. Within the New York/New Jersey/Connecticut area, they can design and install home and commercial playground sets of varying styles and material as well as provide layouts for a gym or other fitness feature. At press time a website was in the works, so stay tuned.

SPECIAL FACTORS: Satisfaction guaranteed; price quote by fax; authorized returns accepted within 15 days for exchange, refund, or credit; minimum order $50.

Creative Health Products

5148 Saddle Ridge Rd., Dept.
WBM
Plymouth, MI 48170

800–742–4478
313–996–5900
Fax: 313–996–4650

Catalog: $2
Pay: check, MO, MC, V, AE, DSC
Sells: fitness testing equipment, health-monitoring
 products
Store: mail order only

Creative Health Products has been selling health/fitness testing and measuring products as well as exercise equipment since 1976, and has some of the best product lines available. Savings run up to 30% on most items, and the company offers a lowest price guarantee, lest you need more incentive to shop here. The 20-page catalog includes such products as exercise bikes, rowing machines, treadmills, blood-pressure monitors, pulse monitors, body-fat calipers, otoscopes, ophthalmoscopes, scales, strength testers, and stopwatches. Creative Health also offers an impressive array of health and fitness books, videos, and training software. Creative Health's knowledgeable staff is ready to answer any questions you have about their products or about how to find the best equipment for your needs. Please note that even with the discounts, the prices are not low; this is professional equipment, after all.

SPECIAL FACTORS: Exercise equipment is not refundable; quantity discounts and institutional accounts available; C.O.D. orders accepted.

Fitness Factory Outlet

2875 S. 25th Ave.
Broadview, IL 60153

800–383–9300
708–345–9000
Fax: 708–345–9772

Catalog: free
Pay: check, MO, MC, V, AE, DSC
Sells: fitness and exercise equipment
Store: same address; Monday to Friday 11–7, Saturday
10–5 CT
Online: www.fitnessfactory.com

Since 1988, Fitness Factory Outlet has been selling aerobic and strength training equipment at factory-direct prices to schools, gyms, and individuals who want the convenience of working out at home. Buying from Fitness Factory Outlet, a serious weight lifter could set up a Basic Pro-Smith gym unit, with additional 210-pound weight stack, for under $1,100. Available here are treadmills and cardio equipment, combination and utility benches, leg machines, various presses, power racks, dumbbells and dumbbell racks, boxing equipment, and Olympic and standard weight plates. Several pages of the 55-page glossy color catalog are dedicated to institutional and commercial-quality machines. Also listed are cable attachment bars, abdominal straps, chinning bars, inversion boots, Olympic and standard bars and collars, rubber flooring, belts, and gloves.

The website is worth a look for its special offers, free fitness tips—including free customized workouts—and links to fitness-related sites; you can also order online here.

SPECIAL FACTORS: Authorized returns (exclusive of shipping and handling charges) are accepted for refund within 31 days if in like-new condition; orders under $50 add $10 service charge.

Fitness Systems Mfg. Corp.

104 Evans Ave.
Sinking Spring, PA 19608

800–822–9995
610–670–0135
Fax: 610–678–9022

Catalog: free
Pay: check, MO, V, MC, DSC, AE
Sells: supplements for bodybuilders and ultra-athletes
Store: mail order only
Online: www.jerron.com/fitness/fsmc

I have to confess that after looking through the catalog from Fitness Systems, I felt puny. This is a company for athletes and exercisers who are majorly devoted to their physiques, strength, and performance—such as beefy bodybuilders one might spot on late-night TV or people who can spare a couple of hours each day to bulk up. In fact, the catalog's inside headline proclaims proudly, "Nation's biggest supplier to convicts since 1985!" So, if you're a convict, or hoping to be one soon, this is a company you should get to know.

If you're looking for vitamin C, this is not your best source. Rather, this company sells supplements—at 40% to 50% off list—that you're not apt to find anywhere else, such as Cymaltex (natural testosterone booster); Maximum Strength and Power Blend; Creatine Monohydrate (an ergogenic aid for maximizing physical power and endurance); anabolic amino formulae; daily vitamin packs; muscular weight gain formulae; 100% egg protein; and many more products designed to enhance your every muscle and movement. The closely printed black-and-white catalog has explanatory text, testimonials, ingredient listings, and other useful information that's not only helpful but necessary. The website contains the same information and products as the catalog, if you prefer to shop online. (To do so you have to print out the order form and then mail or fax in your order; you can't submit the order form electronically.) The manager assures us that all ingredients are herbs or other components you'd find at your local nutrition center. These products, claim the company, are scientifically designed, of the highest purity, are 100% natural, and contain no sugar, starch, artificial colors, flavors, or preservatives. It's always a good idea, however, to consult your physician and trainer before taking these or any other nutritional and vitamin supplements.

SPECIAL FACTORS: Free shipping on orders of $150 or more; special shipping fees apply to international orders; for foreign orders, minimum purchase is $100, payable in U.S. funds.

Related Products/Companies

Athletic endurance enhancers
- East Earth Trade Winds

Biking apparel
- Bike Nashbar

Dance wear
- Dance Distributors

Exercise and how-to videos
- Bear Mountain Books, Video Learning Library

Exercise machines
- Damark, J&R Music

Health-monitoring equipment
- Cotton Scrubs, Tafford

Indoor exercise shoes and clothing
- Dance Distributors, Holabird Sports

Sportswear
- Bart's Water Sports

Swimsuits
- Worldwide Aquatics

Weight-loss formulas
- American Health Food, East Earth Trade Winds

Medications and Vitamins

Prescription and over-the-counter drugs and medications; alternative medicines; and vitamin and mineral supplements

Consider this section of the "Health, Beauty, and Fitness" chapter a print version of a trip to the drug or health-food store. Here you'll find companies selling prescription drugs and other drugstore items by mail, which is not only convenient, but also a great way to save money. Even generic drugs may be cheaper by mail, affording you savings of up to 60% on some commonly prescribed remedies.

Since many people are into less traditional treatments, such as homeopathy, nutritional therapy, and Chinese herbs, I've included several companies that specialize in these as well. When it comes to vitamins and nutritional supplements, you definitely shouldn't pay full price. The companies here can cut your vitamin expenses by more than half.

I find the whole subject of herbs, vitamins, and alternative health approaches daunting. Like most mothers, I've had to become something of an expert. After all, you can't be running to the doctor every time your kid has a runny nose. Just about every bookstore sells a multitude of books on health-related topics. My advice is to read as much as you can—and then read some more. Naturally, you'll need your physician's cooperation when ordering prescriptions by mail. If you're considering nonprescription remedies, it's always a good idea to consult her or him before you start self-treatments.

Some of the companies in this section carry cosmetics and other beauty and personal-care items, but firms specializing in these are found in the section following this one, "Personal Care and Beauty," page 278. For mail-order firms offering prescription glasses and contacts, see "Eye Care and Eyewear," page 258. Refer to the "Related Products/Companies" listing at the end of this section for firms found in other chapters selling health-related products such as medicinal herbs, essential oils, and products for people with limited mobility, impaired hearing, or other health conditions requiring special clothing or aids.

Find It Fast

Alternative Medicines and Remedies
- American Health Food, East Earth Trade Winds, PIA Discount Vitamins

Health-Related Books
- American Health Food, East Earth Trade Winds, PIA Discount Vitamins

Prescription and Over-the-Counter Medications
- Essentials, PIA Discount Vitamins, Preferred Prescription Plan

Seniors Products
- Essentials

Vitamins and Nutritional Supplements
- American Health Food, East Earth Trade Winds, Essentials, Freeda Vitamins, PIA Discount Vitamins, Preferred Prescription Plan

American Health Food

875 W. Roger Rd.
Tucson, AZ 85705

800–858–2143
520–888–8234
Fax: 800–352–0569
Fax: 520–888–0969

Catalog: free
Pay: check, MO, MC, V, AE, DSC
Sells: vitamins and health supplements
Store: mail order only
Online: www.amerhealth.com

Here's a great company for vitamin and health supplement values, in business since 1977. At American Health Food you'll save 20% to 50% on most items; a comparison check with two local health-food stores bore that out. Shipping costs $3.95 regardless of the size of your order, and that includes customers living in Alaska, Hawaii, Puerto Rico, and Canada. The 62-page newsprint catalog features thousands of vitamins and minerals, herbal formulas, powder mixes, and nutritional supplements from the top manufacturers as well as American Health Food's own brand (where you'll find savings up to 60% on some items). American Health lists the retail price alongside their catalog's price so you can calculate your savings at a glance.

There are other health-food-store products here as well, including Bach Flower Remedies by Nelson's Homeopathy, Klamath blue-green algae products, cruelty-free cosmetics by Rachel Perry, essential oils, weight-loss formulas, sunblock, and skin- and hair-care products. Provided you know the specific brand you're looking for, the website can be a quick and convenient way to order, as it's indexed by manufacturer rather than by product type. Also on the website are the smaller, hard-to-find companies and limited-time manufacturers' offers for even deeper discounts. The same postage and handling fee applies when you order online. With orders over $50 you receive a "free gift." At American Health Food there is no minimum order, and if you don't see something you're looking for, ask. They might have it in stock or be able to get it for you.

SPECIAL FACTORS: Flat-rate shipping ($3.95) to anywhere in the U.S., Canada, and U.S. territories.

Chinese traditional medicine is many centuries older than the Western style practiced by U.S. physicians. With the growing Asian population in the U.S. and increasing awareness of the effectiveness of Chinese herbalism by non-Chinese patients and physicians alike, demand for Chinese medicines has soared. If you live in a big city with a Chinatown, you're in luck—sort of. The shopkeeper at the Chinese herb shop may or may not speak English. The product you're looking for may not be fresh or in stock. Parking may be an expensive nightmare. You might be overcharged and not realize it. You won't have any way of verifying the reputability of the manufacturer—do they sell products derived from endangered species, for example, and are their trade practices sound?

Enter East Earth Trade Winds. This company has been in business since 1985 selling unique Chinese herbal products from reputable Chinese and American manufacturers. All of their products are carefully selected by herbalists—not marketers. East Earth's products are inexpensive—much less than their competitors'. The 24-page print catalog offers herbs used for tonics (health-promoting/maintaining formulas) or for treating minor health complaints (cold, flu, indigestion, insomnia, overweight, hay fever, PMS, eczema, etc.). If you're like me and don't know a lot about this revered branch of medicine, you'll find the catalog absolutely fascinating, with detailed descriptions of the products and their ingredients (sea horse genitals, deer antlers, crushed pearls, for example) and what they're used for. You can also call East Earth with questions; they're used to that. This company also carries teapots, incense, tea, and a variety of books relating to Chinese herbs, medicine, and culture. The website shows products, but doesn't feature online ordering.

SPECIAL FACTORS: No products derived from endangered species are stocked; free shipping on orders over $90; no C.O.D. accepted; wholesale buyers should inquire about minimums and policies; satisfaction guaranteed; returns and claims should be made within ten days of receipt.

Essentials

Virginia Retired Persons   800–456–2277
Pharmacy, Inc.   800–260–4452 (Spanish)
P.O. Box 13671, Dept. WBM   Fax: 800–456–7631
Richmond, VA 23286–2616   TDD: 800–933–4327

Catalog: free
Pay: check, MO, V, MC, DSC
Sells: generic drugstore and pharmaceutical items
Store: mail order only
Online: www.rpspharmacy.com

Retired Persons Services, Inc., is an entity that paid AARP (American Association of Retired Persons) a fee to use AARP in its mail-order pharmacy name. It is not affiliated with the well-known seniors' organization. It appears, however, to have some of the same interests—that is, saving seniors and others money on prescription and over-the-counter drugs and drugstore sundries that are a day-to-day necessity for many of us.

The 80-page catalog specializes in generic products—that is, these items have the same active ingredients as common brands such as Tylenol, Preparation H, and Imodium A-D but are sold for much less, sometimes half—under the AARP Pharmacy label. The catalog offers generic vitamins, nutrition formulas, antacids, face creams, sleep aids, toothpaste, sunglasses—just about anything you'd find in a drugstore. Additionally, the Essentials catalog carries products to assist elderly folk with everyday living, featuring items such as elevated toilet seats, heating pads, cholesterol home test kits, humidifiers, and on and on. AARP Pharmacy functions as a full-service pharmacy and can fill any prescription with brand-name or generic medications. Using the latter will net you 30% to 50% savings. See the catalog for details on prescription and other ordering. There's a full-time pharmacist on duty at the main number—8 A.M. to 8 P.M., Monday through Friday ET, and 8:30 A.M. to 5 P.M. Saturday—to answer all of your prescription drug queries. Ostomy customers: Request the special Ostomy products catalog. For your convenience, be sure to look up the website, which features online ordering.

Freeda Vitamins, Inc.

36 E. 41st St.
New York, NY 10017–6203

800–777–3737
212–685–4980
Fax: 212–685–7297
TDD: 800–777–3737

Catalog: free
Pay: check, MO, MC, V, AE, DSC
Sells: dietary supplements and prescriptions
Store: Freeda Pharmacy, same address; Monday to
   Thursday 8:30–6, Friday 8:30–4
E-mail: FreedaVits@aol.com

It's always refreshing to find a family-run business like this one that really cares about its customers. It's obvious that Freeda is just such a place when you read this vitamin company's literature. A leading consumer guide found Freeda to be the most reasonably priced among leading vitamin manufacturers—20% less than everyone else. For over 60 years Philip and Sylvia Zimmerman have kept tight control over their products and quality of service. Today this company has been written up and praised everywhere as one of the only sources for all-natural, *kosher* vitamins that are 100% yeast- and wheat-free. All Freeda vitamins are dated to guarantee freshness; are free from coal-tar dyes, artificial colors, and flavors; and have vegetarian fillers or binders. So if you're someone who has a hard time tolerating commercial vitamins, despair no more.

The 36-page catalog lists vitamins, digestive supplements, nutrients, and nutriceuticals in a wide variety of sizes and strengths. Parents, this is a wonderful source for children's vitamins; all Freeda children's products are found on the Feingold Approved Food List for hyperactive children. Freeda will send your doctor, dentist, chiropractor, podiatrist, or veterinarian their Physicians' Information Packet if you request it.

SPECIAL FACTORS: Courtesy discounts are given to health-care professionals;

most major health plans honored; C.O.D. orders accepted; $10 minimum charge on credit cards; free shipping on orders $100 and above.

PIA Discount Vitamins

708 Saw Mill River Rd.
Ardsley, NY 10502

800-662-8144
914-693-3632
Fax: 914-693-3557

Catalog: free
Pay: check, MO, MC, V, AE, DSC
Sells: supplements, homeopathic remedies, vitamins,
  herbs, books
Store: mail order only
Online: www.piavitamins.com

Everything about this company is appealing. The 32-page print catalog is straightforward, comprehensive, and has just about every type of vitamin, mineral, remedy, and supplement under the sun at an average of 20% off. Even if you're loyal to an obscure brand, as I am, chances are PIA will have it or can get it for you. Now, log on to the website for a real treat. Products are listed by manufacturer's name, or you can search by category. There's even a comprehensive online research library here. I heartily endorse this company and their good product selection and prices.

SPECIAL FACTORS: Satisfaction guaranteed.

Preferred Prescription Plan, Inc.

2201 W. Sample Road
Building 9, Ste. 1a
Pompano Beach, FL 33073

800–881–6325
954–969–1230
Fax: 800–881–6990

Information: price quote and website
Pay: MC, V, DSC
Store: same address, Monday to Friday, 8–5:30
Sells: prescriptions, diabetic supplies, and vitamins
Online: www.prefrx.com

What if you could get your prescriptions filled, have your insurance billed, and receive your medication in the mail—all this without leaving the comfort of your own home while saving as much as 75%? That's the concept behind Preferred Prescription Plan (PPP), a full-service Florida pharmacy that operates a brisk mail-order business. Unlike others, this online pharmacy has no membership fee, and accepts and can bill most insurance companies, Champus and Medicare where authorized (no HMOs). If you need to speak with a customer representative, there are courteous knowledgeable people on the other end of the phone ready to assist you. Before you order, it's worth your while to request a price quote so you'll see how much you're saving. You can do it online at the website with a convenient ready-made form, or by phone, fax, or snail mail. Once you have your price quote, (1) your doctor sends PPP a copy of your prescription via toll-free fax or calls it in via telephone; (2) you fax PPP a copy of your prescription; or (3) you give PPP your doctor's name and phone number and PPP calls for the prescription information. PPP carries thousands of brand-name and generic drugs, diabetic supplies, vitamins, and pet medications. If you don't need your medication today, this may be a good way to cut down on your medical costs.

SPECIAL FACTORS: Preferred Prescription Plan does not dispense medical advice, nor diagnose, nor prescribe medications.

Related Products/Companies

Aromatherapy oils
- Atlantic Spice

Bodybuilding supplements
- Fitness Systems Mfg.

Breast prostheses
- Bosom Buddies Breast Forms

Clothing for children with special needs
- Special Clothes

Dog and puppy vitamins
- Jeffers, KV Vet Supply, UPCO, Valley Vet

Fish supplements
- That Fish/Pet Place

Health-monitoring devices
- Better Health Fitness

Health-related books
- Mountain Ark Trading Co.

Horse vitamins
- Omaha Vaccine

Joint supports, heart-rate monitors
- Holabird

Medicinal herbs
- Atlantic Spice, Caprilands Herb Farm, Rafal Spice

Products for allergy-sensitive people
- National Allergy Supply

Products for people with limited mobility
- Amplestuff, Comfort House

Support hosiery and therapeutic footwear
- Support Plus, The Support Shop

Personal Care and Beauty

Products for skin and hair care; cosmetics; wigs

It's the little things you do for yourself that make a difference in how you feel. Though pampering yourself can be expensive, there's no need to add one more worry line to that face. The companies in this section can save you a solid 50% on everything from cosmetics to wigs to herbal lotions. Refer to "Related Products/ Companies" at the end of this section for many other companies that sell beauty-related products.

Find It Fast

Beauty Products for African-Americans
- Gold Medal Hair Products

Cosmetics
- Beauty Boutique, Gold Medal Hair Products

Skin and Hair Products
- Beauty Boutique, Cal Ben, Gold Medal Hair Products, Kettle Care

Wigs
- Beauty by Spector, Gold Medal Hair Products

Beauty Boutique

6836 Engle Rd.   **440–826–3008**
P.O. Box 94520   **Fax: 440–826–1267**
Cleveland, OH 44101–4520

Catalog: free
Pay: check, MO, MC, V, AE, DSC
Sells: cosmetics and treatment products
Store: mail order only

Can you get terrific bargains on beauty enhancers and still look like a million dollars? That's the concept behind Beauty Boutique's 72-page color catalog, with page after page of name-brand cosmetics, perfumes, costume jewelry, hair products, lingerie, and other skin, hair, figure, hygiene, and oral beauty products, some at savings of 90%. Beauty Boutique also buys up those little fragrance and cosmetics samples from major manufacturers once their promotions end and then resells them to you at great savings.

Having spent the equivalent of a down payment on a computer recently for makeup, I'm painfully aware of the cost of cosmetics. While Beauty Boutique may not have your exact brand and shade, they're likely to carry a less-expensive item that's similar. Some of the ladies' perfumes and men's fragrances are deeply discounted here, and Beauty Boutique also carries famous fragrance "versions" (read: copies) that are a tenth the cost of the original. The product selection is small but eclectic, including strapless bras, anti-itching creams, and even tongue cleaners. This would be a good source for your teenager, who wants at least a dozen shades of eye shadow, lipstick, and nail polish but can't spend more than $7 or $8 in all.

SPECIAL FACTORS: Satisfaction guaranteed; returns accepted for refund or exchange.

Beauty by Spector, Inc.

1 Spector Place, Dept.
BWBM–2000
McKeesport, PA 15134–0502

412–673–3259
Fax: 412–678–3978

Catalog: call (see text)
Pay: check or MO (see text)
Sells: wigs, hairpieces, wig accessories
Store: mail order only

Beauty by Spector, Inc., offers the Alan Thomas line of wigs and hairpieces at savings of up to 50% compared with salon-selling prices. The 32-page color catalog features a number of designer styles for women, modeled in gorgeous full-page photographs. The wigs range from neat, softly coifed shorter styles to the magnificent below-shoulder-length drape "Obsession."

The styles are contemporary and fashionable—pretty, relaxed, and well shaped. Included in the catalog are wiglets, cascades, and extensions that are ideal for everyday wear as well as for dressy occasions (or when you just want to change your image for a night without doing something permanent). There are men's hairpieces here, too, in several styles. Thermal-conductive monofilament and polyurethane are available in the men's pieces for maximum comfort.

The wigs and hairpieces are available in a wide variety of synthetic fibers as well as human hair and are offered in dozens of colors. For color selection, you may purchase a set of actual hair samples, or if you prefer, send a sample of your hair for color matching. You'll also find shampoos, conditioners, hair accessories (turbans and scarves, for example), brushes and combs, and wig stands and mannequins.

Beauty by Spector has been in business since 1958 and is extremely knowledgeable in the field. Wig specialists are on duty 24 hours a day to answer your questions.

Special to WMO readers: Be sure to identify yourself as a *Wholesale by Mail and Online* reader and Beauty by Spector will include the "Wholesale Price List," plus other special offers, with your catalog.

SPECIAL FACTORS: Specify men's or women's styles when requesting information, as added material and flyers pertaining to your gender will be enclosed with the catalog; the price of the catalog was not known at press time, so please call to inquire; pay by money order and receive an additional discount; quantity discounts are negotiable.

Cal Ben Soap Company

9828 Pearmain St., Dept.   800–340–7091
WBM   510–638–7091
Oakland, CA 94603   Fax: 510–638–7827

Catalog: free
Pay: check, MO, MC, V, AE, DSC
Sells: natural, earth-friendly soaps for bath, hair, laundry, and dishes
Store: mail order only

"The third planet from the sun deserves clean air, quality water, and 'pure soap' " according to the exciting, colorful literature sent by Cal Ben Soap Company. Here's a company that believes in environmentally friendly household soaps at great prices. This company has taken a leadership role since 1947 in providing consumers with soaps for laundry, face and body, hair, and dishes that do the job better than their common commercial counterparts, but that also last a lot longer (they're concentrated) and don't harm the environment in any way. Each of the Five Star Soap Products has multiple uses detailed in the accompanying literature. For example, the Seafoam laundry soap can also be used for toilets, greasy driveways, and as an all-purpose household cleaner. The shampoo doubles as a bubble bath, rug shampoo, and delicate-fabrics soap. And on and on.

Since these economical, all-natural products seemed almost too good to be true, I decided on a sample pack so I could try the Gold Star Shampoo Concentrate, the "Pure Soap" bar, the liquid Five Star Dish Glow (I scrubbed my son's leather sneakers with it), and the Seafoam "Destain" automatic dishwashing soap. All were truly wonderful, and I felt excellent about the fact that I wasn't contributing to groundwater pollution. I'm a convert! The prices here are good too. Since the soaps are highly concentrated the savings run about 50% off normal retail. All products come in a variety of sizes, and gift and sample packs are available as well. In addition to soaps, Cal Ben also sells almond hand/body lotion, glass cleaner, crystal deodorant stones, natural scouring pads, and other cleaning/hygiene accessories and products. When the Age of Aquarius begins in the year 2000, Cal Ben may be the clean winner with their old-fashioned values and futuristic vision.

SPECIAL FACTORS: Satisfaction guaranteed; returns accepted for exchange, refund, or credit. Be sure to mention *Wholesale by Mail and Online* when ordering.

Gold Medal Hair Products Co.

One Bennington Avenue   **516–378–6900**
Freeport, NY 11520   **Fax: 516–378–0168**

Catalog: free
Pay: check, MO, MC, V, AE, DSC
Sells: hair and skin products for African-Americans;
   lingerie, music videos, jewelry, etc.
Store: mail order only

Gold Medal Hair Products has been in business for 56 years, catering to the black population with products to fit your different beauty needs and desires. The 36-page color catalog is busy and jam-packed with an eclectic assortment of products, dominated by hair-related products and tools. You'll find tamers, conditioners, shampoos, hair-setting gels, coloring and highlighting agents, perm kits, styling accessories, and hair sprays, as well as wigs, weave sections, and hairpieces—for women, men, and children.

There is also an extensive selection of videos and music cassettes focusing on black culture, from black movies and black history to gospel and comedy. Also available are all kinds of skin products and accessories, figure-controlling (and enhancing) bras, slips, and panties, and even a section on jewelry, vitamins, and cosmetics.

Although the prices are competitive, Gold Medal does offer twofers, specials, and combo items for extra savings. There aren't enough companies like Gold Medal out there, and that's why I'm happy to list them here.

Wholesalers: Minimum order is $250; 40% off. Call for details.

SPECIAL FACTORS: C.O.D. orders require a $10 deposit; satisfaction is guaranteed or you'll be credited or refunded; returned cassettes and videos must remain unopened, and wigs and clothing must be unworn.

Kettle Care

710 Trap Rd., Dept. WBM   **Tel/Fax: 406–892–3294**
Columbia Falls, MT 59912

    Catalog: $1, $2 outside U.S.
    Pay: check, MO, MC, V, DSC
    Sells: natural skin-care and bath products
    Store: mail order only
    Online: www.kettlecare.com

What a lovely woman owns this company, and what lovely products she makes. Breezing through Kettle Care's catalog is like strolling through a Montana field of wildflowers. Since 1984 Lynn Wallingford has grown the very herbs and wildflowers in her garden that go into Kettle Care products. I don't include this company just because I happen to love high-quality, handmade, ecologically sound, all-natural, beautifully packaged personal care products. Compare Kettle Care's products with other high-end companies such as Weleda, Camocare, and Aubrey, and you'll see that on selected items Kettle Care's prices are as much as 50% less. Ms. Wallingford says she hand-blends and personally fusses over each jar and bottle; testimonials from happy customers throughout the catalog confirm that the packaging is beautiful and the products out of the ordinary. Among the products here are moisture creams and lotions, sprays, bath powders, cleansers and soaps, hair products, mineral baths, massage oils, balms and salves (for lips, babies, sore muscles, feet, sunscreen, the delicate eye area, varicose veins, and chapped and callused workers' hands, among others), aromatherapy, and essential and fragrance oils. I liked the "pocket perfumes"—in quarter-ounce screw-top jars so you can apply fragrance wherever you please, in the amount you please. I also liked the handmade Workers Soap, with pumice and clove oil for your tough guy who also wants to smell nice. This is a company that inspires loyalty in its customers. Check out the darling website, where you can order online from the full catalog.

SPECIAL FACTORS: 25-cent refund for returned bottles and jars to recycle; satisfaction guaranteed.

Related Products/Companies

Books on natural beauty and health
- Storey Books

Caswell-Massey products
- Chock

Children's and baby-care products
- Baby Bunz

Handmade soaps, creams, shaving supplies
- Lehman's

Henna
- Sultan's Delight

Herbal toothpaste
- East Earth Trade Winds

Natural cosmetics
- American Health Food, Deer Valley Farm, Mountain Ark

Nonpermanent tattoos
- Dover

Perfume-making supplies and books
- Tom Thumb Workshops

Personal care appliances
- Bernie's Discount, Damark, J&R Music World

Skin, hair, and personal care products
- American Health Food, EDGE Distributing, Essentials, Mountain Ark Trading Co., National Allergy Supply

Skin treatments
- East Earth Trade Winds

Soap-making kits
- Brushy Mountain Bee Farm, Lehman's

Thai deodorant stones
- Chock

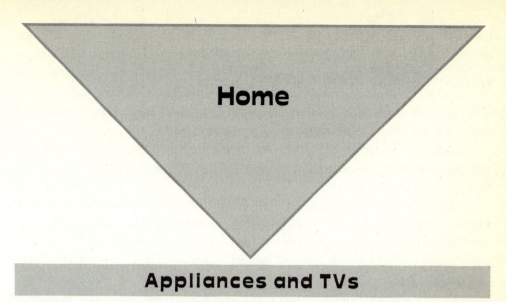

Home

Appliances and TVs

Large and small household appliances, vacuum cleaners, sewing machines, televisions, air conditioners, etc.

The companies featured in this section offer primarily white goods (washers, dryers, refrigerators, microwaves, and ranges), brown goods (TVs, air conditioners, etc.), personal-care appliances, sewing machines, vacuum cleaners, and floor machines.

For companies that specialize in other "pluggables" such as home entertainment systems and audio and/or video equipment, see the "Music, Audio, and Video" chapter. For office machines and computers, see the "Office, Business, and Professional" chapter.

One thing you'll notice about the companies below is that many of them aren't what you'd think of as *mail-order* companies. That is, they may not have a glossy print catalog that comes in the mail each month; they may not have a print catalog at all. But don't let that discourage you. Some of the companies here offer price quotes, which means *you* do the homework and footwork, and they'll reward you for your efforts. You can save hundreds on appliances by shopping this way—up to 70%.

Here's how price quotes work: Shop around locally for the appliance, or log onto the manufacturer's website and get information that way. When you find a model you like, write down the details (make and model numbers, color, etc.), then call the firm. I think you'll be pleasantly surprised at the price you're quoted, even with shipping costs factored in. This is a great way to shop for vacuum cleaners and sewing machines too.

When you've got your choice down to one or two models, you can talk to a sales representative and have him or her send you the manufacturer's brochure.

Or you can obtain this directly from the manufacturer, most of whom will send brochures on specific models upon request. Manufacturers' addresses are usually found on product packaging, and most have websites as well. The consumer contacts and addresses of hundreds of major corporations are also listed in "Consumer's Resource Handbook," available from the Consumer Information Center (see the listing in "Books, Audiobooks, and Periodicals").

If you run into trouble with a major appliance and fail to get it resolved with the seller or the manufacturer, seek help from the Major Appliance Consumer Action Panel (MACAP). MACAP, which is sponsored by the Association of Home Appliance Manufacturers (AHAM), can request action from a manufacturer and make recommendations for resolution of the complaint. (The panel's advice isn't binding, but it resolves over 80% of the cases it handles.) MACAP offers assistance with problems about dishwashers, ranges, microwave ovens, washers, dryers, refrigerators, freezers, garbage disposals, trash compactors, air conditioners, water heaters, and dehumidifiers. If your complaint concerns one of these appliances and your attempts to settle it with the seller and the manufacturer haven't worked, write to Major Appliance Consumer Action Program, 20 N. Wacker Dr., Ste. 1231, Chicago, IL 60606. Your letter should include the manufacturer's name, model number of the appliance, and date purchased, as well as copies of relevant receipts and correspondence. (Call 800–621–0477 for more information.)

For firms in other chapters selling appliances, see "Related Products/Companies" at the end of this section.

Find It Fast

Air Conditioners
- Bernie's Discount Center, Dial-a-Brand, LVT Price Quote Hotline, Percy's

Major Appliances
- Beach Sales, Bernie's Discount Center, Cole's Appliance, Dial-a-Brand, EBA Wholesale, Kaplan Bros., LVT Price Quote Hotline, Percy's

Sewing Machines and Sergers
- Discount Appliance Centers, Sewin' in Vermont, Sewing Machine Super Store

Small Appliances
- Bernie's Discount Center, Sewin' in Vermont, Sewing Machine Super Store

TVs
- Bernie's Discount Center, Cole's Appliance, Dial-a-Brand, LVT Price Quote Hotline, Percy's

Vacuum-Cleaner Repairs
- ABC Vacuum Cleaner Warehouse

Vacuum Cleaners, Rug Shampooers, Floor Polishers
- AAA Vacuums, ABC Vacuum Cleaner Warehouse, Discount Appliance Centers, LVT Price Quote Hotline

AAA Vacuums

1230 North Third St.   800–533–VACS
Abilene, TX 79601   915–677–1311

Information: price quote
Pay: check, MO, MC, V, DSC
Sells: vacuum cleaners, rug shampooers, floor polishers
Store: same address; Monday to Friday 8:30–5
E-mail: aaavacs@aol.com

Save up to 50% on some of the best names in the cleaning biz at AAA Vacuums, in business since 1975. AAA buys in volume, doesn't publish a catalog, spends little on PR, and therefore can pass the savings directly on to the customer. Canister, upright, convertible, and mini vacuum models; rug shampooers; and floor buffers are available from Sharp, Panasonic, Hoover, Sanyo, Fantom, Kirby, Filter Queen, and Tristar. AAA also carries rebuilt Rainbow machines, and supplies and accessories for all of these brands. Whether you're looking for a home model or a commercial model, it'll be well worth your while to call AAA Vacuums for a price quote before you venture out into the crowded stores. A helpful sales rep can quote you current discount prices and provide other product information as well.

SPECIAL FACTORS: All merchandise comes with AAA Vacuum's Parts and Service Contract and/or the original manufacturer's warranty; satisfaction guaranteed; returns accepted within ten days.

ABC Vacuum Cleaner Warehouse

6720 Burnet Rd., BWBM
Austin, TX 78757

800–285–8145
512–459–7643
Fax: 512–451–2352

Information: price list
Pay: check, MO, MC, V, AE, DSC
Sells: vacuum cleaners
Store: same address; Monday to Friday 9–6, Saturday 9–5
Online: www.abcvacuum.com

Once you know about ABC Vacuum Cleaner Warehouse, it would seem silly to go out and buy a machine at a department store. For more than two decades ABC has been purchasing machines from suppliers who are overstocked or going out of business, then selling them to the consumer at greatly discounted prices. You'll find models by Royal, Sanitaire, Oreck, Eureka, Hoover, Kirby, Rainbow, Panasonic, Sanyo, Bissell, Fantom, and others, at amazing prices—some 70% off original list. You won't find prices lower than this, and if you do, tell ABC. They "want to have the lowest prices in America." All machines are new and in the original box, and shipping is a flat rate ($10 when last checked). Most people who buy from ABC have already visited a vacuum cleaner store and know what they want. If you have questions, call ABC to discuss your needs and they'll mail you a price list and product brochures if you request them. One of the features on the website is a questionnaire you can fill out and e-mail if you want ABC to get back to you with their recommendations based on the information you provided online (type of floors, square footage of house, pets, allergies, upright or canister, etc.). The website also features online ordering.

SPECIAL FACTORS: Satisfaction guaranteed; returns accepted within 30 days for exchange, refund, or credit; all machines come with a warranty.

Beach Sales

80 VFW Pkwy.
Revere, MA 02151

781–284–0130
800–562–9020
Fax: 781–284–9823

Information: price quote
Pay: check, MO, MC, V
Sells: major appliances, audio and video components, scanners, film, etc.
Store: same address
Online: www.beachsalesinc.com

Since 1947 Beach Sales has provided the Boston area with major discounts on large and small appliances and electronic items. You can take advantage of these same savings by calling, faxing, or writing to Beach Sales for a price quote on appliances (dishwashers, washing machines, microwaves, dryers, vacuum cleaners, refrigerators, snowblowers, for example), entertainment equipment (VCRs, televisions, car stereos, camcorders, audio and video accessories), and communications items (dictators, fax machines, two-way radios, transcribers, pagers, telephones, word processors). All you need are the manufacturer's name and the model number of the item. There's no catalog, but Beach Sales sells the products of so many major manufacturers that you'd do well to get a quote. Even smaller items such as film and audio- and videotape are available at quantity discounts. The website will give you an idea of what Beach Sales carries, but there's no online ordering.

SPECIAL FACTORS: Returns in their original packaging are accepted for exchange, refund, or credit.

Located in the middle of bustling Manhattan, Bernie's Discount Center has been in the business of selling "pluggables" to consumers by mail at deep discounts since 1947. A pluggable, since you ask, is anything under the sun—large or small—that plugs in. Examples: washing machines, dryers, toasters, microwaves, electric brooms, refrigerators, steam-vacs, vacuum cleaners, ranges, dishwashers, televisions, CD players, answering machines, camcorders, satellite TV systems, food waste disposers, temperature-controlled wine cellars, air conditioners, humidifiers, blenders, water purifiers, portable heaters, fans, personal-care items, countertop kitchen appliances, and on and on. The $1 for the flyer from Bernie's is refundable with your purchase, but shows only a fraction of what Bernie's sells. You're better off calling with the make and model of the pluggable you seek. The owner told me, "We carry everything." Since Bernie's sells everything at 10% to 15% above dealers' cost, that translates into an average of 30% below list price.

Please note: Purchases charged to American Express/Optima cards are shipped to billing addresses only, and MasterCard and VISA are accepted for *in-store* purchases only.

Canadian readers: Orders are chipped to Canada via UPS only.

SPECIAL FACTORS: Store is closed Saturdays in July and August.

Cole's was founded in 1957 with the idea that an educated consumer would be the company's best customer. (Savvy WMO readers have been buying their appliances here for many years.) Cole's sells home electronics (TV and video), appliances, and home furnishings and bedding at discounts of up to 50%. It's a good idea to check out your item locally, write down its make and model, and then call, write, or fax the nice people at Cole's. They'll give you a price quote that will more than likely knock your socks off. If you don't know exactly what you want, the helpful people at Cole's will be happy to give you recommendations, steer you to the right manufacturers, and generally assist you in buying the right appliances for your needs. The following manufacturers are carried by Cole's: Amana, Asko, Dacor, DCS, Frigidaire, General Electric, Hotpoint, Insinkerator, Jenn-Air, KitchenAid, Magic Chef, Maytag, Panasonic, Pioneer, Premier, Speed Queen, Sub-Zero, Tappan, Thermador, Viking, Westinghouse, Wolf, and Zenith, among others. Deliveries are made by Cole in the greater Chicago area, and via UPS elsewhere. Even with the cost of shipping, you'll save a lot by shopping here.

SPECIAL FACTORS: Price quote by phone or letter.

Dial-a-Brand, Inc.

2208 Sunrise Hwy.　　　　516–378–9694
Merrick, NY 11566　　　　Fax: 516–867–3447

Information: price quote
Pay: check, MO, MC, V, DSC
Sells: appliances, TVs, and video equipment
Store: same address; Monday to Friday 9–6, Saturday
9–12

Before I took over as editor of this book in 1997, it never would have occurred to me that one could buy a major appliance through the mail. But all kinds of people do, and that's one of the reasons Dial-a-Brand is still in business after three decades. You'll save from 20% to 40% when you buy your major appliances, TV, or VCR from Dial-a-Brand. They'll give you a price quote right over the phone when you call them with the make and model you seek; you *must* provide the make and model to get a price quote. Most major manufacturers are carried here. Shipping is free if you live in the tristate region of New York/New Jersey/Connecticut. Deliveries elsewhere are made via UPS.

SPECIAL FACTORS: Returns accepted for exchange if goods are defective or damaged in transit.

Discount Appliance Centers

8426 20th Ave., Ste. 100　　　301–559–8932
Adelphi, MD 20783　　　　　Fax: 301–559–1335

Information: price quote with SASE
Pay: check, MO, MC, V, AE
Sells: vacuum cleaners and sewing machines
Store: mail order only

Need a vacuum cleaner or a sewing machine? Here's what you do: Shop around for the make and model you like. Get the best price you can find. Then write to

Discount Appliance Centers (enclose a self-addressed, stamped envelope) with your top one or two choices. Since they sell vacuum cleaners (and vacuum cleaner accessories such as belts, bags, and attachments) and sewing machines from every American manufacturer at just above dealer cost, you're likely to get your item cheaper here than anywhere else (averaging, say, 20% of list), even after you factor in shipping. There's no catalog from Discount Appliance Centers, so it's important that you know the make and model number when you write for a price quote.

SPECIAL FACTORS: Price quote by letter only with SASE; minimum order $49.

EBA Wholesale

2361 Nostrand Ave.   800–380–2378
Brooklyn, NY 11210   718–252–3400
                            Fax: 718–253–6002

Flyer: free
Pay: check, MO, MC, V, DSC
Sells: appliances, audio, video, mattresses, etc.
Store: same address; Monday to Saturday 9–6 EST
Online: www.eba-wholesale.com

"Shop at home!" commands the giant red print on EBA's current catalog. "We cannot be undersold! Wholesale prices! Best service! Nationwide delivery!" Okay, okay, I believe you! Courteous and knowledgeable "sale counselors" will answer your call and offer you a low quote—to the tune of 10% to 40% less than retail price—on hundreds of home appliances and electronics from top-name manufacturers too numerous to list. It's all here, including the kitchen sink: air conditioners, barbecues, boom boxes, camcorders, car stereos, cellular phones, compactors, dehumidifiers, dishwashers, dryers, fans, freezers, heaters, ice makers, microwave ovens, radios, receivers, refrigerators, ranges, stereo systems, telephones, turntables, TV/VCR combos, Walkmans, wall ovens, washers, and more. You can order or get a price quote directly from the website.

SPECIAL FACTORS: Price quote by phone, fax, letter, or e-mail; satisfaction guaranteed.

Kaplan Bros. Blue Flame Corp.

523 W. 125th St.
New York, NY 10027–3498

800–528–6913
212–662–6990
Fax: 212–663–2026

Brochure: free with SASE
Pay: certified check or MO
Sells: commercial restaurant equipment
Store: same address; Monday to Friday 8–4:30

Kaplan Bros. Blue Flame Corp. has been around for nearly half a century, and they've been featured in this book for many years. Why? Because this is the place to shop if you're opening up a bakery or restaurant, or if you want a commercial-grade gas stove in your own house. (I have a couple of friends who own a professional oven and stove; cooking and baking becomes a wonderful experience.) Kaplan Bros. sell stoves, refrigeration systems, fryers, steamers, convection ovens—in other words, large commercial kitchen equipment and appliances—at discounts up to 50%. If you're in the market for this type of item, get the manufacturer's name and Kaplan Bros. will send you manufacturers' brochures on request with a self-addressed, stamped envelope. Blue Flame is best known for Garland commercial stoves and the Dynamic Cooking System.

Please note: Items shipped to addresses within the continental U.S. only; no orders to Hawaii, Alaska, Canada, or APO/FPO addresses.

SPECIAL FACTORS: If purchasing a stove for residential installation, have kitchen flooring, wall insulation, and exhaust systems evaluated—and upgraded if necessary—before ordering; request manufacturers' brochures by name of manufacturer.

Cool. Check out LVT's website and you'll get a good idea of what this company is about. There you'll have access to LVT Brands Links, a page of website links and 800 numbers of major manufacturers such as Amana, At&T, Bosch, Brother, Canon, Frigidaire, GE, Hitachi, Hoover, Hotpoint, Jenn-Air, JVC, KitchenAid, Maytag, Panasonic, RCA, Samsung, Sharp, Sony, Tappan, Toshiba, Westinghouse, Whirlpool, Zenith, and others. Go directly to the manufacturer to get product information on major appliances (dishwashers, washers and dryers, freezers, and ranges), dehumidifiers, vacuum cleaners, microwave ovens, televisions, air conditioners, camcorders, video equipment, telephones ad telephone equipment, calculators, typewriters, breadmakers, and fax machines. When you've specked out the make and model you want, request a price quote by mail, phone, fax, or right on the website. Be sure to specify make, model, and choice of color if applicable. Not only will you receive a low price quote that reflects savings averaging 30%, but LVC picks up all shipping costs and processes your order within 48 hours. No wonder this company has been written up and featured in so many consumer magazines. The website, if you have the time, has some useful information such as articles about product recalls and other consumer-related issues.

SPECIAL FACTORS: Shipping (UPS), handling, and insurance charges are all included in quotes; manufacturers' rebates honored; all sales are final; all goods have manufacturers' warranties; minimum order $100.

Percy's, Inc.

19 Glennie St.
Worcester, MA 01605

800–922–8194
Fax: 508–797–5578

Information: price quote
Pay: MO, MC, V, DSC
Sells: large appliances, home and car audio, TV
  components, video, computers, etc.
Store: same address; Monday to Friday 10–9, Saturday
  10–6
Online: www.percys.com

Founded in 1926, Percy's, Inc., is a discount seller of major appliances (washers, dryers, ranges, refrigerators, freezers, dishwashers, dehumidifiers, trash compactors, water purifiers, microwaves, etc.), computers, audio and video equipment, TVs, satellite dishes, car audio systems, tapes, and more. Please note that Percy's does not sell small appliances (toasters or blenders, for example) and that there's no print catalog. However, you can go online to search an extensive list of name-brand products—by model, description, or brand—or you can call or e-mail for available models and items not appearing at the website. Once you know your make or model, call, fax, or e-mail for a price quote. Percy's aims to be competitive and will try to match competitors' prices if you provide all the pertinent information regarding the item, the seller who's offering it, and so forth.

SPECIAL FACTORS: Prices quoted by e-mail, fax, or phone; domestic shipping only; 2% surcharge added to subtotal of all credit card purchases; authorized returns accepted within seven days less 10% restocking fee.

Sewin' In Vermont

84 Concord Ave.   802–748–3803
St. Johnsbury, VT 05819   Fax: 802–748–2165

Brochure: free
Pay: check, MO, MC, V, DSC
Sells: sewing machines and accessories
Store: same address; Monday to Friday 9:30–5, Saturday
9:30–1

Sewin' in Vermont celebrated their twentieth year in business in 1998. It's no wonder they've survived so long. Their prices are "just down-to-earth excellent. No sales. No gimmicks." Here you'll find machines for home and professional sewers: sewing machines by Necchi, Jaguar, and Singer; sergers by Singer and Juki; specialty machines such as blind hemmers, rufflers, and walking-foot machines; and presses. Sewin' in Vermont also sells sewing and craft supplies: threads (embroidery, serger, quilting, etc.); embroidery supplies such as memory cards and computer design discs, embroidery needles, and stabilizers; quilting supplies such as batts, rotary cutters, rulers, and cutting mats; and sewing supplies that include everything form scissors to bobbin boxes. The 24-page catalog also has a good selection of books.

SPECIAL FACTORS: If paying by check, wait 15 days for check to clear before order will be shipped.

Sewing Machine Super Store

9789 Florida Blvd., Dept.
WBM
Baton Rouge, LA 70815

800–739–7374
504–923–1285
Fax: 800–866–1261
Fax: 504–923–1261

Information: price list
Pay: check, MO, MC, V, AE, DSC
Sells: sewing machines, sergers, and embroidery and
  knitting equipment, and accessories
Store: same address; Monday to Friday 9–6 CT
Online: www.allbrands.com

Sewing Machine Super Store, established in 1976, offers its online shoppers such a comprehensive inventory of home and industrial sewing-related machines, important product news, and valuable customer service information that you'll be delighted and eager to deal with the firm, which also happens to have the lowest prices available. When it comes to buying sewing machines (portables or industrials), knitting machines, embroidery machines, irons and presses, and other equipment, you can assume products are new, unless a different status— refurbished (R), demonstrator (D), or closeout (C)—is indicated in the model number, where super deals arc possible. Sewing Machine Super Store also sells cabinets, needles, rotary cutters, shears, dress forms, and design software. Some models come with how-to-use videos or workbooks; other informational materials are available (manufacturers' brochures, product comparisons, consumer reports, and details about warranties, accessories, and parts) by snail mail if you request them. Got a broken Singer? Sewing Machine Super Store is a nationally authorized service center for Singer, Brother, White, Juki, Ba Elna, Passap, Studio, and Toyota sewing, embroidery, and knitting machines. Your order will ship either from inventory or be drop-shipped from the manufacturer or distributor within the U.S. and Canada. International shipping is available, but C.O.D. is available only in the continental U.S.

SPECIAL FACTORS: No minimum order; small orders accepted; all sales final; returns accepted for warranty service and repairs; no exchanges.

Related Products/Companies

Humidifiers, air cleaners
  • Essentials, National Allergy Supply

Major kitchen appliances
- Peerless Restaurant Supplies

Personal-care appliances
- Bennett Brothers, Damark

Sewing machines, sergers, irons
- Atlanta Thread & Supply, Bennett Brothers, Solo Slide Fasteners, Thread Discount Sales

Shortwave radios
- Hidalgo

Small kitchen appliances
- American Health Food, Bennett Brothers, Colonial Garden Kitchens, Comfort House, J&R Music

Televisions
- Crutchfield, J&R Music

Vacuum cleaners, replacement bags
- Bennett Brothers, The Cleaning Center, Damark, J&R Music

Bed, Bath, and Table Textiles

*Soft goods for bedrooms, bathrooms, and tables;
bed and bath accessories*

I have a friend who's always had great sheets—even in the days when we were struggling waitresses fresh out of college. Her sheets had to be of the finest cotton, maximum thread-count per inch, and coordinated with her bedspreads and curtains. I used to think her sheet fetish was extravagant. But now that I'm older—and especially now that I know about the companies in this chapter—I won't sleep on any old sheets myself.

You too will love the firms listed here, which can save you 40% and more on soft goods for your bathroom (towels, shower curtains, toilet seat covers, bathmats), bedroom (sheets, comforters, duvet covers, blankets, bed ruffles, mattress pads, pillow shams), and dining room (place mats, tablecloths, table runners, cloth napkins). For other firms that sell household textiles, such as upholstery fabric and curtains, see "Wall and Window Treatments, Decorator Fabrics" page 378, as well as the "Related Products/Companies" listings at the end of this section.

Find It Fast

Bedspreads and Blankets
- Bates Mill Store, BedandBath.com, Eldridge Textiles, Harris Levy, J. Schachter

Custom-Made Soft Goods
- Harris Levy, J. Schachter

Down Comforter and Pillow Refurbishing
- J. Schachter

Sheets
- Bates Mill Store, BedandBath.com, Harris Levy, J. Schachter

Table Linens
- Bates Mill Store, BedandBath.com, Eldridge Textiles, Harris Levy

Towels and Bathroom Soft Goods
- Bates Mill Store, BedandBath.com, Eldridge Textiles, Harris Levy, J. Schachter

Bates Mill Store

P.O. Box 591
Lewiston, ME 04232-0591

207-784-7626
800-552-2837
Fax: 207-784-2598

Brochure: free
Pay: check, MO, MC, V
Sells: cotton bedspreads, blankets, sheets, throws, towels, etc.
Showroom: Bates Mill Complex on Canal Street, Lewiston; Monday to Friday 9-4, Saturday 9-1
Online: www.batesbedspreads.com

The Bates textile mill was built in 1850 in Lewiston, Maine. The first bedspread was woven in 1858, and since then Bates has become world famous for their bedspreads, still made by old-fashioned standards of quality using the best of old and new weaving methods and technology. Because you're buying directly from the factory, you'll save a lot on these bedspreads, as well as other items they manufacture such as coverlets, blankets, sheets, towels, table linens, and more.

The full-color glossy brochure shows the current line of cotton bedspreads, among them "America's First," fashioned after the aristocratic woven bedspreads found in Colonial American mansions; "Elizabethan Court," a true matelassé reproduction of a museum piece from the Elizabethan era; and "Heritage," a 19th-century design with a puffed pattern like the originals that were padded and stitched by hand. There's also a beautifully plain 100% cotton bedspread called the "Ripplet"—a real bargain and a perfect year-round blanket cover. Describing these bedspreads hardly does them justice. Bates considers their more elaborate bedspreads so special that they issue a certificate of ownership guaranteeing authenticity and keep the owner's name in a permanent registry. All bedspreads are machine washable and come in the standard four mattress sizes and in a variety of colors. If you're looking for the deal of the century, look into the bedspread seconds, available in most styles and marked down about 40% from the already outstanding prices. Swatches for all bedspreads are available on request. The brochure shows bedspreads only, but Bates also manufactures other woven goods, such as 250-thread-count cotton sheets, tablecloths, towels, and other soft goods, about which they welcome inquiries. The website has some photographs of bedspreads that you might want to check out, but there's no online ordering.

SPECIAL FACTORS: No exchanges or credits given on merchandise kept over 14 days that's been used or washed; shipments made via UPS.

BedandBath.com

12817 Preston Rd., Ste. 128	800–945–7714
Dallas, TX 75230	972–239–5336
	Fax: 972–239–8542

Information: website only, no print catalog
Pay: V, MC, AE, DSC
Sells: bed and bath textiles
Store: Juncture of Preston Road and LBJ Freeway (US
   635), Monday to Saturday 10–8, Sunday 12–5 CT
Online: www.bedandbath.com

I love websites that feature consumer feedback. At BedandBath.com you'll get a sense of glowing consumer contentment with the goods, quality of service, and prices offered here. This is an online merchant that sells bedroom items (bedding ensembles, sheets, comforters and comforter sets, bed ruffles, bed pillows, mattress pads and covers); bathroom items (fashion bath ensembles, towels, bath rugs, shower curtains, mirrors and other accessories); window treatments (kitchen curtains, panels, hard window treatments, top treatments, window hardware); kitchen and tabletop goods (tablecloths, place mats and runners, kitchen towels); and home decor items (decorative pillows, candles, area rugs, lamps) at prices as low as I've seen anywhere.

The merchandise—all top-name brands—is beautiful and easily viewed by clicking on broad category, or by searching by brand or by product type. Bed andBath.com guarantees their prices are lowest or they'll refund the difference plus 5%. In addition to the great selection at discounted prices, the website features clearance items and "Deal of the Week" goods that are stupendous values. Here's an online shop definitely worth checking out. And there's a real Bedand Bath.com store and warehouse in Dallas, with human beings who can answer your questions when you call during business hours.

SPECIAL FACTORS: Satisfaction guaranteed or you may return your purchase for a refund for any reason within 60 days of receipt.

Eldridge Textile Co.

17 E. 37th St.
New York, NY 10016

212–925–1523
Fax: 212–219–9542

Catalog: $3, refundable
Pay: check, MO, MC, V, DSC
Sells: bed, bath, and window textiles
Store: same address; Sunday to Friday 9–5
Online: www.eldridgetextile.com

Since 1940 Eldridge Textile Company has been selling fashions for the home—linens, comforters, curtains, towels, and other bed and bath textiles such as mattress pads, throw pillows, bed skirts, and upholstered headboards—at the guaranteed lowest prices, and well below white sale prices. You can save up to 40% on goods by major manufacturers such as Croscill, Wamsutta, Laura Ashley, Veratex, Bonjour Linens, Royal Sateen, Bay Linens, Martex, Charisma Sheets and Towels, Royal Velvet, Thomasville, Westpoint Stevens, Regal, Ellen Tracy, Fieldcrest Towels, and Crown Crafts, among others. The gorgeous $3 catalog is refundable with your first order. Or you can check out the website, which features monthly specials and promotions, has online ordering, and includes color photographs and detailed product descriptions. If you don't see what you're looking for in either place, call. Eldridge will do their best to accommodate all requests.

SPECIAL FACTORS: Price quote by phone or letter with SASE; return of unused goods accepted within 30 days for refund or credit.

Harris Levy, Inc.

278 Grand St., Dept. WBM
New York, NY 10002

800–221–7750
212–226–3102
Fax: 212–334–9360

Catalog: $2, refundable
Pay: check, MO, MC, V, AE
Sells: luxury bed, bath, and table linens; bath, kitchen, and
closet accessories
Store: same address; Sunday to Friday 9–5
E-mail: harrislevy@aol.com

Harris Levy, a revered firm that's been around since 1894, sells exceptionally fine bed, bath, and table linens at prices up to 60% less than what they sell for at luxury linen stores. This company searches the world over for one-of-a-kind items that will last a lifetime in your home. One might characterize Harris Levy's goods as "luxury for less" or "upscale on sale." We're not talking about sheets you buy at the mall; the soft goods here are items such as heirloom tablecloths from Ireland, imported bed linens from France, and fine kitchen towels from England. Custom sewing, embroidery, and custom-sized sheets, bedding, and tablecloths are a specialty here. Mail-order shoppers can call or write for the catalog, or call for price quotes on bed and bath linens from the major manufacturers. The catalog gives a sampling of Harris Levy's large selection of towels, pillows, down comforters, tablecloths, place mats, cocktail napkins, decorative pillows, mattress pads, bath and clothes accessories, shower curtains, and rugs.

SPECIAL FACTORS: Information and price quote by phone, fax, or letter; swatch and thread color sent by mail when available.

J. Schachter Corp.

5 Cook St.
Brooklyn, NY 11206

800–INTO–BED
718–384–2732
Fax: 718–384–7634

Information: price quote
Pay: check, MO, MC, V
Sells: down-filled bedding, linens, and custom services
Store: same address; Monday to Thursday 9–5, Friday 9–1

J. Schachter has been manufacturing high-end down comforters and pillows for the bedding industry and refurbishing old ones since 1919. We're not talking about $99 mass-produced comforters; the ones manufactured here are lifelong investments. Off the record the owner told me which stores buy his comforters to resell under their labels. I'm sworn to secrecy, but I can tell you they're the crème de la crème of New York's department stores; the same $700 comforter at one of those stores can be bought factory-direct under the J. Schachter label for at least 40% less. Before the advent of the yuppies' throwaway culture, people used to spend a lot on best-quality down comforters and pillows. These "old-timers" still return to J. Schachter to have their pillows, sofa cushions, and comforters restuffed while they wait; the cost is far less than buying a new one of the same quality.

The other portion of Schachter's business is being a dealer of sheets, towels, and bedding (yes, this includes inexpensive down comforters manufactured by others) from the major U.S. linen mills, including but not limited to Fieldcrest, Cannon, Stevens, Wamsutta, Burlington, Palais Royal, Hudson Bay, Sybil Shepard, Thomasville, Nacy Koltes, Faribo, Fino Lino, and many others. Since there's no print catalog, shop around in your local stores. When you see what you want, call, fax, or write to J. Schachter with the brand, size, and color or pattern and they'll be glad to give you a price quote. J. Schachter's price will save you 25% to 40% off retail. This type of shopping takes more time than just looking at a catalog and making one call. On the other hand, if you're making some major purchases for your bed and bath, the extra legwork could end up saving you hundreds of dollars on a large purchase. It's well worth your while to call the nice people at J. Schachter. They've been in the biz for a long time and know how to deliver old-fashioned value in a highly competitive market.

SPECIAL FACTORS: Know the brand and style of goods before you call for a price quote; store closed Saturdays and Sundays.

Related Products/Companies

Acrylic bathroom and household accessories
- Plexi-Craft

Allergen-free pillows and bedding
- National Allergy Supply

Baby sheets and blankets
- Baby Bunz, Chock, Rubens & Marble

Bath and sleeping aids
- Comfort House

Bed and bath organizers
- Colonial Garden Kitchens

Bedding feathers
- Gettinger Feather

Bedspreads
- BMI Home Decorating, Shama Imports

Cardboard tubes for storing tablecloths wrinkle-free
- Yazoo Mills

Custom fabric lamination for tablecloths
- Hancock's of Paducah

Custom-made headboards
- BMI Home Decorating

Extra-wide blanket flannel
- Gohn Bros.

Mattresses
- Cole's Appliance and Furniture, EBA Wholesale, Loftin-Black, Priba Furniture, Quality Furniture Market, Southland Furniture Galleries

Old-fashioned bathroom fixtures
- Baths from the Past

Pillow ticking and pillow forms
- Buffalo Batt and Felt, Gohn Bros., Hancock's of Paducah

Sheets, pillows, blankets, down comforters
- BMI Home Decorating, Clothcrafters, Damark, Gohn Bros., National Allergy Supply, Sierra Trading Post, The Ultimate Outlet

Sleeping bags
- Campmor, Sierra Trading Post

Table pads
- Factory Direct Table Pad Co.

Table skirting and table linens
- Clothcrafters, Kitchen Etc., Peerless, Shama Imports

Towels
- Clothcrafters

Waffle-foam bed pads
- Essentials

Wool and mohair throws and blankets
- Mangham Manor Fiber Farm

Building, Renovation, and Upkeep

Materials for designing, improving, maintaining,
and cleaning your home

This section features all kinds of great companies every home owner will want to know about. Whether you're looking to build a new home, spruce up your old one, or just find a way to keep your house clean, you'll find firms here that sell house plans, plumbing supplies, old-timey bathroom fixtures, screen doors and shutters, cleaning supplies and gadgets, and more. If you're up against a project and wish you had a handy uncle you could call for advice, log onto www.readers digest.com and "Ask the Family Handyman." There are hundreds of free articles you can read with tips, tips, and more tips on just about every subject you can come up with related to home renovation and maintenance. Great!

Be sure to refer to this section's "Related Products/Companies" for more firms that sell handyman supplies such as shop tools, plumbing supplies, wood-working hardware and tools, house paints, fence panels, wood flooring, and more. And if you're focusing on the interior of your house, all the other sections of this "Home" chapter will have what you're looking for: flooring, furniture, appliances, kitchen accessories, lighting, wallpaper, shades, upholstery fabric, and tableware.

Thinking of building a home? The Shelter Institute in Bath, Maine, offers a wide variety of classes for individuals and couples who want to do it themselves. (It's a great way to combine learning with a gorgeous summertime getaway.) The Institute leads hands-on courses of varying length on just about every aspect of home design and building. For more information on the Institute, visit their website (www.shelterinstitute.com); call them at 207–442–7938; or write to Shelter Institute, 38 Center St., Bath, ME 04530.

Find It Fast

Bathroom and Kitchen Hardware and Fixtures
- Baths from the Past, The Faucet Outlet

Cleaning Supplies
- The Cleaning Center

Doors, Windows, Glass Panels, and Components
- Arctic Glass, Oregon Wooden Screen Door

Floor-Plan and 3-D Model Kits for Building
- Design Works

House Plans and Kits
- GeoDomes Woodworks

House Shutters and Shutter Supplies
- Shuttercraft

Arctic Glass & Window Outlet

565 County Rd. T
Hammond, WI 54015

800–428–9276
715–796–2291
Fax: 715–796–2295

Catalog: $4, refundable
Pay: MO, MC, V, DSC
Sells: exterior doors, windows, skylights, sunroom glass
Store: I–94 at Hammond Exit, 35 miles east of St. Paul,
MN; also 1232 W. Clairemont Ave., Eau Claire, WI;
Monday to Thursday 8–8, Friday 8–5, Saturday 9–5

Behind every company there's an interesting tale or two. When you receive a catalog from Artic Glass & Window, you'll also get to read the whole charming story, "How We Got Here." I won't give up all the good parts, but the gist of it is this: When the Bacons moved from Alaska to western Wisconsin, one thing led to another, and they ended up with a truckload of surplus glass. More than two decades later, the Bacons' family-owned business has customers in 49 out of the 50 states. "We supply the highest quality product available at the lowest possible price," according to their brochure. They also offer free design advice if you need it, as well as generous returns and warranty policies.

Arctic Glass & Window sells tempered insulated glass panes that can be used in workshops, sunrooms, offices, storefronts—even barns and chicken coops. Besides bringing in more sunlight, which is known to help fight wintertime depression, these glass units contribute passive solar heat. In the Bacon's own home, heated by wood stove, their wood consumption went from 15 cords per year down to three when they added their sunroom. You can buy both seconds and surplus panes here. The surplus panes have no defects; the seconds have minor visual imperfections, such as a fingerprint between the panes or a slight dimple or scratch, imperceptible from five feet away. Both units carry the same ten-year seal warranty. In addition to glass, the Outlet also sells Kolbe & Kolbe aluminum-clad doors and Velux roof windows and skylights. The brochures you'll receive have clear instructions and detailed information about storing, transporting, and installing, and the staff is willing to answer any other questions.

SPECIAL FACTORS: Quantity discounts available; minimum crating charge is $40; returns accepted up to a year after sale for full refund or credit, provided panes have not been installed and are in salable condition.

Baths from the Past, Inc.

83 E. Water St.
Rockland, MA 02370

800–697–3871
781–871–8530
Fax: 781–871–8533

Catalog: free
Pay: check, MO, MC, V, DSC
Sells: bathroom and kitchen hardware
Store: same address; Monday to Friday 9–5

Is your bathroom the most ignored room in your house? Thumbing through the 40-page color catalog from Baths from the Past, I was struck by how little it would take to jazz up my old claw-foot tub or pedestal porcelain sink.

Baths from the Past makes it affordable to buy authentic-looking brass faucets, porcelain showerheads, telephone-style tub fillers, or old-fashioned shower systems at prices up to 30% below other sources for comparable quality. Whether you're going for Deco Edwardian or Victorian, you'll find a sink, commode, tub, faucet, bath accessories, shower fittings, and other related items to complete or enhance the look you're after. Baths from the Past has been in business since 1981, and offers warranties on all items and finishes (details outlined in catalog).

SPECIAL FACTORS: Satisfaction guaranteed; returns accepted for refund or exchange within 30 days of receipt, but see catalog for details.

The Cleaning Center

P.O. Box 39, Dept. WC
Pocatello, ID 83204

208–232–6212
Fax: 208–232–6286

Catalog: free
Pay: check, MO, MC, V, DSC
Sells: cleaning tools and products
Store: 311 S. 5th Ave., Pocatello, ID; Monday to Saturday 9–6
Online: www.cleanreport.com

Everyone has a gift. Don Aslett, president of The Cleaning Center, has found his niche as "America's number one cleaning expert" and travels the media circuit donning his famous toilet briefcase and preaching cleanliness. Author of many best-selling books on every aspect of cleaning, organizing, and decluttering, Mr. Aslett is a motivator, which you'll immediately grasp from the perky catalog text. You'll be treated to delightful prose on the company's history, the full selection of Aslett's books, and an inventory that includes the best in buckets, sponges, cleaning cloths, gloves, dusters, squeegees, vacuums, mops, cleaning-supply organizers, brushes, and of course his famous brand cleaners for everything from toilets to rugs to tiles to wood. All of the cleaning products are highly concentrated and, therefore, extremely economical if used correctly. The gadgets and items have all been hand-selected by Aslett, who appears to know more about this subject that anyone else. Price checks on similar items show The Cleaning Center to be 20% or more less than comparable name-brand products.

SPECIAL FACTORS: Satisfaction guaranteed; returns accepted for exchange, refund, or credit.

Design Works, Inc.

11 Hitching Post Rd.   **413–549–4763**
Amherst, MA 01002

Information and Flyers: free (see text)
Pay: check, MO, MC, V, AE
Sells: reusable peel-and-stick furniture and architectural
   symbols and 3-D model kits for home-building
Store: mail order only
Online: www.homeplanner.com

If you've ever tried to plan a new home, addition, or remodeling project, you know the hardest parts are organizing the floor plans and visualizing your ideas in three dimensions. Design Works has come up with a unique (and inexpensive) solution. In business for close to two decades, owner Dan Reif has developed two ingenious products. With the Home Quick Planner, for $22.95, you receive 700 precut, reusable, peel-and-stick furniture and architectural symbols, plus a quarter-inch floor plan grid, to plan a home up to approximately 2,000 square feet. Go ahead: Knock down walls, move furniture and fixtures, put in too many windows and bathrooms—you can always change your mind later for free. A Deluxe version for $10 more has additional symbols that make the Planner suitable for floor plans up to approximately 5,000 square feet. There are also separate Quick Planners just for Kitchen, Bathroom, Office, or Interior Design.

The 3-D Home Kit ($33.95) lets you visualize your dream house, sunroom, or new wing in three dimensions. You can use the kit's printed posterboard building materials—from brick, stone, siding, roofing, and decking to windows, doors, skylights, kitchen cabinets, and appliances—to construct a detailed quarter-inch scale model of your own design up to approximately 2,000 square feet. There are also materials for interior walls, stairs, floor plan—even scale people and pets! (The Deluxe version of the 3-D Home Kit has materials for up to 5,000 square feet and costs $43.95.) Both 3-D Home Kits include a "Hands-on Design and Math" booklet to help you solve some common design problems: for example, how to calculate the minimum size for windows, design the roof and calculate its slope, and determine the amount of paint, paneling, or concrete needed. Whether you're teaching architecture to students or daydreaming about how you'll spend that lottery win, this will be a fun and illuminating project.

The website is really fun to visit but also helpful if you're having trouble conceptualizing how these kits are used. There you'll get to see photographs of actual house plans and models assembled, and see other examples of how one might use the kits for interior design, educational projects, and decorating. You can order the kits right on the website.

SPECIAL FACTORS: Shipping and handling is $4.00 for the basic Quick Planner, $5 for all other kits; call for information, or visit the website.

The Faucet Outlet

P.O. Box 547   800–444–5783
Middletown, NY 10940   Fax: 914–343–1617

Catalog: $2 (see text)
Pay: check, MO, MC, V
Sells: bathroom and kitchen fixtures
Store: mail order only; phone hours Monday to Friday 8–6
   ET
Online: www.faucet.com

The Faucet Outlet publishes a 32-page catalog featuring a sampling of products and providing service information and a lowest-price guarantee. But to browse the *entire* inventory of price specials, clearance items, and new products, you might want to visit the website, which also offers a link to another discount product site, The Lighting Outlet. Either site offers an e-mail subscription to *Light Talk* or *Faucet Talk*.

The Faucet Outlet specializes in faucets, fixtures, and home-improvement products for kitchen and bath including fans, intercoms, medicine cabinets, bath cabinets, whirlpools, and door chimes. On the website you'll find clearance items that are a whopping 35% below list price. Keep in mind that plumbing fixtures must meet local code requirements and be compatible with plumbing you already have.

Special to WMO readers: Your catalog will be $2 rather than $4 if you mention this book.

SPECIAL FACTORS: Authorized returns accepted; everything sold is covered by manufacturers' warranties; price quotes by phone, letter, or e-mail; mention WMO when requesting catalog.

GeoDomes Woodworks

6876 Indiana Ave.
Box 4141, Division W
Riverside, CA 92514–4141

909–787–8800
Fax: 909–787–7089

Catalog and Planning Guide: $15
Pay: V, MC (for catalog)
Sells: color-coded geodesic-dome Custom Home Kits
Store: website and mail-order only; phone hours Monday
to Friday 9–5 PST
Online: www.geodomesinc.com

Did you know that a GeoDome Custom Home—the designs of which are based on the geodesic dome invented by Buckminster Fuller—has 30% to 50% less surface area, and thus saves its inhabitants 50% or more on heating and cooling costs? Add to this the dramatic savings you'll reap by building your own home using color-coded kits made by GeoDomes Woodworks and you've got yourself a real deal. So inspired was I by the photographs of actual homes, thoughtful text, and interesting variations on floor plans presented on the website that I'm seriously considering one of these kits for myself.

Don't be ready to dismiss a GeoDome before you look at the examples shown on the website. There you'll see that this ingenious company has created designs that are pleasing, practical, permanent, and can be assembled just like Tinker Toys. Each GeoHub flange is color-coded to correspond to the correct framing member. Simply by matching colors and bolting the framing members to the GeoHubs, your new home takes shape before your very eyes. The plans range from elegant multiple-dome clusters to simple vacation homes. Fully original plans can also be developed for you. The first step is to order the "GeoDomes Catalog and Planning Guide": For $15 you receive a 150-page catalog that presents stunning interior and exterior photos, planning information, specifications on energy efficiency, and retail pricing including cost per square foot of each model offered, custom options, and all material specifications. Included in the package is the "GeoDomes Architectural Plans Book" showing dozens of floor plans from 400 to 10,000 square feet, one- and two-level, with or without basement, etc. You also get the 20-page "GeoDomes Product, Options, and Services" booklet with detailed illustrations of the GeoDome shell, five package levels to choose from, and line-by-line material listings. There's more, but my advice is that you visit the website first, then call or e-mail if you have more specific questions. As the folks at GeoDomes say, it doesn't cost anything to answer your questions. There's a form right on the website to leave your e-mail address or phone number so a rep can get back to you.

SPECIAL FACTORS: GeoDomes Woodworks maintains on-staff architectural ability and has the capability to certify for all 50 states.

Oregon Wooden Screen Door Company

2767 Harris St., Dept. WBM   541–485–0279
Eugene, OR 97405   Fax: 541–484–0353

> Brochure and Price List: $3
> Pay: check, MO, MC, V
> Sells: wooden screen and storm doors
> Store: same address

The specialty of Oregon Wooden Screen Door Company is obvious in its name. That dedication to wooden screen doors has created 30 door styles in categories dubbed "Ornamental," "Classic," "Muscular," and "Designer's Collection," any of which can be modified with spandrels, brackets, and other hardware. Doors have their own character depending on their design, be it simple or more ornate and complex. The doors sold here are constructed of quarter-inch-thick vertical-grain fir, strengthened and made warp resistant with mortise-and-tenon and dowel joinery. For seasonal changes, screen and storm inserts (both wood-framed) are available, primed with wood preservative in a finish of your choosing. The final touch—solid brass hardware—can be ordered from Oregon Wooden Screen Door or from your favorite shop. Prices for doors range from $200 for a kit to several hundred. To custom-order a door or to discuss questions you may have about choosing a design, give the staff a call.

SPECIAL FACTORS: Authorized returns accepted.

Shuttercraft, Inc.

282 Stepstone Hill Rd., Dept.　　**203–453–1973**
WBM　　　　　　　　　　　　**Fax: 203–245–5969**
Guilford, CT 06437

　　Brochures and Price Lists: free
　　Pay: check, MO, MC, V
　　Sells: interior and exterior house shutters and hardware
　　Store: same address; Monday to Friday 9–5
　　Online: www.galaxymall.com/shops/shuttercraft.html

Details, details. What makes your house different from every other one on the block? Details such as authentic exterior wood shutters with movable louvers. You can get them by mail through Shuttercraft at prices well below those charged elsewhere for custom-milled shutters. Shuttercraft offers wood shutters for the exterior and interior of your house, both with movable louvers. The exterior shutters, made of western red cedar, are appropriate for restoring vintage homes, public buildings, or dressing up your new house. Because they're naturally venting they won't cause the wood behind them to rot. The interior shutters, also known as plantation style, are made of both pine and poplar parts; oil- and water-based stains can be applied to these. Interior shutters are popular for living and dining rooms, sunrooms, porches, and as room dividers. Shuttercraft also sells raised-panel shutters and fixed-louver shutters for exteriors, combination panel/louver models, shutters with cut-out designs, shaped panels (gothic arches, half-circle tops, etc.), shutters designed for fabric-panel inserts, and all sorts of shutter hardware practical and decorative. Sample shutters are available for $20, refundable upon return. The website is worth a look because there you'll be able to view much of the inventory, get a good idea about Shuttercraft's commitment to quality and value, and e-mail the company for a brochure or to get fast price quotes on your windows.

SPECIAL FACTORS: Free shipping on shutters 60 inches and under; painting services available; 50% deposit required when ordering; price quotes by phone, fax, or e-mail.

Related Products/Companies

Bamboo and other tropical fencing
* Frank's Cane and Rush

Cabinetry and other hardware
- William Alden, Camelot Enterprises, H&R Company, Tool Crib of the North, Woodworker's Supply

Central vacuum systems
- ABC Vacuum Cleaner Warehouse

Cleaning supplies
- Cal Ben Soap Company, Colonial Garden Kitchens, Defender, EDGE Distributing, Enco Manufacturing, Drs. Foster & Smith, Jaffe Bros., Jeffers Pet Supply, KV Vet Supply, Lehman's, National Allergy Supply, Omaha Vaccine, Reliable, That Fish/Pet Place, UPCO

Cotton and flannel cleaning cloths
- Clothcrafters

Do-it-yourself books and manuals
- Poor Man's Catalog, Reader's Digest, Woodworkers Discount Books

Electric-free water heaters, solar panels and components, composting toilets, etc.
- Lehman's

Floor-care machines and supplies
- AAA Vacuums, ABC Vacuum Cleaner Warehouse

Garbage disposals
- Percy's

Greenhouse supplies
- Bob's Superstrong Greenhouse Plastic, Mellinger's, Turner Greenhouses

Home safes
- Discount Safe

House paint and supplies
- Pearl Paint

Lighting and wiring supplies
- All Electronics

Lumber, wood paneling, molding, flooring inlays
- Beaver Hardwood, Prestige Carpets

Plastic sheeting for storm windows, pool covers, greenhouses, etc.
- Bob's Superstrong Greenhouse Plastic

Professional shop and handyman tools
- William Alden, Enco Manufacturing, Harbor Freight Tools, Tool Crib of the North

Replacement parts for chandeliers
- King's Chandelier

Screen doors and window screens
- Coppa Woodworking

Sheepskin wash and dust mitts
- Sheepskin Station

Sliding pet doors
- Patio Pacific

Swimming pool maintenance supplies and equipment
- Water Warehouse

Teak-care products
- Defender

Weathervanes
- Cook's

Wood-burning furnaces and heaters
- Lehman's, Manufacturer's Supply

Flooring

Hardwood flooring, Oriental and other area rugs, carpeting, vinyl floor coverings, padding, and tiles

How is it possible to save money by purchasing a huge item such as carpeting or hardwood flooring by mail? Here's how: Many of the firms in this section are either flooring manufacturers themselves or get their goods directly from the mill. Special relationships with trucking companies allow them to move very large items at low cost to you. You're saving on tax as well as the normal retailer markup, and all of this can translate into savings of 50% on large rugs and wall-to-wall carpeting, normally one of the biggest single expenses in redecorating a room. Whatever your flooring preference—from gorgeous colonial-style plugged cherry-and-walnut floors to handwoven Oriental runners—you'll find it here for a lot less.

For information on carpet installation, maintenance, and stain removal call The Carpet and Rug Institute's toll-free information line at 800–882–8846. Their website is exceedingly useful too (www.carpet-rug.com). Not only are there great articles about the care and maintenance of rugs, how to choose carpet, carpet and the environment, and more, but here you'll find the Spot Removal Computer. This is a real find. Search for a stain in the alphabetized list of hundreds and then click on it. You'll get a succinct but detailed, step-by-step solution to your particular rug or carpet stain. It's a gold mine of free information.

For more firms selling flooring and related supplies, read "Related Products/ Companies" at the end of this section.

Find It Fast

Carpeting and Area Rugs
- Bearden Bros., Prestige Carpets, S&S Mills, Warehouse Carpets

New and Antique Oriental Rugs
- Charles Jacobsen, Wall Rug & Carpets

Vinyl Flooring
- Bearden Bros., Prestige Carpets, Warehouse Carpets

Wood Flooring
- Beaver Hardwood Flooring, Prestige Carpets

Bearden Bros. Carpet & Textiles Corp.

4109 S. Dixie Hwy., Dept.   800–433–0074
BWBM   888–BEARDEN
Dalton, GA 30721   Fax: 706–277–1754

    Catalog: $4 (see text)
    Pay: check, MO, MC, V, AE, DSC
    Sells: carpeting, rugs, padding, and vinyl flooring
    Store: same address; Monday to Friday 8:30–6

Family-owned and -operated Bearden Brothers Carpet is in Dalton, Georgia, the "Carpet Capital of the World." This company offers a wide selection of carpets, vinyl, tile, and wood floor coverings, as well as carpet cushion—all from the best-known manufacturers, factory-direct to you. The savings are substantial, and they'll ship door-to-door. The shipping fees, estimated in one of the brochures I reviewed, are surprisingly inexpensive—averaging 60 cents a square yard, depending on where you live.

Here's how it works. If you find and price a carpet or vinyl locally, call Bearden Brothers and they'll get you the identical product and price it for you when you call their toll-free number. Just provide them with the manufacturer and style number, as well as the square yards needed. You can also send a sample and they'll try to match it. They can send carpet samples to you or a catalog with beautiful color photographs, regularly $4, but only $2 for WMO readers who mention this listing. The catalog features area rugs—hand-hooked, woven, Oriental, braided, and more. Bearden has thrived in the competitive carpet business by providing top-quality goods and by saving customers a "considerable amount off any retail price, guaranteed!"

SPECIAL FACTORS: Payment must be received prior to shipment; satisfaction guaranteed; all floor coverings come with factory warranties; quantity discounts available.

Beaver Hardwood Flooring Systems

1182 South Service Road West   877–693–WOOD
Oakville ON, L6L 2X8 Canada

Information: website only, no print catalog
Pay: check, MO, AE, V
Sells: prefinished hardwood flooring
Store: mail order only
Online: www.beaverfloor.com

Beaver Hardwood Flooring Systems, a manufacturer of prefinished hardwood flooring, sells and ships BeaverFloor directly to you, the consumer, thus eliminating two middlemen: the regional flooring distributor and the local flooring retailer, whose presence results in twice-inflated prices. Why *prefinished?* Simple, according to the company. The quality and clarity of the finish they apply is unsurpassed and impossible to replicate by sanding and finishing hardwood flooring on site. They liken it to the beautiful finishes applied at the factory to automobiles, with controlled atmospheric conditions that create clear and flawless coats. You'll find flooring made of ash (stained chestnut, golden, walnut, or white-washed), cherry (stained brandywine, chestnut, or walnut), hard maple (stained golden, natural, or whitewash), red oak natural, and white oak stained chestnut. Beaver also manufactures gorgeous authentic colonial-style plugged floors (cherry, red oak, or maple with walnut plugs; or walnut with maple plugs) and engineered flooring. Besides great products at great prices, what more could you ask for? How about free samples, excellent customer service, and consumer-friendly guarantees? The hardwood flooring Beaver produces is sourced from mills that practice sustained harvest techniques; the urethane, stains, and sealers used are water-based and environmentally friendly. To find out more about this company and their prefinished hardwood flooring, and to read testimonials by happy customers from California to New Jersey, check out the excellent website. There you can also e-mail an order for free flooring samples and read about the durability and economy of Beaver's hardwood flooring.

SPECIAL FACTORS: See website for warranty policies; all shipments made from Buffalo, NY; all funds in U.S. dollars; phones are manned 24 hours a day.

Charles W. Jacobsen, Inc.

Learbury Center
401 N. Salina St., Dept.
BWBM
Syracuse, NY 13203–1773

315–422–7832
Fax: 315–422–6909

Catalog: free
Pay: check, MO, MC, V, DSC
Sells: new and antique Oriental rugs
Store: same address; Monday to Saturday 10–5, Monday
   and Thursday 10–8; also 268 Broadway, Saratoga
   Springs, NY, Tuesday to Saturday 9–5, Thursday 9–8,
   Sunday 12–5
Online: www.jacobsenrugs.com

This employee-owned company has been selling fine Oriental rugs since 1924 at prices kept surprisingly low. The beautiful 26-page catalog shows photographs of dozens of rugs from the more than 8,000-rug collection. Jacobsen buys the rugs directly from the countries where the rugs are woven, then imports them to his Syracuse showroom. Doing business this way eliminates the middleman; coupled with large-volume sales, the net effect saves the consumer money.

You'll find genuine, handwoven rugs of recent vintage from India, Pakistan, Turkey, Afghanistan, Iran, Nepal, and China. Sizes vary depending on the type of rug, but range from 2 by 3 feet to some as large as 12 by 20 feet. Both the catalog and website include lots of information about the unique characteristics of different rug-making regions and styles, history of rug-weaving, parts of an Oriental rug, information on looms and design, the ins and outs of judging rug quality, and more. Since Jacobsen wants you to be satisfied, you'll fill out a questionnaire, after which a company representative will write you back with details and colored slides of rugs available that seem to fit your needs. Once you've made your selection, you can have the rug sent on approval to see how it fits in its new surroundings. At the website you can also view Rugs on Sale, which are further discounted around 20%.

SPECIAL FACTORS: Satisfaction guaranteed; rugs sent on approval require you to first fill out a credit form and/or submit a deposit.

Prestige Carpets, Inc.

P.O. Box 516
Dalton, GA 30722

800–887–6807, ext. 100
706–217–6640
Fax: 706–217–2429

Brochure: free
Pay: check, MO, MC, V, AE, DSC
Sells: carpeting, vinyl and wood flooring, area rugs, and
   padding
Store: mail order only

Prestige sells its own line of residential and commercial carpeting that's guaranteed against stains and wear just like the national brands—all at wholesale prices. Carpet samples are available showing the range of colors, fiber content, guarantees, and so on for each style. They also offer custom area rugs, which can be produced to match wallpaper and furniture. In addition to their own brand, Prestige has access to about 95% of all carpet mills and flooring manufacturers to get you great deals on carpet, vinyl, and wood lines at prices up to 80% below those charged at retail outlets and department stores. Your best bet is to contact Prestige by phone, fax, or mail once you've decided on your flooring and get a price quote. You'll need to provide the manufacturer's name, the style number and name, and square yardage. Padding, adhesives, and tack strips for installation are also available. Prestige doesn't publish a catalog, but at press time they were promising a website would be up and running soon.

SPECIAL FACTORS: A deposit is required when you place your order, and final payment must be made before shipment (common carrier is used); both residential and commercial carpeting needs are served here; phone hours are Monday to Friday 8–6.

S&S Mills

P.O. Box 1568
Dalton, GA 30722

706–277–3677
800–241–4013
Fax: 706–277–3922

Catalog: free
Pay: check, MO, V, MC
Sells: carpet and padding
Showroom: 200 Howell Dr., Dalton, GA; Monday to Friday
8–5 EST

S&S Mills Carpet manufactures carpeting and sells and ships it factory-direct to consumers. The stunning 32-page color catalog shows plushes, berbers, and high-traffic commercial carpeting in beautiful colors and styles. Helpful text describes the pros and cons of different carpet styles, how to choose the right cushioning, trade secrets regarding carpeting materials and workmanship, and other information for novice carpet shoppers. Once you've looked at the catalog, a free sample book is a toll-free call away, and carpet specialists can answer your questions every day of the week. S&S is committed to saving you time and money, and to making carpet-buying a convenient, hassle-free experience.

SPECIAL FACTORS: Satisfaction guaranteed; all carpeting comes with a warranty; free Installers Referral Network available for your area; toll-free phone is manned 24 hours, seven days/week.

Wall Rug & Carpets

3719 Battleground Ave.
Greensboro, NC 27410

800–877–1955
336–545–6899
Fax: 336–545–6524

Brochure: free
Pay: check, MO, MC, V
Sells: reproduction Oriental rugs
Store: same address

Wall Rug & Carpets is the distributor for Mastercraft Imports, Ltd. and Karastan—two of the finest machine-made area rug lines in the world. These rugs combine the beauty of classic Oriental design with the long-lasting comfort and performance of New Zealand wool. Best of all, these stunning reproductions are priced affordably—about 50% less than the handwoven versions—so as to be available to regular consumers and not just the world's nobility.

Great care is taken in the manufacture of these rugs to make them as close to the originals as possible. The Karastans, for example, start with 100% worsted New Zealand wool, the traditional fiber of fine Orientals, and each color is individually skein-dyed in the yarn. The modern-day looms are designed to capture the luxury of the handwoven originals. Once woven, the rugs are "lustre-washed" in much the same way the native weavers of antiquity washed their creations; finally, the damp rug is buffed with the "Sultan's Slipper," bundles of old wool drawn across the surface to impart a rich patina to the finish. The beautiful rugs sold by Wall Rug & Carpets are above all practical, unlike their priceless, handwoven counterparts, with warmth, comfort, dirt resistance, wearability, and affordability at the forefront.

SPECIAL FACTORS: All rugs are guaranteed; inquire about return policy; call to get price quotes and delivery information.

Here's another example of a place that rewards consumers who do some of the footwork themselves. Warehouse Carpets has been around for more than 15 years and specializes in serving mail-order customers through direct home delivery. They ship only first-quality carpets from the following manufacturers: Queens Carpet, Mohawk, Shaw Salemcarpets, Diamond Rug and Carpet, Coronet Carpets, Horizon, Downs, and Mannington, among others. There's an informational brochure that basically tells you to shop around for the carpet you want, then call Warehouse Carpet's toll-free number, or fax or write them, with the manufacturer's name and the style name to receive a price quote. Savings on carpeting here run up to 50%, so it's worth the trouble.

SPECIAL FACTORS: A 50% deposit is required when order is placed, with the balance due before shipment; all carpet shipped via common carrier.

Related Products/Companies

Area rugs and carpeting
- BedandBath.com, Carolina Interiors, Ellenburg's Furniture, The Furniture Patch of Calabash, Harris Levy, Priba Furniture, Southland Furniture, The Ultimate Outlet

Carpet-stain removers
- The Cleaning Center

Floor stencils
- Stencil House of N.H.

Rug-weaving supplies and equipment
- Great Northern Weaving

Sheepskin rugs
- Leather Unlimited, Sheepskin Station

Steerhide rugs
- Steerhides

Vacuum cleaners, rug shampooers, floor polishers
- AAA Vacuums, ABC Vacuum Cleaner Warehouse, Discount Appliance Centers, LVT Price Quote Hotline

Furnishings

Household furniture and accessories of all types for house and patio

The companies listed here give new meaning to the term "armchair shopper." You can save as much as 50% on the suggested retail price of furniture of all kinds by sitting back and ordering it directly from North Carolina, the manufacturing center of the furniture industry. Discounters like the ones in this section don't take the staggering markups that make furnishings and home accessories prohibitively expensive in department and furniture stores. So great are the deals in this part of the country that it's not uncommon for people to plan their vacation around furniture shopping. After a week at the North Carolina golf resorts, they hit the showrooms and have a truckload of new furniture shipped home.

Unless you're planning a trip to the area, your choices as a savvy consumer include: finding furniture you like locally and then calling these firms for price quotes, or consulting with the company sales reps for guidance. Most of the firms listed here can supply brochures and swatches, give decorating advice over the phone, and take orders for furniture and accessories from hundreds of manufacturers. Some have gorgeous and elaborate catalogs, the cost of which are refundable when you purchase, others have interactive websites, still others operate solely by price quote. All will deliver real value.

Speaking of delivering, many offer "in-home delivery service"—your furniture will be uncrated exactly where you want it, and if there are damages, you'll see them right away and can contact the company while the shipper is there to find out what to do. In-home delivery is usually made either by the company's own truck or with a moving-van service that's accustomed to handling furnishings. Understand that these companies couldn't be in business if they didn't make buying from them worth your while. You'll pay a lot less here—including shipping—than you will at the local strip mall furniture outlet.

There are also lots of other goodies this section, such as beautiful and functional radiator covers, custom-made table pads, high-tech acrylic bathroom accessories, hand-made wooden baskets, and even steerhides for wall hangings, throw pillows, and rugs.

There are also handsome desks, bookshelves, and other furnishings for the home office here. But if you're specifically looking to furnish your office space, consider the companies listed in the "Office Furnishings" section of the "Office, Business, and Professional" chapter. Many of the companies below sell lighting as well. Companies that *specialize* in lighting, however, are grouped in their own section, "Lighting," page 360.

As always, don't forget to check out the "Related Products/Companies" listings at the end of this section.

Find It Fast

Acrylic Furniture and Accessories
- Plexi-Craft

Children's Furniture and Accessories
- Coppa Woodworking, Fran's Wicker and Rattan, Marion Travis

Country-Style Tables, Chairs, and Accessories
- Coppa Woodworking, Genada Imports, Marion Travis

Home and Office Furniture
- Blackwelder's, Carolina Interiors, Ellenburg's, The Furniture Patch of Calabash, Loftin-Black, Priba Furniture, Quality Furniture, Shaw Furniture, Sobol, Southland

Knickknacks and Home Decor
- Tender Heart Treasures

Modern and Contemporary
- Genada Imports

Radiator Enclosures
- ARSCO, Monarch Radiator Enclosures

Steerhides and Steerhide Pillows
- Steerhides

Table Pads
- Factory Direct Table Pad Co.

Unfinished Furniture
- Marion Travis

Victorian- and French-Style Furniture and Accessories
- Heirloom Reproductions

Wicker and Rattan Furniture and Accessories
- Ellenburg's, Fran's Wicker & Rattan

Wooden Baskets
- West Rindge Baskets

Does your home or office suffer from naked radiator syndrome? Oh no! Actually, naked radiators are more than just unsightly. Here are some of the benefits of installing a radiator enclosure by ARSCO: enhances your decor; saves fuel by preventing outside wall heat absorption; increase comfort by circulating warm air directly into the room; protects drapes, walls, and ceilings from airborne dust; and protects occupants from burns. ARSCO's prices are a solid 35% below those charged by local sources for the same kinds of enclosures.

If you live within 600 miles of Cincinnati, ARSCO can send someone to measure your conventional steam radiator, fan coil unit, or fin tube (baseboard) heater. Or you can do it yourself with the easy measuring guide provided in the ARSCO literature. Standard sizes run up to 42 inches high and 96 inches long. There are 14 very pretty stock colors of baked enamel, and other options include special notches, doors, or cutouts for valve access, a built-in humidifier pan, insulated tops, and adjustable legs for uneven floors. Once you get the enclosure, you can assemble it in about 20 minutes. ("If you can put together a simple 5-piece puzzle, your can assemble our enclosures," says ARSCO's literature.) The brochure and flyers from ARSCO make the whole process clear and easy. This is one of those household details that you can't live without once you see it. By the way, the website has product information but no online ordering.

SPECIAL FACTORS: Since all enclosures are custom-made, they aren't returnable; ARSCO does, however, guarantee the workmanship and durability of the enclosures.

Blackwelder's Industries, Inc.

294 Turnersburg Hwy.　　704–872–8921
Statesville, NC 28625　　Fax: 704–872–4491

Catalog: $19.45, refundable (see text)
Pay: check, MO, MC, V, AE, DSC
Sells: home and office furniture and accessories
Store: phone hours Monday to Friday 9:30–5:30
Online: www.homefurnish.com/blackwelders

Since I spend a lot of time thumbing through mail-order catalogs, it's always a pleasure to come across a high-quality company like Blackwelder's, founded in 1936. From the well-organized, clearly written catalog to the very hip website, this fine-furniture firm is doing a lot of things right.

The key to Blackwelder's success is volume, cost control, and service. Located close to most of the major furniture manufacturers down South, Blackwelder does business in high volume, which allows lower profit margins. By keeping advertising costs down and relying on word of mouth and good press, Blackwelder can sell pieces below what you'd pay elsewhere. Trust me when I say that the 82-page glossy "Furniture Resource Book" will make you want to redo your house one room at a time. The book costs $19.45, but is refundable with purchase within 90 days of receipt, and includes a $30 gift certificate. The selection is marvelous, and savings run as high as 60%. The website (in both Japanese and English) showcases hundreds of home furnishings not shown in the catalog, and features secure online ordering. Both catalog and website describe delivery and other consumer policies. Even with shipping costs, which are surprisingly low, you'll still save money here.

International customers, please note: Blackwelder's is experienced in shipping worldwide. Transportation charges to Europe, the Middle East, and Japan are "very modest" in container loads. No minimum sale required.

SPECIAL FACTORS: Satisfaction guaranteed; shipments made by common carrier; authorized returns are accepted within 30 days (a 25% restocking fee applies) for exchange, refund, or credit.

Carolina Interiors

115 Oak Ave.   704–933–1888
Kannapolis, NC 28081   Fax: 704–932–0434

Brochure: free
Pay: check or MO
Sells: home furnishings and accessories
Store: same address (I–85, Exit 63); Monday to Saturday
9–6
Online: www.cannonvillage.com

Imagine strolling through a showroom the size of a city block lavishly furnished with furniture and accessories for dining rooms, living rooms, and bedrooms, complete with wall coverings, floor coverings, rugs, and bedding. That's what you'd find if you could visit Carolina Interiors, 30 miles north of Charlotte. Carolina Interior's central location (in the heart of America's furniture-manufacturing belt) and high sales volume permit them to offer an outstanding selection from the finest furniture manufacturers at 30% to 60% off suggested retail prices. The brochure and website list some of the best-known names of over 350 manufacturers you can choose from. Chances are that bedroom ensemble, desk, or dining-room set you're in love with can be gotten for less at Carolina, so do give them a call when you know what you want. Provide them with the manufacturer's name; they'll give you a price quote and discuss the cost of having the furniture delivered right to your door. (Even factoring in shipping costs, you still end up saving a bundle when you furniture shop this way.) The brochure explains Carolina's deposit requirements.

SPECIAL FACTORS: Price quote by phone, fax, letter, or e-mail; satisfaction guaranteed.

Coppa Woodworking, Inc.

1231 Paraiso Ave.　　　　**310–548–4142**
San Pedro, CA 90731　　　　**Fax: 310–548–6740**

Catalog: $1
Pay: check, MO, MC, V
Sells: Adirondack furniture, screen doors, windows, etc.
Store: same address; Monday to Friday 8–5

If you've shopped around for Adirondack chairs lately—those classic American wooden chairs with the fan-shaped backs and broad flat arms on which to rest your summertime gin and tonic—you know they're not cheap. But Adirondack chairs are the specialty at Coppa Woodworking, and you can get them for up to 50% less from here than from several other places I checked. The eight-page catalog shows chairs made in two different styles, the classic Fanback and the traditional Westport. You can also find Adirondack loveseats, children's chairs, footrests, and end tables. All are made of unfinished pine and come unassembled, but assembling them is easy. For $10 more you can have your piece stained with a semi-transparent color. Coppa manufactures other wood furniture as well, including coffee tables, wooden magazine baskets, a full line of wood screen doors, dressing screens, butcher block tables, and bar stools. If you go to the website you'll be able to see the entire inventory, but you can't order online.

SPECIAL FACTORS: Satisfaction guaranteed; returns accepted except on custom orders.

Ellenburg's Furniture

I-40 & Stamey Farm Rd.   704–873–2900
P.O. Box 5638   Fax: 704–873–6002
Statesville, NC 28687

Catalog: $6.50, refundable
Pay: check, MO, MC, V, DSC
Sells: home furnishings
Store: same address
Online: www.ellenburgs.com

Ellenburg's Furniture is a family-owned and -operated business committed to saving you 40% to 60% off the suggested retail cost of fine furniture. They say they'll "go the extra mile" when their larger competitors will not. The $6.50 catalog fee (refundable with purchase) brings you a list of manufacturers Ellenburg's represents, as well as a collection of tasty little brochures from some of the best furniture-makers. Flipping through these will definitely get you started thinking about the decorating style you favor. Ellenburg's staff is ready to help you in any way they can, whether by discussing your preferences and sending you more information on a certain style or manufacturer, sending you fabric swatches, or giving you a price quote on a line that's not listed in their catalog. The website is fun in that it shows some best-selling and clearance items, but there's no online ordering.

SPECIAL FACTORS: Price quote by phone or letter; returns of damaged and defective goods only are accepted; call for shipping and deposit details.

Factory Direct Table Pad Co.

1501 W. Market St.
Indianapolis, IN 46222

800–428–4567
Fax: 317–631–2584

Prices and Samples: $1
Pay: check, MO, MC, V, AE, DSC
Sells: custom-made table pads
Store: mail order only; phone hours Monday to Saturday
8–8:30
Online: www.tablepads.com

Factory Direct Table Pad Company, Inc., has been helping us protect our treasured dining table, server, coffee table, desk, piano tops, end tables, and other wood pieces from scratches, heat, stains, spills, burns, dents, and watermarks for over 20 years. All table pads are custom-made to fit any surface. They have a heavy-duty, washable, leatherette top surface, a cushiony cotton bottom, and fold for easy handling and storage. The fiberboard core is unaffected by humidity, doesn't bow when stored upright, and is lighter in weight than most other table pads. Since about half of the cost of a custom-made table pad is the fee paid to the person who measures your table, you'll save a lot by doing it yourself using the free measuring kit or by getting assistance from the highly accurate "phone measuring service." And since this company manufactures and sells the pads factory-direct, you're saving even more money. Do check out the excellent website if you have Internet access, as it presents the company's products complete with color charts, photographs, and measuring instructions, and includes forms where you can e-mail the company for a kit or a price quote.

SPECIAL FACTORS: Inquire about return policy.

Fran's Wicker & Rattan Furniture, Inc.

295 Rt. 10E   973–584–2230
Succasunna, NJ 07876   Fax: 973–584–7446

Catalog: $2
Pay: check, MO, MC, V, AE, DSC
Sells: wicker and rattan furniture and accessories
Store: same address; Monday to Friday 9–5:30,
   Wednesday and Thursday 9–8:30, Saturday 9–6, Sunday
   12–5
Online: www.franswicker.com

There's something calming, almost leisurely, about furniture made of wicker, whether natural or painted, and of high-quality rattan. Even such baskets, no matter what they hold, add warmth to a room. Fran's Wicker & Rattan Furniture, Inc., a family-run business for over three generations, offers a great selection of furniture and accessories in its 64-page color catalog, along with a "lowest price" guarantee. Fran's is a factory-direct importer—which means no middleman to inflate the prices. Here you can get great discounts on major national-brand wicker and rattan furniture.

You can choose seating and table sets styled with Victorian curves or modern lines for your patio and porch, living room, dining room, home office, bedroom, children's room, bathroom, and breakfast area. Also available are office furniture, trunks, plant stands, lamps, mirrors, bookcases, magazine racks, and hampers, as well as children's furniture (bassinets, changing tables, rockers, etc.). The catalog presents many choices in cushion coverings, and Fran's has a full-sized swatch book with over 100 of the most popular swatches for you to choose from. I'd recommend checking out the website. Even though you can't order products online, you can view a lot of what Fran's has to offer, see web specials, and obtain a print catalog.

SPECIAL FACTORS: Satisfaction guaranteed.

The Furniture Patch of Calabash, Inc.

Dept. WBM
10283 Beach Dr. SW
P.O. Box 4970
Calabash, NC 28467

910–579–2001
Fax: 910–579–2017

Brochure: free
Pay: check or MO
Sells: furniture, lighting, accessories
Store: same address; Monday to Saturday 9–5:30

Over 60% of all furniture manufactured in the United States is produced within 200 miles of central North Carolina. There in the midst of it all is The Furniture Patch of Calabash. Offering savings up to 60% off list prices on home and office furnishings (as well as lighting, mirrors, rugs, decorator fabric, and decorating accessories), The Furniture Patch of Calabash, Inc., sells by mail and from its Myrtle Beach showroom. Sales staff knowledgeable in home and industrial design will answer your questions and quote prices on specific products by phone, fax, or mail. The brochure presents only some of the well-known names in furniture design, so giving a call is a good idea. If you're shopping in the continental United States, you can order in-house delivery and setup as well.

SPECIAL FACTORS: Prices quoted by phone, fax, or letter; goods damaged during shipping accepted for repair or replacement.

Genada Imports

P.O. Box 204, Dept. W–00   **Tel/Fax: 973–790–7522**
Teaneck, NJ 07666

Catalog: $1
Pay: check, MO, MC, V
Sells: Danish, modern, and contemporary furniture
Store: mail order only

Since 1968 Genada has been importing Danish-design furniture from Europe and selling it factory-direct to Americans at significant savings. I really liked the 48-page black-and-white catalog with photographs and descriptions on every page. What is it about this style of furniture? It's 50s retro and futuristic chic at the same time: clean, classic lines, beautiful wood, form and function in harmony, comfort without pretense. Here you'll find armless chairs, sofas, and divans; convertible foam furniture (couch or chair into guest bed); sectional corner couches; tables (end, coffee, card, dining room, stackable, snack, etc.), leather office chairs straight out of the Jetsons; bookcases including foldable designs; computer and office furniture; bunk beds and captain's beds; and much more. The unifying element here is design and quality of materials (teak, rosewood, walnut, etc.). If you've a flair for design, or just want some well-made, affordable pieces that will go with anything, Genada Imports is a wonderful source.

SPECIAL FACTORS: Full money-back guarantee; specify upholstery and finish preferences when ordering.

Walking through my grandmother's house was like strolling through a museum of Victoriana. She had ladies' chairs, a red velvet camelback sofa, a chiming clock on the marble mantel, and gorgeous hurricane lamps dripping with crystal baubles and hand-painted with pastel flowers. Heirloom Reproductions can help you achieve that same look in your own home with their collection of New Victorian reproductions shipped to you directly from the factory at savings of 40% to 55%. They represent the top names in the industry: Kimball, Victorian Classics, Carlton McLendon, and Victorian Lighting, to name a few. The color catalog (its $10 cost is refundable with your first purchase) and the website present chairs (ladies' and gents'), parlor sets, fainting sofas, marble-top tables, dining sets, beds, dressers, armoires, hall trees, clocks, display cabinets, grandfather clocks, hurricane lamps, and much more. I liked the website because it allows you to view just about everything in the print catalog, although you can't order online. Heirloom Reproduction's helpful staff will answer questions you might have regarding your decorating scheme, fabric choices, shipping, and the company's sales policy.

SPECIAL FACTORS: Price quote by phone or letter; swatches are available on request; orders shipped from factory in insured truck.

Loftin-Black Furniture Co.

111 Sedgehill Dr.   910–472–6117
Thomasville, NC 27360   Fax: 910–472–2052

Brochure: free
Pay: check, MO, MC, V, DSC
Sells: furnishings, bedding, and accessories
Store: same address; Monday to Friday 8:30–5:30,
   Saturday 8:30–5; also 214 N. Main St., High Point, NC
   (910–883–4711)

Located in the furniture capital of the world, Loftin-Black has been serving customers throughout the U.S. since 1948. How'd they stay in business so long? By representing some of America's finest furniture-makers, and by discounting the furniture they sell by 35% to 50%. Loftin-Black's brochure lists the manufacturers for which they're the factory-authorized dealer, as well as details on ordering. To shop here and take advantage of the great savings, you must be prepared to provide the manufacturer's name and the style number (when known). This company will provide in-home delivery and setup, although you can engage a common carrier if you prefer. If you're in the Thomasville area, be sure to visit one of Loftin-Black's two showrooms.

SPECIAL FACTORS: A 50% deposit is required when ordering; price quote by phone or letter; telephone inquiries answered in 24 hours.

Monarch Radiator Enclosures

P.O. Box 326, Dept. BWBM   **201–507–5551**
111 Kero Rd., Ste. 236   **Fax: 201–438–2820**
Carlstadt, NJ 07072

Brochure: $1, refundable
Pay: check, MO, MC, V
Sells: all-steel radiator enclosures
Store: mail order only
Online: www.monarchrad.com

What could be more money-saving than turning your ugly radiator into a functional piece of furniture that also happens to save on energy costs? That's the idea behind Monarch's stock and custom radiator covers. Don't let exposed radiators spoil the charm of your home. For little money you can get a steel cover that's easy to assemble and install, that comes in several colors, and has an attractive grill front for maximum air circulation. The units are designed for safety; not only will your radiator protect your walls, drapes, and children from burns, but you can now use the insulated top as a surface for plants, books, and knickknacks. Monarch's custom radiator enclosures are even more tempting, with built-in bookshelves, hinged tops, concealed humidifiers, and designer colors and grill styles among some of the features available. The two brochures you'll receive—one for stock, the other for custom models—explain in detail all the features of these nifty products and guide you step-by-step through the task of measuring your radiator for the right cover. If you have online access, visit the website, which offers online ordering and features photographs, information, and a price chart for the stock enclosures.

SPECIAL FACTORS: Most enclosures can be shipped by UPS; larger enclosures are shipped via common carrier.

Plexi-Craft Quality Products Corp.

514 W. 24th St., Dept. BWBM   212–924–3244
New York, NY 10011–1179   Fax: 212–924–3508

Catalog: $2
Pay: check, MO, MC, V
Sells: Plexiglas and Lucite home furnishings and
  accessories
Store: same address; Monday to Friday 9:30–5
Online: www.escape.com/~plexi

Plexi-Craft Quality Products Corp. manufactures Lucite and Plexiglas furniture and household accessories that are available direct from the factory at about 50% less than what they'd cost at department stores. The 16-page print catalog, which can be viewed in its entirety on the website, includes tables (Mandarin, Parson, coffee, console, vanity, TV, etc.), a variety of table bases of unusual shape and design, display cases, futuristic-looking stools and chairs, and lots of practical accessories such as telephone caddies, pedestals (for plants or art), coat racks, wine racks, place mats, and towel bars. These Lucite/Plexiglas pieces are shatterproof and durable, built to last a lifetime, and will add practicality with a minimalist flair to any surroundings. Never, *ever* use window cleaner; Plexi-Craft recommends and sells a special cleaner that will keep your furniture looking new with just an occasional wipe. Tabletops come in a variety of sizes, shapes, and thicknesses, in glass or acrylic; cushion colors are white or beige. Plexi-Craft welcomes custom orders.

SPECIAL FACTORS: Price quote by phone, fax, or letter on custom orders; no returns accepted without prior written permission.

Priba Furniture Sales & Interiors

P.O. Box 13295
Greensboro, NC 27415–3295

336–855–9034
Fax: 336–855–1370

Brochure: free
Pay: check, MO, MC, V, DSC
Sells: furniture, accessories, bedding, rugs, etc.
Store: 210 Stage Coach Trail, Greensboro, NC; Monday to
Friday 9–5:30, Saturday 9–5
Online: www.pribafurniture.com

Priba Furniture Sales and Interiors wants to make you a customer for life. So determined are they that if you come to visit their Greensboro showroom, Priba will arrange transportation from the airport, and will credit 1% of your total order toward lodging (hotel/motel receipt required)! If visiting North Carolina isn't on your agenda, shop around your own neighborhood until you find the furniture, lamps or accessories, fabrics, carpet, wall coverings, or bedding you want. To take advantage of Priba's discounts (which run up to 48% on over 300 lines of furniture and accessories) you'll need the manufacturer's name and style number. For upholstery get the fabric and grade name or number. Both the print brochure and the website list the manufacturers Priba represents. If you're not quite sure what you want, Priba can help narrow your preferences and then send you photographs or brochures of a particular manufacturer's items. Priba uses van-line service so your furniture will be uncrated and set up in your home.

SPECIAL FACTORS: Credit cards accepted for deposit only; a 30% deposit required when you place your order; 150-pound minimum for shipment.

Quality Furniture Market

2034 Hickory Blvd. S.W.　　　828–728–2946
Lenoir, NC 28645　　　　　　Fax: 828–726–0226

> Information: price quote
> Pay: check, MO, MC, V, DSC
> Sells: furnishings, bedding, and accessories
> Store: same address; Monday to Saturday 8:30–5

Quality Furniture Market, in business since 1955, takes its name seriously: You're invited to check the firm's ratings with Dunn and Bradstreet, the Lyons listing, and the Lenoir Chamber of Commerce (800–737–0782) before you buy. The firm's magnificent selection is offered at prices that are 20% over cost, compared with the usual 110% to 125% markups. The company has been recommended as a "great price" store by Oprah Winfrey and *Woman's Day* magazine.

Quality Furniture sells indoor and outdoor furniture, bedding, and home accessories by literally hundreds of firms. The list of brands is given in the brochure, as well as terms of sale and other conditions. Readers have written to say they were very pleased with Quality's prices and the firm's in-home delivery service. If you're traveling near Lenoir, drop by and get lost in the three floors of furniture galleries and display rooms.

SPECIAL FACTORS: Price quote by phone or letter with self-addressed, stamped envelope; all orders must be prepaid before shipment; shipment is made by common carrier or in-home delivery service.

Shaw Furniture Galleries, Inc., national sellers of top-brand furniture for the home and office, some at savings up to 50%, carries furnishings by over 300 manufacturers and has been in business for over 57 years. Log on to the website and you'll get a taste of some of what they carry—beautifully photographed in color. But you still have to call or e-mail the store for a price quote as there's no online ordering at this writing. If you know the name of a collection, you can call to request a color brochure, and if you have questions, you can speak to a sales associate. Customer service is important at Shaw Furniture Galleries, which delivers throughout the continental United States—via Executive Delivery Red Carpet Service—and provides free home setup.

Shaw Furniture Galleries occupies the original Randelman School as well as a spacious showroom facility housing beautiful furniture galleries. If you're in Randelman, North Carolina, Shaw invites you to stop by.

SPECIAL FACTORS: Prices quoted by phone, e-mail, or letter (with a SASE); a Shaw credit card is available.

Sobol House

Richardson Blvd.
P.O. Box 219
Black Mountain, NC 28711

704–669–8031
Fax: 704–669–7969

Brochure: free
Pay: check or MO
Sells: home and office furnishings
Store: same address; Monday to Friday 9–6:30, Saturday
9–5:30, Sunday 12–5 (June to October)

Sobol House was a pioneer in the mail-order furniture business. Since 1970 this company has been offering first-quality modern and traditional furniture at savings of 40% to 50% to customers in places as far flung as Saudi Arabia. Like other companies of this sort, Sobol asks that you do some of the work: Visit showrooms in your area; compare brand names, cost, and quality; take notes. When you find the furnishings you like, call Sobol with the manufacturer's name, the model number, and finish or fabric. Sobol will give you a price quote and answer any other questions you might have about the hundreds of manufacturers they represent. The money you'd spend on sales tax will pay a major portion of your freight cost. In-house delivery and setup are available, or you can have the furniture delivered to your sidewalk, which is more economical. "All we ask," says the brochure, "is the chance to give you a competitive bid!" Okay, so give 'em a chance.

SPECIAL FACTORS: Price quote by phone, fax, or letter.

Southland Furniture Galleries

1244 Highway 17
P.O. Box 1837
Little River, SC 29566

843–280–9342
Fax: 843–249–4527

Brochure: free
Pay: check or MO
Sells: home furnishings and accessories
Store: same address; Monday to Saturday 9–5:30

When you stop in to Southland Furniture Galleries or call, a professional interior designer or sales consultant will answer all of your questions about manufacturers, colors, styles, fabrics, and frames. Southland represents hundreds of major furniture and accessory lines. Once you've gotten a price quote and placed your order, Southland will schedule your furniture on the next available truck to your area. It's that simple, and you'll save up to 40% here off the price tag you'd pay locally. As with other mail-order furniture companies, it's best to have all the pertinent information at hand before you contact the company, since they don't have a catalog but rather a list of manufacturers with whom they deal. Since Southland is near Myrtle Beach, they suggest you plan your vacation and furniture shopping together!

SPECIAL FACTORS: Sales policy is detailed in the brochure; price quote by phone, fax, or letter.

Steerhides

M. C. Limited, Dept. BWBM   800–236–5224
P.O. Box 17696
Whitefish Bay, WI 53217

Brochure and Price List: free
Pay: check, MO, MC, V
Sells: steerhides and hide pillows
Store: mail order only

I once met an Irish-American living in Woodstock who had been named an honorary Lakota. His teepee floor was adorned with black-and-white cow skins. Being a cow fanatic, I'd always wondered where he'd gotten them. Imagine my thrill when I opened up M. C. Limited's Steerhides brochure and saw eight color photographs of natural and printed steerhides! The company offers processed skins in full hides (36 square feet on average, five to six feet wide by seven to eight feet long) in six natural colors, as well as stenciled animal prints (zebra or leopard). The natural steerhides are nearly 40% below prices by two New York City leather suppliers for comparable skins. M. C. Limited also makes steerhide pillows with suede backs, which are offered in the six natural colors and stenciled zebra or leopard, plain or with silver beads and fringes on the corners. Sizes range from 12 to 24 inches square. M. C. Limited notes that all of its hides are byproducts of the beef industry and are not claimed from animals raised primarily for their skins. A special new tanning process is reputed to render the hides "soft and beautiful" as they age, so they won't stiffen, dry out, and lose hair.

SPECIAL FACTORS: Satisfaction is guaranteed; authorized returns (except pillows) are accepted (a restocking fee is charged) within 30 days.

Tender Heart Treasures, Ltd.

10525 J St.
Omaha, NE 68127-1090

800-443-1367
402-593-1313
Fax: 402-593-1316

Catalog: free
Pay: check, MO, MC, V, AE, DSC
Sells: "country" home decor and gifts
Store: mail order only
Online: www.tenderheart.com

Tender Heart Treasures specializes in "country" home accents and seasonal displays and decorations at prices that are a solid 30% to 50% below retail. The 72-page color catalog features hundreds of gifts, display pieces, and seasonal decorations: bears of all types in costume and the buff, "welcome" signs and hospitality plaques, dolls and figurines, angels, electrified kerosene lamps, bent-wire decorations, nesting baskets, picture frames, birdhouses, doll furniture, planters, wooden apples and other fruit, wreaths, miniatures, terra cotta discs to keep your brown sugar moist, and lots more. In addition to terrific prices, Tender Heart Treasures makes ordering a breeze—there's no minimum, and shipping charges are easy to compute to any destination. The website, which shows current best-selling products and clearance items, will give you a good idea of what this company is about, but there's no online ordering.

Wholesale inquiries should be made to 800-443-1367; a copy of your resale tax certificate will be required with your first order.

SPECIAL FACTORS: Satisfaction is guaranteed; quantity discounts are available; authorized returns are accepted within 30 days for exchange, refund, or credit; C.O.D. orders are accepted.

Marion Travis

P.O. Box 1041　　　　　　　**704–528–4424**
Statesville, NC 28687　　　**Fax: 704–528–3526**

Catalog: $1
Pay: check, MO, MC, V
Sells: reproduction Early American chairs, benches, and
  tables
Store: 354 S. Eastway Dr., Troutman, NC; Monday to
  Thursday 8–3:30, Friday 8–12

The owner of Marion Travis tells a little story that demonstrates what this company is all about. Years ago he bought property that had a run-down house on it. From the shambles he salvaged an intriguing old chair. A well-made example of 1800s craftsmanship, the chair inspired him to create a modern-day reproduction, the Lillie Ladderback, one of his best sellers to this day. When the people at Marion Travis say their Early American reproduction chairs last a lifetime, they mean it. This is furniture collectors will be collecting a hundred years from now. But you can collect them now and spend 25% to 50% less than you'd pay elsewhere for furniture of this caliber.

The skilled craftsmen of Marion Travis construct the chairs—of ash, oak, maple, and other hardwoods—in such a way that the natural contraction of the wood, only partially seasoned, causes the joints to grow even stronger and tighter with the years. The 12-page black-and-white catalog from Marion Travis shows beautifully made ladderback chairs with handwoven cord seats, bar stools, tables, rockers, children's chairs and rockers, porch swings, foot stools, and much more. Seats are made with cord, wood slats, and palm cane rush; furniture can be unstained (machine sanded) or finished in natural, walnut, or golden oak. If you're in the vicinity of Troutman and can pick up your furniture unboxed, you'll get an additional 25% off.

Wholesale customers: Request the wholesale catalog and price list from Shaver Woodworks, P.O. Box 946, Troutman, NC 28166. Minimum wholesale order is 12 pieces.

SPECIAL FACTORS: Minimum order is two pieces of furniture; authorized returns of defective goods accepted within 30 days.

West Rindge Baskets, Inc.

47 W. Main St.　　　　　　　　Tel/Fax: 603–899–2231
Rindge, NH 03461

Brochure: free
Pay: check or MO
Sells: handmade, handwoven wooden baskets
Store: same address; Monday to Thursday 8–4 (all year),
Friday to Saturday 10–4 (May 30 to Christmas)

West Rindge has been making baskets from local New Hampshire wood since 1925. The baskets here start as rough-cut, slab-edge white birch or oak from local forests, and are handmade, handwoven, and individually inspected for flaws. Don't be expecting the $5 made-in-Asia basket you'd buy in a dime store. West Rindge baskets are upscale, impeccably made baskets to keep over a lifetime. The color brochure shows the selection—40 in all—which includes baskets for shopping, pie and cake holders (including a double pie holder), picnic baskets, baskets designed for apple picking, wine-toting, planters, wastebaskets, barbecue utensils, French bread, and many more, including ones with swing handles, stiff handles, and hinged lids. The baskets here sell for less than what you'd pay for items of comparable quality in a gourmet shop or decorator store. The prices are very reasonable—averaging around $25. This is a very nice, family-run business.

Wholesale Buyers: West Rindge has a wholesale price list at about 30% less, which you can request if you're a reseller. In New Hampshire, a "reseller" is not required to have a resale number. The only requirement is that you purchase a minimum of $100 on your first wholesale order.

SPECIAL FACTORS: Satisfaction is guaranteed; C.O.D. orders accepted for an additional charge.

Related Products/Companies

Air conditioners
 • Bernie's, Dial-a-Brand, LVT Price Quote Hotline, Percy's, Sound City

Antique historic prints and maps
 • American Maps & Prints

Antique and reproduction telephones, posters
 • Phoneco

Bed and bath organizers
- Colonial Garden Kitchens

Bee-themed rugs, flags, and other decor
- Brushy Mountain Bee Farm

Books on furniture-making and upholstery
- The Caning Shop, Frank's Cane and Rush Supply, Woodworker's Discount Books

Ceiling fans
- Golden Valley Lighting, Main Lamp/Lamp Warehouse

Cherrywood tables
- Cook's

Children's furniture
- Toysmart.com

Cloisonné vases
- House of Onyx

Custom fabric lamination for patio furniture
- Hancock's of Paducah

Custom-upholstered headboards, ottomans, footstools
- Eldridge Textile

Danish furniture and woven seat repair books and materials
- The Caning Shop, Frank's Cane and Rush

Decorator picture frames
- American Frame, Graphik Dimensions

Fruit crate and other labels
- Original Paper Collectibles

Furniture kits
- Frank's Cane and Rush Supply

Hammocks and deck chairs
- Defender

Home furnishings
- BedandBath.com, Bennett Brothers, Cole's Appliance and Furniture, Damark, The Ultimate Outlet

Lawn furniture
- RV Direct

Leather-care products
- Leather Unlimited, UPCO, Weaver Leather

New, antique, and reproduction posters and prints
- American Prints and Maps, Desperate Enterprises, Hake's Americana, Miscellaneous Man, PosterNow

Patio furniture covers and canopies
- RV Direct

Pet-repellent mats for furniture, pet doors, and gates
- Drs. Foster & Smith, Jeffers, KV Vet Supply, Valley Vet

Pool and billiards tables and game-room decor
- Mueller Sporting Goods

Ready-made chair and cushion covers
- Shama Imports

Reproduction and antique tin signs, cannery labels, switch plates, refrigerator magnets
- Desperate Enterprises

Safes and fireproof files
- Discount Safe Outlet

Saunas
- Better Health Fitness

Sliding pet doors and windows
- Patio Pacific

Upholstery hardware and tools
- The Caning Shop, Newark Dressmaker Supply

Upholstery stain remover
- The Cleaning Center

Wicker repair materials
- Frank's Cane and Rush

Wooden shutter room dividers
- Shuttercraft

Woodstoves, fireplace accessories
- Lehman's

Kitchen Equipment

Small kitchen appliances and gadgets, cookware, bakeware, chef's knives and utensils

These firms sell everything from measuring spoons and butcher's knives to bread-making machines and cappuccino makers, frequently at 30% to 50% less than you'd pay retail. For large kitchen appliances such as refrigerators, stoves, and ovens, see the section entitled "Appliances and TVs," page 285. As long as you'll be creating culinary masterpieces, you'll want to set an impressive table for your guests. See "Tableware," page 365, for flatware, glassware, and china; and "Bed, Bath, and Table Textiles" for tablecloths, place mats, and napkins, page 299. And be sure to look at "Related Products/Companies" after the company listings in this section for other firms that carry kitchen- and cooking-related items.

Find It Fast

Cleaning Supplies
- Colonial Garden Kitchen

Cookware and Bakeware
- Broadway Panhandler, ChuckWagon Outfitters, Colonial Garden Kitchen, Kitchen Etc., Peerless, Professional Cutlery, Zabar's

Cutlery
- Broadway Panhandler, Kitchen Etc., Peerless, Professional Cutlery

Food Storage and Kitchen Organizers
- Colonial Garden Kitchen, Peerless

Kitchen Gadgets and Utensils
- Broadway Panhandler, Colonial Garden Kitchen, Peerless, Professional Cutlery

Large Kitchen Appliances
- Peerless

Small Kitchen Appliances
- Broadway Panhandler, Colonial Garden Kitchen, Kitchen Etc., Peerless, Zabar's

Broadway Panhandler

477 Broome St. 212–966–3434
New York, NY 10013 Fax: 212–966–9017

Information: price quote
Pay: check, MO, MC, V, AE, DSC
Sells: cookware, cutlery, kitchenware, bakeware, and
  tabletop accessories
Store: same address; Monday to Friday 10:30–7, Saturday
  11–7, Sunday 11–6

When it comes to cookware and all its accoutrements, the more products the better, for there's excitement in a store's kaleidoscopic mix of materials and textures, shapes and culinary promise. Hold that image in mind when you call or write Broadway Panhandler for quotes on appliances and professional equipment (there's no catalog); manufacturers include All-Clad, Bodum, Bourgeat, Braun, Calphalon, Chicago Metallic, Le Creuset, Cuisinart, Kaisar, KitchenAid, Krups, Omega, Pavoni, Pelouze, and Vollrath. They also carry knives by such notables as Global, Lamson & Goodnow, Sabatier, and Wüsthof-Trident; for the cutlery, price lists and manufacturers' brochures may be available. There is a physical shop, and since most roads lead to New York City you'll want to stop in for cookbooks, serving pieces, kitchen linens, baskets, and assorted gadgets. You can expect savings up to 30% on varying items, especially on open-stock cutlery and selected lines of cookware.

SPECIAL FACTORS: Price quotes by phone or letter.

ChuckWagon Outfitters

250 Avila Beach Dr.
San Luis Obispo, CA 93405

800–543–2359
805–595–2434
Fax: 805–595–7914

Catalog: free (see text)
Pay: check, MO, MC, V, AE, DSC
Sells: cast-iron cookware, accessories
Store: same address
Online: www.chuckwgn.com

In business since 1992, ChuckWagon Outfitters specializes in cast-iron cook-ware—notably the Lodge brand of ironware—and accessories. This family-run establishment started out selling Dutch ovens—available in two styles, flat bottomed and footed, for stovetop and campfire use, respectively—and today offers fryers, skillets, kettles, baking tins, and camp gear. In keeping with ChuckWagon's history, the catalog includes extra-deep ovens that can roast a whole turkey. In addition, if the concept of Dutch-oven cooking is foreign to you—as well it might be in certain regions—the catalog offers books and cookbooks.

ChuckWagon Outfitters can also be your source for flat griddles, cast-iron tea kettles, and classic favorites: ranch chimes (triangles), sad irons, trout andirons, enamelware chamber pots, and Volcano cookers. As readers of this book, you can receive the 20-page catalog at no charge, so be sure to mention WMO. Their homepage is pretty cute, with directions to their store and photographs of their showroom, but no online ordering.

For wholesale purchasers, the minimum order to open an account is $300, and subsequent minimum orders are $75. Call 805–595–2434 to request a price list and terms of sale.

SPECIAL FACTORS: Satisfaction guaranteed; returns accepted for exchange, refund, or credit.

Colonial Garden Kitchens

Dept. CGZ4182　　　　　　　**800-323-6000**
Hanover, PA 17333-0066

Catalog: $2
Pay: check, MO, MC, V, AE, CB, DC, DSC
Sells: kitchen equipment and household helps
Store: mail order only
Online: www.cgkcatalog.com

Colonial Garden Kitchens sells name-brand kitchen appliances, specialty cookware, serving and entertainment equipment, and many useful smaller items for kitchen and bath. Over a third of the goods are regularly on sale for 20% to 40% below regular prices. The catalog contains items such as commercial oven mitts, bed and bath organizers, bread-makers, and even deep fryers. A company of Hanover Direct, Inc., Colonial carries an assortment of handy gadgets and items that make kitchen tasks and cooking easier. All of these items can be found and ordered on their website.

SPECIAL FACTORS: Satisfaction guaranteed; returns in new or like-new condition accepted for exchange, refund, or credit.

Kitchen Etc.

32 Industrial Dr., Dept.
BWBM
Exeter, NH 03833–4557

603–773–0020
Fax: 603–778–9328

Catalog: free
Pay: check, MO, MC, V, DSC
Sells: tableware and kitchenware
Store: locations in CT, MA, NH, and VT; see catalog for
  locations
Online: www.kitchenetc.com

You can save from 20% to 50% when you buy your china, stemware, small appliances, flatware, kitchen gadgets, pots and pans, baking accessories, and other kitchen supplies through Kitchen Etc. This company has been around since 1983 and offers a fat catalog overflowing with great buys, color photographs, and product descriptions to make this a one-stop shopping experience for culinary-related goods. One half of the catalog is devoted to fine and casual tableware, stemware, and flatware from the best names in the biz including Dansk, Mikasa, Noritake, Pfaltzgraff, Waterford, Wedgwood, and many others. It's a great selection and the discounts are deep. The other half of Kitchen Etc.'s catalog is devoted to everything else one might need for the kitchen, from exotic—ravioli-makers and bread machines—to basic supplies—turkey roasters and chef's knives. You'll find top-name manufacturers' goods here for a lot less than you'd pay at your local kitchen supply store. Kitchen Etc. also maintains a bridal registry. The website, by the way, is well organized and very easy to use. You can view a lot of the inventory here, see the fantastic savings, and then order by toll-free number (there's no online ordering).

SPECIAL FACTORS: Satisfaction guaranteed.

Peerless Restaurant Supplies

1124 S. Grand Blvd., Dept.
BWBM
St. Louis, MO 63104–1090

800–255–3663
314–664–0400
Fax: 314–664–8102

Catalog: $10
Pay: check, MO, MC, V
Sells: commercial cookware and restaurant equipment
Store: same address; Monday to Friday 9–5
Online: www.prls.com

If you're setting up a small catering business, sidewalk bar/café, or bakery, Peerless is a great source for commercial restaurant supplies. But even individuals find lots to like in the mammoth 226-page catalog. For a $10 investment, you'll get the annual Peerless catalog, which is well organized, descriptive, and has a fantastic selection. The prices here are at least 40% below suggested retail, and there's no minimum order.

Here's a tiny sample of the kinds of items you'll find in the catalog: plain, restaurant-grade tableware (including adorable art deco pastels from Fiesta); plastic and glassware for poolside, bar, or table; stainless flatware; tablecloths, table skirts, and reversible table mats; ice sculpture molds; cutlery; serving trays, chafers, punch bowls, and urns; everything for the kitchen, from lettuce slicers to vacuum-packing machines; bussing utility carts and open-wire shelving; garbage containers; and large appliances such as fryers, mixers, and ranges. Get the picture? Peerless also has amazing deals on used equipment; if you register your special need with Peerless's used equipment "Wish List," they may be able to save you a bundle. (Used equipment comes with a 30-day parts and labor guarantee.)

Those who live in the St. Louis area would be well advised to stop in to the Peerless showroom and visit the "Bargain Room," where everything is drastically reduced. Food-service professionals should note that Peerless also provides 3-D design services for professional kitchens and interior decorating design services for restaurants and bars. See catalog for details. The website features secure online ordering, but had very little inventory at this writing.

SPECIAL FACTORS: Minimum credit card order is $25; quantity discounts available; authorized returns are accepted within 30 days of receipt (see catalog for return policy).

Professional Cutlery Direct

Dept. BWBM
170 Boston Post Rd., Suite 135
Madison, CT 06443

800–859–6994
203–458–5015
Fax: 203–458–5019

Catalog: $3, refundable
Pay: check, MO, MC, V
Sells: kitchen cutlery, cookware, cookbooks, etc.
Store: mail order only, phone hours Monday to Friday 9–8,
   Weekends 10–3, EST
Online: www.p-c-d.com

Professional Cutlery Direct specializes in commercial-quality equipment for at-home cooks who take cooking seriously. The nearly 70-page catalog features cutlery of high-carbon stainless steel, as well as hardwood cutting boards, bakeware, cookware and utensils, grills and griddles, chef's attire, knife accessories such as sharpeners and steels, specialty tools, cookbooks, cookware racks, butcher block carts, and more. Discounts range between 20% and 30%, with special discounts just under 50% off list. Don't fret if you're new to the kitchen; the catalog gives enough information to help you choose your cutlery wisely. If you'd rather shop online, the website displays an extensive inventory and at press time was being renovated to include online ordering.

SPECIAL FACTORS: Prices quoted by phone or letter; quantity discounts on some items; returns accepted within 30 days for exchange, refund, or credit; minimum order $10.

Zabar's

2245 Broadway
New York, NY 10024

212–496–1234
Fax: 212–580–4477

Catalog: free
Pay: check, MO, MC, V, AE
Sells: gourmet food, cookware, and housewares
Store: same address; Monday to Friday 8–7:30, Saturday
8–8, Sunday 9–6; housewares mezzanine Monday to
Saturday 9–7, Sunday 9–6
E-mail: info@zabars.com

Considered by many to be New York City's ultimate deli, Zabar's offers the better part of North America a sampling from its famed counters and housewares mezzanine via a 64-page color catalog. Zabar's has been around since 1934 selling name-brand kitchenware at 50% off normal retail and gourmet food items at competitive prices.

Past catalogs have offered smoked Scottish, Norwegian, and Irish salmon, plum pudding, peppercorns, Bahlsen cookies and confections, pâtés, mustards, crackers, escargot, Lindt and Droste chocolate, Tiptree preserves, Dresden stollen, olive oil, prosciutto and other deli meats, and similar gourmet fare. (Perishables are packed in ice and shipped via next-day air.) The cookware section features the finest names in pots and pans of every kind, coffee and espresso makers, and baking accessories. The housewares section has more cookery, small appliances such as toasters and food processors, steam presses and irons, sewing machines, vacuum cleaners and sweepers, blenders and mixers, and more. Zabar's distinguishes itself among kitchenware vendors for the enormous selection of goods and the substantial discounts. The catalog features a representative selection from the store, and price quotes are given over the phone—if you don't see it in the catalog, just call. With any catalog order over $25, receive a pound of Zabar's coffee for $3 ($3.50 for decaf).

SPECIAL FACTORS: Minimum order is $15; minimum shipping fee is $5.50; no orders are shipped to APO/FPO addresses, Canada, or Puerto Rico; orders shipped to Alaska and Hawaii must go second-day air; phone orders are accepted Monday to Saturday 9–5.

Related Products/Companies

Acrylic wine racks, kitchen organizers
- Plexi-Craft

Aprons and kitchen towels
- Clothcrafters

Apron-making kits
- Oppenheim's

Cake-decorating equipment
- Party Wholesaler

Camping cookware and equipment
- Campmor, Sierra Trading Post, The Sportsman's Guide

Catering supplies
- Paper Wholesaler

Cheese-making kits
- New England Cheesemaking Supply

Cleaning soaps and supplies
- Cal Ben Soap Company, The Cleaning Center, EDGE Distributing

Cookie cutters
- Current

Cutlery
- Bennett Brothers, Cutlery Shoppe, Lanac

English tea towels
- Harris Levy

Ethnic/exotic cooking utensils, ingredients, and equipment
- A Cook's Wares, The CMC Company, Mountain Ark Trading, Sultan's Delight

Food and spice containers
- Brushy Mountain Bee Farm, Rafal Spice

Food storage bags for everything
- Plastic BagMart

Food-themed posters
- Jessica's Biscuit Cookbooks, PosterNow

Gourmet cookware and bakeware
- Bennett Brothers, A Cook's Wares

Hard-to-find nonelectric cooking gadgets
- Lehman's

Herb scales, mortar and pestle
- East Earth Trade Winds

Household and homemaking tips
- Reader's Digest, Storey Books

Kitchen accents, knickknacks, ad organizers
- Caprilands Herb Farm, Cook Bothers, Current, Lanac, Tender Heart Treasures

Kitchen tools, utensils, and gadgets
- Clothcrafters, Cook Brothers, A Cook's Wares, Johnny's Selected Seeds, Pinetree Garden, Rafal Spice

Kitchen tools for persons with limited eyesight or mobility
- Comfort House, Independent Living Aids, The New Vision Store

Left-handed kitchen equipment
- The Left Hand

Picnic, wine-toting, pie, bread, and other baskets
- West Rindge Baskets

Professional-size aluminum foil and plastic wrap
- Party Wholesaler

Small kitchen appliances
- American Health Food, Bennett Brothers, Bernie's Discount, A Cook's Wares, Lanac, LVT Price Quote Hotline, Percy's, Nat Schwartz, Sound City

Wine-, beer-, mead-, liqueur-making supplies
- Beer and Winemaking Supplies, Brushy Mountain Bee Farm, E. C. Kraus

Lighting

Indoor and outdoor lighting fixtures, crystal chandeliers, lamps and shades

I have a friend who must have fifty lamps in her small house. But it's not the quantity one notices. Rather, it's the warm, inviting pools of mellow light that entice one to curl up in an overstuffed chair with a book and a cup of chai. She's got a special talent for choosing the right lamps and shades for her country home.

But for many, including myself, successful lighting is a big design challenge. None of the firms listed here can tell you how to light your home, but you'll find the basics in interior design textbooks and decorating manuals, and you'll definitely be inspired by the fabulous catalogs.

The companies below sell lighting for the home—lamps, ceiling fixtures, bathroom and kitchen fixtures, patio and walkway lighting, building lanterns, etc.—and related electrical accessories, shades, and replacement parts. Some also sell ceiling fans and attachments. Discounts average about 30% to 40% on name-brand goods, and the firms that manufacture their own fixtures sell at competitive prices as well.

Find It Fast

Ceiling Fans
- Golden Valley, Main Lamp/Lamp Warehouse

Chandeliers
- Brass Light Gallery, King's Chandelier

Lamps, Light Fixtures, Sconces
- Brass Light Gallery, Golden Valley, Main Lamp/Lamp Warehouse

Outdoor Lanterns and Pendants
- Brass Light Gallery, Golden Valley

Brass Light Gallery

131 S. 1st St., Dept. BWBM   800–243–9595
Milwaukee, WI 53204   Fax: 414–271–7755

Catalog: $6, refundable (see text)
Pay: check, MO, MC, V
Sells: lighting fixtures
Store: same address; Monday to Friday 9–5, Saturday
10–4
Online: www.brasslight.com

After you've seen the fixtures from Brass Light Gallery, you'll know why you've held off buying from other sources. Not only are the materials and workmanship here of superior quality, but the designs have that satisfyingly "right" quality that's so often lacking in lighting fixtures. The Goldenrod and Continental Collections showcase classic architectural styles for kitchens, bathrooms, bedrooms, and other interior spaces. The Alabaster Collection offers timeless chandeliers, sconces, and table lamps in natural alabaster, at prices often lower than those charged for the originals from the 1920s and 1930s—when you can find them, intact and unchipped, in antique stores. The Prismatic Collection features authentic vintage glass pendants (ribbed glass), suitable for kitchen and loft spaces. The Arts & Crafts Collection has interior and exterior lanterns and pendants to complement the architecture and design of homes and furniture styled after that eponymous movement in America. There's also a Prairie School Collection, à la Frank Lloyd Wright, with table lamps, ceiling fixtures, and lanterns, and the Classic Exteriors Collection, with great items to enhance your exteriors and landscape. Most of the fixtures are offered in a choice of metal finishes and/or choices of glass shade color or style, allowing you to customize each fixture to your room's decor.

The Brass Light Gallery's catalog—over 100 pages of lighting, plus technical specifications—has been designed for use by home owners, interior designers, and architects. (The catalog costs $6, refundable with purchase, but a 12-page color brochure is free on request.) Prices here average 20% below retail, but the fixtures are better quality than those being sold by many of Brass Light Gallery's competitors. There's no online ordering at Brass Light's website.

SPECIAL FACTORS: Satisfaction is guaranteed.

Golden Valley Lighting

274 Eastchester Dr., #117A
High Point, NC 27262

800-735-3377, ext. 280
336-882-7330
Fax: 800-760-6678
Fax: 336-882-2262

Catalog: free to WMO readers (see text)
Pay: check, MO, MC, V, AE, DSC
Sells: lighting fixtures and ceiling fans
Store: mail order only
Online: www.gvlight.com

Golden Valley Lighting, America's oldest and largest "lighting by mail" catalog retailer, has won the hearts of many loyal customers over the years by providing an excellent inventory of classy lamps and lighting fixtures at 30% to 50% below retail. Now they've created a fantastic website with the full 80-page catalog online, complete with secure online ordering. Golden Lighting welcomes e-mails with any special requests or questions you have about lighting. You'll never have to visit another lighting store again.

Tiffany fixtures (hanging shades, table lamps, standing lamps); traditional, casual, Victorian, and contemporary styles of chandeliers, wall sconces, lamps, and ceiling fixtures; outdoor lights; miniature lamp shades; and framed mirrors are some of what you'll find at Golden Valley Lighting. If by some remote chance this company doesn't have exactly what you're looking for, you can call them with a manufacturer's name and style number and Golden Valley will give you an attractive price quote on that item. Best of all, there's no shipping charged here on catalog orders, so your savings just keep adding up. Be sure to mention you're a WMO reader when you call for a print catalog; it's free to readers of this book.

SPECIAL FACTORS: International orders welcome; returns accepted (see catalog for details).

King's Chandelier Co.

P.O. Box 667, Dept. WBM
Eden, NC 27289–0667

336–623–6188
Fax: 336–627–9935

Catalog: $5, $8 outside U.S.
Pay: check, MO, MC, V
Sells: Czech, Venetian, and Strass crystal chandeliers
Store: 729 S. Van Buren Rd. (Hwy. 14), Eden, NC; Monday
to Saturday 10–4:30
Online: www.chandelier.com

It's nice to know that quality has staying power. That goes for businesses like King's Chandelier Company, owned and operated by the same family for over 60 years, as well as their products—elegant crystal chandeliers, sconces, and candelabras that are instant heirlooms. Discount chandeliers, you ask? Compare King's crystal lighting fixtures with others' and you'll see that their prices are close to wholesale. The reason is because King's Chandelier Company is the manufacturer, so you're getting these goods direct from the factory without retailer mark-ups. The full-color catalog shows all 120 designs dripping with cut crystal, glowing with soft light, and shining in silver or brass finishes. The styles range from extravagant and complex designs fit for royalty to more understated old-timey Victorian. King's imports the finest materials such as Austrian Swarovski crystal, and has artisans who create each piece as it's ordered. The company claims the full beauty of these crystal wonders can't be captured in photographs, so they invite customers to come visit their North Carolina showroom. Barring that, however, you can have a videocassette made with up to six designs of your choosing. The VHS is $20, refundable when you place your order.

SPECIAL FACTORS: An additional 15% discount is extended to designers, decorators, and contractors; satisfaction guaranteed; returns accepted within 15 days (see catalog for details).

Main Lamp/Lamp Warehouse

1073 39th St.   718–436–8500
Brooklyn, NY 11219   Fax: 718–438–6836

Information: price quote
Pay: check, MO, MC, V, AE, DSC
Sells: lighting fixtures and ceiling fans
Store: same address; Monday, Tuesday, and Friday
9–5:30, Thursday 9–8, Saturday and Sunday 10–5

If you're not accustomed to shopping by price quote, maybe it's time you changed. Why? Because companies like Main Lamp/Lamp Warehouse will reward you for your footwork by saving you up to 50% off normal retail prices. Here's how it works. Shop around for lamps, lighting fixtures, ceiling fans—anything having to do with lighting. When you've found the goods that turn you on, give Main Lamp/Lamp Warehouse a call. Since they represent just about every lighting manufacturer, big and small, they can offer you a price that will save you a lot. Buying your lighting this way means you do most of the work: You need to provide the manufacturer's name and the product style number. Main Lamp/Lamp Warehouse will do the rest.

SPECIAL FACTORS: Please note there is no catalog; price quote by phone or letter when you enclose a self-addressed stamped envelope; store closed Wednesdays; minimum order $100.

Related Products/Companies

Kerosene lanterns
- Campmor

Lamp parts and lamp-making kits and supplies
- Aftosa, Axner Pottery, Bailey Ceramic, Glass Crafters, Warner-Crivellaro

Lamp switch enlargers
- Comfort House

Lamps and lighting
- BedandBath.com, Blackwelder's, Carolina Interiors, Fran's Wicker Warehouse, Furniture Heirloom Reproductions, Patch of Calabash, Priba, Southland, Tender Heart Treasures, The Ultimate Outlet

Lava lamps
- Cook Brothers, Sportsman's Guide

Lighting and electrical supplies
- All Electronics

Light-switch plates
- Desperate Enterprises

Magnifying lamps and special lamps for the visually impaired
- Comfort House, Damark, Independent Living Aids

Oil lamps
- Lehman's

Party lights and lights on a string
- Sally Distributors

Soccer-themed lamps
- Soccer International

Themed lamps for pool and billiards game rooms
- Mueller Sporting Goods

Tableware

Silverware and stainless flatware, everyday glasses and crystal, fine and everyday china, hollowware, and giftware

Don't pay full price for fine china, stemware, and flatware—period! Every discounter in this section can save you lots—up to 50%—on active patterns of tableware. And if your wedding china, like mine, is a pattern that's *discontinued*, don't worry. There are firms here that have replacement pieces for your pattern at great prices too. The same is true for silverware and crystal. Some of the companies below are also great sources of fine giftware for less. Luxuries at a discount? Why not!

Remember that many of the companies in the "Kitchen Equipment" section, page 350, also carry tableware, albeit of the more everyday variety. See also "Bed, Bath, and Table Textiles," page 299, for linens, cloth napkins, and table mats to complete your dining table's well-dressed look.

Find It Fast

China and Other Dishware
- Barrons, Michael C. Fina, Lanac, Replacements, Rogers & Rosenthal, Rudi's Pottery, Nat Schwartz, Silver Warehouse

Creamware
- Alberene Royal Mail

Crystal
- Alberene Royal Mail, Michael C. Fina, Replacements, Rogers & Rosenthal, Nat Schwartz, Silver Warehouse

Custom Engraving
- Michael C. Fina, Lanac, Nat Schwartz

Estate Sterling
- Beverly Bremer, Coinways, Replacements, The Silver Queen, Silver Warehouse

Figurines and Collectibles
- Alberene Royal Mail, Replacements, Ltd., Nat Schwartz

Flatware
- Barrons, Beverly Bremer, Coinways, Michael C. Fina, Kaiser Crow, Lanac, Replacements, Rogers & Rosenthal, Rudi's Pottery, Nat Schwartz, The Silver Queen, Silver Warehouse

Silverware Repair Services
- Silver Warehouse

Alberene Royal Mail

P.O. Box 902, Center Village   800–843–9078
Harrisville, NH 03450   603–827–5512

Brochures: free
Pay: check, MO, MC, V, AE, DSC
Sells: Creamware, Edinburgh crystal, misc. Scottish foods,
  videos, music, etc.
Store: showroom at 435 Fifth Ave., 3rd Floor, New York
  City

Perhaps this company should be called "Everything Scottish." You'll find terrific deals on wonderful Creamware here, that ivory-colored earthenware that looks as though it's been crocheted around the edges, popularized by Wedgwood a century ago and more recently by such upscale yard-salers as Martha Stewart. Alberene pares up to 35% off the going rate, making these pretty pieces affordable. They also carry Edinburgh crystal—the largest selection of Thistle outside of Britain—at 25% to 35% lower than elsewhere. There's more, although for the following items you'll pay about what you would in a store (if you could find them!): teas by Brodies of Edinburgh, Wallace Scotch Whisky Cake, preserves, honey, fudge (all Scottish, of course), Scottish pub glasses, Scottish books, videos, music CDs and cassettes, and even fantastic true-to-life miniatures of European architectural treasures by Fraser Creations, including Stonehenge, Westminster Abbey, and the Anne Hathaway Cottage. Best of all, Alberene doesn't charge shipping to addresses within the U.S., which saves you even more.

SPECIAL FACTORS: Satisfaction is guaranteed; returns are accepted for exchange, refund, or credit.

Barrons

P.O. Box 994
Novi, MI 48376–0994

800–538–6340
Fax: 800–523–4456

Catalog: free
Pay: check, MO, MC, V, DSC
Sells: dinnerware, giftware, and home accessories
Store: mail order only
Online: www.barronsdinnerware.com

Since 1975 Barrons has been selling steeply discounted, name-brand tableware, crystal and giftware, and home accessories for people who like the convenience of shopping at home. There's a print catalog, or you can check out the website to view some, but not all, of the inventory and even order online. With thousands of patterns in stock, Barrons offers well-known lines of china, flatware, and serving pieces. If you know what you're looking for, you're likely to find it through Barrons at "amazing savings."

SPECIAL FACTORS: Satisfaction guaranteed; returns accepted within 30 days for exchange, refund, or credit.

Beverly Bremer Silver Shop

3164 Peachtree Rd., NE,
Dept. WBM
Atlanta, GA 30305

800–270–4009
404–261–4009
Fax: 404–261–9708

Information: inquire (see text)
Pay: check, MO, MC, V, DSC
Sells: new and estate sterling flatware, hollowware, gifts, etc.
Store: same address; Monday to Saturday 10–5

Nicknamed the "Silver Belle," Beverly Bremer presides over her glistening eponymous Georgia shop, which has more than 1,200 sterling flatware patterns in stock, including American, English, Italian, French, and Danish designs. Her new and nearly new sterling silver flatware is priced up to 75% off regular retail. If you're missing a piece of your pattern, chances are you'll find it here, including active, discontinued, antique, and hard-to-find patterns.

You can request, by phone or mail, an inventory of your silver patterns showing the pieces in stock. If you don't know the name of the pattern, send along a photocopy or sketch (be sure to sketch any identifying marks on back of the handles). Ms. Bremer says that, unless noted, there are no monograms on the old silver she carries. (She doesn't sell silver on which monograms have been removed, either.) Beverly Bremer also offers a wide selection of new and antique, investment-quality hollowware, new and antique sterling gifts, and a sterling appraisal service. Here's a great place to buy a wedding gift, a romantic gift, or an instant heirloom (antique sterling pieces make good investments), and Beverly Bremer will wrap and ship it to your specifications.

SPECIAL FACTORS: Complete customer satisfaction guaranteed.

Coinways/Antiques Ltd.

475 Central Ave.
Cedarhurst, NY 11516

800–645–2102
516–374–1970
Fax: 516–374–3218

Information: price quote
Pay: check, MO, MC, V, AE, DSC
Sells: new and used sterling flatware
Store: same address; Monday to Friday 10:30–5:30,
Wednesday 10:30–7:30, Saturday 11–5

Today it's salad bars and plastic forks, but decades ago oven-cooked food actually traveled from plate to palate on beautifully patterned, desirably heavy sterling flatware. Since 1979, Coinways/Antiques Ltd. has been selling vintage, as well as new, flatware by the piece and in full sets. Silver manufactured by major names in the flatware business can be bought at savings up to 75% on suggested retail or market prices. Here's a tip from Coinways: When you're trying to replace a piece from an old pattern, look for one made in the same year as your set; the amount of silver in the replacement piece and, hence, its weight, will match the rest of your set. To get a price quote, include in your letter or fax the name, length, and shape of the piece, and a photocopy of the design if the pattern name is in doubt.

SPECIAL FACTORS: Orders shipped worldwide.

Michael C. Fina

545 Fifth Ave.
New York, NY 10017

800–BUY–FINA
718–937–8484
Fax: 718–937–7193

Catalog: free
Pay: check, MO, MC, V, AE, DSC
Sells: jewelry, tableware, and giftware
Store: 3 W. 47th St., New York, NY; Monday to Friday
9:30–6, Thursday 9:30–7, Saturday 10:30–6

In business since 1935, Michael C. Fina has been known locally as a great place to buy jewelry at substantial savings—10% to 50% below list. But Manhattanites, visitors, and mail-order shoppers alike can also choose from an exhaustive roster of name-brand manufacturers of tableware and flatware way too numerous to list here. If there's a particular maker of china, stemware, or flatware you seek, chances are excellent that this company stocks it. A bridal registry is maintained, and sterling silver, stainless steel, and silver-plate gift items are available. The sales staff are fluent in French, Italian, Russian, and Spanish.

SPECIAL FACTORS: Satisfaction guaranteed; returns accepted within three weeks for exchange, refund, or credit (except for engraved and personalized items).

Kaiser Crow, Inc.

14998 W. Sixth Ave., #500
Golden, CO 80401

800–468–2769
303–215–1111
Fax: 303–215–1115

Brochure: free
Pay: check, MO, MC, V, AE, DSC
Sells: Oneida stainless flatware
Store: mail order only
Online: www.kaisercrow.com

Here's a nifty company. Kaiser Crow has been around since 1985 and sells Oneida stainless flatware at prices more than 50% below suggested list price. The color catalog shows the current patterns of Oneida stainless, Oneida Golden Accents (stainless accented with 25-karat gold electroplate), and service pieces (butter knives, sugar spoons, gravy ladles, pie servers, etc.) in every pattern. I like the website, which features website-only specials, lists and photographs of active and discontinued patterns to purchase as sets or individual replacement pieces, and free shipping on all orders placed online. Coming soon to Kaiser Crow, according to the website: Oneida dinnerware.

SPECIAL FACTORS: Satisfaction guaranteed; returns accepted (see catalog or website for details).

Lanac Sales Company

500 Driggs Avenue
Brooklyn, NY 11211

718–782–7200
Fax: 718–782–1313

Catalog: free
Pay: check, MO, MC, V, AE, DSC
Sells: fine tableware, home accents, jewelry, and
  engraving
Store: same address; Monday to Thursday 9–6, Friday
  9–2, Sunday 10–5, closed Saturdays
Online: www.lanacsales.com

Since 1957 Lanac Sales Company has been selling tabletop items and giftware at unbeatable savings—up to 50% off normal retail prices is not unusual—and offers a lowest price guarantee if you can find the same item elsewhere for less. This is welcome information if you're shopping for china, crystal, or silver for your own home or as a wedding gift. (Lanac Sales maintains a bridal registry that you can set up over the telephone or online.) Porcelain or stoneware settings by major designers and manufacturers are available, as are stainless, plate, and sterling silver. (Lanac sells a full line of storage cases for your silver, too.) In addition, Lanac carries gift, home accents, and entertaining accessories such as hinged boxes, fine jewelry, snifters, decanters, and silver tea services, as well as a limited selection of small kitchen appliances (coffeemakers, juicers, food processors, and cappuccino machines). A sampling of major manufacturers represented here includes Aynsley, Baccarat, Gorham, Lenox, Mont Blanc, Ralph Lauren, Royal Doulton, Spode, Waterford, and Wedgwood. Although the website is fun to browse and offers online ordering, the selection there isn't as comprehensive as Lanac's print catalog, at least at the time of this writing. With over 25,000 items in stock, chances are Lanac will have the fine tableware or stemware you seek. You can get a price quote by phone or letter. Custom engraving is available.

SPECIAL FACTORS: Satisfaction guaranteed; prices quoted by phone or letter; closed Saturdays.

Replacements, Ltd.

1089 Knox Rd.
Greensboro, NC 27420

800–737–5223
336–697–3000
Fax: 336–697–3100
TDD: 800–270–3708

Information: website and price quotes only, no print
  catalog
Pay: check, V, MC, DSC
Sells: replacement china, crystal, and silver, and
  collectibles
Store: mail order only; phone hours 8 A.M. to 12 midnight
  EST, seven days a week
Online: www.replacements.com

"We replace the irreplaceable," says the banner at the top of Replacement, Ltd.'s Internet home page. This is a great company that I can vouch for firsthand. My Wedgwood china pattern has been discontinued. I'd be sad if it weren't for the fact that I've been able to replace a broken coffee cup and a soup bowl through Replacements, Ltd. My "new" pieces are indistinguishable from the originals and cost a fraction of the original price. Replacements carries over 100,000 patterns of china, crystal, and silver (flatware and hollowware) from such manufacturers as Lenox, Royal Doulton, Wedgwood, Noritake, Mikasa, Spode, Oneida, International Silver, Pfaltzgraff, Gorham Silver, Towle Silver, Franciscan, and hundreds more. Replacements also carries a large selection of collectibles including plates, bells, and figurines by makers such as Hummel, Royal Doulton, Lladro, Lenox, Precious Moments, Franklin Mint, Swarovski, and others. The website is very informative and allows you to register your pattern so that Replacements can inform you when sales are happening or special pieces have come in. Online you can also identify your pattern, read about manufacturers' histories, browse current specials, and more. Since the inventory is large and ever-changing, this company doesn't publish a print catalog. They're ready, however, to answer your phone inquiries and will even fax or mail you an inventory listing of your pattern.

SPECIAL FACTORS: 30-day, no-questions-asked returns policy; satisfaction guaranteed.

Rogers & Rosenthal, Inc.

2337 Lemoine Ave., Suite 101   201–346–1862
Fort Lee, NJ 07024–0212   Fax: 201–947–5812

    Information: price quote
    Pay: check or MO
    Sells: tableware
    Store: mail order only

Rogers and Rosenthal, two recognizable names in the china and silver trades, have been in the business of providing customers with fine table settings at up to 60% below list price since 1930. They don't have a fancy website. They publish no highfalutin catalog. But if you know the pattern of china, flatware (stainless, silver-plate, or sterling), crystal, stemware, hollowware, or pewter you're looking for by just about any top-name manufacturer, write down the maker and style and leave the rest to Rogers & Rosenthal. Please call or write for a price quote (written requests should be accompanied by a SASE); you'll be glad you did.

    Canadian readers, please note: Only special orders are shipped to Canada.

SPECIAL FACTORS: Price quote by phone or letter with a long self-addressed, stamped envelope; returns accepted for exchange.

Rudi's Pottery, Silver & China

282 Rt. 17 North   800–631–2526
Paramus, NJ 07652   201–265–6096
                        Fax: 201–265–2086

    Information: price quote
    Pay: check, MO, MC, V, DSC
    Sells: tableware
    Store: same address and 357 Rt. 9 S., Manalapan, NJ;
      Monday to Saturday 10–5:30

Rudi's Pottery, Silver & China sells the best names in china, crystal, and flatware at savings up to 60% on list prices. Since Rudi's doesn't send out a regular catalog, when you find a pattern of stemware, for example, that you like, call Rudi's for a price quote. You'll be pleasantly surprised. You can also write them for a price quote if you enclose a self-addressed stamped envelope when you do. Although tableware has been Rudi's mainstay since 1968, they also carry limited-edition Christmas ornaments and collectibles.

SPECIAL FACTORS: Prices quoted by phone or letter (include self-addressed stamped envelope).

Nat Schwartz & Co., Inc.

549 Broadway, Dept. LIB18   800–526–1440
Bayonne, NJ 07002   Fax: 201–437–4903

Catalog: free
Pay: check, MO, MC, V, AE, DSC
Sells: tableware, giftware, and housewares
Store: same address; Monday to Friday 9:30–6, Thursday
    9:30–8, Saturday 10–5

Nat Schwartz & Co., Inc., sells fine china and giftware by almost every name-brand designer or manufacturer you can think of at 10% to 50% below normal retail prices. Belleek, Bing & Grøndahl, Dansk, Fabergé, Lenox, Royal Crown Derby—the list goes on and on, and the 32-page catalog is just the beginning! You'll find crystal, flatware, and housewares as well, all by recognized names: Baccarat, Noritake, Val St. Lambert, and Waterford, for crystal; Boda Nova, Empire, Oneida, and Wallace, for flatware and hollowware; and Braun, Le Creuset, and Krups, for housewares. Nat Schwartz's available services include coordination of silver, crystal, and china patterns, hand engraving, a bridal registry, and a corporate gift program.

SPECIAL FACTORS: Satisfaction guaranteed; prices quoted by phone, fax, or letter; 20% deposit required on special orders (refundable only if order is canceled while on back order); undamaged returns (except engraved items) accepted within 30 days (restocking fee may apply).

The Silver Queen Inc.

730 N. Indian Rocks Rd.   **727–581–6827**
Belleair Bluffs, FL 33770   **Fax: 727–586–0822**

Catalog: free
Pay: check, MO, MC, V, AE, DSC
Sells: estate silver flatware, and new flatware, china, and crystal
Store: same address; Monday to Friday 9–5, Saturday 9:30–5
Online: www.silverqueen.com

When I was setting up my first apartment, I used to go to second-hand stores to buy silver-plated flatware, which I could usually afford. Having grown up with real silverware, I couldn't bring myself to eat off stainless steel. Too bad I didn't know about The Silver Queen. Since 1973, the Silver Queen has specialized in estate sterling flatware. With over 1,500 patterns in stock, they have one of the largest inventories of active and discontinued patterns in the U.S. They obtain their flatware from estate collections and jewelry buyouts and pass the savings on to you. You can view many of these on The Silver Queen's website, where the estate patterns listed next to the new ones prove if you're willing to buy "like-new" flatware rather than brand new, you'll save 25% or more on perfectly restored estate silverware. If there's a pattern you're interested in, you can also call to get the latest computerized list of prices and availability. Either way, you'll need to call, since the website doesn't offer online ordering. The Silver Queen also has a 24-page color catalog offering new and estate sterling silverware, stainless flatware, silverplated flatware, hollowware, baby gifts, and new china and crystal, many of these priced below normal retail by as much as 40%.

SPECIAL FACTORS: Price quote by phone or letter.

Silver Warehouse

4311 NE Vivion Road, 3rd
Floor
Kansas City, MO 64119–2890

816–454–1990
Fax: 816–454–1605

Information: online catalog, no print catalog
Pay: check, MO, V, MC
Sells: silver, stainless, and pewter flatware, china, crystal,
hollowware, etc.
Store: same address, 10–6 daily, closed Wednesday and
Sunday
Online: www.silverwarehouse.com

Silver Warehouse, founded in 1970, has the largest selection of silverware world-wide, offers active and discontinued patterns, and is a full-service company for sterling silver, stainless, silverplate, Dirilyte, and pewter flatware and hollowware as well as crystal and china. The website reminds shoppers that Silver Warehouse also buys, sells, and repairs silverware and hollowware, offering professional knife reblading and garbage disposal damage repair. Here you can also get free pattern identification and free pattern search to supplement those missing spoons. A bridal registry is maintained, and a no-interest layaway is available. The attractive website allows you to order online or view the inventory, which includes lots of tableware, flatware, china, and stemware in addition to books on silver care, polish, storage chests and cloths, and then phone in your order. The Silver Warehouse site permits a search/order of china and an identification and match of silverware patterns, both current and discontinued. The same information can be obtained by sending a business-sized stamped and self-addressed envelope for a price quote form.

SPECIAL FACTORS: Returns accepted within 30 days for full refund, less shipping charges, provided an e-mail is received indicating which pieces are being returned.

Related Products/Companies

Everyday china
- Kitchen Etc., Peerless

Fine china
- Bennett Brothers, Kitchen Etc.

Glassware
- Peerless, Stumps

Miscellaneous tableware
- Broadway Panhandler, Peerless

Pewterware
- Bennett Brothers

Plastic and paper tableware for catering/entertaining
- M&N International, Party and Paper Worldwide, The Party Wholesaler, U.S. Toy

Serving pieces
- Kitchen Etc.

Silverware and gold-plated flatware
- Bennett Brothers, Cook Brothers

Stainless steel flatware
- Damark

Stoneware
- Caprilands Herb Farm

Tea cups and tea pots
- East Earth Trade Winds

Wall and Window Treatments, Decorator Fabrics

Wallpaper, wall stencils, curtains, shades, and blinds; upholstery, drapery, and other interior-decorating fabric

It turns out that companies that specialize in window treatments such as shades and blinds also often carry wallpaper. And companies that specialize in wallpaper often carry decorator fabric. Well, it makes sense if you think about it. If you want to pull a room together, what better way than to coordinate your curtains or shades with your wallpaper and upholstery? So here they are together: wall and window treatments and decorator fabric. The firms in this section carry all the fabrics and materials you'll need to create window ruffles, throw pillows, fabric room dividers, and coordinated upholstery. There's also every kind of shade and blind as well as the hardware you'll need. And if you've the energy for hanging wallpaper or stenciling a border around your room, you'll find these here too. The companies listed below can save you as much as 80%.

Decorator Fabrics and Trim
- BMI Home Decorating, The Fabric Center, Hancock's of Paducah, Harmony Supply, Homespun Fabrics & Draperies, Marlene's, Robinson's Wallpaper, Shama Imports, Silk Surplus

Decorator Stencils
- Stencil House of N.H.

Hand-Embroidered Crewel Fabrics
- Shama Imports

Wall Coverings and Related Supplies
- American Blind and Wallpaper, BMI Home Decorating, Harmony Supply, Robinson's Wallpaper

Window Treatments and Hardware
- American Blind and Wallpaper, BMI Home Decorating, Harmony Supply, Homespun Fabrics & Draperies, Smith & Noble Windoware, Wells Interiors

American Blind and Wallpaper Factory

909 N. Sheldon Rd.   **800–735–5300**
Plymouth, MI 48170   **Fax: 800–403–2293**

Catalog: free
Pay: check, MO, MC, V, AE, DC, DSC
Sells: wallpaper and blinds
Store: mail order only
Online: www.abwf.com

Why pay more than you have to for blinds and wallpaper? American Blind & Wallpaper Factory claims to have the largest selection of national brand special-order blinds and wallpaper in the U.S. You can save up to 80% by buying here.

This company offers product selections from over 62 national brand manufacturers, and has access to wallpaper patterns from over 5,000 special-order wallpaper books. You can browse the wallpaper catalog, which features hundreds of the most popular patterns, or log on to the website to view thousands of patterns in their Wallpapery Gallery. If you need a closer look at a pattern, they'll send you a free sample just for the asking. The free American Blind Sample Kit, which you can request, has the complete assortment of mini, micro, pleated, cellular, vertical, and wood blinds, as well as directions for mounting and measuring. With either blinds or wallpaper, if you shop your local decorating store and write down the brand, color, and pattern number, a quick call or e-mail to the company will get you an express quote. American Blind & Wallpaper guarantees the lowest prices anywhere, and offers a free lifetime guarantee against product defects.

SPECIAL FACTORS: Satisfaction guaranteed; free shipping in the continental U.S.

BMI Home Decorating

6917 Catalpa Ct.   815–675–3703
Spring Grove, IL 60081   Fax: 815–675–3603

Information: price quote
Pay: check, MO, MC, V, AE
Sells: decorator fabric, wall coverings, and window
  treatments
Store: mail order only

If you're preparing to do some major decorating and know what fabrics and wall coverings you want, BMI Home Decorating can save you 35% or more on these, depending on the amount ordered and other criteria. As a friend of mine always says, "It doesn't hurt to ask," especially since you've already done the hard part, which is the footwork. So here's what you do: Call or write BMI with the manufacturer's name and/or number, and the book name (for wall coverings). They'll give you a price quote that may make you glad you waited to buy your material. BMI can give you access to almost any fabric from hundreds of manufacturers, including many limited to the trade. In addition to fabric, BMI offers wall coverings, drapery hardware, and can custom-make pillows, bedspreads, and headboards to order.

SPECIAL FACTORS: Price quote by phone or letter.

The Fabric Center, in business for 66 years, buys first-quality fabric in volume from the leading mills and then passes those savings on to you at discounts close to 50% off retail. The 164-page catalog from The Fabric Center is like sitting down with your own personal decorator. Page after page of luscious photographs show these decorator fabrics used in context: as pillow shams in elaborate settings with matching tablecloths, as upholstery for Victorian fainting couches, adorning windows with complementary bedspreads. Fabric and pattern specifications are given, including material content, widths, vertical repeat, price, and a usage code to help you determine the appropriate use in your home (bedspreads, windows, upholstery, etc.). The catalog also has a section devoted to tassels, lace, and other trim for finishing touches. The Fabric Center has been in business for a long time and there's a good reason for it: They make it easy for you but offering samples for pennies (a 3″ × 4″ fabric sample is 15 cents; larger swatches are slightly more) and by having customer reps on the other end of the phone line who can answer all your questions.

SPECIAL FACTORS: Minimum order one yard.

Hancock's of Paducah

3841 Hinkleville Rd., Dept.
BWBM
Paducah, KY 42001

800–845–8723
502–443–4410
Fax: 502–442–2164, 3152

Catalog: $2
Pay: check, MO, MC, V, DSC
Sells: home-decorating fabrics, quilting fabrics, pillow
forms, quilting supplies, etc.
Store: same address; Monday to Friday 9:30–7, Saturday
10–6, Sunday 1–5
Online: www.hancocks-paducah.com

Down in Paducah, Kentucky, is "America's largest quilting and home-decorating store," Hancock's of Paducah. For over three decades this company has operated a brisk mail-order business serving two primary markets—home decorators and quilters—by offering goods priced 50% lower than anywhere else. Some other nice features include a custom laminating service (great for patio furniture, table-cloths, place mats, rain gear, and more) and an inexpensive sample service.

The full-color 64-page "Fabrics for the Home" catalog features hundreds of fabrics for bedding ensembles, window treatments, upholstery, and decorative pillows, along with accessory items such as cords, tassels, fringes, and drapery hardware. The catalog for quilters has thousands of fabrics appropriate for quilting, along with tools, notions, and other supplies that are often hard to find, especially in less-populated areas. Both quilters and decorators would be well served to check out Hancock of Paducah's website, where you can view fabric samples, check out specials, and order online.

SPECIAL FACTORS: Free shipping within continental U.S. when you order online; satisfaction guaranteed; see catalog for returns policy.

Harmony Supply Inc.

P.O. Box 313
Medford, MA 02155

781–395–2600
Fax: 781–396–8218

Information: price quote
Pay: check, MO, MC, V, DSC
Sells: wall coverings, window treatments, and decorator
 fabrics
Store: 18 High St., Medford, MA; Monday to Saturday
 8–5:30, Thursday 8–9

In business since 1949, Harmony Supply has been helping folks like us save money when it's time to redo curtains, upholstery, blinds, and wallpaper, offering discounts up to 70%. Harmony carries over 2,500 designs and patterns of wallpaper, grass cloth, and string cloth, including all the top sellers and in-vogue lines of coordinating fabric. Harmony also sells all kinds of window treatments—made-to-measure mini, micro, and vertical binds, including wood, and pleated shades and blinds. Everything Harmony sells is first quality. Since the company doesn't have a catalog, it's necessary to scope out the goods locally, then call or write Harmony for a price quote.

SPECIAL FACTORS: Satisfaction is guaranteed; returns (except custom blinds and fabrics) are accepted within 30 days (a 25% restocking fee is charged on special-order goods).

Homespun "10-Foot Wide" Fabrics & Draperies has a solution to some of the biggest drapery headaches—bulkiness, sun rot, the expense of dry cleaning, and the hassle of pleater hooks among them. Homespun Fabrics sells all-cotton material that's ten feet wide, or about 105 to 109 inches after shrinkage. The fabric includes homespun, hobnail, barley, and monkscloth weaves, in white and natural. The width makes the fabric perfect for "seamless draperies," and even eliminates some of the finishing work. Homespun Fabrics manufactures all styles of draperies (suitable to the fabric) and can also custom-make "Fan Pleat" draperies. These operate on a track system that's hung from the ceiling or mounted on the wall, with a buckram header tape with nylon tabs that engage the track. The drapery folds are four or five inches deep, so the stackback (the area covered by the curtain when it's drawn back) that would be 37 inches deep with conventional pinch-pleat draperies is only 11 inches deep with the Fan Pleat system. Made in Homespun Fabrics' heavyweight cottons, this system produces handsome, neutral window coverings that give you maximum glass exposure. They have a crisp, tailored appearance that's ideal for modern decor and office settings, and are machine washable and dryable and guaranteed against sun rot for seven years. An added bonus: The fabric can be tolerated by people with chemical sensitivities, as one such customer enthused in a letter to the company.

Besides draperies, Homespun also carries bedcovers and throws, roman shades, tablecloths and napkins, bedskirts, and more, not to mention the hardware for accessorizing your drapes (fanwood poles and decorative ends of all kinds). Some of the fabrics even lend themselves nicely to labor-saving and attractive wall coverings, hiding ugly plaster and old wallpaper. In addition to the heavy cottons, Homespun Fabrics offers open-weave casement fabric, wide muslin, and both regular-width and ultra-wide semi-sheers—batiste, voile, and bouclé slub, in lots of colors. Homespun can create the draperies, or you can do it yourself— and you'll find helpful books on home decorating and guides to making fan pleat draperies, slipcovers, bedspreads, table linens, and accessories.

SPECIAL FACTORS: Returns are accepted within ten days for exchange, refund, or credit; $5 cutting fee on orders of five or fewer yards.

Marlene's Decorator Fabrics

301 Beech St., Dept. 2J 201–843–0844
Hackensack, NJ 07601

Flyer: free with SASE
Pay: check, MO, MC, V, AE
Sells: decorator fabrics
Store: mail order only; phone hours Monday to Friday
9:30–6 EST

The brochure from Marlene's is about as straightforward as one could be. It lists the manufacturer names of first-quality fabrics and trims with which Marlene's deals. If the decorator fabric you seek is on that list, you're in luck, because this company can get it to you at 35% to 50% off retail prices as long as you can meet the minimum yardage requirement (five-yard minimum on some, 15-yard minimum on others). Write or call for a price quote, or send a self-addressed stamped envelope with a sample if you're not sure of the manufacturer name or pattern number, or to request a brochure. Specify the yardage needed and whether you're interested in upholstery, drapery, or other decorator fabrics.

SPECIAL FACTORS: Minimum orders apply; no returns unless damaged by UPS or manufacturer.

Robinson's Wallpaper Interiors

225 W. Spring St., 8LY   800–458–2426
P.O. Box 427   Fax: 814–827–1693
Titusville, PA 16354–0427

Catalog: $2
Pay: check, MO, MC, V, AE, DSC
Sells: wallpaper, borders, decorator fabrics, and
  accessories
Store: same address; also 3506 Liberty Center, Erie, PA,
  and 1720 Wilmington Rd., Rt. 18, New Castle, PA
Online: www.robinsonswallpaper.com

How has Robinson's Wallpaper Interiors been in business since 1919? They've survived and excelled in the competitive home decorating industry by offering a fabulous selection of wallpapers and borders at unbeatable prices—up to 60% off any pattern from nearly any book. If you browse the print catalog you'll find formal patterns for stately dining rooms, cozy kitchen designs, and designs for everything in between, from the library to the bathroom to your child's nursery. The photographs show actual papered rooms and walls so you can see how these designs look when installed. If there's a pattern you love that you don't see in the catalog, simply call Robinson's and tell them the book name and manufacturer, pattern number and page number, and they'll quote you a bargain price. Other offerings include wallpaper supplies and tools; free samples of any pattern; free shipping on orders of six rolls or more; and a helpful measuring guide. At press time the website was promising to have a complete online showroom soon, but it also featured how-to books on wallpapering that you could order online.

SPECIAL FACTORS: Satisfaction guaranteed; returns accepted within 30 days for exchange or refund; excess unopened rolls are returnable.

Shama Imports, Inc.

P.O. Box 2900, Dept. BWBM   **248–478–7740**
Farmington Hills, MI
48333–2900

Brochure: free
Pay: check, MO, MC, V
Sells: hand-embroidered crewel fabrics and accessories
Store: mail order only

If only I could attach a fabric swatch to this paragraph so you could see the beauty and uniqueness of Shama Imports' hand-made crewel fabric. This company specializes in hand-embroidered wool on hand-loomed cotton backgrounds that comes directly to Shama from craftsmen in Kashmir, India, eliminating both the middleman and the normal markup. Thus, you can buy bedspreads, tablecloths, seat and cushion covers, fabric for upholstery, drapes, or even wall hangings directly from Shama Imports for 50% less than you'd pay elsewhere. But don't believe me. Believe the dozens of ecstatic customers' testimonials included in the literature sent by Shama.

The fabric can be hand-washed or dry-cleaned and comes in serpentine flower-and-vine motifs and other distinctive classic designs embroidered in a variety of very tasteful color choices, all on an off-white background. I'm certain it would be impossible to find anything this beautiful at a fabric or design store at these fantastic prices. At the time of this writing, for example, the 52-inch-wide fabric averaged around $30 per yard, and ready-made items were equally reasonable, from a $11 cushion cover to a $80 round tablecloth. Fabric samples are available for $1 each; those showing one-fourth of the complete pattern cost $5 (refundable). The brochure lists the pattern repeats for all of the designs.

SPECIAL FACTORS: Satisfaction guaranteed; uncut, undamaged returns accepted within 30 days for refund or credit.

Silk Surplus

1127 2nd Ave.
New York, NY 10022

212–753–6511
Fax: 212–753–0463

Information: price quote
Pay: check, MO, MC, V, AE
Sells: discontinued decorator fabric and trim
Store: same address; Monday to Saturday 10–6; two other
NY locations, call for directions

All good things—even decorator fabrics—come to an end. Luckily, there's Silk Surplus to rescue discontinued Scalamandré and Boris Kroll fabric as well as silks, cottons, velvets, woolens, chintzes, brocades, damasks, and other weaves at savings up to 75%. Since 1962, Silk Surplus has welcomed walk-in shoppers to its stores, now totaling three. Since there's no catalog, mail-order customers must know in advance the exact discontinued Scalamandré or Boris Kroll fabric and color they want. Serious mail-order buyers can query by mail and enclose fabric samples. Design professionals should inquire about additional trade discounts.

SPECIAL FACTORS: Prices quoted by phone or letter (with a SASE); free sample cuttings; all sales final; minimum order three yards.

Smith & Noble Windoware

P.O. Box 1838
Corona, CA 91718

800–248–8888
Fax: 800–426–7780

Catalog: free
Pay: check, MO, MC, V, AE, DSC
Sells: shades, blinds, and shutters
Store: mail order only
Online: www.smithandnoble.com

The 60-page "Windoware Sourcebook" from Smith & Noble made me want to dress up all my windows with shades, blinds, curtains, and shutters. Ordering direct from Smith & Noble means you can save from 20% to 70% off store prices.

The carefully laid out catalog walks you through all the options with beautiful color photographs and good, descriptive text. You'll find shades (natural Roman, honeycomb, roller, Duette insulated, Parisian, pleated, and soft), blinds (wood, Optica, vertical, Duraflex, and metal), shutters, cornices, panels, hardware, scarves, and sconces. Detailed instructions for measuring and installing will help you feel confident; customer service people can answer any other questions you might have. If you need fabric swatches, you can order up to ten for $5, which is refundable with any order over $100 made within 90 days. The Smith & Noble website does not feature online ordering at this time.

Please note: Since all window treatments are specifically custom-crafted for your windows, items are nonreturnable except for warranty repair.

SPECIAL FACTORS: All custom orders must be made in writing and mailed or faxed; free shipping within the continental U.S.

Stencil House of N.H., Inc.

P.O. Box 109, Dept. BWBM   603–625–1716
Hooksett, NH 03106

Catalog: $4, refundable with first order
Pay: check, MO, V, MC
Sells: decorator stencils
Store: mail order only
Online: www.isystems.com/stencil

Jan Gordon's husband is afraid to turn his back on his wife, president of Stencil House of N.H. "If I see a plain surface, I want to stencil it," she says. The 20-page color catalog from Stencil House offers a dazzling array of decorator-quality stencil designs at craft-store prices. While common craft stencils are one-piece designs, Stencil House's designs are multilayered to allow for two or more colors. The current catalog has over 230 different designs appropriate for walls, floors, stair risers, fireboards, wooden furniture, fabric, and more.

The stencils come precut or "uncut"; you can save an average of $2 to $3 on each by cutting out the designs yourself. Most of the stencils are under $10, and all are one-of-a-kind items, designed by Gordon, although the starred items in the catalog are modeled after authentic stencil designs found in museums and old homesteads. There are quaint country motifs, such as a bird with birdhouse and a laundry line; Shaker-inspired designs; Penn-Dutch stylized vines, flowerpots, hearts, birds, and flowers; themes for children, such as Teddy bears, animals, and alphabets; berries, fruits, and flowers galore; and much more. Stencil House can also custom-design stencils to go with your wallpaper and fabric. If you send in a fabric sample, they'll help you match the paint color and give other color and design advice for free.

Stencil House sells various stencil supplies, including paints (two different paint charts are offered), stencil brushes, brush cleaner, stencil adhesive that won't damage the surface when the stencil is removed; varnish; floor cloth; and unprinted Mylar sheets (for making your own stencils). Stencil House has a "frequent stenciler's plan"—when you've ordered five stencils (no time limit) you get one stencil for free. See catalog for details. The website is worth a peek. There you can view some of these stencil designs as well as order a print catalog.

Wholesale customers: Please inquire about wholesale prices and policies.

SPECIAL FACTORS: All payments in U.S. funds. Custom designing and sizing available; no returns on custom orders.

Wells Interiors Inc.

7171 Amador Plaza Dr. **800–547–8982**
Dublin, CA 94568 **Fax: 510–829–1374**

Catalog: free
Pay: check, MO, MC, V
Sells: window treatments and accessories
Store: 19 locations in CA, NV, and OR; see catalog for
locations

Wells says, "We will beat any competitor's advertised price on any identical product we carry, right down to our cost." Since 1980, Wells Interiors, "The Window Covering Experts," have been selling mini-blinds, verticals, wood blinds, Venetian blinds, pleated shades, silhouette blinds, honeycomb shades, specialty blinds, and shutters by mail at amazing prices. Discounts can run up to 85% on some items. The catalog includes a guide to the lines currently available and has instructions on measuring your windows and installing the blinds. A Wells Interiors website was under construction at this writing.

SPECIAL FACTORS: Limited lifetime warranty on all products purchased from Wells (see catalog for details); written confirmation required on all phone orders.

Related Products/Companies

Cowhide pillows and cowhides for wall hangings
- Steerhides

Curtains
- BedandBath.com, Eldridge Textile

Custom embroidery
- Harris Levy

Decorator fabrics
- Furniture Patch of Calabash, Priba Furniture, Quality Furniture Market

Drapery hardware
- Atlanta Thread & Supply, BedandBath.com

Interior house shutters
- Shuttercraft

Interior wall paint
- Pearl Paint

Leather
- Weaver Leather

Supplies and tools for marbleizing, faux finishes, and gilding
- Jerry's Artarama, Pearl Paint

Upholstery books
- Frank's Cane and Rush

Upholstery stuffing
- Buffalo Batt & Felt

Upholstery supplies
- The Button Shop, The Caning Shop, Frank's Cane and Rush, Newark Dressmaker Supply

Upholstery-weight silk fabric
- Utex Trading, Thai Silks

Vintage product labels for papering walls
- Original Paper Collectibles

Wall coverings
- Priba Furniture

Wall, floor, and fabric stencils
- Glass Crafters, Vanguard Crafts

Window screens
- Coppa Woodworking

Luggage and Leather Goods

Luggage, briefcases, computer bags, handbags, backpacks, etc.; leather by the piece and leather-crafting tools and supplies

The luggage discounters here can deliver big savings on everything from suitcases, attaché cases, and rolling garment bags to smaller items such as travel kits, handbags, and backpacks. Some of the firms also sell cases for musical instruments and artist portfolios. You'll also find firms that sell leather by the piece, leather-care products, and leather-craft tools. For other firms that sell luggage, leather goods, and related supplies, see "Related Products/Companies" at the end of this chapter.

Find It Fast

Briefcases and Luggage
- Ace Luggage, Airline International, Al's Luggage, Leather Unlimited, The Luggage Center, Santa Maria

Handbags
- Ace Luggage, Al's Luggage, Leather Unlimited

Leather-Craft Supplies
- Leather Unlimited, Weaver Leather

Leather Desk Accessories and Gift Items
- Ace Luggage, Airline International

Luggage Repair
- Airline International, Santa Maria

Ace Luggage and Gifts

2122 Ave. U
Brooklyn, NY 11229

800–DIAL–ACE
718–891–9713
Fax: 718–891–3878

Catalog: $2, refundable with first order
Pay: check, MO, MC, V, AE, DSC
Sells: luggage and leather goods, fine pens, etc.
Store: same address; Monday to Saturday 10–6, Thursday
  10–7 (extended hours in December), Sunday 12–5
E-mail: aceluggage@aol.com

Established in 1961, Ace Luggage sells luggage, briefcases, handbags, travel items, desk accessories, Swiss army knives, and fine writing instruments. You'll find all of these in their 36-page color catalog. But the real deal here is on the luggage and briefcases, which are discounted to the tune of 40%. Ace carries over 40 brands of leather and luggage goods, including top names such as Samsonite, Ricardo, TravelPro, Atlantic, Delsey, Lucas, Andiamo, Dakota, Jansport, Lesport-sac, Timberland, Hugo Bosca, Jack Georges, Sacoche, Lodis, and many more. If you don't see the brand you're looking for in their catalog, or if you just want to get a price quote before making the investment, call, fax, or e-mail Ace with the manufacturer's name and the style number. Ace welcomes such inquiries and the opportunity to show you how much money you can save.

SPECIAL FACTORS: Price quote by phone, fax, or e-mail (please have make and model number ready).

Airline International Luggage & Gifts, Inc.

8701 Montana Ave.
El Paso, TX 79925

800–592–1234
915–778–1234
Fax: 915–778–1533

Catalog: free
Pay: check, MO, MC, V, AE, DSC
Sells: luggage and leather goods, gifts, etc.
Store: same address; Monday to Saturday 9:30–6,
  Thursday 9:30–7, Sunday 11–5; also Sunland Park Mall,
  El Paso, TX; Monday to Saturday 10–9, Sunday 12–6
Online: www.airlineintl.com

In 1978 Airline International got its start as a luggage-repair business serving airlines in the El Paso area. Since then it has expanded to offer luggage from every major manufacturer, including attaché cases, briefcases, overnighters and suitcases, laptop cases, backpacks, and other pieces. The 36-page color catalog also presents gift and desk items such as clocks, calculators, jewelry boxes, Swiss watches, collapsible umbrellas, pens, and more. But you'll save big on the luggage, where discounts average 25% off regular retail prices. And if you're not part of today's throwaway culture and have an old leather suitcase you're sentimental about that's in need of repair, send it to Airline International and they'll make it as good as new for you. The website is very user-friendly and offers online ordering, so check it out.

SPECIAL FACTORS: Price quote by phone or letter; returns accepted for exchange, refund, or credit.

Al's Luggage

2134 Larimer St.	303–295–9009
Denver, CO 80205	303–294–9045
	Fax: 303–296–8769

Catalog: $2, refundable
Pay: check, MO, MC, V, AE, DSC
Sells: Samsonite leather goods and luggage
Store: same address; Monday to Friday 9–5:30, Saturday
  9–5

My very first suitcase was a Samsonite—I got it as a present just before leaving for college. I still have that suitcase, many *many* years later! Since 1948, Al's Luggage has been *the* source for Samsonite luggage steeply discounted—to the tune of 35% to 50% savings. The catalog and flyers you'll receive show wardrobes, cosmetics cases, portfolios, briefcases, suitcases, camcorder carrying cases, and other assorted Samsonite luggage. If you love Samsonite, don't shop anywhere else.

SPECIAL FACTORS: Price quotes given by phone or by letter with a self-addressed stamped envelope; C.O.D. orders accepted.

Leather Unlimited Corp.

7155 Cty. Hwy. B, Dept.	920–994–9464
BWBM	Fax: 920–994–4099
Belgium, WI 53004–9990	

Catalog: $2, refundable
Pay: check, MO, MC, V, AE, DSC
Sells: leather-crafting supplies and equipment and
  finished products
Store: same address; Monday to Friday 7–4

In business since 1970, Leather Unlimited issues a 92-page black-and-white catalog with photos and line drawings depicting everything from finished leather products to raccoon skins. Leather crafters will find hardware, tools, and kits; every conceivable kind of skin (caribou, rattlesnake, impala, curly sheep, rabbit, coyote, and more); leather for garments, upholstery, and belts, including dyed leather; and books galore. Interested in Native American craft? You'll find feathers, drum parts, beads, porcupine quills, warrior headdresses, horsehair, tomahawks, replica animal talons, claws, and teeth, looms, silver buttons and conchos, and other items for making modern-day Native American–style clothing, ritual objects, jewelry, and weapons. Cowboys, Hell's Angels, and Vermont soccer moms will all find something they need among the finished items sold here: cycle gear and clothing, Western chaps and saddlebags, ladies' handbags, wallets, and cigarette cases, hats, mittens, slippers, briefcases and computer bags, bicycle seat covers, luggage tags, earrings, and more. Everything in the catalog is 30% to 50% off retail, and there is no minimum order. Extra discounts are given for quantity purchases, detailed in the catalog.

SPECIAL FACTORS: Authorized returns are accepted within ten days of receipt; no minimum order; satisfaction guaranteed.

The Luggage Center

960 Remillard Ct.　　　　800–450–2400
San Jose, CA 95122　　　 408–288–5363
　　　　　　　　　　　　Fax: 408–998–2536

Information:　price quote and website
Pay:　MO, MC, V, AE, DSC
Sells:　luggage, business cases, and travel accessories
Store:　call for 30 locations in California
Online:　www.luggagecenter.com

The Luggage Center specializes in helping leisure and business travelers save money on luggage and business cases. They carry all the major luggage brands, from Ampac to Zero Halliburton, and many items for the business person, such as attachés, book bags, catalog cases, computer cases, portfolios, and rolling business cases. They claim to have the largest selection of Samsonite in the USA, sold at discounts of 33% to 50% off. Among the travel essentials The Luggage Center offers are agendas, clocks, disposable cameras, earplugs, hair dryers, eye shades, manicure sets, laundry items, electrical items, and much more. But the best prices are on the luggage and business cases. It used to be that you had to visit one of their 30 stores in California or Washington, or else call for a price quote. But now The Luggage Center has a website that offers convenient online ordering. The website also features hot buys where some of the closeout items (last year's discontinued models, for example) are up to 60% discounted. You can still call or write for a price quote on an item you've seen locally to see how The Luggage Center's price compares; when you do, have the make and model number handy.

SPECIAL FACTORS: Returns accepted within 30 days.

Santa Maria Discount Luggage

125-F E. Betteravia   888–832–1201
Santa Maria, CA 93454   Tel/Fax: 805–928–2252

     Information: price quote and website
     Pay: check, MO, MC, V, AE, DSC
     Sells: luggage and travel accessories
     Store: same address; Tuesday to Friday 10–6, Saturday
       10–5; also San Luis Luggage, 1135 Chorro St., San Luis
       Obispo, CA
     Online: www.luggageman.com

Santa Maria Discount Luggage offers first-quality travel and business bags and cases at up to 60% off suggested retail prices. If you have Internet access, log onto the website, where you can click on a major brand name and view pictures and descriptions of the full line of offerings. Some prices aren't listed on the website so you still have to call Santa Maria's toll-free number for a price quote. When I did this, I discovered that Santa Maria's price was $5 less than another online luggage store promising "lowest prices." There are some truly amazing sale items on the website for those looking to buy an entire set of brand-new luggage from last year's stock, and other incentives such as free shipping on certain lines. What's good about this company is that they've been around the block a few times and are endorsed by the Better Business Bureau and other consumer organizations. If you don't have web access, you can still call Santa Maria if you've seen a bag you're considering buying. Provide them with the maker's name and model number so they can quote you a price.

SPECIAL FACTORS: Satisfaction guaranteed; returns accepted within 30 days for exchange, refund, or credit.

Weaver Leather

P.O. Box 68
Mt. Hope, OH 44660

330–674–1782
Fax: 330–674–0330

Catalog: free
Pay: check, MO, MC, V
Sells: leather and leather-working and saddlery supplies, parts, and tools
Store: mail order only; phone hours Monday to Friday 7:30–7 ET
Online: www.weaverleather.com

Founded as a small family shoe repair business in 1973 by Harry and Sarah Weaver, Weaver Leather is still family-run but now employs 180 people. Professional leather workers and saddlery shops know Weaver Leather for its selection of leather, hardware, leather-working and leather-crafting tools, oils, dyes and finishes, webbing, machinery and equipment, and much more ("over 2,900 supplies") at excellent prices. Weaver Leather, which runs monthly unadvertised specials that you can hear about through a service rep who will call you (if you like), invites orders on large lots of leather and bulk nylon for additional discounts.

The 118-page color catalog's leather section features shoulders, sole bends, saddle skirting, strap, tooling, shearlings, rawhide, latigo, lace, harness, bridle, patent, nubuck, deer, upholstery, garment, suede, and more. Convenient precut suede fringe and belt blanks as well as custom fringe- and strap-cutting services save you time. But if you've decided to buy your own machinery and equipment, Weaver Leather's full selection includes sewing machines, riveters, skivers, bevelers, strap cutters, grommet fasteners, and more. Hardware, including sleigh bells, buckles, snaps, rings, loops, squares, chain, harness hardware, and harness ornaments and silver by Montana Silversmiths make every project shine. The website is informative and comprehensive, but doesn't offer online ordering.

SPECIAL FACTORS: Satisfaction guaranteed; authorized returns accepted for exchange, refund, or credit; minimum order $50; quotes given on large leather lots; C.O.D. orders accepted.

Related Products/Companies

Cowhides
- Steerhides

Duffel bags and gear bags
- Defender

Flight bags
- Aircraft Spruce & Specialty

Leather-care products
- Bailey's, State Line Tack, UPCO

Leather gloves
- Gohn Bros.

Luggage
- Bennett Brothers, Cook Brothers, Damark, J&R Music World

Luggage carts
- Bennett Brothers

Luggage for equestrians
- State Line Tack, Valley Vet

Replacement luggage-weight zippers
- A. Feibusch Corporation

Saddles, tack, chaps, and gloves
- KV Vet Supply, Omaha Vaccine, State Line Tack

Sheepskin car seats and other sheepskin items
- Sheepskin Station

Small leather goods
- Bennett Brothers, Huntington Clothiers, J&R Music World

Wallets
- Cook Brothers

Luxuries

Rare gourmet foods;
investment-grade jewels,
wedding rings and jewelry;
perfumes; flowers; faux furs; cigars

Webster's defines *luxury* as "a condition of great ease or abundance." Now while your idea of a luxury may be different from mine, I'm sure we can both agree that a human being doesn't *need* a diamond in order to survive. Nor is caviar or a fine cigar likely to sustain us through hard times. And yet, some of the items you'll find in this chapter aren't really very expensive, so one needn't feel guilty about indulging a bit. Would having a dozen fresh roses on your sunny desk make you a happier and more productive person? Then my advice is by all means *go for it*. Not only will you avoid inflated prices on the goods in this chapter, but in some cases you'll save as much as 90% off the usual retail price. Is it possible to enjoy a state of abundance at bargain prices? Absolutely. Read on, and don't forget to check out the "Related Products/Companies" listings at the end of this chapter for a selective listing of luxuries found elsewhere in the book. For fine crystal and silver items, be sure to see the companies in the "Tableware" section of the "Home" chapter.

Find It Fast

Caviar and Gourmet Foods
- Caviar and Imported Gourmet Foods Warehouse

Cigars
- New Global Marketing

Faux Furs
- Fabulous-Furs

Fragrances
- Essential Products, Fragrance International, Perfumax

Fresh-Cut Flowers
- Evergreen Farms, Hand-tied Flowers

Jewels and Jewelry
- Diamonds by Rennie Ellen, Eastern Jewelry, House of Onyx, Simply Diamonds, Wedding Ring Hotline

Caviar and Imported Gourmet Foods Warehouse

888–889–1949

Information: website only, no print catalog
Pay: MC, V, AE, DSC
Sells: caviar, mushrooms, truffles, foie gras, smoked
  salmon, and other imported gourmet foods and gifts
Store: website only, phone hours Monday to Friday 8–5
  EST
Online: www.freshcaviar.com

I'll admit that I'm fairly ignorant when it comes to caviar. But a visit to the Caviar and Imported Gourmet Foods Warehouse (CIGFW) website was illuminating. There I learned how long caviar lasts (caviar's total shelf life is two to three weeks, which means it's important you buy caviar from a reputable store that orders it fresh and sells large volumes), why it's sold in colored tins or jars (color determines the type: Beluga's packed in blue; Osetra in yellow; Sevruga in red, for example), and how it's processed (the *ikrjanschik*, or Russian caviar-maker, has to apprentice 15 years before he's allowed to process caviar on his own, a delicate procedure involving running the large sac, or roe, over a fine mesh screen until the tiny eggs separate out). But the most important thing for readers to know is that this is America's largest importer of fine gourmet foods, which results in prices that are well below those of his competitors—about 30% to 40% below. If you're addicted to this expensive stuff, get ready to indulge yourself.

CIGFW sells caviar in many different styles, grades, and sizes; smoked salmon and other preserved gourmet fish (e.g., kippers, trout, and mackerel); mushrooms (morels, chanterelles, porcini, shitake, oyster, and more); exotic imports such as Spanish squid ink, saffron, and French prunes in Armagnac; foie gras of many types; truffles aplenty; and gift items including mother-of-pearl caviar sets. The Caviar Man even has an in-house Executive Chef who can help you plan a meal or recipe using any of these exotic products. Perishable gifts are shipped Federal Express overnight at $25 (you should consume your caviar within two to three days); nonrefrigerated gifts are shipped UPS 2nd Day. Believe it or not, even with shipping factored in The Caviar Man is still far ahead of the pack in terms of price. So don't shop for luxury foods anywhere else until you've checked out this website.

SPECIAL FACTORS: Wholesale inquiries welcome.

Diamonds by Rennie Ellen

15 W. 47th St., Rm. 401　　　212–869–5525
New York, NY 10036　　　　　Fax: 212–869–5526

Catalog: $3
Pay: check, MO, teller's check, bank draft
Sells: stock and custom-made jewelry
Factory: visits by appointment only

Rennie Ellen, a gem-cutter since 1966, not only designs rings, pendants, and earrings with diamonds of all shapes, sizes, and qualities, but also offers them at savings up to 75% on prices charged elsewhere for similar jewelry. She specializes in engagement and wedding rings, and opens the factory to customers on an appointment-only basis. This way she can give her clients, many of them soon-to-be newlyweds, the personalized attention they deserve. The proprietress, who's a real gem herself, peppers her conversations with "honey" and "darling," and likes doing business the old-fashioned way—no high-tech websites for her. Gals: this company is a real find.

SPECIAL FACTORS: Prices are quoted by phone or letter; each purchase receives a detailed bill of sale; returns are accepted within five working days; the minimum charge on shipping (registered mail), handling, and insurance is $15; for an additional charge, orders can be shipped overnight via Federal Express.

Anyone who loves the elegant look and feel of gold and jewels in classic, distinctive designs is going to flip over this company. All of the earrings, brooches, bracelets, necklaces, pendants, and rings in Eastern Jewelry's collection are made with 14-karat gold over sterling silver, and most of the jewels are genuine. Eastern is really a jewelry wholesaler but will sell to individuals too (there's no minimum, but orders under $100 are charged a $5 surcharge); the prices here reflect radical discounts from the usual retail price.

You could go to a Fifth Avenue jeweler and buy a bracelet dripping with diamonds set in 14-karat gold for thousands—or you could buy the same design from Eastern, albeit in gold over sterling silver with smaller diamonds, for $46 (retails for $189). You get the same effect as the movie stars and princesses without the cost or the worry. When you call for information, you'll receive a pack of about 70 loose-leaf pages in a folder with prices, descriptions, and pictures. Color sheets are extra. By press time, Eastern should have CD-ROMs to send out to customers as well.

Among the hundreds of pieces here, you'll find diamond circle brooches made with green agate, amethyst, sapphires, blue topaz, garnets, and mixed-color gems ranging from $14 to $26. There are dozens of bracelet designs to choose from, including bangles with inset jewels and continuous-link designs with a single jewel set in each link. The earrings range from the classic dangling rows of rubies, diamonds, garnets, etc., to tasteful flowers, hearts, and geometric designs; most of the earrings are under $20 a pair, and many are closer to $10. The rings, necklaces, and pendants reflect the same tasteful aesthetic and good value. If you're looking for Judaica or crosses, you'll find them here too. Don't just stop with one piece; you can buy dazzling jeweled necklace-and-earring sets for much less than you'd pay for a single piece elsewhere (starting as low as $22 per set), and you'll look like you're ready for a night at the Oscars. All jewelry comes in a gift box and has a certificate of authenticity. The owner speaks Hebrew, Bulgarian, Russian, Romanian, and Spanish, but understands many other languages as well!

Wholesalers, corporate/promotional gift buyers: Eastern Jewelry offers attractive quantity discounts.

SPECIAL FACTORS: Quantity discounts available; $5 handling charge added to orders under $100; returns accepted on manufacturer-damaged goods only.

Essential Products Co., Inc.

90 Water St., Dept. WBM   212–344–4288
New York, NY 10005–3587

    Price List and Sample Cards: free with SASE (see text)
    Pay: check or MO
    Sells: "interpretation" fragrances
    Store: same address; Monday to Friday 9–6

"We offer our versions of the world's most treasured and expensive ladies' perfumes and men's colognes, selling them at a small fraction of the original prices"—so states the literature from Essential Products Co., Inc. Ralph Nader, in his *Buyer's Market,* praised this company as being consumer-friendly with good-quality products and great value. How do they do it? They don't spend a lot of money on fancy packaging, royalties for the couturier's name, or international advertising—which are what contribute to the incredibly high cost of most perfumes.

Essential Products was founded in 1895 and markets its interpretations of famous perfumes under the brand name of "Naudet." The company stocks 50 different copies of such costly perfumes as Beautiful, Boucheron, Chanel #5, Coco, Giorgio, Joy, L'Air du Temps, Opium, Paloma Picasso, Passion, Poison, Shalimar, White Diamonds, and Ysatis, as well as 23 "copycat" colognes for men, including Drakkar Noir, Eternity, Obsession, Polo, and Joop. A one-ounce bottle of perfume is $20 (half an ounce, $11.50), and four ounces of any men's cologne costs $11.

When you write to Essential Products, please identify yourself as a WMO reader, which entitles you to five free "scent cards" of Essential Products' bestselling fragrances. The sample cards give an idea of how closely the Naudet version replicates the original, but you should try the product to evaluate it properly.

You must also enclose a long, stamped, self-addressed envelope for the set of samples.

SPECIAL FACTORS: Satisfaction is guaranteed; returns are accepted within 30 days for refund; minimum order is $20.

Evergreen Farms Inc.

11769 Nubbin Drive	**205–333–1234**
Coker, AL 35452	**Fax: 205–333–1236**

Information: website only, no catalog
Pay: check, MO, V, MC
Sells: fresh-cut lily and snapdragon bouquets
Store: mail order only; phone hours 8–5 Monday to Friday
Online: www.evergreenfarms.com

What could be more luxurious than having fresh flowers delivered to your door (or to the door of your surprised mother, employee, or girlfriend)? I recently bought a bouquet of tulips for my male companion and he was thrilled, so don't think women are the only ones who love blossoms adorning their table. How I wish I had known about Evergreen Farms! This company is a gem and I'll tell you why. When you buy flowers from a florist, not only are the flowers seven to ten days old by the time you buy them, but the florist is acting as middleman, thus adding to the price tag of the flowers. Evergreen Farms, the largest grower of greenhouse-cut fresh flowers in the deep South, harvests their lilies and snapdragons daily, and ships them out within 36 hours of harvest. These will be the freshest, longest-lasting flowers you've ever received. And because they're coming straight from the grower, they'll also be the cheapest. Evergreen offers fresh-cut Asiatic lilies and snapdragons (their specialty), a refreshing change of pace from the usual roses, in my opinion. They can drop-ship your order to that special someone and enclose a card with a note from you. Each order contains over 30 stems of snapdragons giving you well over 100 blooms or ten stems of lilies giving you 30 to 40 blooms. There's also a combination bouquet. All orders are shipped the day they receive them by UPS Next Day Air service. At this writing a bouquet was $29.95 plus $12 shipping. When I looked at smaller bouquets from a few FTD florists—with many less blooms, lots of filler green, and frou-frou stuff you don't need or want—I found their prices a lot higher than Evergreen's. You can order online, by phone, or by fax, whichever is most convenient for you. The website, in addition to offering online ordering, has an interesting section on do's and don'ts for handling and preserving your fresh-cut flowers.

SPECIAL FACTORS: Orders received after 3 P.M. CT on Friday will be shipped on Monday, for Tuesday delivery; wholesalers should inquire for terms.

Fabulous-Furs

20 W. Pike St.   800–848–4650
Covington, KY 41011   606–291–3300
                           Fax: 606–291–9687

Catalog: free
Pay: check, MO, V, MC, DSC
Sells: faux fur coats, hats, and accessories
Showroom: same address; Monday to Friday 9–4:30; call
  for Saturday hours
Online: www.fabulousfurs.com

My grandmother, who was born in 1896 and grew up in rural Illinois, always wished she could own a mink stole. My grandfather bought her one for her sixtieth birthday, one of the happiest days of her life. Fast forward to the year 2000. Modern women want the luxurious look and feel of fur, but let's face it: We're animal lovers. And besides, that level of outrageous materialism is out of sync with our other values. Enter Fabulous-Furs. Founded by Donna Salyers, this company sells faux furs combining the beauty, warmth, and luxury of animal fur with exquisite design details and fabrics so real that Ms. Salyers tucks a few Fab-Furs business cards into every package in case you need to fend off outraged animal rights people.

The 24-page color catalog features long coats, jackets, stoles, and vests made to look like sable, chinchilla, arctic fox, white mink, coyote, Mongolian lamb, Asian raccoon, beaver, leopard, and other furry friends. Although some are most appropriate for formal occasions such as attending the opera, there are plenty of darling examples of more casual coats and jackets appropriate for skiing, shopping, and even cheering at your son's soccer games. You'll also find fun accessories such as muffs, hats, throws, decorative pillows, and even a few surprises such as faux-leopard thong sandals (I have some; they're great!), a faux-fur Barbie costume, and a rug for your dog. Some of these coats aren't cheap, but even the most expensive one is more than $39,000 less than its $40,000 counterpart, a savings of almost 98%! On the other hand, there are quite a few coats here that are really affordable—cheaper, in fact, than my own full-length wool coat cost me, and vastly more elegant. If you're curious, log on to the website, where many of these faux furs are pictured. There you can get more information about this wonderful, future-sighted company and read about the famous people who own these coats. If you're in the Cincinnati vicinity, stop by the showroom, which offers 20% to 40% off showroom models.

SPECIAL FACTORS: Satisfaction guaranteed (see catalog for returns policy).

Fragrance International, Inc.

398 E. Rayen Ave.　　　　800–543–3341
Youngstown, OH 44505　　330–747–3341
　　　　　　　　　　　　　　Fax: 330–747–7200

Information: price quote
Pay: check, MO, MC, V, DSC
Sells: men's and women's fragrances
Store: mail order only, phone hours Monday to Friday
　8:30–5:30 EST (see text)
E-mail: fii@cisnet.com

Fragrance International has been featured in this book for a number of years for their comprehensive selection of fragrances at discount prices—28% to 33% below retail. If you're like me and happen to be hooked on an expensive perfume, Fragrance International should be able to save you a lot of money. Their inventory has grown so huge that they no longer publish a print catalog. Instead, this company maintains a massive database updated daily of just about every line of fragrance one could imagine—from brand-new hot items to the hard-to-find old brands and everything in between, including mass-market lines. Give them a call with your fragrance brand, and they'll quote you a price over the phone. If you call after hours, an answering machine is on duty to take your order or message. A helpful representative will get back to you on the next business day.

SPECIAL FACTORS: Orders under $50 are charged a $5 handling fee.

Hand-Tied Flowers

888–563–8880

Information: website only, no print catalog
Pay: V, MC, AE, Electronic Check
Sells: long-stemmed roses and other fresh flower bouquets
Store: website only; phone hours 8:30–11:30 A.M. PST
Online: www.hand-flowers.com

If you're a rose lover, I hope you're sitting down. Hand-Tied Flowers sells greenhouse-fresh roses ("grower-direct") over the web at close to 50% off what you're used to paying. Even with overnight shipping factored in, you'll spend about the same here for two dozen roses that you're used to paying for one dozen locally! And these flowers last and last. Just read the testimonials from happy customers on the website. Because they're shipped to you shortly after they've been cut at the greenhouse, you not only benefit in terms of freshness, but also cost—there's no middleman hiking up the price for profit. In addition to long-stemmed roses (your choice of white, yellow, pink, red, peach, lavender, or mixed), Hand-Tied also sells Gerber Daisy, Dendrobium Orchid, Protea and Lily, Iris, Delphinium and Roses, Sunflowers, Wildflowers, Carnations, and Bird of Paradise bouquets, among others. Each stem comes with its own water source; the flowers are tied in a bunch—you do your own arrangement. The website has color photographs, a section on flower care, the aforementioned customer testimonials page, and secure online ordering 24 hours a day. If you prefer to use the phone, there's a toll-free customer service number you can use instead.

SPECIAL FACTORS: Flowers delivered Federal Express via next-day delivery nationwide when you order by 2 P.M. EST.

House of Onyx

120 N. Main St.
Greenville, KY 42345–1504

800–844–3100
502–338–2363
Fax: 502–338–9605

Catalog: free
Pay: check, MO, MC, V, DSC
Sells: investment-grade stones, jewelry, and gifts
Store: same address; Monday to Friday 9–4
Online: www.houseofonyx.com

Begun in 1967 as the first quality importer of Mexican onyx, House of Onyx has expanded to include high-grade investment-quality gemstones, imported gifts, jewelry, cloisonné vases, and more while maintaining their stock of Aztec onyx chess sets, statuettes, paperweights, ashtrays, bookends, and candlesticks—all at 50% to 60% less than you would find elsewhere. The owners, Fred and Shirley Rowe, stand behind their products 100%, and happily give advice on investing in gems, politics, and the economy! Fred is recognized worldwide as an expert on gemstones and their values, and he and his wife have traveled the world gathering information about them.

The House of Onyx has a complete GIA-equipped laboratory with five full-time GIA graduate gemologists on staff for positive identification of all gemstones. Couple this with their absolute commitment to client satisfaction and their "buy-back" policy that insures your investment, and you could not find a more worry-free place to purchase gemstones. The catalog also includes carved soapstone, rose quartz, tiger's eye, semiprecious bead necklaces, cameos, freshwater and cultured pearls, diamond and gemstone rings, gold and jeweled watches, earrings, and pendants, all ranging from inexpensive to rare and unusual pieces. Gems are offered, from actinolite to zoisite, minerals from aragonite to smoky quartz crystal, and the fossils they offer range from ammonites to trilobites, and include dinosaur eggs and teeth! Their website shows clear full-color photographs of the gems, diamonds, fossils, jewelry and cloisonné that they sell. You will also find deeply discounted gem videos and encyclopedias, which are useful for the budding enthusiast and collector alike.

International readers, please note: The House of Onyx is not able to ship catalogs or any merchandise to addresses outside of the U.S., but they invite you to visit them and will happily arrange for your hotel accommodations and transportation.

SPECIAL FACTORS: Satisfaction is guaranteed; investment gemstones are sold with an unlimited time return guarantee and a "100% purchase price refund" pledge; other returns are accepted within 30 days; minimum order is $25.

New Global Marketing

P.O. Box 652   914–687–2033
Stone Ridge, NY 12484   Fax: 914–687–9357

Information: online or print catalog (see text)
Pay: check, MO, V, MC, AE, DSC
Sells: cigars, humidors, wine racks, coffee and tea, etc.
Store: mail order only, phone hours Monday to Friday 9–6
  EST
Online: www.newglobal.com

No discussion of luxuries would be complete without mentioning a hot trend of the late 1990s: cigars. Word of New Global Marketing's website, named one of the top three cigar sites on the web, is spreading like wildfire through cigar-lovers' chat rooms, and it's no surprise. New Global purchases the major brands, including many of the smaller boutique lines that have come out over the last few years, then resells them with only a small markup. This company also seeks out brands that aren't top sellers, but are of good quality and at a price they consider a great deal for you. Fabulous prices resulting in high-volume sales means that the cigars you buy here are really fresh.

The website, frequently updated to reflect the latest price fluctuations, lists hundreds of cigars alphabetically along with their near-wholesale price tag. There are no fancy photographs or descriptions, so this is a great place to shop if you already know cigars. However, if you're looking for some friendly guidance, the nice people at New Global assured me they're happy to field phone calls and answer questions. ("It happens all the time," says the owner.) You can order online, by phone, or download an order form, fill it out by hand, and fax it in. New Global Marketing also sells cigar accessories such as humidors, along with an eclectic mix of wine accessories, world music CDs, coffee, and tea. If you don't have Internet access, a print catalog is available by request.

SPECIAL FACTORS: New York State residents must pay the appropriate tobacco and sales taxes; a $5 surcharge is waived if you order two or more items or if your order totals $100 or more.

Perfumax

Bush Terminal Station   800–789–7373
P.O. Box 320154   Fax: 888–755–7373
Brooklyn, NY 11232–0154

   Catalog: free
   Pay: check, MO, MC, V, AE, DSC
   Sells: name-brand perfumes
   Store: mail order only
   Online: www.perfumax.net

Here's a company with a simple concept: Stock nothing but perfumes, and sell them at a discount. The prices here are excellent—up to 25% off list. Perfumax stocks over 200 fragrances—even hard-to-find items—many of which are listed in the 16-page color catalog. If you don't see what you want, call; they probably stock it or can get it for you. The catalog has tips about how to find your "pulse points," the difference between "top notes" and "heart notes," and other useful perfume trivia. The website lists the current specials, but there's no online ordering.

SPECIAL FACTORS: Perfumax will gift wrap your order for free if you request it. Complete satisfaction guaranteed; returns accepted within 30 days for a full refund.

Simply Diamonds

P.O. Box 682, Dept. A
Ardsley, NY 10502–0682

800–552–2728
914–693–2370
Fax: 914–693–2446

Information: inquire
Pay: check, MO, MC, V, AE, DSC
Sells: diamond jewelry
Store: mail order only
E-mail: 75224.1032@compuserve.com

If there's one thing I've learned through researching and writing this book, it's that dispensing with some of the niceties of typical mail-order shopping can save me a lot of money. Why? Because certain companies offer products at amazing discounts by cutting down on or eliminating their overhead. In many cases that means no fancy website, no slick catalog or brochure, not even a storefront or retail shop. When you find such a company, you're in luck. Simply Diamonds is just such a place, only better: less like a mail-order company and more like having an uncle in the diamond biz who's your personal broker. This husband-and-wife team will walk you through the extremely scary and perilous process of buying a diamond. They've been doing it for decades and know every facet of New York City's diamond district, including all the tricks and traps. To best use the services of Simply Diamonds, they encourage you to do some shopping first. Get an idea of the type, size, and price range you want. When you're serious about buying a diamond, call Simply Diamonds. They take pride in personally talking to you, answering all your questions, giving advice, but above all finding exactly the diamond you seek at a price that's well below retail. Simply Diamonds mounts your gem in a very basic setting; once it's yours, you can pick out a setting at a jeweler's. This is a great source for people like me who don't know much about diamonds and would make easy targets for unscrupulous dealers. All pieces are backed by GIA, EGL, and IGI certificates (available on request).

SPECIAL FACTORS: Satisfaction guaranteed on every purchase; returns are accepted within seven days of receipt for exchange, refund, or credit.

Wedding Ring Hotline

172 Rt. 9   **732–972–7777**
Englishtown, NJ 07726   **Fax: 732–972–0720**

Brochure: free
Pay: check, MO, MC, V, AE, DSC
Sells: wedding bands, diamonds, and engagement rings
Store: same address (by appointment)
Online: www.weddingringhotline.com

A division of Bride & Groom's West, Inc., Wedding Ring Hotline makes it possible for you to buy wedding bands, diamonds, and engagement rings factory-direct at savings from 30% to 70%. Manufacturer of its own line of classic-style rings, Wedding Ring Hotline offers selections in yellow and white gold, as well as Comfort-fit wedding bands. Sizes range from widths of 2 mm to 12 mm, with a choice of plain and milgrain edges (milgrain is the technical term for the tiny beading lining the rims). Rings are available in 10-karat, 14-karat, and 18-karat gold and in platinum. You can request a free brochure, but I'd recommend the website instead, which has stunning photographs of the various rings so you can really see what you're getting. The website also features charts detailing ring features, sizes, and prices. Ordering is done by phone, and you are invited to call for price quotes on name-brand rings and information on custom-made jewelry. Engraving is available, and if your order is over $200, there's no engraving charge.

SPECIAL FACTORS: 100% money back guarantee within 30 days; prices quoted by phone and letter; returns accepted within 30 days for exchange, refund, or credit; engraving free on orders over $200.

Related Products/Companies

Antique prints and maps
  • American Prints and Maps

Brand-name perfumes and "imposter" fragrances
  • Beauty Boutique, Cook Brothers

Cruise vacation packages
  • Vacations to Go

Crystal chandeliers
  • King's Chandeliers

Designer clothing
- DesignerOutlet

Fake exotic animal skins and real steerhides
- Steerhides

Fine writing instruments
- Fountain Pen Hospital

Gourmet chocolates
- Make Us An Offer

Grand pianos
- Altenburg Piano House

Hand-made lotions and herbal balms
- Kettle Care

Imported fine linens
- Harris Levy

Inflatable boats
- SOAR Inflatables

Investment grade pearls and precious stones
- Fire Mountain Gems, Hong Kong Lapidaries

Jewelry and executive gifts
- Bennett Brothers

Kit airplanes
- Aircraft Spruce and Specialty

Liqueur-making ingredients and kits
- E. C. Kraus

Monogrammed men's shirts
- Huntington

Oriental Rugs
- Charles W. Jacobsen

Perfume-making supplies and books
- Tom Thumb Workshops

Pet cologne
- UPCO

Safes
- Discount Safe Outlet

Top-of-the-line down comforters
- J. Schachter

Wild-game tours and safaris
- Bowhunters Warehouse

Music, Audio, and Video

Audiocassettes, CDs, LPs, and Video

Music, instructional, and entertainment recordings of all kinds

The companies in this section sell music of all types, in all forms—from old-fashioned vinyl LPs to high-tech CDs—and audio selections that include old-time radio dramas and music instruction. Don't forget that music never gets old. If you're willing to buy used CDs, for example, or last year's titles, you can build an enormous music library for yourself for up to 80% less than the cost of buying everything brand new and hot off the press. You'll also find music, movie, stand-up comedy, and educational videos in every conceivable category, including vintage, alternative, documentary, self-help, and many hard-to-find selections.

For books on cassette, see the "Books, Audiobooks, and Periodicals" chapter. And since many of the other companies in this book sell videos—on animal training, cooking, exercise, art and craft technique, and much more—don't forget to read the listings in "Related Products/Companies" section at the end of this chapter.

Find It Fast

Educational and Instructional Videos
- Homespun Tapes, Video Learning Library, Video Yesteryear

LPs
- Berkshire Record Outlet, CDnow, Harvard Square, Record-Rama, Upstairs Records

Music and Entertainment Videos
- CDnow, Harvard Square Records, Video Yesteryear

Music CDs and Audiocassettes
- Adventures in Cassettes, CDnow, Upstairs Records

Used CDs and Audiocassettes
- Audio House, Berkshire Record Outlet, Harvard Square, Record-Rama

Vintage Radio Audiocassettes
- Adventures in Cassettes

Vintage TV/Cinema Videos
- Video Yesteryear

Adventures in Cassettes

A division of Metacom, Inc.　　**800–328–0108**
5353 Nathan Lane, Dept.　　**Fax: 612–553–0424**
BWBM
Plymouth, MN 55442

Catalog: free
Pay: check, MO, MC, V, AE, DSC
Sells: audiotapes and music CDs
Store: mail order only
Online: www.aic-radio.com

There was once a funny little guy I worked with years ago in an all-night typography shop who loved radio crime thrillers. He used to lend me cassettes he'd listen to on his Walkman, which I'd listen to when I got home from my lobster shift as proofreader at 3 A.M. I loved lying in the dark listening to *The Green Hornet*, imagining how it must have been years ago before people had televisions and computers. Adventures in Cassettes offers hundreds of audiotapes featuring just about any radio classic one could think of: *Abbott and Costello, Amos 'n Andy Show, The Bickersons, Burns and Allen, Captain Midnight, Crime Classics, Dimension X, Dragnet, The Falcon,* and many other favorites, from science fiction to westerns to melodramas. The free 36-page print catalog has good descriptions, but if you can go online I'd recommend the website, which describes and lists everything alphabetically, features vintage-radio links, has a section of special buys, and allows you to order online. You can also order by mail, phone, or fax if you prefer.

SPECIAL FACTORS: Satisfaction guaranteed; returns accepted within 30 days for exchange, refund, or credit.

Audio House

8105 Hawk Crest Dr.   810–695–3415
Grand Blanc, MI 48439   Fax: 810–695–1753

Catalog: $3, refundable (see text)
Pay: check, MO, MC, V, AE, DC, DSC
Sells: used music CDs
Store: mail order only
Online: www.audiohousecd.com

What's the difference between a new CD and a used CD? The answer, according to Audio House owner Terry Duffy, is "the price." Unlike their vinyl ancestors, CDs don't wear. So instead of paying between $10 and $20 for a new CD, Duffy suggests you buy them from him instead, at between $5 and $10.

You can order a copy of the Audio House catalog, issued once every two months, for $3, which is refundable with your first order. Or better yet, log onto the world wide web and download or just view Audio House's searchable up-to-the-minute inventory. Since the selection is always changing, this is your best bet. Audio House has a wide range of music CDs in three rather broad categories—Popular, Jazz, and Classical—arranged alphabetically. If you want to save even more money, you can sell your own unwanted CDs for cash or credit. Selling used CDs to Audio House is also a great way to raise money for your PTA or local charity. Details on how to do this are in the print and online catalog.

SPECIAL FACTORS: Satisfaction guaranteed; returns accepted within 30 days for exchange, refund, or credit.

Berkshire Record Outlet

R.R. 1, Rte. 102 Pleasant St.   413–243–4080
Lee, MA 01238–9804   Fax: 413–243–4340

> Catalog: $2 cash; $5 check or credit card
> Pay: check, MO, MC, V
> Sells: classical recordings on LP, CDs, and cassettes
> Store: same address; Saturday 10–5:30
> Online: www.berkshirerecoutlet.com

Berkshire has been selling classical music since 1974, long before online shopping became a reality. Whether you're like my father, who still has a mint-condition turntable and collector-quality LPs, or own a state-of-the-art CD player, Berkshire has classical recordings in your preferred form, including also audiocassettes. While you can pay the small fee to receive a hard copy of their big catalog, viewing the 290 pages is probably easier and more fun by accessing the catalog online. The 500 title sections are broken down into 50 ten-title pages, offering LPs, tapes, and compact discs at prices starting as low as $1.99 and $2.99. Every conceivable classical label is here, from Abbey to Xenophone, with new arrivals flagged separately for the convenience of frequent shoppers. There's even an easy-to-use online Search and Shopping Cart where knowing only part of a title or of a composer's name or a label will still get you the information you seek. Berkshire also has a selection of sound tracks, books about classical music, videotapes, and folk and ethnic music titles.

Japanese readers, please note: This website can be viewed in Japanese.

SPECIAL FACTORS: Minimum order, inclusive of shipping, is $15.

CDnow

Jenkins Court, Ste. 300　　　**800–595–6874**
610 Old York Rd.　　　**215–885–8471**
Jenkintown, PA 19046　　　**Fax: 800–461–9232**

Information: website only, no print catalog
Pay: check, MO, MC, V, AE, DSC
Sells: music CDs, movies, and music videos
Store: online only
Online: www.cdnow.com

CDnow carries almost every album currently in print in the United States. Their prices are 30% and more below other CD stores—as a "cyberstore" they don't have to pay for floor space. The site is laid out for maximum usability. The music inventory at CDnow is separated into rock/pop, jazz/blues, urban/electronic, classical, country/folk, world/new age, and children. You can search by artist (when you do, you'll be able to see everything he or she has recorded that's still in print, as well as a listing of "Not Available" titles), by album, or by song title. There's lots here for the browser—in-depth reviews and interviews, ratings, artists' biographical information, discussion groups, sound samples, and music-related links galore. The classical section allows you to search by composer, title of album or composition, performer or soloist, conductor, record label, genre, and several other elements. The site runs regular specials on titles, such as Grammy and American Music Award winners, at 50% off list. CDnow also sells vinyl LPs and CD imports, movies, music videos, Japanese import videos, DVDs (digital video discs), music-related books, T-shirts, and more.

SPECIAL FACTORS: Any item can be returned within 30 days of delivery for full refund, except Japanese imports, vinyl, and T-shirts (unless defective); see website for details.

Harvard Square Records, Inc.

P.O. Box 381975-BWBM
Cambridge, MA 02238

617–868–3385
Fax: 617–547–2838

Catalog: $2 U.S.; $3 Canada; $5 international
Pay: check, MO, MC, V
Sells: out-of-print LPs, audiotapes, and videotapes
Store: mail order only
Online: www.lpnow.com

Harvard Square Records, Inc., in business since 1985, has a 10,000-title catalog of sealed rare and out-of-print vinyl LPs. Called cut-outs, the record-industry version of remainders, these discontinued records are categorized under jazz and easy listening, gospel, children's music, R&B and dance, blues, rock, country, world and traditional, spoken word, sound effects, soundtracks, classical, and others. Prices range from $5 to $20, depending on the title and whether it's an import. The website, where you can order online, has an Audiophile category of higher-priced titles that are hard to find elsewhere (How I wish I had saved my Rolling Stones "Sticky Fingers" album with the zipper! Now it's worth a fortune!). To make shopping easier, Harvard Square issues three catalogs: "Vinyl," "Cassettes," and "Video," with free shipping on cassette orders of $50 or more. Be sure to indicate which catalog you want when making your catalog request. Stock in all categories moves quickly, so if you see what you want, order promptly since items cannot be put on hold. If your title is sold out when you order, a refund check or a merchandise credit will be issued (specify which on the order form).

SPECIAL FACTORS: Returns (defective, unplayable goods) accepted within 14 days for replacement or merchandise credit.

Homespun Tapes

Box 340, Dept. WH   914–246–2550
Woodstock, NY 12498   Fax: 914–246–5282

Catalog: free
Pay: check, MO, MC, V, DSC
Sells: music instruction videos, audiocassettes, CDs, and
 books; and miscellaneous recording and music supplies
Store: mail order only
Online: www.homespuntapes.com

If the best way to learn is by doing, then pick up that banjo, flute, or accordion collecting dust in your corner and start playing. Have no fear, because Homespun Tapes, founded in 1981 by Jane and Happy Traum (the latter of the folk/blues duo Happy and Artie Traum), will guide you through the learning or mastering process with their unique instructional music tapes. If you've been wanting to take lessons but have been too busy or broke, these tapes will restore your confidence and save you money at the same time.

Homespun's 72-page catalog features instructional videotapes, audiocassettes, and CDs by the very best musicians in their fields. You can learn guitar arrangement from Patty Larkin; jazz piano from Warren Bernhardt; singing techniques from Maria Muldaur; fingerpicking and flatpicking from Doc Watson; banjo from Pete Seeger; Appalachian dulcimer from Lorraine Lee; and on and on. There are instructional tapes for children and tapes for musicians at all levels of expertise. The tapes are created with close-ups and split-screen imaging techniques, three-camera systems, good studios, and top camera operators to present the clearest possible angles. There are about 250 titles in the current catalog, spanning accordions to whistling, averaging in price from about $15 to $40. Homespun Tapes also has a small selection of musician supplies, such as study recorders, Keith tuners, and slides and strings, as well as scores of books. But the real bargain here is the time and money you'll save by taking lessons from a pro right in your own home.

Special to readers of this book: If you mention WMO, Homespun Tapes will take 20% off your initial instructional videotape, audiocassette, or CD order. By the way, Homespun's new website features new releases, important updates, in-depth listings of all the lessons, and online ordering, so check it out.

SPECIAL FACTORS: Overseas customers can wire money directly into Homespun's bank account or pay by credit card or in U.S. funds; returns are accepted, but see catalog for more details; wholesale orders are available (call Hal Leonard at 800–554–0626).

Record-Rama Sound Archives

4981 McKnight Rd.   412–367–7330
Pittsburgh, PA 15237–3407   Fax: 412–367–7388

Information: price quote
Pay: check, MO, MC, V, AE, DSC
Sells: vintage 45s, LPs, and CDs; phonograph needles and
   deejay supplies
Store: same address; Tuesday to Saturday 10–6, closed
   Sunday and Monday
Online: www.recordrama.com

When word reached the Library of Congress that a retired paper goods salesman was claiming to have the country's largest known collection of 45s, a curator was sent over to check it out. Sure enough: Record-Rama Sound Archives, which shares a building with the local post office, holds the record with 1.5 million oldies on 45s, plus a million LPs. Paul C. Mawhinney's collection began with his youthful purchase of Frankie Lane's "Jezebel," and an obsession was born.

Mr. Mawhinney isn't sitting on this national treasure; he has created *Music-Master: The 45 RPM Singles Directory*, the ultimate reference on 45s produced from 1948 to 1996. The *MusicMaster*, organized by artist and title, is now the most-used reference in the New York Public Library, and a must-have for any library or serious collector. Record-Rama offers the MusicMaster Database and other directories—the CD–5 Singles Directory and the 45 RPM Christmas Singles Directory, both by artist/title. (Call for current directory prices.)

If you check out the website, you'll see that Mr. Mawhinney's CD collection currently numbers over 300,000, and he has amassed a large selection of CD-ROMs as well. If you're looking for a CD or LP title, he probably has it—just call and ask. Better yet, use the Record-Rama "World Search" online database that allows you to search for an artist and access his or her entire discography on the web, as well as place orders right from your computer. You'll also find maintenance products for LPs and CDs, as well as over 10,000 phonograph needles and other supplies for deejays.

Please note: Just mention WMO and get an additional 10% discount on any record and any single disc CD (multiple discs and boxed sets are excluded).

SPECIAL FACTORS: Calls are not accepted on the weekends; phone quotes are limited to two requests per call.

Upstairs Records

140 58th St., Dept. WBM,   718–567–3333
Ste. 6W   Fax: 718–567–2310
Brooklyn, NY 11220–2521

Catalog: free
Pay: check, MO, MC, V, AE, DSC
Sells: DJ equipment, sound, lighting, and recordings
Store: 2968 Avenue X, Brooklyn, NY; Monday to Thursday
  9–7, Friday 9–5, Sunday 10–5, closed Saturdays
Online: www.upstairsrecords.com

A one-stop source of deejay equipment, club gear, and hip-hop music is Upstairs Records, which stocks the sometimes hard-to-find music of small independent labels. Inventory is routinely priced at 35% below comparable retail prices, and the catalog details a "low price guarantee" to ensure competitive pricing. There's also a deejay equipment trade-in program (see catalog for details). To keep up on the latest releases, you can take advantage of the "Vinyl Record Pool," which offers a standing-order service for new hard-core rap, dance, reggae, and hip-hop, and the "Vinyl Fax Club," which sends you each month a list of 12-inch singles and vinyl LPs in stock, as well as special discounts and giveaways.

Upstairs Records publishes two catalogs, one for equipment and one for music, which makes sense when you consider how much inventory there is of each. The 65-page equipment catalog is loaded with four-track recorders, drum machines, effect processors, full-size mixers, microphones, CD players, powered speakers, fog machines, cassette decks, CD cases, processing gear, digital samplers, lighting, and much more—everything for a club, bar, or restaurant. Upstairs Records can help you design a system if you fax the blueprints and a description of what you have in mind in terms of sound and lighting. The music catalog will get you started and keep you going with hundreds of CDs and cassettes in a range of music categories, not only club sounds (for example, comedy, gospel, Latin, and sound tracks). The website is the place to check out for the latest information on music charts, specials, closeouts, and industry info. You can also place your orders online.

SPECIAL FACTORS: Authorized returns accepted within 30 days (see catalog for restrictions and limitations); call for prices on some items.

Video Learning Library

15838 N. 62nd St., Dept. 702
Scottsdale, AZ 85254

888–383–8811
602–596–9970
Fax: 602–596–9973

Catalog: $29.95
Pay: check, MO, V, MC, AE, DSC
Sells: how-to, self-help, hobby, and educational videos
Store: mail order only
Online: www.videomarketplace.com

The Video Learning Library is the brainchild of James Spencer, editor and publisher of the massive 750-page reference entitled *Complete Guide to Special Interest Videos.* What a great idea! Suppose, for example, you want to learn ballroom dancing, floral design, Vietnamese cooking, chi gong, pet grooming, or get some fishing instruction, bowling tips, or hints on giving yourself a home perm. You could either enroll in an expensive course or buy a video from Video Learning Library. There are over 13,000 titles in the current edition selected for their usefulness, uniqueness, and availability. The videos are arranged by broad subject categories (for instance, automotive, home improvement, travel and adventure, photography, games and magic, and languages, to name a few) and indexed in the back by specific subject. The individual listings include brief descriptions or reviews and plenty of user-friendly icons denoting closed captioned for the hearing impaired, star ratings by independent media consultants and reviewers, videos available in PAL (European) format, and titles endorsed by Kids First! for their kid-friendly content. If you're like me, scanning the catalog or the website evokes an "Oh, wow!" response, as in, "Oh, wow, maybe I should get that feng shui tape and fix up my house differently." This is a wonderful source for teachers looking to enhance a classroom presentation, documentarists looking for subject material, administrators needing training materials, camp counselors or elder-care workers wanting to educate and/or entertain, newly retired people seeking a hobby, or just folks on a never-ending quest for self-improvement. The *Complete Guide* is a worthwhile investment, and includes coupons for a free video and a $5 certificate toward your first purchase of videos, books, or CD-ROMs listed in the catalog (see catalog for details). You can also view and order video titles right on the website.

Special to WMO readers: When you order *by phone or fax,* mention this book and you'll receive 20% off.

SPECIAL FACTORS: Shipping charges are $4 for the first tape and $1.50 for each additional.

Video Yesteryear

Box C, Dept. BWBM   800–243–0987
Sandy Hook, CT 06482   Fax: 203–797–0819

Catalog: $4.95 and $3.95 (see text)
Pay: check, MO, V, MC, AE, DSC, CB, DC
Sells: ancient and obscure cinema videotapes
Store: mail order only
Online: www.yesteryear.com

"Why would anyone in his right mind buy video cassettes by mail?" so begins the introduction in Video Yesteryear's 362-page catalog. Here's why: Video Yesteryear offers hard-to-find videos—including many foreign films, nostalgia movies, silent films, and old TV shows—at great prices. If you're a movie or old TV buff, you know that very few video stores carry these titles. The phonebook-sized, black-and-white catalog is filled with thousands of titles in categories that include comedy/cartoons, music, drama, adventures, crime/mystery/horror, westerns, serials, sword and sandal, documentary/exploitation/avant-garde/propaganda, and golden age of television. This company even has films dating back to 1896! Whether you're a teacher looking for an illuminating documentary on the U.S. government's campaign to kindle the fires of patriotism among Negroes during World War II (*The Negro Soldier,* produced by Frank Capra in 1944); a parent wishing to introduce her child to 1930s cartoon classics; or a hostess throwing a silent movie party for friends, this is a great source.

So vast is Video Yesteryear's inventory that they've produced two catalogs,

Volume 1 ($4.95) and Volume 2 ($3.95). Each catalog has an index that covers the entire Video Yesteryear inventory. The website will give you a sampling from which you can order online, but it's not as extensive as the catalogs. (You can also request a shorter, abbreviated catalog that's free.) The prices at Video Yesteryear are very reasonable when you take advantage of the "buy three and get one free" offer, as well as the discounted videos listed in a separate section of the large catalog. If you order 13, you'll get an additional 10% off. Videotapes are available in VHS, BETA, and 8 mm formats, as well as European formats. On the website you can view the entire inventory, but there's no online order form.

Wholesalers: Please inquire about resale prices and minimums.

SPECIAL FACTORS: Wholesale orders available; products guaranteed to be free of manufacturing defects or defective merchandise replaced (company will not exchange one title for another); Internet customers: call or see website for special ordering instructions.

Related Products/Companies

Alternative and underground culture videos
- Essential Media

Animal-care and training videos
- Drs. Foster & Smith, KV Vet, That Fish Place/That Pet Place, Valley Vet

Art-related videos
- Jerry's Artarama, The Potters Shop

Aviation videos
- Aircraft Spruce & Specialty

Craft and hobby instructional videos
- Axner Pottery Supply, Baron Barclay Bridge Supply, Brushy Mountain Bee Farm, Glass Crafters, Sewin' in Vermont, Weaver Leather, Woodworker's Discount Books

Documentary and educational videos
- Essential Media, The Scholar's Bookshelf, Shar Products

Do-it-yourself instructional videos
- Reader's Digest, Woodworker's Discount Books

Entertainment videos
- Amazon.com, Barnes & Noble, Bear Mountain Books, Gold Medal Hair Products

Equestrian-subject videos
- State Line Tack

Exercise videos
  • Amplestuff, Bear Mountain Books, Reader's Digest

Fishing videos
  • Defender

Language audiotapes
  • Dover Publications

Music CDs and audiotapes
  • Anyone Can Whistle, Barnes & Noble, Bear Mountain Books, Daedalus, Damark, Essential Media, Gold Medal Hair Products, Reader's Digest, Shar Products

Music instructional videos
  • American Musical Supply, Elderly Instruments, Musician's Friend, Shar Products

Sports-related videos
  • The House

Survival and hunting videos
  • The Cutlery Shoppe

Home Audio and Video Equipment

Stereo and speaker systems, CD players, radios, VCRs, camcorders, home entertainment systems

Whether you're a regular Joe wanting a pair of good speakers for your car or a sound nut who can't stand to listen to R&B CDs without a subwoofer, the firms in this section will please you with audio supplies and equipment up to 80% off regular retail. Some of these companies also sell video equipment such as camcorders, VCRs, and all-around home-entertainment systems. Between the price of technology going down and the good discounts offered by these companies, you'll find some amazing deals here.

For firms that sell related goods, particularly professional sound equipment for stage, studio, and deejay, as well as electronic instruments and supplies, see the section following this one, "Musical Instruments, Accessories, and Sound Equipment," page 436. And refer to "Related Products/Companies" at the end of this section for other firms that sell audio, sound, and recording equipment as well as video-related goods.

Find It Fast

Audio Equipment
- CAM Audio, Crutchfield, J&R Music World, Sound City

Blank Audio- and Videotapes
- CAM Audio, Wholesale Tape and Supply

Duplicating Services for Audio- and Videotapes
- Wholesale Tape and Supply

Phonograph Parts and Supplies
- Lyle Cartridges

Speaker Kits
- Gold Sound

Speakers
- Audio Concepts, Crutchfield, J&R Music World

Used, Demo, and Closeout Audio and Video Equipment
- Gold Sound

Video Equipment
- CAM Audio, Crutchfield, J&R Music World, Sound City

Audio Concepts, Inc.

901 S. 4th St., Dept. BWBM   608–784–4570
La Crosse, WI 54601   Fax: 608–784–6367

Catalog: free
Pay: check, MO, MC, V, AE
Sells: ACI speakers
Store: mail order only
Online: www.audioc.com

If you're a speaker aficionado, you're no doubt familiar with the legendary Sapphire III and Titan, made by Audio Concepts, Inc. (ACI). What if I told you that you could buy these and other ACI products at up to 50% off the suggested retail price? Well, it's true. The best way to find out about this company is to log on to the website, where you can read about and view all the products, including ACI speaker systems, do-it-yourself speaker kits, ACI home theater packages, audio accessories such as speaker stands, passive high-pass filters, speaker cables, and interconnects, and more. There's an excellent FAQ section that gives detailed information on various ACI products, an audio glossary, a page of demos and specials, audio-related links, and much more. You can submit your order via e-mail or else call or fax it in. The free print catalog is very basic: a black-and-white listing of products, prices, and policies.

SPECIAL FACTORS: Satisfaction guaranteed; authorized returns in new condition sent in the original packaging are accepted within 15 days for exchange, refund, or credit.

CAM Audio, Inc.

Missionary Tape and
Equipment Supply
2210 Executive Dr.
Garland, TX 75041

800–527–3458
972–271–0006
Fax: 972–271–1555

Catalog: free
Pay: check, MO, MC, V, AE, DSC
Sells: audio and video equipment, blank tapes, duplication
  services, etc.
Store: same address; Monday to Friday 8:30–5
Online: www.camaudio.com

Cam Audio is celebrating three decades in business as a consumer-friendly supplier of audio and video equipment and supplies at 40% and more off suggested list prices. The major manufacturers of every conceivable recording media are represented here with a broad selection of products: audio- and videocassettes (including bulk), professional audio reel tape, labels and storage boxes for all of the preceding, digital audio recorders, minidisc recorders, digital audio tape, every kind of cassette recorder, microphones, PA systems, duplication equipment, projectors, VCRs, camcorders, monitors, power sources, audio furniture, speakers, mixers, cases, stands, screens, headphones, and much more. CAM has services as well, including repair, duplication, printing, loading, and packing. CAM is also a leading supplier of discount-priced church equipment through its Missionary

Tape division. There's a print catalog, but if you have Internet access I'd recommend the website, which features the entire inventory and online ordering as well.

SPECIAL FACTORS: Price quote by phone or letter.

Crutchfield

1 Crutchfield Park, Dept. WH   800–955–9009
Charlottesville, VA   Fax: 804–817–1010
22911–9097   TDD: 800–388–9753

Catalog: free (see text)
Pay: check, MO, MC, V, AE, CB, DSC
Sells: audio and video components, home theater, car
stereos, telephones and pagers, and digital satellite
systems
Store: Rio Hill Shopping Center, Charlottesville, and
Market Square East Shopping Center, Harrisonburg, VA;
call for hours
Online: www.crutchfield.com

Whether you're a novice at car stereos or an audio/video expert, Crutchfield has bridged the gap. If there's one phrase I'd use to describe Crutchfield's amazing 148-page catalog and comprehensive website it's "information-intensive and consumer-driven." Some of the features that make Crutchfield attractive for consumers: 25% off retail price on many products, sales advisors well-versed on technical details, complete specs on all products for easy comparison, free consumer guides on subjects ranging from speaker placement to basic camcorder techniques, free kits pertaining to the installation of DSS dishes and car stereos, a free "Crutchfield Audio/Video Reference Kit" with purchase of any home audio component, free tech help, secure online ordering, two-day delivery, and more.

Products for the car include receivers, speakers, subwoofers, radar detectors, amp power cables and hardware, car security items, and related accessories from top-name manufacturers. The home offerings include two-way radios, telephones, home theater, receivers, turntables, CD players, cassette decks, VCRs, speakers, TVs, WebTV, DVD players, and many other items. By the way, the website receives frequent positive reviews from a variety of consumer and media groups for its consumer-friendly approach.

A note to WMO readers: The catalog is free to readers of this book, so be sure to identify yourself as such.

SPECIAL FACTORS: Satisfaction guaranteed; returns accepted within 30 days.

Gold Sound

4285 S. Broadway, Dept.   303–761–3652
BWBM   Fax: 303–762–0527
Englewood, CO 80110

Catalog: free
Pay: check, MO, MC, V, AE, DSC
Sells: high-end speaker kits; used, demo, and closeout
    home and professional audio equipment
Store: same address; Monday to Friday 10–6, Saturday
    11–5

If you thought you had to spend thousands to get high-end speakers, think again. Gold Sound has designed and sold quality speaker kits for home and professional use since 1976. Speaker kit advantages include: (1) better sound, deeper bass, greater clarity; (2) lower cost (up to 80% savings!); (3) greater flexibility in size, wood finish, and appearance, plus space-saving units you can build into walls, ceilings, and furniture; (4) easy upgrades for newer technologies (you can dramatically improve your existing 25-year-old speakers); and (5) they're educational and fun! *Stereo Review* has praised Gold Sound speakers as the high end of the high end; they've won the International Consumer Electronics Show's Innovation Design Award; and they're used by NASA, Boeing, and scores of institutions and corporations.

In prebuilt speakers, you pay mainly for labor, advertising, overhead, and store markup. Use your time and only pay for what makes sound: the working parts. A Gold Sound $299 kit has better parts and sound, says owner/designer Ron Gold, than $1,000 assembled units. All kits use high-quality European- and U.S.-made components, yet several cost under $200. The kits include detailed, easy-to-follow plans. Kits with completely built cabinets need as little as one evening to assemble. The kits are also available without cabinets, for people who prefer to make their own. Home kits for stereo or home-theater use include subwoofers, satellites, bookshelves, towers, centers, surrounds, and in-wall models. Pro models are popular for clubs, musicians, deejays, schools, and churches. The catalog lists and describes in detail each Gold Sound Kit, and also has some amazing deals (up to 70% off retail) on closeouts, demos, and used units, including receivers, amplifiers, CD players, turntables, tuners, tape decks, mixers, microphones, and pro equipment from well-respected makers. If you're in the area, stop by Gold Sound's Denver showroom, where you can hear many assembled kits.

SPECIAL FACTORS: Speaker kits have a 30-day money-back guarantee and a two-year replacement warranty; quantity discounts are available.

J&R Music World

59–50 Queens-Midtown   **800–221–8180**
Expressway, Dept. BWBM   **Fax: 800–232–4432**
Maspeth, NY 11378–9896

Catalog: free
Pay: check, MO, MC, V, AE, DSC
Sells: audio, video, computers, music, small appliances,
   etc.
Store: Park Row, New York, NY; Monday to Saturday
   9–6:30, Sunday 10–6
Online: www.jandr.com

When tourists visit New York, they inevitably go to see the Statue of Liberty, the Empire State Building, and Rockefeller Center. Then they visit J&R Music World in downtown Manhattan. This store has become a destination for foreigners looking for home entertainment and computer equipment at unbeatable prices. (J&R has a "meet or beat" price policy on everything they sell.) There are two ways to shop here by mail. You can get a free copy of the print catalog or visit the store online, which features the whole inventory as well as online ordering.

J&R sells entertainment products such as home audio equipment (amps, CD players, headphones, tuners, speakers, etc.), portable audio (boom boxes, shortwave radios, DAT and mini-disc players, etc.), car stereos, and video equipment (camcorders, DVD players, video editing units, laser disc players, etc.). The other half of J&R's business is home/office equipment including PC computers, Macintosh computers, software, and office equipment such as answering machines, cordless telephones, videophones, fax machines, and more. There's also a selection of large and small home appliances such as refrigerators, microwave ovens, water filtration systems, and fans. One has to ask, what *doesn't* J&R sell? Don't say videos, music CDs, watches, and radar detectors, because they do sell these items, and many others too numerous to list here. The best thing to do is see for yourself.

SPECIAL FACTORS: Satisfaction guaranteed; all products brand-new and factory fresh; authorized returns accepted (see catalog for details).

Lyle Cartridges

115 S. Corona Ave., Dept.
BWBM
Valley Stream, NY 11582

800–221–0906
516–599–1112
Fax: 516–599–2027

Catalog: free with SASE
Pay: check, MO, MC, V, AE, DSC
Sells: phono cartridges, replacement styli, turntables, tone arms, and phono-related accessories
Store: same address; Monday to Friday 9–5, Saturday 10–1 (October to May)
E-mail: lylemax@aol.com

In business since 1952, Lyle Cartridges is *the* source for those of you who can't bring yourself to give up your perfectly wonderful turntable for a CD player. As LPs have become harder to find, so too have the products and services needed to enjoy them. This is Lyle's specialty. At Lyle you'll find phono cartridges and replacement styli (factory original), turntables and tone arms, and other phono-related accessories such as headphones and record cleaners at 60% less than anywhere else. Lyle's black-and-white catalog has photographs, minimal descriptions, and price lists, but if you're unsure or need more help, call the friendly folks at Lyle for more personalized attention. These are people with whom you'll have a lot in common.

SPECIAL FACTORS: Authorized returns are accepted; defective goods replaced; minimum order is $15, $25 with credit cards.

Sound City

58 W. 45th St., Dept. BWBM   212–575–0210
New York, NY 10036   Fax: 212–221–7907

Information: price quote
Pay: check, MO, MC, V, AE, DSC
Sells: audio and video equipment, and home-office
  products
Store: same address; Monday to Friday 8:30–7, Saturday
  9–6

"Discover something you never thought possible," says the PR material from
Sound City. What they're talking about is a smallish company that carries more
brands of audio, video, TV, personal electronics, home theater, and home office
products than the megastores; a place where "you can always talk to the boss";
customer-friendly policies such as special products for overseas companies and
delivery anytime, anywhere; and Manhattan salespeople who don't have attitudes,
to name a few. But I forgot to mention price: Sound City sells audio equipment
from major manufacturers including RCA, Sony, Panasonic, Bose, Yamaha, Pro-
Scan, Mitsubishi, JVC, Paradigm, Harman/Kardon, and Technics—all at a discount. If you don't like Sound City's price, "talk to the boss." "Whatever it takes,"
he says, "we want to make you happy." Don't look for a flashy website or slick
catalog here. You'll need to call or write for a price quote, as there's no print
catalog. Once you've done so, you may become one of Sound City's many loyal
customers.

SPECIAL FACTORS: Returns accepted within seven days (inquire for details).

If you've ever been on television, you know that it's important to have videotape copies of your 5-, 10-, or 15-minute segment to send out as PR. But where do you find tapes of this length? The answer is Wholesale Tape and Supply. When you need quantity duplication of audio- or videotapes or CDs, Wholesale Tape and Supply Company offers professional duplicating and fulfillment services. If you have your own equipment or want to buy some, or you need audiovisual supplies, Wholesale Tape, in business since 1977, sells blank audio- and videocassettes, AV accessories, and high-speed audio duplicating equipment. Cassettes come with a choice of housings (clear, white, black) and tape lengths from 12 to 122 minutes. Custom-ordered tape lengths and cassette colors are available, as are custom labels and shell imprinting. You can also purchase cassette boxes, audio equipment for albums, shipping envelopes, and storage units from Wholesale Tape. At press time Wholesale Tape's website was under construction, so check it out.

SPECIAL FACTORS: Satisfaction guaranteed; quantity discounts offered; C.O.D. orders accepted; minimum order $30.

Related Products/Companies

Car audio systems
- Bernie's Discount, Crutchfield, Percy's

CD players and other audio components
- American Musical Supply, B&H Photo-Video–Pro Audio, Beach Sales, Bernie's Discount, Crutchfield, Damark, EBA Wholesale, Percy's, Upstairs Records

Digital recording equipment
- American Musical Supply, Wray's Music House

Internet shopping agent for home electronics
- KillerApp

Radios
- Defender Industries

Sound systems
- Sam Ash

Surplus audio/video parts
- All Electronics, H&R Company

Video equipment
- B&H Photo-Video–Pro Audio, Beach Sales, Bernie's Discount, Cole's Appliance, Crutchfield, Damark, EBA Wholesale, LVT Price Quote Hotline, Percy's, Porter's Camera Store

Musical Instruments, Accessories, and Sound Equipment

New and used musical instruments and musician supplies; sheet music; professional sound and recording equipment for stage, recording studio, and deejay

Whereas the firms in the previous section carry goods primarily for people who *listen* to music, this section features companies that cater to those who *play* or *produce* music. The firms listed here sell top-quality instruments—everything from school band recorders to grand pianos. Professional musicians rarely pay full price for their instruments, and if you buy from the same sources they use, neither will you. You'll also find electronic equipment and supplies for professional or at-home studio recording, as well as stage electronics, deejay equipment, and even karaoke machines. Get ready to save up to 75% from some of these firms.

Find It Fast

Accordions and Concertinas
- Accordion-O-Rama

Band Instruments
- Giardinelli Band Instruments, Interstate Music Supply, National Educational Music Co., Swords Music Companies, West Manor

Brass and Woodwinds and Accessories
- Discount Reed, Kennelly Keys

Children's Musical Instruments and Music-Related Toys
- Anyone Can Whistle

Electronic Keyboard
- Interstate Music Supply, Kennelly Keys, Musician's Friend

General Musical Instruments
- American Musical Supply, Anyone Can Whistle, Sam Ash, Elderly Instruments, Giardinelli Band Instrument, Interstate Music Supply, National Educational Music Co., Swords Music Companies, Thoroughbred Music, West Manor

Guitars, Stringed Instruments, and Accessories
- Interstate Music Supply, Kennelly Keys, Mandolin Brothers, Metropolitan Music, Musician's Friend, Shar Products, Weinkrantz

Musical Chimes
- American Musical Supply, Anyone Can Whistle

Percussion Instruments
- Anyone Can Whistle, Interstate Music Supply, Kennelly Keys

Pianos and Organs
- Altenburg Piano House

Songbooks and Sheet Music
- Elderly Instruments, Patti Music Company, Shar Products, Wray's Music House

Stage and Studio Electronics and Equipment
- Sam Ash, Interstate Music Supply, Musician's Friend, Thoroughbred Music, Wray's Music House

Used Instruments
- Altenburg Piano House, Elderly Instruments, Mandolin Brothers, Wray's Music House

Accordion-O-Rama

307 Seventh Ave., 20th Fl.,
Dept. BWBM
New York, NY 10001

212–675–9089
Fax: 212–206–8344

Catalog: $1 (see text)
Pay: check, MO, MC, V
Sells: accordions, accessories, and services
Store: same address; Tuesday to Friday 10–5, Saturday
  11–3 (may be open longer; call)

So you're in the market for an accordion. Where do you go to find the widest selection of new and rebuilt instruments, personalized service, and specialists in tuning, repairs, and electronics? Accordion-O-Rama is your place. Accordion-O-Rama is a specialty store for accordions, if you couldn't tell by the name, whose staff will help you select the best one for your taste and budget. The current set of flyers at the time of this writing featured a number of famous-name models marked down from suggested retail price to the tune of 25% to 35%. There are several ways you can go about finding the right squeeze box. If you call or write, the staff will ask that you give them detailed information about what you're looking for so they can best respond. The color catalog is $1; the black-and-white catalog is free. Or you can take a video "Demonstration" tour of Accordion-O-Rama for $25, or receive an instructional video on "The Basics of MIDI," also $25 (or get both videotapes for $45).

SPECIAL FACTORS: Trade-ins are welcomed; wholesale prices based on volume.

Altenburg Piano House, Inc.

1150 E. Jersey St.　　　　908–351–2000
Elizabeth, NJ 07201　　　Fax: 908–527–9210

Brochure: free
Pay: check, MO, MC, V, AE, DSC
Sells: pianos and organs
Store: same address; Monday to Friday 8–7, Saturday
　8–5, Sunday 12–5; also Asbury Park and Trenton, NJ

The Altenburg family knows pianos and organs, having been in the business of selling pianos since 1847. Altenburg sells pianos and organs by "almost all" manufacturers, including various one-of-a-kind pianos and Altenburg's own models (recommended by Franz Liszt and other luminaries). Besides personalized attention and knowledgeable salespeople, Altenburg has great prices as well: nearly 35% below everyone else's. If you call for literature, you'll receive information and specifications on Altenburg's own line of upright, grand, and console models, including details on encasing, action, workmanship, and warranty. Be sure to stop by if you're in the vicinity of Elizabeth, New Jersey, where you can stroll around the art deco showroom and tickle the ivories of an authentic Altenburg.

SPECIAL FACTORS: Inquire for information.

American Musical Supply

600 Industrial Ave.
Paramus, NJ 07652–3607

800–458–4076
320–796–2088
Fax: 201–262–3332

Catalog: free
Pay: check, MO, MC, V, AE, DSC
Sells: musical instruments and recording equipment
Store: Victor's House of Music, 762 Rt. 17 N., Paramus,
 NJ; open Monday to Thursday 10–9, Friday 10–7,
 Saturday 10–6
Online: www.victors.com (store);
 www.americanmusical.com (catalog)

I like companies like this one, where service and customer satisfaction are high priorities. American Musical Supply is a musician's discount catalog that offers the hottest brands at the lowest guaranteed prices, in addition to some super deals (up to 60% off on some items) by way of closeouts, "dent & scratch" specials, and "nonfactory boxed blowouts." They offer a 45-day money-back guarantee, free one-year extended warranties on many items, extended payment plans, two-day express shipping at no extra charge, seven-day-a-week phone hours, and more.

Among the hundreds of products at American Musical Supply are microphones and mic accessories, studio and recording equipment, studio furniture, speakers and amps, guitars and basses, guitar accessories, drum sets and percussion accessories, keyboards, MIDI gear, books and videos, and more. Color photographs and well-written text make it easy to navigate through this catalog. AMS is the mail-order division of Victor's House of Music, a third-generation family business. The full catalog is online, with online ordering available, so check it out!

SPECIAL FACTORS: C.O.D. orders are accepted, but must be paid with a postal money order and are $7.50 extra.

Anyone Can Whistle

323 Wall St.
Kingston, NY 12401–4407

800–435–8863
914–331–7728
Fax: 914–339–3301

Catalog: free
Pay: check, MO, V, MC, AE, DSC
Sells: Woodstock Chimes, exotic and novelty musical instruments, gifts, music CDs, etc.
Store: same address; Monday to Saturday 10–6
E-mail: anyone@chimes.com

Anyone Can Whistle (ACW) was founded in 1991 by the creator of the famous Woodstock Chimes. The philosophy behind the store and mail-order business is that anyone, regardless of training or past experience, can enjoy the act of creativity. The current mini-catalog gives you just a taste of what Anyone Can Whistle carries. (If there's an exotic instrument you're seeking, just call and ask; chances are they'll have it or can get it.) At Anyone Can Whistle you'll find unusual instruments such as German concertinas, Australian didgeridoos, African udu drums, English pennywhistles, Mexican rainsticks, Swiss music boxes, American folk instruments, Calypso steel drums, and waterfall pentatonic bamboo xylophones from Southeast Asia. There are also children's instruments, such as a "Kiddy Keys" Baby Grand piano (for children three and up, with color-coded keys for that emerging Mozart), "lollipop" drums, and a children's accordion. ACW also carries party favors and unique, creative gifts that you and your children will love, including puppets, world music CDs, juggling sets, and tiny whistles that do things when you blow: an alligator's jaws pop open, a caged canary flutters before a cat, race cars zoom around a tiny track. And, of course, Anyone Can Whistle sells Woodstock Chimes, from tiny magnetic refrigerator chimes to the 56-inch baritone "Gregorian Chimes." Don't miss this store if you're visiting Kingston, New York. You and your children won't ever want to leave.

Special to WMO readers: Anyone Can Whistle has a specific selection of goods that they'll offer to you for 20% to 40% off if you mention that you're a WMO reader.

SPECIAL FACTORS: For Canadian and international shipping rates, please inquire; no C.O.D. orders accepted.

Sam Ash Music Corp.

P.O. Box 9047, Dept. BWBM   800–472–6274
Hicksville, NY 11802   908–572–0263
                             Fax: 908–572–7138

Catalog: free
Pay: check, MC, V, AE, DSC
Sells: instruments and electronics
Store: locations in CT, FL, IL, NY, NJ, OH, PA, and CA; call
   main number or see website for addresses
Online: www.samash.com

In 1924 Sam and Rose Ash had to pawn Rose's engagement ring for $400 to make the first down payment on the first Sam Ash Music Store, eventually to become known as "The Musical Instrument Megastore" 75 years later. Today there are nearly two dozen Sam Ash stores scattered around the United States famous for their wide selection of musical instruments at the lowest prices anywhere. In addition to the regular discounts, Sam Ash runs frequent half-off sales and "Deals of the Month"; will give you money for your trade-in guitars (acoustic and electric), basses, tube amplifiers, drums, brass and woodwind instruments, and electronic equipment; and pledges to beat any price that's lower. On the website you can fill out a form to request information on the pricing and availability of guitars, basses, and amps; keyboards and sound modules; drums and percussion; brass and woodwinds; recording and effect units; and live sound, deejay, and lighting equipment. Someone at Sam Ash will contact you by e-mail, phone, or fax, whichever you prefer. You can also see the latest and greatest products from the best names in the business in the "Sam Ash Savings Guide," the company's 100-plus page full-color catalog, or you can call toll-free with a specific product request.

Please note: For a Spanish-speaking sales representative, call 212–719–2299 (NY) or 305–628–3510 (FL).

SPECIAL FACTORS: Minimum order $25; returns on certain items accepted within 15 days of receipt, but inquire for details.

Carvin Corp.

12340 World Trade Dr.   **800–854–2235**
San Diego, CA 92128   **619–487–1600**
                               Fax: 619–487–8160

Catalog: free
Pay: check, MO, MC, V, AE, DSC
Sells: Carvin guitars, basses, and accessories
Store: same address; Monday to Friday 9:30–6, Saturday
   10–4; also Hollywood, Santa Ana, and West Covina, CA,
   locations. Call for addresses and hours.
Online: www.carvin.com

What do James Brown's band, Mariah Carey's guitarist, and YES all have in common? Duh—I *know* they're all musicians! Besides that, though, they all have a soft spot for Carvin guitars and basses. Award-winning Carvin manufactures its own line of instruments and equipment, then offers them to consumers at factory-direct prices from the catalog and website. The 64-page color catalog features photographs, detailed descriptions, specifications, and prices that are up to 65% off list. The website has the same features, with secure online ordering. All Carvins are "Born in the USA."

In addition to guitars and basses of every type and description, Carvin offers such equipment as power amps, mixers and sound systems, loudspeakers, monitors, mics and cables, pickups, amplifiers, racks and stands, and speaker parts. In the current catalog are raves from both customers and professional reviewers, including *Bass Player* magazine and *Pro Audio Revue*. You'll also find a small selection of instructional books and videotapes.

Please note: Order toll-free during phone hours, Monday through Friday 7–6 and Saturday 10–4 PT.

SPECIAL FACTORS: Money-back guarantee if you're not completely satisfied within ten-day trial period; one-year warranty against manufacturing defects.

Discount Reed Co.

24307 Magic Mountain Pkwy.,   **800–428–5993**
#181   **805–294–9437**
Valencia, CA 91355   **Fax: 805–294–9762**

Price List: free
Pay: check, MO, MC, V, DSC
Sells: reeds for musical instruments
Store: mail order only
Online: www.discountreed.com

Discount Reed specializes in clarinet and saxophone reeds, many of them at savings up to 50% off retail prices. The eight-page catalog chronicles one deeply discounted product after another: from Rico Jazz sax reeds to Mitchell Lurie clarinet reeds to hand-selected clarinet and sax reeds from France. The reeds here come in a variety of canes, strengths, cuts, and even coatings—the Rico Plasticover, used by Tom Scott, has a coating that significantly reduces moisture absorption, allowing the reed to be played longer. The huge in-stock reed inventory includes Grand Concert Select, RKM, Peter Ponzol, Dave Guardala, Fred Hemke, a Vandoren selection, E. Rousseau, and Marca, plus synthetic reeds by Fibracell and Bari. There is also a limited selection of reeds for oboe and bassoon. Accessories include a Pisoni reed knife, Qwik-Time metronome, Hodge silk swabs, Claricord elastic clarinet neckstrap, Kiwi NeckPak, Blue Note sax straps, bore and key oils, and reed cases, guards, and trimmers. The website offers specials on accessories such as Yamaha cleaning paper (said to be much better than dirty dollar bills!) and Pack a Stand, which folds to fit into the bell of a clarinet for storage in the case. Online catalog viewing and ordering through e-mail are available.

SPECIAL FACTORS: School purchase orders accepted; minimum order $20 on credit cards.

Elderly Instruments

P.O. Box 14249-BWBM
Lansing, MI 48901

517–372–7890, ext. 123
Fax: 517–372–5155

Catalog: free (see text)
Pay: check, MO, MC, V, DSC
Sells: new and vintage musical instruments, books, audio-
and videotapes, and music CDs
Store: 1100 North Washington, Lansing, MI; Monday to
Wednesday 11–7, Thursday 11–9, Friday and Saturday
10–6; mail order hours Monday to Saturday 9–5
Online: www.elderly.com

Since 1972 Elderly Instruments has been known for its huge selection of new and used guitars, basses, amplifiers, effects, banjos, ukuleles, mandolins, fiddles, dulcimers, harmonicas, accordions, bodhrans, and other instruments at terrific prices. Concertinas, autoharps, folk harps, bowed psalterys, harmonicas, kalimbas, recorders, didgeridoos, flutes and fifes, Andean pipes, pennywhistles, steel drums, bongos, and tambourines are among the many instruments you'll find. Many of these instruments need parts and supplies, cases, and accessories, all available here, and while it might not be a necessity, there's also a sliding "rocking" chair, designed without arms, for easy picking and relaxing. For electronics users, Elderly's catalog details specifications for home recording equipment, microphones, wireless systems, amps, overdrive and distortion effects, foot pedals, processors, and much more.

For different musical interests, Elderly prepares several catalogs: "Instruments and Accessories," "Books and Videos," and "CDs and Cassettes," in addition to a monthly subscription newsletter, *Vintage and Used Instrument List* (a sample copy is available by request). Book subjects include instrument building and repair, songbooks (country, gospel, folk, Irish, Christmas, bluegrass), self-instruction for every instrument sold (with the possible exception of kazoo!), biography, and recording techniques. Elderly's website is worth checking out, where among other things you can scan the amazing selection of Elderly's hard-to-find CDs and cassettes and see the current Cheapo Depot specials and closeouts; you can also order online.

SPECIAL FACTORS: Satisfaction guaranteed (see catalog for policies); unused, authorized returns accepted within five days.

Giardinelli Band Instrument Co., Inc.

7845 Maltlage Dr.
Liverpool, NY 13090

800–288–2334
315–652–4792
Fax: 800–652–4534
Fax: 315–652–4534

Catalog: free, $7 outside U.S.
Pay: check, MO, MC, V, AE, DC, DSC
Sells: brasses, woodwinds, string, percussion, and
accessories
Store: same address; Monday to Friday 8:30–5, Saturday
9–1
Online: www.giardinelli.com

When you see the high school band parade and the school orchestra perform, it's likely they're playing instruments from Giardinelli Band Instrument Co., Inc., a seller of fine brasses and woodwinds since 1947. Over the years the catalog offerings have been expanded to include violins, violas, cellos, and basses, and electronic and portable keyboards, electric guitars and basses, and amplifiers. Giardinelli describes its prices as "thrifty," which is a term of modesty; prices here dip as low as 45% off suggested retail.

The more than 200-page newsprint catalog is easy to use with inventory categorized by instrument (woodwind, brass, concert and marching percussion, orchestral, guitars, and keyboards), accessories (mouthpieces and mutes; reeds, caps and ligatures; cases, covers and gig bags; metronomes and tuners; stands), and care and maintenance. Forty-five pages are dedicated to publications, notably methods books and music for flute, clarinet, tuba, bassoon, trumpet solos, trombone solos and ensembles, and brass ensembles. Many additional name-brand products available from Giardinelli are not listed in the catalog, so calls are invited. If you have the six-digit product number from your mail-order catalog, you can place orders online; there are also significant web-only specials, so be sure to visit the store online.

SPECIAL FACTORS: Satisfaction guaranteed; returns accepted; institutional accounts welcome.

Interstate Music Supply

P.O. Box 510865
13819 W. National Ave.
New Berlin, WI 53151

800–982–BAND
414–786–6210
Fax: 414–786–6840

Catalog: free (see text)
Pay: check, MO, MC, V, DSC
Sells: instruments, electronics, and accessories
Store: Cascio Music Co., same address; Monday to Friday
8–8, Saturday 8:30–5 CT; also 11010 North Port
Washington Rd., Mequon, WI; Monday to Thursday 10–8,
Friday 10–5:30, Saturday 10–4
Online: www.execpc.com/~ims

How does one company top another? Interstate Music Supply claims to have "the lowest prices on the planet." Unless you're from Mars, you won't do any better than to shop here for everything from acoustic basses to zonda reeds. The 363-page "School Discount Catalog" has every kind of musical instrument for band or orchestra, including children's instruments; sound, stage, lighting, and recording equipment; parts and accessories for every type of instrument; storage units; stage furniture and riser setups; and much, much more. As the catalog name suggests, this is a major source for schools and other institutions looking to fully equip their departments and musicians. But you don't have to be an institution to enjoy 60% off list prices on these products. Individuals get the same savings. And the catalog features closeouts, blowouts, and other great sale items where savings are even greater. IMS also publishes specialty catalogs: "Guitars" (guitars/bass instruments), "MIDI, Keyboard, and Revording" (including keyboard and computer software), and "Drums" (percussion instruments and accessories). The website has mostly general information, but you can order a print catalog online.

SPECIAL FACTORS: Satisfaction guaranteed; returns accepted within ten days for exchange, refund, or credit; institutional accounts available; minimum order $25.

Kennelly Keys Music, Inc.

20505 Hwy. 99
Lynnwood, WA 98036

425–771–7020
Fax: 425–670–6713

Information: price quote
Pay: check, MO, MC, V, AE, DSC
Sells: musical instruments and accessories
Store: same address
Online: www.musicconnect.com

Since 1960, Kennelly Keys Music, Inc., has been selling brass and woodwind, string, percussion, and electronic instruments and accessories at discounts up to 40%. Kennelly also carries PA equipment (mixing boards, microphones, speakers), combo gear (guitars, amps, effects processors), and electronic equipment (keyboards, digital pianos, MIDI equipment). Inquire by phone or fax for prices; if you want information on specific models and product lines, brochures are available in lieu of a catalog. Better yet, log on to the website, which is a well-designed, full-functioning online store where you can view prices and models right away and see Kennelly's discounted prices listed alongside the normal list prices so you can calculate your savings.

SPECIAL FACTORS: Institutional accounts available; authorized returns accepted; minimum order $25.

Mandolin Brothers, Ltd., inspired a lovely Joni Mitchell lyric about going to Staten Island to buy a mandolin, and prompted the *Boston Globe* to call this "one of the best guitar shops in the world." Since 1971, Mandolin Brothers has been the home for vintage, new, and used American fretted instruments at reasonable prices; new products sell at discounts up to 35% off list.

Vintage guitars, mandolins, mandolas, banjos, ukuleles, and other stringed instruments are featured in the 75-page catalog along with such new equipment as electronics, guitars, and accessories. In stock are pickups, cables, strings, straps, frets, books, videos, and more. In addition to instrument repairs, Mandolin Brothers offers written appraisals of instruments, maintains a "want list" service for individuals, and has an online and print newsletter, *Vintage News,* offering comprehensive listings of available vintage instruments (subscription to print version of monthly newsletter is $15/year). The website will give you a good idea of what this company is all about, what they sell, and the great specials they're currently running, but there's no online ordering; you still have to phone, fax, or mail in your order. In-stock as well as vintage instruments can be shipped on a three-day approval basis.

SPECIAL FACTORS: Satisfaction guaranteed; returns accepted within three days.

Metropolitan Music Co.

P.O. Box 1415
Stowe, VT 05672

802–253–4814
Fax: 802–253–9834

Catalog: $1.25
Pay: check or MO
Sells: stringed instruments and accessories
Store: mail order only

Since 1928, Metropolitan Music Co. has been a source for stringed instruments and accessories primarily for professional and otherwise experienced musicians. The 40-page catalog includes violins, violas, cellos, basses, and bows by Ibex, Resonance, and J. Uzek, among others. In stock are such parts as bridges, pegs, chin rests, and shoulder rests. Wood and tools are also available, as are books on the repair and construction of instruments. Catalog prices are 30% to 50% less than you'd pay retail.

If you need overseas delivery, Metropolitan Music will refer you to worldwide distributors.

SPECIAL FACTORS: Prices quoted by phone or letter, with self-addressed stamped envelope; minimum order $15.

Musician's Friend, in business since 1981, calls its inventory of professional recording equipment and electronics "gear" and dubs itself "the world's largest direct-mail music gear company delivering the best for less." The color catalog offers everything for guitar and bass, including amps and combos, effects processors, pedals, pickups, stands, straps, strings, tubes, tuners, and cases and gig bags; everything for keyboards and MIDI—more amps, more stands, more cases and gig bags, plus software, sequencers, samplers, and synth and sound modules; and everything for stage and studio: acoustic foam, cables, CD players and recorders, cassette decks, compressors, drum machines and drums, microphones, mixers, rack accessories, speakers, and wireless systems. Prices are lowest on the most popular gear, with additional savings available on back-of-the-catalog closeouts. The website offers online ordering, good web-only specials, and a free online newsletter subscription.

SPECIAL FACTORS: Satisfaction guaranteed; price quote by phone; authorized returns accepted within 45 days.

National Educational Music Co., Ltd.

1181 Rte. 22, Dept. BWBM
Mountainside, NJ 07092

908–232–6700
Fax: 908–789–3025

Catalog: free
Pay: check, MO, MC, V, AE
Sells: instruments and accessories
Store: mail order only
Online: www.nemc.com

National Educational Music Company, NEMC for short, offers an excellent selection of band and orchestra instruments at up to 60% off suggested list price. These are brand-new, first-quality instruments—no damaged goods or manufacturer's seconds. The savings improve if you can buy in quantity, and NEMC makes it attractive for schools and other institutions to do so through a coupon program that enables frequent or large buyers to earn free instruments.

Every type of band and orchestra instrument is available here, from alto horns to xylophones—all well-known, top-quality brands. NEMC sells accessories too: amplifiers, carriers and cases, drum hardware, reeds, sound systems, and tuners, for example. By the way, NEMC's offers the best warranty coverage in the industry at no additional cost (except for fretted instruments). Their website does not feature online ordering, but is still worth taking a look at for more information.

SPECIAL FACTORS: Eligible returns accepted within seven days (a restocking fee may be charged).

Patti Music Company

P.O. Box 1514, Dept. 39
Madison, WI 53701–1514

800–777–2884
Fax: 608–257–5847

Catalog: $2
Pay: check, MO, MC, V, DSC
Sells: sheet music, music books, teaching methods and
aids, metronomes, etc.
Store: 414 State St., Madison, WI; Monday to Friday
9:30–5:30, Saturday 9:30–5
Online: www.pattimusic.com

People at all ages and stages of life study or teach piano and organ, and for them Patti Music Company sells sheet music, methods books, MIDI diskettes, teaching aids (flash cards, dictionaries, manuscript paper), and instructional videos, always below list price, sometimes at discounts up to 30%. The hefty newsprint catalog (nearly 190 pages) offers popular standards by The Beatles, Billy Joel, and Elton John, and scores from Broadway shows and movies. The piano methods section, running 24 pages, presents annotated entries on all the major instructional methods currently available, detailing levels and grades and availability of instructor's handbooks. Teachers and musicians can choose music from piano collections, libraries, National Federation Junior Festivals selections, piano solos and ensembles, and organ methods and repertoire. There are excellent books for parents who want to help their children develop musically, as well as general-interest titles about composers and performers. Piano furniture is also offered toward the back of the catalog, as are music stands, lamps, and gifts. If you have online access, orders can be placed using information from *the print catalog* since no online catalog is available. The print catalog, however, can be requested online.

SPECIAL FACTORS: Discounts are available through the catalog only; catalog fee waived for teachers and music professionals.

Shar Products Company

P.O. Box 1411
Ann Arbor, MI 48106

800–248–7427
313–665–7711
Fax: 800–997–8723

Catalog: free
Pay: check, MO, MC, V, DSC
Sells: sheet music, stringed instruments, videos, accessories
Store: 2465 S. Industrial Hwy., Ann Arbor, MI; Tuesday to Friday 9–6, Saturday 9–5; also Toronto, Ontario (call for location and hours)
Online: www.sharmusic.com

Since 1962, Shar has been "proudly serving the needs of string players" and is still setting the trend for bowed string instruments. This family-owned business has a wide selection, prices up to 35% off retail on many items, and excellent customer service. In the 64-page color catalog you'll find violin, viola, cello, and bass instruments and outfits, bows, strings, and general accessories such as rosin and instrument cleaners/polish, chin and shoulder rests, metronomes, tuners, pitchpipes, tuning forks, and more. There's a separate print catalog for sheet music with over 7,000 titles (string music, chamber music, jazz, Christmas, fiddle, Broadway, etc.) that also carries such items as manuscript paper, educational materials, and really wonderful and innovative music games; the online version features an easy-to-use search engine for music titles, which doubles as an excellent reference for teachers and students. The website, which has online ordering, is arranged by the proficiency level of the musician. In other words, the instrument offerings are grouped by beginning players and instruments, intermediate, advancing, and advanced and professional players, since a cello for a student would be a very different instrument from that needed by a world-class recording artist. In addition to products, Shar offers services for bowed-instrument players: instrument and bow appraisal, restoration services, and a personal consultant program to help you identify the ideal stringed instrument for your specific needs.

SPECIAL FACTORS: Satisfaction is guaranteed; sheet music not in catalog can be special-ordered.

Swords Music Companies, Inc., has been offering savings up to 50% on all sorts of musical instruments since 1969. Here's a company without a fancy catalog or website. But if you're looking for just about any type of instrument from one of the major manufacturers—including Kroc, Ovation, Ibanez, AKG, Tama, Guild, Yorkville, Akai, Vito, Crate, Gibson, Jackson, Fostex, Roland, Alvarez, B. C. Rich, Martin, DigiTech, Tascam, Marshall, Fender, Pearl, Ludwig, and many others— call Swords toll-free and ask for a price quote. While you're there, ask about Swords' "meet-or-beat" pricing.

SPECIAL FACTORS: Price quote by phone or letter with a self-addressed stamped envelope; returns accepted within 14 days for exchange or credit (inquire about policy details); minimum order $50.

Thoroughbred Music, Inc.

7726 Cheri Ct.
Tampa, FL 33634

800–800–4654
Fax: 800–818–9050
Fax: 813–881–1896

Catalog: free
Pay: check, MO, V, MC, AE, DSC
Sells: musical instruments, music electronics, and
  accessories
Store: five locations in Tampa, Orlando, Clearwater,
  Sarasota, and Bradenton, FL; call for addresses and hours
Online: www.tbred-music.com

If they don't know about it already, serious rock musicians and studio engineers should see the 146-page color catalog from Thoroughbred Music, which showcases amps, CD and digital audiotape players and recorders, drum machines and effects boxes, MIDI equipment, special-effect lighting, matador timbales, and hundreds of other electronics and instruments (guitars and bass, banjos, keyboards, mandolins, drums, etc.). The top-name manufacturers are represented here, and Thoroughbred backs up their great prices with a "lowest price guarantee." Suggested retail prices and Thoroughbred's prices are listed side by side, the latter averaging 20% to 25% less. The catalog includes a number of pages of instructional books, tapes, and videos.

If you don't see what you're looking for, call—it may be available. And be sure to visit the website, with over 150 pages featuring online ordering, giveaways, music resources, information, contests, web-only specials and closeouts, and over 600 links.

SPECIAL FACTORS: Satisfaction is guaranteed; price quote by phone or letter.

Weinkrantz Musical Supply Co., Inc.

870 Market St., Suite 1265   800–736–8742
San Francisco, CA 94102–2907   415–399–1201
                                    Fax: 415–399–1705

Catalog: free
Pay: check, MO, MC, V
Sells: stringed instruments and accessories
Store: same address; Monday to Friday 9–5, PST

Since 1975, Weinkrantz Musical Supply Co., Inc., has been devoted to selling stringed instruments, accessories, and supplies. Prices usually range from 30% to 50% below retail, and you can call or write if you're looking for instruments produced by limited-run small workshops. The 40-page catalog offers strings, violins and violas, basses, and cellos. Instruments are available as part of outfits, or you can purchase bows, cases, rosin, and other equipment separately. Metronomes, tuners, bridges, chin rests, bow hair, and instrument bags and cases are all sold at discount.

SPECIAL FACTORS: Satisfaction guaranteed (special policy on strings; see catalog).

West Manor Music

831 E. Gunhill Rd.   718–655–5400
Bronx, NY 10467   Fax: 718–655–1115

Price List: free
Pay: check, MO, MC, V
Sells: musical instruments
Store: same address; call for hours

West Manor Music has been supplying schools and institutions with musical instruments since 1956, and it offers a wide range of equipment at average discounts of 45%. The 16-page catalog lists clarinets, flutes, piccolos, saxophones, oboes, English horns, cornets, trumpets, flugelhorns, trombones, French horns, euphoniums, tubas, violins, violas, cellos, string-bass, electric and acoustic guitars, snare drums, drum sets, cymbals, xylophones, timbales, marimbas, orchestra chimes, congas, tambourines, bongos, and other instruments. Drum stands and heads, strings, reeds, cases, music stands, metronomes, mouthpieces, amplifiers, music books, manuscript pads, cases, and other supplies and accessories are sold. All of the instruments are new and guaranteed for one year. West Manor also offers an "overhaul" service for popular woodwinds and brasses, and it can perform repairs as well.

SPECIAL FACTORS: Quantity discounts are available; minimum order is $25, $100 with credit cards.

Wray's Music House

326 Market St.   888–761–8222
Lemoyne, PA 17043   717–761–8222
    Fax: 717–731–0568

Information: price quote
Pay: check, MO, MC, V, AE, DSC
Sells: musical instruments and electronics
Store: same address; Monday to Friday 10–7, Saturday
    10–5
Online: www.wrays.com

Wray Music House, seller of musical instruments and electronics, promises a "Best Price Guarantee" at its website, which offers drums, keyboards, guitars (new and used), and deejay and other professional audio equipment. Founded by a former door-to-door salesman of upright pianos in the Harrisburg, Pennsylvania, area, Wray Music carries lines by Gibson, PRS, Ovation, Marshall, Mesa-Boogie, Takamine, Ensoniq, Roland, and many others, with 400 guitars in stock at all times. The website features "Internet Specials" with discounts up to 50% off list prices (you can submit an order via e-mail, but there's no online ordering). Wray carries amps, effects, synthesizers, MIDI, and recording equipment as well. Owned and operated by professional musicians, this store offers something others can't—personalized advice and service. If you're in the greater Harrisburg area, stop by. Or you can call, e-mail, or fax them with specific questions.

SPECIAL FACTORS: Satisfaction guaranteed; returns accepted for exchange, refund, or credit.

Related Products/Companies

Deejay equipment
- Upstairs Records

Duplication for audiotapes, videotapes, and CDs
- Wholesale Tape and Supply

High-performance earplugs
- Aircraft Spruce & Specialty

Horsetail hair
- Mangham Manor Farm

Keyboards, stereos, mirror balls
- Cook Brothers

Miscellaneous musician supplies
- Homespun Tapes

Phonograph needles and deejay supplies
- Record-Rama

Stage and recording studio equipment
- B&H Photo-Video–Pro Audio, Upstairs Records

Office, Business, and Professional

Computer Hardware and Software

PC and Macintosh computers and peripherals, business software, computer games, and computer accessories

I don't know about you, but just because I spend inordinate amounts of time in front of my computer at the office, have a portable I tote home with me each night, and own still another desktop PC in my living room for my young son to play educational games on, I wouldn't call myself techno-savvy, especially when it comes to buying a new computer or upgrading the one I have. Like many of you, I find the whole competitive world of computer vendors overwhelming. If you compare prices, which I've done quite a bit while researching this section, you'll find that one company can be cheaper by $200 to $300 on one model, but more expensive by the same amount on another product. Thankfully, the advent of the World Wide Web has brought help to consumers like us in the form of "computer shopping agents."

What are they? They're sites you can log onto *for free*, type in the product you're looking for, and the shopping agent scans their database to list all the stores that sell that product and the price at which they sell it. Two I'd highly recommend are Killer App (www.killerapp.com) and Price Scan (www.pricescan.com). Unlike some shopping agents on the web, these two are unbiased; in other words, there's no relationship between their advertisers and who gets ranked in their database. The only criterion is low price. Both sites are updated regularly, and both Killer App and Price Scan list businesses that have online stores as well as those that don't.

When I tested out these two computer shopping agents, the range was stunning: The same product was selling for half as much in one place as another! I definitely advise you to use a web shopping agent before investing large sums of money. If necessary, use the computer at your public library if you don't have Internet access at home. You'll be glad you did.

Meanwhile, the companies in this chapter are all good firms that have managed to survive in the vicious dog-byte-dog world of technology by offering good products at a discount. Because competition is so fierce in this industry, there's absolutely no need for us consumers to pay full price for computer hardware and software. Many of the companies in other chapters, by the way, also sell computer-related goods. See "Related Products/Companies" at the end of this chapter for a listing. For computer workstations and other computer furniture, be sure to check out the section following this one, "Office Furnishings," page 470. And for many computer-related supplies such as printer paper and diskettes, see "Office Supplies and Machines," page 479.

Find It Fast

Business Software and Computer Games
- Computer Discount Warehouse, Dartek, MicroWarehouse, Multiple Zones, NECX, Recycled Software, Shoplet.com

Computer Books and Manuals
- Computer Discount Warehouse, Multiple Zones

Computer Furniture and Organizers
- Dartek

Hardware
- Computer Discount Warehouse, Dartek, MicroWarehouse, Multiple Zones, NECX

Macintosh-Compatible Products
- Computer Discount Warehouse, MacWarehouse (under MicroWarehouse), MacWholesale (under Dartek), Multiple Zones, Shoplet.com

Networking Equipment
- Computer Discount Warehouse, Dartek, Data Comm Warehouse (under MicroWarehouse), Multiple Zones, NECX

Online Computer Auction
- Multiple Zones

Printer Supplies
- Computer Discount Warehouse, Dartek, Multiple Zones, NECX

Used Software for IBM-Compatibles
- Recycled Software

Computer Discount Warehouse

CDW Computer Centers, Inc.   847–465–6000
200 North Milwaukee Ave.   Fax: 847–465–6800
Vernon Hills, IL 60061

Catalog: free
Pay: check, MO, MC, V, DSC
Sells: computer hardware and software, peripherals, etc.
Store: showrooms in Chicago and Vernon Hills, IL; call for
   hours and addresses
Online: www.cdw.com

CDW offers more than 30,000 computer hardware, peripheral, and software items at discount prices. In business since 1982, this company publishes a comprehensive 98-page color print catalog, seven specialty catalogs, and has one of the best computer-related websites around.

CDW takes advantage of "every possible discount and special purchase opportunity" to get the lowest possible prices. You'll find the hottest name brands, the latest technology, and a solid foundation of service from CDW. Customer service by trained professionals (all graduates from CDW University!), custom configurations, toll-free technical support for the life of your product, manufacturer warranties, leasing options, fast delivery, and a comprehensive selection of everything under the sun that's computer-related keep CDW winning praise in the consumer media year after year. My advice is to skip the print catalog and go right to the website.

International customers, please note: There's a $25 handling fee charged on all orders shipped outside the U.S.

SPECIAL FACTORS: Phone hours for ordering and technical support are Monday to Friday, 7 A.M. to 9 P.M., Saturday 9 A.M. to 5 P.M. CT; 30-day return policy, with some restrictions (see website or catalog).

Dartek Computer Supply Corp.

175 Ambassador Dr., Dept.
BWBM
Naperville, IL 60540

800–832–7835
630–355–3000
Fax: 800–808–1106

Catalog: free
Pay: check, MO, MC, V, AE, DSC
Sells: PC and Macintosh supplies and equipment
Store: mail order only
Online: www.dartek.com and www.macwholesale.com

Dartek, for PC users, and its sister company MacWholesale (800–531–4MAC), for Macintosh people, can save you up to 60% on the equipment you need to make the most out of your PC or Mac. This company has been around since 1978 serving the ever-changing needs of technophiles with a wide range of products including hardware, software, printers, modems, supplies and accessories, computer furniture, and much more. I found the print catalog to be more user-friendly than the online versions, which didn't always have photographs or descriptions to accompany the product listings. Nevertheless, the prices were good, and the sites do feature closeout items and "Hot Deals" of the week, which make logging on worth your while.

SPECIAL FACTORS: Satisfaction guaranteed; quantity discounts available; authorized returns accepted within 45 days (see catalog or website for policies).

MicroWarehouse, Inc.

P.O. Box 3014, Dept. BWBM   **800–285–7080**
1720 Oak St.   **Fax: 732–905–5425**
Lakewood, NJ 08701–5926

Catalog: free
Pay: check, MO, MC, V, DSC
Sells: computers, components, software, and accessories
Store: mail order only
Online: www.warehouse.com

MicroWarehouse is a one-stop shopping experience, by print or online catalog, for computers and related goods at savings that can reach up to 50%. This company has made it easy for consumers by offering three different divisions—one for PC people (MicroWarehouse), another for Mac-heads (MacWarehouse), and a third for your networking, connectivity, and communications needs (Data Comm Warehouse). If you're not hooked up to the World Wide Web, request the catalog that best suits your needs.

Browsing this company's products online is an excursion into technological abundance. If you're expecting to find only computing products, get ready for fax machines and supplies, laminators, copiers, fax furniture, and more. Online you can search for products by name or manufacturer. You can also request print catalogs, sign up for the free e-mail buyers' guide *Online Advantage*, take advantage of special sales and blowouts, find discontinued or refurbished items deeply discounted, and visit MicroWarehouse's international sites. Best of all, you can go shopping for products by such manufacturers as Adobe, Canon, Corel, IBM, Iomega, Kodak, Microsoft, and Toshiba and get some of the best prices around.

SPECIAL FACTORS: Authorized return of defective items accepted within 120 days for exchange, refund, or credit; institutional accounts available; C.O.D. orders accepted.

Multiple Zones International

707 South Grady Way   **425—430—3000**
Renton, WA 98055—3233   **800—248—9948**

Catalog: free
Pay: V, MC, AE, DSC
Store: mail order only
Sells: PC and Mac hardware and software
Online: www.zones.com

Click onto the Zones.com site and you'll be met with the slogan "Expect the Best!" This online superstore comprises PC Zone and Mac Zone, and is regularly rated one of the top web-merchant sites. Whether you have a PC or a Mac, one click will take you to the appropriate site where you'll be met with a clutter of coupons, discounts, super blowout sales, promotions, and much more. But even the regular items here are very competitively priced—they have to be with all the competition out there. Prices can go as low as 50% off suggested list prices.

Some of the non-Mac and -Apple manufacturers represented here include AMS, Compaq, Fujitsu, Hewlett-Packard, Hitachi, IBM, Toshiba, and Performantz. Both the Mac and PC sites feature hardware, software, accessories, and peripherals and make shopping feel friendly, albeit a bit noisy and crowded. Don't like the web? Then you can request a print catalog for free for the same good selection and service.

Multiple Zones is also an Authorized Education Reseller for publishers and manufacturers, with the kind of product and manufacturer access that allows for institutional discounts up to 70% compared to retail prices. There are separate telephone numbers, listed online and in the catalog, for international, corporate, education, and government buyers.

By the way, if you're into online auctions, Multiple Zones had just added, at press time, a live auction site where you can bid for amazing deals on hardware, software, and accessories. Very cool.

SPECIAL FACTORS: Authorized returns accepted; corporate and business accounts available.

NECX

Four Technology Dr.   978–538–8356
Peabody, MA 01960   Fax: 978–538–8751

Information: website only, no print catalog
Pay: check, MO, MC, V, AE, DSC
Sells: computers and peripherals
Store: online, phone, and fax orders only
Online: www.necx.com

Ask your favorite computer wiz what's his or her best source for computer hardware and peripherals, and "NECX" will likely be the answer. My best computer buddy, for whom I have endless respect, recommended this company, so, of course, I checked it out. NECX, the oldest and largest website for computer shoppers, guarantees the lowest prices. It's continually top-ranked by BizRate, which means that actual customers have had excellent experiences time and time again.

NECX sells a wide array of computer parts and components, from high-end graphics accelerators to complete computer systems, motherboards, and modems. A combination of complete product descriptions, specifications, and product reviews allows you to make informed decisions. Departments include home and office computer center, memory express, and an area for corporate accounts. There's also a "Bargains and Rebates" page, where NECX searches the web for all current manufacturer rebates on products they carry, then lists them for consumers. You either receive the rebate with your product or can print out the rebate coupon from your own computer. Be sure to check out the "Outlet Center," where end-of-line, open-boxed, demonstration models, or special deals will net you even more savings. To keep processing costs—and therefore customer costs—low, Outlet Center purchases may only be made online—not over the phone. You can order online or by phone or fax on all other items.

SPECIAL FACTORS: Institutional accounts are available; satisfaction guaranteed; unopened, original purchases may be returned for a refund; see website for complete returns policy.

Recycled Software, Inc.

P.O. Box 33999
Las Vegas, NV 89133–3999

800–851–2425
Fax: 702–655–5662

Price List: free
Pay: check, MO, MC, V, AE, DSC
Sells: used computer software
Store: mail order only; phone hours Monday to Friday 7–4
 PT
Online: www.recycledsoftware.com

Contrary to popular belief, most software can be resold or transferred to a new owner, determined by the manufacturer's agreement that's included with the software. Recycled Software took this concept and built a successful mail-order business around it that benefits all of us. The software sold here (IBM compatible) can be had at amazing prices—up to 80% off. So who cares if it was preowned? The current price list can be viewed and downloaded on the website, which is updated weekly, but there's no online ordering. Or you can have a free print version mailed to you. You'll be happy to see the original price listed next to Recycled Software's deeply discounted prices.

The categories here include popular titles of all kinds—antivirus and backup, business/contact managers, computer-aided design, communication, databases, desktop publishing, financial and statistical, flowcharting tools, graphics and design, integrated packages, online/web utilities, operating systems, print utilities, and much more. Many titles have not been preregistered, which means you'll be able to register them in your own name and get all the accompanying perks: technical support in many cases, warranty services, reduced-rate upgrades, etc. Recycled Software sells only fully documented, non-OEM software, English version as sold in the U.S., guaranteed to be free of viruses or defects.

International customers, please note: Recycled Software honors prohibitions on sale of programs outside the U.S. when such restrictions are imposed.

SPECIAL FACTORS: Satisfaction guaranteed; returns accepted within 30 days for refund, exchange, or credit.

Shoplet.com

Information: website only, no print catalog

Pay: V, MC, AE, DSC

Sells: software titles, computer games, software
  e-downloads, hardware, books, etc.

Store: online only

Online: www.shoplet.com

Wow. If you're looking for a one-stop shopping experience on the web for software and computer games, this is it. Shoplet.com is a virtual minimall with several online stores contained within it: Internet Software Outlet, CD-ROM Outlet, DownloadOutlet.com, and three others that sell books, computer hardware, and toys.

Internet Software Outlet calls itself "the world's largest online software superstore." Here you'll find nearly 23,000 software titles, at this writing, discounted anywhere from 20% to 70%. There's an easy-to-use index as well as a search engine that makes it a snap to find just about any type of software you seek.

CD-ROM Outlet is a great source for CD-ROM games, games, and more games, with over 8,000 Macintosh and Win/95 titles in stock at the lowest prices anywhere. This site has been named the best source for multimedia software by the likes of NetGuide, Excite, and *MacWorld Magazine*. My own price checks bore that out; CD-ROM Outlet charged less on the three items I compared than one of the best-known software discounters on the web.

Finally, a trip to Shoplet.com will lead you to the fascinating DownloadOutlet.com. I say *fascinating* because no matter how technologically learned I become, it never ceases to amaze me that one can download information off the web. For that matter, the telephone still amazes me! Anyway, DownloadOutlet.com was launched on the basis of a simple concept: There's no reason to pay for the box. In other words, software, being a digital product, can come directly to your computer digitally—at three in the morning when you need that tax software! There's no reason to pay extra for the packaging and shipping costs, only to have that overdesigned software box take up space on your office bookshelf long after you've downloaded its contents. How much money can you save? At the very least you'll save $9.95, or the cost of the box. Savings reach 38% off in-store retail price on some items that are more deeply discounted. You don't have to be a computer expert to buy software this way; a customer service team will answer your questions and will guide you through the downloading process.

All in all, Shoplet.com is a place you'll want to bookmark whether you're seeking discount educational computer games for your child or spreadsheet programs for your office.

SPECIAL FACTORS: 24-hour customer service line; 30-day money back guarantee; institutional and government accounts welcome (inquire).

Related Products/Companies

Astronomy software and CD-ROMs
- Orion Telescope

Business software
- OfficeMax

Computer software for the visually impaired
- Independent Living Aids

Computer supplies
- Quill, Reliable Corp., Viking Office Products

Computers and computer accessories
- Damark, Defender Industries, J&R Music

Dance CD-ROMs
- Dance Distributor

Digital imaging components
- B&H Photo-Video–Pro Audio

General software
- Barnes & Noble, Bear Mountain Books, J&R Music, Reader's Digest

Horse and pony CD-ROMs
- State Line Tack

Horse-themed mousepads, clip-art, and screen savers
- Valley Vet

Leather laptop-computer cases
- Airline International Luggage

Left-handed keyboards and computer accessories
- The Left Hand

Surplus computer components
- H&R Company

Vinyl pages, pockets, and binders for storing CDs
- Store Smart 20th Century Plastics, University Products

Weather and navigation software
- Aircraft Spruce & Specialty, Defender

Web design, desktop publishing, computer graphics books, and CD-ROMs
- Fidelity Products, Print Bookstore

Office Furnishings

Functional furniture and furnishing accessories for home offices, professional settings, reception rooms, storerooms, hospitals, churches, schools, day-care facilities, etc.

Whether you're looking for an inexpensive, ergonomic desk chair for home or computer workstations for two dozen employees, these companies will have what you need. Many of the firms here carry furnishings for institutional settings—church pews, stacking cafeteria chairs, gymnasium bleachers, chalkboards—while others are more focused on the needs of small businesses. Every company listed here will save you significant amounts of money.

Some of the companies that carry office machines and shipping supplies also sell office furniture, shelving, and other furnishings for your stockroom or office, so be sure to see the listings in the next section, "Office Supplies and Machines," page 479.

Find It Fast

Children's Institutional Furniture
- Alfax, Business & Institutional Furniture Co., Dallas Midwest

Office Furnishings
- Alfax, Business & Institutional Furniture, Dallas Midwest, Factory Direct Furniture, Frank Eastern, K-Log, National Business Furniture

Other Institutional Furniture
- Alfax, Business & Institutional Furniture, Dallas Midwest, Factory Direct Furniture, Frank Eastern

Safes and Fireproof Files
- Discount Safe Outlet

Alfax Wholesale Furniture

Dept. C–1501   **800–221–5710**
370 Seventh Ave., Ste. 1101   **212–947–9560**
New York, NY 10001–3981   **Fax: 212–947–4734**

Catalog: free
Pay: check, MO, MC, V, AE
Sells: office and institutional furniture
Store: mail order only

If you're opening a day-care center, refurnishing a school or religious institution, or looking to update your company's offices, Alfax Wholesale Furniture sells the institutional furniture you need at quantity-discount prices. The furniture and equipment, such as file cabinets, literature storage systems, lockers, and heavy steel shelving, are designed for heavy use, with many products suitable for the home as well. Prefabricated office and computer stations; nursery and child-care furnishings (cots, play centers); park benches; pulpits and lecterns; cafeteria and library furnishings; conference-room seating; and miscellaneous fixtures such as PA systems, trophy cases, hat racks, and lockers can be ordered from the 116-page catalog.

SPECIAL FACTORS: Satisfaction guaranteed; institutional accounts and leasing available.

Business & Institutional Furniture Company

Box 92039
Milwaukee, WI 53202–0039

800–558–8662
414–272–6080
Fax: 800–468–1526
Fax: 414–272–0248

Catalog: free
Pay: check, MO, MC, V, AE, DSC
Sells: office and institutional furnishings
Store: mail order only; phone hours Monday to Friday 7–6,
  Saturday 8–12 CT
Online: www.bi-furniture.com

Between telecommuting and the trend toward lifestyle downscaling, more people are choosing to set up office right in their own homes. If you're looking for the perfect company to help you do so, this is it. B&I has been helping individuals, companies, and institutions set up their workplaces with a comprehensive selection of high-quality furnishings, good prices, and special attention to their customers that's built customer loyalty over the years. B&I's knowledgeable sales representatives can help you plan your workspace to achieve the look you want with the most efficient use of space and money. In-house designers will even provide computer-generated floor plans to help you visualize a new office setup.

For individuals and businesses there is the "Business" catalog, which has office furniture including desks, files, bookcases, credenzas, and panels and panel systems (for office partitioning). The seating ranges from stacking lunchroom chairs to leather-upholstered executive models. There are data and literature storage units, computer workstations, locking cabinets, waste cans, announcement boards, and much more. Spot checks on several items in this catalog compared with other office furniture discounters showed B&I's prices to be lowest. The catalog itself is well designed and may inspire you to get organized and rearrange your workspace.

B&I also puts out four other catalogs: "Health Care," "School," "Church," and "Government." If you work in one of these areas, B&I has attractive and appropriate furnishings for these settings—all at a discount.

The website allows you to track the progress of your order and shows a small selection of their products, but doesn't feature online ordering. You can, however, order one of the five print catalogs through the website.

SPECIAL FACTORS: "15-year, no-risk warranty"; volume discounts are available.

Dallas Midwest

4100 Alpha Rd., Ste. 111	972–866–0101
Dallas, TX 75244	Fax: 972–866–9433

Catalog: free
Pay: check, MO, MC, V, AE
Sells: office and institutional furniture
Store: mail order only
Online: www.catalogcity.com

Dallas Midwest sells office, school, church, and other institutional furniture at discounts of 30% to 50% off list prices, with special savings offered on orders over $1,000. The catalog presents furnishings and fixtures such as executive desks and chairs, conference furniture, partitions and dividers to create cubicles, and wooden and metal files. Stacking chairs, folding chairs, and folding and adjustable worktables are available, as are post and rope systems for managing crowds, mobile stages and risers, and indoor and outdoor signboards.

The catalog devotes sections to school and day-care equipment for indoor (classroom desks, chairs, wooden storage units for toys and books, activity tables) and outdoor use (sandboxes, slides, seesaws, playground sets). The section on church furnishings features pulpits, kneelers, credence and communion tables, and stands. School and church furnishings available in unfinished wood are detailed in a separate catalog, available on request.

Park and other recreation-oriented items are also sold by Dallas Midwest. A sampling includes park benches, bike racks, and picnic tables. Dallas Midwest carries so much standard furniture and so many related institutional goods that the nearly 100-page catalog is a must-see. Their website allows you to view the entire catalog, although there's no online product ordering.

For qualifying institutions, terms are net 30 days; a 2% discount is applied to orders paid by check.

SPECIAL FACTORS: Price quotes by phone; quantity discounts given; authorized returns accepted for exchange, refund, or credit; institutional accounts available.

Discount Safe Outlet

P.O. Box 67, Dept. BWBM   **888–444–2135**
Leonia, NJ 07605

> Catalog: free
> Pay: check, MO, MC, V, AE, DC, DSC
> Sells: Sentry safes, fireproof files, media safes, and
>   storage chests
> Store: Discount Safe Outlet, 117 Grand Ave., Palisades
>   Park, NJ; Monday to Friday 9–5, Saturday 9–1
> Online: www.mediasafes.com

When I think of wall safes, I think of 1940s black-and-white hard-boiled detective flicks. But these days if you're an embezzler and blackmailer, keep in mind that it's not stacks of hundreds you'll need to stash but more likely your computer data. While paper records can withstand temperatures to 350° F, computer media is damaged beyond use by temperatures about 125° F and 80% humidity. That's where Discount Safe Outlet steps in. They've been selling safes for home and office use for two decades. With shipping free in the continental U.S., expert advice, a size for every need, customized interiors appropriate for your specific items, lifetime product warranties, and the lowest prices, this is the place to shop for fireproof files, safes (wall, floor, cash-drop, store, office, electronic "digital" push-button, and gun), and diskette chest/files. The website at this writing was mainly an advertisement for the company. Your best bet is to call toll-free for a free catalog.

SPECIAL FACTORS: Shipping free in 48 contiguous states.

Factory Direct Furniture

P.O. Box 92967   800–972–6570
Milwaukee, WI 53202   414–289–9770
                             Fax: 414–289–9946

Catalog: free
Pay: check, MO, MC, V, AE
Sells: office furniture and institutional equipment
Store: mail order only
Online: www.factorydirectfurniture.com

If you're in the market for office furnishings, Factory Direct Furniture's (FDF) claim, "We will not be undersold," and discounts of 50% and higher off manufacturers' list prices are just the enticements you've been waiting for. With the manufacturer's 15-year guarantee, items such as a sturdy executive swivel and tilt chair by Globe ($250 list; FDF's price $149.50, or $139.50 if you order more than two) become irresistible. Most products are available "factory in-stock," which means there's no undue waiting. Sharp color photos in the 80-page catalog detail important aspects of every piece of value-priced office furniture including bookcases, organizers, panels, reception seating, tables, and, of course, chairs, desks, and computer furniture. The website offers additional product selections of chair mats, hand trucks, bulletin boards, office electronics, and conference room furnishings. Online shoppers can also sign up for e-mail notice of specials updates. You can request fabric swatches and wood chips to help make your selection, and if your order is likely to exceed $1,000, you're invited to phone for a price quote, since additional discounts of 2% to 18% apply to larger orders.

SPECIAL FACTORS: Satisfaction guaranteed; quantity discounts available; Factory Direct Furniture's own ten-year guarantee (except for normal wear and tear) applies to everything it sells.

Frank Eastern Co.

599 Broadway   800–221–4914
New York, NY 10012–3258 212–219–0007
                           Fax: 212–219–0722

Catalog: free
Pay: check, MO, MC, V, AE
Sells: office, institutional, and computer furniture
Store: same address; Monday to Friday 9–5
Online: www.belowcost.com

You're familiar with all the office megastores, and probably get barraged with their blowout, blockbuster sales flyers too often. Then there's Frank Eastern Co. This company may not have instant name recognition, but once you've thumbed through the 80-page color catalog it's not a name you'll soon forget. The reason is that Frank Eastern sells office, computer, and institutional furniture at savings up to 60% on list.

Since 1946 Frank Eastern had it in their minds that ergonomic products could help people be more productive. These include desks, chairs, filing cabinets, bookcases, storage units, computer workstations, and wall systems and panels, all of which are shown and described in the catalog, with their suggested retail price listed alongside Frank Eastern's price. Seating seems to be Frank Eastern's specialty; you'll find ergonomic, executive, clerical, drafting, waiting room, conference, folding, and stacking models in wood, leather, chrome, and plastic. There's a task chair with air-lift seat adjustment and an adjustable back that's way cheaper than I've seen it anywhere. You'll even locate the hard-to-find Hag balans vital chair here—a stool/knee rest combo that helps align your spine while you work. Don't overlook the good buys on solid oak bookcases, wall organizers, lateral filing cabinets, and mobile computer workstations.

SPECIAL FACTORS: Satisfaction guaranteed; quantity discounts available; minimum order is $75 with credit card.

K-Log

P.O. Box 5   800–872–6611
Zion, IL 60099–0005   847–872–6611
                                    Fax: 847–872–3728

Catalog: free
Pay: check, MO, MC, V
Sells: office, A/V, and computer furniture and equipment
Store: mail order only
Online: www.k-log.com

Luckily for mail-order shoppers, all discount furniture enterprises are not created equal, and the differences are what set them apart. K-Log clearly excels in its inventory of training/hospitality, utility, folding, and activity tables, and other conference room furniture that ranges from boat-shaped, slab-base tables to traditional plinth-base tables to modular conference and computer tables. For a less institutional feel, there are solid American red oak and oak-veneer furniture lines, a classic cherry executive series, and, for computer work, a traditional-style oak set, all in a variety of configurations, with most products up to 50% off. K-Log can equip school audiovisual and computer labs with two-student stations, split-top workstations, and computer lab desks with space for both computer and desk work. Electric-lift adjustable workcenters allow for computer work while standing or sitting, and tower workstations accommodate multiple monitors for LAN systems or video editing. The glossy 68-page color catalog allots ten pages to audiovisual equipment that includes overhead projector tables, locking consoles, TV mounts, deluxe presentation screens, big screen video projectors, LCD projection panels, lecterns, and hands-free PA and cordless sound systems. K-Log also stocks chairs, floor and wall displays, bookcases, steel and wire shelving, coat rack systems, storage cabinets, and fireproof files. The website offers monthly superspecials, but watch for expiration dates before reaching for the phone. There's no online ordering at the website.

SPECIAL FACTORS: Satisfaction guaranteed; quantity discounts available; prices quoted by phone or letter; authorized returns accepted for exchange, refund, or credit (restocking fee may apply); institutional accounts available.

National Business Furniture Inc.

735 N. Water St.
P.O. Box 92952
Milwaukee, WI 53202

414–276–8511
Fax: 414–276–8371

Catalog: free
Pay: check, MO, MC, V, AE
Sells: office and computer furnishings
Store: mail order and outside sales staff (see text)
Online: www.catalogcity.com

Established in 1975, National Business Furniture (NBF) sells quality office furniture at wholesale prices including standard or reinforced libraries, conference room tables, bookcases, cabinets, leather chairs, traditional chairs with classic button-tufting, wood-grain organizers and desk toppers, and radius-style desks. Savings reach as high as 50% on many items. NBF's 180-page catalog includes products not seen in some other furniture dealers' catalogs, namely portable partitions to create instant rooms, acoustic panels to screen out distracting noises, low-decibel lockers to conveniently and quietly store personal belongings, and olefin floor mats to wipe shoes and reduce water tracking on tile. Most top-name manufacturers are represented in the 13,000-item catalog, and complete manufacturers' product-line brochures are available by calling NBF, as are fabric swatches and wood chips, and answers to your space-planning questions. Local sales reps in branch locations (Atlanta, Boston, Chicago, Dallas, Los Angeles, Milwaukee, and New York) are available for office consultations. NBF provides a 15-year guarantee on products (except for normal wear and for chairs used on a 24-hour basis), and will adjust, repair, or replace them if there are problems with workmanship or quality. You can electronically view the entire print catalog as well as order a copy on the website.

SPECIAL FACTORS: Prices quoted by phone or letter with self-addressed stamped envelope; quantity discounts available; leasing plans available to qualifying companies.

Related Products/Companies

Acrylic literature stands and office accessories
- Plexi-Craft

Bookends
- Barnes & Noble

Computer and graphic-design furniture
- Fidelity Products, Pearl Paint, Daniel Smith

Display cases and shelving
- University Products

Executive desk accessories
- Ace Luggage, Bennett Brothers, Fountain Pen Hospital

Fax furniture
- MicroWarehouse

Home office furniture
- Bennett Brothers, Damark, Reliable Corp.

Office furniture and accessories
- Blackwelder's, Dartek, Fran's Wicker & Rattan, The Furniture Patch of Calabash, Genada Imports, Quality Furniture, Quill, Reliable Corp., Shaw Furniture, Sobol House, Viking Office Products

Safes
- OfficeMax

Shelving for computer workstations
- Woodworker's Hardware

Wooden woven wastebaskets and magazine baskets
- West Rindge Baskets

Office Supplies and Machines

General office supplies, office machines, presentations materials and services, and shipping supplies

If you're still using a single source for your office needs, check out the vendors listed here, then pull your last few supply invoices. When you compare prices—especially on items your firm uses in bulk—you'll no doubt find that you're paying more than you should. And many of the discounters listed here offer the same perks you've been getting: open accounts, quick shipment, special orders, and custom services. You'll find virtually everything you need in this section to keep your office humming—from paper clips to copiers.

For firms specializing in computers, computer-related hardware such as printers and modems, and computer software, see "Computer Hardware and Software," page 460. For furniture such as desks, workstations, chairs, shelving, and the like, see "Office Furnishings," page 470. The section following this one, "Printing and Stationery," page 499, features companies that can custom-print logos, payroll checks, business cards, invoices, rubber stamps, letterhead, and other items for you and your business, although many of the firms in this section offer some of these services as well. And if you're looking for promotional items, corporate gifts, or clothing imprinted with your company's logo, see the last section of this chapter, "Uniforms and Promotional Products," on page 505. As always, check out the company listings in "Related Products/Companies" for other firms that sell furniture, supplies, and services of use to small businesses and home offices.

Find It Fast

Bags
- Associated Bag, Plastic Bagmart, U.S. Box

Binders and Organizers for Business and Photos
- Store Smart, 20th Century Plastics, University Products

Cash Registers
- Affordable Photocopy, Business Technologies

Commercial Arts Supplies
- Fidelity

General Office Supplies and Office Machines
- Affordable Photocopy, Fidelity, OfficeMax, Quill Corp., Reliable Corp.

Presentations Materials and Services
- Visual Horizons

Printer/Computer/Copy Machine Supplies
- Affordable Photocopy, DCS, Viking

Resale Packaging and Retail Displays
- U.S. Box

Shipping Supplies
- Associated Bag, Fidelity, ULINE, Yazoo Mills

Writing Implements
- Fountain Pen Hospital

Affordable Photocopy Inc.

11010 SW 62nd Avenue
Portland, OR 97219

888–293–8071
Fax: 503–977–2522

Information: online and print catalogs (see text)
Pay: check, MO, V, MC, AE, DSC
Sells: photocopiers, fax machines, printers, cash registers,
  and parts and suppliers
Store: website only; phone hours Monday to Friday 9–5 PT
Online: www.photocopiers.com

I always wished I had a photocopier. I use my fax machine to make single copies, but for multiple copies I go to the local copy shop, where the owner always manages a smile for me, as well she should: I've probably put her child through a year of college. What if ordinary people like me could afford a photocopier? Well now we can. Affordable Photocopy Incorporated, aptly named, has been selling major-brand copiers, faxes, printers, multifunction copier/fax/printer/scanner machines, and the parts and supplies to keep them running since 1987. All of this is supplied to the public at wholesale prices: 60% off suggested retail. Add to that free shipping (on business-grade machines) and no sales tax and you're looking at some serious savings.

Some of the manufacturers represented here include Canon, Sharp, Ricoh, Minolta, Copystar, Xerox, Gestetner, Mita, Monroe, PitneyBowes, Panasonic, Savin, Toshiba, and Hewlett Packard. At the website, if you have the right-version browser, you can navigate around by price, brand, or category. If not, just click onto the directory, which lists different product categories, to view the current offerings, complete with detailed color images, descriptions, product specifications, suggested list and API prices, and other details. Besides the above-named machines, Affordable Photocopy sells computerized cash registers, as well as a good selection of parts for your printer, fax, and copier. There are some excellent features about the website, including informative text about consumer fraud vis-à-vis warranties, closeouts and monthly specials, a toll-free number you can call with questions, and secure online ordering.

Note: If you do not have Internet access, API will mail you a print catalog on request.

SPECIAL FACTORS: All products come with full factory warranty; free shipping on business-grade office machines; minimum order $50; unopened, authorized returns accepted within 15 days of receipt; wholesale orders accepted (inquire about terms).

Associated Bag Company

400 W. Boden St.
Milwaukee, WI 53207-7120

800-926-6100
800-926-4600 (Spanish)
Fax: 800-926-4610
TDD: 800-926-4611

Catalog: free
Pay: check, MO, MC, V, AE
Sells: poly bags, shipping and packaging supplies
Store: mail order only
Online: www.associatedbag.com

If only the world were as straightforward and direct as this company, in the packaging and shipping business since 1938. If you need to wrap, box, or ship something, they sell it: bags, boxes, bubble wrap, tape, labels, packaging materials, sealing materials, envelopes, and so on.

The well-organized 117-page color catalog has poly bags, bag-closing devices, envelopes, shipping/packaging products, industrial covers and liners, static control products, and safety/cleanup supplies. From Junior's lunchtime sandwiches to radioactive waste, Associated has the right size and material bag to contain it. Besides a fantastic array of containers and other products, Associated Bag offers pricing that's competitive, even more so when you order in volume. The staff is trained to deal with just about any packaging problem you or your business can come up with, and free product samples are available. This is a great source for small businesses or large projects such as moving.

SPECIAL FACTORS: Satisfaction guaranteed; products for special applications can be made to order; quantity discounts available; returns accepted; same-day shipping on orders placed by 7 P.M. CT.

Business Technologies

3350 Center Grove Dr.   319–556–7994
Dubuque, IA 52003–5225   Fax: 319–556–2512

Catalog: free
Pay: company check, MO, MC, V
Sells: cash registers and related supplies
Store: same address; Monday to Friday 8:30–5

If you'd like to open a retail shop and start small, you don't want to spend a lot for a cash register. Business Technologies has a simple solution: don't. This company sells Sharp electronic cash registers and cash register supplies (paper rolls, inking supplies, extra tills, etc.) at discount prices—to the tune of about 30% off list. The one-page brochure shows the basic models with features listed for each. But a telephone call once you've seen the selection will hook you up to Business Technologies' helpful salespeople and support staff who'll walk you through the pros and cons of different models, and will stand by you after you've made the purchase with technical support, a one-year warranty, and free programming.

SPECIAL FACTORS: Price quote by phone, fax, or letter; minimum order is $25.

DCS

6501 State Rte. 123 N.	800–735–3272
Franklin, OH 45005	513–743–4060
	Fax: 513–743–4056

Catalog: $3, refundable
Pay: MC, V, DSC
Sells: toner cartridges, diskettes, cables, printer ribbons, etc.
Store: same address; Monday to Friday 8–5
Online: www.dcsusa.com

Since 1979, DCS (the new name for the old Dayton Computer Supply) has been selling name-brand and house-brand supplies for computers, printers, copiers, and other office machines. If finding great deals on the priciest office supplies leaves you exalted, get ready. I called to price a toner cartridge for my office's laser printer and discovered that DCS's price was 35% less than my regular supplier. What's more, if I send in my old, used-up toner cartridge that's been sitting in a box with three others waiting to be recycled, DCS will recondition it and send it back to me at even greater savings. DCS's comprehensive selection includes, but is far from limited to, diskettes and other data storage media (available in bulk packages for house brands), cabling supplies and accessories (switch boxes, surge protectors, "mice" and mouse supplies), and printer stands.

As one of the top 50 toner cartridge remanufacturers in the United States, DCS produces cartridges for hundreds of laser printer and copier models; new cartridges from original manufacturers are also in stock. If you need replacement ribbon, especially the hard-to-find item, DCS is a good bet. By the way, this company recently did a comprehensive price comparison with the national office supply superstores and came out ahead. On the DCS website you can view the products and read descriptions of them, but online ordering is not available.

SPECIAL FACTORS: Satisfaction guaranteed; price quotes given by phone; discounts available; C.O.D. orders accepted; institutional accounts available.

Fidelity Products Co.

5601 International Pkwy.
P.O. Box 155
Minneapolis, MN 55440–0155

800–328–3034 (office supplies)
800–326–7555 (graphics supplies)
Fax: 800–842–2725

Catalog: free
Pay: check, MO, MC, V, AE, DSC
Sells: office and shipping supplies, graphics products
Store: mail order only

For over 36 years, Fidelity Products Co. has filled the packing and shipping needs of companies, small businesses, and individuals with standard and custom-sized products at factory-direct prices from their Fidelity Direct catalog. The 86-page illustrated color catalog abounds with savings—40% off list prices—on such business staples as shipping boxes, packaging tape, hand trucks and utility carts, poly bags, Kraft paper, storage files, bin boxes, scales, packing list envelopes, pallet wrap, loose fill, strapping systems, racks, and literature organizers. Products manufactured at Fidelity's own plant offer the greatest opportunities for saving and the assurance that products are available when you need them. Packing materials sold by the roll can be cut to custom widths, and if you're not sure about measurements, the catalog includes a metric/imperial conversion chart. An indication of Fidelity's commitment to customer service can be seen in a margin feature called "Practical Answers," which helps buyers choose, for example, the right tapes and poly bags (you can also ask for a free copy of "Packaging Tape Bulletin F11000"). For office shopping convenience, Fidelity also carries task chairs, desktop laminators, time clocks, soap dispensers, various Uni-San maintenance products, Kleenex and other brand paper products, protective eyeglasses and back support belts, lockers, and a carton-sealing gun.

The other catalog published by Fidelity is the "Graphics" catalog, which offers tools and supplies for architects, engineers, contractors, and anyone doing desktop publishing and computer-aided design. The goods here are priced below retail—averaging 30% off or more.

SPECIAL FACTORS: Satisfaction guaranteed; price quotes by phone; quantity discounts available; returns in original carton accepted within 30 days for exchange, credit, or refund (Fidelity pays shipping).

Fountain Pen Hospital

10 Warren St.
New York, NY 10007

800–253–PENS
212–964–0580
Fax: 212–227–5916

Catalog: free
Pay: check, MO, MC, V, AE, DSC
Sells: fountain pens, writing instruments, and repair
 services
Store: same address; Monday to Friday 8–5:45
Online: www.fountainpenhospital.com

There are certain items you don't expect to find at good prices: fine writing implements, for example. But Fountain Pen Hospital, in business since 1946, has "the world's largest selection" of modern and vintage writing instruments at great prices. Price comparisons with several other fine-writing-instrument companies showed that Fountain Pen Hospital offers the best deals by far with prices 20% to 40% less than everyone else's. The 64-page catalog includes some of the best names in the biz: Montblanc, Aurora, Waterman, Namiki, Parker, and many others. This family-run business specializes in new pens as well as vintage instruments made between the 1880s and 1960s. Recent catalog offerings included a collection of limited-edition pens by Silver Eagle, the only manufacturer of fine silver and 18-karat-gold vermeil overlay instruments (20% off list), a zigzag ballpoint collection by Jean Lepine with colorful metallic accents resembling modern jewelry (also 20% off list), and Montblanc's Meisterstück Ramses II collection, offering a lapis lazuli and vermeil pen with an 18-karat-gold nib and piston filling system (26% off list). You'll also find wood and leather pen cases and trunks, matching pens and lighters, Filo-fax organizers, and more. Retail prices are listed alongside Fountain Pen Hospital's price so you can readily see the discounts.

Owners Steve and Terry Wiederlight apply lots of TLC to pen repair (call for mailing procedure) and to maintaining their subscription publication *Vintage Pens Quarterly*, which lists about 150 items of interest to the serious investor and vintage collector ($10/year; $25/3 years). For more on the firm's history, latest product arrivals, bargains in very limited quantities, a link to Pen Collectors of America, and an invitation to sell your vintage pens, visit the excellent website, which at press time was promising to offer online buying very soon.

SPECIAL FACTORS: Satisfaction guaranteed; price quote by phone or letter; returns accepted within seven days for exchange, refund, or credit.

OfficeMax Inc.

3605 Warrensville Center Rd.   800–788–8080
Shaker Heights, OH   Fax: 800–995–9644
44122–5203

Catalog: free
Pay: check, MO, MC, V, AE, DSC
Sells: office supplies, computers and office machines, and
  printing services
Store: stores nationwide (call for nearest location)
Online: www.officemax.com

The 353-page catalog from OfficeMax represents over 8,000 office supplies, machines, and equipment for your home office or business at savings of up to 70%. Among the many product categories to shop from are paper products, binders and filing supplies, basic office supplies, calendars and personal organizers, business machines and accessories, computers and printers and their accessories, office furniture and lamps, art, drafting, and presentation supplies and books, break-room supplies, and safes. The CopyMax division allows you to order digital printing from your own computer (using a free CopyMax Link disc).

The website lists thousands of software titles, details the services of the custom print shop, offers online specials, and invites shoppers to register as OfficeMax members. Members are entitled to express-order templates for frequently ordered items, a record of previous orders, online modification of billing and shipping information, and special member-only savings. Online ordering is available.

SPECIAL FACTORS: Satisfaction guaranteed; shipping free on orders of $50 or more within designated store areas.

Plastic Bagmart

900 Old Country Rd.
Westbury, NY 11590

800–343–BAGS
516–997–3355
Fax: 516–997–1836

Catalog: free with SASE
Pay: check, MO, MC, V
Sells: plastic bags
Store: same address; Monday to Friday 9–5, Saturday 9–3
Online: www.bagmart.com

The little eight-page catalog from Plastic Bagmart has just the right bags for your business, home, or industry and offers discounts up to 60% below supermarket prices. In the print catalog as well as online you'll find reclosable zipper bags; flat, heat-sealable poly bags; trash liners; take-out bags for merchants; rolls of poly tubing; FDA-approved bags for food and packaging; cellophane bags; handy bags on a roll; printed ice bags; foldover shirt bags; heavyweight storage bags; doorknob and newspaper bags; garment bags; disposable poly gloves; packing list envelopes; and sealing equipment. There's a bag here for just about every need and in just about every size imaginable. Quantity discounts apply, and you can mix and match cases to earn them. By the way, the online catalog shows the whole inventory, but you still have to order the old-fashioned way: by phone or fax.

SPECIAL FACTORS: Satisfaction guaranteed; prices quoted by letter with SASE; returns accepted within ten days; minimum order one case; prices include shipping.

Quill Corporation

100 Schelter Rd.   800–789–1331
Lincolnshire, IL 60069–3621   Fax: 800–789–8955

Catalog: free (see text)
Pay: check, MO, MC, V, AE
Sells: office supplies and equipment
Store: mail order only
Online: www.quillcorp.com

In business since 1956, Quill Corporation is one of those immediately recognized names among business managers, institutional buyers, and individuals purchasing office supplies and equipment at the best prices; savings can reach as high as 83% off list. In addition to the mega 600-page master catalog, Quill publishes smaller special-interest catalogs that you can request to make shopping easier for your more targeted needs. Catalog subjects include computer supplies, professional services (financial, accounting, legal), health care, business furniture, school supplies, warehouse express (shipping, janitorial, safety equipment), and Quill's CD-ROM catalog.

I liked the website, where you can order your office supplies online, take advantage of specials, and get a good sense of all the products this company sells. With more than 14,000 products to handle, the Quill website is surprisingly easy to navigate.

SPECIAL FACTORS: Satisfaction guaranteed; institutional accounts available; returns accepted; goods shipped only within the U.S.; minimum order $20.

Reliable Corp.

P.O. Box 1502
Ottawa, IL 61350–9914

800–359–5000
Fax: 800–326–3233

Catalog: free
Pay: check, MO, MC, V, AE, DSC
Sells: office supplies and equipment
Store: mail order only
Online: www.reliable.com

Reliable Corp., also known as Reliable Office Solutions, sells thousands of office supply products and furniture items at 50% to 80% off suggested retail prices. By phone, fax, and online you can request one or more free catalogs for "General Office Supplies," "Computer Supplies," "Business Furniture," "Home Office," "Electronics," "Shipping and Warehouse," or "Printers Row." If you want to receive up-to-the-minute sales announcements, simply provide your e-mail address when you place your catalog request.

Among Reliable's inventory are paper and pens, presentation folios, binders, computer furniture, workstations, cleaning supplies, media storage, leather chairs, cordless phones, fax machines, corporate gifts, lamps, task chairs, breakroom supplies, shipping supplies, imprinted goods, specialty items, and designer laser paper. Your savings increase even more if you can buy in quantity. This firm ships products within an hour of receiving your order, with free delivery standard on all in-stock items. Reliable offers an unconditional guarantee with a 30-day free trial that includes computers and electronics. At press time Reliable's website promised to have online ordering soon, so check it out. If you log on to the website, be sure to read the glowing letters from ecstatic customers, which make you want to shop here too.

SPECIAL FACTORS: Satisfaction guaranteed; institutional accounts available; minimum order $25.

Store Smart

180 Metro Park	**800–424–1011**
Rochester, NY 14623	**716–424–5300**
	Fax: 800–424–5411
	Fax: 716–424–5313

Catalog: free
Pay: check, MO, V, MC, AE
Sells: clear vinyl adhesive-backed pockets
Store: same address; Monday to Thursday 9–5:30,
   Saturday 9–5
Online: www.storesmart.com

Store Smart is a sister company of Visual Horizons, also listed in this section. Click onto the website, or order the free eight-page catalog, and you'll be greeted with a selection of about 250 different-sized vinyl, adhesive-backed pockets. Business is booming at Store Smart as customers discover that these pockets have hundreds of uses. Stick them onto proposals, bulletin boards, telephones, computers, file cabinets, and more. You'll find sizes to fit business cards, CD-ROMs and three-inch computer disks, coins and slides, 8 by 11-inch pages, all the way up to 26 by 38 inches. You can customize just about anything with Store Smart pockets. They act as a permanent protector of the material, yet the material can easily be removed and replaced. The prices are excellent if you can order in large qualities. Order online, over the telephone, or by fax or mail.

SPECIAL FACTORS: Satisfaction is guaranteed; rush service available.

20th Century Plastics, Inc.

P.O. Box 2393
Brea, CA 92822–2393

800–767–0777
Fax: 800–786–7939

Catalog: free
Pay: check, MO, MC, V, AE, DSC
Sells: photo albums and accessories, binders, organizers,
  scrapbooks, etc.
Store: mail order only
Online: www.20thcenturydirect.com

If you collect tabloid-sized newspapers, 20th Century Plastics, with 45 years' experience, has the perfect scrapbook with screw bindings to help you protect your collection up to 25 pages. This company specializes in helping people organize, display, and archive their treasured images. For more typical archival or storage needs—family photos and videos, baseball cards, stamps, periodicals, and recipes—20th Century Plastics carries photo and slide storage sheets and albums, binders, report covers, video- and audiocassette portfolios, and filing systems, with savings running between 20% and 33%. Certain products such as Crown linen albums, oversize photo binders, and library albums come with free gold imprinting. The 60-page catalog of office and photo organizers (there's also a 48-page photo catalog) includes sections of disk storage and CD storage products including double-capacity static-guard diskette pages, mini-display disk binders, poly or vinyl CD safety sleeves, and CD zipper travel cases. For sorting, identifying, and handling signs, letters, and schedules, there are heavyweight vinyl envelopes in 22 sizes, with pricing for silk screen color logo imprinting, when you supply the camera-ready color-separated art. Foil stamping and deluxe personalization are available for other products as well. When you request your catalog, you can also request by product number a complimentary sample of any photo page or sheet protector. A good sampling of the inventory can be viewed on the website, which didn't feature online ordering at press time.

SPECIAL FACTORS: Satisfaction guaranteed; returns accepted within 30 days for exchange, refund, or credit.

ULINE

2200 S. Lakeside Dr.
Waukegan, IL 60085

800–295–5510
Fax: 800–295–5571

Catalog: free
Pay: check, MO, MC, V, AE, DSC, DC
Sells: shipping supplies
Store: mail order only
Online: www.uline.com

Whether you're running a mom-and-pop business out of your home or are in charge of a warehouse, ULINE is the source for every kind of packing need. This family-run, reader-recommended business has warehouses in Illinois, Minnesota, New Jersey, and California; orders are shipped from the location nearest you to ensure the quickest and most cost-effective service. The 208-page catalog features anti-static products, bags and bag sealers, boxes, bubble and cushioning material, tape and tape dispensers, envelopes, foam, labels, mailers, packing list envelopes, strapping, stretch wrap, tags, tubes—everything from aerosol products to vermiculite. And ULINE has over 500 different box types in stock—one of their biggest advantages over other shipping-supply houses. At ULINE, the more you buy, the more you save—there are quantity price breaks on all items. ULINE's website features limited inventory but does provide online ordering. You can also access product information from your print catalog and then submit your order online. Free offers—NBA, NHL, MLB, and NFL hats or jumbo insulated mugs—are available to online purchasers of products totaling $250 or more.

SPECIAL FACTORS: Satisfaction guaranteed 100%; returns must be made within 30 days; C.O.D. orders not accepted.

University Products, Inc.

517 Main St.
Holyoke, MA 01041–0101

800–628–1912
Fax: 800–532–9281

Catalog: free

Pay: check, MO, MC, V, AE, DSC, DC

Sells: archival-quality materials for conservation,
restoration, and preservation

Store: mail order only

Online: www.universityproducts.com

For over 30 years University Products, Inc., has been a leader in providing archival-quality materials for conservation, restoration, and preservation as well as library and school furniture and supplies. The "Archival Quality Materials Catalog" of over 200 pages details standard archival products such as conservation paper and boards, tapes and adhesives, photo supplies, framing and matting supplies, display materials, and conservation tools and equipment. But you can also discover unexpected or hard-to-find items such as solid aluminum and bookcase time capsules, unbuffered acid-free tissue paper, archival hatboxes, artifact/specimen storage cartons and trays with clear-view covers, and museum pest kits that are pheromone traps and lures for controlling clothes moths, cigarette beetles, and cockroaches. Disaster supplies, which can serve institutions and home owners, include a sensor-activated Water Alert, newsprint paper for drawing spills away from documents, and Rescube for transporting water-soaked books. Professionals or hobbyists who rely on slides, prints, and negatives in their work can choose from storage boxes, enclosures, envelopes, folders, preservers, marking pens, mounts, a mounting press, inspection gloves, and slide sorter.

There's also a "Library and Media Center Sourcebook," 200 pages of processing and circulation supplies, multimedia and audio-visual equipment, computer workstations, literature displays, and library shelving and furniture. In the "feel good" department, it's wonderful to know that University Products sponsors a $5,000 annual award for distinguished achievement in conservation of cultural property, and that its product line, designed specifically to meet the needs of museums, brings that same high quality to individuals. New products and monthly specials can be viewed at the website and online ordering is available.

SPECIAL FACTORS: Satisfaction guaranteed; quantity discounts available; institutional accounts available.

U.S. Box Corp.

1296 McCarter Hwy.   973–481–2000
Newark, NJ 07104   Fax: 973–481–2002

Catalog: free
Pay: check, MO, MC, V, AE
Sells: resale packaging
Store: mail order only
Online: www.usbox.com

U.S. Box Corp. has been selling retail and gift packaging since 1948. This is primarily a business-to-business firm, but it offers products that consumers use routinely: wrapping paper, tape, gift boxes, ribbon, and mailing bags, for example. Prices are as much as 60% lower here than those charged for comparable items in variety and stationery stores. Additional discounts of 5% apply to orders over $500, and up to 15% on totals of $2,500 plus. Samples of the goods may be purchased at unit cost plus $2 shipping; this is recommended, since returns are not accepted.

U.S. Box Corp.'s 148-page color catalog showcases their dizzying inventory, beginning with every conceivable type of box: cotton-filled jewelry boxes from plain gold or silver to leopard and other designs, as well as velvet-lined suede and leatherette jewelry boxes; custom plastic boxes; wooden-slat boxes; boxes designed for watches, ties, apparel, breakables, plates, cakes, candy, etc.; gift boxes shaped like rabbits, houses, and sleighs; heavy-duty shipping boxes and mailers. You'll also find paper bags, gift bags, party bags, net bags, shopping bags, tins, drawstring bags; labels of every size, shape, and description, from functional to fancy; bows, ribbons, and other box decorations, such as bells, roses, animals, and metallic elastic; packing and decorative fillers, such as shredded Mylar and plastic in every color; tissue sheets and gift wrap in indescribable choices; poly/cello bags and rolls—patterned, colored, and clear; plastic storage containers for anything you could think of; jewelry displays, plastic tray liners for small items of every shape and size, and more. Consolidate your packaging needs or go in with a friend and you'll easily meet the $150 minimum order.

SPECIAL FACTORS: Samples available at unit cost plus $2 shipping; returns not accepted; minimum order $150.

Viking Office Products

950 W. 190th St.
Torrance, CA 90502

800–248–6111
Fax: 800–762–7329

Catalog: free
Pay: check, MO, MC, V, AE
Sells: office supplies, furniture, computer supplies, stationery
Store: mail order only
Online: www.vikingop.com

With your first order from Viking Office Products, established in 1960, you'll receive the 564-page full-line catalog of over 12,000 office products at discounts easily over 50%. Offerings in sale catalogs are priced at discounts as high as 79%, savings that add up when you consider how quickly supplies get depleted. Rely on Viking for great deals on printers, ribbons, and cartridges; computer furniture; computer paper and labels; diskette data cartridges; myriad office supplies; and business machines. With competition in the office supplies industry so fierce, Viking has learned to excel by offering great prices and exemplary customer service. The website, where you can order online, lists over 500 products, conveniently arranged in alphabetical product groupings, with *Your Favorite Coffee* comprising the entire Y section (Z, unbelievably, has no products!).

SPECIAL FACTORS: Satisfaction guaranteed; institutional accounts available; shipping free on orders over $25 (continental U.S. only).

Visual Horizons

180 Metro Park   716–424–5300
Rochester, NY 14623   Fax: 716–424–5313

Catalogs and Samples: free
Pay: check, MO, V, MC, AE
Sells: business presentations material, equipment, and
   services
Store: same address; Monday to Thursday 9–5:30,
   Saturday 9–5
Online: www.visualhorizons.com

Visual Horizons is a company devoted to helping you make the best business presentation possible, with services and products to help you create, deliver, or publish memorable, eye-catching presentations at less cost than you'd incur if you hired a PR consultant and a graphic designer. Their "Powerful Presentations Source Book" is a 56-page color catalog peppered throughout with testimonials from happy customers, and well-designed photo layouts and descriptions of the products and services that made them that way. Presentation formats the company supports are LCD panels and screen shows, slides and overheads, computer disks and CD-ROMs, video, and flip charts. You'll find imaging equipment, slide projectors, slide scanners, wall screens, light tables, overhead projectors, communication boards, audiovisual furniture, label printers, and much more.

In business for 25 years, Visual Horizons has a staff of people who can provide all kinds of services, from slide duplicating to designing logos to creating your entire presentation. They have 300 dynamic graphic images you can choose from—with or without words, in many languages—if you don't want to design your own, or they can custom-design graphics for you. Their free imaging software enables you to send computer files through your modem, and their host computer will transform those images into slides. The prices get good when you order in quantity, and there are special deals on certain services. Visit the website for more details, or call. "Advice is free," they say.

SPECIAL FACTORS: Satisfaction is guaranteed "110%."

Yazoo Mills, Inc.

305 Commerce St.
P.O. Box 369
New Oxford, PA 17350

800–242–5216
717–624–8993
Fax: 717–624–4420

Catalog: free
Pay: check, MO, MC, V, AE, DSC
Sells: shipping tubes
Store: mail order only

Everything comes from somewhere—the name for Yazoo Mills comes from a town in Mississippi, and those tubes you find inside rolls of fax paper come from Yazoo Mills. Yazoo also makes carpet cores, cable reels, heavy blast casings for mining companies, and shipping tubes for posters and other works on paper. An ex-boyfriend of mine, a painter of very large pictures, used to search the dumpsters of Manhattan for gigantic carpeting tubes, perfect for rolling up his unstretched canvases for storage. If only he'd known about this gem of a company. Shipping tubes, which range in length from 12 to 85 inches and in diameter from 2 to 12 inches, are sold by the case with plastic inserts for plugging the ends—at discounts up to 80% below art-supply shop prices. For custom sizes and colors, or for acid-free stock, call for a price quote; Yazoo routinely does job-specific manufacturing.

SPECIAL FACTORS: No shipping charges; minimum order, one carton of stock tubes; C.O.D. orders accepted.

Related Products/Companies

Antique telephones
- Phoneco

Attaché cases, briefcases, computer bags, leather portfolios
- Ace Luggage, Airline International Luggage, Al's Luggage, Bennett Brothers

Books on the graphic arts
- Print Bookstore

Calendars
- Barnes & Noble, Current, Dover

Commercial artist/design supplies
- Pearl Paint, Daniel Smith

Information relevant to small businesses
- Consumer Information Center, U.S. Government Superintendent of Documents

Office and shipping supplies for the visually impaired
- Independent Living Aids, The New Vision Store

Office cleaning supplies
- The Cleaning Center

Overhead projectors
- Cheap Joe's Art Stuff

Power generators
- Harbor Freight Tools, Northern Hydraulics

Shredders, calculators, fax machines, scanners, laminators, and other small office machines
- Beach Sales, Bernie's Discount, Damark, J&R Music, LVT Price Quote Hotline, MicroWarehouse

"Talking" clocks, calculators, and other desk accessories for the visually impaired
- Independent Living Aids, The New Vision Store

Telephones
- Beach Sales, Crutchfield, EBA Wholesale, J&R Music, LVT Price Quote Hotline, Sound City

Writing implements
- J&R Music, Pearl Paint

Printing and Stationery

Stationery, invitations, letterhead, logo design, check printing, business cards, and other custom-printing services

Jazz up your company image with some new letterhead and business cards. Increase efficiency and save time and money with preprinted business checks, invoices, and shipping forms that you can feed through your printer. Need a rubber stamp to identify your child's books, some monogrammed stationery, or customized invitations? Some of the firms here can do that too. Don't pay full price for printing services! All of the companies in this section can save you lots of money. For other firms that offer discount custom stationery and other printing services, see "Related Products/Companies" at the end of this section.

For a really great Internet site that allows you to send—via e-mail—customized, animated greeting cards complete with sound, check out Blue Mountain Arts (www.bluemountain.com). I sent my delighted parents a Bon Voyage electronic message and they thought I was a genius. (All I did was write the message and pick out the adorable animated card that Blue Mountain had designed.) It's free! Don't ask me why!

Find It Fast

Business Cards and Address Labels
- Brown Print, Checks in the Mail, Invitation Hotline, Lighthouse Colorprint, Mr. Z's

Check-Printing Services
- Checks in the Mail

General Printing Services
- Mr. Z's

Invoices, Statements, and Other Business Forms
- Mr. Z's

Personalized Cards and Stationery
- Mr. Z's, Invitation Hotline

Wedding Invitations
- Invitation Hotline

Brown Print & Co.

P.O. Box 935   626–286–2106
Temple City, CA 91780

   Price List and Samples: $2
   Pay: check or MO
   Sells: custom-designed business cards
   Store: mail order only

In a world of electronic clip-art and templates for every occasion, Brown Print & Co. offers a mail-order alternative for the individual who prefers a memorable or quirky design or special format (such as foldovers) for stationery and business cards. Brown Print will send, upon request, an assortment of paper samples—from the sophisticated and sassy combination of glossy stock and iridescent foil to the stalwart black-and-white raised-ink business card. Meeting the client's design challenge to create "effective visual concepts" is Brown Print's specialty, as unique as its proprietor, Mr. Brown.

SPECIAL FACTORS: Quantity discounts available; 250- or 500-card minimum.

Checks in the Mail, Inc.

2345 Goodwin Ln.　　　　800–733–4443
New Braunfels, TX　　　　Fax: 800–822–0005
78135–0001

Brochure: free
Pay: check, MO, V, MC, AE, DSC
Sells: check-printing services
Store: mail order only, phone hours Monday to Friday 7–7
　CT
Online: www.checksinthemail.com

The designs offered by Checks in the Mail are among the liveliest available from the big check-printing firms. The Anne Geddes line, for example, features those now-famous photos of real babies as potted sunflowers, pea pods, cabbages, and others. Why you'd want these on your checks is one question. *Why not?* is another. There are scores of designs for personal checks, offered in wallet and carbonless duplicate styles, and in three-to-a-page desk sets. Other options such as logos, designer typestyles, and message lines are also available. Business checks are available in a choice of formats and designs, in continuous-feed and laser-printer styles.

Prices begin at $5.99 for 200 wallet-style personal checks and run up to $30.99 for a desk set of 300 duplicate checks. The checks are guaranteed to be printed to your bank's standard, and confidentiality of your bank data is assured. You'll also find personalized address labels and business cards offered here. See brochure or website for details. The website, by the way, is lots of fun because you can view all of the designs. But you still need to phone, fax, or mail in your order.

SPECIAL FACTORS: Satisfaction is guaranteed; checks can be ordered on U.S. banks only.

Invitation Hotline

68 Hawkins Rd.
Manalapan, NJ 07726

800–800–4355, ext. 921
732–536–9115
Fax: 732–972–4875

Flyer: free
Pay: check, MO, MC, V, AE, DSC
Sells: printed wedding invitations, business and social
stationery, favors, holiday cards, etc.
Store: by appointment only; phone hours Monday to Friday
9–5
E-mail: invhotline@aol.com

An invitation to a wedding or Bat Mitzvah tells the guests a lot about you, whether you like it or not. But to send the right message, must you pay a lot? When you're budgeting for a big event, Invitation Hotline can trim the cost of invitations, reply cards, wedding stationery, birth announcements, favors (matches and napkins, for example), programs, and other printed items (letterhead stationery and business cards, for example) by 25% or more (save more on volume and multiple orders). Invitation Hotline says they'll "beat any store's price."

Here's how it works. Go to your local print shop or card store and ask to look through their stationery albums. These large books put out by card and stationery manufacturers feature page after page of samples. When you find a style you like, write down the book and style numbers, then call Invitation Hotline. They'll get it to you for a lot less than if you ordered it locally. Accuracy is guaranteed or Invitation Hotline will replace it for free. If you need advice, or don't have access to the manufacturers' books, feel free to call Invitation Hotline. They understand everything about the selection process and can help you find the right item for your taste, needs, and budget, including composing the wording, custom design work, foreign-language orders, and even hand-addressed calligraphy envelopes. The one-page flyer lists some of the manufacturers Invitation Hotline discounts, but since they're adding new manufacturers every day, it's best just to call.

SPECIAL FACTORS: Complete satisfaction guaranteed; price quote by phone or letter.

Lighthouse Colorprint

P.O. Box 465, Dept. WBM
Saint Joseph, MI 49085-0465

616-428-7062, ext. 2
Fax: 616-428-0847

Order Kit and Samples: $5, refundable (see text)
Pay: check or MO
Sells: color printing services
Store: mail order only
Online: www.lighthousecolorprint.com

Studies show that full-color business cards are held longer and generate more sales than traditional print-only business cards; in other words, an image is worth a thousand words. Lighthouse Colorprint can create business cards, postcards, rack cards, brochures, sell sheets, and other marketing materials that your clients won't soon forget, using 200-line screen photographic images at levels 33% to 50% higher than the printing industry standard. This resolution is comparable, for example, to the photo quality found in *National Geographic* magazine.

Lighthouse Colorprint's pricing includes typesetting, layout, photo scanning, color separations, and full-color proofs. They say they'll try to meet or beat your best price; "the larger the order, the lower the price per piece." For example, a standard photographic business card job goes from 22 cents each for 1,000 to 4 cents on orders of 15,000 or more; 4 by 6-inch postcards drop from 33 cents each at 1,000 to 6 cents at 15,000. The $5 fee Lighthouse charges for the "Custom Order Kit" brings you price lists, order forms, sample business cards, postcards, brochures, and rack cards, and a $25 gift certificate on your first order. Another option is to check out the website, where you can view the samples online. Either way, expect some back-and-forth on type specs and color, options, proofs, and other details—just as you would a walk-in printer.

Wholesale buyers, please note: a resale number is required for the wholesale discount of 20% on regular rates.

SPECIAL FACTORS: Price quote by phone, e-mail, or letter; quantity discounts available; minimum order 1,000 pieces.

Mr. Z's Print Services

P.O. Box 3368   352–683–5683
Spring Hill, FL 34611   Fax: 352–688–3922

Information Pack and Samples: free
Pay: check, MO, MC, V
Sells: business-card and general printing services
Store: 12549 Spring Hill Dr., Spring Hill, FL; Monday to
    Thursday 8–4, Friday 9–12

I love this company. There's nothing hidden or phony about what they do and how they charge. Mr. Z's is an actual family-run printer—not a printer broker—that has been serving mail-order clients since 1984. The company specializes in raised-print business cards, but they also print letterheads, envelopes, flyers, tickets, invoices, statements, carbonless forms, menus, Rolodex cards, memo pads, postcards, door hangers, and all other types of promotional materials at wholesale prices—which means savings of 50% or more to you. Basic bright-white raised business cards start at $13.95 for 500 (the normal retail price is close to $23). When you request information, you'll get tiny strips of actual card stock in different colors and textures as well as samples of business cards. You can either provide a current business card sample for Mr. Z to match, or choose one of the typefaces provided and follow the enclosed instructions as to color, design, and layout. If something is unclear, Mr. Z's will call you; they won't print your order without contacting you first if it appears to have an error or poor artwork. To sweeten the deal, shipping is free.

SPECIAL FACTORS: Orders to Alaska, Hawaii, and Puerto Rico, add $6.50; free shipping within the continental U.S.

Related Products/Companies

At-home digital printing services
- OfficeMax

Braille embossing services
- The New Vision Store

Check-printing services
- Current, Reliable Corp.

Custom printing (rubber stamps, stationery, business cards, etc.)
- OfficeMax, Quill Corp., Reliable

Design-your-own greeting cards and postcards
- Dover, Ott's Discount Art Supply

Greeting cards and themed stationery
- Current, Party & Paper Worldwide

Labels
- University Products

Logo design services
- Visual Horizons

Logo screen-printing on mugs, pens, and other corporate gifts
- Best Impressions, Nelson Marketing

Logo silk-screening and embroidery for clothing and uniforms
- Cheap Aprons/Allstates Uniforms, Cotton Scrubs, Tafford Manufacturing

Personal GOCCO printing presses
- Think Ink

Uniforms and Promotional Products

Uniforms and institutional workwear and miscellaneous promotional goods—with and without custom logos

The firms listed in this section specialize in clothing and other products that can be screen-printed, embroidered, or embossed with your company's name or logo. Some of the clothing is quite specialized—for people in the restaurant, catering, or medical professions. Other clothing is more all-purpose—janitorial jumpsuits, polo-style shirts, and baseball caps, to name a few. If your business requires uniforms other than suit and tie, you're apt to find what you need here at good discounts. Speaking of uniforms, if you're looking for school uniforms, see the listing for Iuniforms.com in the "Babies and Children" section of the "Clothing" chapter.

Businesses looking to strengthen employee loyalty, up their name recognition with clients, or reward good customers will be interested in the firms below offering good deals on items of all kinds—from golf balls, totes, and key rings to pens and clocks—all custom-printed with your company's name, of course.

Find It Fast

Custom Logo Design Services
- Cheap Aprons/Allstates Uniforms, Tafford

Food Industry Clothing
- Cheap Aprons/Allstates Uniform

General Work Clothing and Casual Apparel
- Cheap Aprons/Allstates Uniform, Nelson Marketing

Medical Industry Clothing
- Cotton Scrubs, Tafford

Miscellaneous Promotional Products
- Best Impressions, Nelson Marketing

Best Impressions Promotional Products Catalog

P.O. Box 802   800–635–2378
LaSalle, IL 61301

    Catalog: free
    Pay: check, MO, MC, V, AE, DSC
    Sells: business-promotion products
    Store: mail order only
    Online: www.bestimpressions.com

What are promotional products? They're items like coffee mugs, pens, or mouse-pads with your company's logo, designed to inspire employees, reinforce a positive company image with clients, and spur new sales leads. Or put another way, they're for people like me who love to get free stuff. The Best Impressions catalog features items for every company's budget: mugs, glasses, sports bottles, balls, balloons, bean-bag buddies, fortune cookies, pocket knives, key chains, calendars, address books, digital desk clocks, holiday ornaments, candy jars, picture frames, calculators, notepads, and of course pens and pencils. Savings can run up to 50%, depending on the item and quantity ordered, and prices include execution of your design in one color in one imprint area (additional colors are extra). Camera-ready artwork is required or can be produced by the firm's art department for $30 per item. Each product has a minimum order—48 baseball caps, 24 umbrellas, 500 Post-it notes are typical examples—but many minimums can be lowered (surcharges apply). And selected products are available for accelerated shipment, at no extra charge—see the catalog or website for details. At this writing, the website is for information and catalog requests only; it does not have online ordering.

SPECIAL FACTORS: Price quote by phone; quantity discounts are available; institutional accounts are available; minimum orders vary by item.

Cheap Aprons/Allstates Uniform

Catalog Sales, 599 Canal St.   800–367–2374
Lawrence, MA 01840   Fax: 978–689–2483

Catalog: free
Pay: check, MO, V, MC, AE
Sells: monogrammed or screen-printed apparel, uniforms, hats, etc.
Store: same address for showroom; Monday to Friday 9–5, Saturday 9–1
Online: www.cheapaprons.com

If you own a restaurant, are a caterer, run a business, or even have a weekend bowling team that needs a morale booster, you should know about Cheap Aprons and Allstates Uniforms, sister companies supplying workwear and casual apparel that's custom-monogrammed or screen-printed with your logo. Cheap Apron's 32-page color catalog offers aprons of every kind (wrap, café, bib, full-length bistro, waist, etc.), button-down shirts in plain and patterned, bow ties and neckties, polo shirts and T-shirts, tuxedo shirts, chef's apparel, table linens, baseball-style caps, sweatshirts, and more—all at reasonable prices that include a one-color screen-printed logo. Cheap Aprons offers quantity discounts on every item, and there are additional deals in the catalog as well as website-only specials. The website gives you a good idea of this company's offerings, complete with photographs and descriptions, but there's no online ordering.

In Allstates Uniform's 16-page catalog you'll find other types of workwear—work jackets, coveralls, waterproof rain suits, utility smocks, T-shirts, caps, and tank tops among them. The screen-printing is included in the good prices, and quantity discounts are listed here as well.

SPECIAL FACTORS: Satisfaction guaranteed; see catalogs for returns policy; custom logo design is available; specify which catalog you want when you request it.

Cotton Scrubs & Co.

104 Park Dr.　　　　　　**888–225–7160**
P.O. Box 1014
Montgomeryville, PA
18936–1014

Catalog: free
Pay: check, MO, MC, V, AE, DSC
Sells: all-cotton scrubs for medical professionals
Store: three locations in Pennsylvania; call for addresses
and hours

Doctors, nurses, veterinarians, techs—these and other medical professionals spend their time and energy helping us and our loved ones feel better. Cotton Scrubs and Co. is a newish venture of Tafford (see listing this section) dedicated to helping the caregivers feel comfortable as well. Imagine a surgeon dressed in a gaily decorated cartoon alligator print being the first person your child sees when he comes out of anesthesia. The styles, colors, and prints offered here make the whole experience more human. And medical professionals will jump for joy at the all-cotton fabric that breathes and is easy to care for, in cuts that provide a soft, natural fit. Since these items come directly to the consumer from the manufacturer, you'll save an average of 20% (retail prices and Cotton Scrubs' prices are listed side by side so you can calculate the discounts). In addition to the good selection of scrubs (drawstrings and tops, tunics, skorts, scrub dresses, etc.) there are a number of amusing and useful items here: themed and matching earrings, pendants, and pins, comfort shoes and socks, color-coordinated stethoscopes, and more. Sizes run from XS to 4X.

SPECIAL FACTORS: Custom embroidering available; unworn garments may be returned within 30 days for refund or exchange.

Nelson Marketing

P.O. Box 320
Oshkosh, WI 54902–0320

800–722–5203
Fax: 800–355–5043
TDD: 800–642–2076

Catalog: free
Pay: check, MO, MC, V, AE, DSC
Sells: business-promotion products and apparel
Store: mail order only
Online: www.nelsonmarketing.com

According to Dick Nelson, president of Nelson Marketing, employees, friends, members, and donors of your company all have one thing in common: the need for appreciation and recognition. Nelson Marketing was founded on this idea. This mail-order company offers businesses like yours hundreds of high-quality imprinted promotional or corporate-identity products at the lowest prices. They back up this latter claim with a "lowest prices or double the difference" guarantee.

Nelson puts out two different catalogs: one for corporate apparel and sportswear, the other for general merchandise. The 24-page apparel catalog features a variety of polo shirts (all cotton, various weaves and textures, solid colors, tricolored, long- and short-sleeved, etc.), neckties, oxford-style shirts, rugby shirts, turtlenecks, rain gear, sweat suits, jackets (denim, parka, Polartec, etc.), caps, and more—all imprinted with your company's logo. The 64-page general merchandise catalog has just about everything else you can imagine—from auto accessories, clocks, and glassware to magnets, mugs, and watches.

Both catalogs include detailed text about how to order. A one-color design is included in the price, and if you check out the website you can even click on a product to receive a free sample. There are also web-only specials you'll want to check out.

SPECIAL FACTORS: Goods guaranteed to be delivered exactly as ordered, or order will be rerun, refunded, or credited; quantity discounts available; institutional accounts available.

Tafford Manufacturing, Inc.

104 Park Dr.

P.O. Box 1001

Montgomeryville, PA 18936

800–697–3321

Fax: 215–643–4922

Catalog: free

Pay: check, MO, MC, V, AE, DSC

Sells: uniforms, shoes, and accessories for the medical professional

Store: three retail locations in PA; call for addresses and hours

Compared to the average catalog of uniforms for health-care professionals, Tafford has the best fashion buys for the dollar around. The firm manufactures its own uniforms, which means you beat at least one markup, and the size selection is great—from XS to 6X, petite to tall. The 72-page color catalog shows mostly women's clothing, although most of the scrubs and warm-ups are unisex. Say good-bye to the intimidating doctor or nurse dressed in clinical white. You'll find many colors, prints, and styles here—even jumpsuits and matching baseball-style caps—designed to suit every figure type, including maternity styles. The catalog also shows cardigans, jackets, shoes (from traditional "nurse" styles to clogs and Birkenstocks), emblem pins, reference books, and brightly colored basic equipment—stethoscopes, blood pressure kits, scissors, otoscopes, etc. Both the retail and the discount prices of the clothing are given so you see how much you're saving—usually 20% or 30% on the regular retail. Consult your colleagues before ordering, because if you buy as part of a group Tafford also offers special services such as swatches and samples, volume discounts, and custom embroidery and logo silk-screening.

SPECIAL FACTORS: Satisfaction is guaranteed; unworn, undamaged, unwashed returns are accepted within 30 days for exchange, refund, or credit.

Related Products/Companies

Barber's capes, aprons, chef's hats and kitchen whites
- Clothcrafters, Professional Cutlery Direct

Corporate logos imprinted on golf clubs and equipment
- Discount Golf Superstore

Imprintable clothes and accessories for corporate promotions
- WearGuard

Party goods and events decor with your logo
- M&N International

Work clothing
- Cahall's Work Wear

Special Needs

Clothing, tools, gadgets,
and home and office accessories
for children and adults with
special physical or medical requirements

If you're fortunate enough to be youngish, of average size, in excellent health, with no disabilities, then you probably take for granted, as I often do, all the little activities and pleasures in life that come easily and naturally. The companies in this chapter provide all kinds of products to restore dignity, help out, and make life more fun for people who are extra large, visually impaired, have limited strength or mobility, or have physical conditions requiring special clothing, furniture, or personal accessories. From seat belt extenders to seat-lift chairs, braille playing cards to all-cotton bedding, left-handed baseball mitts to support hosiery, you'll find a lot here that you and your loved ones will appreciate.

Find It Fast

Clothing for Disabled Children
- Special Clothes

Post–Breast Surgery Products
- B&B Company (Bosom Buddy)

Products for Extra-Large People
- Amplestuff

Products for Miscellaneous Post-Operative or Medical Conditions
- Comfort House, Special Clothes

Products for the Allergy-Sensitive
- National Allergy Supply

Products for the Elderly or Those with Limited Mobility
- Amplestuff, Comfort House

Products for Left-Handed People
- The Left Hand

Products for the Visually Impaired
- Independent Living Aids, The New Vision Store

Amplestuff

P.O. Box 116, Dept. PP
Bearsville, NY 12409–0166

914–679–3316
Fax: 914–679–1206

Catalog: free
Pay: check, MO, MC, V
Sells: products and books for plus-size and supersize
  people
Store: mail order only
E-mail: amplestuff@aol.com

One evening Amplestuff president Bill Fabrey received a call from a 540-pound man across the country in the hospital for an emergency appendectomy. His most serious suffering was caused by humiliation for lack of a hospital gown that fit him. Bill made sure the very next morning there were four hospital gowns waiting for the grateful patient when he woke up. There aren't many businesses with this kind of concern and personal rapport with their customers. Amplestuff's motto is "make your world fit you," and its 34-page catalog is devoted to products that big people all over the world will surely appreciate, many of them appropriate for anybody with movement restrictions. Items such as airline seat belt extenders, fanny packs ("you shouldn't have to be slender to wear a fanny pack"), large-size socks, silver- and gold-plated bangles in eight, nine, or ten-inch sizes, extra-large clothes hangers, extra-large bath towels, reach extenders, a portable bidet, ten-inch car steering wheels (for more leg and stomach room), blood pressure kits, personal fans, and more are offered, with photographs and descriptions of each. There are also size-friendly videos and books, including exercise videos, art books, and a resource guide to the best books related to the larger-size population.

Bill Fabrey says half of his business dealings are in communications, since there are very few sources out there knowledgeable about improving the lives of ample-size people. You can also subscribe to the *Ample Shopper*, a 12-page newsletter chock full of news, reviews, ratings, information, how-to articles, Q&A, consumer activism, and more. The review issue at the time of this writing spoke to the hazards of automobile airbags for larger-size people. The newsletter is $15 for a year, U.S. and Canada ($22 elsewhere). Amplestuff's voicemail is often on, but the staff always returns calls promptly.

Wholesalers: Inquire for terms.

SPECIAL FACTORS: U.S. funds only; quantity discounts on some items; satisfaction is guaranteed; orders by phone, fax, and mail—no e-mail orders.

Bosom Buddy Breast Forms

2417 Bank Dr., Dept. WC01
P.O. Box 5731
Boise, ID 83705–0731

800–262–2789
208–343–9696
Fax: 208–343–9266

Brochure: free
Pay: check, MO, MC, V, DSC
Sells: Bosom Buddy breast prostheses
Store: mail order only, phone hours Monday to Friday 9–5
   MST
Online: www.bosombuddy.com

B&B Company has been producing and selling the "Bosom Buddy Breast Form" by direct mail since 1976. Founder Melva Smith found a way to turn her own experience with breast cancer into something positive with the invention of an all-fabric external breast prosthesis that's helped thousands of women around the world. The Bosom Buddy costs about 50% less than other breast forms on the market, and is a more-comfortable alternative to the hot and heavy silicone versions. It's ideal for active women—golfers, joggers, swimmers, and the like.

The Bosom Buddy is made from luxurious nylon softened with fiberfill, backed with 100% cool cotton next to your skin. The unique design incorporates the use of smooth, tiny glass beads cushioned in fiberfill pillows to give the form weight and balance. The shape and balance can be adjusted, and the breast forms are interchangeable (fit both left and right sides). The forms fit into a regular bra from size AAA to DDD, and come in two different shapes and three different skin-tone shades. The brochure has all the details, but if you still have questions, call B&B's staff and they'll be glad to help. The attractive and easy-to-use website features the same information as the brochure, complete with pictures, and offers online ordering.

Wholesale customers: The minimum order is three breast forms or $100.

SPECIAL FACTORS: Satisfaction guaranteed; returns accepted; Medicare-approved.

Comfort House

189-WM Frelinghuysen Ave.   973–242–8080
Newark, NJ 07114–1595   Fax: 973–242–0131

Catalog: $2, refundable
Pay: check, MO, MC, V, AE, DSC
Sells: all-around helpful tools and gadgets
Store: mail order only
Online: www.comforthouse.com

Here are 24 pages of products designed to make the little things easier for everyone, beginning with the catalog itself, which is printed in a big, clear typeface. Comfort House, in business since 1991, also has a website where you can order online and view the full inventory. This company sells things such as cleaning tools with extension poles that anyone might find useful, as well as electric vegetable peelers, lamp switch enlargers, zipper pulls, and seat-lift chairs designed specifically for those with limited strength and mobility. There are doorknob turners, dressing aids, various gripping devices, exercisers, sleeping and bathing aids, travel accessories, gardening tools, and much more. Comfort House is not a discount catalog, although a couple of price checks showed savings of over 30% on some of the body-care products; this is simply a great collection of products that can help people perform everyday tasks more easily and more safely, as well as coping with changed conditions.

In addition to what's shown in the catalog, Comfort House accepts special orders for any of thousands of products for general personal care, incontinence, mobility assistance, or needs associated with orthopedics, ostomy, laryngectomy, mobility, and urology.

Wholesale terms are available to drug, medical, and surgical-supply stores only. Inquire on company letterhead for terms and pricing.

SPECIAL FACTORS: Satisfaction is guaranteed; returns in unused condition are accepted within 30 days.

Independent Living Aids

27 East Mall
Plainview, NY 11803

800–537–2118
516–752–8080
Fax: 516–752–3135

Catalog: $1
Pay: check, MO, V, MC
Sells: aids for the visually impaired
Store: mail order only
Online: www.independentliving.com

For 20 years ILA has been distributing unique and hard-to-find aids to people who are visually handicapped. The 72-page color catalog features hundreds of items to help individuals with special needs live more comfortably and safely. A sampling of their products includes large-face watches and desk clocks, magnifiers (handheld and clip-ons for eyeglasses), desk lamps, floor lamps, and other lighting to enhance visibility, recorders, calculators, and all kinds of "talking" items—from clocks, telephones, and bathroom scales to thermometers and money identifiers. You'll find canes and walkers, writing guides for checks and envelopes, large-face playing cards and other games in braille, including bingo and Trivial Pursuit, and much more. There are personal care items (mirrors, for example), cooking aids such as tactile meat thermometers, bath and shower items such as the Gentle Jet Bidet that attaches easily to any toilet seat, a whole section on accessories for diabetic care, books about and for the visually impaired (such as large-print cookbooks), and computer software that adapts to any computer. The prices on most items are very reasonable, but Independent Living Aids also runs specials and has a wholesale division, where savings generally run over 20%. The real plus with this company is that they offer hard-to-find items, many of which would be useful for the rest of us and our aging parents as well. The website is really terrific and allows you to view a lot of the catalog offerings, but doesn't have online ordering.

SPECIAL FACTORS: Wholesale customers must have a resale number; returns must be made within 30 days.

The Left Hand

P.O. Box 3263
Bethlehem, PA 18017–0263

800–462–5338
610–923–0677
Fax: 610–923–0678

Catalog: $2
Pay: check, MO, V, MC, AE
Sells: left-handed tools, sports gear, and other products
    for children and adults
Store: mail order only; phone hours Monday to Friday
    12–4 EST
Online: www.thelefthand.com

If you're right-handed and have ever tried to use scissors with your left, you know it's nearly impossible. Now consider that everything from cars to clothes to kitchens are designed with the right-handed person in mind. When Ross Perot, Bill Clinton, and George Bush were running for the presidency a few years back, I remember thinking how very odd it was that all three were lefties. The truth is, there are millions upon millions of left-handed people, but few consumer products designed with their special needs in mind.

The Left Hand intends to correct that. Owners Carolyn and John Williams have put together an eclectic selection of items—some whimsical, others necessary—geared to the needs of left-handed children and adults. You won't find most of these items in stores, and everything carried at The Left Hand has been hand-picked, and family-tested and -approved. The online catalog offers baseball items (pitcher, catcher, baseman, and fielder gloves); books on subjects ranging from left-handed calligraphy to guitar instruction, including children's titles; computer accessories (keyboards with numeric and arrow pads positioned on the left, ergonomic mouse models, joysticks for lefties); hand tools (tape measure, Swiss army knife, ergonomic pruner); products for kids (notebooks, scissors, coloring books, rulers, handwriting helpers); kitchen and cooking implements (can opener, peeler, corkscrew, measuring cups, knives of all kinds, pastry servers); scissors (manicure, pinking, household, barber, etc.); and more. The website offers the full inventory, offers online ordering, and features helpful links to other websites with products and information of relevance to lefties.

SPECIAL FACTORS: Satisfaction guaranteed; returns accepted within 30 days of receipt for refund, exchange, or credit.

National Allergy Supply, Inc.

4400 Abbott's Bridge Road
Duluth, GA 30096

800–522–1448
Fax: 770–623–5568

Catalog: free
Pay: check, MO, MC, V, AE, DSC
Sells: nondrug products to avoid allergens
Store: mail order only
Online: www.natlallergy.com

National Allergy Supply is the nation's largest discount allergy products supplier. The "Allergy Relief Catalog" is a 24-page color catalog designed for people who suffer from sneezing, runny nose, swollen and itchy eyes, coughing, wheezing, postnasal drip, and many other allergy and asthma symptoms. Ryner Wittgens started this company nine years ago as a result of his daughter's being diagnosed with six different airborne allergies. He made it his goal to find the best products out there for people like his daughter, for whom ordinary household environments full of pet dander, dust mite allergen, dust mold, chemical gassing of carpets, and toxins from household cleaners make life difficult if not dangerous. Even if you're not allergy-prone, there are lots of ways to make your environment cleaner and healthier. You'll find all-cotton bedding, nondown comforters, air cleaners, carpet treatments, vinyl and cotton gloves for people with chemically sensitive skin, household cleaners, skin- and hair-care products, floor dusters, vacuum cleaners specially designed to eliminate 99.97% of allergens, in-home asthma treatments, respiratory masks, breathing and sleeping aids, window fans, and much more.

The catalog is not overwhelming. One gets the sense that the company has selected only the best one or two manufacturers in each category, and explanatory text accompanies each product with descriptions about its benefit to allergy-sensitive people. There are plenty of testimonials from happy customers, and the company offers a 100% satisfaction guarantee on all their products. National Allergy Supply keeps a staff of highly trained reps who are available to answer all of your questions. By the way, at the website you'll be able to check out some of the products, but there's no online ordering.

Special to WMO readers: Identify yourself as a reader of this book and National Allergy will send you a free video about allergen avoidance in your home, a $9 value. Mention offer FVID when calling.

SPECIAL FACTORS: Satisfaction guaranteed; Canadian customers must pay by credit card; phone hours are 24 hours a day, Monday through Saturday.

The New Vision Store

919 Walnut St., 1st Fl.　　　　　215–629–2990
Philadelphia, PA 19107

> Product List: free
> Pay: check, MO, MC, V, DSC
> Sells: products to aid the visually impaired
> Store: same address; Monday to Friday 10–4

Bill Ankenbrant understands the challenges faced by visually impaired persons. Visually impaired himself, he launched his store and mail-order company to "provide products that promote hope and independence for every customer wherever possible." The eight-page typewritten product list, which also comes out in braille twice a year, presents a variety of necessary but hard-to-find items, some of which are discounted, others discounted 20% if you buy in small quantity, but all at reasonable prices. The New Vision Store offers such products as canes (auto-fold, rigid fiberglass, folding support canes, and others); flame-retardant oven mitts; raised-number timers, clocks, and calculators, as well as large-print, talking, and braille versions; magnifiers of all kinds; labeling supplies, such as kits, labeling guns, braille-embossing guns, as well as tapes for clothing, magnetized tapes, and labels of every kind; bill organizers; talking thermometers; a variety of sunglasses; small electronics such as Walkmans, desk recorders, and desk radios; mailing supplies including free-matter-for-the-blind labels and two- and four-cassette mailers; a variety of user-friendly watches; desk accessories such as rulers and pens, as well as signature guides and slates of different sizes for note-writing; and much more. Send in a greeting card to New Vision and they'll emboss it for you in braille for $3.

SPECIAL FACTORS: If you have a product not found in the catalog, The New Vision Store will find it for you; mail-order hours are the same as store hours; request in writing for shipping Free Matter for the Blind; see company literature for other shipping fees and policies.

Special Clothes, Inc., was founded in 1987 by Judith Sweeney, whose interest in developing adaptive designs was inspired by her experiences as an educator involved with children with special needs. Special Clothes has two catalogs—one for children, one for adults—to help people for whom dressing is a daily struggle. Because the company prices the clothing by size, pricing is not inflated, and there are quantity discounts that enable you to cut costs further. All garments of knit, fleece, or denim are 100% cotton, most garments are latex-free, and functional features such as snap crotches, bib fronts, and G-tube access are inconspicuous. The 40-page children's catalog is for toddlers to size-18 teens. (There's a handy sizing chart included that helps you choose the right size for your child.) Among the clothing and accessories offered are all-cotton bodysuits with snap crotches and optional gastrostomy-tube access (Special Clothes will conceal the access opening with a stitched-on pocket), available in solid colors and a variety of styles; snap-on bodysuit extenders that add four inches to the torso length; a travel bag to carry catheterization items safely, easily, and discreetly; all-cotton absorbent briefs and nylon protective pull-ons; feeding bibs; knit jumpsuits; denim and chambray overalls; jeans, trousers, and dress pants; shirts and skirted leggings; heavyweight flannel diapers; swimwear, socks, slippers, mittens, and more. All clothing is available in a variety of colors, closure options, G-tube access, length, etc. Special Clothes' Birthday Club will give your child a greeting card and a 15%-off coupon when you send in your child's name and birth date.

The adult catalog offers bodysuits, sleepers, jumpsuits, knit pants, and wheelchair jackets and ponchos, and includes a sizing chart to accommodate small to extra-large adults. The catalogs include some helpful incontinence and parent resources, as well as lists for sale ($1 each) of other manufacturers of adaptive clothing for adults, health-care supplies, special needs publications, and service organizations.

Wholesale buyers and institutions: Please inquire about Special Clothes' terms and pricing.

SPECIAL FACTORS: See catalog for returns policy; custom orders are available (but not returnable).

Support Plus

99 West St., Dept. BWBM   800–229–2910
Box 500   508–359–2910
Medfield, MA 02052   Fax: 508–359–0139

Catalog: free
Pay: check, MO, MC, V, AE, DSC
Sells: women's support hosiery, supportive footwear,
   undergarments, and daily living aids
Store: mail order only
Online: www.catalogcity.com

Support Plus has been in business since 1972 offering products geared toward the older woman (although men can use many of these products as well). Here you'll find an extensive selection of medical and support hosiery; aids to daily living (magnifiers, large-print playing cards, bio curve pens, back-support products, reachers, travel chairs and cushions, walkers with baskets), supportive shoes; health-care products for feet, skin, arthritis, and back pain; safety products for your bathtub and shower; incontinence products; and undergarments. The website, which features online ordering, shows much but not all that's in the print catalog, so if you don't see something, call. Although discounts here aren't deep—sale items may run from 15% to 25% off regular prices—Support Plus nevertheless is a good company to know about because of their solid customer-relations policies and the thoughtful selection of products.

SPECIAL FACTORS: Unscuffed shoes can be returned for refund or exchange; price quote by phone for quantities in excess of 12 pairs.

The Support Shop

370 Wall Street
Princeton, NJ 08540

888–339–1689
888–395–HOSE
Fax: 908–874–5051

Catalog: free
Pay: check, MO, V, MC, AE
Sells: men's and women's therapeutic support hosiery
Store: mail order only; phone hours Monday to Friday 9–5 EST
Online: www.supportshop.com

Did your doctor tell you to buy support hose? Then you know how expensive they can be. The Support Shop sells compression stockings at 35% to 50% below retail. Authorized dealers for Jobst, Juzo, Medi, Sigvaris, and Venosan. The Support Shop also sells their own manufactured brand, RxFit, where you can reap the most savings; this "house brand" is the same high-quality product sold in retail stores under more famous brand names. You'll appreciate the prices here on support products including sheer support (pantyhose, thigh highs, knee highs), men's socks, maternity pantyhose, 20–30 and 30–40 surgical weight (pantyhose and thigh highs), anti-embolism stockings, and diabetic socks. The Support Shop is so sure you'll love their products that they let every new customer try out any product risk-free, and they'll charge no shipping on your first order (see website or call for New Customer information). The website has size charts, and offers secure online ordering if you wish, or you can call, mail, or fax in your order. The site also has a valuable FAQ page with lots of articles and information on pregnancy and varicose veins, swollen legs, the benefits of compression hosiery, and more, written by the likes of Dr. Andrew Weil and the Mayo Clinic. You've suffered enough; now give your pocketbook some relief.

SPECIAL FACTORS: 100% satisfaction guaranteed; authorized returns accepted within 30 days of receipt for refund, credit, or exchange.

Related Products/Companies

Adult incontinence products
• Diaper Warehouse

Audiobooks
• Bargain Book Warehouse, Blackstone, The Family Travel Guides Catalogue

Bathroom fixtures for disabled persons
- The Faucet Outlet

Blood-pressure and other health-monitoring equipment
- Cotton Scrubs, Creative Health Products, Essentials, Tafford Manufacturing

Braille medicine labels
- Essentials

Closed-caption decoders
- Sound City

Cookbooks for diabetics, allergy sufferers, and dieters
- Jessica's Biscuit Cookbooks

Custom-made nonallergenic comforters
- J. Schachter

Disability rights literature
- Consumer Information Center

Left-handed stringed instruments
- Mandolin Brothers

Mail-order catalogs in braille and/or audio
- Essentials

Mastectomy bras
- Lady Grace, The Smart Saver

Neutriceuticals for hyperactive children
- Freeda Vitamins

Office workstations with wheelchair access
- Dallas Midwest, K-Log

Post-mastectomy swimwear
- Lady Grace, World Wide Aquatics

Slightly irregular support hosiery
- No Nonsense Direct

Snap-up-the-back nightgowns
- Chock

Special-needs assistance for travelers over 55
- Elder Hostel

Special-needs books
- Bargain Book Warehouse, Blackstone Audiobooks, The Family Travel Guides Catalog, Reader's Digest

Sugar-free candy and confections
- Bulkfoods.com, Mountain Ark

Tack for differently abled equestrians
- State Line Tack

Wigs
- Beauty by Spector, Gold Medal Hair Products

Sports and Recreation

*Clothing, footwear, and
equipment for all kinds
of indoor and outdoor sports
and recreational activities*

No matter what your sport—scuba diving, kite flying, golf, soccer, kayaking, swimming, tennis, etc.—you'll find clothing, footwear, and equipment to be in full gear from the companies in this chapter. If organized sports are your thing, there are firms here that specialize in outfitting whole teams. Discounts of 40% and more are routine here. And if you don't mind buying last year's ski equipment, for instance, savings can run as high as 60% or more.

For camping, survival equipment, or hunting, see the section following this one, "Camping, Hunting, and Survival," page 548. For firms that offer foul-weather gear, swimwear, and clothing for athletes and nature lovers, see the "Clothing" chapter, page 84. For companies that sell boating and marine supplies, see "Auto, Marine, and Aviation," page 26. For workout equipment, see the "Fitness and Exercise" section, page 265, of the "Health, Beauty, and Fitness" chapter. And for various other firms throughout the book that offer sports- and recreation-related items, see the listings at the end of this chapter under "Related Products/Companies."

Find It Fast

Billiards, Table Tennis, Darts
- Mueller Sporting Goods

Boats and Water Sports
- Bart's Water Sports, Berry Scuba, Central Skindivers, The House, Mohawk Canoe, Overton's, Performance Diver, SOAR Inflatables, Water Warehouse, World Wide Aquatics

Cycling
- Bike Nashbar, Performance Bicycle

Golf
- Discount Golf Superstore, Golf Haus, Virtual Fairway

Kites
- BFK Sports

Racquet Sports
- Holabird

Skiing and Snowboarding
- Al's Ski Barn, The House

Soccer
- Acme Soccer, Soccer International

Volleyball
- Spike Nashbar

Acme Soccer and Widget Works

P.O. Box 811
Carrboro, NC 27510–0811

800–333–4625
Fax: 919–644–6808

Catalog: free
Pay: check, MO, MC, V, AE, DSC
Sells: soccer gear
Store: mail order only

Soccer moms: Stop despairing at the coming of spring. Sure, your kid has outgrown her shin guards and needs some new cleats. But Acme Soccer knows this, and that's why the company purchases manufacturers' overstocks of soccer gear and can sell it to you at prices that are 50% to 60% off the regular retail price. The 32-page color catalog has items for kids and adults, including soccer shorts; T-shirts with cool slogans and pictures, as well as plain ones and the designer logos the kids flip for; soccer shoes of every type and style, designed for indoor courts as well as muddy fields; socks; knit hats and visor caps; gloves; shin guards; equipment bags; single-color team shirts; nylon windbreakers and other jackets; and soccer accessories and gifts.

Note to Spanish-speaking customers: Acme welcomes your calls and has Spanish-speaking reps to assist you.

SPECIAL FACTORS: Acme recommends that you call before placing your order, since some of the items are stocked in limited quantities; returns accepted on clean, unused, or defective merchandise (see catalog for details); no C.O.D. orders.

Skiing is an expensive sport, but it just got cheaper. Al's Ski Barn is a virtual ski shop that acquires surplus ski equipment or equipment from outfits that are going out of business, and then sells it directly to you off their website—at savings that reach up to 60% and more. All equipment is still warranted by the manufacturer, but it may be last year's stock. (Next year your brand-new equipment will be last year's model anyway!) When you visit Al's user-friendly, uncomplicated website, you'll see what they currently have in stock. The stock changes periodically when new equipment comes in, so if you don't find what you're looking for right away, check back. Next to each item is the retail price and then Al's Ski Barn price. The savings are *really* significant. Al's carries top-name skis, boots, and bindings from such famous makers as Atomic, Blizzard, Dynastar, Head, K2, Kastle, Lange, Look, Marker, Nordica, Salomon, Tyrolia, and Volkl. Don't forget to check out the "Bargain Stall," where the drastically marked down sale items will blow your boots off. If you don't find what you're looking for right away, check back or join Al's Ski Barn's e-mailing list to receive e-mail when new inventory is added. Need the current snow, weather, or avalanche conditions? You can find these at Al's too.

SPECIAL FACTORS: Returns are negotiable; all equipment warranted by manufacturer; all items shipped from MN warehouse.

Bart's Water Sports

P.O. Box 294-WBM
North Webster, IN 46555

800–348–5016
219–834–7666
Fax: 219–834–4246

Catalog: free, $5 outside U.S.
Pay: check, MO, MC, V, AE, DSC
Sells: water sports, marine/boating, and personal
  watercraft goods
Store: Hwy. 13, North Webster, IN; Monday to Saturday
  9–6
Online: www.bartsports.com

In 1976, Bart Culver, a recent undergraduate in biology from University of Indiana with a love for water sports, started selling water skis by mail. Decades later, Bart's Water Sports is still housed in little ole North Webster, Indiana (population 885!), but now boasts a state-of-the-art facility, employs a staff of distinguished experts who can answer all your water sports questions, and maintains a loyal worldwide customer base. This company has weathered the uncertain wakes of commerce by selling everything related to water sports at discount prices—up to 40% on many items, with savings even greater on closeouts, "scratch and dent" specials, and BLEMs (factory-new goods with a minor cosmetic blemish that won't affect performance). "Betty Price Beater" will help you get the absolute lowest prices on every item Bart's stocks, including wakeboards, PWC, boating and marine equipment, water skis, wetsuits, kneeboards, vests, sportswear, snorkel gear, children's pool toys and floats, videos and interactive media, gear bags, deck and pool accessories, and much more. I liked the website, where you can search for a product by category, order online, and check out the latest closeouts, for which 60% or more off isn't uncommon.

SPECIAL FACTORS: Satisfaction guaranteed; quantity discounts available; returns accepted within 60 days (including closeout items); minimum overseas order is $250.

Berry Scuba Co.

6674 N. Northwest Hwy.,
Dept. WBM
Chicago, IL 60631

800–621–6019
773–763–1626
Fax: 773–775–1815

Catalog: free
Pay: check, MO, MC, V, AE, DSC
Sells: scuba-diving gear
Store: same address; also Lombard and Palatine, IL, and Atlanta, GA
Online: www.berryscuba.com

Berry Scuba is a good source for all underwater explorers looking for new equipment at savings that run up to 40%. The oldest, largest, and best-known direct-mail scuba firm in the country, Berry carries everything for the snorkeler and diver, including fins, snorkels, and masks, regulators, hoses and hose accessories, dive computers, dive jackets, wet suits, boots, gloves, duffels, books, videos, and more. Berry's factory-trained service department in Chicago can also repair your equipment and service regulators, gauges, dive computers, BCDs, valves, wet suits, and accessories. Call or fax the Chicago facility for service rates.

SPECIAL FACTORS: 30-day satisfaction guarantee on all purchases.

BFK Sports, Inc.

19306 Windrose Dr.   **626–912–9696**
Rowland Heights, CA 91748

Catalog: free
Pay: check, MO, MC, V, AE, DSC, JCB
Sells: kites and kiting supplies
Store: same address; Monday to Saturday 11–6, Sunday
12–5
Online: www.kitestore.com

Have you ever packed up the kids—or gathered a few friends—for an afternoon of kite-flying only to have the day fizzle for lack of wind? A glance at the catalog and website for BFK Sports, Inc., and you'll see the folks there know all about the thrills and agonies of kite-flying and which kites will maximize your recreational pleasure or competitive success. BKF Sports turns novices into savvy shoppers by providing a thorough introduction to kites that answers commonsense questions without the Q&A format. Once you've read the intro, you can confidently shop for a single- or dual-line kite—perhaps a Super Ultralight, no wind kite—or a starter package. The website presents a wind chart (using the Beaufort scale) to help competitors choose the right sports kite with kites ranging from $18 to $500 apiece, and packages available from $100 to $300 for professional equipment. The wind-related inventory, including small items such as boomerangs and gliders, will rekindle your childhood or poetic interests in wind, especially if you find your heart's desire among the discontinued or closeout items—at savings up to 50% off list prices. You can also order a free print catalog from the site.

The BFK Sports website also features a string product of a more grounded sort, the yo-yo, under the heading YoYo Store (yoyostore.com). They carry 50-plus models by Yomega, Playmaxx, Tom Kuhn, Duncan, and other manufacturers. Because of volume purchasing, BFK can offer special Yomega deals and products. And there's no need to embarrass yourself in front of friends as you struggle to master the yo-yo. BFK's YoYo Store also sells an instructional video!

SPECIAL FACTORS: Satisfaction guaranteed; new, unused returns (some exceptions) accepted within 15 days for exchange, refund, or credit; C.O.D. orders accepted.

Bike Nashbar

4111 Simon Rd., Dept. WBM   **800–NASHBAR**
Youngstown, OH 44512–1343   **Fax: 800–456–1223**

Catalog: free
Pay: check, MO, MC, V, DSC
Sells: bicycles, accessories, apparel and equipment
Store: same address; call for hours
Online: www.bikenashbar.com

Bike Nashbar is one of the country's top sources for casual and serious cyclists, and publishes a 70-plus-page catalog that runs from seat bags to glow-in-the-dark wind vests—all sold at "guaranteed lowest prices." In business since 1973, Bike Nashbar sells its own line of road, touring, and ATB bikes, which have features usually found on more expensive models. You'll find full lines of parts and accessories, including saddles, gears, brakes, chain wheels, hubs, pedals, derailleurs, and handlebars. Panniers and bags, racks, helmets, protective eyewear, gloves, tires and tubes, wheels, toe clips, locks, handlebar tape, grips, tire pumps, lights, and other accessories are offered. Bike Nashbar also features a large selection of cycling clothing and shoes. Check out the website for online ordering and specials.

SPECIAL FACTORS: Satisfaction is guaranteed; technical advice available.

Central Skindivers

160–09 Jamaica Ave.   **718–739–5772**
Jamaica, NY 11432–6111   **Fax: 718–739–3679**

Catalog: free
Pay: check, MO, MC, V, AE, DSC
Sells: scuba-diving equipment
Store: same address; Monday to Saturday 10–6:30

Since 1952, in Jamaica, New York, just outside Manhattan, Central Skindivers has been selling diving gear to adventurous souls called by profession or recreational urge to explore watery depths firsthand. Today Central Skindivers offers savings of up to 40% on tanks, regulators, suits, masks, fins, gauges, watches, timers, and computers—state-of-the-art equipment that old-timers could never have imagined needing! Central Skindivers "will not be undersold" so call for price quotes on products by most major manufacturers, or to request a catalog.

SPECIAL FACTORS: No shipping charges; minimum order $50.

Discount Golf Superstore

888–394–4653
425–957–3626
Fax: 425–778–2679

Information: website only, no print catalog
Pay: cashier's check, MO, V, MC, AE, DSC, JCB
Sells: golf equipment
Store: online only; phone hours are Monday to Friday 6–6,
 Saturday 8–4, Sunday 9–4 PT
Online: www.golfdiscount.com

If you love to surf (the Internet, that is) as well as to golf, then Discount Golf Superstore (DGS) is the place for you. Discount Golf Superstore—"your Internet source to the lowest prices on the best names in golf!"—brings 20 years experience in the golf retail business to golf enthusiasts looking to pay about 20% less than they would at retail. There's a page of fan e-mail from satisfied customers (quite a few of whom were left-handed golfers ecstatic to have found southpaw-friendly clubs), which is always heartening to see. This site carries clubs by the top-name manufacturers—including Cobra, Ping, Callaway, Taylor Made, Top Flite, Power Bilt, Cleveland, La Jolla, Titleist, Armour, Adams, Odyssey, Wilson, Nicklaus, and many others—as well as putters, bags, travel covers, and even golf shoes by Dunlop, Etonic, Reebok, Foot-Joy, and Bite.

Straightforward and easy to use, this site has something too many other online shops lack: customer service. If you have questions, you can call and speak to a helpful sales rep who will even find the clubs you're looking for if DGS doesn't happen to be showing them at present on their site. You can also chat live online, if that's your thing. The site is changed and updated frequently, so the selection will vary. All merchandise comes with the manufacturer's warranty.

Corporate clients: DSB provides imprinting. You can have your corporate logo on golf balls, caps, shirts, and other items. Call toll-free 888–394–4653 for more information.

SPECIAL FACTORS: Satisfaction guaranteed; returns accepted within 30 days, but customer pays shipping; no personal checks accepted.

Golf Haus

700 N. Pennsylvania   517–482–8842
Lansing, MI 48906   Fax: 517–482–8843

Price List: free
Pay: check, MO, MC, V
Sells: golf clubs, apparel, and accessories
Store: same address; Monday to Saturday 9–5:30

"If we can't save you money, we don't deserve your business!" The folks at Golf Haus are earnest all right, which I like in a company. They specialize in one thing—saving you money on golf-related gear and equipment—and they do it well. The price list Golf Haus sends out is so frequently updated that it almost makes more sense to call. Here you'll find the lowest prices—up to 70% below list—on clubs, bags, putters, balls, and other golf equipment and accessories by major manufacturers including Powerbilt, Cobra, Goldwin, Wilson, Titleist, Taylor Made, Ping, Spalding, Mizuno, and many others. In addition, recent offerings have included such items as Gore-Tex rain suits, spikes, airline travel bags (holds clubs and bag), and gloves. If you have a golf fanatic in the family, you'll do well to call Golf Haus before making any major purchases.

Special to WMO readers: Golf Haus is offering a free set of head covers with an order of a complete set of clubs (wood and irons) to readers who mention this book.

SPECIAL FACTORS: Free shipping and insurance on orders within the continental U.S.; minimum order $50.

Holabird Sports

9220 Pulaski Hwy.   410–687–6400
Baltimore, MD 21220   Fax: 410–687–7311

Brochure: free
Pay: check, MO, MC, V, AE, DSC
Sells: racquet sports equipment and athletic footwear
Store: same address; Monday to Friday 9–5, Saturday 9–3
Online: www.holabirdsports.com

Holabird Sports, established in 1981, carries equipment, clothing, and accessories for a good number of sports, but its specialty is rackets—prestrung, unstrung, and custom strung—for tennis, squash, and racquetball. Prices here are good—sometimes as much as 40% off suggested list. The eight-page monthly flyer lists racquet models by all the major brands, plus Best Buy racquet specials in limited quantities. Holabird has a staff of professionals to custom-string rackets, but racquets can be purchased unstrung (deduct $4 from price) for stringing by do-it-yourself kit.

Since you won't find detailed product specifications or photographs here, only product names and great prices, you'd do well to take the catalog with you to a local retailer to see firsthand which products you like best. Holabird stocks over 3,000 items, among them a large selection of shoes (in regular and junior sizes) for golf, aerobics, tennis, soccer, racquetball or squash, walking, boating, running, cross training, and basketball, as well as rugged boots for hiking or work. You'll also find portable stringing machines, ball hoppers, ball machines, and wind screens (many of these large items ship free of charge), and an eclectic assortment of other racquet-sport-related goods: reflective gear, Teva Wet Climber sandals, ladies clogs, joint supports, heart-rate monitors, videos, sports bags (including backpacks and fanny packs), sports gloves, eyeguards, socks, watches, visors, and personal sports radar gadgets. The website is easy to use and features online ordering.

SPECIAL FACTORS: Authorized unused returns accepted within seven days; small additional shipping charge outside continental U.S. and to APO addresses; call for price quotes.

The House

300 S. Owasso Blvd., Dept.
WBM
St. Paul, MN 55117

651–482–9995
Fax: 651–482–1353

Catalog: free (see text)
Pay: check, MO, MC, V, AE, DSC
Sells: snowboarding and sailboarding equipment and
accessories
Store: same address; Monday to Friday, 10–7, Saturday
9–2
Online: www.the-house.com

The House, established in 1983, is as much a philosophy as it is a business, being "dedicated to no rip-off pricing so you can ride more!" Buying directly from manufacturers enables The House to save you from 20% to 50% off the price of sailboards, rigs, sails, snowboards, device step-in boots and bindings, custom boots, clothing, accessories, and more. Whether your venue is wind or water, you'll reap the greatest savings by buying the H-Brand merchandise. The House issues two catalogs—one for sailboarding, the other for snowboarding. Be sure to specify which one you're interested in. Each catalog gives important board specs for both H-Brand and "name brand" products, along with recommendations for choosing the best board based on such factors as rider weight and foot size. The House also sells equipment and clothing for children. The website, ever expanding, lets you enter either world—snowboards or sailboards—and view some of the inventory and current specials, as well as order online.

SPECIAL FACTORS: Satisfaction guaranteed; authorized returns accepted within 20 days.

Mohawk Canoe

963 North C.R. 427
Longwood, FL 32750

800–686–6429
407–834–3233
Fax: 407–834–0292

Catalog: free
Pay: check, MO
Sells: canoes and canoe accessories
Store: same address; Monday to Friday 8:30–4:30,
   9–noon Saturday
Online: www.mohawkcanoes.com

Canoes are not inexpensive, but if you take care of them right they'll last a lifetime. Mohawk Canoe, in the manufacturing business for 36 years, builds quality canoes and offers them factory direct to paddlers at 30% below suggested retail price. One of the reasons Mohawk can sell their canoes at these discount prices is that they don't spend a lot of money on advertising, fancy catalogs, and PR. This company has a fully functioning website, where you can browse the models, prices, and company policies; check out related links; read about such subjects as "canoes vs. kayaks" and "kids and canoes"; or just obtain a print catalog. Although you can't submit your order electronically, you can download a form and then fax or mail it in.

These gorgeous canoes are made of Royalite and Royalex, a lightweight, durable material, and come in beautiful colors with high-quality webbed or caned ash seats and yokes. There are solo models, tandem models, and short white-water play-boats designed for river rodeos and extremely challenging rivers. Mohawk also sells accessories such as paddles, life jackets, canoe hardware, seat cushions, car racks, and more. The literature has helpful charts that compare Mohawk canoes with other manufacturer's models, as well as ratings compiled by *Backpacker* magazine, so you can see how Mohawk stacks up next to the leading competitors when it comes to stability, tracking and turning, speed, portaging, and construction quality.

Wholesalers, please note: For wholesale rates, the minimum order is six canoes.

SPECIAL FACTORS: No credit cards accepted; due to packing and shipping requirements, Mohawk cannot accept returns.

Mueller Sporting Goods, Inc.

4825 So. 16th St., Dept. 60
Lincoln, NE 68512

800–925–7665
Fax: 402–423–5964

Catalog: free
Pay: check, MO, MC, V, DSC
Sells: billiards, table tennis, and darts equipment
Store: 20th and Highway 2, Lincoln, NE; also 5705
 Hickman Rd., Des Moines, IA; Monday to Saturday 9–6,
 Sunday 1–5
Online: www.mueller-sporting-goods.com

When you think Mueller Sporting Goods, think indoor, rec room pastimes such as table tennis, billiards, darts, casino games, foosball, air hockey, shuffleboard, and bumper pool. And think savings between 40% and 55% off retail prices, which the catalog lists alongside Mueller's discount prices. For billiards buffs there's an extensive inventory of cues, cue cases, engravable brass cue chalkers, ball and table accessories such as cone talc holders and leather shake bottles, billiard lights, and wall and floor racks. Mueller maintains a professional cue repair service that will replace butt and shaft collars, reface joints, and install inlays on existing cues. Cue butts can be rewrapped in Irish linen or leather, and can also be engraved. For creating billiard hall atmosphere, there are cleverly worded signs, neon posters, clocks, oak spectator chairs, and numbered pool ball bar stools. For dart lovers, the glossy 180-page catalog reserves nearly 75 pages to dart sets, custom darts, shafts, flights, cases, portfolios, and miscellaneous gifts and accessories. All manner of rec room supplies, equipment, and novelties— refrigerator magnets, note cubes, mugs, T-shirts—from name-brand manufacturers are available from Mueller Sporting Goods. Mueller is also interested in buying old billiard tables and accessories. At press time the website was under construction, so check back.

SPECIAL FACTORS: Quantity discounts available; returns accepted within 30 days for exchange, refund, or credit (except personalized and custom orders); see catalog for lowest-price guarantee.

Overton's Sports Center, Inc.

P.O. Box 8228, Dept. 57612
Greenville, NC 27835

800–334–6541
252–355–7600
Fax: 252–355–2923

Catalog: free
Pay: check, MO, V, MC, AE, DSC, JCB
Sells: boating accessories and water sports goods
Store: 5343 S. Boulevard, Charlotte; 111 Red Banks Rd.
 Greenville; and 3062 Wake Forest Road, Raleigh, NC
Online: www.overtons.com

When Overton's Sports Center, Inc., self-proclaimed "World's Largest Water Sports Dealer," offers its online shoppers a "power search" of the entire database of inventory, power is what the shopper gets. You can search for boating, water-skiing, and snorkeling equipment by a long or a short product description, by part number, and by vendor. Here you'll find top manufacturers of hundreds of products including apparel (belts, eyewear, footwear, ladies' swimwear, men's shorts, rain gear, etc.); boating accessories (boat covers, heaters, lights, mooring hardware, navigation equipment, fuel systems, toilets, flags); gifts and gadgets (kids' floating trampolines, boat telephones, remote-control toy boats); personal water craft (PWC) apparel and accessories; SUV/truck accessories; and water sports gear and equipment (diving equipment, kneeboards, pool accessories, wet-suits, flotation vests). The website also has great bargain basement deals on goods in every category, so check here first. If web-surfing isn't your thing, you can request one of Overton's three print catalogs ("Water Sports"; "Swimwear and Apparel"; and "Discount Boating Accessories"). Overton's lowest price guarantee states that if you find a published price that's lower than theirs, they'll refund your money plus 10%.

SPECIAL FACTORS: Satisfaction guaranteed; quantity discounts available; unused returns accepted within 30 days for exchange, refund, or credit; C.O.D. orders accepted.

Performance Bicycle Shop

P.O. Box 2741   **800–727–2453**
Chapel Hill, NC 27514   **Fax: 800–727–3291**

    Catalog: free
    Pay: check, MO, MC, V, DSC
    Sells: bicycle parts and cycling apparel
    Store: retail outlets in CA, CO, IL, MD, NC, OR, PA, VA,
      and WA
    Online: www.performancebike.com

If it's good enough for the U.S. Cycling Team, it should be good enough for the rest of us. I'm talking about the technical clothing and bicycle parts and accessories sold at Performance Bicycle. If you have access to the Internet, I strongly advise you to check out the online catalog, where you can not only view hundreds of products—books/videos, car racks, glasses, helmets, indoor storage hardware, lights, locks, pumps, saddles, wheels, tools/lubes, packs, and much more—but also check out weekly specials and clearance items that offer unbelievable deals on last season's goods—some as low as 70% off; hop to other bike-fanatic web links; and order online. If you prefer, there's also a 70-page color print catalog. This company, in business since 1981, will give you a price that's lower than anyone else's—a promise they back with a guarantee.

SPECIAL FACTORS: Satisfaction guaranteed; returns accepted for refund, credit, or exchange (see print or online catalog for details).

Performance Diver

P.O. Box 2741, Dept. WBM   800–933–3299
Chapel Hill, NC 27514   Fax: 800–727–3291

Catalog: free
Pay: check, MO, MC, V, DSC
Sells: scuba equipment and apparel
Store: mail order only
Online: www.performancediver.com

Performance Diver offers savings up to 50% on comparable retail prices by sell-ing, *under the Performance name*, scuba equipment, apparel, wet suits, regulators, gauges, and accessories, manufactured by name-brand companies. Savings are also possible because Performance, in business since 1990, sells only by mail order, emphasizing the latest in technological design and construction for optimal performance, comfort, and safety. The catalog also features T-shirts, name-brand watches, duffel bags, and other beach-related products. The website offers weekly specials and online ordering, as well diving-related links, subscription to an e-mail newsletter, and membership to the Dive Club, where you earn points on each purchase that can be applied to later discounts.

SPECIAL FACTORS: Satisfaction guaranteed; returns accepted for exchange, refund, or credit.

SOAR Inflatables

20 Healdsburg Ave.
Healdsburg, CA 95448

707–433–5599
800–280–SOAR
Fax: 707–433–4499

Catalog: free
Pay: check, MO, V, MC
Sells: inflatable boats and accessories
Store: mail order only
Online: www.soar1.com

There are only three other companies in the world, according to SOAR Inflatables owner Larry Laba, who make inflatable canoes, and his are less expensive because he manufactures and sells them factory-direct to the consumer. The boats are 12-foot ($1,300), 14-foot ($1,425), and 16-foot ($1,550). Why spend that much when a regular canoe could cost as little as $500 (or up to $3,000)? Because, says Laba, his boats can be rolled up to fit into a backpack, a car trunk, an RV, and any airline storage unit. You can't do *that* with a rigid canoe. For regular (noncommercial) use, your SOAR Inflatable will last a lifetime. And these canoes handle virtually any condition a rigid canoe can, including Class 3 white water—this, from a customer who did it. (Incidentally, Outward Bound of Colorado uses SOAR Inflatables and hasn't had any complaints as of this writing.) SOAR Inflatables are fun and reliable, as witness the dozen or more testimonials from happy customers in the flyer that comes with the eight-page color catalog. These customers range from urban apartment dwellers to families with children to professional river guides, and they all echo the same themes: easy maneuverability, extreme ruggedness, versatility, and convenience.

Rolled up, the canoes weigh between 52 and 67 pounds, and they come with two seats, a double-action hand pump, straps to keep your inflatable tightly rolled, and a repair kit. Other items available in the catalog include collapsible paddles (and kayak paddle converters), duffel bags, padded seats with backs, a pump that hooks up to your car battery, and more. The catalog provides details for canoe aficionados, such as abrasion resistance, buoyancy, and drag. For more about these remarkable boats, visit the website, where you can read all about them, sign SOAR's guestbook, get on the mailing list for the most recent brochure, and read testimonials from SOAR owners. SOAR offers quantity discounts to businesses, ranging from 10% to 30% off, depending on the numbers purchased.

Special to WMO readers: Mention that you're a reader of this book and SOAR will take 20% off your boat.

SPECIAL FACTORS: Satisfaction guaranteed, with a 30-day trial; limited five-year warranty.

Soccer International

P.O. Box 7222, Dept. WBM   703–524–4333
Arlington, VA 22207–7222

Catalog: $2
Pay: check or MO
Sells: soccer gear, accessories, books, videos, and gifts
Store: mail order only; phone hours 8:30–10 seven days a
   week
Online: www.soccerinternational.com/soccerintl

Soccer International, founded in 1976 by an avid soccer buff, publishes an 18-page color catalog of soccer necessities including balls, nets, goals, cones, flags, and other equipment; jerseys, socks, vests, shin guards, and uniforms; referee accessories; books and videos; and even novelty items such as games, jewelry, and piñatas. The website has all of this too, as well as the most current specials. You can print out an order form, but you still have to phone or mail in your order if using the website. Savings at Soccer International average about 20% less than some of the other "discounters" I price checked.

APO/FPO readers, please note: Orders are not shipped to APO/FPO addresses during November or December.

Institutional buyers, please note: Catalog prices are mainly for single items, but Soccer International's specialty is sales to teams, leagues, clubs, and schools. If you're buying in multiples for a group, let the company know when you request the catalog.

SPECIAL FACTORS: Minimum order is $15; shipping is not charged on orders over $35 sent within the contiguous U.S.; quantity pricing available.

Spike Nashbar, Inc.

4111 Simon Rd., Dept. WBM   **800–SPIKE–IT**
Youngstown, OH 44512   **Fax: 800–456–1223**

Catalog: free
Pay: check, MO, MC, V, DSC
Sells: volleyball gear and apparel
Store: same address (Nashbar Outlet Store); call
  330–782–2244 for hours
Online: www.spikenashbar.com

Spike Nashbar, established in 1990, has competition volleyball gear, clothing, and accessories, and offers deals on some items if you buy in quantity or select from the "special buys" merchandise available in limited quantities and sizes. The 32-page color catalog has nets and balls for indoor and outdoor play, volleyball pumps, indoor and outdoor clothing and undergarments for men and women, shoes, kneepads, wraps and braces, sunglasses, and volleyball-related books, videos, novelties, and jewelry. Spike Nashbar will custom print, embroider, and number your team's logo onto clothing. And don't miss the website—you can order a print catalog, order from the online catalog, or check the closeouts and bargains while you're there. This company offers a lowest price guarantee.

SPECIAL FACTORS: Satisfaction is guaranteed; quantity discounts are available; returns are accepted for exchange, refund, or credit.

Virtual Fairway

26581 San Torini Road   948–348–6947
Mission Viejo, CA 92692   Fax: 948–348–6967

Information: website only, no print catalog
Pay: check, MO, V, MC
Sells: used golf balls
Store: mail order only
Online: www.virtual-fairway.com

Sometimes the simplest, least complicated things in life are the best. Virtual Fairway is just such a company. Three years ago Cindy Carpino and her husband started a business so that Cindy could be a working mom at home with their children. Her husband, a golf fanatic, came up with the idea of a company that would sell nothing but used golf balls over the web, and the rest of the story is a happy one for both the Carpinos and their satisfied customers.

Golf balls are expensive. Period. And quality, high-grade, used golf balls at 50% less than they cost brand new is the solution. For low-handicap and scratch golfers, used golf balls are great for practice. For mid- and high-handicap golfers as well as beginners, used golf balls will save money as you perfect your stroke. The inventory changes at Virtual Fairway, but past specials have included Titleist HP2 Distance balls at $10 a dozen and Precept EV Extra Distance balls at $11 a dozen. Among the selections were Top Flite Strata Tour (90 or 100) for $17/dozen, Wilson Titanium Spin (90 or 100) at $16/dozen, Titleist Professional (90 or 100) for $16/dozen, all the way down to Top Flite Hot XL ($8), AA Grade ($6), and A Grade ($3). The selection regularly features a half-dozen leading brands in a spectrum of choices. If the prices don't snag you, the e-letters from happy Virtual Fairway customers from all over the world will. Whether you're golf-obsessed or merely a novice, this is an address you'll want to visit. Virtual Fairway offers 10% off if you order 200 dozen, but the prices are already deeply discounted. You can order by phone, fax, mail, or right on the site.

SPECIAL FACTORS: Satisfaction is guaranTEED; special orders welcomed.

Water Warehouse

6950 51st St.
Kenosha, WI 53144

800–574–7665
Fax: 414–605–1080

Catalog: $2
Pay: check, MO, MC, V, DSC
Sells: swimming pool supplies and equipment
Store: mail order only
Online: www.waterwarehouse.com

"America's Swimming Pool Experts," in business for more than 30 years, carry not only the pool equipment and chemicals you'd expect, but also innovative products such as solar blankets (guaranteed for six years), Kreepy Krauly's automatic cleaners and Arneson's Aqua Critter, high-rate sand filter systems, and pool alarms. Water Warehouse guarantees that their prices are lowest. Whether your pool is in-ground or aboveground, standard or custom-size, in a one-season or four-season climate, Water Warehouse has the necessary sanitizing chemicals, algaecides, test kits, water purifiers, and floating chlorinators (in decorative duck, swan, and turtle designs). If you don't yet have a pool, you're invited to consult by phone with knowledgeable staff about a variety of Muskin above-ground pools including the family-size portable SimPool, do-it-yourself in-ground pool kits, and any other pool-related questions, especially those pertaining to custom and install-it-yourself pools (call the custom hotline, 800–574–7946, for free measuring installation packet, how-to video, price sheet, and installation guide). Shop the Water Warehouse for diving boards, aquatic exercise equipment and games, pumps, liners—everything but the water! By the way, the website was under construction at press time, but promised to offer web-only discounts and online shopping.

SPECIAL FACTORS: Satisfaction guaranteed; returns accepted within 30 days.

World Wide Aquatics

Dept. WBM
10500 University Center Dr.,
Ste. 295
Tampa, FL 33612-6462

800-726-1530
813-972-0818
Fax: 813-972-0905

Catalog: free, $2 outside U.S.
Pay: check, MO, MC, V, AE, DSC
Sells: swimwear and accessories
Store: mail order only
Online: www.worldwideaquattics.com

Since 1972, World Wide Aquatics has been the mail-order source for competitive swimmers, triathletes, water aerobics and water exercisers, fitness swimmers, water polo players, lifeguards and all other water enthusiasts! The catalog presents products by Speedo, Kie, Tyr, Dolfin, Plus, Ocean Pool, Hind, Aquajogger, Danskin, Ironman, Competitor, Mikasa, Zura, Hyro-Fit, Ocean, Quintana Roo, and others at supercompetitive prices. Here you'll find swimsuits, trunks, shorts, cover-ups, pool equipment, swim caps, goggles, fins, kickboards, triathlon gear, and fitness gear for men and women. Women's sizes run to 24, with a post-mastectomy line available; men's to 40-inch waist. Children's suits are also available. Books and additional equipment are also available. For multiple orders on suits, as for a swim team, greater discounts are offered, so call or consult the catalog for details. The website features a full online catalog with electronic ordering, a free e-newsletter, a water sports library, clearance corner, and more. Check it out.

SPECIAL FACTORS: Satisfaction guaranteed; except for books and videos, new, unused items with hang tags and labels attached are accepted for return (in original packaging) for exchange, refund, or credit.

Related Products/Companies

Archery supplies
• Bowhunters Warehouse

Auto-racing safety equipment and gear
• Racer Wholesale

Biking shorts
• No Nonsense Direct

Boats, boat clothing and shoes, and boating supplies
- Defender Industries

Boxing equipment
- Better Health Fitness, Fitness Factory Outlet

Car racks for kayaks, canoes, skis, surfboards, etc.
- Car Racks Direct

Children's snowboard and ski equipment and clothing
- Campmor

Equestrian sports gear
- State Line Tack

Exercise equipment
- Damark, J&R Music

Fitness and exercise equipment
- Better Health Fitness, Creative Health Products, Fitness Factory Outlet

Folding bicycles
- Aircraft Spruce

Gymnastics shoes and dancewear
- Dance Distributors

Leather duffels and sports bags
- Al's Luggage, Leather Unlimited

Left-handed golf and baseball equipment
- The Left Hand

Miscellaneous sporting equipment
- Bennett Brothers

Muscle-relief balms, athletic endurance enhancers
- East Earth Trade Winds

Playground equipment
- Better Health Fitness

Pool covers
- Bob's Superstrong Greenhouse Plastic, Defender Industries

Saddlery supplies
- State Line Tack, Weaver Leather

Sheepskin bicycle seats
- Sheepskin Station

Ski gloves
- Cook Brothers

Snow and ski equipment
- Sierra Trading Post

Snowmobiles and ATVs
- Manufacturer's Supply

Sports bras
- The Smart Saver

Sport-themed belt buckles
- Leather Unlimited

Swimwear
- Lady Grace, The Ultimate Outlet

Camping, Hunting, and Survival

This section is for people who enjoy camping, fishing, hiking, wilderness back-packing, and hunting. The companies in this section have everything one needs for outdoor living and survival, from camp stoves and heavy-duty rain tarps to brush-clearing machetes and state-of-the-art bows and arrows. There are some truly wonderful deals on camping equipment and surplus goods, up to 70% off in some cases. If you're uninspired as a city slicker, you should be able to gear up and turn into Daniel Boone in no time.

Find It Fast

Hunting Supplies
- Bowhunters Warehouse, Cheap Shot, Cutlery Shoppe, The Sportsman's Guide, Wiley Outdoor Sports

Camping and Survival Gear and Equipment
- Campmor, Cutlery Shoppe, Don Gleason's, Sierra Trading Post, The Sportsman's Guide, Wiley

Outdoor Clothing
- Bowhunters Warehouse, Campmor, Sierra Trading Post, The Sportsman's Guide, Wiley Outdoor Sports

Bowhunters Discount Warehouse, Inc.

1045 Ziegler Rd.   800–306–2697
P.O. Box 158   717–432–8611
Wellsville, PA 17365   Fax: 717–432–2683

Catalog: free
Pay: check, MO, MC, V, DSC
Sells: equipment for bow-hunting, hunting, and archery
Store: same address; Monday, Wednesday, and Friday
  10–8, Tuesday and Thursday 10–6, Saturday 10–4
Online: www.bowhunterswarehouse.com

If you automatically equate hunting with firearms, think again. There's a whole culture of hunting aficionados out there who prefer state-of-the-art bows and arrows to guns. And if you're one of these sportsmen, Bowhunters Warehouse, in business since 1974, is your kind of place, offering a wide selection of archery supplies and related gear at "the best possible price." Monthly specials listed at the website (where there's no online ordering) as well as a page of hundreds of sale items in each catalog puts shopping here right on target.

The 192-page color catalog offers bows (compound, traditional, compound youth, longbows, recurves, and take-down bows), arrows and shafts—custom-built to your specifications if you like, as well as arrow-building supplies, and everything else you can think of related to the sport of bow-hunting. This includes arrow rests, camo clothing (for adults and children), quivers, sights, tree stand accessories, wrist slings, computer software, videos, books, and more. Bowhunters Warehouse serves as agent for selected outfitters, whose ads for African safaris, Idaho bear treks, and Maryland turkey hunts in the back of the catalog will quickly transport you into the bowhunter's world and mind-set.

SPECIAL FACTORS: A $10 minimum applies, $75 minimum for international customers; authorized returns accepted; C.O.D. orders accepted.

Campmor

P.O. Box 700   800–230–2151
Saddle River, NJ 07458–0700   201–445–5000

Catalog: free
Pay: check, MO, MC, V, AE, DSC
Sells: camping gear and supplies
Store: 810 Rt. 17 N., Paramus, NJ; Monday to Friday
  9:30–9:30, Saturday 9:30–6, closed Sunday
Online: www.campmor.com

Since 1978 savvy mail-order shoppers have turned to Campmor for savings up to 50% on gear and equipment for outdoor activities and recreation. You'll be thrilled to know that when I did a price comparison with another major camping discounter recently on backpacks, tents, and sleeping bags, Campmor came out way ahead on all three. Most of the offerings in the 240-page newsprint catalog cater to the needs of campers, hikers, and backpackers of all ages, with special sections for "kids" (for example, children's outerwear and snowboard and ski accessories). You'll find major manufacturers represented even in the super-discount sections of the catalog and website, with items such as packs (back, fanny, day, dog, internal and external frame), boots and snowshoes, fleece clothing, underwear, rain wear, hats and balaclavas, and gloves and mitts. Equipment is plentiful, including compasses, first aid/wilderness medicine kits, lanterns, flashlights, stoves, cook sets, water filters and purifiers, and watches. You'll also find tents, sleeping bags, inflatables, mountain racks, reflective vests, flotation pet vests, antifog lens cleaner, a portable urinal, and an assortment of survival items (survival cards, waterproof matches, ten-mile signal mirror, 120-hour candles). What's so delightful about this catalog, in addition to the informative line drawings and detailed product specifications, are the unusual products and savings tucked in among the major items. For example, among children's fleece clothing in a recent review catalog were two items: *How Come?*, a book that answers a child's most frequently asked questions, and a 50%-off closeout offer on Bell Traverse Pro helmets.

The website boasts a catalog of more than 10,000 items and Web Specials priced below catalog prices (you must mention the website to get the lower price when you call). Past specials have included men's and women's turtlenecks, infant fleece booties, a folding armchair, and snowshoes. Additional savings are available by clicking on Products of the Week and Hot Deals, where name-brand manufacturers offer drastically reduced items. The links to related sites are broad and useful, covering parks and recreation, outdoor organizations and clubs, and outdoor magazines available on the Internet. To receive up-to-the-minute sale and new-product information, sign up for Campmor's TrailMail.

SPECIAL FACTORS: Returns accepted for exchange, refund, or credit; $20 minimum order on credit cards; institutional purchase orders accepted (minimum order $200); additional discounts available for nonprofit organizations.

Cheap Shot, Inc.

P.O. Box 685
1797 Rt. 980
Canonsburg, PA 15317

724–745–2658
Fax: 724–745–4265

Catalog: free
Pay: check or MO
Sells: ammunition
Store: Gun Runner, 950 S. Central Ave., Canonsburg, PA;
   Monday to Friday 8–8, Saturday 8–5, Sunday 10–4

You can shop a hunting catalog for ammunition, but Cheap Shot, Inc.'s discounts will be better. Cheap Shot, a volume buyer, specializes in ammo and reloading components (no neon vests or thermal gloves here). The slim catalog, from "shooters serving shooters since 1976," tells you all you need to know about savings (33% and up off customary prices), building a "reloading library," and meeting federal regulations for the purchase of ammunition.

SPECIAL FACTORS: Authorized returns accepted; with a 25% deposit, C.O.D. orders accepted.

Cutlery Shoppe

390 E. Corporate Dr.   **800–231–1272**
P.O. Box 610   **208–884–7500**
Meridian, ID 83680–0610   **Fax: 208–884–7575**

Catalog: free
Pay: check, MO, MC, V, AE, DSC
Sells: cutlery, knives, sharpeners, etc.
Store: same address
Online: www.cutleryshoppe.com

I don't think there's a person reading this who won't find something to love in the Cutlery Shoppe's current catalog. This company specializes in knives—sport, military, kitchen, self-defense, and survival. Besides high-quality knives there are lots of tools and neat gadgets here as well. And you'll like the discounts, which run as high as 35% on many items.

The well-designed, 64-page color catalog features photographs and descriptive text of items that appeal to a wide range of people, from chefs to survivalists, from old-time whittlers to jungle explorers, from Navy SEALs to handimen. The Cutlery Shoppe also sells flashlights, self-defense items such as pepper spray that fits on your key chain, Leatherman Super Tools, Swiss army knives, knife sharpeners of every type and description, kitchen utensils, and more. I really appreciate companies that specialize in one type of product—and do it right. The new website offers ordering by e-mail, and at press time was in the process of being greatly expanded. A print catalog of only kitchen knives was being created at press time also, so stay tuned.

Please note: Consult your local ordinances regarding the purchase, possession, and use of weaponry and personal-protection devices.

SPECIAL FACTORS: Satisfaction guaranteed; volume discounts available; returns accepted within 30 days for exchange, refund, or credit.

Don Gleason's Campers Supply, Inc.

9 Pearl St., P.O. Box 87   413–584–4895
Northampton, MA 01061–0087   Fax: 413–586–8770

Catalog: free
Pay: check, MO, MC, V, DSC
Sells: camping supplies and equipment
Store: same address; Monday to Friday 9–5:30, Thursday
    9–8:30, Saturday 9–5
Online: www.gleasoncamping.com

Don Gleason's Campers Supply is a family-owned business started in 1958 by Don, and run today by sons John and Dan Gleason. This company has one of the largest selections of family camping, backpacking, and hiking equipment. Their prices are comparable to other camping discounters, but what I really liked here beyond the good value was the selection. In addition to the usual tents; tarps; sleeping pads, mattresses, and bags; camp furniture; camping equipment such as stoves and lanterns; and backpacks—all from top-name manufacturers—Don Gleason's carries unusual and hard-to-find items: a pocket knife sharpener, an inflatable sink, safety fork for campfire roasting (the sharp prongs point safely toward the handle), fold-up trip kits, and a waterproof outdoor notebook among them. The 64-page black-and-white catalog reminded me of an old-fashioned general store, with lots of goodies tucked in the back on closely printed pages with line-drawn illustrations. Lest you think everything here is old-fashioned, including the family's commitment to good service, check out the website, where you'll find lots of products of the week, web bargains, and hot deals, in addition to full online ordering from the extensive electronic catalog that's state-of-the-art and easy to use.

Special Factors: Satisfaction guaranteed; quantity discounts available; returns accepted for exchange, refund, or credit; minimum order $10 with credit card.

Sierra Trading Post

5025 Campstool Rd., Dept.
WBM
Cheyenne, WY 82007-1802

307–775–8000
Fax: 307–775–8088

Catalog: free
Pay: check, MO, MC, V, DSC
Sells: outdoor clothing and equipment
Store: same address; Monday to Saturday 9–6, Sunday
   12–6; also 2000 Harvard Way, Reno, NV; Monday to
   Saturday 10–7, Sunday 11–5
Online: www.sierratradingpost.com

Since 1986, Sierra Trading Post has been buying the best clothing, footwear, outerwear, and home furnishings from name-brand manufacturers at low overstock, closeout, and irregular prices so catalog shoppers can enjoy 35% to 70% savings off retail prices. Quantities on all products are, understandably, limited, so Sierra encourages phone orders since orders are filled on a first-come, first-served basis. Greatest savings come under the Super Clearance category, which is a boxed item appearing at the bottom of some pages. For example, in a recent catalog a first-quality Aussie merino wool bush pant in limited sizes retailing for $135 sold for $19.95. A lined denim chore coat that regularly would sell for $65 was available for $25. Sierra's inventory of high-quality clothing, outdoor gear, and home furnishings includes terry-cloth robes, cotton boxer shorts, combed-cotton underwear, socks in various fibers, Polartec outerwear, Tekware henleys, down parkas, down comforters, dress wool slacks, cashmere scarves, adult and kids' snowshoes, ski goggles, winter sports boots, and Gore-Tex pants and bibs. The offerings change frequently, so begin receiving your seasonal catalogs and start saving. Or log on to the website, which has an extensive online catalog, really fantastic deals, and online ordering as well.

SPECIAL FACTORS: Satisfaction guaranteed; insured, prepaid returns accepted for exchange or refund.

The Sportsman's Guide

411 Farwell Ave., Dept. WBM   800–888–3006
So. St. Paul, MN 55075–0239   Fax: 800–333–6933

Catalog: free
Pay: check, MO, MC, V, AE, DSC
Sells: outdoor clothing and footwear, hunting and
    camping gear, military surplus, etc.
Store: mail order only
Online: www.sportsmansguide.com

For more than 20 years, The Sportsman's Guide, brainchild of Gary Olen, has been selling outdoor gear (and plenty of indoor products) at prices 68% below what others sell it for. New items receive deep discounts from the get-go, close-outs are priced even lower, and special buys do better than closeouts. If you join the Buyer's Club ($29.99) for one year you save an additional 10% and receive notice of special Members Only bargains. What could The Sportsman's Guide have for you? How about thermal underwear, flannel-lined denim shirt, Thinsulate swampwalker boots, handheld CB radio, women's Crystal Lake Pac boots, women's Timberland leather slip-ons, and side-zip boots available in big and wide sizes. Inventory holdings vary with each shipment so one time you might catch a deal on a tree stand or a reconditioned Harmon Kardon surround-sound receiver and new Sherwood six-speaker system, and another, luck into some Ray-Ban X-Rays sport sunglasses. There's a tempting section of government surplus gear and clothing with specials on such items as new British military tennis shoes, West German military issue parkas with removable pile liner, and French military issue hip bags. You can't predict what The Sportsman's Guide will offer you next—which is why it's called "The Fun to Read Catalog"—but you can always count on low prices. The website is every bit as much fun as the catalog, with more than 2,500 products and "Deals of the Day," as well as online ordering capability.

SPECIAL FACTORS: Satisfaction guaranteed; returns accepted for exchange, credit, or refund; see catalog for restrictions on ordering and shipping of certain goods.

Wiley Outdoor Sports, Inc.

P.O. Box 99, Dept. WBM
Decatur, AL 35602

800–494–5397
256–382–2553
Fax: 256–837–4017

Catalog: free
Pay: check, MO, MC, V, DSC
Sells: hunting, camping, and outdoor gear and equipment
Store: 1808 Sportsman Lane, Huntsville, AL; Monday to
   Friday 9–6, Saturday 9–4:30
Online: www.wileyoutdoorsports.com

Since 1953, hunters have relied on Wiley Outdoor Sports, Inc., for a full range of outfitting gear and equipment at savings that run 30% on certain lines. Today's hunter or outdoorsman can access detailed product, pricing, and online ordering information at Wiley's website, which features extensive listings by product and manufacturer's name. Pop-up menus make browsing and ordering simple.

Wiley sells optics (binoculars, spotting scopes, rifle slings, telescopes, and night-vision products such as infrared illuminators and lens accessories), hunting equipment (archery, knives, ammunition, firearms), camping gear and equipment, boy scout gear, outerwear for men, women, and children, outdoor sports equipment (fishing, paddlesports), and footwear—all from top-name manufacturers. "Red Moose Specials" are a regular feature here, with some of the best deals on overstocks, closeouts, new product specials, and general good deals.

SPECIAL FACTORS: Satisfaction guaranteed; unused returns accepted within ten days for exchange, refund, or credit; minimum order $25; C.O.D. orders (UPS only) accepted.

Related Products/Companies

Black powder supplies
- Leather Unlimited

Child-friendly outdoor recreation and vacation guides
- The Family Travel Guides Catalog

Extra-large fanny packs
- Amplestuff

Fishing gear
- Bennett Brothers

Gun safes
- Discount Safe Outlet

Hunting and camping gear
- ChuckWagon Outfitters, Mass. Army & Navy, RV Direct

Kitchen and cooking equipment for camping
- RV Direct

Mosquito netting, gun-cleaning cloths, sleeping bag liners
- Clothcrafters, Gohn Bros., Newark Dress Supply

RV equipment
- RV Direct

Snowshoes
- Lehman's

Swiss army knives
- Ace Luggage, Lens Express

Tarps and tent-floor liners
- Bob's Superstrong Greenhouse Plastic, RV Direct

Telescopes, binoculars, spotting scopes, etc.
- Ewald Clark, Mardiron Optics, Orion Telescope

Weather instruments
- Mardiron

Wineskins
- Leather Unlimited

Woodsman tools
- Bailey's

Y2K nonelectric appliances and supplies of every kind
- Lehman's

Zippers for tents and sleeping bags
- The Button Shop, A. Feibusch, Newark Dressmaker Supply

Tools, Hardware, and Shop Machines

*Hand, power, and
machine-shop tools,
machine parts, hardware,
and related supplies*

If power tools are to grown-ups what toys are to kids, then this chapter will make you happy. The firms here offer the do-it-yourselfer, woodworker, hobbyist, woodsman, professional machine-shop worker, and small-time mechanic a wealth of hand and power tools, hardware and parts, electronics and abrasives, and heavy-duty machinery—much of it at rock-bottom prices. Here you'll find replacement parts for lawnmowers, trimmers, garden tractors, snowmobiles, snow throwers, blowers, go-carts, and minibikes. The tools run from hex wrenches and fine wood chisels to complete work benches and professional machinery, and the hardware includes hard-to-find specialty items as well as nuts and bolts. There are even plumbing and electrical supplies here. See "Related Products/Companies" at chapter's end for other firms that also carry tools and various hardware-store items.

Find It Fast

Abrasives and Related Tools
- Econ-Abrasives, Red Hill Corporation

Hardware, Tools, and Machines
- William Alden, Camelot Enterprises, Coastal Tool, Enco Manufacturing, Harbor Freight Tools, Northern Hydraulics, Tool Crib of the North, Tools on Sale, Wholesale Tool, Woodworker's Hardware, Woodworker's Supply

Hobbyist Tools
- William Alden, Hot Tools, Micro-Mark, Tool Crib of the North, Wholesale Tool, Woodworker's Supply

Machine Parts
- Manufacturer's Supply

Online Auction of Tools and Machines
- Harbor Freight Tools

Surplus Electronics Components, Tools
- All Electronics, H&R Company

Tool-Building Manuals
- Poor Man's Catalog

Woodcutter/Logger Equipment and Supplies
- Bailey's, Manufacturer's Supply, Northern Hydraulics

William Alden Company

27 Stuart St.	**Tel/Fax: 800–249–8665**
Boston, MA 02116	**Tel/Fax: 508–824–1259**

Catalog: free
Pay: check, MO, MC, V, AE, DSC
Sells: tools for contractors, woodworkers, general handy
 work
Store: mail order only; phone 24 hours, seven days a week
Online: www.williamalden.com

Woodworkers, contractors, do-it-yourselfers, take note: William Alden Company has first-quality tools and equipment from leading manufacturers at "super-low prices." What does this mean? It means that you can buy certain products at 25% to 35% below list, or as the catalog brags, "We sell retail at wholesale prices."

The 180-page color catalog has everything one needs to equip a professional or home workshop: generators, planers, saws, sanders, routers, drill presses, power tools, work tables, measurers, levels, wet-dry vacs—you name it. The hobbyist will find wood-burning tools, hand chisels, miniature woodworking tools, and other necessities for doing fine, detailed work. But there's lots here for the average home putterer as well, such as garden tools, compost bins, hand tools, safety equipment, tarps, wood-finishing products, woodworking project plans, and more. I liked the collection of books on everything from making birdhouses and wooden toys to restoring Victorian furniture and designing ergonomic kitchens. The website, by the way, has great specials and also features online ordering.

SPECIAL FACTORS: Satisfaction guaranteed; returns accepted within 30 days for exchange, refund, or credit; 24-hour order line; orders shipped within 24 hours.

All Electronics Corp.

P.O. Box 567, Dept. WBM   800–826–5432
Van Nuys, CA 91408–0567   818–904–0524
                            Fax: 818–781–2653

Catalog: free, $5 outside the U.S.
Pay: check, MO, MC, V, AE, DSC
Sells: surplus electronics and tools
Store: 905 S. Vermont Ave., Los Angeles, CA; Monday to
    Friday 9–5, Saturday 9–4; also 14928 Oxnard St., Van
    Nuys, CA; Monday to Friday 9–6:30, Saturday 9–5
Online: www.allcorp.com

If you're an electronics nerd and want to get your hands on such items as a geophone vibration sensor, a 110-watt switching supply, a socket connector, a miniature bullet camera, or a deluxe crimp tool, you've just found a great resource. Inventors, technicians, and hobbyists will find all sorts of treasures here for making robotics, building computers, repairing antique radios, restoring electric trains, creating remote-control toys—in short, any project that requires common and hard-to-find electronic devices. All Electronics has been offering new and pre-owned electronics for over 30 years, keeping pace with the ever-changing needs of technology. If you're a web shopper, check out the reader-friendly website, which features the current specials, product photographs and descriptions, and online ordering. Keep in mind that because much of the stock is surplus, the products are always changing.

SPECIAL FACTORS: Satisfaction is guaranteed; returns accepted within 30 days of receipt in original condition for a full refund or exchange.

Bailey's

44650 Hwy. 101

P.O. Box 550

Laytonville, CA 95454

800–322–4539

Fax: 707–984–8115

Catalog: free, $6 outside U.S.
Pay: check, MO, MC, V, AE, DSC
Sells: "woodsman" supplies
Store: same address; Monday to Friday 7–6, Saturday
   8–1; also 196 Edwards Dr., Jackson, TN; Monday to
   Friday 7–6, Saturday 8–1
Online: www.bbaileys.com

Bailey's bills itself as "The World's Largest Mail Order Woodsman Supplies Company—Selling at Discounted Prices." While it may not be the fanciest motto, you won't hear the lumberjacks, log-home builders, and chain-saw guys loyal to this company complaining. Thumbing through the 100-page color catalog transported me into a different world, a world where Wild Ass Tin Pants, chain grinders, tree saddles, and competition throwing axes are everyday items. The serious woodsman will find all types of chain saws and related parts, equipment, and accessories; logging tools and gear; fire-fighting equipment; forest management supplies; and of course a complete selection of outdoor clothing and boots designed for safety and durability for rough-hewn types. The catalog also offers books and videos on everything from tying knots to tree-climbing techniques, as well as themed gift items and real wood business cards. Bailey's good prices are further discounted if you buy in quantity. The website features online ordering of selected products.

SPECIAL FACTORS: Satisfaction guaranteed; authorized returns accepted within 90 days of receipt (see catalog for details).

Since 1983 Camelot Enterprises has been selling "quality fasteners, hardware, and tools direct to the craftsman" at savings of up to 60%. The 32-page catalog is jam-packed with garage and workshop necessities such as a full range of nuts (hex, K-lock, wing, stop, etc.), bolts (hexhead, machine, carriage), screws (wood, lag, drywall, machine), washers, grease fittings, turnbuckles, eyebolts, solderless electrical terminals, cotter pins, anchors, and other hardware. And you don't have to buy by the pound to get wholesale prices—Camelot packages the hardware in counts of 10, 25, 50, 100, etc. Camelot's tools include screwdrivers, punches, air tools, pliers, snips, rasps, and other hand and power tools for hobbyists and machinists by major manufacturers. Shop equipment, Excalibur fastener sets, Marson pop rivets, and Camelot's own twist drills and fasteners are also sold at competitive prices.

Wholesale buyers, please note: If your business is in Illinois, Indiana, or Wisconsin, you must provide a copy of your resale certificate to buy wholesale from Camelot.

SPECIAL FACTORS: Satisfaction guaranteed; price quote by letter only; returns accepted within ten days for replacement, refund, or credit.

Coastal Tool & Supply

248 Sisson Ave.
Hartford, CT 06105

860–233–8213
Fax: 860–233–6295

Catalog: free
Pay: check, MO, MC, V, AE, DSC
Sells: hand, power, and air tools
Store: same address (Exit 46 off I–84); Monday to Friday
8–5, Saturday 8–4
Online: www.coastaltool.com

Proclaiming "power tools, air tools, hand tools at everyday low, low, discount prices," the 32-page, jam-packed catalog from Coastal Tool draws you in like a cluttered warehouse filled with bargains. All merchandise here is brand new and first quality, in the original factory packaging with factory warranties, yet priced up to 50% less than you'd pay retail. Because Coastal's customers range from state agencies to professional builders to home woodworkers, the staff people are used to fielding a wide range of requests. Call them if you don't see what you're looking for in the catalog, or visit the website, where you'll find over 500 power tools you can order online, a free factory service locator, an e-newsletter you can subscribe to, and "Tool Doctor," who can answer your toughest power tool questions.

SPECIAL FACTORS: Satisfaction guaranteed; returns (in condition received) are accepted for exchange, refund, or credit.

Econ-Abrasives

P.O. Box 1628, Dept. WBM   800–367–4101
Frisco, TX 75034   972–335–9234
                             Fax: 972–377–2248

Catalog: free
Pay: check, MO, MC, V, DSC
Sells: abrasives and related products
Store: mail order only

If you only need sandpaper once in a while, you can stick to shopping at your local hardware store. But when volume purchases of sanding belts, sheets, blocks and disc bases, and drums are in order, Econ-Abrasives can save you money on its mail-order line of industrial-grade abrasives for home and professional use. The free 32-page catalog is chock-full of data on product materials, specifications, and uses; and since Econ manufactures what it sells—if the grit you need, for example, doesn't appear in the catalog—Econ can make it for you. The company also carries specially shaped forms for sanding crevices, recesses, turnings, and the like. You can also order handheld scrapers, router and drill bits, wood chisels, sanding wheels, steel wool, safety gear, and many more sanding-related products. In case you're embarking on a new aspect of woodworking or using a new tool, the catalog provides a glossary of common abrasive terms and suggestions for the best tools for different jobs.

SPECIAL FACTORS: Price quotes by phone or letter; $25 minimum on orders using credit cards.

Enco Manufacturing Company

5000 W. Bloomingdale Ave.,   **800–USE–ENCO**
Dept. WBM   **Fax: 800–965–5857**
Chicago, IL 60639

Catalog: free
Pay: check, MO, MC, V, DSC
Sells: machining tools and hardware
Store: same address; also 12 locations in AZ, CA, FL, GA,
   IL, MN, OH, TX, and WA (see catalog for locations or call
   800–873–3626)
Online: www.use-enco.com

Enco Manufacturing Company, in business over 56 years, grew from a tiny manu-facturer of lathe accessories into one of the largest industrial distributors of name-brand tools in the United States. And yet among the thousands of products in the 500-page catalog, many are suitable for home owners, amateur woodworkers or hobbyists, artists—basically anyone who needs easy-to-handle portable power tools or has a shop where whey can set up more heavy-duty items such as sand-blasters. Savings between 30% and 50% off list price are common, with the best prices available on Enco's own line of products.

The product index, a whopping ten pages long, kicks off with abrasives, air tools, and arbors, rolls into blades, calipers, and clamps, dives into dust-collector accessories, fasteners, and gauges, and barrels full speed through micrometers, pliers, safety gear, and sheet metal equipment—with many products to be discov-ered. Enco's centralized Parts Department can ship most parts from stock, and Enco's reference library carries handbooks and multivolume titles on subjects ranging from blueprint-reading to rapid automated prototyping to harnessing the power of AutoCAD. With 13 branches, Enco automatically routes your call to the nearest location, and undoubtedly has the large or small items you need for indus-try or home.

SPECIAL FACTORS: Quantity discounts and institutional accounts available; C.O.D. orders accepted; minimum order $25.

H&R Company

16 Roland Ave.
Mount Laurel, NJ 08054-1012

609-802-0422
Fax: 609-802-0465

Catalog: $5/year's subscription, refundable
Pay: check, MO, MC, V, DSC
Sells: new and surplus electromechanical, robotic, and
optical components
Store: mail order only
Online: www.herbach.com

If you've got an imagination, H&R (Herbach & Rademan) Co.'s 112-page catalog will spark it. Established in 1934, this company sells a fascinating mix of surplus bargains—chiefly electronics, robotics, scientific equipment, optics, and mechanical devices. Past catalogs have featured power supplies, CCTV cameras, monitors, switchers, stepper motors, security equipment, gear-head motors, blowers, synchronous motors, robotic kits and components, relays and contactors, compressors, instruments and tools, transformers, magnets, laser devices, switches, infrared devices, timers, motion detectors, heating and cooling devices, and lots more. Even if you're not a mad scientist, electronics nerd, or genius inventor, there's lots of stuff here anyone, electromechanically inclined or not, can use: microscopes, wire strippers, educational kits, phone accessories, digital scales, heavy-duty outlet strips and surge suppressers, model trains and cars, goggles, compasses, cabinet slides, parts bins, tool cases and cabinets, battery chargers, inkjet printers, weather balloons, and reference books on technical topics. H&R also runs closeout and "grab bag" sales—and will purchase large quantities of your surplus current, quality electromechanical components, optics, relays, computer peripheral devices, and other similar items. Smaller quantities of special items are also purchased. Call to inquire. The website, by the way, has featured products, the current closeouts, and allows you to download your order form and then call, fax, or mail in your order.

SPECIAL FACTORS: Satisfaction guaranteed; price quote by phone, fax, or letter; returns with original packing materials are accepted within 30 days; minimum order is $25, $50 on open account, $100 on orders outside the U.S. and Canada.

Harbor Freight Tools

3491 Mission Oaks Blvd.   800-444-3353
P.O. Box 6010   Fax: 800-905-5215
Camarillo, CA 93011

Catalog: free
Pay: check, MO, MC, V, AE, DSC
Sells: tools, hardware, industrial equipment, machinery
Store: same address; also 40 other locations in AZ, CA,
   KY, NV, OR, and UT
Online: www.harborfreight.com

Harbor Freight Tools can save you up to 70% off list prices on home tools and industrial equipment, machinery and hardware, and unexpected products that are the delight of seasoned catalog shoppers—namely, a 26-inch all-terrain adjustable-frame tricycle (with a rear tow hitch for pulling), kids' Big Foot and panel wagons, and a Victorian mailbox. Harbor Freight's reputation, however, has been built on equipment and accessories used in welding, woodworking, automotive work, and outdoor maintenance.

The catalog experience is akin to wandering through a hardware shop where you find something you need at every turn. Among the products featured in the 116-page color catalog are laser tools, air compressors, air fastening tools, concrete mixers, lawn and garden tractors, motors, pumps, storehouses, tarpaulins, power and hand tools, propane stoves, generators, and shop and safety equipment. Additional specials can be found at the website, which is really fun. It features, among other things, an online auction that invites shoppers to bid on hand and power tools, gardening equipment, and many other products; a clearance center; and online ordering of selected items in categories that include auto shop, metal shop, wood shop, painting supplies, great outdoors (camping equipment), recon shop (great deals on factory reconditioned items), and more. You can also place an order from your print catalog online. If you need another incentive to shop Harbor Freight, remember: Shipping is free on orders over $50.

SPECIAL FACTORS: Free shipping on orders over $50 delivered within continental U.S.

Hot Tools

P.O. Box 615   781–639–1000
Marblehead, MA 01945   Fax: 781–631–8887

Flyers: free
Pay: check, MO, V, MC
Sells: wood-burning tools and accessories
Store: mail order only
Online: www.mmnewman.com

If you're a sail-maker, kite smith, bird carver, or woodworking hobbyist, you're caught between a rock and a hard place when it comes to wood-burning tools and hot knives. You can go for the really cheap, handheld junkers that are available in craft shops, inexpensive but not made for heavy-duty use; or you can spring for the second tier—the sophisticated, professional versions that will set you back several hundred dollars. M. M. Newman, the parent company of Hot Tools, has solved this problem by creating and manufacturing affordable, high-quality wood-burners and passing the savings directly to the consumer without a middleman. Unlike the hobby-shop models, the Hot Tool has a generous 64-inch cord and slim design, is lightweight, has a handle that stays cool, and features a heat shield, slide-on changeable tips, and heating elements under the tip. When you call or fax Hot Tools (or contact them through their website), they'll send you several pages of flyers with photographs and detailed descriptions of their products. The Hot Tool with standard tip is priced at $29.95. You'll also find #8 needle tips, reshapable blank tips, feather tips, multigroove tips, and buttons tips, as well as circle and round tips from $^{1}/_{16}$ inch to $^{3}/_{16}$ inch—all for $4.95 each, except for the two multigroove tips ($11.49 each). The helpful text gives step-by-step instructions on how to carve realistic feathers and do other fine work.

Other offerings include a heavy-duty wood-burner that heats up to 1,050° F and sells for $45.95; a hot knife tip, blank tip, and standard tip for the heavy-duty model are $10.95 each. You'll also find the Hot Knife, intended for cutting and melting synthetic materials such as sailcloth, spinnaker cloth, indoor/outdoor carpeting, etc. It's $44.95, and its three tips (Hot Knife, blank, or standard) are $10.95 each. You'll find wood-burner stands, the Dial-Temp precision temperature controller, stencil-makers, a Lacquer Burn-In Knife ($30.95), library marking tools, metallic marking foils, and other items here. These tools are good values, great quality, and will last a long time. Wholesale prices are offered on purchases of 12 or more items; resale number is required for wholesale. The website is informational only; no online ordering is available.

SPECIAL FACTORS: Hot Tools will gladly replace any defective product; C.O.D. orders are accepted.

Manufacturer's Supply

P.O. Box 167, Dept. WBM   800–826–8563
Dorchester, WI 54425–0167   Fax: 800–294–4144

Catalog: free
Pay: check, MO, MC, V, DSC
Sells: replacement parts for chain saws, lawnmowers,
   snowmobiles, ATVs, minibikes, etc.
Store: mail order only
Online: www.mfgsupply.com

For 35 years Manufacturer's Supply has been a leading supplier of parts for all-terrain vehicles, chain-saw/harvester/logging equipment, go-karts and minibikes, lawnmowers, snowblowers, snowmobiles, trailers, harvesters, and all other kinds of small engines, at savings up to 50% off retail prices. The seemingly endless inventory has pretty much everything you need to get any motorized vehicle or power implement humming again. The beauty of shopping Manufacturer's Supply is that within the 200-plus pages of the catalog, at the website, and via phone, fax, and e-mail, you have access to parts and accessories by major manufacturers for every imaginable make and model. The award-winning website provides referrals to companies that carry go-karts and minibikes, provides snowmobile stud patterns and an installation guide, has a section where you can contribute your expertise to the FAQ pages, features online ordering, has product specifications and information, and much more. Definitely check it out.

SPECIAL FACTORS: Authorized returns (except special orders and electronic components) accepted within 30 days (10% restocking fee may apply); C.O.D. orders accepted; shipping $4.99, within contiguous U.S., except on freight shipments or special orders.

Micro-Mark

340–2314 Snyder Ave.   800–225–1066
Berkeley Heights, NJ   908–464–2984
07922–1595   Fax: 908–665–9383

Catalog: free
Pay: check, MO, MC, V, AE, DSC
Sells: model-building tools and supplies
Store: mail order only; phone hours Monday to Friday 9–5
EST
Online: www.micromark.com

If your hobby or profession is building models, making miniatures, toys, musical instruments, dolls, or other small-scale items, then you must check out Micro-Mark, "the Small Tool Specialists." Both selection and prices are great here, and if you're a web shopper, you'll love the convenience of shopping at home online. (There's also an excellent print catalog.) Micro-Mark sells over 2,500 tools and supplies at a discount—up to 40% off retail on adhesives, cleaners, and lubes; clamps, jigs, and specialty tools; electronic items, files and sanders; hand tools; kits; knives and cutters; measuring, marking, and vision products; model ship and railroad items; organizers and display cases; painting, weathering, and decaling tools; power tools and accessories; resin, wood, and metal; scenery; soldering and electrical supplies; and even books and videos. You'll also find special offers regularly posted on the website.

SPECIAL FACTORS: Wholesale rates to qualified individuals and businesses; satisfaction guaranteed; returns accepted within 30 days of receipt for refund or credit.

Northern Hydraulics Inc.

P.O. Box 1499, Dept. 24619
Burnsville, MN 55337–1499

800–533–5545
Fax: 612–894–0083

Catalog: free
Pay: check, MO, MC, V, DSC
Sells: do-it-yourself items, power tools, etc.
Store: 33 outlets in FL, GA, IA, MN, NC, SC, TN, TX, VA,
  and WI
Online: www.northern-online.com

Do-it-yourself items and power tools from Northern Hydraulics, Inc., are perfect for use by farms, garages, and rental stores, as well as in the home workshop and light industrial operations. The nearly 150-page catalog, with discounts up to 50%, features such heavy-duty machinery and equipment as gas engines; generators; painting, welding, and sandblasting equipment; hoists and presses; log splitters; hydraulic pumps; and tillers, mowers, and lawn tractors. Northern also sells air compressors and air tools, lawn and garden equipment (trimmers, cultivators, garden carts, blowers, sprayers), protective gear, and boating accessories. You'll find trailer parts, go-karts and parts, tires, casters and wheels, and such up-to-the-minute items as cordless phones, solar or electronic fences, and security lights and alarms—all discounted. At press time the website was informative and easy to use, and featured online ordering on a partial inventory that included pressure washers, generators, and small engines, with the promise that more products would be available online soon.

SPECIAL FACTORS: Authorized returns accepted for exchange, refund, or credit.

Poor Man's Catalog

7000 20th St., #930   **561–778–1807**
Vero Beach, FL 32966–8878

> Catalog: $1
> Pay: check, MO
> Sells: U-Build plans for power tools
> Store: mail order only

Every once in a while you discover someone out there offering something totally unique that's a real find. Poor Man's Catalog is just such a company. Johnny Blackwell, a mechanical wizard, has written scores of books and handbooks on low-cost tool-building and has been written up and praised by national media luminaries. The 28-page catalog is mind-boggling and made this baby boomer wish she were retired or had more time to tinker. Machinists and metal-workers take note: Building your own machines and power tools saves you between 50% and 90% off what the purchased item would cost! Every U-Build plan is designed for low-cost building in the home shop using mostly recycled materials. Among the eclectic selection of U-Build plans found in recent catalogs were a sheet metal brake, a vacuum dust collector for routers, a micrometer work holder for a bench grinder, an ARC-welding gun, an emergency power generator, air coolers, power saws, power sanders, wood-turning lathes, flood lights, photographic enlargers, a mulcher, a lawn trimmer, a fruit press—even a lie detector! There are also fun projects for the hobbyist, including a model boiler for any model steam engine, a replica of the 1832 Atlantic locomotive that runs under the power of a tiny perma-nent-magnet located in the boiler, and a Civil War Parrott rifle model.

The single-tool plans are inexpensive, ranging from $8 to $14. But you can order three for $19.95, six for $37.95, or ten for $56.95 (wonderful for educational institutions). There's also a six-page catalog of book offerings on subjects devoted to photographic equipment ("build everything from your own simple coffee-can camera that develops its own pictures, to a precision telephoto lens made from a piece of plumbing, and loads in between"), lawn and garden tools, woodworking tools and accessories, power sanders and accessories, and more. These subject books are more expensive than the U-Build plans ($34.95 for *Photographic Equip-ment,* for example), but very reasonable when you think of the alternative: taking an extension class or buying the equipment new.

SPECIAL FACTORS: Satisfaction guaranteed; quantity discounts available; extra postage applies on Canadian and overseas orders.

Red Hill Corporation

P.O. Box 4234
Gettysburg, PA 17325

800–822–4003
717–337–3038
Fax: 717–337–0732

Catalog: free
Pay: check, MO, MC, V
Sells: abrasives and refinishing products
Store: Supergrit Abrasives, 1540 Biglerville Rd.,
  Gettysburg, PA
Online: www.supergrit.com

Founded in 1978, Red Hill Corp. specializes in the gritty side of life: namely, abrasives of all kinds. Red Hill is able to pass great savings on to the customer by purchasing huge quantities of first-quality closeouts from manufacturers and distributors, and by scanning the inventory of manufacturers in 14 other countries to find the best deals. You'll reap savings of up to 50% here on flap wheels (great for irregular-shaped surfaces or for removing paint or rust); sanding gel (for removing fine scratches from nonporous surfaces); sanding sticks (for hard-to-get areas); discs of every size and description; paper rolls; buffing pads and bonnets; grinding discs; cloth shop rolls; sanding sheets; sand screen; scuffing pads; and much more. Whether you've got a heavy-duty, industrial-size job or fine work in your hobby shop, Red Hill will definitely have the product you're looking for in the 28-page color catalog. In addition, the catalog offers sander parts and accessories, auto-body refinishing products, masking tape, tack cloths, a stick for cleaning sanding belts when the grit gets clogged, a selection of glue guns and glue sticks, and more. The website shows current specials, but there's no online ordering.

SPECIAL FACTORS: Price quote by phone or letter on special order sizes; quantity discounts are available; minimum order $25; C.O.D. orders are accepted.

Tool Crib of the North

P.O. Box 14040
Grand Forks, ND 58208

800–358–3096
Fax: 800–343–4205

Catalog: free
Pay: check, MO, MC, V, DSC
Sells: tools and hardware
Store: Duluth, MN, and Fargo, Grand Forks, and Minot,
ND; see catalog for locations
Online: www.toolcribofthenorth.com

From a small motor repair shop in 1948, Tool Crib of the North has grown into five retail tool stores and a tool distribution center occupying 70,000 square feet, to serve the product needs of woodworkers, contractors, and do-it-yourselfers. Tool Crib works closely with manufacturers to maintain full-line product availability, stocking portable power tools and machines beyond those featured in the catalog. In addition to new tools, the 108-page color catalog offers limited-time specials on factory-reconditioned, fully warranted cordless saws, hammer drills, air compressors, belt sanders, portable planers, miter saws, electronic plunge routers, joiner kits, and framer's saws with the blade on the left (prices range from $15 to $100 off new). Products are categorized by manufacturer—Delta, Porter Cable, DeWalt, Bosch, Biesemeyer, Makita, Panasonic, Milwaukee, Powermatic, Hitachi, Jet, Freud, Jesada, Ryobi, Senco, and Fein—and function—pickup supplies, lighting, metal working, clamps, router tables and jigs, heaters, drywall tools, framers tools, and flooring, cutting, caulking, and door-hanging tools. The book selection is short but pithy, including *The Contractor's Legal Kit,* the 480-page *Pocket Ref* (with tables, charts and maps), and *Code Check: A Field Guide to Building a Safe House.* Not surprisingly, the website is as comprehensive as the print catalog, with the advantage of offering current specials and hot-selling items. There you can order online, search for products new or reconditioned, and request a print catalog.

SPECIAL FACTORS: Free shipping on orders over $500.

Tools on Sale

Seven Corners Hardware, Inc.
216 W. Seventh St.
St. Paul, MN 55102

612–224–4859
Fax: 612–224–8263

Catalog: free
Pay: check, MO, MC, V, AE, DSC
Sells: tools for contractors, masons, and woodworkers
Store: same address; Monday to Friday 7–5:30, Saturday
  8–1 CT
Online: www.7cornershdwe.com

The 520-page newsprint catalog from Tools on Sale, in business since 1933, doesn't have to be glitzy to be *very exciting*. Every page features six to eight products, illustrated by black-and-white photos, fully described, and clearly stating the manufacturer's name and the model number. The breathtaking part appears at the end of each item: a shocking difference between the list price and the sale price—up to 50% difference! Many items are further discounted, but require that you call for prices. This is all in keeping with Tools on Sale's philosophy: "We want to be your only source for the items that we sell." The folks at Tools on Sale are constantly negotiating with manufacturers to get you prices lower than anyone else's.

Designed to address the shopping needs of contractors, professional woodworkers, and hobbyists, the catalog includes well-placed page guides to related products. If you're shopping for a recipro saw, you'll be reminded, "for heavy cutting, use a 12 ga. extension cord found on pages 425–427," the kind of pointer a top-notch salesperson would offer. There's nothing you won't find here: glue bottles and mallets, pockethole jigs, saws (chop, chain, pull, circular, jig, miter, slide compound, worm drive, bench top, plus beam cutter attachments), blades (diamond, circular, Teflon coated, dado, metal cutting, carbide tipped), drills, Makita Quad-Drivers, Stabila and electronic levels, angle finders, insulated tools, vises, Master padlocks, and van and pickup truck racks. You'll also find a comprehensive guide to choosing the proper ladder (by duty rating), safety tips for optimal use of your selection, and advice for deciding among the many wood, aluminum, and fiberglass ladders. Tools on Sale has gone to such pains to anticipate a shopper's concerns that virtually every product question can be answered from the catalog, making shopping and ordering with confidence easy and simple. For in-depth study of tools, techniques, and machinery, there are 14 pages of books and a small selection of videos (15% off list prices; 20% off for three or more) that include Taunton's *Fine Homebuilding* series and many paperbacks amply illustrated with color photos. At the well-designed website you can order a print catalog, view many products, check out specials, and more—but there's no online product ordering.

SPECIAL FACTORS: Prepaid freight on orders shipped within the 48 contiguous U.S.; authorized returns accepted; institutional and government accounts available.

Wholesale Tool Co., Inc.

P.O. Box 68, Dept. WBM   810–754–9270
12155 Stephens Dr.   Fax: 810–754–8652
Warren, MI 48089

Catalog: free
Pay: check, MO, MC, V, DSC
Sells: tools, hardware, and machinery
Store: same address; also six other locations in FL, IN, MA,
   NC, OK, and TX; see catalog for locations
Online: www.wttool.com

Established in 1960, Wholesale Tool Co., Inc., publishes an 800-page easy-to-use catalog of industrial tools and supplies of value to the professional contractor, woodworker, and surveyor as well as the weekend handyperson. Here you'll find, at discount prices of about 30% off list, the usual roundup of name-brand tools (saws, drills, lathes, routers, drill presses, grinders, sanders, and air tools) and the supplies that go with them (blades, bits, pads, dies, spindles, wheels, back plates). In addition there are indicator and base sets, micrometers, tachometers, calipers (five pages), digital readout systems, indexable mills, mill accessories, deburring tools, tool holders, knurls, and knurling tools, reamers, countersinks, metric broaches, parts washers, sprayers, vacuums (wet/dry), coolant systems, skimmers, angle plates and tables, thread repair systems, phase converters, motors (single and three phase), torches, and welding equipment—a collection of products not often seen together in a catalog. The do-it-yourselfer or small business owner can count on Wholesale for socket sets, hammers, wrenches, pliers, power tools, abrasives, safety gear, casters and wheels (also in sets), drawer slides, storage bins, tool boxes, cleaning equipment, brooms, screwdrivers, staplers, magnets and demagnetizers, etching tools, tags and stencils, magnifiers, and automotive tools. For materials handling there are work positioners, portable electric lifts, light duty scissor lifts, post lift tables, machinery moving kits (to handle up to 60 tons), pallet trucks, hand trucks, drum stacking racks, dollies, utility carts, self-dumping hoppers, wheelbarrows, and crossover truck boxes for full-size trucks. The 12-page index is sure to list what you're looking for. If not, inquire by phone. The website lists manufacturers and product categories, but there's no online ordering.

SPECIAL FACTORS: Authorized returns accepted within 30 days (10% restocking fee may apply); minimum order $25.

Woodworker's Hardware

P.O. Box 180   800–383–0130
Sauk Rapids, MN 56379   Fax: 800–207–0180

Catalog: $3, refundable (see text)
Pay: check, MO, MC, V, DSC
Sells: cabinet and furniture hardware
Store: mail order only; phone hours September to April:
    Monday to Friday 8–8, Saturday 8–noon; May to August:
    Monday to Friday 8–5, closed Saturday

If today's homes and apartments serve our needs so well, a major reason is the hardware used on or in cabinets, dressers, computer tables, entertainment centers, and storage areas, the very hardware Woodworker's Hardware specializes in. The $3 cost of the 216-page catalog is offset by a $5 coupon good for your first purchase. The catalog offers more than 4,500 items including hinges, knobs, slides, pulls, latches, and supports. Woodworker's also carries specialty bins (wastebaskets that slide out of sight) and shelving, wire organizers, lazy susans, caddies, and items you might not expect but certainly could use such as keyboard trays, strip lighting, putties, fasteners, glue, and brass rail fittings. If you don't see what you need in the catalog, call for product availability and prices. Prices here are 20% below other woodworker's supply discounters.

SPECIAL FACTORS: Satisfaction guaranteed; prices quoted by phone or letter; quantity discounts available; authorized returns (unused, undamaged goods) accepted within 30 days.

Woodworker's Supply, Inc.

5604 Alameda Pl. NE
Albuquerque, NM 87113

800–645–9292
Fax: 800–853–9663

Catalog: $2
Pay: check, MO, MC, V, DSC
Sells: woodworking tools and equipment
Store: same address; Monday to Friday 8–5:30, Saturday 9–1; also Graham, NC; Casper, WY; and Seabrook, NH

For nearly 30 years, Woodworker's Supply has been "where the experts buy their tools," often at savings up to 30% on comparable goods sold by other supply houses. The 155-page color catalog has a major advantage over some of the heftier tools catalogs of similar products: If you're *not* an expert but rather a novice or hobbyist, the inventory will seem more accessible and suitable for smaller projects. There are shelf pins and shelving supports; audio-video hardware; kitchen and decorative hardware; shellacs and stains; wood fillers and putty; casters and tee-molding; furniture, computer, and table hardware; caning and chair seats; glues and gluing tools; tung oil, varnish, and Danish oil; and woodworking books and plans. Woodworker's Supply has an ample selection of hand tools, power tools, carving, turning, scraping, and wood-burning tools, bench components and clamps, shop and drilling accessories, spray equipment and lacquers, sanding tools and accessories, air nailers, and machinery accessories. Woodtek's line of machinery is offered at the back of the catalog in a dedicated section featuring widebelts, machine stands, a belt/disc machine, large convertible sanders, a heavy duty 36-inch radial drill press, dust collectors, overarm router, hollow chisel mortiser, and more. Woodworker's Supply can bring you the "tools of the trade" with the cozy atmosphere and personalized attention of a local shop.

SPECIAL FACTORS: Satisfaction guaranteed; returns accepted.

Related Products/Companies

Axes
- Cook Brothers

Bathroom and kitchen hardware and fixtures
- Baths from the Past, The Faucet Outlet

Books and videos on woodworking
- Woodworkers' Discount Books

Do-it-yourself books and online answers
- Reader's Digest

Doors, windows, glass panels, and components
- Arctic Glass, Oregon Wooden Screen Door

Electrical surplus
- American Science and Surplus

General tools
- American Science and Surplus, Damark, Cook Brothers, Lehman's

Generators, pressure washers
- RV Direct

Heavy-duty work clothes, boots, and caps
- Cahall's

House plans and kits
- GeoDomes Woodworks

Knobs and hardware, furniture plans
- Turncraft Clocks

Left-handed hand tools
- The Left Hand

Marine hardware
- Defender Industries

Musical-instrument-making tools
- Metropolitan Music

Peel-and-stick floor plans
- Design Works

Screen-door, shutter, and window hardware
- Coppa Woodworking, Shuttercraft

Shop aprons and tool belts
- Clothcrafters

Storage equipment
- Fidelity

Toolbags and pocket tools
- Aircraft Spruce & Specialty

Toys, Games, and Party Supplies

*Toys and games for children
and adults; party supplies,
favors, and decorations;
gift wrapping and holiday decor*

Parents know that one of the biggest annual expenses is the Birthday Party. Somehow the guest list keeps getting bigger, the party favors more elaborate. If you're throwing a kid's party, you'll find great sources here: companies that supply piñatas, balloons, penny candy, party favors, and more at tremendous savings compared with your local mall superstore. Likewise, if you're hosting an event, say, a fund-raiser, retirement party, or a Super Bowl get-together, you'll want to check out the party suppliers here for themed decor, custom-imprinted items such as napkins and matchbooks, and great catering supplies.

This chapter also features firms that sell discounted games and toys for children from one to one hundred. Every year around holiday time a favorite media topic is what to buy for your kids, which toys are dangerous, what's the hot toy, and other tiresome topics. But I'll add my two-cents' worth to the mix and recommend a great website, Dr. Toy (www.drtoy.com). Sponsored by The Institute for Childhood Resources, a not-for-profit organization, Dr. Toy has reviews of good toys and games for children, categorized by age. This is a good source for parents like me who don't want to shop at that backward R place or give in to the latest fad toy. The items Dr. Toy recommends are chosen for their educational and entertainment qualities, as well as their ability to stay outside of or at the very top of the toy chest. I always get terrific ideas from this site.

Be sure to see the listings under "Related Products/Companies" at the end of the chapter for relevant items found in other parts of this book.

Find It Fast

Bridge Supplies
- Baron Barclay

Children's Party Favors and Decor
- Kaye's Holiday, Oriental Trading Company, Party & Paper Worldwide, Sally Distributors, U.S. Toy

Holiday Ornaments
- Kaye's Holiday

Party and Event Decor and Supplies
- M&N International, Oriental Trading Company, Paradise Products, Party & Paper Worldwide, The Party Wholesaler, Sally Distributors, Stumps, U.S. Toy

Stickers
- Oriental Trading Company, Stickers 'N' Stuff, Toysmart.com

Toys and Games
- Cheapass Games, Constructive Playthings, Toysmart.com

Baron Barclay Bridge Supplies

3600 Chamberlain Lane, Suite 230 Louisville, KY 40241–1989

800–274–2221 502–426–0410 Fax: 502–426–2044

Catalog: free
Pay: check, MO, MC, V, AE, DSC
Sells: bridge playing and teaching materials
Store: mail order only; phone hours Monday to Friday 8–5:30 EST
Online: www.baronbarclay.com

"The World's Largest Bridge Supply Company" has everything you might need—whether you're a novice or experienced player—at discounts of up to 50%. Playing cards are only the beginning here. Baron Barclay stocks electronic bridge games, bridge software, instructional videotapes, card holders, teaching manuals and texts, books on strategy, history, and reference texts. For the bridge fanatic, there are card-design earrings and pins, "I Love Bridge" pens, rhinestone jewelry, tote bags, key rings, and more. Half of the 64-page catalog focuses on hundreds of instructional books, many written by well-known bridge teachers. If you have Internet access, Baron Barclay's website is especially friendly, with the constantly updated full catalog available online, bridge articles, links to other sites of interest, witty bridge quotes, and online ordering.

SPECIAL FACTORS: Satisfaction is guaranteed; quantity discounts are available;

returns are accepted within 30 days for refund, exchange, or credit (videotapes and software for exchange only).

Cheapass Games

2530 East Miller St.   **206–324–6728**
Seattle, WA 98112

    Information: website and print catalog (see text)
    Pay: check or MO
    Sells: original dice, card, and board games and
      accessories
    Store: mail order only; phone hours Monday to Friday 9–5
     PST
    Online: www.cheapass.com

When I first discovered Cheapass Games on the web, I wanted to add my own kudos to the growing list of reviewers who've also discovered this little gem of a company, which sells original board, card, and dice games at incredibly inexpensive prices with names like Falling, Kill Doctor Lucky, Ben Hvrt, Huzzah!, Give Me the Brain!, Hong Kong Spree!, Devil Bunny Needs a Ham, and Button Men. At this writing the most expensive game was $9.95, with many starting at $2! How is this possible? Because, as founder James Ernest rightly reasons, most of us already own—or can cheaply obtain—the dice, the play money, the pencils, and the pawns needed for any game. What Cheapass does is invent and design their own games, print them out in black ink on colored card stock (the boards for the board games are cut into sections for you to reassemble), and then mail them to you with instructions. "You don't need to pay forty bucks for a game that's overproduced and underdesigned," he adds. All games are fully described on the website.

Cheapass has recently started selling some of the game pieces as well, such as multicolored dice and 4-, 6-, 8-, 10-, 12-, and 20-sided solid and transparent polyhedra. At the website you can also get free games, join the "Players Club," which allows you to pay one sum and then get games mailed to you as soon as they're released, and check out accessories such as Cheapass buttons and comics. Cheapass as of this writing takes no credit cards, and all transactions are done by mail or phone (see hours, above), although you can download an order form off the website. Even though these games target the 25- to 35-year-old population for the most part, I smell a teenage cult trend in the making (à la Magic Cards and Pogs in the 1990s). If you don't have Internet access, you can request a print catalog.

SPECIAL FACTORS: Resellers/wholesalers should inquire for terms; overseas customers call for shipping fees.

Constructive Playthings

U.S. Toy Company, Inc.
13201 Arrington Rd.
Grandview, MO 64030–2886

816–761–5900
Fax: 816–761–9295

Catalog: free (see text)
Pay: check, MO, MC, V, DSC
Sells: toys and educational products
Store: CA, CO, FL, IL, KS, PA, TX; call for address
Online: www.ustoyco.com

It doesn't take long for your innocent toddler to get sucked into the materialistic vortex of toy marketing, TV show and movie linkage, and fast-food/toy cobranding. It's nice to know there's a company out there that specializes in wholesome, growth-oriented toys that children will love, despite the fact that they're "educational." Constructive Playthings offers a "lowest price guarantee" on everything they sell and carries the kinds of items you won't easily find in the mega kids' stores. (If you've ever tried to find wooden building blocks at the mall, you know what I'm talking about.) Since 1953 Constructive Playthings has been in the business of selling classic toys for less, with an emphasis on early educational toys: musical playmats, real steel tool sets, kid-friendly furniture, giant tumble books, tapes, videos, and outdoor playthings such as teepees and sand diggers. The products here are built to last and designed to promote creative, safe play. At the website you can order print catalogs and view a small sampling of the merchandise, but there's no online ordering.

Please note: If you operate a day-care center or teach in a school, request the 200-page "School Catalog" ($3), where the focus is more on group play and institutional settings.

SPECIAL FACTORS: Satisfaction guaranteed; returns accepted for exchange, refund, or credit; institutional accounts available.

Kaye's Holiday

1991 Fays Ln., Dept. BWBM   630–466–0009
Sugar Grove, IL 60554   Fax: 630–466–0008

Catalog: free with large SASE
Pay: check, MO, MC, V
Sells: holiday ornaments and small decor
Store: mail order only
Online: www.shophere.com/kaye

Kaye's Holiday, in business since 1982, is a closeout dealer selling holiday ornaments and tiny gift items. What does that mean? It means that everything at Kaye's is 20% to 70% off the original retail price. Four times a year Kaye's issues sales flyers that offer European glass ornaments, porcelain hinged boxes, wooden themed ornaments (Christmas, Easter, Halloween, etc.), small pins, and various other gift items. The flyer and website, where you can order online, have photographs of the current inventory, which could include anything from a blown-glass golfer to hang on your Christmas tree to a patriotic wooden teddy bear pin. Grab Bag specials allow you to sample different ornaments (Kaye's choice) at low prices. Name brands include Midwest Importers, Lefton, Silverstri, Eddie Walker, and Enesco.

SPECIAL FACTORS: Order as early as possible for the best choice.

M&N International, Inc.

P.O. Box 64784, Dept. WBM　　　800–479–2043
St. Paul, MN 55164–0784　　　　**Fax: 800–PARTY–ON**

Catalog:　free, $6 outside U.S.
Pay:　check, MO, MC, V, DSC
Sells:　party supplies
Store:　mail order only
Online:　www.mninternational.com

For inspiration on your next party, prom, dance, or shower at very affordable prices, take a look at M&N's "bright idea" book. You'll find anything and everything you might need to make your event memorable, and the variety will send your imagination flying. The color catalog is published in the spring and fall, and each edition features seasonal themes rounded out with year-round party staples. The fall/winter catalog has decorations and supplies for back-to-school, Halloween, Thanksgiving, Hanukkah, Christmas, and the New Year, as well as for sports parties, Oktoberfest, Chinese New Year, Bastille Day, south-of-the-border fiestas, Old West, Hawaiian luaus, Mardi Gras, and much more. Best of all, they guarantee the lowest prices possible on everything, so you can't go wrong by shopping here. Birthdays, anniversaries, weddings, and every other reason to celebrate are covered in this catalog as well, with banners, party hats, festive tablecloths, party favors, and more. In the "caterer's corner" you'll find items that will help make serving easier and more elegant, such as place cards, centerpieces, serving platters, candles, warming racks, chef hats, and special carry-home containers. M&N also offers promotional materials for your company, and will engrave wine glasses, pens, wooden nickels, and more with your company insignia. An online order form is available on their website, but their products are not listed, so you'll need a print catalog in order to use this feature.

SPECIAL FACTORS: Satisfaction is guaranteed; quantity discounts are available; authorized returns are accepted for exchange, refund or credit; institutional accounts are available; C.O.D. orders are accepted.

Oriental Trading Company, Inc.

P.O. Box 3407, Dept. 868
Omaha, NE 68103

800–228–0122
Fax: 800–327–8904

Catalog: free
Pay: check, MO, MC, V, AE, DSC
Sells: party goods, novelties, etc.
Store: mail order only
Online: www.oriental.com

In business since 1932, the "World's Biggest Toy Box" sells everything a novelty shop would sell—at prices up to 50% below what you would normally pay in a store. In this toy box you will find everything from porcelain dolls dressed in period costumes to black tissue-paper Halloween cats—with a great deal in between, including jester hats for both adults and children, feather masks, red devil horns, angel costumes for dogs, fairy princess costumes complete with magic wand, clown shoe, funny eyeglasses, sparkly wigs, plastic Viking helmets and swords, gorilla costumes for adults, and much, much more! They also sell many year-round items such as stickers, party hats and decorations, and party favors. Many items are sold singly, but others are sold by the dozen, gross, or pound. On the website, you may order a catalog and view a selection of their many fun products, but you must request a print catalog to order.

SPECIAL FACTORS: Quantity discounts available; authorized returns (except food, candy, and costumes) are accepted after contacting customer service within five days of receipt of goods.

Paradise Products, Inc.

P.O. Box 568, Dept. WBM   800–227–1092
El Cerrito, CA 94530–0568   Fax: 800–258–5333

Catalog: free bulk mail, $3 first class
Pay: check, MO, MC, V
Sells: party paraphernalia
Store: mail order only
E-mail: paradise-party@worldnet.att.net

This is one company worthy of its name! As you flip through the pages of this catalog, you'll soon realize this company sells everything you might need to turn your next party or event into a fun-and-savings paradise. With savings of 50% below typical retail prices, you'll be able to pull off a memorable and festive event without emptying your wallet. Paradise Products sells decorations and supplies for over 60 different themes, including the big holidays of Halloween, Thanksgiving, Christmas/Hanukkah, and New Year, and others such as Mardi Gras, Fourth of July, St. Patrick's Day, Valentine's Day, and Mother's Day. Glitzy streamers, golden crowns, ice-sculpture molds, and tissue centerpieces will give your event that exciting touch, while matching dining accessories, candles, and aprons will help the event go off with ease and flair.

SPECIAL FACTORS: Goods are guaranteed to be as represented in the catalog; shipments are guaranteed to arrive in time for the party date specified (terms are stated in catalog); minimum order is $20 or a $3 service charge applies.

Party & Paper Worldwide

800-631-3310

Information: website only, no print catalog
Pay: V, MC
Sells: party supplies
Store: website only; phone hours Monday to Friday 8–6,
  Saturday 10–6
Online: www.partypro.com

I like companies like this online party supply store: What you see is what you get. Party & Paper Worldwide buys direct from the manufacturers, which saves you from 15% to 60% off normal retail. Secure online ordering, free shipping on orders over $30, and a customer service department reachable by phone (toll-free) make this an easy place to like.

The online catalog has thousands of items in fourteen departments: anniversary supplies, balloons, candles, cards and stationery, centerpieces, dinnerware, gift wrap supplies, graduation supplies, party favors/decorations, party themes, scrapbooking, seasonal party supplies, signs/banners/flags, and wedding supplies. If you've thrown a party lately you know how much little things add up, such as the tablecloths and dinnerware. Imagine a 54 by 108-inch white tablecloth for 99 cents! Wrapping paper is available here for 13 cents a foot (40 inches wide). Gorgeous piñatas shaped in many whimsical designs from mermaids and unicorns to ballet slippers, fish, and basketballs are only $9 at this writing, and Party & Paper Worldwide also sells the piñata filler (party favors and candy). Check out other items, such as 39-cent greeting cards and decorative gift bags for $1.49, and you'll become a party animal.

SPECIAL FACTORS: Free shipping within the continental U.S. on orders over $30; complete satisfaction guaranteed or your money fully refunded.

The Party Wholesaler

2638 SW 28th Lane   305–443–0042
Miami, FL 33133   Fax: 305–442–2689

Catalog: $3
Pay: check, MO, MC, V, AE, DSC
Sells: party supplies, restaurant disposables
Store: (warehouses) same address; also call for four other
     warehouse locations in FL
Online: www.partywholesaler.com

Whether you're looking to decorate for an important event or seeking catering supplies that will give your event that special touch, search no further than the Party Wholesaler. This company sells decorative paper and plastic dinnerware, place mats, cocktail napkins, garlands, centerpieces, and more to make your event beautiful, and catering essentials such as serving trays, punch bowls, spring-form pans, plastic containers, deli paper, bakery boxes, and roasting pans, among other items, at savings of up to 40% off typical retail prices. The Party Wholesaler also sells reception necessities—creamer, sugar, salt-and-pepper packets, as well as coffee, tea, hot chocolate, and bar needs such as salted almonds, peanuts, and fancy stirrers. You can also fill your gift-wrapping needs here: foil gift wrap in 17 colors, tissue paper, cellophane, ribbons, gift boxes, bows, and tulle. And if your child is having a birthday party, the Party Wholesaler can supply children's-theme paper plates, napkins, balloons, and party favors. At his writing the website was under construction, so be sure to check it out.

SPECIAL FACTORS: Satisfaction is guaranteed; returns of unopened goods are accepted within 30 days for exchange, refund, or credit.

Sally Distributors, Inc.

4100 Quebec Ave. N.
Minneapolis, MN 55427

800–472–5597
612–533–7100
Fax: 800–575–1453
Fax: 612–533–0141

Catalog: free, $5 outside U.S.
Pay: check, MO, MC, V, DSC
Sells: party goods, toys, novelties, seasonal items, etc.
Store: same address; Monday to Friday 8–5, Saturday 8–12
E-mail: sallydist@sallydist.com

Since 1921, Sally Distributors has been saving its customers an easy 40% off typical retail prices on party goods, decorations, and fun extras. Anything you might need for any celebration is sold in this full-color catalog, from patriotic decorations to purely whimsical things. You could fill a room with balloons, stuff bags with fun party favors, or hand out feather masks to your guests for a masquerade ball without stretching your budget too far. If you're looking for playful items such as insect finger puppets, illuminated silk roses, rubber chickens, glow-in-the-dark alien keychains, boxes of candy, or large plush cartoon characters, this is the catalog for you. But don't forget to check out Sally's more practical items, which include gift bags, wrapping paper, Mylar and latex balloons, disposable wedding cameras, ticket rolls, and more!

SPECIAL FACTORS: Quantity discounts available; authorized returns accepted for exchange, refund, or credit; institutional accounts available; $2 surcharge imposed on orders under $30.

Stickers 'N' Stuff, Inc.

P.O. Box 430, Dept. WBM   **303-604-0422**
Louisville, CO 80027-0430   **Fax: 303-665-8779**

Catalog and Samples: $2
Pay: check, MO, MC, V
Sells: novelty stickers
Store: mail order only

Stickers, stickers, stickers! What child doesn't like to see a sticker next to a good grade on a test? Teachers love to give stickers as much as kids love to get them, and this company makes it easy for every teacher to give stickers, with prices as low as 6 cents for stickers that usually cost 25 cents! The wide variety of stickers here includes prisms (rainbow effect), chrome (foil background), hologram, pearlescent, velvety fuzzies, and glowing neon. Smiley faces and stars are just the beginning here—designs include bunnies, butterflies, clowns, monkeys, bears, rainbows, horses, angels, ice cream cones, unicorns, snakes, and airplanes. Stickers 'N' Stuff also offers some wonderful collections, with the least expensive being their 410-sticker grab bag. Other collections include an endangered species set, holiday and seasonal stickers, a unicorn grab bag, and economy paper stickers. You'll find heart-shaped adhesive bandages, "liquid crystal" jewelry, sticker "earrings," and sticker-collecting books here too.

SPECIAL FACTORS: Satisfaction guaranteed; quantity discounts available; returns accepted for exchange, refund, or credit; minimum credit card order is $10.

Stumps

One Party Place
P.O. Box 305
South Whitley, IN 46787–0305

800–348–5084
219–723–5171
Fax: 219–723–6976

Catalog: free
Pay: check, MO, MC, V, AE, DSC
Sells: party goods, display items, etc.
Outlet store: downtown South Whitley on the west side of
  ST 5; Wednesday 10–4, Thursday and Friday 10–5:30,
  Saturday 8–12, closed Sunday through Tuesday
Online: www.stumpsparty.com

Stumps, founded in 1926, introduced the first full-color catalog featuring themed prom kits such as "Starry, Starry Night" and "A Night in Venice" in 1960. This company may very well be responsible for thousands of first kisses! This mail-order party-supply company sells Mylar balloons (nonhelium), buttons, car decorations, candles, centerpieces, columns, crowns, curtains, favors, flowers, fund-raising candy, garters, lights, float and parade materials, photo albums, sashes and scepters, stickers, streamers, tiaras, and more to make large-scale events—for schools, theaters, weddings, reunions, and holidays—memorable and festive. And, yes, Stumps' prices are wholesale (up to 50% below retail) and the main "Prom & Party" catalog nearly exhaustive, weighing in at 400-plus pages. (Stumps also has six other specialty party catalogs.)

But where Stumps excels, beyond selling thematic decorations at great prices, is in service. The website offers prom planning guides, one for committees and advisors, another for students (select "for guys" or "for girls"). These online easy-access guides (click PromNet) not only list everything needed to create or enjoy a prom; they offer charts for creating budgets, tips for prioritizing expenditures, and sage advice for dealing with the whole prom experience. (For sports and team participants, there's CheerNet to get the school spirit going.) Stumps also has a free on-staff party planner who can offer everything from wedding tips to decorating advice (see hours above).

After the popularity of the movie *Titanic*, Stumps added "My Heart Will Go On" to its roster of theme kits (Mardi Gras, Hollywood, Manhattan Mystique). The Titanic theme is built around a 25′ × 8′ silhouette ship with 475 twinkling lights (about $125), three six-foot-high glitter-sprayed icebergs (about $40 per set), and centerpieces (about $23 per set of four). The theme can be announced, and remembered, with custom-imprinted items, such as invitations.

SPECIAL FACTORS: Satisfaction guaranteed; quantity discounts and institutional accounts available; authorized returns, except worn clothing and imprinted or customized items, accepted within 15 days for exchange, refund, or credit (15% restocking fee possible); minimum order $15.

Toysmart.com

781–788–6000
800–462–1232

Information: website only, no print catalog
Pay: MC, V, AE, DSC
Sells: educational toys and resources
Store: website only
Online: www.toysmart.com

If you're familiar with Holt Educational Outlet, a leading discount retailer of childhood developmental and educational toys, then you'll be thrilled to learn that they've launched an online store for parents to find thousands of the best educational toys and learning tools at 10% to 50% less than anywhere else, as well as a large selection of articles, resources, and information. There's even a special teachers' section that includes curriculum guides, teacher resources, classroom decorations, and art supplies.

The website allows you to search in a number of ways (by manufacturer, category, etc.) or seek further assistance from the "Toy Detective." This encyclopedic site has toys—trains, planes, automobiles, construction, imaginative play, indoor/outdoor play, stuffed animals and dolls, science and nature, software/electronic learning, activity kits; games and puzzles—board and card games, preschool and family puzzles; items for infants—crib toys, blankets, board books; children's furniture; arts and crafts supplies, projects, and kits; audio/video/music products, and of course books. There's lots more here, such as specials, giveaways, and toy reviews, but I'd advise you to sit back with a cup of cocoa, log on, and discover it yourself. Most of what you need is explained on the site, but if you have additional questions there's a toll-free customer service number you can call.

SPECIAL FACTORS: All goods shipped via Federal Express, unless a P.O. box is specified; Toysmart.com cannot ship to APO/FPO addresses; returns accepted (see website for policies).

U.S. Toy Co., Inc.

1227 E. 119th St.
Grandview, MO 64030–1117

800–255–6124
816–761–5900
Fax: 816–761–9295

Catalog: $3
Pay: check, MO, MC, V
Sells: novelties and fund-raising items
Store: Garden Grove, CA; Englewood, CO; Apoka, FL;
  Skokie, IL; Leawood, KS; North Wales, PA; and Carrollton,
  TX; see catalog for locations
Online: www.ustoyco.com

If you're a parent, teacher, day-care or camp director looking for inexpensive, imaginative party materials, the prices in this catalog will make you smile. Some of the party toys and decorations are priced as low as a penny apiece! U.S. Toy Co. offers a vast array of carnival/party and seasonal decorations, masks, novelty toys, costumes, festive tableware, stuffed animals, grab-bag prizes, balloons, and many more items developed for their exclusive sale. Prices at U.S. Toy are up to 70% lower than retail, and the variety is outstanding, with literally thousands of items to choose from. There are decorating supplies for just about every holiday and occasion. Some of these products are sold by the case or in large quantities, but most items are available singly or in fewer quantities. More information is available on their website, but you still must call or fax your order in.

SPECIAL FACTORS: Institutional accounts are available; minimum order is $25.

Related Products/Companies

Adult puzzles and games
- Airline International Luggage & Gifts

Amish games
- Gohn Bros.

Baby toys
- After the Stork, Baby Bunz, Chock

Batteries
- Porter's Camera Store

Breyer horses
- State Line Tack

Candle- and soap-making kits
- Brushy Mountain Bee Farm

Casino-game computers
- Mardiron

CD-ROM computer games
- Shoplet.com

Children's bee-themed games and activities
- Brushy Mountain Bee Farm

Children's musical instruments, toys, party favors, and sheet music
- Anyone Can Whistle, Shar Products

Children's travel games
- Dover, Family Travel Guides Catalog

Comic book storage bags
- University Products

Craft kits
- The Artist's Club, The Caning Shop, CR's Bear and Doll Supply, Frank's Cane and Rush, Gramma's Graphics, Vanguard, Warner-Crivellaro Stained Glass

Craps, blackjack, shuffleboard, darts, foosball, and other rec-room games
- Mueller Sporting Goods

Dog training board game
- Jeffers

Doll buggies
- Fran's Wicker & Rattan

Dollhouse plans
- Woodworker's Supply

Dolls and toy-making supplies and parts
- CR's Bear and Doll

Educational toys and dolls
- Cook Brothers

Game books, stickers, cut-and-assemble projects
- Current, Dover Publications

Grower-direct fresh flowers
- Evergreen Farms, Hand-Tied Flowers

Grow-your-own-butterfly and other educational kits
- American Science and Surplus

Karaoke machines
- Upstairs Records

Kid's pedal plane
- Aircraft Spruce & Specialty

Kites and kite-building kits
- BFK Sports

Miniatures
- Lehman's

Onyx chess sets
- House of Onyx

Peel-and-stick kits for educational projects
- Design Works

Penny candies
- Bates Bros., Bulkfoods.com

Pet toys
- Drs. Foster & Smith, Jeffers Pet Supply, KV Vet, Omaha Vaccine, State Line Tack, That Fish/Pet Place, UPCO, Valley Vet

Playground equipment
- Alfax, Better Health Fitness

Simpson's chess/checkers sets
- Sunway

Sleds, toboggans, tricycles, go-carts
- Lehman's, Northern Hydraulics, RV Direct

Toy chests
- Fran's Wicker & Rattan

Toys
- Make Us An Offer

Travel chess game
- RV Direct

Water toys
- Overton's

Yo-yos
- BFK Sports

Travel

*Money-saving travel
and moving services
of various kinds for all ages*

I had a lot of fun researching this chapter. This section includes firms that in one way or another could save you money on your next move, airline ticket, cruise, or cross-country or European trip. Travel is a big industry, so there's a lot of information out there, as well as a mind-boggling number of choices. If you have the creativity—and in some cases, flexibility—to nail down your itinerary in a slightly unconventional way, there are lots of ways to save money and benefit personally in other ways.

One newsletter I'd recommend if you travel a lot—or wish you could—is *Consumer Reports Travel Letter (CRTL),* produced by Consumers Union. This is a well-regarded publication for both business and recreational travelers. *CRTL* conducts in-depth comparisons of accommodations and prices in the U.S. and abroad, and does regular features on airline food, travel scams, travel agents, airline booking systems, and more. Each monthly issue of *CRTL* runs around 24 pages; a year's subscription costs $39 at this writing, or $59 for two years. Call 800–234–1970, or write to Circulation Department, *Consumer Reports Travel Letter,* P.O. Box 53600, Boulder, CO 80322 for information.

In addition to the company listings in this chapter, here are some basics to get you started with saving money.

Consolidators/Bucket Shops

Consolidators, also known as bucket shops, are companies that buy cruise slots, blocks of rooms, and plane seats from airlines, hotels, and charter agents at wholesale prices, and then resell them for less than the hotels, airlines, or often the charter operators themselves could. Although travel agents are the main customers of consolidators, individuals may buy from some of them too, saving as much as 20% to 30% on APEX fares and much more on full economy tickets.

Unitravel Flights for Less, one of the oldest consolidators in the business, books mainly international flights, sells directly to individuals, and can save you up to 35% off typical prices. Contact Unitravel at least a month before you want to leave and allow for some flexibility, as tickets might not be available until shortly before the day of departure. The toll-free number is 800–325–2222 for more information, or write to 11737 Administrative Dr., Ste. 120, St. Louis, MO 63146. You can also get automated fare quotes on their website (www.flightsfor less.com).

Council Travel, a leader in student, youth, and low-priced airfares, has offices in over 27 states and districts. This is a good source for obtaining student IDs and getting set up in a language program for work or study abroad. This student-friendly company also has information on youth hostels, home stays, and other economical accommodations for young people. For more information, call toll-free 800–2COUNCIL, or visit the website (www.counciltravel.com).

STA Travel, "the world's largest student travel organization," is another bucket shop that deals with individuals. STA has offices in major California cities, as well as in the District of Columbia, Chicago, Boston and Cambridge, New York City, Philadelphia, and Seattle; call 800–777–0112 for the location nearest you.

Nouvelle Frontiers is an off-price travel broker that sells to consumers as well as to travel agencies. For information, call 212–779–0600 or 800–366–6387. You can also try *Travac Tours and Charters,* at 212–563–3303 or 800–872–8800.

Hotel Brokers

If you have a credit card, belong to an automobile club, use a discount telephone long-distance service, or are otherwise listed somewhere on the American infor-mation grid, you've no doubt been solicited to join a dining and travel club. Depending on how frequently you travel, the annual membership, if there is one, might be worth it for the discounts.

Another way to save on your hotel stays, however, is to book through a hotel broker, who may work like a consolidator or an independent agent, providing reservations and confirmations, often at a discount. Many of these services require prepayment to the service for the room and stay. The services listed below act as agents and allow you to pay the hotel in the customary way:

Quikbook has connections with great midpriced hotels at great prices in seven cities; you can save up to 60% by booking through them. The cities are New York, Boston, Atlanta, San Francisco, Washington, DC, Chicago, and Los Angeles. Quikbook can be reached at 800–789–9887 or 212–532–1660; at their website (www.quikbook.com); or through the mail, Quikbook, 381 Park Ave. South, New York, NY 10016.

Central Reservation Service handles reservations in the following cities: New York, Chicago, Boston, Atlanta, New Orleans, San Francisco, Miami, Washington, DC, and Orlando. If you book through them, you'll save from 10% to 40%. The very friendly staff speaks both Spanish and English. Call 800–548–3311 or 407–740–6442; the address is Central Reservation Service, 220 Lookout Pl., Ste. 200, Maitland, FL 32751.

Home Exchanges

One of the cheapest ways to save on hotel bills, especially if you're traveling with children, is to stay in someone else's home. *International Home Exchange Service/Intervac* is an organization that compiles three directories a year listing thousands of homes worldwide (most are outside the U.S.). The apartments and houses in this directory are available for exchange and rent, so you don't necessarily have to exchange your own home to take advantage of a good deal. For more information, write to International Home Exchange Service/Intervac, 30 Corte San Ferrando, Belvedere Tiburon, CA 94920, or call 415–435–3497. The web address is www.intervac.com.

In a city such as New York, where every single hotel room may be booked for the weekend, it's nice to know that there are thousands of vacant apartments available for less than a hotel would cost—with a number of advantages, namely more space, use of a full kitchen, and no doubt better ambiance. These are listed under "Bed and Breakfasts" in the yellow pages of the local phone directory or weekly entertainment newspaper classifieds. Just about every major city has companies that make their business out of connecting owners with overnight guests.

Free, or Nearly Free, Rides

Remember hitchhiking? It used to be a great way to get around the U.S. cheaply. In Woodstock, where I live, it's not all that uncommon to see a hopeful soul meandering by the side of the road, thumb stuck out. Personally, I've gotten to the age where I neither hitch nor pick up hitchers. However, there's an ingenious website called E-Hitch (www.e-hitch.com) that acts as a sort of national rideboard. If you're looking for a driver or a rider, simply fill out the information and submit the form. E-Hitch has a search engine that lets you fill in your destination state and access all the riders or drivers going there. It's free! E-Hitch takes no responsibility for your experience; this website merely serves to hook the two of you up. It's your job to get a sense of who you're dealing with when you get in touch with your rider/driver. At this writing E-Hitch was setting up a related service for linking skiers and snowboarders (Snow-Hitch). Run by a couple of smart, idealistic brothers, E-Hitch gets an enthusiastic thumbs up (thumb out?) from me for its democratic and constructive use of the information superhighway.

Last-Minute Bookings

There's so much cool (and free) information on the web. I've got to pass along a site I recently discovered called Webflyer (www.webflyer.com), which compiles all the cyber deals the airlines, hotels, and car rental companies are offering for last-minute travel and then posts them once a week. You get to access this information for *free*. You'll find these in Webflyer's section called "Deal Watch." Deal Watch allows you click on the first letter of the city you want to fly from, stay in, or rent a car in. For example, I clicked *N* for New York. For that following week some of the airfare options included a round trip to Nashville on American for $39 plus 13,000 miles; round-trip from New York to Seattle on Continental for $29 plus 17,500 miles; and round-trip from New York to Caracas, Venezuela, on United for $264. Departure and return times and dates vary and are restricted for each trip. The above two domestic flights, for example, were for an extended weekend (you had to leave between certain times on Friday and not return until Monday or Tuesday). When you find a good deal, you're responsible for calling the airline to make the reservation—and you'd better do it quickly! International air deals are posted at 3 P.M. on Mondays. Domestic deals for airfare, car, and hotel deals are updated at 3 P.M. on Wednesdays. An FAQ page answers most questions. This is a *great* way to book spontaneous and extremely affordable trips to see your long-distance friends and loved ones.

Cheap Intra-Europe Travel

If you're traveling around Europe, the following two options work in basically the same way: You pay one flat fee for a span of time (30 or 60 days, for instance), which entitles you to nearly unlimited travel within that time span. Deals vary depending on your age and itinerary. If you want to hop around Europe by bus, Eurolines claims to be the cheapest mode of travel in and around the European countries. Their website address is www.eurolines.com. Then of course there's the most famous mode of all: via romantic European trains where you're apt to fall in love with a mysterious Italian over a glass of wine. Go to the Eurailpass website for more information (www.eurailpass.com) or call them toll-free at 888–RAIL–888.

Find It Fast

Automobile Transporting Services
- A2B Automobile Moving

Discount Cruise Packages
- Vacations to Go

Discount Outdoor Vacations by Bus
- Green Tortoise

Learning or Community Service Travel Packages
- Elderhostel, Volunteers for Peace

Lowest-Price Travel Bids
- TravelBids

Low-Fare, Unbooked Airline Seats
- Airhitch

Moving Service
- Help-U-Move

Online Travel Services
- Microsoft Expedia

Up-To-Date, Comprehensive Courier Travel Information
- International Association of Air Travel Couriers

A2B Automobile Moving

888–274–4722

Information: website only, no print catalog
Pay: bank check, MO, MC, V, AE
Sells: automobile, pickup, and van transport services
Store: online and telephone only
Online: www.choicemall.com/shipacar

Moving? Save time, money, and mileage—and reduce your overall stress—by having A2B Automobile Moving transport your car, van, or truck to your new home. A2B can save you 20% to 40% over moving van rates. They have daily pickups in more than 100 major cities nationwide and can promptly deliver your vehicle to your new location anywhere in the continental U.S. This company, founded in 1995, has specially designed trucks and licensed insured carriers. Major corporations recommend A2B for relocating employees, as do individuals, whose letters pepper the website with tried-and-true testimonials. You can get a free quote right on the website, or call or send e-mail with your questions.

SPECIAL FACTORS: Vehicle transportation within the continental U.S.; for Canadian destinations, inquire; member of the Better Business Bureau.

Airhitch

2641 Broadway, 3rd Fl.
New York, NY 10025

212–864–2000
800–326–2009
Fax: 212–864–5489

Information Packet: free
Pay: MC, V
Sells: low-fare, unbooked airline seats
Store: same address; Monday to Friday, 10–5; Saturday
   noon–3; also offices in Paris, Los Angeles, San Francisco,
   Amsterdam, Berlin, Prague, Madrid, and Rome
Online: www.airhitch.org

On any given day, hundreds of seats go empty between the U.S. and Europe, as well as on domestic flights. Airhitch takes advantage of these empty seats by putting people in them for low fares. "The Airhitch system was created for the free-spirited, independent, and resourceful traveler who does not have a rigorous schedule, and enjoys seeing different places even when en route to his/her final destination." Here's how it works, in brief: When you call Airhitch you'll be given an information packet and will then be asked to register. The staff will fax you a form to fill out and fax back, ask you to register online, or if the former two options are not available to you, they will mail you an information packet and registration form. Once registered, you let Airhitch know your target date of departure and your destination (including a region of departure and three destination options). The "date range" for your departure must be a span of five days minimum, and you must be prepared to leave on any flight, on any day within your date range. (A "call-in" date is assigned for you slightly before the beginning of your date range.) Airhitch staff will help you design a strategy for prioritizing from among available flight alternatives to maximize the chances of getting you as close as possible to where you want to go, when you want to go.

Note that this is a one-way transaction only. You need to go through the procedure again for the return flight. There are reps overseas who can assist you. Sound complicated? Ponder this: You can go across the Atlantic for $175, and from the East Coast to the West Coast for about $119. If you're not rigid about travel times and dates, this is definitely a great bargain way to travel.

SPECIAL FACTORS: Pay by credit card only.

Elderhostel

| 75 Federal St. | 877–426–8056 |
| Boston, MA 02110–1941 | TDD: 877–426–2167 |

Catalog: free (see text)
Pay: varies (see text)
Sells: inexpensive travel/learning packages for seniors
Office: same address; Monday to Friday 9–9
Online: www.elderhostel.org

"I can't imagine an Elderhostel-free retirement"—so says one of the many happy clients whose life has been enriched by this wonderful organization. If you're 55 years or older and you want to see the world without spending your children's inheritance, Elderhostel is the way to travel. Imagine studying the literature of Jane Austen in the White Mountains of New Hampshire; traveling to Greece to explore the spectacular art and architecture; or conducting field research in Belize to save the endangered dolphin population. Elderhostel was started in 1975 with 200 participants and a few programs; now it offers 10,000 programs in 70 countries every year plus 300 service programs that bring volunteer energy to worthy causes around the world. The cost for programs is low, ranging from $390 for a weeklong program in the U.S., which includes meals, rooms, instruction, and field trips, to $2,600 for two and a half weeks in Europe, which includes airfare. And since Elderhostel is a 501(c)(3) organization, expenses incurred to participants are generally tax-deductible! When you call Elderhostel or visit the website, you'll be asked to choose which of four catalogs you want: "U.S.," "Canada," "International," or "Service." The website has a great FAQ section for first-time visitors that answers everything from whether you have to have a roommate ("no": 65% of Elderhostel travelers request and get single rooms) and whether those with special physical needs can be accommodated ("yes": most of the time).

Note to Canadian readers: Please contact Elderhostel Canada at 613–530–2222.

SPECIAL FACTORS: Specify which catalog you want when ordering; forms of payment accepted vary depending on which travel program you book.

Green Tortoise

494 Broadway
San Francisco, CA 94133

800–867–8647
415–956–7500
Fax: 415–956–4900

Catalog: free
Pay: traveler's check, MO, U.S. bank draft
Sells: adventure bus tours in North and Central America
Office: same address as above, daily 8–8 PT
Online: www.greentortoise.com

Ready for an adventure? Green Tortoise is a San Francisco–based company that organizes "adventure" tours to some of the most remote and beautiful places in North and Central America. This isn't the type of bus tour where elderly blue-haired people sit in air-conditioned, perfumy seats and look out the window at the scenery passing by. Green Tortoise travelers ride in one of the "legendary sleeper coaches." They don't sit up all night with their heads against the window; the seats convert to mattresses (with fitted sheets) on raised platforms and bunk beds. In the morning you've usually arrived somewhere incredible. By day you "swim, cook breakfast, explore caves, climb mountains, raft downstream, stand under waterfalls, walk through forests, cook dinner, build campfires, visit towns, meet people, or just plain take it easy." Green Tortoise trips aren't for everyone. In fact, the website, which has the same information as the print catalog, has a section on the type of people who *shouldn't* travel on Green Tortoise. These might include people who don't enjoy the outdoors, those who can't tolerate diversity and togetherness with strangers, rabid teetotalers, people with young children, and those unwilling to do some work. (Meals and meal preparation and cleanup are cooperative.) Because of the style of travel, Green Tortoise trips are amazingly inexpensive. Destinations include Alaska, Baja, Costa Rica, Grand Canyon, Death Valley, Yosemite, the Mayan ruins in Mexico, and many others. There's lots more to learn here, so I suggest you check out the website.

SPECIAL FACTORS: No personal checks accepted; travel with children must be preapproved through main office.

Help-U-Move, Inc.

131 Bishopwood Drive　　　　888–851–3273
Jupiter, FL 33458　　　　　　561–625–6683

Information: website only, no print catalog
Pay: MO, MC, V, AE, DSC, Electronic check
Sells: you-pack-they-drive moving services
Office: same address, Monday to Friday 9–6 EST
Online: www.helpumove.com

Let's say you're a debt-burdened graduating college student who needs to move his dorm or apartment furniture to a city two states away to begin a new job. Or let's say your elderly mother is moving out of the family home into an assisted-living situation, and she wants you to have the family heirlooms in your home—halfway across the country. As common as these situations are, the options until now haven't been satisfactory. One option: Hire a mover, which is prohibitively expensive; another option is to pack up the things yourself and drive the stuff in one of those run-down, dangerous rental trucks. Help-U-Move offers a third alternative that's low cost and hassle-free. Help-U-Move delivers a 28-foot-long semi-trailer (called a *pup*) to your dorm, apartment, or house and allows you adequate time to load your belongings. They return when you're finished loading and deliver the pup to the new location for you to unload. Once you're finished unloading, you call them and they remove the pup. It's easy. Best of all, you save money by packing the stuff yourself, and you're only charged for the actual footage you use. Even if you hire someone to help you load and unload, you'll still end up paying less here. The pup can hold a large house full of furniture (28′ × 8′ × 8½′), but you can rent as little as three feet of the pup.

Help-U-Move's informative website has answers to most of your questions, has a section of testimonials from satisfied customers, and allows you to track your shipment online. At the website you can obtain a free price quote by e-mail; you can also get a quote over the phone. Help-U-Move wants your business; if you get a cheaper quote from another company, give them a chance to beat it.

SPECIAL FACTORS: Help-U-Move does not perform same-state moves, local moves, or moves under 250 miles; free price quote by e-mail or phone; member Better Business Bureau.

International Association of Air Travel Couriers

P.O. Box 1349

Lake Worth, FL 33460

561–582–8320

Fax: 561–582–1581

Information packet: free

Membership: $45 for one year (see text)

Pay: check, MO, V, MC

Sells: up-to-the-minute courier travel information

Office: same address, Monday to Friday, 9–5; another

location in UK

Online: www.courier.org

International Association of Air Travel Couriers (IAATC) is the premier clearing-house for consumers who wish to travel as couriers to foreign destinations. Being a courier is a superdiscount way to travel, but it's not easy to find out whom to book with and how to do it. After speaking with a company representative, I learned some of the many pitfalls of the courier industry, and it became clear to me why one would want and need to join IAATC. For one thing, courier companies (of which there are hundreds) come and go, sometimes weekly. You could book with a company and find yourself out of luck come travel day. For another thing, new flights and opportunities spring up hourly, and some of these last-minute deals are unbelievably cheap. You won't be able to get this hard-to-find information from anyone as accurately as from IAATC, which specializes in customer service. The IAATC "does not sell tickets or profit in any way from your courier flight. Its mission is to provide up-to-date information on all courier travel opportunities available to couriers, while working to support air courier travel as a way to see the world on a shoestring."

Courier flights work like this, in short: Companies need to send packages overseas. If they send them cargo, the packages might spend two to three days in customs before even getting on the plane. If companies want to send packages on regular flights (getting overseas in a few hours), airline regulations require that they be accompanied by a live body. That's where you enter in. You take the packages as your check-in luggage and hand over the package to the waiting representative when you arrive at the destination airport. You might have to give up some of your carry-on luggage allotment, which is the downside. The upside is that your fare will be up to 85% less than you'd pay otherwise! The U.S. cities from which air-courier flights originate as of this writing were New York, Los Angeles, San Francisco, Miami, Chicago, Newark, and Washington, DC.

A one-year membership to IAATC is $45, which entitles you to telephone support, 24-hour access to their fax-on-demand system, IAATC's online access system for couriers, and a bimonthly subscription to both *The Shoestring Traveler* and the *Air Courier Bulletin.*

SPECIAL FACTORS: Information is for foreign destinations only; no domestic travel service; customers must pay in U.S. funds or British pounds.

Microsoft Expedia

Information: website only, no catalog
Pay: V, MC, AE, DSC, CB, DC
Sells: travel information and services
Store: online only
Online: www.expedia.com

I tried out quite a few travel sites before I hit upon Expedia. As the name suggests, it's fast and easy to use. Some of the virtual travel agents have quick fare-finders that only work if you happen to be traveling between two of the major cities they've included in their calculations. Others allow you to go to the trouble of entering in all the information about your trip, only to inform you that no such flight exists. At Expedia, you sign up (for free), then you're off on a fun-filled adventure in finding (and booking, if you wish) your own flight. You choose the departure and destination cities or airports and the times and dates on both ends of your trip. Expedia's "Travel Wizard" will search any or all airlines, sort them by price or by schedule (those that fall closest to your specifications), and then list them, complete with connecting flights if applicable, exact times of departure/arrival, price, airline, and any restrictions that apply. You don't have to reserve the flight in order to get the full details. (How many times have you asked an airline rep to give you a quote, only to have her go through the whole booking routine?) Further, you can list your itinerary in "Fare Tracker" to receive weekly updates of the lowest fares available between those cities. When you book a flight through Expedia, as I did recently, it allows you to also make your own seat assignment.

Other features that make Expedia a good travel site include the Expedia "Travel Network," which informs you about cruises, vacation packages, resorts, special interest vacations, and more; loads of travel news and feature articles;

listings of hotels worldwide; a currency converter; maps, driving directions, weather updates, and much more. Will Expedia find you cheaper fares than other travel sites? A recent survey done by Internet Shopper of online travel bookers compared the top ten sites. Expedia produced the second cheapest fare out of the ten, but it definitely ranked best in terms of user-friendliness.

SPECIAL FACTORS: Ticketing and travel restrictions may apply; refer to your particular itinerary for details.

TravelBids Travel Discount Auction

4800 Riverbend Road   **Fax: 303–443–4705**
Boulder, CO 80301

Information: $5 per bid; website only, no print catalog
Pay: V, MC, AE
Offers: lowest-price bids on travel reservations
Store: online only
Online: www.travelbids.com

Online bidding is the new big thing, but there are quite a few tricks and traps that can snag the unsuspecting consumer, especially when it comes to travel auctions. Fortunately, TravelBids, an online auction that allows travelers to save money by having many different travel agents bid for their business, has been around for a while and distinguishes itself from competitors in a few important ways.

Here's how it works: The customer makes a reservation (but not a purchase) for a flight, cruise, hotel room, etc., and then registers it on the TravelBids site. The registration is a one-time fee of $5, and the first listing is free. After that, each additional listing is $5, presumably to keep nonserious travelers from posting trips that they're not really going to take, thus taking up the time of the travel agent bidders. The travel agents then have a specified amount of time to make bids on that listing, from one to 72 hours (customer sets the time limit). The minimum bid amount is 6% of your ticket cost, but bids usually run higher. Travel agents are willing to give up all or part of their commission because the consumer has done 99% of the work in making the travel arrangements. There are two other bidding variations on the above scenario, both involving the winning travel agents making your reservations. All three options are $5, and they're detailed on the website.

Don't be fooled by other travel auction sites until you've examined all their policies. Some differences between TravelBids and other travel-bidding services: TravelBids allows *many* travel agents to bid on your business; all bids are visible; you set the bidding price; you can include or exclude any airlines you wish; you get to set a specific range of travel times for your travel; TravelBids can be used for either business or leisure trips; you can accumulate frequent flyer miles with a ticket you got through TravelBids; changes to your ticket can be made if needed (with the usual change fees); the cost of the service is $5—there are no hidden fees. There's a place on the website where you get to see the most recent bids, and the savings are impressive. For five bucks, I don't see any reason *not* to use this service if you're going to be researching your own tickets anyway. (If no travel agent bids on your ticket, which is unlikely, you won't be charged the $5.) In essence, TravelBids will try to beat your lowest price, so you don't have anything to lose.

SPECIAL FACTORS: Registration requires a signed fax sheet from the consumer.

Vacations to Go

1502 Augusta Drive, Ste. 415　　800–338–4962
Houston, TX 77057　　　　　　　713–974–2121
　　　　　　　　　　　　　　　　　Fax: 713–974–0445

Catalog: free
Pay: major credit cards (see text)
Sells: cruises
Store: same address; Monday to Friday 8:30–5:30

There's a lot of fierce competition out there between travel agents looking to book your dream vacation. Vacations to Go calls itself "America's premier discount cruise specialist," and I was impressed with their no-nonsense approach. They claim to offer the lowest prices available on cruises 99% of the time, which they accomplish by being one of the largest sellers. This means that they have access to discounts and special fare programs that aren't available to the rest of the nation's travel agents. If the prices go down after you've booked your trip, they'll refund the difference (see catalog for details). Besides their regular low fares, here are some tips on how to save even more with Vacations to Go: (1) Book your trip in the fall; fall departures are traditionally less popular, and you'll get some great deals. (2) Take advantage of their group discounting program. You'll get a group rate (great for small family reunions) that's anywhere from 25% to 60% off the regular price, and if you book 15 full-fare people, the sixteenth gets to go for free—this on top of the group discount. (3) Take advantage of last-minute specials. Luckily, "last minute" to a cruise line means three months from departure, so that's plenty of time to plan. Vacations to Go has been in business since 1984, and their "cruise counselors" are easy and pleasant to talk to. Details on booking, cancellations, paying, etc., are in the catalog, or you can call for more information.

SPECIAL FACTORS: The type of credit cards accepted is determined by the cruise line on which you'll be traveling; quantity discounts available; smoke-free cruises available.

Volunteers for Peace

3 Tiffany Rd.　　　　　　**802–259–2759**
Belmont, VT 05730–0202　　**Fax: 802–259–2922**

Newsletter: free
Pay: MC, V, AE
Offers: placement service in short-term international
　workcamps
Online: www.vfp.org

You're an idealistic person with a strong commitment to social change. You yearn to travel to faraway places, but don't have a lot of money. You love people and you're not afraid of hard work. Does this describe you? If so, you should get hooked up with Volunteers for Peace. Volunteers for Peace is a Vermont nonprofit 501(c)(3) membership organization that's been coordinating International Workcamps since 1982. VFP is a member of the Coordinating Committee for International Voluntary Service (CCIVS) at UNESCO and works in cooperation with Service Civil International (SCI), the Alliance of European Voluntary Service Organizations, and the International Youth Action for Peace (YAP). Their services include providing consultation and a placement service for workcamp hosts and volunteers, linking people with programs that foster international education, voluntary service, and friendship worldwide.

　　The type of work you might be doing in a VFP workcamp is construction and restoration of low-income housing or community buildings; environmental projects such as trail-building, park maintenance, and organic farming; social services such as working with children, the elderly, physically or mentally handicapped, refugees, minority groups, drug/alcohol recovery, AIDS education and arts projects; and historic preservation and archaeology. Work projects can be of any type because they arise from the needs of the local host community. Generally, 10 to 20 people from four or more countries arrive on a given day in a host community, and you'll be housed in a school, church, private home, or community center. Living arrangements are cooperative, like a family, with volunteers coordinating and sharing the day-to-day activities such as food preparation, work projects, and recreation. The registration fee (beginning at $195 as of this writing) covers room and board and insurance; you pay airfare. Anyone 18 and up can volunteer. Most workcamps occur June through September and are two to three weeks in duration. The free newsletter gives a good overview of VFP and includes photos from some of the more recent workcamps.

The website, which has a wealth of information about VFP, allows you to order the free newsletter and a variety of other books and material online. If you decide to join VFP ($15/year) you'll receive the *International Workcamp Directory*, which lists and describes the more than 1,200 programs in over 70 countries from which you can choose. If you can find a cheap way to get to the host country, Volunteers for Peace will then provide you with an unbeatable opportunity to serve, to learn, and to discover at a bargain price.

SPECIAL FACTORS: No foreign language proficiency is required.

Related Products/Companies

Airline animal carriers
- UPCO, Valley Vet

Car racks and strapping for transporting large items
- Car Racks Direct

Family- and children-oriented travel guides
- The Family Travel Guide Catalog

Foldover shirt bags for wrinkle-free packing
- Plastic BagMart

Inflatable boat that fits in airline luggage compartment
- SOAR Inflatables

Luggage and travel accessories
- Ace Luggage, Airline International Luggage, Al's Luggage, The Luggage Center, Make Us An Offer, Santa Maria Discount Luggage

Packing materials and bags of every size and description
- Associated Bag

RV accessories
- RV Direct

Summer home-building workshops in Maine
- The Shelter Institute

Travel tips brochures
- Consumer Information Center, U.S. Gov't Superintendent of Documents

12-volt kitchen and bath appliances
- RV Direct

The Gift Guide

I have a friend who's a gifted gift-giver. Somehow she always comes up with the perfect item for the perfect occasion. Her gifts are appropriate, never extravagant, often highly creative and imaginative, and almost always touching. When I, on the other hand, wrack my brain to come up with the right present, my ideas flow naturally to "What does he *need?*" The gifts I give are infuriatingly practical, unromantic, and, well, boring. (I gave my sister a case of her favorite, hard-to-find shampoo one year. See what I mean?)

That's why I'm delighted to present "The Gift Guide." I've had a blast looking through so many hundreds of mail-order catalogs in print form and on the web. I no longer feel ungifted and uninspired when it comes to shopping for others. In fact, I feel confident now that I could find something for everyone on my gift list that he or she would absolutely love. Of course, the difference between me and you is that you've only got this book as a reference, while I have about 600 physical catalogs that I've read and studied and thoroughly know.

Wouldn't it be fun, I said to myself, if I could pick out some of my favorite products and present them in the form of gift ideas? I hope this highly opinionated guide gives you inspiration next time you're stuck. Below are gift ideas—most of the items $40 or under—that jumped out at me from different companies I researched, as well as the people for whom they might be appropriate. In many cases it's not the gifts that inspired me half as much as the company, which impressed me for one reason or another and made me want to share my enthusiasm with readers. As you're looking through this for ideas, please don't limit yourself to the categories I've suggested. Gender, age, relationships—these are all highly subjective.

If beautiful packaging isn't your forte, it never hurts to ask the company if they'll gift-wrap your purchase for you. Many will! Another option is to request a copy of the print catalog from **Current** (or better yet, visit their website). Current is a company that specializes in paper goods, although they carry an unusually interesting selection of household and gift items as well. Current offers cards for every occasion, gift wraps, gift bags that you can just plunk the present into, gorgeous curling ribbons, bows, giant festive bags (for jumbo gifts, such a doll-houses), labels, rubber stampers, jewelry boxes, gift boxes that double as tree ornaments, and much more.

Another *amazing* source of boxes and wrappings is **U.S. Box.** It's likely that you'll never look at packaging materials quite the same way again after you've seen the catalog from this company. This is a particularly good source if you need to save money by making candy or confections as gifts, but want these little presents to look like a million dollars. You'll find spectacular boxes and decorative display materials at U.S. Box that will probably be more unforgettable than what you packed in them.

A Gift for the Gift-Giver

I have a friend who only buys books as gifts—year after year. He has a knack for buying strange and quirky subject matter for the wrong people, but somehow it's endearing nevertheless. I have a similar idea that falls into the one-gift-for-all category, from an innovative company that I promise you'll fall in love with. It's called **Video Learning Library**. Invest in their catalog, which is under $40 at this writing, and you'll have gifts for all, for every occasion, *forever*. I'm not kidding. Every once in a while someone comes up with a great idea. This company has compiled thousands of video titles on every conceivable subject concerned with self-help, how-to, hobby, and educational subjects. Give videos as presents. You'll end up buying many for yourself as well once you own the catalog.

The Perfect (and Easiest) Present

Gift certificates, of course, are the best presents you can give, particularly if the receiver is unusually fussy or someone you don't know very well. Gift certificates are *not* no-brainers. I consider them to be among the most thoughtful of all presents since the type of vendor you choose can reveal a lot about how you feel. The amount of the gift certificate, of course, is up to you. Here are some really stand-out companies I can heartily recommend.

- *Ace Luggage & Gifts*
  for your favorite frequent traveler. Is her computer bag falling apart? Are you embarrassed by her raggedly makeup kit? This nifty company specializes in leather and luggage, especially geared for the executive. It's a can't-go-wrong present.
- *CD-ROM Outlet*
  for your favorite computer-gamer. The kid will really like that you didn't buy him something "educational." He'll definitely find a great game here to show off to his friends.
- *Daylily Discounters*
  for your favorite flower gardener. This is the gift that keeps on giving. A handful of daylily bulbs will bloom forever, multiply, and will always

remind the recipient of you at least once a year. Not too many gifts can accomplish all that!

- *Fire Mountain Gems*
for your favorite artsy-craftsy teenaged girl. Every page of this jewelry-making catalog has things I would have died for as a teen. She'll be able to design her own earrings that'll be the rage among her friends. And who knows? It may get her interested in a lucrative hobby.

- *Holabird*
for your favorite tennis or racquetball nut. This company offers great buys on an eclectic assortment of top-name merchandise for every type of racquet sport.

- *The Left Hand*
for your favorite southpaw. This catalog of tools, games, gifts, and accessories for left-handed people has something for everyone: from your six-year-old to your grandpa, including hand tools, kitchen items, computer accessories, sports equipment, and whimsical gifts.

- *New Global Marketing*
for your favorite closet cigar smoker. He (she?) will like this hip little company that scans the world for the best deals on cigars, both brand-name and lesser-known boutique lines. Best of all, he or she won't have to sneak them.

- *State Line Tack*
for your favorite horse fanatic. This wonderful catalog has all kinds of fun as well as practical items for equestrians.

- *That Fish Place*
for your favorite aquarist. Since you don't know whether he'll want real plants, fake coral, or a miniature shipwreck to decorate his aquarium floor and to provide intellectual stimulation for his guppies, give him a gift certificate and let him decide for himself.

- *Tools on Sale*
for your favorite man who's tool-crazy. This may end up being an expensive gift, but at least you'll know he's finally gotten what he really wanted.

- *Toysmart.com*
for your favorite kid. Is there a kid in the world who wouldn't think you were the *absolute coolest* after getting this gift certificate to one of the best toy stores on the Internet?

- *Valley Vet*
for your favorite DINK (Double Income, No Kids) couple. When you're at their house for dinner, they ask you politely about your son's progress in school, and then light up when you ask *them* how Fluffy is acclimating to the new puppy. They'll find doggie toys and cutesy cat items galore here.

College-Aged Kids, Gen-Xers, and Adult Children

Antique broom labels collection

for your twenty-something daughter who's just gotten her own place. These pretty labels feature original American commercial art picturing flowers, birds, cats, sailors, Indians, and more, and make adorable decorations for any kitchen. Collection of 30 different broom labels, $12 plus postage. (Original Paper Collectibles)

Sterling silver serving fork and spoon

for your daughter-in-law, whose friends gave her sculptures and poems as presents instead of consulting her wedding registry. She's scraped together service for six of her wedding pattern. But if she's into entertaining, she'll appreciate having a large silver fork, pie server, gravy ladle, etc. to match her flatware. $ varies. (Beverly Bremer)

Streetwise Guide: Chinese Herbal Medicine

for your recent college grad who's interested in alternative medicine. This is a valuable introduction to the subject written simply and clearly. $11.95. (East Earth Trade Winds)

Thai cookbook and "Bare Essentials" box of Thai ingredients

for your daughter who loves to cook. Every famous Thai restaurant specialty is included in *The Elegant Taste of Thailand-Cha Am Cuisine,* and the ingredients package has the necessary basics to get started: Thai fish sauce, red and green curry pastes, lemon grass powder, Laos powder, tamarind paste, Sriracha sauce, canned coconut milk, and Kaffir lime leaves. Now maybe she'll invite you to dinner. Cookbook: $22; "Bare Essentials": $27 (The CMC Company)

"Trio" cheese and sausage gift box

for the homesick, Midwestern gen-Xer who's moved to the big city. Comes with 1 pound of aged cheddar, 1 pound of medium cheddar, and 9 ounces of beef summer sausage. Enough to share with friends who are crashing out on the couch indefinitely. $12. (Gibbsville Cheese)

Vintage pink princess rotary phone

for your college girl who's just moved off campus. Retro is in, daddy, and she'll think you're the greatest for giving her such a fun housewarming present that's also a collectible. $ varies. (Phoneco, Inc.)

Zoom spotting scope

for your urban-dwelling grad-school kid who shares an apartment with two buddies and likes to look out the window at, ahem, birds. Should you be encouraging this kind of behavior? I bet you wish you had one of these, small and light enough to carry around in a backpack, with its own mini tripod. $149. (Orion)

Fathers, Uncles, Fathers-In-Law, and Grandfathers

Campfire pie iron

for dad who loves to sit by a fire out back, sip a brewsky, and watch the kids running around on an August evening. Who says Dad can't cook? Put a favorite filling between two buttered slices of bread, close, and toast over the open fire for a melted, delicious treat. Made of cast iron, with a 21-inch handle. $19.95. (Lehman's Non-Electric Catalog)

Cashmere men's hosiery

for your favorite man who has it all. If he's into luxury, he'll think you're the greatest for indulging in these handsome socks made of Merino wool and cashmere. They're machine washable. $23.50. (Huntington)

Chimes of Kyoto

for your aesthetic father-in-law, who's been in touch with his feminine side ever since he had that big medical scare a few years back. He'll enjoy relaxing on the patio listening to the graceful, soft sounds of these famous, hand-crafted Woodstock Chimes. $42. (Anyone Can Whistle)

Coffee-table art book

for your father-in-law. He'll think you spent a lot of money, he'll be impressed with your inside knowledge about his favorite artist (his son, of course, tipped you off), and it'll even make him look good in front of his friends. $ varies. (Hacker Art Books)

Manual of Traditional Wood Carving

for Grampa the Whittler. If he loves to carve little animals for the grandkids, he'll appreciate this classic book full of refinements on the subject as well as hundreds of interesting projects and ideas. $12. (Woodworkers Discount Books)

Pocket-sized pillbox with built-in alarm

for dear old dad, who has to take his meds four times a day—but can never remember. This nifty little pillbox can be programmed to beep up to 19 times every 24 hours, and it's small enough to fit into his change pocket. $13.95. (Comfort House)

Sheepskin seat covers

for your uncle, who loves you just a little bit more than his car. These slightly irregular sheepskins are so affordable that you can probably afford one for his passenger seat as well. Starting at $29. (Sheepskin Station)

SwissCard

for your uncle, who loves gadgets. This is a Swiss army–type tool—complete with straight pen, toothpick, nail file with screwdriver tip, tweezers, ballpoint pen, scissors, and knife—that fits together to become the size of a credit card! Wow! $19.95. (Cutlery Shoppe)

Friends, Siblings, and Significant Others

Armful bouquet of fresh-cut snapdragons

for yourself. Well, okay, for someone else. These babies come straight from the greenhouse that grows them, and they'll last longer and be more beautiful than any other flowers you've ever purchased. (I know; I got some for myself!) $41.95, includes next-day delivery. (Evergreen Farms)

"Carvin Bolt" kit guitar

to placate your boyfriend's "inner teenager." He can make his own Carvin, knock down some cold ones with his buddies in the garage, alienate the neighbors, and claim to be in the company of such greats as James Brown's band, YES, and Michael Bolton's and Mariah Carey's guitar players—all Carvin aficionados. $329.95, least expensive kit. (Carvin)

Chocolate-lover's cookbook

for your favorite chocoholic. There are scores to choose from, and they're all deeply discounted. $ varies. (Jessica's Biscuit Cookbooks)

Cinnamon Cider Syrup

for your earth-mama friend whose baby wears cloth diapers, eats homemade organic baby food, and listened to Joni Mitchell while still in the womb. Your girlfriend will love the "story" behind the family who makes this delirious stuff, and she'll also appreciate the many ways it can be used in cooking as an out-of-the-ordinary natural sweetener. $7.75/pint. (Wood's Cider Mill)

Counterculture book

for your favorite tattooed, body-pierced, cross-dressing, vegan friend. He'll feel you're being sensitive to his lifestyle, and you'll get a tremendous kick out of shopping from the catalog and website that feature a variety of shockable but smart counterculture media items. $ varies. (Essential Media)

Cracker Jack reproduction tin sign

for your favorite overeater's kitchen. "The More You Eat, The More You Want," announces Little Jack in sailor suit accompanied by his black-and-white mutt. This gift will add nostalgic class and humor to any kitchen decor. $12. (Desperate Enterprises)

Earth-friendly household cloth products

for your friend who's had a compost pile going since 1969. Make up your own combination from the many catalog items, but here's a nifty start: 100% Cotton Coffee Filter Baskets (two/$6)—to substitute for those throwaway store-bought paper filters; Salad Bags (six/$5)—100% cheesecloth bags that keep your lettuce fresh longer than plastic ones; and Plastic Bag Sleeve ($4)—hanging cotton sleeve that you stuff full of plastic bags at the top, and pull out at the bottom so they get reused. (Clothcrafters)

Hand-dyed silk velvet muffler

for your sophisticated girlfriend from college who's now living in the city, making big bucks, and hobnobbing with the rich and famous (she still loves you the best, though). These two-hued textured scarves somehow straddle the fence between artsy and elegant, and come in somber, classy colors such as black and gray. $35. (Holly Raal Textiles)

Her favorite perfume

for your not-so-little sister. Every woman who loves perfume wishes someone else would buy it! Buy it discount, have it gift-wrapped for free, and she'll forgive you the ten years of noogies and Indian rope burns you delivered. $ varies. (Perfumax)

Laminated decorator-fabric place mats

for your best friend's new country house. You don't have to be a genius to pick out a gorgeous fabric (you can even do it online), have part of it custom-laminated, then sew that fabric into rectangles (for place mats) and the untreated fabric into squares (for matching napkins). $ varies. (Hancock's of Paducah)

Mini-collection of Betty or Carlene Carter

for your girlfriend, who heard the singer for the very first time last week on NPR, and flipped. (Which planet has she been inhabiting all these years anyway?) But don't buy these CDs new. Get them pre-owned and you'll be able to buy her several so she'll have an instant collection. Cost varies, but most used CDs are under $8. (Audio House)

Mini vacuum-attachment kit

for your lovable computer geek whose idea of great exercise is web-surfing. This little gadget vacuums tiny places—such as computer keyboards. $8.95. (Newark Dressmaker Supply)

Misto

for your health-conscious wife who's succeeded in decaffeinating you, and is now determined to lower your cholesterol and weight too. This is a gourmet olive-oil sprayer you fill half-full with your favorite oil, pump the cap to pressurize, and then without propellants or chemicals it sprays onto salads, pasta, meats, veggies, and pizza. $19.99. (A Cook's Wares)

Old-fashioned, cast-iron cornbread molds

for your friend who aspires to be a chef. He's going to treasure these, which create baked goodies in the shape of corncobs or cacti, and look great hung on the kitchen wall between uses. $5.85. (ChuckWagon Outfitters)

100% cotton coverlet

for your brother and sister-in-law's weekend home. Is there anyone who wouldn't love a solid-color, woven bedspread that's perfect year-round? You won't believe the prices at this old-fashioned Maine mill, especially on the "seconds." $ varies. (Bates Mill Store)

Pottery book

for your talented ceramicist friend. The books here range from nifty treasure troves filled with ceramic craft ideas to elegant coffee-table books that showcase the best examples of pottery styles and techniques. $ varies. (Aftosa)

Rush-woven stool

for your big brother whom you adore. This little stool comes in a kit and you weave the rush yourself. He'll love that you made him something, and it makes a great footstool or plant stand for his bachelor pad. $15.50. (Frank's Cane and Rush)

Russian Caviar Sampler

for your gal or guy who has everything. You'll get three 1-ounce jars each of Beluga, Osetra, and Sevruga caviar, a mother-of-pearl spoon, and a package of caviar toast. $100 (includes overnight shipping). (The Caviar Man)

Small woodland management kit

for that city-slicker couple who've just purchased a dozen acres of land in the country and don't have a clue. These kits include a how-to video, management calendar, resource directory, workbook, and more—in short, everything new landowners need in order to protect their land from natural disasters such as fire and pestilence; manage their property; and improve the beauty and health of their trees. Customized by state. $99.00 (Bailey's)

Sunshower III

for your favorite camper. Hang this 3.9-gallon pouch outside in the sun and get a nice warm shower at day's end. The Sunshower III features a shampoo pouch, pipe handle for carrying ease, heavy-duty 4-ply construction, and thermal indicator to monitor water temperature. $21.50. (Defender Industries)

Trunk organizer

for your slob of a boyfriend whose flashlight, umbrella, window-washing fluid, and cylindrical tools are always rolling around in his trunk at every wild turn. This attractive bag has interior pockets, moveable interior dividers, and double web handles. After you organize his car trunk, Velcro strips on the bottom allow you to secure the whole thing down so *it* will never tip over. $37.99. (William Alden Company)

Undyed silk boxers to tie-dye

for your terminally hip husband. Tie-dye him a pair for his birthday. $7.95/pair. (Dharma Trading Co.)

Volleyball net

for you and your gang of friends renting the beach house this summer. About $85. (Spike Nashbar)

Worker's Soap

for your beloved grease monkey whose hands are always hopelessly black just when it's time to get romantic. Okay, so he pays a little bit more attention to his cars than to you. But he'll appreciate this triangular bar of soap that's handmade with pumice and scented with clove oil. The woman who makes it says it's one of her best sellers—and men love it! $3. (Kettle Care)

Kids and Teens

Battery-operated kids' pottery wheel

for your young potter. Think of the hundreds of tiny bowls and ashtrays she'll be able to give as presents! About $29. (Ott's Discount Art Supply)

A Cheapass game

for your clever but slightly rotten prepubescent son. He'll definitely thank you for introducing him to the coolest game his gang of feet-smelling pals has ever played. These original games are smart, fun, offbeat, and *way cool.* Best of all, they're cheap—so you can get him two or three. Under $10. (Cheapass Games)

Color Your Own Hanukkah Postcards

for your granddaughters who need an excuse to write. After they detach the cards from a small book and color or paint youngsters with menorahs, dreidels, Stars of David, and more, would it kill them to send their dear old grandma a short letter for a change? Oy vey, kids today! $1 (Dover Publications)

Incredible! or Musopoly music-oriented games

for your big and little Von Trapps. Since musical talent runs in genes, these games will provide your whole familial gang with great and innovative fun, ages six and up. $17.50 and $22.95, respectively. (Shar Products Company)

Miles of Smiles or 52 Fun Things to Do on the Plane

for your kids, aged four and up, just as soon as you're pulling out of the driveway to begin vacation. The former has 101 great car games and activities, and is a book one enthusiastic user called "the ultimate solution for back seat squabbling." The latter is a colorfully decorated card deck that easily fits into a purse or pocket with games and activities for bored kids. *Miles of Smiles,* $8.95; *52 Fun Things,* $6.95. (The Family Travel Guides Catalog)

Pretend grocery check-out collection

for your two- to seven-year-old children. All children love to role-play, and this setup includes a realistic cash register, moving conveyor belt and scanner that beeps and flashes, play money, shopping basket, and miniature groceries. A great way to encourage social skills, creative play, and math. Set $29.95. (Constructive Playthings)

Ready-to-paint nesting boxes

for your favorite artsy niece. If the two of you decorate a set of three papier mâché boxes—oval, round, heart-shaped, or hexagonal—together, she'll treasure them always. $10.99 a set. (Artists Club)

Sioux war bonnet kit

for the seven-year-old kid who loves 1950s shoot-'em-ups and always sides with the Indians. This kit has imitation eagle feathers, base fluffs, tip plumes, red felt, leather for loops and crown, brow band, glue, sinew lace, horsehair, and complete instructions. $19. (Leather Unlimited)

Sports hero poster

for your preteen to plaster the last empty space of his bedroom ceiling with. There are lots of great posters to choose from (movies, comics, etc.) so don't stop with one. About $7. (PosterNow)

Teen magazine subscription

for your teenage nephew who pretty much hates everything. He'll like the fact that his aunt or uncle was hip enough to buy him his own nonacademic reading material. And once it starts arriving with his name on it, he can rag on Mom and Dad for reading his mail. Besides, you'll save about 80% off the normal cover price if you buy it here. $ varies. (Below Wholesale Magazines)

Whimsical-shaped adhesive bandages

as a stocking stuffer for your little one who always seems to have a scraped knee or elbow. Let a heart-shaped bandage take the sting out of his next "ouchie." $5 for 33. (Stickers 'N' Stuff)

Mothers, Aunts, Mothers-In-Law, and Grandmothers

Carry-all easel box

for your Sunday-painter mom who likes to stroll to the Village Green and paint the blossoming apple trees in front of the old library. This little wooden box holds a 16 by 20-inch canvas, has adjustable side tray for brushes and paints, and a sliding T-top. $33.39. (Utrecht Art Supply)

Cordials from Your Kitchen

for your favorite aunt who loves to nip at the bottle from time to time. This book has recipes for 100 easy, elegant liqueurs she can make at home at a fraction of the cost of commercial ones. Tiny, decorative bottles of homemade cordials make great gifts too. $14.95. (Storey Books)

4X pendant magnifier

for your mother, who can never seem to locate her reading glasses when she needs them. What a great idea: an attractive 2-inch-diameter magnifier that looks like a piece of jewelry, hangs from a 35-inch black silk cord, and is always there when she'll need it—at the grocery store, when the afternoon mail arrives, in the kitchen, etc. $10.95. (Independent Living Aids)

Gift-wrap organizer

for your aunt, who's always sending little gifts to everyone under the sun. Now you can send her one that she'll really use. She'll appreciate this ingenious little item, which allows one to store rolls of gift wrap, ribbons, decorative bags, and other wrapping items such as scissors and tape all in one place. $5.99. (Current)

Grandloving: Making Memories with Your Grandchildren

for your children's creative grandma before you drop the kids off to spend a week with her. This book, endorsed by such notables as Bil Keane, creator of *The Family Circus* cartoon, offers over 200 inexpensive and innovative activities grandparents can do with their grandkids, and is full of anecdotes and little jewels of wisdom from around the world. $14.95. (Gramma's Graphics)

1950s radio dramas

for your great-aunt who still loves the radio but mourns the fact that there aren't as many good stations as there used to be. She'll be thrilled to sit back in her rocker and listen to a collection of her old favorites on a tape player. Around $15. (Adventures in Cassettes)

Outdoor light

for that special woman who loves her garden paths, landscaped lawns, and never lets you leave without a sack full of fresh greens. Trust me when I tell you that the lighting designs from this company are artistic masterpieces. $ varies. (Golden Valley Lighting)

Photographic insurance record book

for your aging parents as they're getting ready to make that move to Florida with a lifetime of heirloom antiques. Includes a Deluxe Record Book, one roll double-stick tape in dispenser, and the pamphlet "Making a Photo Inventory of Your Home." $14.95. (Porter's Camera Store)

Scissors block

for your favorite serious seamstress. This hardwood scissors block (looks like a knife block) holds five pairs of scissors, from 8-inch pinking shears to the small 4-inch embroidery size. Neat. $10.95. (Atlanta Thread & Supply)

Teapot basket

for your mother, who loves to sit by the fire, knit, listen to classical music, and drink tea. This little gift basket includes a tea sampler (four 2-ounce bags of tea), a mesh tea infuser, plus a six-cup English Brown Betty teapot. From $29, depending on tea sampler. (Northwestern Coffee Mills)

Two crewel hand-embroidered cushion covers

for your mother's new room at the retirement home to class up her minimal furnishings. Anyone who sees it will love this luscious fabric that's handmade in India. About $11 each. (Shama Imports)

Thank-You Gifts

Blue Velvet Gift Box

for your favorite New Age-y hostess. She burns incense, drinks green tea, and knows how to make tempeh taste like bacon, so give her a sample of these all-natural, earth-friendly products—dish, hair, bath, and laundry soaps, and almond lotion. She'll thank you that it's not one of those frilly, perfumed soap-and-bath-oil gift baskets from the convenience mart. $10.00. (Cal Ben Soap Company)

Custom-made teabags

for your neighbors, children's teachers, school bus driver, postman, etc. Made from nonirradiated bulk teas and self-seal tea bags, you can customize little thank-you gifts without spending much money. Teas, about $6.95/pound; tea bags, $1.90/50. (Atlantic Spice Co.)

Custom fortune cookies

for the retiring executive's farewell party. 500-count with your own personal message inside. 500, 29 cents each. (Best Impressions Promotional Products)

Handmade wood-slat lunch basket

for your favorite secretary who's so frugally brought her lunch with her all these years. She'll love this little basket, even if she decides to keep it at home for a million other uses. $21. (West Rindge)

Pound of organic coffee

for three different hostesses. Anyone who loves coffee will appreciate this gift, and since there's a three-pound minimum to qualify for the stupendous price, stick a bow on each pound and keep the extras in your freezer for emergency hostess gifts. (Guests bearing gifts are always invited back!) $5.80. (Catskill Mountain Coffee)

A Guide to
Buying by Mail

Catalogs and Price Quotes

Catalogs

Print catalogs, which most of the firms in this book issue, range from glossy tomes laden with color photos to a few photocopied pages listing products and prices. Some are free; others cost up to $5, a fee more intended to weed out frivolous requests than to offset publishing costs. To receive a print catalog, you must request it, although if you're a recent customer, some companies will automatically send you the latest catalog.

Online Catalogs. An intangible catalog that is gaining in popularity is the online catalog, located at a company's website. Depending on the size of the company, the site can present select items intended to prompt an online or telephone request for a print copy of the catalog (without an ordering option), or it can detail every product in stock and provide for online and traditional forms of ordering. An advantage of using the online catalog is a feature known as Online, or Web, Specials, where new sale items are listed daily or weekly.

"Refundable" Catalogs. Companies *want* catalog shoppers to place orders from the catalog they requested. Therefore, as an incentive, they offer to deduct the catalog fee from the first order, which should be placed within six months of receipt of the catalog, unless a specific time limit is stated. Reimbursement can be done a number of ways. Two common methods are: (1) to deduct the catalog fee from the *grand total* of the order (the order *plus* tax, if applicable, and shipping charges), adding the words "less catalog fee" beside the deducted amount; and (2) to submit a company-issued refund coupon with the order, deducting the coupon amount from the *product total.* If you don't place any orders from the catalog, you do not qualify for a refund of the fee.

Sending for Catalogs. The easiest way to get a catalog is to call and request one. If you choose to make your request in writing, for free catalogs, a postcard is enough as long as it states your name, address, the catalog you want, and how you learned about it (in this case, from *Wholesale by Mail and Online 2000*). If there's a charge for the catalog, you'll need to send a letter, with the same information mentioned above, and payment in the form of a check, money order, or, for small amounts, a dollar bill or two secured inside two pieces of cardboard. (For sums so small, it's unlikely a company would accept credit card payment for just a catalog.) When sending checks, always note the company's name, address, and telephone number in the memo section and in your check register. Finally, if a firm asks for "an SASE" (self-addressed, stamped envelope), you must also enclose a #10 (business size) envelope, addressed to yourself, with one first-class stamp affixed.

Receiving Catalogs. To be realistic, you should expect receipt of your catalog within six to eight weeks of placing your request. Long as that seems, it's not unreasonable when you consider that catalogs are published seasonally or annually and that if a company runs out, reprinting takes time. More likely, though, if a catalog is available, you'll receive it in under two weeks—when buying is still on your mind!

Price Quotes

When stock moves in and out quickly—as it can at outlets and at companies that sell discontinued or deeply discounted products—goods are sold on a price-quote basis, rather than by catalog. Another reason companies sell by price quote is because they can avoid excessive overhead. Their "store" may consist of nothing more than an office, where a staffperson acts as agent between manufacturer and customer. There's no inventory, no showroom, no print catalog, small staff. Name-brand products sold this way include appliances, electronics, cameras and similar equipment, tableware, furniture, carpeting, perfume, bedding, and sporting goods. (Price quotes are also given when the customer seeks an item not found in the company's catalog.) A price quote, simply put, represents the cost of a specific item from a company at the time of the quote, and can usually be obtained by phone, letter, fax, and e-mail.

Advantages to Price Quotes. I didn't know much about buying by price quote until I began researching this book. Now it's one of my favorite ways to shop. Why? Because vendors will reward me in the form of deep discounts for all the hard work I did for them. To request a price quote, the shopper needs to know some standard information: the manufacturer's name; the product's model number; and the color or pattern name or code. The quote is usually honored for a limited time or until stock is gone. Find out if the price you receive includes, or is exclusive of, tax, shipping and handling, insurance, and other charges.

Finding the Information. One of the reasons mail-order prices are low is that you, the shopper, do your own product research *before* seeking a price quote. You need to get the name of the company that manufactures the product you're interested in, the *manufacturer's* product code (also called model number or style number or pattern name), and in some cases, the product's size and color. Maybe you saw the item in a catalog, a magazine, an ad, or in a friend's home or office. Since those sources won't always provide the detailed, current, and accurate information you need, it's a good idea to check factory cartons or product tags in local stores as well as manufacturers' product brochures, sometimes available in stores.

Prices Quoted by Letter. If you are the organized sort who likes information to be written in a consistent format, you can request price quotes by letter. This seems a quaint method in the age of e-mail, but if you're engaged in a long-term search for a hard-to-find item, tracking which firm does or doesn't have what you need can be easier by letter. *Make sure you enclose an SASE with your request.* If you don't, no matter how much product information you provide, no quote will be given. That said, your request should include all the information that would help a sales rep identify the product. Limit your request to three items, and draw lines next to each item where the price and estimated shipping can be written in. To prevent misunderstandings, make sure your request is dated, and ask how long the quoted prices will be in effect.

Prices Quoted by E-mail. Some companies have both website and e-mail addresses. Some only have an e-mail address to which shoppers are invited to send comments and questions. If you seek a price quote by e-mail, include the usual product information. Some discounters, in apparel, for example, will respond to more general queries, such as whether a line by a particular designer is in stock. E-mail correspondence automatically includes when and from what address the query was sent; if you want the company's response to go to a *different* e-mail address, say so, and give the address. Response time varies, so be patient before sending a repeat query.

Prices Quoted by Phone. The preferred way of giving quotes, for most companies, is by phone. For distance callers, there's often a toll-free number (800–, 888–, or 877–). If a firm is in your area, use the local number if one is given. When you call, be ready to write down what the salesperson tells you, and ask for the person's name in case you need to refer to the call at a later date. Be considerate of the sales rep's hectic pace by having the product information—organized and readable—at hand. If your information is unclear, getting the right quote becomes more difficult.

How to Order

Our reasons for shopping by mail or online vary from person to person—for convenience, lowest price, the excitement of getting a package at home. What matters is that your shopping experience be satisfactory and that products meet your expectations.

Cost Comparisons

If your prime reason for shopping by mail or online is to get the best price, then you need to do some comparing and contrasting between retail and mail-order firms. When considering retail shopping, factor in time, for traveling and shopping; cost, for the item and for travel (gas, tolls, parking, or bus fares); taxes, which you often don't have to pay if ordering by mail; and convenience or lack thereof, as in crowds, long lines, and unavailable sales help. If the product would need to be delivered, add in delivery charges and time spent waiting for the item to arrive. When considering shopping for the same product by mail or online, look at price, which may include tax and probably shipping; time, between placing the order and receiving it; the availability of customer service, at the time of ordering and in case of problems; and policies regarding returns, which can include restocking fees and time limits, which usually do not apply at large retailers.

If the item is a gift, you can place an order and have it shipped to the recipient without leaving your home. If you're buying in quantity, discounts are available from many of the vendors in this book.

After weighing the costs and intangible differences between the two forms of shopping, you'll know which is better for you. A final tip, here: Catalog descriptions of furniture, exercise equipment, and appliances give product dimensions so you can see, before ordering, if the item will fit the space you have in mind. Always make sure the product you want will be able to fit through doorways (interior and exterior), stairways, hallways, and the like, or onto a shelf or counter space if that is the ultimate destination.

Ordering by Mail

Always order from a company's most recent catalog. If you have an older one but you know the products are fairly consistent, call to confirm that the product is available and what the current price is. If you order from an out-of-date edition, you risk delaying delivery if the firm has to contact you about price differences and payment. Generally speaking, you'd do better to request a new catalog.

Place your order using the form in the catalog, making sure to affix your preprinted address label to the indicated space on the form. If your catalog is a pass-along, without an order form, write up the order on your own paper, using a form from another catalog as an example of the kinds of information to include. You'll need to know code numbers, item names, quantity of each item being ordered, price per item, tax if applicable, and shipping charges. Take your time so you don't forget such important information as your name, delivery address, and phone number; the name and address of the firm you're ordering from; payment information (see "Payment," page 630) and special information such as an additional address if the item is being shipped as a gift or if the order is being billed to someone other than yourself. Respect any minimum-order requirements. Attach a *copy of the order* to the catalog and file it.

Second Choices and Substitutions. Indicating a *second choice* on the order form means that you will accept a different color of the same product if the first color is not available. Indicating that you will accept *substitutions* means that if the product you want is out of stock, you will accept an available product comparable in function, quality, and price to the one you originally wanted. If that kind of substitution is fine with you, say so on the order form or letter. Companies are prohibited by law from making substitutions without the buyer's *written* authorization. If neither a second choice nor a substitution is acceptable to you, write in red *on the order form,* "NO SECOND CHOICES OR SUBSTITUTIONS ACCEPTED."

Ordering by Phone

Giving an order by phone can be easier and faster than mailing in an order. If you opt to order by phone, you'll need to have the same information you would include in a mail order. Therefore, you should fill out the order form *before* placing your call—including the address label, which has encoded information the operator might ask for, and home and business telephone numbers. Your phone order, however, will probably be processed more quickly than a mail order would, and if an item is out of stock, the customer service rep probably will be able to tell you at the time of your call.

When you're ready to call, have before you the completed order form, your credit card, and note-taking materials. The operator will facilitate the steps of placing the order. You, in turn, should obtain the following information from the person taking your call:

- the operator's name and/or operator number
- the policy on returns, in case your product carries exceptions to terms listed in the catalog
- when new stock will arrive if an ordered item is not currently available
- expected shipping date
- how the order will be shipped (items together or separate)
- the grand total that will be charged to your credit card
- your order number

Before the transaction ends, the customer service rep may tell you about additional products on special discount. Give a listen in case there's something you've been meaning to pick up when the price was right. If you do add a product to your order, be sure to jot it down, including the price, and ask for the final total. Add the date of the call to your notes, and attach the record to the catalog for safe keeping.

Buying at Wholesale

A wholesale buyer operates, or represents, a business that intends to resell the purchased items as they are or in another form. If your order or your business qualifies, you can buy at true wholesale from the firms in this book that have a star icon among the symbols. Wholesale orders are subject to any one of the special sales terms below:

> *Letterhead or Business Card:* to show you're acting as a company, not as an individual.
>
> *Resale Number or Business Certificate:* to show your activity is part of a business enterprise registered with local authorities and to qualify for exemption from sales tax.
>
> *Bank and Credit References:* to obtain invoice billing or to open an account.
>
> *Limited Options of Payment:* to protect the vendor's interest. Payment could be limited to a check or money order or include credit card.
>
> *Minimum Order:* to qualify as a wholesale purchase. Minimums can be stated as dollar amounts, number of items, yardage—whatever applies to a particular type of product.

How companies handle wholesale and retail catalog requests varies, from sending out the same catalog, with a discount price schedule attached to the wholesaler's catalog, to issuing separate catalogs for retail and wholesale buyers, with different products available to wholesalers. Although wholesale catalogs give a pared-down version of product information compared to retail catalogs, they do make sample orders available. Also, they charge less for shipping than retail buyers would pay. At such price breaks, it's not unreasonable to be charged a restocking fee of 10% to 25% if merchandise is accepted for return. Likewise, the savvy wholesale buyer will stay away from orders labeled "final sale, no returns accepted."

For some firms in this book wholesale buyers' terms are indicated in the text. If wholesale orders are accepted, make sure you honor the company's terms when you place your order.

Payment

The Federal Trade Commission (FTC) Mail or Telephone Order Rule may not mean anything to you now, but in the event you are due a refund on an order placed by mail or phone, it will come into play. Did you pay for your order on *credit* using a credit card, or did you *prepay*, using a check or money order or debit card?

Prepaid Orders. Orders paid for using checks (personal, certified, bank, teller's, cashier's), money orders (bank, postal), and debit cards are considered *cash* payments under the FTC Mail or Telephone Order Rule. Each form of payment has its pluses and minuses.

Personal checks are convenient, inexpensive, and accepted by most firms. The canceled check serves as a receipt for the purchase, and it is automatically returned to you with your bank's monthly statement of checking account activity. The "memo" portion of the check, filled out when you placed the order, keeps a record of the firm's address and telephone number. On the downside, a firm will usually wait for your check to clear before shipping your order, adding a delay of up to two weeks to your delivery date. Also, if omitted or underpaid charges must be added to your total, a second check might have to be sent to make up the difference, adding to the delay.

A *certified check* is a *personal* check that has been marked "certified" by the bank on which the check is drawn. A "certified" stamp means that the bank has frozen in your account the amount indicated on the check, thereby guaranteeing the availability of the funds to the vendor. This guarantee eliminates payment-related delays. The fee for a certified check ranges from $5 to $9; like a personal check, this check is returned to you in the monthly checking account statement. If a firm requires a certified check, common when fulfilling a first order, it is likely to accept a bank check, a teller's check, or a cashier's check, each of which represents a guarantee of funds.

Both banks and the U.S. Postal Service (through post offices and postal carriers in rural areas) sell *money orders.* A bank will charge between $1 and $3, with no cap on the amount. At 80 cents each, a postal money order costs less, but it is limited to a maximum of $700. Both come with receipts attached, either a copy underneath the money order or a stub that should be filled out with the company's name and address and the money order amount. If the date of the money order is not automatically printed on it, be sure to add the date when you fill in the name of the firm and your name and address.

You won't automatically receive proof of a money order's having been cashed, the way you would with a check, but a bank money order can be traced, payment can be stopped, and a refund can be issued. A postal money order can be replaced if it is lost or stolen (as long as you have the receipt), and copies of a cashed money order can be obtained from USPS within two years of its being cashed. A reminder: *Immediately* fill in the blanks on a money order, and separate it from the receipt when you're done. If the money order is stolen or lost, you can't get a replacement if you don't have the filled-in receipt.

Credit, Charge, and Debit Cards. Let's start with *debit cards* since they are a hybrid of the more familiar credit card and personal check. When you pay with a debit card, your bank receives an invoice for your purchase and electronically deducts the total of the invoice from your account (checking, savings, money management). That payment is viewed as a cash payment by the FTC, not a credit card payment.

Credit and charge cards are not identical creatures, but when you use one or the other to make a purchase, the procedure is the same. You must provide the vendor with the account number of the card (make sure the firm accepts that card), the expiration date, your phone number, and your signature, if ordering by mail. The advantage to using these cards, besides getting to pay later for a product you enjoy now, is that any unforeseen or overlooked charges, such as shipping costs, can be added to the card, thereby preventing a shipping delay. You're probably wondering what distinguishes the two cards. Simply this: a credit card (MasterCard, Visa) allows you to carry a balance from month to month and requires only a minimum payment while charging interest on the total unpaid balance; a charge card (American Express) requires you to pay the entire balance on each statement. Because *vendors* incur charges (from the card-issuing companies) when they accept credit and charge cards, their minimum-order requirement is usually higher than it would be for a prepaid order.

Return Policies

Policies differ among companies, so you should check on a policy *before* you order (the "Special Factors" entry in the text often addresses this). Catalog firms will accept returns within 10 to 30 days of receipt of the order (a couple of exceptions are as short as 7 and as long as 90!). Products purchased on a price-quote basis (that is, when a catalog is not offered) usually are not returnable unless defective. Certain items not covered by general return policies include those that have been personalized, logoed, or monogrammed; custom-made; or purchased as surplus or on final sale. Likewise if you ask a company to special-order a product. Returns of undergarments and swimsuits are generally not accepted, but there are exceptions, especially if a package is unopened (see "Returns," page 641).

Finally, before you spring for an expensive item with lots of moving parts, ask the firm to fax you a copy of the manufacturer's warranty. Then take a look at "Evaluating Warranties," page 646, for help in deciding whether the warranty holds any value for you.

Canceling Your Order

By ordering goods or services by phone or mail, you create a *contract of sale* between yourself and the firm providing them. According to the FTC rule, you cannot cancel that order or stop payment on a check or money order simply because you have changed your mind about the purchase. (Remember, *you* contacted the company; it did not phone or knock on your door to solicit a purchase from you.) Contract law varies from state to state, but rescinding an order could open you up to legal action by the firm.

What if your concern is that the company is about to fold, taking your money with it and not delivering the goods? Then stopping payment might be a prudent step. But barring such a situation, keep in mind that most catalog firms guarantee satisfaction (they want your repeat business) so goods can be sent back when they arrive. If you *really* don't want to go through with an order you've already placed, speak to representatives of the firm *first*. For whatever reason, they might be able to work with you to everyone's satisfaction.

Shipping, Handling, Insurance, and Sales Tax

A *major* consideration when weighing the advantages and disadvantages of shopping by mail, phone, and online is the combined cost of shipping, handling, insurance, and tax. (See also "Cost Comparisons," page 627.)

Shipping

Shipping costs discussed in this section apply to purchases that are made from U.S. firms *and* that are being delivered to addresses in the U.S.

Shipping Computations. One reason for confusion among mail-order shoppers trying to tally their own orders is that shipping charges can be computed a number of ways.

Postpaid. This method is simplest for consumers because the shipping and handling costs are incorporated into the price of the item. The price, therefore, is *not* subject to an additional shipping charge. (Tax is another matter, covered below.)

Itemized. This method is also simple but not necessarily cost efficient. The firm indicates the cost of shipping in parentheses at the end of the product description or after the product price or code number. The amount you pay might not match the meter strip on the delivered package, though. Perhaps the amount you were charged included handling and packing, or maybe the company uses the charge as a means of taking in some extra bucks. If you sense *too large* a difference between actual cost and the amount you paid, you can discuss it with the company and see what happens, if anything.

Numeric. In an effort to get consumers to order several items at one time, rather than one here, one there, some companies charge shipping based on *the number of items* you order, not on their cost or weight or destination. The charge on the first item is usually the highest, with successive items costing less: "$1.50 for first title, $.75 for each additional book." Sometimes after a specified number of items, charges are eliminated entirely!

Flat order fees. Here's another easy-to-calculate method since one charge is applied to an entire order no matter how many items are included or how much they weigh. Too good to be true? Yes, if your selection is exceptionally heavy or fragile or is not a standard size. Read the catalog for exceptions, which can also apply to orders sent to more than one address.

Free shipping. Is it possible? Could shipping actually be "free"? Yes, if the cost or quantity of your order meets a standard stated in the catalog. For example, orders "over $100" might not be charged shipping; likewise, for multiple units (say, two dozen) of one color, style, or size. Such an arrangement is common among smaller companies and is usually contingent upon shipping to *one* address.

Purchase amount. With this method, the shipping charge based on the *total purchase amount* of an order is determined using a two-column table found on the catalog order form. Locate the *total cost* of your *purchases* in the left column; then look across to the corresponding shipping charge in the right column. For example, if your total purchase amount is between $25.01 and $50, your shipping charge is $6.95. If your purchase total is $300.01 and over, your charge is a maximum of $14.95. This method seems unfair if your order consists of a $400 ring, as opposed to a heavy $150 microwave oven. In such cases, a company might apply itemized shipping charges; and most set a maximum limit on the cost of shipping, generally, below $20.

Weight and distance. This is the method that tempts buyers to "forget" to add in shipping because figuring out the charges seems complicated. It involves using a chart of weight and/or distance, doing arithmetic, and rereading catalog product descriptions for notes about trucking. In a "simple" case, you would total the *weight* of your purchases, locate the zone or area you live in on the chart, and then figure out the shipping charge. But some products are "trucked," and you have to know if one of yours fits that category. Usually the catalog codes will tell you with an extra letter at the end. If your catalog does not have a rate chart, or if computing the charge is more than you bargained for, you have options. The best is to pay by credit card so the company can simply add the shipping to the total without delaying your order. Next best is to phone the shipping department of the firm. Add the figure they give you to your order. The last way, which could cause a shipping delay, is to send a check for the order and request to be billed for the shipping.

Saving on Shipping Costs. If placing a large order appeals to you because of potential savings on shipping, invite like-minded friends and associates to order when you do, especially if a holiday is coming up and shipping to one address is convenient for all. If ordering solo, avoid placing an "after-thought" order: give yourself a day's "cooling-off" period after filling in the order form, in case you decide in favor of an item you were on the fence about.

Carriers. Regardless of how firms arrive at shipping charges, they tend to ship goods by UPS, USPS, trucks, and overnight delivery services (sometimes called "Air Delivery").

United Parcel Service (UPS): For mail order, many businesses prefer to use UPS because overall it costs less than USPS and automatically insures each package up to $100. One possible disadvantage from a customer's view is that delivery is made only to street addresses, not post-office boxes.

United States Postal Service (USPS)/Parcel Post (PP): Parcel Post (fourth-class mail) delivers to post-office boxes, an advantage in favor of the higher charge, compared to UPS's rate. If Parcel Post delivery is imperative, do the following two things: (1) Across the top of the *order form*, in large red letters, write,

"DELIVER BY PARCEL POST ONLY; UPS NOT ACCEPTABLE." (2) In a conspicuous place on *your check*, write "GOODS TO BE DELIVERED BY PARCEL POST ONLY." By cashing the check the firm agrees to honor this arrangement and, therefore, should ship by Parcel Post.

Truck: Here's that term for a tricky form of shipping mentioned earlier, "Truck." It means that an item, because of its size or its location in a *manufacturer's* warehouse (not the mail-order firm's premises) must be shipped by truck, not UPS or USPS/PP. If your order includes some items that can go by mail and some that *must* go by truck, the whole order might ship by truck. How do you know which products require trucking when you place your order?

The catalog will contain the following terms if a product requires shipment by truck: "FOB" (free on board) or "freight," followed by "warehouse" or "manufacturer" or the city from which the goods will be trucked. What, then, does "FOB manufacturer" mean? It means that trucking charges are billed from the *manufacturer's* location, not the mail-order firm's warehouse. A product coming to you from the manufacturer is most likely being drop-shipped to you en route to another, nearby destination. You can ask the mail-order firm if your item is being drop-shipped, and if so where the manufacturer's warehouse is so you can estimate trucking costs. If quick delivery is important to you, ask the mail-order firm to find out before you order if the manufacturer has the item in stock and if it does, if it can ship by overnight service.

Trucking presents additional considerations: The charges, collected *upon delivery*, must be paid in cash or by certified check. They mount if you've ordered something heavy traveling from far away. Deliveries are usually left on the sidewalk in front of your home or business, not inside the door. Sometimes, for additional cash fees, drivers will carry the delivery inside, but not always, especially if you're in a nonelevator building. Additional fees come into play if you require advance notice of delivery or your order is not part of a larger trucking shipment. Sometimes, because of trucking charges, you might do better to buy appliances or heavy-duty equipment from a local retailer that delivers.

Handling

Sometimes a fee for "handling"—the processing and packing of your order—is charged as a part of the "shipping and handling" cost. Sometimes it's a separate fee of $1 to $5. Whether applied alone or in tandem with shipping, handling—and shipping, for that matter—it can be subject to state tax.

Insurance

When should you pay for it? If your order is being delivered by USPS ("the mail"), ask to have it insured, since insurance is not automatic. Charges are usually quite reasonable at 85 cents for goods valued at $50 and below, and $1.85 for shipments valued from $51 to $100. If the contents of your package are valued at more than $500 but less than $25,000, the shipment must be registered too. Note, also, that not all goods are insurable by the U.S. Post Office (some edibles, for example, or extremely fragile and valuable antiques). If your purchase is uninsurable, ask the mail-order firm to use a service that will insure it.

UPS *automatically* insures packages for up to $100. UPS's charges for each $100 worth of insurance on the same package get added into the shipping charge. If you encounter an order form that says shipments are made by UPS, yet there's an insurance charge printed on the form, don't pay it—insurance is already part of the UPS shipping.

Insurance claims occur most frequently because goods are lost or damaged during shipping. As soon as you notice damage to your shipment, call the customer service department of the firm *you ordered from*, and ask what the procedure is for making a claim. The answer will depend on how your goods were shipped and on the policy of the mail-order company. However, if you have documentation of having received and/or insured the order (a signature in a UPS log, an insurance receipt from USPS), the company has enough to verify and process your claim, and eventually to reimburse you or issue a replacement order. If the goods do not arrive and you cannot prove that they were insured, the firm might send a replacement order anyway. If you paid for your purchase with a credit card, you might qualify for a charge-back, provided you follow the *creditor's* procedure for obtaining one. (See "The Fair Credit Billing Act," page 651, for information on this.) If you are unable to resolve your claim to your satisfaction after persistently using all the options, contact the agencies listed in "Obtaining Help," page 650, and present your case to them.

Sales Tax

For years one of the joys of shopping by mail was that purchases were exempt from sales tax if they were shipped to an address *outside the state* where the mail-order firm (or its branch offices or its representative) was located. Those unfortunate enough to live in the same state as the mail-order firm or its branches and representatives paid tax on goods as well as on handling, shipping, and packing.

These days, more of us are being numbered among "the unfortunates" as state governments seek to benefit from the success of mail-order shopping (what will happen regarding online shopping is not yet known) by imposing a "use" tax on orders shipped *into* a state! No matter how you feel about paying a sales tax on a mail order, if the order form says "Add applicable taxes for shipments to WY, WV and ID addresses only," and you live in one of those states, you must calculate and add in the correct percentage of sales tax. If the form says "Add applicable sales tax for your state," you must do so. If you have questions about purchases that you expect to deduct or take depreciation on, speak to an accountant or a local tax authority.

Shipments Abroad

If you would have your order shipped outside the continental U.S.—*before you order*—find out from the catalog, the website, or a customer service representative about policies and regulations that could affect your shipment.

Shipments to and from Canada. The North American Free Trade Agreement (NAFTA) has eliminated some but not all tariff problems. Also, some products are not allowed to be shipped out of the country. The maple leaf icon in the symbol row indicates which mail-order companies will ship to Canada, but to be sure all items in your order can go there, speak to the vendor's reps.

Shipments to APO/FPO Addresses. Let's start with the carriers that *do not* ship to these addresses: UPS and Federal Express. Not surprisingly, USPS will ship to an APO/FPO address but not on a C.O.D. basis. USPS, the carrier used by most mail-order companies for this kind of shipping, uses parcel airlift (PAL) to a military dispatch center, which, in turn, ships packages overseas on a space-available basis (SAM, space available mail). Packages cannot exceed 70 pounds and must be no larger than 108 inches combined length and girth (the same restrictions that apply to regular first-class mail). Firms that ship to APO/FPO addresses—indicated by the American flag icon—might charge additional handling fees, so you might want to get a shipping estimate before you place an order.

Shipments Worldwide. The globe in the symbol row indicates that a company ships worldwide. But such shipping is not a simple matter for the consumer: Import restrictions, duty rates, and conversion rates are important concerns for the mail-order shopper. Experts in these areas should be consulted before you place an order to an address outside the U.S. and Canada (Israel, Japan, Europe, for example). Also, before sending any money, read a company's catalog closely or have the firm, if it sells on a price-quote basis, mail you a shipping quote.

Receiving Your Order

Mail-order shopping is a two-way street with rights and responsibilities falling to both the consumer and the vendor. Here are some guidelines on how to handle your order when it arrives and what to do if it doesn't.

Accepting Deliveries

First of all, when the order arrives from the trucking service, UPS, or USPS, inspect the crate, box, or bag for *extensive* damage. If you think the packaging has been through too much—and therefore suspect damage to your order—you don't have to sign for or accept the delivery. (If someone else is accepting the delivery for you, advise that person to make the same inspection.) See "Returns, Guarantees, and Warranties," page 641, for details about returning shipments.

If the box, crate, or bag seems fine, sign for it. While you should not put off opening the delivery, neither should you tear into it with excitement. Open the package with care, paying attention to any instructions on the box, and put aside the packing materials. Retrieve a copy of your order form or an invoice from inside the box or from the plastic envelope attached to the shipping carton. If none is enclosed, get the copy you filed away with the catalog and begin to inspect the contents.

What are you checking for? Damage to goods, an incomplete ("short") order; substitutions you did not authorize; errors in size, color, style, or model; missing parts; instruction sheets or booklets; warranty forms. If the item was customized (printed, engraved, monogrammed), check wording and spelling slowly and out loud, letter by letter. If you ordered an ensemble, make sure all the pieces were shipped: belts, hats, scarves, vests, ties, ascots. If you ordered a tool or something electronic, use it—after reading instructions carefully—as soon as possible to make sure it works as it should and does what you were expecting it to do. Check the item for signs of use to make sure you were not sent a demonstration, reconditioned, or returned item as "new." (If you were, you could return it or negotiate for a lower price.) Don't mail in the warranty card until after you've tried out the item. See "Returns, Guarantees, and Warranties," page 641, on what to do if you decide to return an item.

If goods are *damaged*, inform the seller right away. Speak calmly and politely as you describe the condition of the order and how you think the problem could be corrected. If the damage seems to have occurred during shipping, the seller will ask you to file a complaint with the delivery service. In that case, ask the seller for the following information: the *seller's* shipping address, the date of shipment, the seller's account number with the delivery service, relevant shipment codes, and any other information you might need. Then, *file the claim with the delivery service*, and send a copy of the complaint to the seller. If you think photos will help your cause, enclose them with the original complaint. Sometimes purchases made with a credit card are entitled to extended warranties, so contact the issuer of your credit card if you used it to purchase the damaged goods.

Should you receive a short shipment, don't get upset. The seller might have included a notice saying that the pieces will be shipped separately. Check also for an option notice which would be sent if an item were out of stock. (See "The Option Notice," page 640, for information on this.) If a company doesn't back order, it will enclose a refund check with the order or send a refund check under separate cover or, if you paid by credit card, bill it for the adjusted total. What if you don't find a notice about the missing items? Look in the catalog to find out if certain items get shipped from the manufacturer or separately by the vendor. If no such information is apparent, call the firm right way.

Contact the firm immediately if customized products have errors in them—even if a special occasion is months away.

Delayed Shipments

What feels like a long time to you may not constitute an actual delay in the legal sense as outlined in the FTC Mail or Telephone Order Rule. However, if a company does delay shipping your order, you need to know your basic rights and obligations.

The FTC Mail or Telephone Order Rule. This federal rule was created to address the problem of late delivery as it concerns mail-order shopping. The Rule contains certain principles that the mail-order consumer ought to know, as well as exemptions to its protection and *obligatory* actions on the part of the buyer when there are problems. When state or local laws exist for purposes similar to the functions of the FTC Mail or Telephone Order Rule, whichever law affords the *consumer* the most protection is the law that takes precedence.

General Terms of the Rule. An important term to understand is the word *ship.* The Rule states that a seller must *ship*—not "deliver"—goods within 30 days of receiving an order that is properly completed, unless the firm, in its catalog, advertisement, or promotional material, asked for more time. A "properly completed order" means that the check or money order sent as payment is good and made out in the proper amount; your credit is good if an order is charged; and all necessary information for processing the order is available. The 30 days start counting as soon as the firm receives your payment, but the count stops if the payment is dishonored. For credit card payments, the countdown starts when the seller receives valid account information, *not* when it puts the charges onto the card.

If there are any problems with the order, the 30-day clock does not begin until they are fixed. Problems could include any of the following: your check or money order is dishonored by the bank or made out for less than the total cost of the order; your credit card does not receive authorization from the issuer; the order is missing such information as your address, the color you want—anything that stands in the way of completing the order. Once the problem is eliminated—proper payment is received or credit is approved or missing data is supplied—the 30-day countdown begins. Therefore, to prevent delay, you should be attentive to details when you write up your order and, if placing it by phone, be as organized as possible to avoid making errors.

Exceptions to the Rule. To every rule there are exceptions. If a firms asks you to allow more than 30 days for shipment—"allow 6 to 8 weeks for delivery"— then the 30-day limit does not apply. In addition, some goods and purchases do not receive protection under the Rule: seeds and growing plants; C.O.D. orders; purchases that require you to say "no" to prevent shipment, such as book and record clubs (also called negative-option plans); and subscriptions to magazines and other "serial deliveries." The Rule applies to catalogs that require payment or compensation, but it does *not* apply to gifts that really are "free."

The firms you order from know all about the FTC rule. Therefore, if your order is covered under the Rule, the firm knows there's a specified procedure it must follow if it cannot ship your order within 30 days. Likewise, to protect your rights under the terms of the Rule, you must know what they are. The next few sections will tell you.

The Option Notice. If you submit a properly completed order, and the seller cannot ship within 30 days of receiving your order or by the time specified in its catalog, ads, or promotional material, it is obligated to send you an *option notice.* An option notice, to comply with the Rule, tells you that there is a delay in shipping the item you requested. A new shipping date might be mentioned. If it is, and the date is *up to* 30 days later than the original deadline or another date specified by the firm, you should be given the choice of consenting to the delay (accepting the new delivery date) *or* of canceling the order and receiving a refund. (See below for orders shipped *over* 30 days after the original date.) The option notice, under the Rule, must state that if you do *not* respond to the notice you are giving your implied consent to the delay. (That means, if you get an option notice and you don't respond to it, the delay is okay with you.) If you choose to cancel the order—and it is definitely your right to do so under this circumstance—the cancellation must reach the firm *before* it ships the order. That's why, again, acting immediately is important when dealing with mail-order issues.

If the seller gives you a new shipping deadline that is *over* 30 days *after* the original date, or it cannot give you any revised shipping date, the option notice must clearly say so. Read the following statement carefully, since it describes a procedure different from the one in the paragraph above: the notice must say that your order will be *automatically canceled* unless (1) the seller receives, within 30 days of the *original shipping date,* your *consent* to the delay, and (2) the firm *is* able to ship the order *within* 30 days *after* the original deadline and has not received cancellation of the order from you as of the time of shipping.

Notices must be sent by first-class mail with a cost-free way to respond to the notice, such as a prepaid business-reply envelope or postcard (the ones that say "Postage will be paid by" or "No postage required if mailed within the United States"). Reply immediately, especially if you want to cancel your order. For protection, photocopy the cancellation order (the card, letter, or form that you send), and send it "return receipt requested" so you'll know the exact date it was received. If the order goes out any time after the date the firm received your cancellation order, and you have proof, you can refuse to accept delivery, sending the order back to the seller at the seller's expense and claiming a prompt refund or credit.

The Renewed Option Notice. Let's say a firm has sent you an option notice stating a revised shipping deadline. If the firm cannot meet the *revised* shipping deadline, it must send you, *before the date of the revised deadline,* a renewed option notice. This second notice, and any that come after it, must state that if you do not consent *in writing* to a new shipping date or to an indefinite delay, the order will be canceled. According to the Rule, the consent to the second delay must reach the seller *before* the first delay period ends, or the order must be canceled.

Even if you agree to an indefinite delay, you have the right to cancel the order at any time before the goods are shipped. Note, also, that the *seller,* if it is unable to ship within the delay period, may cancel the order and that it must cancel the order under various circumstances.

The Rule and Refunds. Under the terms of the Rule, how you paid for your order determines the time-frame within which you receive a refund should you or the firm cancel the order. Regardless of how you paid for the order, however, the Rule provides for a prompt refund. For prepaid orders the firm must send you a refund check or money order by first-class mail within seven business days after the order was canceled. If you used a debit card tell the firm at the time of cancellation because it needs to treat that payment as cash, the way it would for a money order or check. It must reimburse your *account* within seven working days *or* send a refund check. According to the Rule, payments made by credit card must be refunded (credited to your account as a void of the charges made for the goods) in one billing cycle. Firms cannot substitute credit vouchers for their own goods in lieu of making a reimbursement.

Returns, Guarantees, and Warranties

A lasting mail-order relationship depends on satisfied customers, and firms know that sometimes delivering satisfaction means accepting customer returns. To do that, sellers have policies that spell out the procedures and conditions for making a return. The customer's right to return products also depends on the nature of the problem, the conditions under which the return is made, and laws made at local, state, and federal levels. For general information, see "Return Policies" and "Accepting Deliveries." Many goods purchased by mail are covered by written or implied product warranties. For information on all types of warranties, see "Guarantees and Warranties," starting at page 643.

Returns

Before you order by mail, read the catalog carefully because it tells you the firm's policy on returning items, including how soon after receipt they must be returned, whether you need authorization from the seller, reasons for which returns can be made, and which types of goods are nonreturnable. Generally, special orders, "final sale" items, truly wholesale purchases, intimate apparel, bathing suits, hats, and custom-made items are *not* returnable. However, if the firm made an error or the product was defective, some "nonreturnables" will be accepted for exchange. "Implied Warranties" provide information on laws that apply to product performance and to the rights of consumers beyond those stated in catalogs, so it's wise to read them.

Obtaining Authorization. The phrase "authorized returns accepted" appears frequently in the "Special Factors" sections of WMO listings. An authorized return is a return you have called the company about and for which you have received an authorization number (also called an "RMA"). The company expects you to use that number on all correspondence pertaining to the return and on the outside of the package when you ship it back. Before sending back goods, you should check for packing inserts that detail the return procedure; if no inserts are found, read the catalog for instructions. Also, the back of the order statement sent with your goods might have a return form printed on it. If it does, use that for your correspondence, filling it in completely and correctly. If it doesn't, write a straightforward, *factual* letter that states (1) the reason you're returning the item, (2) the price and the order number of the item, (3) the date the package was delivered to you, and (4) how you would like the situation resolved. For example, do you want a refund check, an exchange, a repair, a credit to your charge account, a store credit toward a future purchase? Avoid wordiness, threats, and emotional arguments at this point. Keep a copy of the correspondence, be it a letter or the company's return form, and notes of your phone conversation with the company, especially the authorization number and the person you spoke to.

Restocking Fees. A restocking fee offsets the company's cost to rehandle a product when returning it to inventory. Fees are stated in catalogs and range from 10% to 15% of the cost of the item (some items such as frames may go as high as 25%). Pay attention to catalog notes about fees when buying furniture, electronics, and appliances. If an item is returned because of a defect or shipping error, a restocking fee usually is not charged.

Sending the Item. Under "Accepting Deliveries," page 637, we advised setting aside packing materials until the contents of the package had been examined. If an item needs to be returned, package it in those same materials, if feasible or requested by the firm, and make sure any insurance coverage equals the full value of the item (see "Insurance," page 635). Before sealing the package, enclose the return form or your *dated* letter, double checking that you included your name and address, the product's order number, the authorization number and/or name of the person who approved the return, and what you would like done (repair, exchange, refund, or credit). File a copy of the correspondence, any notes, and your invoice with the catalog.

Refunds and Credits. By reading the catalog before you order, you will know *in advance of returning a product* what a company will and will not do when it accepts a return. Knowing this is important when you state in your letter what you would like done. To ask for a refund from a firm that only offers a choice of replacement or repair will delay resolution of the problem. However, many firms *do* have refund policies, so if you want a credit to your charge account, include the necessary information in your letter, and if you want a refund check, specify the mailing address that should be used.

Exchanges. If you are exchanging the returned product for an identical item (without the defects) say so in your correspondence. But if you are exchanging the product for a completely different item, provide the same information you would give if you were ordering the item new: the code number from the catalog, the size and color, the price, and other relevant information. It's best to talk to a customer service representative before exercising this latter option, as a difference in price between the two items could be problematic.

Postage Reimbursement. Generally, firms do *not* pick up the customer's cost of shipping and insuring a return. A few exceptions, however, will accept "postage collect" returns or hire UPS to pick up the package at no charge to the buyer. Others will reimburse their customers for shipping and insurance. Since *federal* law does not require reimbursement of these costs—even when the seller makes a mistake—companies tend not to reimburse for them. However, since the buyer benefits from the law that offers the most consumer protection, state and local laws should be checked in case they provide for reimbursement.

Guarantees and Warranties

People use the terms "guarantee" and "warranty" interchangeably, but they are somewhat different. In "Special Factors," the expression "satisfaction guaranteed" represents a firm's pledge to stand behind the products and services it sells. That promise is backed up by each firm's policy on returns (see "Return Policies," "Returns," and "Implied Warranties"). In contrast, a warranty is a written policy covering the performance of a specific product, and, like a guarantee, it is available without charge. An "extended warranty," however, is a *paid service contract* for a particular product.

Since warranties are regulated by state and federal laws, you have certain rights with regard to achieving product satisfaction. Therefore, it pays to know the terms of each policy so you can get the best warranty value for your product and avoid paying for services (such as repairs or replacement) that ought to be paid for by another party (for example, the manufacturer or the seller).

The Warranty Act. Before we get to the terms of the Magnuson-Moss Warranty—Federal Trade Commission Improvement Act ("the Warranty Act"), a word about oral promises made by salespeople. An oral "warranty" that assures product performance and customer satisfaction has no value *unless it is also given in writing.* The Warranty Act, enacted in 1975, regulates printed warranties. It requires that all terms and conditions of warranties be expressed in "simple and readily understood language"—in other words, plain speech. For products costing over $15, a copy of the warranty must be available to the buyer *before* purchase. Stores are supposed to post warranties on or near their products or keep them on-premises in a binder of warranties, posting a conspicuous notice about its location. Mail-order firms honor the law by making copies of warranties available to potential customers *upon request*. Therefore if, along with a price quote, you ask to receive a copy of a warranty, you're entitled to have your request fulfilled.

The party making the warranty (the warrantor) is required by the Warranty Act to describe the policy using the terms "full" and/or "limited." Sometimes multiple warranties will apply to a single product if it has parts that are covered differently. The warranty covering each of those parts can be designated as full *or* limited.

Full warranties. A full warranty provides for the repair or replacement of the product at *no cost* to the buyer. This provision includes removing and reinstalling the item, if applicable. A full warranty exists for a certain amount of time, which must be stated, and its provisions must be transferable to another party for the full term of the policy. So, if a relative passes a small appliance on to you during the term of the warranty, you are entitled to the benefits of the warranty should you need them within the covered time. The duration of *implied* warranties (see page 645) may not be limited by the terms of the full warranty and may last, under some state laws, up to four years.

After you inform the seller of a problem, repair should be made within a "reasonable" amount of time. If a reasonable number of attempts have been made to repair the product, and it still doesn't work properly, a "lemon provision" entitles you to replacement of or refund for the product.

For marketing research and product development purposes, many firms enclose registration cards with their products, inviting consumers whose products are covered by a full warranty to register them with the warrantor. Such registration is a voluntary act and should be so stated on the card. Registration is *not necessary* to protect your rights under the warranty.

Limited warranties. A limited warranty offers fewer benefits (less coverage) than does a full warranty, and is not subject to the "lemon provision." Under a limited warranty, the buyer can be held responsible for some costly aspects of product repair or replacement: removal, transportation, and reinstallation of the product and labor costs for repairs. In order to validate the policy, the buyer can be required to return the warranty card to the firm. Also, the warrantor *can limit* the terms of the policy to the original purchaser and make a prorated refund or credit for the product.

There is also something called an *implied* warranty (see "Implied Warranties," page 645), the duration of which can be limited by the warrantor, but not shortened. If the implied warranty time is limited, the warranty must state: "Some states do not allow limitations on how long an implied warranty lasts, so the above limitation may not apply to you." However, the warrantor may not put a limit on the extent of the protection you are entitled to under an implied warranty.

An informed buyer has more leverage in attaining product satisfaction than one who has no knowledge of consumer protections and seller obligations under the law. Here are some additional provisions of the Warranty Act:

- If a firm receives your complaint within the warranty period, it must take action to remedy the problem according to the terms of the warranty.
- If a product comes with a written warranty, the warrantor can't exclude the product from protection under implied warranties.
- A warrantor is allowed to exclude or limit consequential damages from coverage under both full and limited policies provided the warranty states: "Some states do not allow the exclusion or limitation of incidental or consequential damages, so the above limitation or exclusion may not apply to you." See "Implied Warranties" and "Consequential Damages" below and on the following pages for more information.
- All warranties must tell you whom to contact, where to take or mail the product, and how to reach the warrantor (name, address, or toll-free phone number).
- Both full and limited warranties must state: "This warranty gives you specific legal rights, and you may have other rights that vary from state to state."

Implied Warranties. Unlike the Warranty Act, which is a federal law, an implied warranty is a *state* law that offers protection against major hidden product defects. Every state has implied warranties covering every sale *unless* the seller states that the product is being sold "as is," a declaration that means no warranties or guarantees are offered. However, even if a firm sells a product under a no-guarantee policy ("as is"), if that product comes with a written warranty, the implied warranty of the *buyer's* state is valid on that item. Although states vary in some aspects of the terms of the implied warranties, many offer similar kinds of provisions.

Warranty of merchantability. This common implied warranty means that a product must work properly when used in its customary fashion. For example, a toaster should toast at varying degrees of lightness and darkness; a vacuum cleaner should pick up ordinary household debris—or liquids if that's its function. If a warranty of merchantability exists in your state, and you have purchased a product that doesn't do what it's supposed to do, most likely you will be entitled to a refund for that product.

Warranty of fitness. This warranty applies to cases in which the seller has identified or recommended a particular purpose or use for a product. So, if the seller indicates that a sleeping bag is appropriate for use in sub-zero temperatures, it should offer warmth in that situation. You should still check the product literature to verify such a claim. If none is available, call the manufacturer. Whether through product ignorance or misguided good intentions or a profit motive, the seller might not be entirely accurate. The manufacturer should have reliable information about product fitness.

Consequential Damages. Consequential (incidental) damages result when the malfunction of a product causes *other* property to become damaged or destroyed. According to the FTC's example, consequential damage has occurred if the use of faulty antifreeze causes a crack in an engine block. Likewise, an incidental damage has occurred if a properly installed home aquarium begins leaking at its seams and damages the carpet.

Although written warranties usually entitle the buyer to consequential damages, warrantors are permitted to exclude this provision under both full and limited warranties. If such damages are exempted, the warrantor must still state: "Some states do not allow exclusion of limitation of incidental or consequential damages, so the above limitation or exclusion may not apply to you."

There are two important consumer entitlements in the provisions for consequential damages: (1) compensation for the damage or loss of the property, and (2) repair or replacement of the defective product. You can see why, given something as costly to repair or replace as an engine block, a seller might declare an exemption of damages. And if your state *allows* exclusion of limitation of incidental damages, the value of the product and its warranty will be greatly reduced from the buyer's point of view.

Evaluating Warranties. With so many products at competitive prices and similar features, a buyer must also weigh the value of a warranty *before* making a purchase. As you read the warranty—and you really should *read* it—pay attention to what you know about yourself as a product user (are you rough on gadgets? careless about or attentive to maintenance?) and what you know about the type of product in general. For example, what usually goes wrong with a cassette player or a VCR? Do you have reason to be concerned about being able to get such an item repaired or replaced, based on your experiences? You can also review the warranty in terms of the following questions:

- Is it a full or a limited warranty?
- Is the whole product covered or only specific parts?
- From date of purchase, is the warranty period a number of days (30, 45, 90 days) or months (6 months) or years (one, two, five)?
- Whom do you contact for repairs: the manufacturer? the seller? a service center? (And note where each is located.)
- Who is responsible for removing, delivering, and reinstalling the product? (Especially important for large appliances.)

- Must repairs be made by an "authorized" service center or representative? Where is the closest one located?
- Is a temporary replacement provided while your product is being repaired or serviced?
- Are consequential damages excluded? If so, would malfunction of the product lead to considerable damage and loss?
- How is reimbursement on a pro rata basis calculated (according to time, use, or price)?
- If the product can't be repaired, are you entitled to a refund or a replacement?

To evaluate a warranty, consider (as if you were in a horror film) *all* that could go wrong with a product and how soon after purchase things could go wrong. Then determine how much loss, inconvenience, and expense you could bear concerning this particular product. Your answers will help you decide if the product and its particular warranty are worthwhile for you.

Complying with Warranty Terms. By virtue of being human, we all mean to do things we should do, but often we don't actually do them—following instructions and reading contracts, for example. Here are some reminders to help you take advantage of the protections in warranties and fulfill the obligations of any buyer.

- Read the warranty card—or have someone read and explain it to you.
- Read the instructions or operating manual *before* using the product, even if you are sure you know what to do. There could be some delightful feature you don't know about, or less optimistically, an important warning, such as "Do not turn on unit until compartment is filled with water."
- Follow the instructions for using the product.
- Understand the conditions that void a warranty: misuse, mishandling, and neglect of the product; improper installation; repair or service by an unauthorized party; commercial use of a noncommercial model; and use of the product at the wrong voltage. Anyone who uses your property should know how to operate it.
- Keep the warranty and dated proof of purchase together, in a spot reserved for such records.
- If you must send in proof of payment to qualify for a rebate, photocopy the receipt and store it with the warranty.
- Maintain the product as suggested in the manual, and resist the impulse to perform do-it-yourself repairs. Improper maintenance or tampering with the product could void the warranty.

When in doubt, let the manufacturer or service center answer questions about maintenance and use—because if you violate the terms of the warranty, it will become void and the cost of repairs will fall to you.

Obtaining Service. If your product stops working or malfunctions, don't panic. Try following these suggestions:

- Refer to the operating manual or instructions, specifically the troubleshooting section. Make sure you're not trying to get the product to do something it wasn't intended to do.
- Speak to a friend who may have knowledge about common problems or who can run through your product's setup procedures, to make sure you installed the item correctly.
- Contact the warrantor—unless the seller offers service under the warranty—from information on the warranty card.
- Describe the problem, state when it occurred, and indicate whether you want a repair, replacement, refund, and/or consequential damages. If you visit a service center, bring a copy of the warranty and proof of payment; include the same if you send a letter. Your rights and the form (and extent) of compensation will vary depending on the terms of the warranty and the laws for your area.
- If you drop off a product or the repair service picks it up, get a signed receipt with the date the item should be ready, approximately how much the repairs will cost, and the serial number of the product, if it has one.
- Any product you ship out for repairs should be insured for its full value, and a letter enclosed stating the problem, the date it occurred, and what you would like done.
- If you call or visit the warrantor or the seller, follow up with a letter stating what was said during the conversation. Photocopy the letter, and send it by certified mail to the person or agency you talked to.
- Log the actions taken in the process of your honoring the warranty: indicate dates of phone calls, visits, and actions as well as expenses for them.
- If, after three to four weeks, you have not heard from the seller or the manufacturer in response to your letter, write again. Ask for a reply within four weeks, enclose a photocopy of the *first* letter, and mail the second correspondence using certified mail. Address the letter to the person you've been dealing with; if you don't have a specific contact, send the letter to the attention of the warranty department or the head of customer relations.
- Deal with one party at a time: the manufacturer *or* the seller, not both. If one does not resolve the issue, then contact the other. Neither can afford to do business with a party that doesn't hold up its end of the relationship.
- Before you accept a product that has been repaired, have it demonstrated. If you recognize quirks that repairs should have eliminated, point them out. Better to have the problem checked there than to take the item home and go through the procedure again.

- When you pay for the repairs, get a guarantee on parts and labor. This will protect you from paying for repairs again if the items malfunctions shortly after you start using it.
- Under the "lemon provision," if the product repeatedly malfunctions after being repaired, and it is covered by a full warranty, you can most likely get a replacement or a refund. In a letter to either the manufacturer or the seller, detail the history of the problems and the repairs, ask for a replacement or a refund, and enclose a copy of the warranty. If the warranty is limited, not full, the terms may still entitle you to a replacement or a refund. Send the same correspondence as for a full warranty to either the seller or the manufacturer.
- Your state's laws covering implied warranties and consequential damages may provide protections not given in the product warranty. Find out what the laws in your state are.
- If a malfunctioning product has caused you physical injury, contact the appropriate attorney.
- For problems that have not been resolved to your satisfaction, despite your good-faith actions and the passage of a reasonable amount of time, your local consumer-protection agency can provide advice.
- Other agencies and organizations exist to help consumers with unresolved product disputes. See "Obtaining Help," page 650.

Complaints

Complaint Procedures

Telling a company that you received a defective product is not complaining; neither is pursuing your rights under a warranty. But what if you have acted in good faith to resolve a problem, only to end up with unsatisfactory results? Then it's time to make a formal complaint, which involves writing a complaint letter.

The Complaint Letter. No matter how angry or frustrated you feel over the matter, keep your letter neat, formal, assertive, and respectful. Follow proper letter-writing format to include the date of the letter, your name and address, and reference to your customer account number. Give accurate and complete product and payment information: the order (or product) number or code, descriptive details, and payment data (credit card information, debit account number, etc.). State your specific complaint ("I have not received a reply"; "The appliance still does not work"; "No refund check has been received"), and provide a *brief* history of the problem. Mention that you are enclosing *copies* of previous letters (both to and from various parties), the warranty, proof of payment, proof of repairs, and other relevant documents. (Later, be sure to enclose them, and return all originals to your file.) State what you think would be a fair resolution to the problem, and indicate that you are offering the firm one last chance to settle the issue before seeking outside help. Explain that if a reply is not received or a resolution reached within 30 days, you will report the firm to the appropriate agency or agencies (the U.S. Postal Service, Better Business Bureau, Direct Marketing Association, Federal Trade Commission, and/or other group). (See "Obtaining Help," below.) If after 30 days, the matter has not been resolved, take the promised action.

Obtaining Help

The challenge consumers face when trying to get help is not knowing what kind of help they need and which agency to turn to. One great resource is the *Consumer's Resource Handbook*, published by the Consumer Information Center. Log onto www.pueblo.gsa.gov for more information about this guide, which provides advice, consumer tips, names, addresses, and phone numbers for every organization and agency out there who can help with all your consumer complaints.

Regardless of which organization helps you, you'll need to provide a copy of your final complaint letter along with copies of the documentation you enclosed. (Keep the originals for your file.) The agencies described below have their own ways of handling consumer mail-order problems, so be understanding if the help they *can* provide falls short of your dream solution. Some groups will investigate individual complaints while others will accumulate complaints until they have enough to take action.

Consumer Action Panels (CAPs). CAPs offer third-party dispute resolution programs for specific industries. In addition to investigating consumer complaints, they provide consumers with service information and members with suggestions for improving consumer service. For example, the Major Appliance Consumer Action Program (MACAP) helps with problems involving major appliances. Call 800–621–0477 for information, or write to MACAP at 20 N. Wacker Dr., Ste. 1231, Chicago, IL 60606.

Better Business Bureaus (BBBs). Business and professional firms fund the self-regulatory agencies known as Better Business Bureaus. They maintain files on firms, which are useful for answering consumer inquiries about a firm's selling history; monitor business practices such as advertising and selling; and make service information available to consumers. Since most BBBs have programs for mediation and arbitration, and the power to make awards (binding arbitration), they really can assist in resolving consumer complaints.

If you want to contact a BBB, look for an office closest to the *company* you're concerned about. You can call to request a directory of offices (703–276–0100) or write to the Council of Better Business Bureaus, Inc., 4200 Wilson Blvd., Ste. 800, Arlington VA 22203–1804. Be sure to enclose a self-addressed stamped envelope with your request. (You can also visit the Better Business Bureau website at www.bbb.org.) Once you've located the appropriate office, write to request either a "consumer complaint" form or a "consumer inquiry" form.

Direct Marketing Association (DMA). A trade organization of direct marketers and mail-order companies, the Direct Marketing Association is the largest and oldest organization of its sort, with more than half its membership comprised of non-U.S. firms. The DMA maintains a Mail Order Action Line (MOAL) to assist in resolving nondelivery problems involving *any* direct-marketing firm, not only member firms. You can seek help by *writing* to MOAL. Send a copy of your complaint letter and all the documentation to Mail Order Action Line, DMA, 1111 19th St. NW, Ste. 1100, Washington, DC 20030–3606. After your complaint is received, the DMA will contact the firm and attempt to resolve the problem, making a request that you allow the firm 30 days to act.

If you get too many direct mailings and solicitation calls, the DMA's "Telephone Preference Service" and "Mail Preference Service" can reduce them. Your name will be kept on the DMA's lists for five years, lists that most reputable firms consult before sending out a mail campaign. You can reduce *mail* by writing to Mail Preference Service, DMA, P.O. Box 9008, Farmingdale, NY 11735–9008. Give your name and home address (this procedure won't work for business addresses), state that you don't want direct mail, and write "HOME" on your request. You can reduce *solicitation calls*, by writing to Telephone Preference Service, DMA, P.O. Box 9014, Farmingdale, NY 11735–9014. Give your name, home address, and *home* telephone number, state that you don't want solicitation calls, and write "HOME" on your request. If you continue to receive calls, speak to the marketer directly, and if a third party seems to be using another firm's list of customers, tell the referring company that you want the practice stopped.

The Federal Trade Commission (FTC). This law-enforcement agency protects the public against business practices that are anticompetitive, unfair, and deceptive. It accepts complaint letters that form the basis of files on firms. If a large number of complaints is received or the problems are of a serious nature, the FTC may decide an investigation is appropriate. They may seek court injunctions and/or the imposition of fines as stiff as $10,000 for each day the violation continues. Your letters about firms that do not follow FTC regulations are important, so report them.

The Fair Credit Billing Act (FCBA). The FCBA was passed in 1975 as part of the FTC's Consumer Protection Act to give mail-order shoppers who pay with credit cards some recourse in the event of nondelivery problems. The FCBA created a procedure for consumers to settle billing errors such as, but not limited to, charges for goods and/or services that were not accepted or not provided or delivered as agreed. Read the entire procedure carefully, as it includes deadlines and steps that should not be overlooked.

1. To activate FCBA protection, you must *write to* the "billing error" address that appears on your monthly statement. Do not call the customer service telephone number on your bill.

2. In your letter, give your name, address, and account number; the dollar amount of the error; and reason you think the error occurred.
3. This letter must reach the creditor *within 60 days* after the first bill with the error was mailed to you. Send the letter by certified mail, return receipt requested.
4. The creditor is obligated to acknowledge your correspondence in writing and within 30 days of its receipt, unless the problem is corrected before then.
5. While an amount is being disputed under this procedure, it does not have to be paid. Neither does the related portion of the minimum payment nor the related finance charges have to be paid.
6. If the creditor finds an error, the creditor must send you a letter explaining the correction, credit the disputed amount to your account, and remove related finance charges. If the creditor finds that you owe *a portion* of the disputed amount, the finding must be explained in writing.
7. If the creditor finds the bill correct, it must send you a letter explaining the reasons and stating the amount you owe. When this is the outcome, you are liable for missed minimum payments and finance charges that accrued pending resolution.
8. If your state laws allow you to pursue the matter against the *seller* rather than the creditor, you can further dispute the amount. Within ten days of receiving the creditor's justification of the charge, send the *creditor* a letter saying that you still refuse to pay the disputed amount. At this point the creditor can begin collection proceedings against you. Therefore, it might be wise for you to contact a local consumer protection agency for options to handle the problem.

If state law allows withholding of payment from a seller, then under the FCBA you can dispute the *quality* of goods or services. This coverage holds for credit-card purchases over $50 made in your state of residence or within 100 miles of your mailing address. If the credit card used was issued by the seller, the limits do not apply. Before doing anything, contact a local consumer protection agency for advice.

The United States Postal Service (USPS). Another organization to turn to for help is the USPS, which has a reputation for resolving around 85% of the complaints it acts on. Under provisions of the U.S. Code, the USPS has the power to go to court, obtain a restraining order, and withhold mail delivery to a company—a debilitating circumstance, surely, for a mail-order firm. To enlist the support of the USPS you have two options: send a copy of your final complaint letter and documentation to the Chief Postal Inspector, U.S. Postal Service, Washington, DC 20260, or write directly to the Postmaster of the post office serving the firm with which you're in dispute.

Bankruptcy Courts. How can a bankruptcy court help? It might be able to offer information on orders and refunds that seem to have gone astray. You should contact a bankruptcy court if letters to a company have gone unanswered for an inordinately long time and attempts to reach it by phone have yielded only disconnect messages. Tell the clerk at the U.S. Bankruptcy Court nearest to the firm the reason for your call. If the company has filed for reorganization under Chapter 11, ask for the case number and any information or forms you need to file a claim. Under Chapter 11, a hierarchy of creditors exists to protect a business against its creditors' claims. Your claim will join the roster after claims by suppliers, utilities, banks, and others. Filing does not guarantee that you'll get your money back, but it is an option available to you, so why not use it.

If you are especially dissatisfied with—or gratified by—a service you've received from a company appearing in this book, we would like to know. To find out how to reach us, see "Feedback," page 655.

Feedback

Your suggestions, complaints, and comments help us to shape each edition of *Wholesale by Mail and Online*. When you write, please use the guidelines that follow:

Firms. If you think your company qualifies to be included in this book, we'd like to hear from you. Have your marketing director send The Print Project a copy of your current catalog, literature, or web address along with an explanatory cover letter and a way for us to contact you.

Consumers. If you wish to make suggestions for the next edition, send a postcard or letter to the address below.

The Print Project
P.O. Box 703
Bearsville, NY 12409

Company Index